A HISTORY OF THE CROCKETT FAMILY

OF CROCKETT'S RIDGE, NORWAY, MAINE

A HISTORY OF THE CROCKETT FAMILY

OF CROCKETT'S RIDGE, NORWAY, MAINE

BY

JENNIFER WIXSON

EDITED BY
YVETTE YOUNG

Copyright © 2024 by Jennifer Wixson

All rights reserved.

No part of this book may be reproduced or transmitted in any form or by any means, electronic or mechanical, including photocopying, recording or by any information storage or retrieval system – except by a reviewer who may quote brief passages in a review to be printed in a magazine, newspaper, or blog – without permission in writing from the publisher.

For more information contact:

whitewavepublishing@gmail.com

10 9 8 7 6 5 4 3 2 1

ISBN 978-0-9962237-2-0

eBook ISBN 978-0-9962237-3-7

All images in the book used with permission (as noted) or are in the public domain.

Cover images: Ephraim and Sally (Wentworth) Crockett. (Tintypes courtesy of Joyce Palmer.) Background: Colorized postcard, "Maine Logging Camp and Saw Mill near Norway, Me." (Robbins Brothers, Boston, MA and Germany) and map of Pennesseewassee Pond (from H.F. Walling's 1858 map of Oxford County, Maine).

"One of the primary results—and one of the primary needs—of industrialism is the separation of people and places and products from their histories. To the extent that we participate in the industrial economy, we do not know the history of our families or of our habitats or of our meals."

—Wendell Berry
From *The Art of the Commonplace: The Agrarian Essays of Wendell Berry*

This book is dedicated to my grandmother, Winona (Young) Palmer, who received me into her home on Crockett's Ridge in 1978 and proudly shared with me our family's history.

Four (plus) Generations: Winona (Young) Palmer holds her great-granddaughter Emily Louise McFarland, while behind her stands daughter Rowena Palmer (the author's mother) and granddaughter Cheryl Wixson (Emily's mother and the author's sister). This photo was taken circa 1992 in the parlor of the old Crockett homestead. Tintypes of our Norway ancestors—Ephraim and Sally (Wentworth) Crockett (Winona's great-great grandparents)—hang on the wall above the fireplace, behind the four generations of their descendants.

Table of Contents

Introduction	xiii
List of Photographs, Maps, Postcards, Deeds, and Illustrations	xvii
Source Material Abbreviations	xxiii
Chapter 1 – The Settlement of Norway, Maine, and Lee's Grant	1
The Settlement of Norway	1
The Story of Lee's Grant	8
The Lees and the Little Family	14
Old Family Land in Lee's Grant	25
Chapter 2 – Ephraim Crockett, Jr. and Sally (Wentworth) Crockett	29
Our Norway Crockett Ancestor	29
Ephraim, Jr.'s Early Years in Pejepscot	33
The Peculiar History of Lot 45 in Lee's Grant	36
Sarah "Sally" Bartlett Wentworth and the Wentworth Family	41
Ephraim Crockett, Jr.'s Service in the War of 1812	48
"Like Brothers" – Ephraim Crockett, Jr. and Nathan Morse, Jr.	53
Ephraim and Sally's Family, and Life in Norway	64
Conclusion to Chapter 2	77
Chapter 3 – The Crocketts and the Penleys	83
Real Estate, Lumber, and Weddings	83
The Penley Family	85
William Robinson Crockett and Lydia Stetson	89
Weaving Together the Story of the Second Generation in Norway	92
Death of John Penley, Jr. and Upheaval in the Family	113
William Robinson Crockett and His Father Build the Brick House	120
A Walk to the Big Hill Field	125
Overlapping Generations	127
Another Death in the Second Norway Generation and More Family Losses	129
Crocketts and Penleys in the Civil War	130
Concluding Synopses – Crocketts and Penleys	138
The Move to Norway Pine Grove Cemetery	161
Chapter 4 – Emma Tuell (Crockett) Young Harding – Last Crockett Standing	171
The Last of the Crocketts on the Ridge and the Age of Industrialization	171
A Cocoon of Security	172
B.F. Spinney & Co.	181
George P. Young	186
Emma and George	197
Family Scandals Come to the Aid of Emma	201
Life of the Newlyweds in Norway Village	210
A Tipping Point for the Crockett Homestead	212
Fair View Farm	213
An Heir Is Born	215

The Purchase of the John Penley Farm and the Shoe Factory Is Threatened with Closure	219
Norway's Centennial	224
Compounding Troubles for George	229
Life After George	242
John Aberdeen Harding	250
Warren E. Crockett in the Spanish American War	254
Family Updates and Leasing the Crockett Homestead	256
Purchase of the Original Nathan Morse Farm	258
The Call to Evangelism and Spreading the Good News	261
Grandchildren and a New Barn for Fair View Farm	264
Death of John Harding and Emma's Financial Difficulty	267
Extended Family Summaries and Emma's Final Years	268
Emma's Importance in Our Family History	276
Chapter 5 – Bill and Addie (Chaplin) Young	279
A Bride for Bill	279
Luella Batchelder and Willis B. Chaplin	282
Bill and Addie Young – The Early Years	290
The New Barn	297
Addie and the Heywood Club	299
Family Life	302
Mellie and "Gram" Dunham	311
Death of Bill's Stepfather and Emma Returns to Crockett's Ridge	315
The New Barn Burns	316
Young's Turkey Farm Rises From the Ashes	318
George, Winona, and Bud	322
The Grandchildren at Young's Turkey Farm	325
Expanding the Turkey Business	328
Addie's Sales and Marketing Genius	336
Bill and His Other Livestock	344
Overdue Taxes and Black Growth Timber	347
The Maine State Turkey Growers Association and Civic Duties	349
A New Well – Finally!	354
Open House at Young's Turkey Farm	357
The End of Young's Turkey Farm and the Birth of Young's Cottage Lots	361
Conclusion to Our History of the Crockett Family of Crockett's Ridge	370
Acknowledgements	375
Appendix	381
List of Appendix Items	381
Bibliography	405
Original Records	405
Family Histories and Genealogies (Published and Unpublished)	410
Magazines, Periodicals, Other Printed Materials and Websites	411
Books	416

Family Recipes and Remedies	419
Introduction	419
Recipes	421
Remedies	425
"Will the Real Crockett's Ridge Please Stand Up?" By Jennifer Wixson	427
Crockett Genealogy By Robert B. Johnson	431
Index	445
About the Author	466
Other Books by Jennifer Wixson	466

Author Jennifer Wixson in the tie-up of the old Crockett barn.
Photo taken circa 1984, when she was living with her grandmother Winona (Young) Palmer.

Introduction

The great American essayist and environmental activist Wendell Berry suggests that much of the malaise in the modern world can be traced to our disconnection from the land, from our own family histories on that land. If we do not know where we come from—if we do not understand how those who lived before us not only shaped their lives, but also our own—it can be difficult to find a solid foundation upon which to build our own personal stories. This history is the culmination of my nearly half-century quest to discern who I am and where I belong. In effect, writing this history of the Crockett family of Crockett's Ridge, Norway, Maine, was for me the writing of my own personal story.

In 1978, while living in Escondido, California, I had a vision of my home state of Maine. At the time, I was standing upon a sun-drenched cliff in the Cuyamaca Mountains, contemplating Life. My heart did a little back flip of excitement as I realized what I needed to do for myself. I needed to return to Maine where our ancestors had lived for hundreds of years and where my roots sank deep into the rocky, hardscrabble soil. So, I telephoned my remaining living grandparent—my maternal grandmother, Winona (Young) Palmer—and boldly asked if I could move in with her.

Winona ("Nonie" to us grandkids) resided in the dignified brick house in Norway in which she had been born and lived most of her life. Our family life and that of our relatives had for generations centered around this historic home. We had been told as children by our mother (and others) that the house and land had been in our family for nearly two hundred years. As a child I heard about our original ancestor, Ephraim Crockett, Jr., for whom the Crockett Ridge Road was named, and who had settled the land with his wife Sarah "Sally" Wentworth in 1814.[1]

I was twenty-one when I arrived on Winona's doorstep from California with boxes of books, some juvenile scribblings, and a strong desire to return to the state of my birth to make a new life for myself as a Maine writer. Winona was seventy-two, a retired supervisor of elementary education, former school teacher, and used to living alone. By then, so was I.

I never asked Winona why she allowed me to move in with her. (I was not her

---
1. Ephraim first purchased the land in 1812.

favorite grandchild.) Whatever my grandmother's reasoning, her risk paid off and after a few rough patches we settled into a comfortable groove. Winona cooked for both of us (Bakewell Cream biscuits, roast chicken, raspberry and strawberry-rhubarb pies, and fudge). I would have gained twenty pounds that first year had I not been kept busy around the homestead, mowing lawns and hand trimming, stacking wood, scraping and painting woodwork, and basically doing all the odd jobs and chores on Winona's "To Do" list. Weekends, we played cards with my childhood playmate, Pam (Young) Williams, Winona's niece, who with her husband Lloyd lived next door on another piece of old family land. It was a good life.

My favorite hours with my grandmother were those Winona and I spent revisiting the history of our family on Crockett's Ridge. On slow summer afternoons, when the scent of hay was in the air and the leaves on the trees barely moved, Winona, like a proud museum director, ushered me around the house showing off all the treasures and antiques from prior generations. She introduced me to the ancestors whose photographs hung on the walls, and, later, when tuckered out and wanting to retire to the couch, she gave me the green light to peruse the ancient books in the bookcases, including the prized Wentworth Genealogy (Ephraim Crockett's wife Sally was a Wentworth) and encouraged me to delve into the built-in drawers in the upstairs landing where hundreds (if not thousands) of old family letters had accumulated over the past century and a half. Likewise, on snowy winter days when we were house-bound Winona had me drag out boxes of old photographs and we went through them together one by one, Nonie explaining who each person was and his or her connection to the family. Best of all, after dinner or while driving around the backroads of Norway to admire the fall foliage, Winona regaled me with endless family stories, some of which turned out to be very personal in nature. I never forgot them.

So enthralled was I by what I learned that first year living with my grandmother, I wrote a twenty-page Crockett family history, *It All Began with Ephraim*. The little booklet, which I had photocopied and presented to Winona and her descendants in 1979, included Crockett genealogy, historical research, family recipes, stories, and more. Winona and I had fun working together to collect the source material and the recipes for *Ephraim*. (See "Family Recipes and Remedies" in the back of the book.) I also spent many enjoyable hours at the Oxford County Registry of Deeds researching old land records.

Introduction

Unfortunately, some of the facts in my little family history have proved over the years to be inaccurate. Now, forty-six years later, it is time to correct the record. In addition, my longing to know *more* about our ancestors on Crockett's Ridge—where they themselves came from, who their ancestors were—borders on an obsession as I find myself approaching the age my grandmother was when, in 1978, I picked up the phone from my home in California and dialed the old standard number—Pilgrim 3, 2882[2]—and asked Winona if I could move in with her.

My grandmother passed away in 1993 and my mother built a new home upon thirty-four acres of family land her mother willed her. Mom died in 2017, and her home and land are now in a family trust for the benefit of her children, grandchildren, and great-grandchildren. In addition, in the spring of 2019, I purchased eleven acres of land that had become separated from the original Crockett purchase—in fact, the ridge of land for which Crockett's Ridge was named. Not long after acquiring the property I wryly realized that I did not own the land—the land owned me. I had unconsciously developed a sense of love and obligation for this land during the fifteen years I resided off-and-on with my grandmother. I suspect now Winona knew exactly what she was doing on that fateful day in 1978 when she allowed that, yes, I could move in with her!

Today I offer this updated family history to the descendants of Ephraim and Sally Crockett, as well as to other interested parties. Although our family can lay claim to no particular fame, the Crocketts in Maine represent the ordinary men and women who flocked to the New World in the 17th century seeking opportunity and land; who fought the Native Americans, the French, the British, and the Great Proprietors for that land; who settled the backcountry of Maine, in Pejepscot and on Lee's Grant in Norway; and who voted to separate from Massachusetts, becoming the twenty-third state in the Union. The fact that much of the land Ephraim Crockett, Jr. and the extended family purchased in Norway has remained in the family for more than two hundred years speaks to the strength of our ancestors' love for this land which they passed down to us.

My brother Bill, when informed of this new history, bade me: "Don't make it boring, Jennifer." As a result, I wrote my history so the story can be read on two levels. The first level is the regular text, which I tried to make as interesting as possible without delving too far into the historical weeds. For those who like fishing in the

---

2. The old telephone number is still in the family.

pickerel weeds, however, the footnotes that run with the text offer a second, deeper level of information and understanding. If I had to recommend the best way to read this history, I would recommend reading the top text first and then re-reading the entire history, regular text and running footnotes together.

I hope that my history proves not only informative and interesting, but also provides a living link to the past for us Crockett and Young descendants. I would especially like to know that my work helps my nephews and nieces (and someday their children)—as well as the offspring of my Young cousins—to become even more connected to our family land in Norway.

Finally, although I have done due diligence in this history, I realize that over time, and with the development of new technologies (such as genetic testing and the online availability of original sources) new information regarding the Crockett family will come to light. The thought of new discoveries inspires and excites me, and I hope it will inspire and excite the family historian(s) of the next generation. Whoever you are—rise up and correct my mistakes (and there will be mistakes), and carry on!

Jennifer Wixson
Patriot's Day, April 19, 2024
Troy and Norway, Maine

List of Photographs, Maps, Postcards, Deeds, and Illustrations

Chapter 1 – The Settlement of Norway, Maine, and Lee's Grant
Stationery marketing flier for Norway, Maine published by the Board of Trade, 1928.   xxvi
Photo from back of Norway marketing stationery, published by the Board of Trade, 1928.   4
NORWAY, MAINE: Map of 18th Century Land Grants and Purchases.   6
Sketch of Arthur Lee.   10
1785 diagram of the survey of Lee's Grant executed by Amos Davis.   13
Partial plan of Lee's Grant, executed around 1812 by Maine surveyor Alexander Greenwood, assisted by Norway residents Joshua Smith and Uriah Holt.   21
Art postcard, "Pasture Birches, Norway, Me."   27

Chapter 2 – Ephraim Crockett, Jr. and Sally (Wentworth) Crockett
Ephraim Crockett, Jr., 1788-1856.   28
Sarah "Sally" Bartlett (Wentworth) Crockett, 1794–1875.   28
Direct Descendants of Thomas Crockett.   31
Colorized postcard, "Head of Lake Pennesseewassee from Crocketts Ledge, Norway, Me."   32
Order for payment to Ephraim Crockett for labor done on a bridge near James Wagg's dated February 13, 1808.   35
Warranty deed from Edward Little to Ephraim Crockett, Jr. and Josiah Hill, Jr. for Lot 45 in Lee's Grant.   38
Lot 45 in Lee's Grant, purchased by Ephraim Crockett and Josiah Hill, December 26, 1812.   39
Colorized postcard, "Scene near NORWAY LAKE, ME."   41
Authorization by Pejepscot Selectmen to reimburse Samuel S. Wentworth $3.08 for "paying the interest on John Nevens order." December 15, 1800.   46
Authorization by Pejepscot assessors Benning Wentworth and John Witham to reimburse Samuel S. Wentworth $42.04 for paying the town's fine for "not being provided with military stors [sic] as the law directs." February 11, 1809.   46
Stone wall on Ephraim Crockett's land on Crockett's Ridge.   56
Stone wall separating the adjoining properties of Ephraim Crockett and Nathan Morse on Lot 45.   60
Lee's Grant map, Crockett and Morse holdings on Lot 45 and Lot 30 in 1828.   61
Lee's Grant map, Crockett and Morse split their joint property in 1833.   62
Iron pipe in the woods next to the Cross Road. This pipe marked the southeast corner of the Crockett-Morse line when the two men split the south half of Lot 30.   63
Straight up-and-down sash saw marks on board in the shed attached to the old Crockett homestead.   66
Circular saw marks on board in the shed attached to the old Crockett homestead.   67
Colorized postcard, "A New England Road."   77
Ephraim and Sally (Wentworth) Crockett in their later years.   81

Chapter 3 – The Crocketts and the Penleys
"Maine Logging Camp and Saw Mill near Norway, Me."   82
John Penley, Sr.   88

Genealogy Chart - Crockett-Penley Marriages in the 2nd Norway Generation. 93
Lee's Grant lot map showing some of Charles Penley's real estate purchases. 96
Cartoon published during the 1839 Maine-New Brunswick boundary dispute between the United States and Great Britain. 99
Locket tintypes of Ephraim Stanford Crockett and Sally (Penley) Crockett. 104
1846 Lee's Grant lot map showing the location of the Crocketts, Penleys, and Nathan and Mary (Crockett) Morse. 107
Portland businessman Joshua Richardson. 112
Hannah Jordan Crockett 113
Lee's Grant lot map updated to 1850. 118
The cellar hole from the home of John and Betsey (Crockett) Penley, on the south half of Lot 44. 119
Second-generation brick house built in 1850 by William Robinson Crockett and his father. 122
The old Crockett homestead; photo circa 1980, 122
2021 restoration work at the old Crockett homestead. 123
One of my mysterious friends from a summer long, long ago. 127
Three Civil War Soldiers from Norway. 135
No longer a carefree young girl, Hannah Jordan (Crockett) Richardson. 145
Logging right-of-way off the Needham Road, Norway, Maine. 148
Colorized postcard, "Crockett's Bridge, Lake Pennesseewassee, Norway, ME." 149
Trees reflected in the Mill Pond at the site of the former North Pond Dam. 150
Remnant of North Pond Dam where Col. Millett's sawmill (formerly belonging to William Foye) was located. 151
Colorized postcard, "Boat Landing, Lake Pennesseewassee, Norway, Me." 154
Lee's Grant Lot Map updated to 1882, the year of William Robinson Crockett's death. 160
Burial plot of Ephraim Stanford and Sally (Penley) Crockett and family at Norway Pine Grove Cemetery. 162
Original Victorian archway entrance to Norway Pine Grove Cemetery. 164
Adjoining gravestones of William Robinson Crockett and Lydia (Stetson) Crockett. 168
Original gravestone of Ephraim Crockett, Jr. 169

Chapter 4 – Emma Tuell (Crockett) Young Harding – Last Crockett Standing
Emma Tuell (Crockett) Young Harding 170
Lee's Grant map updated to 1874 when Emma Crockett was fifteen, showing the cocoon of family surrounding her. 174
Julia Ann and Edwina Maud Richardson, studio portrait. 178
Tannery of John L. Horne and Horne's Main Street, Norway, residence. 179
"Bottoming Room in Factory of B.F. Spinney & Company, Lynn, Mass." 181
Employees at the newly-open B.F. Spinney shoe factory in Norway, Maine, summer 1873. 185
George P. Young circa 1880. 186
B.F. Spinney employees of the cutting room, 1880. 196
Summary of the divorce record of Martha W. Young and George P. Young. 197
Postcard, "Steep Falls, Norway, ME." 204
Hannah Jordan (Crockett) Richardson Harris, circa 1895–1900 208
Possible photo of Emma Tuell (Crockett) Young in her bridal veil. 209
Close-up of an 1880 Norway Village map showing Danforth and Main Streets. 210
Envelope and letterhead from Fair View Farm, Geo. P. Young, Proprietor. 214

List of Photographs, Maps, Postcards, Deeds, and Illustrations

First two shares of the Norway Shoe Shop Company stock issued January 2, 1886, to E.G. Allen.	223
Colorized postcard, "B.F. Spinney & Co., Shoe Factory, Norway, Me."	223
George P. Young in his International Order of Odd Fellows Encampment regalia.	225
Freelan O. Stanley, circa. 1910.	230
Francis E. Stanley, circa 1882.	230
Colorful poster announcing the 4th of July Horse Trot, 1889.	233
Close-up of the bottom of the poster with more details, including the name of Geo. P. Young, Secretary.	233
Gray Gables, the Marietta, Georgia home of Warren, Ella, Allie and Louisa Crockett.	235
"Lynn Conflagration No. 2, view from high rock during the progress of the fire, November 26th 1889."	236
Leather trunk belonging to George P. Young, and a look inside the trunk.	241
Fatherless Willie Young with bicycle at his mother's Beal Street home in Norway Village.	249
The Rev. John A. Harding	250
"The Newton Theological Institute."	253
Warren E. Crockett escorts President Roosevelt during his trip to Roswell, Georgia, 1905.	255
Lee's Grant lot map updated to 1900.	260
First Baptist Church of Warner, New Hampshire.	262
Three generations: Emma (Crockett) Young Harding seated and holding Winona Young; Adalade "Addie" (Chaplin) Young (rear left) and Addie's mother Luella (Batchelder) Chaplin (right).	265
Emma's grandchildren circa 1913.	266
Wreaths at Arlington National Cemetery, 2005.	269
(Probably) Abel Stetson Crockett and his sister Emma (Crockett) Young Harding.	270
William Felker and his bride, Lydia "Frances" (Crockett) Felker.	271
Emma (Crockett) Young Harding holding her great-granddaughter, Rowena Mae Palmer.	273

Chapter 5 – Bill and Addie (Chaplin) Young

L. Adalade Chaplin and William Foss Young	278
Adalade L. Chaplin's graduation photo from Western State Normal and Training School, 1903.	280
Addie in her wedding dress and the wedding book of Addie (Chaplin) and Bill Young.	281
Willis B. Chaplin and horse.	287
Willis and Luella (Batchelder) Chaplin.	289
Addie with Bill's team of horses.	291
Addie with the family dog on the granite steps of the old Crockett homestead.	291
Bill's cows in the cow lane, headed down to pasture.	292
William F. Young carves a piece of wood in the kitchen of the old Crockett homestead, accompanied by his son, George Willis Young.	293
George Willis and Winona Young	294
Willard Harding Young	294
Albert and Sarah (Penley) Farnham and family.	295
Norway, Maine postcard, "Storm of '07."	297
Fair View Jersey Farm - new barn, circa 1920.	298
The Heywood Club and some of the attendees at the dedication of the new clubhouse July 10, 1907.	301

Poetic invitation to the Heywood Club's 1924 Christmas party and a copy of the menu.	302
Doing chores on the farm circa 1917.	303
Addie and her chickens (and German shepherd) circa 1920.	304
"Aunt Frances." Lydia Frances (Crockett) Felker.	305
The Young family, circa 1922 or 1923.	306
Luella (Batchelder) Chaplin in later years.	309
A visit from the Hobbs family, circa 1932.	311
Neighborhood Christmas dance held in Mellie Dunham's barn.	312
Newspaper photo of Mellie Dunham playing for Henry Ford and "'Mellie' Dunham's Fiddlin' Dance Tunes" songbook.	313
Mellie and Emma "Gram" Dunham on the road.	314
Mellie Dunham in later years.	315
Addie and two of the family's German shepherds.	317
Lee's Grant lot map showing the property Bill Young inherited from his mother in 1937.	321
Willard "Bud" Young and his new bride, Lillian (Hilden) Young.	323
Winona Young, Norway High School graduation photo 1925; and UMO Women's Rifle Club members 1926-27, including Winona Young and Hope Craig.	324
Winona (Young) and Bill Palmer on their honeymoon, at Forget-Me-Not train station in Maine.	325
Bill and Addie's grandchildren, part of the fabric of Young's Turkey Farm.	326
Norman Young, and Paula, Kurt and Rowena Palmer.	327
Paula Palmer and Norman Young (with guns) and Kurt Palmer, kneeling, with Charlie the dog.	327
Addie's new turkey grower house, 1937.	328
1937 Portland Press Herald photo and caption about Addie's new grower house.	329
Young's Turkey Farm newspaper ad touting the state turkey tag.	331
August 19, 1939 *Lewiston Daily Sun* article and photo of Kurt Palmer with axe and turkey.	333
Addie holding one of her Black Diamond turkeys.	334
The author's mother Rowena Palmer with some turkey chicks newly-hatched in the incubator.	335
Bill (center, holding pole) and Addie (right) moving a flock of White Hollands with the help of their son George Young (far left) and grandson, Kurt Palmer (center).	335
Newspaper photo, "Day's Getting Near, Feller."	337
Newspaper photo, "It's Crowded Here—Right Now." Turkeys blocking the Crockett Ridge Road, September 4, 1942.	338
Newspaper article featuring Young's Turkey Farm, likely published in the *Norway Advertiser* around 1939 or 1940.	339
Winona (Young) Palmer and an unidentified youth (possibly son Kurt) standing in front of Bill's new farm truck.	341
1944 newspaper clipping from Young's Turkey Farm scrapbook.	342
A selection of Young's Turkey Farm ads from Addie's scrapbook.	343
Shop window poster for Young's Turkey Farm.	343
Bill Young with some of his cows.	344
One of Bill Young's cows with her new calf.	344
Photo from *Norway Advertiser* article on Bill Young's yellow corn for his pigs.	345

List of Photographs, Maps, Postcards, Deeds, and Illustrations

Bill and his team of horses in front of the old Crockett homestead.	346
Newspaper clipping about Bill's team from Young's Turkey Farm scrapbook.	347
"Musings of a Turkey Grower," op-ed piece written by Addie Young in 1947.	350
Norway Board of Selectman 1948.	351
Top of *Portland Press Herald* article showing Addie preparing for the Heywood Club's Annual Patriots' Day Dinner, April 19, 1951.	352
Bill and Addie on their 45th wedding anniversary.	353
Dilling the new well at Young's Turkey Farm, Spring 1950.	355
Page one of the *American Agriculturalist* story by Harry Packard, May 20, 1950.	357
Open House, Young's Turkey Farm, 1954.	358
Willard "Bud" Young carves up a turkey under the supervision of his mother Addie.	359
Lewiston Daily Sun article about the 1950 Open House and Addie's sale of 50 turkeys to Bangor State Hospital.	360
August 1954 newspaper article and photo from the *Norway Advertiser*.	361
Young's Turkey Farm stationery.	362
A TRUE LOVE MATCH: Postcard Addie Young sent to her husband "Billy" while visiting her ailing mother in North Gorham, March 19, 1912.	363
Four Generations: Addie holding her great-granddaughter Cheryl Wixson, summer 1955.	364
Original Plan of Young's Cottage Lots prepared by E.W. Cummings, C.E., June 2, 1956.	366
The author's sister Cheryl Wixson presents a cake to Addie for her 77th birthday in April 1960.	367
Addie with five of her great-grandchildren.	368
Addie and her granddaughter Paula (Palmer) Johnson in Addie's garden of gladiolus.	369
Bill and Addie enjoying a happy moment together.	370
Aerial view of Young's Turkey Farm circa 1950s.	372
Lee's Grant map, updated to 2024.	373

Acknowledgements

The Four Musketeers (left to right): Rowena Palmer, Norman Young, Paula (Palmer) Johnson, and Kurt Palmer. The cousins grew up together on Young's Turkey Farm.	377
Laundry hanging on the clothesline next to the old barn cellar at the Crockett homestead, Norway, Maine.	379

Appendix

1. Mortgage given to Edward Little for Lot 45 in Lee's Grant by Ephraim Crockett, Jr. and Josiah Hill, Jr., December 26, 1812.	382
2. Quit claim deed from Ephraim Crockett, Jr. and Josiah Hill, Jr. transferring Lot 45 back to Edward Little, September 7, 1814.	383
3. Warranty deed from Edward Little for Lot 45 in Lee's Grant given to Ephraim Crockett, Jr. and Nathan Morse, Jr., signed on February 3, 1816 and backdated to September 7, 1814.	384
4. Mortgage given to Edward Little for Lot 45 in Lee's Grant by Ephraim Crockett, Jr. and Nathan Morse, Jr., December 26, 1815.	385
5. Warranty deed from Josiah Little for the south half of Lot 30 in Lee's Grant given to Ephraim Crockett, Jr. and Nathan Morse, Jr., April 28, 1828.	386
6. Service record of Captain John Wentworth in the French and Indian War and American Revolution. Information from: U.S., Sons of the American Revolution Membership Applications, 1889-1970. James Albert Wentworth.	387

7. Release deed from Ephraim Crockett to Nathan Morse, April 16, 1833. — 388
8. Release deed from Nathan Morse to Ephraim Crockett, April 16, 1833. — 389
9. U.S., Selected Federal Census Non-Population Schedules (Agriculture) 1850 for Ephraim Crockett, Jr. (Line 23.) Norway, Maine, July 15, 1850. — 390
10. Warranty deed from Ephraim Crockett to son Nathan Crockett for his homestead farm on Lots 45 and 30 in Lee's Grant, March 12, 1847. — 391
11. Deed of conveyance (p. 1) from Nathan Crockett to Ephraim Crockett promising to care for his parents in their old age or the property reverts to his father, March 12, 1847. — 392
12. Warranty deed from Nathan Crockett to his brother William Robinson Crockett conveying the Crockett homestead and the responsibilities that went with it, April 2, 1848. — 395
13. Last will and testament (p. 1) of William Robinson Crockett, January 12, 1882. Maine Wills & Probate Records, 1584-1999. Volume 19, Page 467. — 396
14. George P. Young's Wildey Encampment membership certificate, IOOF, Norway, Maine, May 1, 1875. — 398
15. Warranty deed from Abbie Jane Tubbs to George P. Young and Emma T. Young for the John Penley farm, June 24, 1885. — 399
16. Ordination certificate (p. 1) for John A. Harding, Norway Baptist Church, April 16, 1896. — 400
17. Warranty deed from Howard A. Knightly to Emma T. Harding for the Isaiah V. Penley farm, December 24, 1900. — 402
18. Abstract of the will of L. Adalade Young, Nov. 22, 1963. — 403

Source Material Abbreviations

Abbreviation	Source
AGENTBOOK	Record book belonging to an agent of Josiah Little, Pejepscot Proprietor, found in the Danville files at the Androscoggin Historical Society, Auburn, Maine.
AHS	Androscoggin Historical Society. Original notes and historical records of Pejepscot (later, Danville) and her early settlers.
ANDHIST	"History of Androscoggin County, Maine, Illustrated." Edited by Georgia Drew Merrill. Boston: W.A. Fergusson & Co., 1891.
ACROD	Androscoggin County Registry of Deeds.
CANDAGE	"Crockett Genealogy 1610-1988; Some Descendants of Thomas and Ann Crockett of Kittery, Maine (with 1990 Addendum)." Charles Samuel Candage. Rockland: Picton Press. Second Printing, with Addendum, July 2000.
CCROD	Cumberland County Registry of Deeds.
CHAPLIN	"John Chaplin (1758-1837) of Rowley, Mass. and Bridgton, ME, His Ancestry and Descendants." Compiled by Milton Ellis and Leola Chaplin Ellis. Self-published. 1948.
CROCKETT	"The Crockett Family of Maine." Compiled and edited by Donna Hopkins Scott. Provo, Utah: BYU Press, 1968.
DEARPARENT	"Dear Parent: A Biography and Letters of Edward Little." Douglas I. Hodgkin. Auburn: Androscoggin Historical Society, 2017.
DESCENDANTS	"Descendants of Richard Crockett," by Dr. Carol P. McCoy, Including Notes of Dr. David Crockett. Self-published, June 2007.
DINGLEY	"The Life and Times of Nelson Dingley, Jr.," Edward Nelson Dingley. Kalamazoo, Michigan: Ihling Bros. & Everard, 1902. Published by subscription.
DURHAM	"History of Durham, Maine." Everett S. Stackpole. Lewiston, Maine: Press of the Lewiston Journal Co., 1899.
GOOLD	"History of Colonel Edmund Phinney's Thirty-first regiment of foot," Nathan Goold, author. Maine Society Sons of the American Revolution. Portland, Maine: Thurston Press, 1896.
LAPHAM	"The History of Norway, Maine – A reprinting of the 1886 edition on the occasion of the town's Bicentennial Year. Including a new foreword by Rev. Donald L. McAllister." William Berry Lapham. Originally published 1886 by Brown Thurston & Co., Publishers, Portland, Maine 1886. Reprint 1986 by New England History Press in collaboration with the Norway, Maine Historical Society.
LEWISTON	"Frontier to Industrial City: Lewiston Town Politics, 1768-1863." Douglas I. Hodgkin. Topsham, Maine: Just Write Books, Topsham, 2008.
LIBBYNOYES	"Genealogical Dictionary of Maine and New Hampshire." Sybil Noyes, Charles Thornton Libby, and Walter Goodwin Davis. Baltimore: Genealogical Publishing Company, 1928.

---

3. See also Bibliography located at the end of the book for other resources.

LITTLE	"Genealogical and Family History of the STATE OF MAINE," Compiled under the editorial supervision of George Thomas Little, A.M., Litt.D. Little Family. New York: Lewis Historical Publishing Company, 1909.
MASSMILITIA	"Massachusetts Volunteer Militia, Called out by the Governor of Massachusetts to suppress a threatened invasion during the War of 1812-14." Brigadier General Gardner W. Pearson, The Adjutant General of Massachusetts, by a Resolve of the General Court. Original published 1913. Reprint, Baltimore: Clearfield Company, Inc. by Genealogical Publishing Company, 1993.
MEMORIESTIES	"Bound By Memories Ties: A Pictorial History of Norway, Maine." Don A. McAllister. Norway: Twin Town Graphics, 1988.
NHS	Norway, Maine Historical Society. Various genealogies, histories, maps, and other records.
NORWAY40s	"Norway in the Forties." Osgood N. Bradbury. A compilation of stories and newspaper articles written in the 19th century by Dr. Osgood N. Bradbury. Edited by Don L. McCallister. Norway: Twin Town Graphics, 1986.
NOYES	"The History of Norway: Comprising a Minute Account of Its First Settlements, Town Officers, the Annual Expenditures of the Town, with Other Statistical Matters; Interspersed with Historical Sketches and Anecdote, and Occasional Remarks by the Author." David Noyes. Published by the Author, 1852.
OCROD	Oxford County Registry of Deeds.
PENLEY	"Study of the Penley Family." Unknown author who garnered his or her information from Mrs. Harriet J. Ross, the great-great granddaughter of Joseph Penley. Androscoggin Historical Society, Penley genealogy papers.
SETTLERS	"The Settlers of Crockett Ridge." Magazine article by C.F. Whitman, published in the Lewiston Journal, Illustrated Magazine Section. Unknown date.
STARBIRD	Various genealogies of Danville families assembled by historian Charles Starbird, currently in the possession of the Androscoggin Historical Society.
SUMNER	"Centennial History of the town of Sumner, 1798-1898." Charles Handy. West Sumner: Charles Handy, Jr., Publisher, 1899.
WENTWORTH	"The Wentworth Genealogy: English and American." John Wentworth, LL.D. Boston: Little, Brown, and Company, 1878. Three volumes.
WHITMAN	"A History of Norway, Maine, from the Earliest Settlements to the Close of the Year 1922." Charles F. Whitman. Lewiston: Lewiston Journal Company, 1924.
WRIGHT	"Notes and Documents: Norway, Maine." Norwegian-American Studies, Vol. XV. Walter W. Wright p. 219.

NEARLY a century and a half ago five men came to what now is Norway, Maine, and looked on the island-dotted lake, the encircling hills and grand background of mountains, and heard the wind at its eternal business of trying to relate ancient mysteries to the pines towering above their camp. They sent out word this was a beautiful place for home-makers. Families came by ox-team and horse-back. Their children's children's children have found Norway good to live in.

The deeply rutted roads are of the past. Today you travel the town's shaded streets on the smoothest pavement in Maine, or New England. All conditions which made for hardships are gone. But Lake Pennesseewassee is as beautiful to day as when first seen by a white man; and the meadow streams are as fair, and the wind is still trying to tell secrets to the pines. There is no locale in all the wonderful Oxford County Hills more graciously favored by Nature. Woods and hills, sky and water, are as they were in 1786. Those who have heard the call of this ideal vacation land come back year after year. An invitation is now extended to you who are strangers to it. Come.

This Stationery Published 1928, by The Board of Trade, Norway, Maine

Stationery marketing flier for Norway, Maine published by the Board of Trade, 1928.
(Stationery in the author's possession.)

Chapter 1

THE SETTLEMENT OF NORWAY, MAINE, AND LEE'S GRANT

In 1812, twenty-four-year-old Ephraim Crockett, Jr. left his parent's home in Danville and ventured about thirty-five miles northwest to a largely unsettled 6,000-acre tract of land known as Lee's Grant, a part of Norway, District of Maine. Ephraim might have been in the company of Edward Little, a land speculator who owned Lee's Grant and was selling 100-acre lots there. Ephraim, a second son, was in search of a good place to build a homestead and raise a family. (He would marry Sally Wentworth of Danville the following spring.) What he saw during his trip to Lee's Grant Ephraim found agreeable. The day after Christmas in 1812, Edward Little drew up a deed of sale for Lot 45 on Lee's Grant to Ephraim Crockett, Jr. and Josiah Hill, Jr. (Hill would later back out.) From 1812 until this day, much of the land on what came to be known as Crockett's Ridge in Norway—which Ephraim and other members of his family purchased over the years—has remained in our extended family. This book tells the story of how that came to be.

In our family history, we will explore the lives of Ephraim and Sally Crockett (my 4th great-grandparents). We will then follow their descendants down through four more generations, ending with their great-grandson William "Bill" Young and his wife Addie, who operated a turkey farm on the old Lot 45. Bill's mother Emma was the last Crockett bearing the name to live on Crockett's Ridge. Before we begin our tale, however, we will need to take a slight detour to learn the history of the settlement of Norway and establishment of Lee's Grant.

The Settlement of Norway

Quaint as is the story told by the 1928 marketing flier (opposite page) about the 1786 settlement of Norway, the reality was quite different. Those five early-comers to the area who "looked on the island-dotted lake, the encircling hills and grand background of the mountains" had no legal title to the land they claimed. The five men might have enjoyed listening "to the wind at its eternal business of trying to relate ancient mysteries to the pines towering above their camp," but they did so with shifting sands beneath their feet. Ownership of this unappropriated land in the District of Maine (part of Massachusetts) had yet to be finalized by the time of their arrival. Fortunately for them, four of the five original settlers to the Norway area—Joseph Stevens,[1] Jonas Stevens,[2] Amos Hobbs,[3] and Jeremiah Hobbs[4]—were later able to purchase their land from the wealthy men who secured title to large tracts of real estate from the Commonwealth of Massachusetts. George Lessley, a Revolutionary War veteran, never obtained fee simple title to his property, although his sons appear to have done so after his death in 1800.[5]

Even before the Revolutionary War ended, thousands of settlers—many of them Revolutionary War veterans like George Lessley and our ancestor Ephraim Crockett, Sr. (Ephraim, Jr.'s father, who settled on the Pejepscot Claim, now Auburn)—began flocking into the backcountry of Maine, looking for land. Massachusetts, as well as the Continental Congress, created this land rush by promising bounty land to soldiers. On September 16, 1776, the Continental Congress offered a 100-acre bounty to soldiers who enlisted (or reenlisted) for a period of three years.[6] In 1779, Massachusetts also promised 100 acres of land to her soldiers for three years of

---

1. On December 7, 1789 Joseph Stevens purchased Lot 20 in "a New Plantation called Rustfield" from Henry Rust, a wealthy merchant from Salem, Massachusetts. Stevens paid twenty pounds and two shillings for the lot, which was 120 acres. CCROD Book 16, Page 548.
2. On January 2, 1792 Jonas Stevens purchased Lot 19 from Henry Rust, which contained 137 acres in Rustfield. Jonas paid twenty-three pounds, fifteen shillings and five pence. CCROD Book 18, Page 438.
3. On January 2, 1792 Amos Hobbs purchased Lot 21 from Henry Rust, which contained 133 acres in Rustfield. Hobbs paid twenty-two pounds, nineteen shillings and five pence. CCROD Book 18, Page 439.
4. On September 18, 1794 Jeremiah Hobbs purchased from Jonathan Cummings, a blacksmith from Andover, Massachusetts, Lot 1 in the Second Division of "a new Plantation called Cummings Grant." Jeremiah paid Cummings fifteen pounds for 100 acres. CCROD Book 27, Page 367.
5. I can find no evidence in the Cumberland County Registry of Deeds that George Lessley made a land purchase in the Norway area from 1780 to 1800. According to Norway historian Charles F. Whitman (WHITMAN, p. 27) Lessley, a Revolutionary War veteran, died in 1800. His two sons, Amasa and George, lived on the home place and appear to have purchased the property from Jonathan Cummings in 1806 and 1808. See OCROD Book 2, Page 416; Book 3, Page 305; Book 3, Page 308; and Book 5, Page 84.
6. A Resolve passed by Congress later that year, on October 6, 1776, also gave the army a pay-raise and a combined clothing-cash bounty of $40. Enlisted men would receive $6.67 per month for salary, plus $20 in scrip (which would be worthless before the end of the war), and $20 worth of clothing, including "two linen hunting-shirts, two pair of stockings, two pair shoes, one pair breeches, one waistcoat, two pairs of overalls, two shirts, and one leather cap or hat, amounting in the whole to twenty dollars..." GOOLD.

service.[7] When the war concluded (or the men's three years were up) these veterans, many of them landless younger sons, were understandably anxious to claim their bounties. In addition, the Commonwealth briefly offered free land to settlers who would help create new townships in the undeveloped backcountry. This offer of free land did not last long, however. Massachusetts quickly realized that it was a lot smarter to replenish a treasury drained by years of fighting the British by selling large tracts of unappropriated real estate in Maine to investors of means (and consequence) rather than to give or sell small amounts of land to individual settlers. (To say nothing about the accounting logistics of selling small lots of land to thousands of individuals.) According to Norway historian Charles F. Whitman, Massachusetts was left with an enormous debt—$5,000,000—at the end of the Revolutionary War.[8]

After the Revolution, the Commonwealth doled out large tracts of Maine land like real estate cards from the board game Monopoly to important military men and statesmen for their services (including for services during the earlier French and Indian War). The Massachusetts legislature also presented grants of land to preparatory schools in order that the sons of the privileged might be prepared for college (and, one assumes, prepared to take their place in the formation of a new nation). Massachusetts schools that received these grants hired land managers to sell lots of Maine land to the less privileged (many of whom were veterans) who flooded the District seeking a better life for themselves and their families. While our story revolves around one of those grants of land—Lee's Grant, upon which Ephraim Crockett, Jr. and his family settled—this grant was only one of many cards in the Monopoly deck dealt out by Massachusetts from 1780 to 1800.

The town of Norway began its life after the last of the indigenous peoples had decamped to Canada following 1763, the conclusion of the French and Indian War (the last of the four bloody French and Indian wars spanning nearly a century in Maine). In the beginning, the town consisted of a loose web of white settlements upon four large tracts of land that surrounded and encompassed Lake Pennesseewassee.

---

7. "Settling Oxford County: Maine's Revolutionary War Bounty Myth." Jean F. Hankins, Otisfield Historical Society. *Maine History*. Vol. 2, No. 3. October 1, 2005. P. 141. (Via DigitalCommons@UMaine.)
8. I have lost the Whitman reference; however, Jean Hankins of the Otisfield Historical Society also concurs with his estimation that Massachusetts was $5 million in debt at the end of the Revolutionary War. She also points out that the Commonwealth was responsible for its share of the national debt, as well. "Settling Oxford County: Maine's Revolutionary War Bounty Myth." Jean F. Hankins, Otisfield Historical Society. *Maine History*. Vol. 2, No. 3. October 1, 2005. P. 141.

Photo from back of Norway marketing stationery, published by the Board of Trade, 1928.

The four large tracts that later became the town of Norway were: Rust's Purchase, Cummings Purchases (1st and 2nd), Waterford Three Tiers, and Lee's Grant. (See map on page 6 for these four grants/purchases.) Excepting Waterford Three Tiers, the tracts were owned by wealthy men, none of whom lived in Maine.

Charles Whitman goes to great lengths in his history of Norway to prove that the original settlers to the area—including Jonas and Joseph Stevens, and Amos and Jeremiah Hobbs—were not squatters. (He disliked the word "squatter," objecting to the negative connotations the word implies.) Whitman states that these men had made prior arrangements to legally purchase their homesteads from a man named James Stinchfield of Gray.[9] The latter apparently planned to buy a large tract of land on Lake Pennesseewassee and settle families from Gray and New Gloucester there, reselling lots to them.

Whitman's attempt to put a floor under the shifting sands glosses over the fluidity of land ownership in Maine and the capriciousness of the General Court of Massachusetts when it came to land affairs in the District. As it turned out, Stinchfield did not buy the land from Massachusetts as planned. Instead, Captain Henry Rust, a wealthy merchant from Salem, Massachusetts, on February 7, 1787,

---

9. WHITMAN, p. 24-26. The fifth settler, George Lessley, a Revolutionary War veteran, most likely intended to gain title to his land directly from the Commonwealth for his service in the war.

purchased 6,000 acres that included Stinchfield's piece. Rust made the purchase from "a Committee appointed by the General Court of the Commonwealth of Massachusetts, by their Resolves of October 17, 1783, and November 6, 1786 … to sell and dispose of the unappropriated Land of this Commonwealth."[10] Captain Rust, the proprietor of what became known as Rust's Purchase or Rustfield, was instrumental in creating what would become the backbone of the town of Norway. For his 6,000 acres Rust paid "the sum of four hundred and fifty Pounds in Securities of this Commonwealth." Nearly three years after his purchase, Rust signed on December 9, 1789, eight deeds[11] to men who were already living "on a new plantation called Rustfield," including James Stinchfield, to whom he sold 234 acres.

---

10. CCROD, Book 15, Page 447.
11. CCROD, Book 16, Pages 545, 546, 548, 549, 550, and 552. The eight men were: James Stinchfield, Jonathan Abbott, John Parsons, Joseph Stevens, William Parsons, Dudley Pike, Nathan Noble, and Samuel Ames.

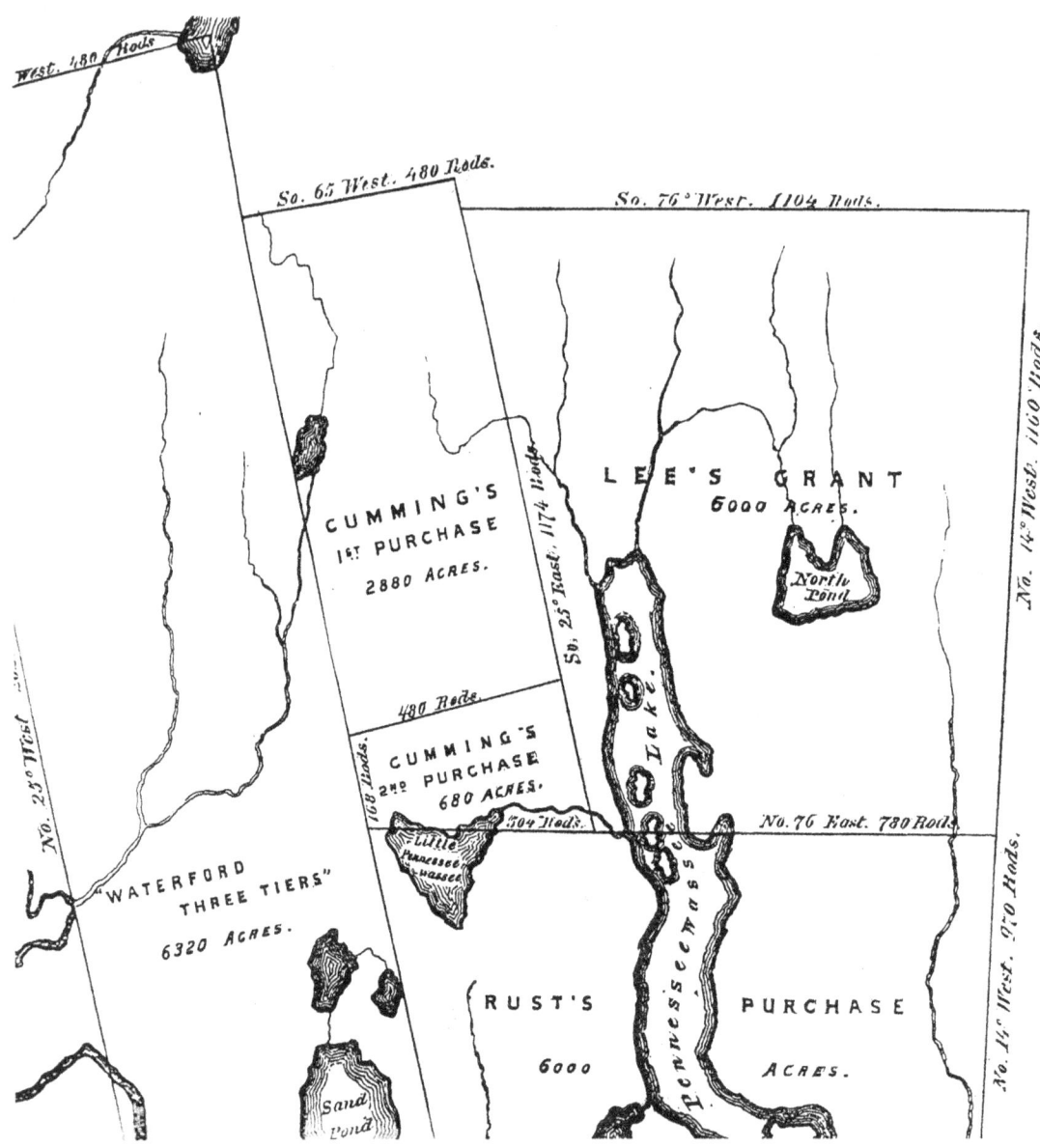

NORWAY, MAINE: Map of 18th Century Land Grants and Purchases.
(Map courtesy of the Norway, Maine Historical Society.)

The next active proprietor of the four tracts later comprising the town of Norway was Jonathan Cummings, who, it is noted in his deed from the Commonwealth, was a blacksmith from Andover, Massachusetts. Cummings appears to have been quite a successful blacksmith because he had pockets deep enough to make two purchases of Maine land. On August 7, 1788, Cummings paid £540 for 2,880 acres from the same Committee appointed to "dispose of" unappropriated land in Maine (his so-called "1st Purchase"), and on April 10, 1790, he bought for £119, 680 acres (his "2nd Purchase").[12] Cummings began selling lots on his tracts April 13, 1790.[13] Jeremiah Hobbs, who was already living on what became Cummings 2nd Purchase, did not buy his lot until 1794, which suggests that there was certainly no prior arrangement between Hobbs and Cummings.[14] George Lessley, as previously mentioned, died without completing a purchase from Cummings.

The story behind Waterford Three Tiers has an interesting twist. This grant for a six-square-mile piece of unappropriated land situated "between the Connecticut and Merrick Rivers" was given in 1735 by the General Court of Massachusetts to some settlers who were "sufferers in the Indian wars."[15] The new township was supposed to be on Commonwealth land; however, Whitman says that after "considerable expense," including money spent on building roads and mills, "it was ascertained that the grant was within the boundaries of New Hampshire."[16] Oops! The group was then given land for a township on unappropriated lands in Maine, which grant came to be known as Waterford Plantation. A survey was run that determined some of the land was in Cumberland County and some in York County. When settlers were ready to petition the Massachusetts legislature for a township, Whitman reports that there was a controversy over the location of a meeting house, which controversy was settled by agreeing to have three ranges or "tiers" of lots—in total 6,320 acres—annexed to Cummings Purchase.[17]

Lee's Grant was the fourth large tract that later became a part of the town of Norway. We will cover the story of Lee's Grant in depth in a bit.

In 1797, settlers on these four tracts—Rustfield, Cummings 1st and 2nd Purchases, Waterford Three Tiers, and Lee's Grant—banded together and petitioned

---

12. CCROD, Book 17, Pages 332 and 333.
13. CCROD, Book 18, Page 86.
14. CCROD, Book 27, Page 367. Whitman claims that Hobbs believed he was settling on the Rust/Stinchfield parcel.
15. WHITMAN, p. 56.
16. WHITMAN, p. 56.
17. WHITMAN, p. 56.

the Massachusetts General Court to incorporate as a new town. They asked the Legislature to have the town named "Norage," a Native American word that translates to "falls" in English. (Steep Falls was situated at the lower end of Norway village, and according to Whitman: "These falls at that period, presented the most striking feature in all the country round about, particularly at a freshet of water.")[18] The Massachusetts General Court, possibly thinking the settlers could not spell correctly, changed the name to "Norway" since the practice of copying European country names (i.e. Paris, Poland, and Naples) for new towns was common at the time.[19] This is how the town of Norway, Maine came to be.

The Story of Lee's Grant

When I was a child, I was fascinated by the story I was proudly told by various relatives of my mother (including my grandmother Winona) that our family land in Norway had been given as a grant from the King of England. Not being historically-inclined at that point, I assumed this grant was given by the King to our ancestor Ephraim Crockett, Jr, for whom Crockett's Ridge in Norway was named. In my early twenties, when I moved in with my grandmother, she showed me what we both believed was the original old land grant deed/map.[20] Winona kept the tattered ancient paper in the "gun closet," an alcove situated between the chimneys in the living room and parlor in the brick homestead, where old guns and other family artifacts and treasures were stored. (Winona told me the document had been kept in the gun closet for more than a century.)

Compelling as that story is, it is nevertheless just that—a story. Rather than being a grant to our ancestor Ephraim Crockett, Jr., the lot our family settled was purchased by Ephraim from a land speculator, who himself had bought Lee's Grant from descendants of the original grantee. The grantor was not the King of England, either. Quite the opposite! The grantor was the Commonwealth of Massachusetts, who in 1780 awarded 6,000 acres of land in the District of Maine to the

---

18. WHITMAN, p. 67.
19. LAPHAM, p. 44 and WRIGHT, p. 219, suggest the name "Norage" or "The Falls" was because of the falls between the outlet of Pennesseewassee Lake and Pennesseewassee Stream. In my opinion, Norage is a much nicer name than Norway, although it was popular at the time to name towns after European countries that had recently thrown off the yoke of tyranny. Most likely this is what the Massachusetts General Court assumed the settlers had meant.
20. Now I believe that this old document might have been marketing material, perhaps a map with lots laid out, given to Ephraim Crockett, Jr. by Edward Little, who had purchased Lee's Grant. The map/deed shown me by my grandmother was not the surveyor's plan at the beginning of this chapter, although it might have been similar. Regrettably, the paper seems to have disappeared over the half-century since I saw it.

Honorable Arthur Lee of Virginia for his services as an American diplomat during the Revolutionary War.

When I first discovered the fact that a wealthy Virginian and not our ancestor had received 6,000 acres of land in Maine, I was shocked (and angered), especially since Ephraim's father—Ephraim Crockett, Sr. of Danville—who served three enlistments during the Revolution, had not received one acre of land from Massachusetts as a reward for his services. (In fact, Ephraim, Sr. was sued by the descendants of Tories for the land he settled and improved on the Pejepscot Claim.)[21] My research on Arthur Lee, however, has helped dissipate some (but not all) of that outrage.

Arthur Lee was born in 1740 into the distinguished Lee family of Virginia. (Arthur's brother Francis Lightfoot Lee was one of the signers of the Declaration of Independence.)[22] He was educated in England and Scotland and became first a physician practicing in Williamsburg; however, in 1766, he returned to London and studied law. Like other members of his family at the time, Lee was an opponent of slavery and an advocate for American resistance against the British.[23] In 1764, he wrote *An Essay in Vindication of the Continental Colonies of America*[24] and later produced many letters and pamphlets advocating the American cause under the pseudonyms "Junius" and "Monitor."[25] In 1770, Lee was proposed as an agent of Massachusetts to "bring the grievance of the colony before the King of England."[26] But Benjamin Franklin was chosen instead, with Lee denoted as Franklin's substitute (or demoted to be Franklin's substitute, as Lee felt). (In "A History of Norway, Maine," historian William Lapham goes into detail about Lee's reported dislike and envy of Franklin and his failed attempts to discredit Franklin.) In 1774, Benjamin Franklin left London, and Lee became the sole agent of Massachusetts there.

But by this time, Arthur Lee's seditious writings, although anonymous, had come to the notice of King George, who, according to historian Lapham, wanted to try the successful London attorney for treason. Fortunately for Lee, the Crown

---

21. The story of Ephraim Crockett, Sr. and his early ancestors is told in my upcoming book, "Into the Maine ~ One Maine Family's Quest for Land, 1630-1830." Ephraim, Sr.'s eldest son David eventually paid the descendants of Tories for the 60-acre lot that his father had settled decades earlier.
22. Confederate general Robert E. Lee was also a descendant of this same prominent Virginia family. Arthur Lee was an abolitionist. General Lee, however, obviously was not.
23. Nash, Gary B. 2008. "The Unknown American Revolution." New York: Viking Penguin. p. 114–115.
24. Chisholm, Hugh, ed. 1911. "Lee, Arthur." Encyclopædia Britannica (11th ed.). Cambridge University Press.
25. LAPHAM, p. 16
26. LAPHAM, p. 16

could not uncover enough evidence against him and Arthur Lee escaped a certain death sentence for treason.

In 1776, the Provincial Congress sent Arthur Lee to Paris as a secret agent to drum up support—political and financial—for the American Revolution. Lee was so successful with this effort and other efforts on behalf of the Provincial Congress (he also unmasked the Secretary to the American legation in Paris, Edward Bancroft, as a British spy)[27] that although he was not involved in any of the actual fighting, he was rewarded for his "services to the country" in 1780 with the large tract of land in the District of Maine that came to be known as "Lee's Grant."

Sketch of Arthur Lee.
Sketch from Whitman's "A History of Norway, Maine," p. 50.

It is doubtful that Arthur Lee ever visited the grant of land in Maine that bore his name, and he probably never profited from it, either. For starters, in 1780, when the grant was awarded, nobody knew where Lee's Grant was, the actual location of the tract being vaguely described by the General Court as "Unappropriated land in

---
27. LEE, Arthur (1740-1792). Biographical Dictionary of the U. S. Congress. Retrieved 22 January 2012.

this State lying eastward of Saco River to be laid out either in one or two pieces, adjoining to Some former Grant or Grants."[28] It took five years before the Committee located a parcel of previously unappropriated state land meeting that description.[29] They found Lee's 6,000 acres between the township of Waterford and another 6,000-acre parcel of backcountry land, the purchase of which was at the same time being negotiated by the formerly-mentioned Captain Henry Rust.

In his Norway history, Whitman writes that it would have made more sense because of Arthur Lee's service to the nation for Lee to have been granted the better of the two parcels of 6,000 acres. After all, Rust's acreage (basically the land around the village of Norway and the southern part of the lake) contained better water access for erecting saw and grist mills, necessary to the creation of a proper settlement. But Rust was a member of the Massachusetts legislature—and Lee was from Virginia—and so Lee ended up with the parcel situated north of Rust's, that land mass in the northeast part of what would later become the town of Norway (as well as part of Greenwood and Woodstock).[30] In a Resolve dated November 8, 1785, the General Court finally declared the boundaries of Lee's Grant to be:

> "Beginning at a Certain 'Berch' Tree thence running North fourteen Degrees West one thousand one hundred and sixty Rods to a Spruce Tree, a corner, trees being well marked about it, thence running South Seventy six [degrees] West Eleven hundred and four Rods to a Cedar Tree, a corner, standing on the easterly side of a Township known by the name of Waterford, trees being well marked about said Corner, thence running South Twenty five [degrees] east eleven hundred and seventy five Rods to a large Pine tree, a Corner, thence North Seventy Six [degrees] East Eighty four Rods to a Pond, then Continuing across the Said Pond one hundred and sixty Rods, then Continuing the Same Course five hundred & Thirty six Rods to the Tree first mentioned."[31]

During the actual hostilities with Great Britain, Arthur Lee wisely removed from London back to Virginia (the reverse of the Tories here who fled to Canada or England), where, in 1781, he was elected to the general assembly and later served in the Continental Congress. After the close of the war, he was appointed to a commission

---

28. WHITMAN, p. 49. Whitman says that the grant was made to Arthur Lee by the Massachusetts General Court in 1780 and was "confirmed" to him in 1785.
29. In his 1789 deposition, surveyor Amos Davis of Lewiston says he performed the work for Arthur Lee. OCROD, Book 8, Page 89.
30. WHITMAN, p. 51.
31. Massachusetts State Archives. Resolve of the General Court of Massachusetts, Nov. 8, 1785.

that attempted to obtain a treaty with Native American tribes in the northwestern frontier.[32] Lee was a busy man and, as mentioned, probably never visited his land in the wilderness of Maine, although he did hire a surveyor from Lewiston, Amos Davis, to survey the grant for him. (See diagram of survey on page 13.) According to a deposition given by Davis on June 26, 1789, the surveyor ran the lines of Lee's Grant in 1785, marking the corners (on trees).[33] (Reading Davis' deposition describing in detail which trees were marked, one can see that the boundaries for Lee's Grant noted above were given after this survey was completed.)

In 1790, Lee purchased from Robert Wormeley III a gracious brick home known as Lansdowne, situated in Urbanna, Virginia.[34] Here the elder statesman lived out his few remaining days. Arthur Lee passed away in 1792. He was reportedly buried in the backyard at Lansdowne with no gravestone.[35] Even as shovels of sod fell onto Lee's coffin, settlers were pushing their way onto his 6,000 acres in the backcountry of Maine.

---

32. LAPHAM, p. 17.
33. OCROD, Book 8, Page 89. Davis also noted in that deposition that there was a mile and a half of unappropriated state land between Lee's Grant and the town of Waterford to the west.
34. LEE, Arthur (1740-1792). Biographical Dictionary of the U. S. Congress. Retrieved 22 January 2012..
35. The lack of gravestone was apparently at Lee's request. In 1974, Lee's home, Lansdowne, was listed on the National Register of Historic Places.

The Settlement of Norway, Maine, and Lee's Grant

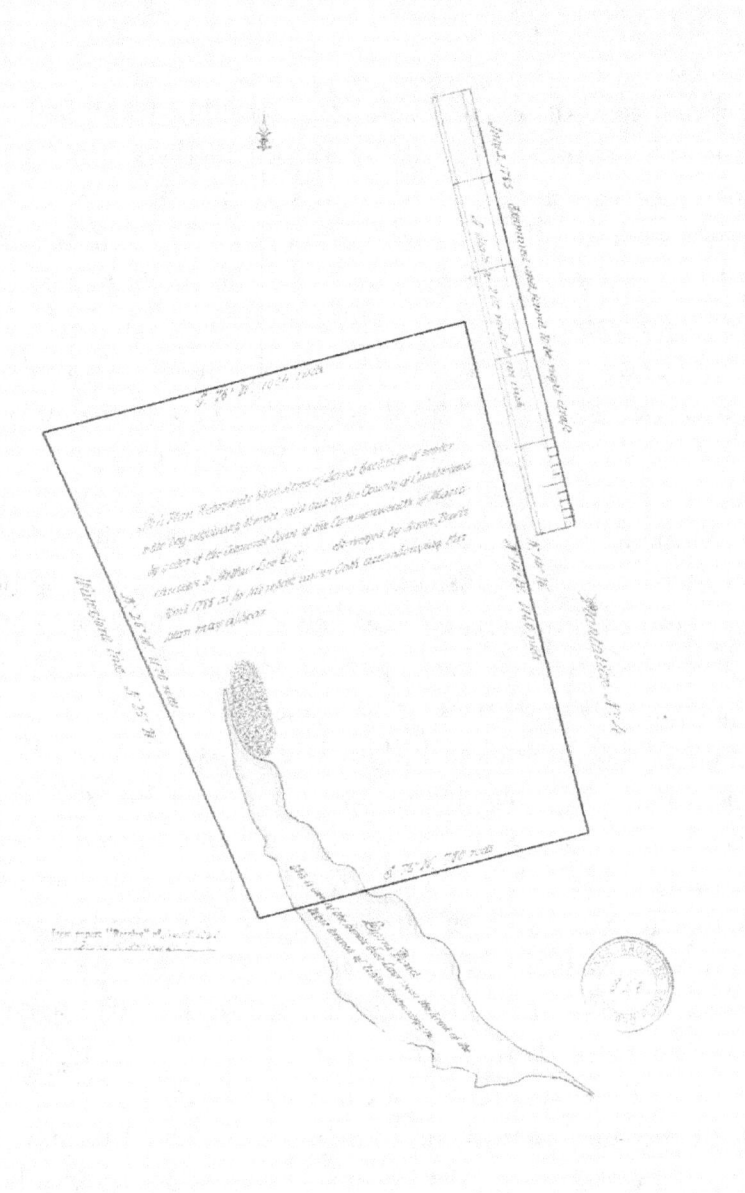

1785 diagram of the survey of Lee's Grant executed by Amos Davis.
Diagram shows Lee's 6,000 acres encompassing the northern half of Lake Pennesseewassee.
Maine State Archives, copied from Massachusetts Archives, Maps and Plans #883.

The Lees and the Little Family

Arthur Lee never married nor had any children. Upon his death, he bequeathed his Maine land grant to his nephew, Francis Lightfoot Lee, the son of Arthur's brother Richard.[36] Francis Lee was a gentleman from Virginia, not a Maine land baron. While he did make a few small attempts to develop Lee's Grant, the attempts were half-hearted at best. At some point prior to 1810 (probably five to ten years earlier), Francis Lee negotiated a bond for a deed with Jacob Tubbs, who had settled on 200 acres of Lee's Grant.[37] The rest of the settlers on Lee's Grant became tenant farmers, likely because the men did not have money enough to make an outright purchase of land (and Francis Lee probably did not want to hold mortgages). As a result, these tenant farmers paid an annual fee to Francis Lee for the lease of their land and were dunned annually for the privilege of improving land they might never own. According to Norway historian Charles Whitman, the settlers' inability to purchase their land freehold created sore feelings, as they "were holding under yearly leases—a very poor and uncertain tenure and one not conducive to much improvements, particularly respecting habitations."[38]

Certainly, compared to the indefatigable Henry Rust, owner of the 6,000 acres to the south of Lee's Grant, Francis Lee's efforts to develop his land were lackluster. The Massachusetts General Court's decision to allocate Captain Rust the better piece of land proved prescient. It was Rust who was responsible for putting in place the framework to which the web of settlements on the four large tracts of land would attach and become the town of Norway.

Rust, when he gained title to his tract, welcomed settlers with open arms—both those settlers who were already there and those who came later to the area. Instead of leasing them land, Rust sold real estate outright at reasonable prices. In addition, Captain Rust provided opportunities for settlers to earn money, paying up to fifty cents per day to workers who helped build his grist and saw mills (situated at the head of Norway Village). That money often went toward the purchase of lots he sold for as little as fifty cents an acre.[39] In other words: "every day's work paid

---

36. LAPHAM, p. 19.
37. OCROD, Book 5, Page 394. This is a release for the bond for a deed, when Francis Lightfoot Lee declares that he has received the entire $1,200 from Jacob Tubbs for the two hundred acres. He also notes that the land has been surveyed and laid out by Aaron Wilkins, who was a housewright in the greater Norway area.
38. WHITMAN, p. 51.
39. Later Norway historian Charles F. Whitman contests Noyes' claim that Rust sold lots for as little as fifty cents per acre. Whitman writes in his Norway history: "The records show that this statement is an error. He [Rust] paid at the rate of thir-

for an acre of land." Captain Rust's goal was to build a town, not to build wealth by indebting the settlers and their offspring. Early Norway historian David Noyes admired Rust and in his book reveals the man's character:

> "Capt. Rust performed many acts of kindness to the settlers on his land, not only by selling his land very cheap, but in trying to add otherwise to their comforts and conveniences. Among other things, he brought down from Salem quite a lot of small six-squared windows of six by eight glass, which he distributed among the settlers, a window or two to each; and this was a valuable present to them, as this was the first glass known in this place."[40]

Settlers, always on the hunt for more land, soon spread out from Rustfield to Lee's Grant on the north. In fact, among the several roads laid out in 1797 by Norway selectmen after the town's incorporation was a road leading from the village up to the height of land at Lee's Grant, where many people were already living.[41]

Somehow, a provision that Lee's Grant should not be taxed for a period of ten years was inserted into the town's 1797 petition for incorporation.[42] Charles Whitman, a later historian than Noyes, is very generous in his history when describing this provision, which preempted Lee's Grant from taxation for at least a decade. Whitman says that the provision was requested "on account presumably of his [Francis Lee] not being ready to take up the matter of its settlement as Captain Rust had done"[43] (which seems a very poor excuse for not taxing someone). But the Massachusetts Legislature, comprised mostly of wealthy, landed men, was inclined to support moneyed landowners. It accepted the included provision, making Lee's Grant exempt from taxation until at least 1807.

Regrettably, the provision for tax exemption ushered in a decade or more of tenant farming on Lee's Grant. Not having any motivation to sell lots (thereby transferring the tax burden to the buyer), Francis Lee, through his agent(s) in the

---

ty-seven and a half cents an acre, reckoning $5.00 to the pound. Money in those times was stated in pounds, shillings and pence. In no case among the records of those examined by the writer [Whitman] did Captain Rust sell any land for less than twice what he paid for it." WHITMAN, p. 28. (Thus, if Rust paid thirty-seven and a half cents per acre, he would have sold it for at least seventy-five cents per acre.) Whitman goes on to conclude in his remarks on Rust's prices: "Captain Rust must have realized a fortune for those times, from his purchase." Clearly, Whitman was not familiar with the $5-$7 per acre that land speculators such as Josiah Little, Edward Little's father, were charging for land in the backcountry of Maine. Compared to the elder Little, Captain Rust's prices were extremely fair and reasonable.
40. NOYES, p. 15-16.
41. WHITMAN, p. 50 and OCROD, Book 5, P. 394. In Francis Lightfoot Lee's deed to Jacob Tubbs, he notes that the road was accepted by Norway at a town meeting held October 25, 1797.
42. WHITMAN, p. 49-50.
43. WHITMAN, p. 49.

area, began negotiating annual leases and collecting rents from the early settlers. According to Whitman, little is known about the period of tenant farming on Lee's Grant. This is because the business transacted on the tract was private, unlike the sale and mortgaging of real estate in Rustfield, which was public. (Property transfers and mortgages were recorded at the Cumberland County Registry of Deeds, until Oxford County was formed in 1805.)[44] The sole exception to tenancy on Lee's Grant seems to have been Jacob Tubbs, the man who settled on 200 acres at the highest point—where the road from the village stopped.[45] Probably because he had money, Tubbs was able to negotiate a bond for a deed with Francis Lee. He agreed to pay $1,200 in three annual installments to Lee for his real estate on Lee's Grant.[46] (Tubbs, therefore, paid $6 per acre for his lot, compared to Henry Rust's $.50-$.75 per acre.) Other than Tubbs, the rest of the settlers on Lee's Grant remained tenant farmers, with no security other than what an annual lease could offer them.

At some point, the wealthy and powerful Little family of Newbury, Massachusetts became involved with the management of Lee's Grant. The most prominent member of the family, Josiah Little, was the father of Edward Little, who sold Lot 45 to Ephraim Crockett. Josiah was the son of Moses Little, a gentleman farmer of Newbury, Massachusetts (enslaved persons performed the actual labor);[47] who in the 18th century was a representative to the General Court and a notorious land speculator. In his early years, Moses was a surveyor of the King's Woods, which opened his eyes to the potential value of backcountry lands.[48] In addition to his Massachusetts real estate, Moses Little invested in large tracts of land in Vermont, New Hampshire, and Maine.[49] After Moses Little's stroke in 1781, Josiah, his eldest surviving son, took over his vast real estate empire.

---

44. The website maineanencyclopedia.com states that the "northern parts of York and Cumberland counties were separated to form Oxford County on March 5, 1805."
45. The road stopped near the old schoolhouse across from the Heywood Club. Bridle paths proceeded from there, according to Whitman.
46. OCROD, Book 5, Page 394. Tubb's 200-acre lot was surveyed in December of 1804 by Aaron Wilkins. On May 7, 1810, Lee released the land to Tubbs for payment of his bond. When Ludlow Lee sold the entire grant to Edward Little in 1812, he excepted the 200 acres that Francis Lee had already sold to Tubbs. OCROD, Box 8, Page 76.
47. LITTLE, p. 5. In 1773, Moses Little sold a slave by the name of "Caesar" to President Eleazar Wheelock of Dartmouth College for twenty pounds. "I have determined to buy the Negro if he proves to be the Slave which you take him to be," Wheelock wrote to Little. According to the Little family historian, most of the leading families of Newbury were slaveholders at that time.
48. LITTLE, p. 4.
49. LITTLE, p. 4. In 1750, thanks to Moses Little's efforts with the Massachusetts General Court, he "succeeded in obtaining for [the proprietors of Bakerstown], a township of land in Maine in exchange for one previously granted and found to be within the borders of New Hampshire." In addition to buying into (and working for) the Pejepscot Proprietors, Little (and his son, Josiah) purchased another large grant of land in Maine, which today is comprised of Poland, Minot, and part of Auburn.

In addition to himself, Josiah's sons Michael and Edward were active in real estate management and speculation in Maine, New Hampshire, and Massachusetts. Michael, the eldest son, was born in 1771. Edward, Josiah's second son, was born in 1773.[50] Both boys graduated from Dartmouth College and became attorneys,[51] which served them in good stead during their land management careers. Edward was also a publisher (specializing in law reports) and a bookseller, who sold stationery, paper, and the like. Without having access to the Lee or Little business records, we cannot know which Little family member collected rents on Lee's Grant for Francis Lee. Considering, however, that all three men—Josiah, Michael, and Edward Little—negotiated real estate transactions in the area, it is reasonable to assume some (or all) of the Littles were involved with Francis Lee.

By 1801, Michael Little was active in nearby Woodstock, then known as Plantation No. 3. Unlike his father who never lived in Maine, Michael was living in Poland as early as 1801.[52] In June of 1802, Michael negotiated a real estate deed of sale[53] for Dummer's Academy of Newbury, Massachusetts, one of the college preparatory schools that received a generous grant from the Massachusetts General Court. The deed Michael negotiated was for the western half of Plantation No. 3.[54] (Those historians who claim that Massachusetts has given more to Maine than vice versa perhaps are not familiar with how much Maine land financed the education of the privileged in the Commonwealth.) Plantation No. 3 abutted Lee's Grant (and Paris, Maine, which was then Plantation No. 4), and it would have been natural for the 6,000-acre Lee's Grant tract to come to the attention of Michael, who, like his father, had become a land speculator. According to the Cumberland County Registry of Deeds, Michael owned real estate in Minot, Poland, and New Gloucester,

---

50. LITTLE, p. 6. When he was twelve, Michael received a gift from his grandfather Moses Little of one hundred acres of land in Baker's Town (a large land grant that included present-day Poland, Minot, Mechanics Falls, and part of Auburn). The gift was "in consideration of his being named Michael to bear up the name of one who late of Newbury (Massachusetts) deceased." (CCROD Book 12, Page 254.) It appears that Michael moved to the Poland-Minot area as early as 1801, when he would have been thirty. (See CCROD Book 36, Page 217.)
51. LITTLE, p. 6. See also CCROD Book 36, Page 217 for Michael's power-of-attorney for his father, Josiah, for a parcel of land in Poland.
52. CCROD, Book 36, Page 217.
53. OCROD, Book 7, Page 121. In this deed Michael Little sells to Daniel Cummings (then of Norway) one hundred acres in Plantation No. 3 for $200.
54. The eastern half of Plantation No. 3 was granted to Gorham Academy by the Massachusetts General Court. See the notice given for non-payment of nonresident taxes for the year 1813, OCROD, Book 12, Page 262A. Gorham Academy in Maine and Dummer's Academy in Massachusetts were two of several preparatory schools to receive grants of land from the General Court. The sale of these lands was to help fund higher education in areas (typically where the affluent lived), where formal education ended around age fourteen. They are called "prep" schools because they prepared the students for colleges, such as Dartmouth.

in addition to the real estate he owned in Woodstock in Oxford County. Michael also managed land in Maine for his father, including some of the Pejepscot Patent.[55]

Edward Little, Josiah's second son, who plays an important role in our family history, also relocated to Maine. He moved to the District after his property at Newburyport was destroyed in "the great fire of 1811."[56] Edward settled first in Portland, where he resumed his law career and continued to publish law reports for the Commonwealth. Edward also set up a bookstore, similar to the one he had operated in Massachusetts, and a circulating library. (The library charged patrons 6¢ for each book they checked out.)[57] Later, in 1826 after Edward Little had taken over most of his father's empire in the Pejepscot Patent, which included mills, logging, farming, and toll bridges in addition to lot sales in Danville, Turner, and other towns, Edward removed with his family to Danville (formerly the town of Pejepscot, and now part of Auburn).[58]

In 2017, Douglas I. Hodgkin, Professor Emeritus of Bates College, and president of the Androscoggin Historical Society, published an excellent book on Edward Little, "Dear Parent: A Biography and Letters of Edward Little."[59] In his book, Dr. Hodgkin states that Edward, who probably would have done fine for himself had he stuck to his law career, entertained romantic and grandiose visions of becoming a wealthy land baron like his father and grandfather before him. These grand visions kept Edward in constant debt. First, he dabbled in the shipping business in Newburyport,[60] which business turned disastrous during the embargo imposed during the War of 1812. (Edward attempted to dig himself out of that debt by selling some of his late father-in-law's real estate.) Land speculation was Edward Little's primary dream, though. He became involved in several real estate deals in Maine prior to his 1812 purchase of Lee's Grant.

One of the deals Edward engaged in was related to Maine land owned by the preparatory school Dummer's Academy (now, The Governor's Academy) of Newbury, Massachusetts. He inveigled his father and brother Michael to include him in

---

55. CCROD, Book 36, Page 217. In this 1801 document Josiah Little gives his son Michael power-of-attorney for some of his land in Maine. Michael later lived in Minot, although whether he moved or the town lines moved, I am not sure. Also, some other early deeds say he was still living in Newbury (or Newburyport).
56. LITTLE, p. 7.
57. DEARPARENT, p. 42. Occasionally borrowers were charged 10¢ per book.
58. DEARPARENT, p. 53-55. See also p. 44.
59. The history of Little also contains the 1826-1830 Letters of Edward Little, which were transcribed by Everett Bertrand, a Wheaton College Summer Fellow who interned with the Androscoggin Historical Society during the summer of 2015. Edward Little had terrible handwriting, which made the letters difficult and time-consuming to transcribe.
60. DEARPARENT, p. 14-15.

their purchase of land in what is now Woodstock, Maine that had been granted to Dummer Academy's. Michael and Josiah Little bought out the Academy's remaining land in Plantation No. 3 (part of which abutted Lee's Grant), paying $6,240 for 11,520 acres, for which they were to pay the school $1,240 plus interest in annual installments. When Edward asked to be cut into the deal, his brother Michael agreed. For his share Edward was to pay Michael one-quarter of the cost of the real estate in Woodstock plus one-quarter of the expenses.[61] In 1816 the Academy quitclaimed their remaining land in Plantation No. 3 to Michael and Josiah Little for full payment of the mortgage given the school by father and son.[62] But it is doubtful that Edward, who was constantly in debt, ever paid for the one-quarter share he "bought" from his brother Michael, although he shared in the profits. Many of the letters between Edward and his father in "Dear Parent" concern issues between the two brothers. The hard feelings between Josiah Little's sons appear to harken back to the Dummer's Academy land purchase.

Hodgkin's book about the younger Little reveals that Edward was not a good money manager. While his father and brother Michael were sharp negotiators and close with their money, earning them few friends in Maine, Edward had a penchant for wanting to be liked by everyone. He wanted to be seen as open-handed, not close-fisted. In addition, Edward was not the same caliber of land speculator as was his father, or even his brother, Michael. For starters, Edward was risk-averse. When in 1808 he decided to step out on his own and buy Lee's Grant, he apparently demanded from Francis Lee an iron-clad title to it.[63] But Francis Lee, who had inherited Lee's Grant from his uncle Arthur Lee, refused to give Edward a warranty deed. At the time, according to Norway historian Whitman, there was some question about the validity of Arthur Lee's will, by which the 6,000 acres were to pass to Francis Lee.[64] Under the instigation of Edward Little, Francis Lee petitioned the Massachusetts legislature in May of 1808 to attempt to get around the problem with Arthur Lee's will. In the petition, Francis Lee asked "that a special act be passed permitting the will to pass the grant to him."[65] Not too surprisingly, the

---

61. DEARPARENT, p. 14.
62. OCROD, Book 12, Page 262A. On November 16, 1816, trustee John Andrews of Dummer's Academy quitclaimed the remaining grant of land to Josiah and Michael Little for full payment of their mortgage (which was most likely recorded at Cumberland County Registry of Deeds, as it is not recorded at OCROD).
63. Edward Little no doubt was influenced by his father's decades-long, but ultimately successful struggle to secure title to the Pejepscot Claim, keeping the land away from the settlers, many of whom were Revolutionary War veterans like our ancestor Ephraim Crockett, Sr.
64. WHITMAN, p. 50.
65. WHITMAN, p. 50.

General Court did not want to get involved with the disposition of the Virginian Arthur Lee's estate and refused Francis Lee's petition. At that point, Edward temporarily backed away from buying this large tract of land in Maine, although he likely continued to act as Lee's agent and collect rents there for Lee.[66]

Edward's passion for owning Lee's Grant did not abate, though. (Probably riding around collecting rents on Lee's Grant only inflamed his desire to own the entire 6,000 acres.) Still unwilling to take a risk that there might be a problem with the title (which Norway historian Whitman says was unlikely), Edward found some Lee family members who were not afraid to gamble on the outcome of Arthur Lee's will. On February 25, 1812, Francis Lee sold via quit claim deed the 6,000 acres he had inherited from his uncle to family members Ludwell and Eliza Lee for $5,000. Three days later, Ludwell and Eliza sold Lee's Grant to Edward Little for $9,000, making a cool profit of $4,000. The only thing the couple had to do for the extra $4,000 was to warrant and defend the title against any claims put forth, not only by their heirs but also by any potential claimants under the will of Arthur Little. Whitman writes:

> "These two deeds coming so near together and from such terms as they contained, we may reasonably assume to be a part of one transaction whereby Edward Little, for some reason not now apparent, could obtain what he considered a better title than by a conveyance from Francis Lightfoot Lee, and was willing to pay $4,000 more for it; yet [Jacob] Tubb's title [for his 200 acres in Lee's Grant] from [Francis] Lightfoot Lee stood the test of time and was never questioned."[67]

After he purchased Lee's Grant, Edward hired Maine surveyor Alexander Greenwood, assisted by Norway residents Joshua Smith and Uriah Holt, to lay out lots on the tract, approximately 100 acres each. Once the lots were plotted, Little went to work selling them. He naturally first targeted the tenant farmers already living on Lee's Grant. No doubt these men were relieved at the chance to switch from renters to fee simple landowners. Of the eighteen deeds Edward Little executed between October 9, 1812 and January 1, 1813, all but two of the grantees

---
66. WHITMAN, p. 50. In his petition to the General Court Francis Lee stated that he had "devoted his care and attention to the preservation and improvement of the said estate," and had also "employed agents for these purposes."
67. WHITMAN, p. 50-51. Given Josiah Little's history, one can assume he would never have paid the extra $4,000 for Lee's Grant. Instead, he would have taken his chances on Francis Lee's title. Had there been title issues in the future Josiah would have badgered the Massachusetts General Court for resolution in his favor, much like he had done for decades until successful with the Pejepscot Claim.

were from Norway (all but one, if you count our ancestor Ephraim Crockett, Jr. who, although then living in Danville, purchased Lot 45 with Josiah Hill, Jr., who resided in Norway).[68] Only one of the buyers, Israel Millett on Lot 15, had actual cash money to pay for his lot. The other seventeen gave a mortgage to Edward Little, typically for the full purchase price plus annual interest. As was common at the time, the mortgages were guaranteed by notes of hand that Edward requested. In the notes, the newly-minted landowners agreed to pay the total due (the purchase price plus interest) in three or four annual installments.

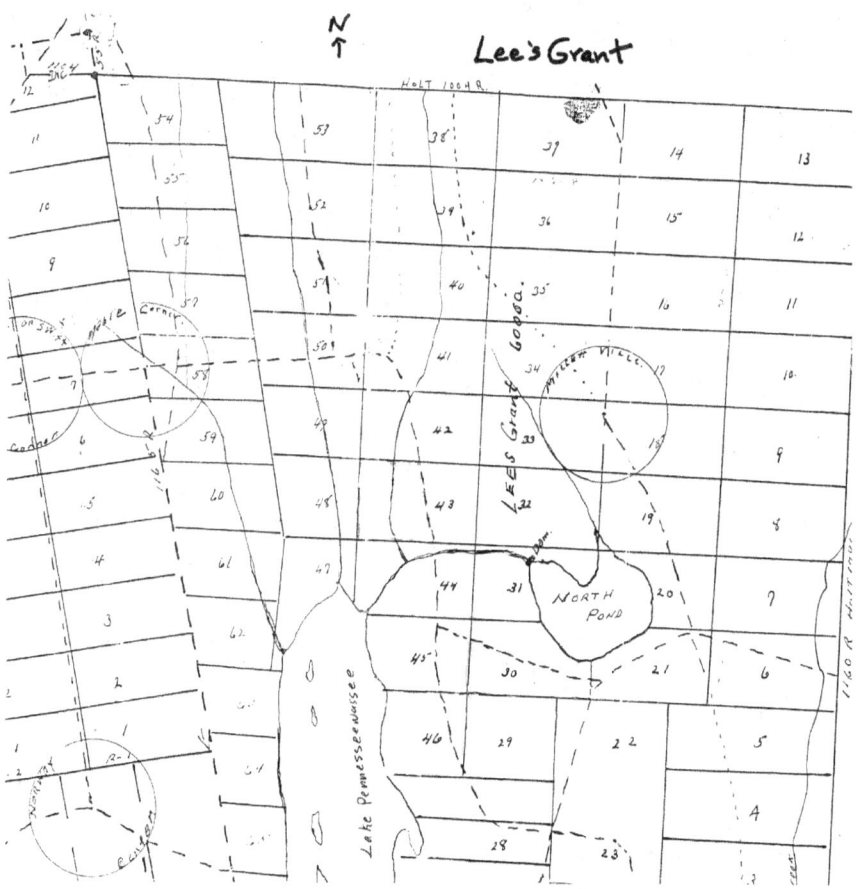

Partial plan of Lee's Grant, executed around 1812 by Maine surveyor Alexander Greenwood, assisted by Norway residents Joshua Smith and Uriah Holt.[69]

---

68. I gleaned this information from the Oxford County Registry of Deeds.
69. This is a partial copy of Greenwood's lot map that I found at the Oxford County Registry of Deeds when I wrote my first little Crockett history in 1979. I am glad I kept a copy, because no one at the registry has ever been able to find the map since.

Edward Little continued to sell lots at a fast pace throughout the years 1813-1816, taking a mortgage on almost all his sales. By 1814, however, some of his early buyers had failed to make their first payments and these buyers were forced to quitclaim their properties back to Little.[70] Unlike Henry Rust, Edward Little had not invested funds to build up a settlement on Lee's Grant or build a sawmill. Nor had he provided settlers with opportunities of earning money to pay for their real estate. In addition, Edward charged high prices for the lots—$6-$7 per acre[71]—which prices were especially onerous compared to the $.50-$.75 per acre that Rust initially charged settlers in Rustfield.

Over time, the lack of access to real money by the settlers on Lee's Grant put another strain on Edward's precarious finances. On May 16, 1822, a notice for back taxes was hung at the public inn of Joshua Smith in Norway. The notice included (among other delinquents) Edward Little as proprietor of Lee's Grant and warned that if Edward failed to pay his 1821 taxes (state, county, town, and road taxes), the town would sell on June 29, 1823, as many lots in the tract as it needed to cover the back taxes.[72] This notice netted Joshua Smith, the innholder, who was also the town treasurer,[73] a rather whiney letter from Edward, who complained not only that the selectmen wanted to tax him on the lots individually and not as one large parcel (taxing one large lot would obviously be cheaper), but also that they did not deduct from taxation for roads, waterways, and bogs, for which he felt he should not be taxed. Edward wrote the following to Smith on April 1, 1822 (just three months shy of the public auction):

> "Dear Sir; I cannot perceive any advantage to be derived to the town or myself from taxing the lots separately; and if the Selectmen should prefer to tax them so it seems that if I give a list which I now own it would be shorter than to give what I have sold. In making the allotments no roads were allowed & when I sold it has been exclusive of roads so that they are to be taken from what is unsold. There should also be large deductions for water, bog(s) & ledge…Why [the land] should be separated any more than any other man I know not & I hope & expect to be taxed in proportion to others."[74]

---

70. See OCROD, Book 17, Page 158; Book 10, Page 379; Book 12, Page 316A; and Book 10, Page 285
71. See for example these mortgages executed by Edward Little for the sale of lots in Lee's Grant: OCROD Book 8, Page 121; Book 8; Page 132; Book 8, Page 133; and Book 8, Page 139.
72. OCROD, Book 21, Page 98. James Crockett, a distant relative, was tax collector in Norway at the time.
73. LAPHAM, p. 631.
74. OCROD, Book 21, Page 377.

After giving a list of the disposition of Lee's Grant lots, Edward notes that the final tax bill should be sent—not to him—but to his father, Josiah Little, "as [the land] is all his." In a surprising turn of events, Edward, a few years prior, had transferred most of his Norway and Woodstock real estate to his father to save it from a large creditor.

It appears that Edward Little, rather than ask his wealthy father to lend him the money to purchase Lee's Grant, instead borrowed the required sum (and more) from Edmund Blunt, a man with whom Edward had significant business dealings in Newburyport, and who later relocated to New York City.[75] (Edward might have suspected—rightly so—that his father would not approve of paying an extra $4,000 for Lee's Grant.) Less than ten years after buying the 6,000 acres from Francis Lee, a writ of execution against Edward Little was issued by the Supreme Judicial Court of Massachusetts for his failure to pay the entirety of his debt to Blunt. Little, who had borrowed more than $12,000 from Blunt, still owed (in November of 1821) $6,242.26. The writ ordered the Sheriff to "take the body of Little and commit him unto either of our gaols in Boston, Portland, Salem, Ipswich, and Newburyport … and retain in your custody in either of our said gaols until he pay the full sums above mentioned…"[76] The writ also directed the Sheriff to have appraised and to attach all of the real estate owned by Edward Little in Woodstock, Norway, and Lee's Grant. Unbeknownst to the court, however, Edward had already, in July of 1817, transferred to his father title to most of the remaining lots he owned in Lee's Grant, as well as his land in Woodstock, for the tidy sum of $7,000.[77] No doubt, the sale was an attempt to raise capital to repay Blunt some of the $12,000 due, but the transaction also protected most of the remaining real estate. When in 1822, on the direction of the Court, Edward Little's Maine real estate was appraised, the value came only to $2,088.92. What real estate was left in Edward's name was attached by the Sheriff for Blunt.[78] In "Dear Parent" Dr. Hodgkin says it is highly unlikely Edward, who at other times in his career had been remanded to jail for unpaid debts,[79] was ever actually imprisoned. Hodgkin surmises that Josiah Little's influence and money would have kept Edward from losing his liberty.

---

75. DEARPARENT, p. 17.
76. OCROD, Book 20, Page 351.
77. OCROD, Book 16, Page 355.
78. OCROD, Box 20, Page 351.
79. Edward Little was arrested on New Year's Eve 1817 for failure to pay his debts related to the Union Canal Lottery, a "device to raise funds for the construction of a canal in southeastern Pennsylvania." The Sheriff, rather than jailing him, gave Edward parole until the next day. Edward wrote to his father begging for financial assistance, which no doubt came

As the result of his disastrous financial affairs, Edward, in the 1820s, took the "poor man's oath" (i.e., he declared bankruptcy), which enabled him to protect his home and personal property.[80] After that, he was completely financially dependent upon his father. In the exchange of letters between father and son that are included in "Dear Parent" covering the years 1826-1830, Edward's debts appear to have been a sore spot between them. Josiah, a hard-hearted man, never let his son forget what he had done for him. These barbs from father to son often hit their mark and occasioned a few resentful replies from Edward, although carefully bookended by affectionate remarks.

Josiah Little died on December 26, 1830[81] (ironically, the same day of the year on which Edward regularly sat down to wrap up his annual land dealings). After the elder Little's death, Josiah's seven living children, including Edward, divvied up their father's vast estate, which included land, farms, mills, and other improved properties (as well as a meeting house and even numerous church pews) in Maine, New Hampshire, Vermont, and Massachusetts. But it was Josiah's daughter Mary, rather than Edward, who selected as hers what remained of the real estate on Lee's Grant, approximately 475 of the original 6,000 acres "with buildings thereon."[82]

After inheriting his one-seventh share of Josiah Little's wealth, Edward became a leading man in Danville (Auburn) and something of a philanthropist. In fact, Edward Little High School is the modern manifestation of an academy he founded. In the spring of 2020, while we were both at the Androscoggin Historical Society offices, Dr. Hodgkin told me that after Josiah Little's death, Edward spent the rest of his life trying to make up for his father's tight-fisted tyranny over the settlers by giving away his father's money. I think it is also possible that Edward finally enjoyed the ability to spend or donate money freely without Josiah Little questioning his every move (or without having to look over his shoulder to see if the Sheriff was coming with a writ of execution).

Perhaps because he could relate to those who were continually behind in their

---

and kept him out of jail. For this debt (and possibly others) Edward had to agree to mortgage his furniture and household goods to his father, including a mahogany desk, bookcase, and dining table; ten yellow chairs; beds and bedding; Liverpool China, children's chairs; a horse-drawn wagon and saddlery, and much more to the extent of $424.66. His father's demand to mortgage Edward's household furnishings was in keeping with Josiah Little's character, and must have been particularly humiliating for his son. DEARPARENT, p. 38-39.
80. DEARPARENT, p. 40.
81. LITTLE, p. 6.
82. OCROD, Page 38, Book 74. This is a disposition of Josiah Little's estate, filed with the Oxford County Registry of Deeds as agreed upon by his seven heirs. Reading the document, one realizes the incredible wealth that Little, through sheer indomitable force and political power, was able to suck out of hardworking men and women and Revolutionary War veterans.

payments, Edward Little, whom we will meet again in the next chapter, *was* a kinder, more understanding creditor than his father. When Edward managed most of Josiah Little's Maine interests, his father regularly pressured him (in very blunt terms) to collect past-due monies owed on real estate transactions. However, Edward sent back excuse after excuse to his father for why he did not lower the boom on debtors. Below are some of Edward's excuses to Josiah Little, which give us insight into the younger Little's character:

> "The circulation of money is very sluggish it is slow collecting. I expect next week to forward some (money) to you ..."[83]
>
> "I do what I can in the way of collections without pressing harder than I suppose you would wish. I have some good hopes that the collections between this + next year will be nearly or quite sufficient to answer your calls."[84]
>
> "I trust it is not necessary to remind me in every letter that you wish to have your debts collected. I have already notified most of your debtors of your wish to have their notes paid + when the notice is neglected + I think it probable that collections can be forwarded by suits I shall prosecute."[85]

Records show that even prior to taking the "poor man's oath," Edward gave settlers on Lee's Grant leeway in making their payments to him,[86] despite putting his own finances in jeopardy as a result. In fact, our ancestor Ephraim Crockett, Jr. was one of those to whom Edward Little appears to have given special consideration, as we will see in the next chapter.

Old Family Land in Lee's Grant

Most of us descendants of Ephraim, Jr. and his wife, Sally (Wentworth) Crockett, who have either lived in the old Crockett homestead or who otherwise have an emotional connection to the farm (or perhaps even own some of the old family land) know that Ephraim and Sally relocated from Danville to Crockett's Ridge in

---

83. Letter of Edward Little to his father dated June 9, 1828. DEARPARENT, p. 139.
84. Letter of Edward Little to his father dated June 18, 1827. DEARPARENT, p. 116.
85. Letter of Edward Little to his father dated October 11, 1827. DEARPARENT, p. 122.
86. In addition to allowing Ephraim Crockett, Jr. time to find a second partner with whom to purchase Lot 45, Little also seems to have given Revolutionary War veteran Daniel Knight extra time to make his payments on the half of Lot 21 where Knight had been a tenant farmer. Knight purchased the westerly half of Lot 21 from Little January 1, 1813. After six years of failing to make what was to be four annual payments, Knight finally quitclaimed his land back to Little on November 24, 1819. OCROD, Book 8, Page 496; Book 8, Page 521; and Book 17, Page 158.

1814. What many do not know, however, is that what we were raised to think of as one large parcel of land belonging to our family since 1812, began as several different lots in Lee's Grant comprised of family farms and woodlots purchased over the course of several generations. These parcels of real estate, owned by various Crocketts and their spouses (most notably the Penleys), were eventually consolidated into one property by Emma Tuell (Crockett) Young Harding (my grandmother Winona's grandmother).

Emma Crockett and her first husband, George P. Young, were the parents of William F. Young (Winona's father), who was their only child. Bill Young and his wife L. Adalade Chaplin ("Addie," as she was affectionately known to everyone) were the ancestors of those of us who are left with a genealogical and physical link to Crockett's Ridge. In effect, we descendants of Emma Tuell Crockett—one of Ephraim, Jr. and Sally's numerous grandchildren[87]—are the last ones standing on Crockett's Ridge. All the other various Crockett (and Penley) families and their descendants have disappeared into the mists of time. In fact, there are no families named Crockett left on Crockett's Ridge. Even the road that runs by the old Crockett homestead has been renamed so that it no longer bears Ephraim Crockett's name.[88] (See my essay, "Will the Real Crockett's Ridge Please Stand Up?" in the back of the book.) No doubt, Crockett descendants can be found close at hand, as some of the Crockett daughters married into other families in the greater Crockett's Ridge neighborhood. Many Crocketts, however, relocated to Maine cities or moved out West, where more and better land became available later in the 19th century. Some Crockett descendants even relocated to Canada. It is not my intent in this history to follow the entire family's footsteps much beyond Crockett's Ridge, although we will take a side trail here and there with some interesting characters.

The following chapters will cover one generation each. We will begin with Ephraim and his wife Sally, the first Crocketts on Lee's Grant. (In that chapter we will also meet Ephraim's younger sister Mary and her husband Nathan Morse, without whose aid and affection Crockett's Ridge might never have been.) After that, we will progress down through four generations, ending our history with Bill and Addie Young.

To make the land acquisitions among the various Crocketts (and their spouses

---

87. When Ephraim, Jr.'s widow Sally died in 1875 (her husband having predeceased her by about twenty years), the couple's descendants numbered "nearly one hundred persons." ANDHIST, p. 713
88. Today, this section of the old Crockett's Ridge Road is officially "Round the Pond Road."

and descendants) as understandable as possible, I have utilized what I believe to be Greenwood's map of Lee's Grant to identify which Crockett (or Penley/Crockett) bought what real estate and who of the family lived where in the subsequent generations. As we progress through this history, I will update the map so that readers can more easily follow along. The old map, which I unearthed decades ago at the Oxford County Registry of Deeds, has been a great help in my historical research. Without the lot notations on the map, I would have had an extremely challenging time figuring out where each of the Crocketts (and Penley/Crocketts) was located. In conjunction with the map, I also used the 200-year-old stone walls on the land to help discern the original boundary lines, and utilized Google Earth and town maps. See you on Crockett's Ridge!

Art postcard, "Pasture Birches, Norway, Me."
(United Art Publishing Co., New York City.)

Ephraim Crockett, Jr., 1788-1856.

Sarah "Sally" Bartlett (Wentworth) Crockett, 1794–1875.

(Original tintypes in possession of Joyce Palmer. Images shared by Yvette Young.)

Chapter 2

EPHRAIM CROCKETT, JR. AND SALLY (WENTWORTH) CROCKETT

Our Norway Crockett Ancestor

Although he was a second son, Ephraim Crockett, Jr. by nature resembled his father and namesake, Ephraim Crockett, Sr., more than did his older brother David, who remained on the family homestead. Ephraim, Jr. was adventurous and ambitious—hungry for a place of his own, as his father had been before him. The senior Crockett, when in his early twenties, relocated from Cape Elizabeth to the uninhabited Pejepscot Claim, a large tract of undeveloped land in the Maine backcountry. A generation later, Ephraim, Jr. relocated from the now-settled town of Pejepscot (soon to be Danville) to Lee's Grant, a 6,000-acre tract of wild land in western Maine, lots of which were just being offered for sale. In addition, the elder Crockett (a Revolutionary War veteran) accompanied his uncle James Wagg, Sr.[1] and cousin James Wagg, Jr. into the backcountry. Similarly, the junior Crockett (a volunteer soldier in the War of 1812) enticed his sister Mary and her husband Nathan Morse, Jr. to move from Pejepscot to Lee's Grant with him and his wife Sally, after the land purchase with Ephraim's prior partner fell through. Like his father before him, Ephraim, Jr. wanted a piece of land—Lot 45 in Lee's Grant—and he did what he needed to do to secure it.

Ephraim Crockett, Jr. was a seventh-generation descendant of Thomas Crockett, the first Crockett to the New World. Thomas Crockett was an Englishman from Stoke Gabriel, county Devon, who arrived on the Piscataqua River around 1630 as part of Captain John Mason's crew. He married Ann _____ (surname unknown, but possibly Lynn or Gunnison). Together Thomas and Ann Crockett

---

1. James Wagg, Sr. was the widow of Mary (Crockett) Wagg, a sister of Richard Crockett III, father of Ephraim Crockett, Sr.

had eight children.[2] (We are descended from their eldest son, the first Ephraim Crockett.) Our Crockett line—from Thomas Crockett to Emma Tuell Crockett (my grandmother Winona's grandmother, the last Crockett on Crockett's Ridge)—is as follows: Thomas-Ephraim-Richard-Richard, Jr.-Richard III-Ephraim, Sr.-Ephraim, Jr.-William Robinson Crockett-Emma Tuell Crockett. (See Crockett genealogy chart on opposite page.)

---

2. CANDAGE, p. 1.

Ephraim Crockett, Jr. and Sally (Wentworth) Crockett

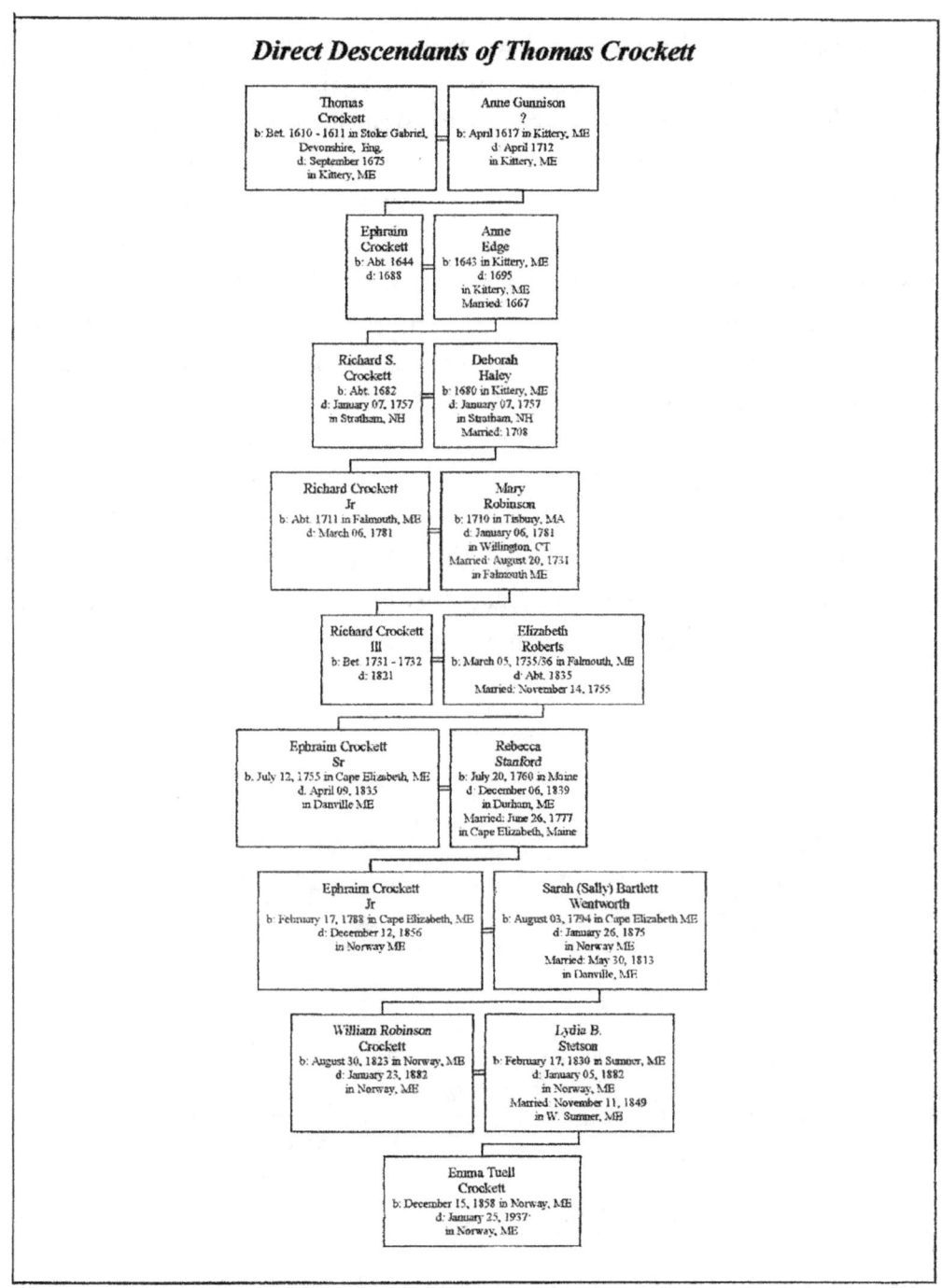

Direct Descendants of Thomas Crockett.
Our direct line from Thomas Crockett to Emma Tuell Crockett
(Genealogy by Robert B. Johnson. See the extended genealogy in back of book.)

Like most early Englishmen who arrived in Maine, the Crockett family was actuated by the desire for land ownership, something not available in the home country except primarily the landed gentry in Great Britain. This reverence for land has been passed down through our family. Much of the land Ephraim, Jr. purchased in 1812 is still owned by his descendants, albeit several different branches of us, none of whom now bear the Crockett name. To date, seven generations of Ephraim, Jr.'s descendants have lived upon the 110 acres of Lot 45 with which he fell in love. More than half a dozen members of the eighth generation of Ephraim and Sally's descendants have been born since I began researching and writing this history in 2019. These days as I stand upon Crockett's Ledge, shielding my eyes from the western sun, I revel in the thought that I am gazing down upon the same sublime view of Lake Pennesseewassee that my ancestor and his family also enjoyed. I wonder whether Ephraim, Jr., as he contemplated this same scene, ever reflected upon those who had preceded *him* to the area, the Native Americans who took their tribal name from the place they christened "Pennesseewassee" or, "where the fruitful land slopes down to meet the shining waters."[3]

Colorized postcard, "Head of Lake Pennesseewassee from Crocketts Ledge, Norway, Me."[4]

---

3. WHITMAN, p. 21. Following a century of warfare between English colonists and the French and their Native American allies, indigenous peoples (those who survived) were pushed north to Canada after the last of the four French and Indian wars. By the time Ephraim Crockett arrived, the Pennesseewassee Indians were long gone.

4. Today I am a temporary steward of the 11 acres of Crockett's Ridge (including the Ledge) that I "own" (or rather, which land owns me).

Our family has two images of Ephraim and his wife Sally Wentworth—the tintypes at the beginning of this chapter, taken in midlife, and a photograph of an old tintype at the end of the chapter, showing Ephraim and Sally in their later years. Both images of Ephraim depict a sober, steady, thoughtful man. This description meshes with the information we have of his character provided by Norway historian Charles F. Whitman, who "boarded around" with several Crockett's Ridge families when he taught at the corner schoolhouse, School District No. 8. Whitman describes Ephraim Crockett, Jr. as a man of "stability, upright in his dealings with others, moral, industrious and frugal."[5]

The face in Ephraim's midlife portrait reveals a hint of sadness, perhaps for hardships and losses already suffered. Resignation, an acceptance of life and its challenges, can also be discerned in his face. In Ephraim's later portrait, his large, arthritic hands, so prominent in the photograph, bear witness to his six decades of physical labor. Ephraim's earthly toils began during his childhood in the Pejepscot Claim and likely did not end until his death in Norway in 1856 at the age of sixty-eight. (By contrast, Ephraim's father was seventy-nine when he died and Ephraim's grandfather, Richard Crockett III was in his late eighties.)

Ephraim, Jr.'s Early Years in Pejepscot

Ephraim Crockett, Jr. was the third child of Ephraim Crockett, Sr. and Rebecca (Stanford) Crockett. He was born February 17, 1788,[6] in Cape Elizabeth. (In 1898, the area in which the Crocketts lived around Long Creek became South Portland.)

Ephraim arrived in the world shortly before the family's relocation from Cape Elizabeth to the Pejepscot Claim near their Wagg relations, who settled there in 1780. (Ephraim, Sr. accompanied his uncle and cousin to the area in 1780 before returning to Cape Elizabeth years later for his wife and family.) Prior to the close of the Revolutionary War and immediately following, veterans who had fought for the creation of a new nation—men like Ephraim Crockett, Sr. and James Wagg, Jr.—flocked to the Maine backcountry from coastal settlements in the District of

---

5. This quote is taken from the Crockett family history located at the Androscoggin Historical Society; however, Whitman uses the same language to describe both Ephraim Crockett and his brother-in-law Nathan Morse (with whom Ephraim purchased Lot 45) in the article he wrote for *The Lewiston Journal Illustrated Magazine Section*, "The Settlers of Crockett Ridge."
6. CANDAGE, p. 36 and p. 85. Candage notes an alternative birth date for Ephraim, Jr. as Feb. 7, 1789; however, most genealogists and family members use the Feb. 17, 1788 date. Records at the Norway, Maine Historical Society also give the Feb. 17, 1788 date.

Maine and from crowded towns in Massachusetts. Some of the veterans (including James Wagg, Jr.) had been promised land in exchange for signing up for three years of service in the War for Independence. Others, especially soldiers such as Ephraim, Sr., understandably believed that land claimed or owned by Tories and confiscated by Massachusetts would later be given or sold to veterans at reasonable rates. Regrettably, that did not happen. Many veterans were forced to buy the land they settled and improved from Tories (or their descendants) who had fled to England or Nova Scotia before hostilities broke out. (Ephraim, Sr. refused to pay Tories for his land, but his son David eventually purchased the property from descendants of Tories.) Some land grants were made to Revolutionary War veterans by the state of Maine, but those came decades too late to be useful.

Ephraim, Jr. was a toddler when the family arrived in the backcountry of the Pejepscot Claim, a large tract of land on the Androscoggin River, the boundaries and ownership of which were in dispute at the Massachusetts General Court. Ephraim's sister Mary, who plays an important role in our family history and whose birth followed his, was born in Pejepscot on April 21, 1790.[7]

When the children were young, settlers on the Pejepscot Claim were focused on survival. The priority was to build a cabin, put food on the table, and prepare for winter. There were no schools in the early days at Pejepscot. Nor did children learn to read and write at the kitchen table, because in most households there were no tables. In addition, there was little free time for study, nor a source of light in the evening other than firelight (a fortunate few had a tallow candle or two). As a result, Ephraim was illiterate when he reached the age of maturity. He signed both a mortgage and quitclaim deed in Norway with his mark.[8] (Ephraim did not remain illiterate, however. The "cannot read or write" question on the 1850 U.S. Census for Norway was not checked, meaning he had learned his ABCs by then.)[9]

There is little doubt but that from a young age, Ephraim, Jr. worked hard to do his share to provide for the increasing Crockett family. (Ephraim, Jr. had nine brothers and sisters.) The pioneering lessons he learned at his father's side about clearing land, planting crops, and hunting game stood Ephraim in good stead when in 1812, at age twenty-four, he purchased land in the backcountry of Lee's Grant.

---
7. CANDAGE, p. 36.
8. See OCROD, Book 9, Page 35 and Book 10, Page 379.
9. 1850 U.S. Census, Norway, Maine. When Ephraim was asked the census question: "Can you read and write?" he must have replied "yes." Ephraim was most likely taught to read and write by his wife, Sally Wentworth, who was one of the fortunate few in the Pejepscot Claim to receive an education, as we will see later in this chapter.

Ephraim was the first settler on his lot in Lee's Grant. This means that twice in his lifetime he would have experienced the challenges of hewing a homestead out of virgin forest—once in Pejepscot and once in Norway. (I never realized this fact until writing this book.) How much easier Ephraim, Jr.'s life would have been had he stayed in Pejepscot, like his older brother David! Pejepscot, soon to be renamed Danville, was growing fast. By 1820, when Maine separated from Massachusetts, Danville boasted stores, schools, roads, bridges, mills, churches, and most importantly—plenty of neighbors. Crockett's Ridge in Norway, by contrast, would offer a handful of neighbors and one mill (a sawmill). The town center of Norway was five miles away.

Ephraim, Jr.'s documented history in Pejepscot during his early adulthood is limited. He is first mentioned in town records in July of 1808 when he was twenty. On February 13, 1808, Pejepscot Selectmen Benning Wentworth and John Witham directed an order for payment to Ephraim Crockett in the amount of $3.75 for "labour done on a Bridge near James Waggs on the County Road."[10] Although the Selectmen do not distinguish whether the payee was Ephraim, Jr. or Ephraim, Sr., I think we can conclude that given their ages—twenty and fifty-three, respectively—the physical labor on the bridge was most likely done by the son. (In addition, David Crockett was also paid $3.75 for work on the same bridge in 1808.)[11]

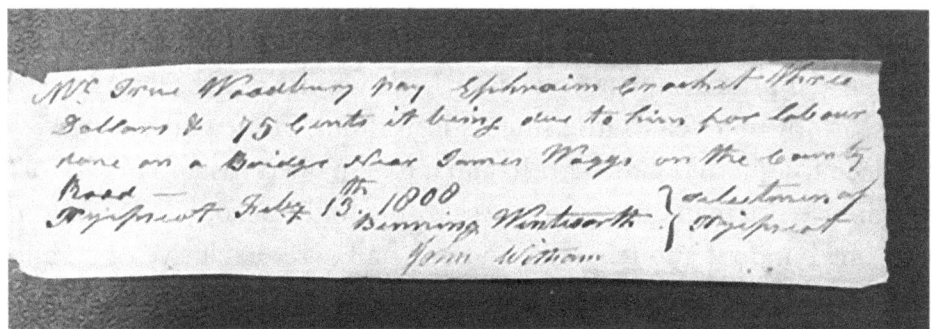

Order for payment to Ephraim Crockett for labor done on a bridge near James Wagg's dated February 13, 1808.[12]
(Photo by Jennifer Wixson.)

---

10. AHS, Pejepscot/Danville folder, "Miscellaneous receipts and assessments." The order for payment was addressed to Pejepscot Town Treasurer True Woodbury.
11. AHS, Pejepscot/Danville folder, "Miscellaneous receipts and assessments." David's order for payment was also dated February 13, 1808.
12. Payment order from AHS, Pejepscot/Danville records of assessments and receipts.

Ephraim, Jr. next appears in a Pejepscot assessment record of 1811. That year Ephraim, now twenty-three, was assessed 27¢ for his poll tax[13] (a "head tax" that was a way of levying taxes on men who were eligible to vote). The assessment and gathering of poll taxes[14] (the same amount for every man), as well as real and personal estate taxes and road taxes, enabled states, towns, and cities to pay their bills. We can assume that Ephraim, Jr. was still living at home in 1811 because he was assessed nothing for real or personal estate taxes that year (just his poll tax).

I found no 1812 assessment records for Pejepscot at the Androscoggin Historical Society. This is unfortunate because 1812 is the year Ephraim Crockett, Jr. first purchased his lot in Lee's Grant. It would have been interesting to know whether Ephraim temporarily relocated to Norway at the end of 1812 (perhaps to build a crude cabin) or remained in Pejepscot. In 1813 he was assessed $2 by the town of Pejepscot for his poll tax. If he temporarily removed to Norway in 1812, he was back in Pejepscot by the following year. In 1813, according to Pejepscot town records, Ephraim was once again assessed nothing for real or personal estate taxes. This information does not mean that Ephraim, Jr. was not attempting to better his situation, however, because he was.

The Peculiar History of Lot 45 in Lee's Grant

The Massachusetts lawyer, publisher, and land speculator Edward Little, who we introduced in the prior chapter, purchased Lee's Grant on February 28, 1812. On December 26th of that year, Little (then still residing in Newburyport) drew up a warranty deed to Ephraim Crockett, Jr. and a man named Josiah Hill, Jr. for Lot 45 in Lee's Grant (see lot map on page 39). According to the deed, Lot 45 contained "by estimation one hundred and ten acres and one half acres exclusive of an allowance for a road of three rods wide across the same."[15] The purchase price for the lot was $663. The parties were not together at the time. The deed culminated a deal that had been agreed to earlier in the year.[16]

---

13. AHS, Pejepscot/Danville records of assessments and receipts.
14. Direct taxation was first introduced in the Massachusetts Bay Colony in 1634, with the first poll tax assessed in 1646. See "The Colonial Roots of American Taxation, 1607-1700." Alvin Rabushka. *Policy Review*. August & September 2002 issue. Published by Hoover Institution, Stanford University. Later in the 19th and 20th centuries in the United States poll taxes were often utilized as a means of voter suppression. A registered voter had to pay his (or her) poll tax before being able to vote. The poll tax was outlawed in 1962 by the Twenty-fourth Amendment to the U.S. Constitution. Unfortunately, the other taxes did not follow suit.
15. OCROD, Book 9, Page 86.
16. Edward Little seems to have had an affinity for dealing with real estate business on December 26. Perhaps it was a

Lot 45 has a peculiar history. For some reason lost in the fog of time, Ephraim purchased Lot 45 twice. We know little about Josiah Hill, Jr., the man with whom Ephraim first purchased Lot 45 in Lee's Grant. Nor do we know how Ephraim became connected with Hill or who the man was. In his book, "The History of Norway, Maine," David Noyes simply notes that Hill was a new immigrant to Norway in 1812.[17]

We do not know which man first became acquainted with Edward Little, Crockett or Hill. Both certainly would have had occasion to know him. Ephraim hailed from Pejepscot, where Edward's father, Josiah Little (one of the Pejepscot Proprietors) was actively engaged in selling, buying, and managing real estate. Edward, who was beginning to handle some of his father's affairs in Maine, most likely marketed his lots in Lee's Grant to second and third sons of original settlers on the Pejepscot Patent. (The eldest son of a settler typically—but not always—purchased the family homestead from his father.) For Hill's part, in 1812, he was living in Norway, where Edward Little publicly offered his lots for sale. It is even possible that Edward Little brought Ephraim Crockett and Josiah Hill together, knowing that separately the two men could not afford to buy the lot. Regardless of how it happened, Crockett and Hill jointly purchased Lot 45 from Little.

Although Edward Little dated his deed December 26, 1812, the instrument was signed by him on May 13, 1813, in Norway.[18] On that same day, Ephraim Crockett, Jr. and Josiah Hill, Jr. were also in Norway and signed a mortgage to Edward Little for Lot 45. The mortgage was also dated December 26, 1812. (See Appendix #1 for a copy of this mortgage.) In the mortgage, the pair agreed to pay Little the purchase price of $663 ($6 per acre) in four equal yearly payments plus interest, with the first payment becoming due in seven months, on December 26, 1813[19] (i.e. a year after the deed was dated, but only seven-and-a-half months after the deed was signed).

---

regular habit with him to sit down the day after Christmas and get his estate organized for the upcoming year. In addition to the warranty deed Little gave Crockett and Hill dated Dec. 26, 1812 he also dated a mortgage on the same lot from Ephraim and Nathan Morse, Jr. on December 26th, three years later, in 1815. See OCROD Book 9, Page 86 and OCROD Book 12, Page 15. The warranty deed and mortgage were signed later than the instruments were dated.

17. NOYES, p. 106. Noyes also notes that a Josiah Hill passed away in Norway in 1845 at the age of 80. We do not know if this was the same Josiah Hill, Jr. with whom Ephraim first purchased Lot 45, or possibly his father. (NOYES, p. 156.) There are no other land transactions through 1845 for Josiah Hill recorded at the Oxford County Registry of Deeds. Norway historian Charles Whitman reports Josiah Hill, Jr. as an "immigrant" to Norway in 1811. WHITMAN, p. 554.

18. The signatures were witnessed by Levi Whitman and Joshua Smith, both of Norway. Smith, in addition to serving as a Justice of the Peace, was one of the town's selectmen in 1814, and Whitman was a representative to the Massachusetts General Court for Norway.

19. OCROD, Book 9, Page 35.

Warranty deed from Edward Little to Ephraim Crockett, Jr. and Josiah Hill, Jr. for Lot 45 in Lee's Grant.
Deed is dated December 26, 1812. Price is $663. Little held a mortgage on the property for the entire amount. See also OCROD Book 9, Page 35.

Ephraim Crockett, Jr. and Sally (Wentworth) Crockett

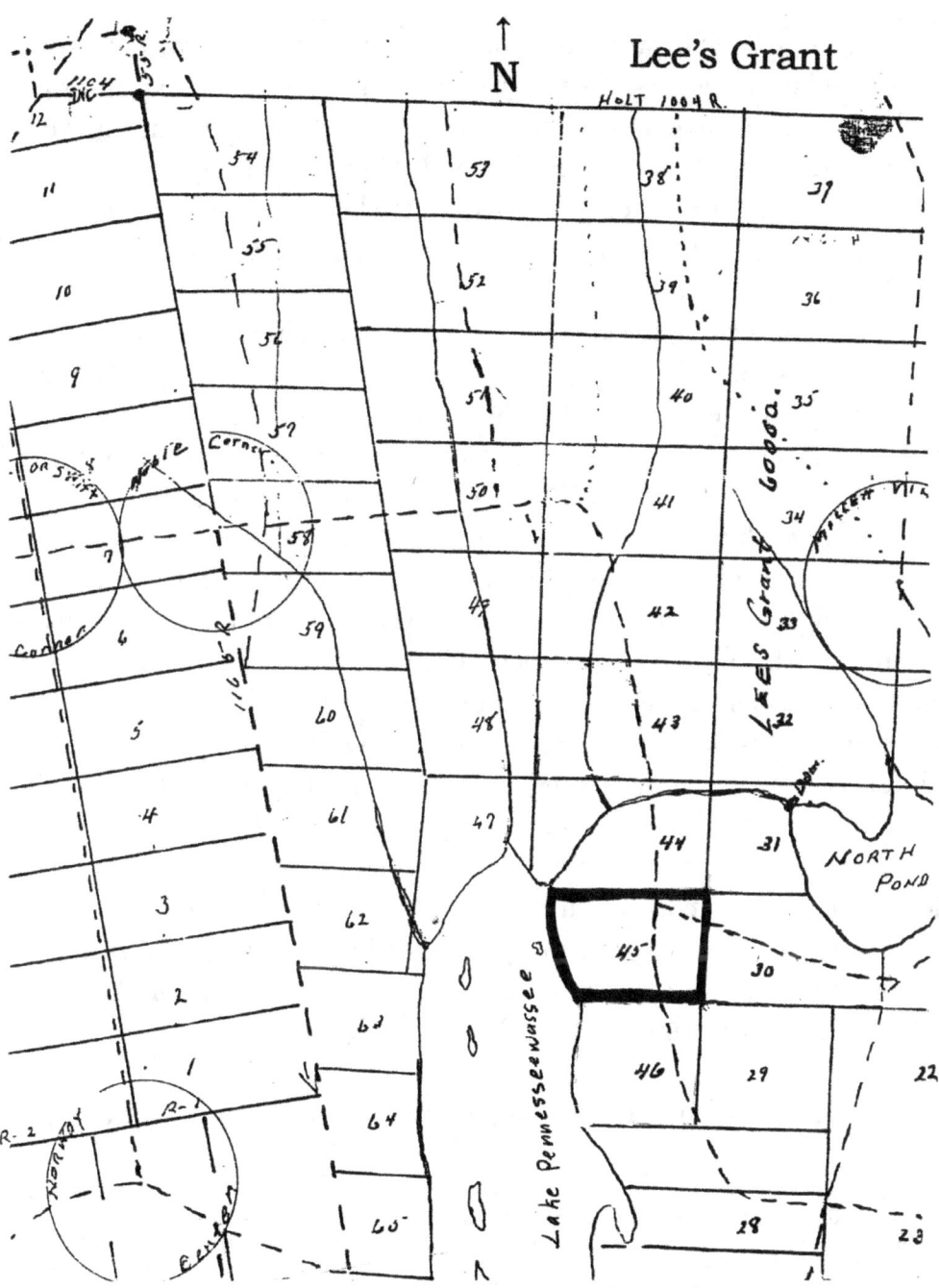

Lot 45 in Lee's Grant, purchased by Ephraim Crockett and Josiah Hill, December 26, 1812. Copy of a (partial) plan of Lee's Grant by Maine surveyor Alexander Greenwood circa 1812. (The dotted lines on the maps indicate roads. For reference, the Heywood Club is now located at the crossroad by lots 28 and 23.)

Without access to Edward Little's personal and financial records, many of which were burned in various fires,[20] we have no way of knowing if Crockett or Hill made their first payment. An educated guess would be that they did not make the payment due December 26, 1813. If money had changed hands, the three payments on Ephraim's second purchase of Lot 45 would likely have been less. The young men's lack of funds at the time might have been an issue or perhaps a lack of commitment on Hill's part.

If Josiah Hill was resigned to give up Lot 45, Ephraim Crockett was not, although he did—sort of. In fact, Ephraim, Sally, and their young daughter Sarah were already homesteading Lot 45 when, on September 7, 1814, Crockett and Hill signed a quitclaim deed releasing Lot 45 to Edward Little.[21] (See Appendix #2 for a copy of this deed.) Sally was pregnant with their second child at the time. (The child, Samuel Wentworth Crockett, was born in Norway on January 15, 1815.)[22] Forty years ago, when writing my first Crockett history, I first discovered this quitclaim deed and conjectured that it must have been very sad for Ephraim and his fledgling family to turn the property back over to Little. I then believed there was a gap in Ephraim's ownership of his land in Norway, and thought how fortunate he was (and we were) that someone else did not swoop in and buy Lot 45 from Edward Little, especially as Little was selling lots fast and furious from 1812-1816. Fast forward to the present, when I now suspect that our ancestor and Edward Little struck a hand-shake deal whereby Little agreed to keep Lot 45 off the market for a certain period until Ephraim could secure another partner with whom to buy the lot.[23] When Little signed a second warranty deed for Lot 45 eighteen months later[24]—to Ephraim Crockett, Jr. and Nathan Morse, Jr. (Ephraim's brother-in-law)—he backdated the deed to September 7, 1814.[25] In effect, the back-dating of the deed to the same day that Crockett and Hill signed the quitclaim deed to Little ensured that there was never a day since December 26, 1812 when Ephraim Crockett, Jr. did not

---

20. The historic and preservation non-profit *Historic New England* has some Little family records available; however, the records of this Edward Little (there were more than one Edward Little) are not among them. In the early years, Edward Little suffered several fires at his places of business in Newbury, Massachusetts and Portland, Maine. See DEARPARENT.
21. OCROD, Book 10, Page 379.
22. Crockett genealogy, NHS. Ephraim and Sally's first child, Sarah Wentworth Crockett, was born in Pejepscot November 11, 1813.
23. Not only could Ephraim probably not afford to purchase Lot 45 by himself, but also it made more sense to have a partner with whom to share the physical work of hewing a homestead in the wilderness.
24. This deed was probably drawn up on December 26, 1815, the same day Edward Little dated the mortgage given to him by Crockett and Morse. Little regularly appears to have wrapped up his land deals on December 26th.
25. OCROD, Book 13, Page 253.

legally own Lot 45. (This act could have been more than goodwill on Little's part. The back-dating of the deed ensured that Ephraim Crockett, not Edward Little, was legally responsible for the taxes on Lot 45 from December 26, 1812 onward.)

Edward Little signed the new deed to Ephraim Crockett and Nathan Morse on February 3, 1816, also in Norway.[26] The sales price was $660 ($3 less than the first time around). Per usual, Crockett and Morse gave Little a mortgage for the entire amount (plus interest), agreeing to pay him $664.20 in three equal payments.[27] (See Appendix #2 & #3 for a copy of this second deed and mortgage.) Although signed the same day as the deed from Little, the mortgage was dated December 26, 1815, which meant the first payment was due in eleven months. Fortunately for all of us, Crockett and Morse made their payments.

Colorized postcard, "Scene near NORWAY LAKE, ME."

Sarah "Sally" Bartlett Wentworth and the Wentworth Family

In the parlance of the 19th century, Ephraim Crockett, Jr. married well. His wife, Sarah "Sally" Bartlett Wentworth, was a descendant of the prominent and

---

26. Joshua Smith, the Norway Town Treasurer, who was also a Justice of the Peace, was one of the witnesses to the mortgage deed, and William Foye, who operated a sawmill at the outlet stream on North Pond, was the other. WHITMAN, p. 168 and p. 543. See also OCROD, Book 12, Page 15.
27. OCROD, Book 12, Page 15.

well-connected Wentworth family of New Hampshire. Her grandfather, Captain John Wentworth, was a military man who distinguished himself in the service of two nations: he fought in the British army during the French and Indian War and fought in the American Continental army during the Revolutionary War.[28]

Sally's great-great-grandfather, also named John Wentworth, was Lieutenant Governor of the Province of New Hampshire and was one of the original Pejepscot Proprietors (the investors who owned the Pejepscot Patent in Maine). But before Sally's father, Samuel Solley Wentworth, and his brother Benning Wentworth settled on the Pejepscot Claim (where Ephraim Crockett, Sr. also settled) the Wentworth share of Pejepscot Patent land had been sold.

Sally Bartlett Wentworth's fifth-great grandfather was Elder William Wentworth, an early settler of New Hampshire, who came to the New World around 1636 or 1637.[29] Elder Wentworth was the progenitor of all the Wentworths listed in the three-volume family history, "The Wentworth Genealogy." One of the first items of historical importance from the old Crockett homestead in Norway that my grandmother Winona showed me when I moved in with her was the family's copy of "The Wentworth Genealogy," in which Sally was mentioned, as well as

---

28. Born in Kittery in 1736, Captain John Wentworth was the son of Captain William Wentworth and Margery (Pepperell) Wentworth. During the French and Indian War, 1754-1763 (the last of the French and Indian Wars, also known in Europe as the "Seven Year's War"), he received a commission as a Lieutenant from his uncle Col. William Pepperell and served in Captain Osgood's company during the 1759 Battle of Quebec (also known as the Battle of the Plains of Abraham), the decisive battle for Canada, which was won by the British. (Not long after this decisive battle France ceded Canada to England.) According to direct descendant Albert James Wentworth in his application for membership in the Ohio Chapter of Sons of the American Revolution, John Wentworth was "near General Wolfe [the British commander] when he fell, and helped carry him to the rock where he died." A famous 1770 painting by American artist Benjamin West depicts Wolfe's death. Although realistic-looking, West reportedly took liberties with the painting, in which some of the soldiers who are painted with Wolfe were not actually present at the battle. John Wentworth, who *was* at hand during the major general's death, is not one of the identified soldiers surrounding Wolfe in the picture, although some of the soldiers remain unidentified.

Both commanders—Major General Wolfe and the marquis de Montcalm, who commanded the French troops—died from wounds they received in the Battle of Quebec. When war broke out between the American colonies and Great Britain, John Wentworth, then forty-years-old, volunteered to serve with American rebels. He was at Ticonderoga and later helped guard General Burgoyne's defeated troops in Boston after the general surrendered at Saratoga, N.Y. (Information on John Wentworth's service taken from Albert James Wentworth's application for membership in the Sons of the American Revolution. See Appendix #6 to read his record of his ancestor's service. See also "A Record of the Commissioned Officers and Enlisted Men of Kittery and Eliot" and WENTWORTH, Vol. 1, p. 517-518.) Captain John was nephew to Benning Wentworth (for whom Sally's uncle Benning was named), long-time Governor of the Province of New Hampshire. Captain John's first cousin Sir John Wentworth, the last Royal Governor of New Hampshire, was a Tory who fled to Halifax at the commencement of the Revolution, where he was later appointed Governor of Nova Scotia.

29. WENTWORTH, Vol. I, p. 71. William Wentworth arrived in the New World *prior* to July 1639 and was a follower of the Rev. John Wheelwright and the spiritualist Anne Hutchinson, who was Wentworth's first cousin. When Wheelwright and Hutchinson were banished by Massachusetts in 1637 for radical religious views that did not align with those of the dour Puritans, William Wentworth went with them. William eventually ended up in Dover, N.H., where he owned a sawmill and was active in town affairs. According to Dr. John Wentworth, the highly regarded Wentworth genealogist, "The office, however, by which William Wentworth was best known was that of *Ruler Elder* of the church at Dover, especially as it resulted in his officiating as preacher in many years of his life."

her children and some of her grandchildren. Winona wanted me to know that the Crockett family had always been proud of their Wentworth roots.[30]

Sarah "Sally" Bartlett Wentworth was a seventh-generation Wentworth in the New World.[31] She was born August 3, 1794,[32] to Samuel Solley Wentworth (the fifth child of Captain John Wentworth and his second wife) and Hepsibah Hanscom. Sally's parents were married in 1793,[33] probably in Cape Elizabeth. In 1794, the couple moved to the Pejepscot Claim, where Sally, their first child, was born.[34]

It appears that Samuel Solley followed his older brother Benning Wentworth to the Pejepscot Claim.[35] Benning had served in the Revolutionary War[36] with their father, Captain John Wentworth (Samuel Solley was too young to volunteer). Like

---

30. "The Wentworth Genealogy," a large tome written by Dr. John Wentworth, chronicles the lives of Elder Wentworth and his many, many descendants, as well as his ancestors in England. Volume I opens with Elder Wentworth's English ancestors from the period of the Conquest (1066), moving forward in time to Elder Wentworth's settlement in the New World. The rest of Volume I and Volume II covers nearly 250 years of the history and family genealogy of Elder Wentworth's descendants, with the last information added by Dr. Wentworth in the 1870s. The three-volume set (Volume III is corrections and additions) was published in 1878; however, a private first edition was printed in 1871 for descendants of Elder Wentworth. Winona told me the copy she owned, which was Volume II, was much-venerated by her Crockett ancestors. Volume II includes vital statistics and other information about Sally's father Samuel Solley Wentworth, as well as Sally and Ephraim's children in Norway, and many of their grandchildren, including Emma Tuell Crockett (my great-great-grandmother), who eventually inherited (most of) the Crockett homestead and later added other family farms to her holdings.
There is little doubt in my mind that the second generation of Crocketts in Norway (including our ancestor William Robinson Crockett, son of Ephraim Jr. and Sally) provided their family information directly to Dr. Wentworth for his genealogy. The different Crockett families in the greater Crockett's Ridge neighborhood most likely also provided him money in advance for copies of Volume II (in which they were mentioned), which would have helped Dr. Wentworth raise funds to publish the book. Unfortunately, that original family copy of Volume II has been lost, so we cannot know whether it was a first edition and/or inscribed by Dr. Wentworth. (I have since purchased my own copy of all three volumes of "The Wentworth Genealogy.") While researching this book I came across a family story on Ancestry.com about Hannah Jordan (Crockett) Richardson, daughter of Ephraim Jr. and Sally, and a younger sister to our ancestor William Robinson Crockett (whose life we will cover in the next chapter). The story told how proud Hannah was of her Wentworth connections, and noted that she, too, possessed her own personal copy of "The Wentworth Genealogy" (which listed herself and her family). This information recently discovered from out of the blue validated what my grandmother had told me forty years earlier—that the Crockett family in Norway revered their Wentworth roots.
31. WENTWORTH, p. 301. If Sally was of the seventh generation of Wentworths, then as her 4th-great granddaughter I am of the thirteenth generation.
32. There has been some confusion about Sally's birth year, due to a mistake made in Crockett genealogy at the Norway, Maine Historical Society. Regrettably, this genealogy was utilized by Charles Candage in his later Crockett genealogy. NHS and Candage have her birth year as 1784, rather than 1794. Given that Sally's parents were not even married in 1784 and that her birth certificate says 1794, I think we can take the later date as accurate. Norway census records for Sally also affirm her 1794 birth.
33. WENTWORTH, p. 301.
34. ANDHIST, Chapter XL.
35. A list of early settlers in the Pejepscot Claim (and the towns from which they came) compiled by Janus Ganville Elder and edited by David C. Young of the Androscoggin Historical Society shows Benning Wentworth arriving in Pejepscot in 1792 and his younger brother Samuel Solley arriving in 1795. (We know Samuel Solley was in Pejepscot in 1794, however, because Sally Wentworth was born there that year.) According to this list Benning relocated from Freeport (to which town he appears to have returned in 1810) and Samuel Solley came from Cape Elizabeth (the Second District of Falmouth), where the Crocketts lived since around 1730.
36. According to his pension application, Benning served three "tours" of duty totaling about 2 years, most of which service was in his father's company. U.S. Revolutionary War Pension and Bounty-Land Warrant Application Files, 1800-1900. Wentworth, Benning.

other veterans who flocked to the Pejepscot Claim (notably, Ephraim Crockett, Sr. and his cousin and uncle James Wagg, Jr. and Sr.) Benning Wentworth was looking for land and opportunity. Unlike Ephraim Crockett, Sr. and the Waggs, Benning probably expected to buy the lot he settled on Great Lot #5 in the Pejepscot Claim. The Wentworth family had once been partial owners of the Pejepscot Patent and it is logical to assume that Benning and Samuel Solley Wentworth would have had great respect for that company's legal ownership—Tory or not.

Whatever their motivation for moving to the Pejepscot Claim, the experience of the Wentworth brothers in purchasing their land was a cut above that of most other settlers. Thanks to their Wentworth connections (I presume), Benning and Samuel Solley Wentworth purchased their real estate at very favorable prices. On September 8, 1803, after having resided on his land for approximately a decade, Benning Wentworth formally purchased from the Tory Pejepscot Proprietor Isaac Royall (via his attorney, since Royall had fled the country) seventy-seven acres in Great Lot #5[37] for $2 per acre.[38] Samuel Solley paid only $1.75 per acre for his seventy-two acres next to his brother's lot.[39] If we contrast the real estate prices the Wentworth brothers paid with the land prices paid by other early Pejepscot settlers—such as the $4.22 per acre paid by David Crockett for his father Ephraim, Sr.'s lot; the $4.91 per acre paid by his uncle James Wagg; and the $7 per acre paid by Revolutionary War veteran William Dingley[40]—we can see how fortuitous it was to have the last name of Wentworth.

Samuel Solley Wentworth and his family settled permanently in Pejepscot. Not much is known about Sally's mother, Hepsibah (Hanscom) Wentworth. She was Samuel Solley's first wife. Hepsibah died in Pejepscot in 1802 when Sally was seven.[41] Hepsibah might have died in childbirth (or from complications as a result of childbirth). She appears to have borne a child every two years from the time of her marriage to Samuel Solley in 1793. Her last living child was born in 1800, making 1802 a probable birth year. (If Hepsibah Wentworth died in childbirth, the child died as well.)

Out of expediency, Samuel Solley, while attempting to make a life in the

---

37. Great Lot #5 was just north of where the Crocketts and James Wagg lived on the Androscoggin River.
38. CCROD, Book 69, Page 408. Thomas Sparhawk of Portsmouth N.H. was the attorney for Isaac Royall. He negotiated the price with the Wentworth brothers and signed their deeds.
39. CCROG, Book 51/Page 130. Sparkhawk dated the Wentworth brothers' deeds the same day, September 8, 1803.
40. Information from my book, "Into the Maine ~ One Maine Family's Quest for Land, 1630-1830." See Chapter 7.
41. WENTWORTH, Vol. II, p. 301-305.

backcountry and finding himself with four young children on his hands—Sarah, age 7; Betsey, 5; William, 3; and Samuel Solley, Jr., 2[42]—married again seven months after Hepsibah passed. Sally would have been around eight at the time of the second marriage, meaning she would have been raised by her step-mother Sally Parker. Sally (Parker) Wentworth bore Samuel Solley five more children. Since our Sally was the eldest child, she was likely one of the important workers in the family, undertaking household chores and providing childcare for her younger siblings. (Sadly, Samuel Solley, Jr. died February 1815 at the age of 15, and the youngest two of Samuel Solley and Sally's children—Esther, born 1812, and Samuel, born 1813—burned to death in the family's house in Danville on April 1, 1819. Our Sally was married and living in Norway at the time of her siblings' deaths.)[43]

Unlike Ephraim Crockett, Sr., whose sole town office in Pejepscot was one year as hog reeve (basically, an animal control officer), Samuel Solley Wentworth (as well as his brother Benning) took an active role in the development of the fledgling town of Pejepscot. Samuel Solley served as a Selectman, as well as Tax Collector.[44] He also seems to have acted as an unofficial banker for the town, perhaps having access to funds when cash was tight. In 1801 he was reimbursed by the Selectmen (one of whom was his brother) "$3.08 for paying interest on John Nevens order."[45]

On another occasion, Samuel Solley Wentworth stepped in and rescued the town from financial difficulty by paying a hefty fine levied by the Commonwealth of Massachusetts (of which Maine was still a part). On February 11, 1809, Town Treasurer True Woodbury was directed by Selectmen Benning Wentworth and John Witham to reimburse Samuel Solley $42.04 "it being due to him for paying the cost and fine brought against the town for not being provided with military stors [stores] as the law dictates."[46]

---

42. WENTWORTH, Vol. II, p. 301-304.
43. WENTWORTH, Vol. II, p. 305. House fires were unfortunately only too common before the advent of fire departments and better building materials and codes. Twenty years after the Wentworth children burned to death, Rebecca Stanford Crockett, widow of Ephraim Crockett, Sr., and mother-in-law of Sally (Wentworth) Crockett, burned to death in her bed in Danville. *The Maine Farmer*, December 28, 1839.
44. AHS, Pejepscot/Danville files. Samuel Solley Wentworth was tax collector in 1808 and was charged with collecting the $472.98 in taxes due for that year.
45. AHS, Pejepscot receipts folder.
46. AHS, Pejepscot receipts folder.

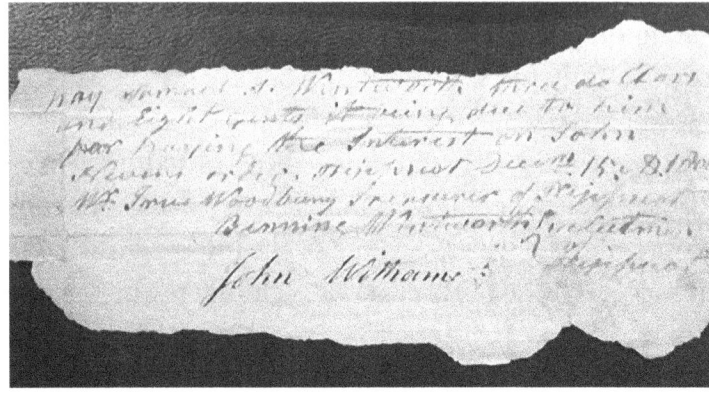

Authorization by Pejepscot Selectmen to reimburse Samuel S. Wentworth $3.08 for "paying the interest on John Nevens order." December 15, 1800.[47]
(Photo by Jennifer Wixson)

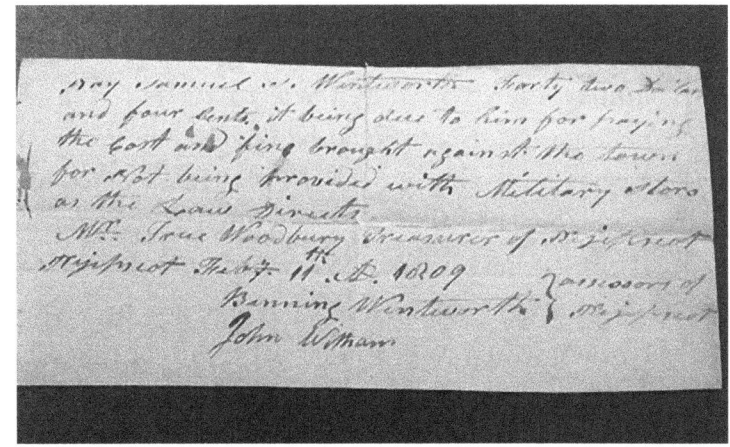

Authorization by Pejepscot assessors Benning Wentworth and John Witham to reimburse Samuel S. Wentworth $42.04 for paying the town's fine for "not being provided with military stors [sic] as the law directs." February 11, 1809.[48]
(Photo by Jennifer Wixson.)

Since there were no schools in Pejepscot, Sally was educated either by her father or, more likely, by her uncle Benning Wentworth, who "…was teaching children in the area before the incorporation of the town."[49] By the time Sally was sixteen, however, that formal instruction ended. Benning Wentworth and his family left the

---

47. AHS, Pejepscot receipts folder.
48. AHS, Pejepscot receipts folder.
49. "Study of the Penley Family," p. 7 (Second Generation). Unknown author or date. Androscoggin Historical Society, Penley Genealogy.

area before 1810.⁵⁰ (Benning relocated to Ohio, where he lived outside Chillicothe the rest of his life and where most of his children also relocated.)⁵¹

Sally Wentworth and her siblings grew up with the children of the Crockett, Wagg, and Dingley families, who had also relocated to Pejepscot from Cape Elizabeth. Friendships and life partnerships developed in their youths (Sally's sister Betsey married Ephraim, Jr.'s younger brother Joseph Crockett),⁵² and a little neighborhood coalesced around the families of these Revolutionary War veterans who settled on the banks of the Androscoggin River on the Pejepscot Claim. Their "connexion" reminds me of the advice English author Jane Austen gave her niece Anna about how to gather her characters for a novel: "Three or four families in a country village is the very thing to work on…"⁵³ This neighborhood lifestyle would later be recreated in Norway on Crockett's Ridge by childhood friends—and later sweethearts—Ephraim Crockett, Jr. and Sally Wentworth.

Ephraim and Sally were married in Pejepscot on May 30, 1813,⁵⁴ by Elder Joseph Roberts, a Baptist clergyman⁵⁵ (and the man to whom uncle Benning had sold his homestead). Ephraim was twenty-five and Sally was eighteen. Their wedding occurred after Ephraim Jr. had already made the first purchase (with Josiah Hill, Jr.) of Lot 45 in Lee's Grant. Ephraim signed the mortgage to Edward Little for Lot 45 on May 13, 1813, about two weeks before the couple's wedding. Ephraim and Sally's first child, Sarah Wentworth Crockett, was born in Danville on November 11, 1813. The rest of the couple's thirteen children were born at their homestead

---

50. Benning Wentworth sold his seventy-seven acres December 14, 1810 to Rev. Joseph Roberts for $890, making a nice profit of $736 on the sale. According to the deed, Benning was living in Freeport at the time of the sale. CCROD Book 63, Page 257. Freeport was the home of his wife, Phebe (Sawyer) Wentworth. WENTWORTH, Vol. II, p. 296.
51. WENTWORTH, Vol. II, p. 296. According to Dr. Wentworth (who received information from Benning himself), Benning Wentworth left Maine for Ohio on September 17, 1816 and arrived on November 2nd at Chillicothe, Ohio, where he remained until his death in 1852.
52. WENTWORTH, Vol. II, p. 304. Betsey (Wentworth) Crockett and Joseph Crockett moved to Chillicothe, Ohio, where her uncle Benning Wentworth and most of her cousins were living.
53. Jane Austen, letter to Anna, August 1814.
54. Maine Marriage Records, 1713-1922. There is some confusion as to whether Ephraim and Sally Crockett were married in March or May of 1813. Wentworth in his genealogy reports the couple was married in March however, he does not give a day. In Sally's application for her husband's bounty land (from Ephraim's service in the War of 1812) their wedding date is clearly spelled out as "the thirtieth day of May A.D. 1813." (The National Archives, Bounty Land File, 267.234, Sarah B. Crockett, widow of Ephraim Crockett, private.)
55. ANDHIST, Chapter XXXIX, "Danville," written by George Thomas Little. Pejepscot, like other wilderness settlements, had difficulty getting settled ministers, which was required by Massachusetts law. Selectmen regularly appointed community members (such as Ephraim Crockett, Sr.'s cousin Samuel Crockett) to go out and attract clergy. This was an expensive proposition and Little reports the situation was alleviated by the arrival of Roberts, who was ordained in December 1808. Elder Roberts later became a representative to the Massachusetts General Court and therefore might have been away for significant periods of time, perhaps delaying Ephraim and Sally's wedding, and explaining why Sally appears to have been three or four months pregnant when the couple was married.

on Crockett's Ridge, as the height of land above the northeast edge of Lake Pennesseewassee came to be known.

Ephraim Crockett, Jr.'s Service in the War of 1812

The War of 1812 affected every Maine family, including the Crocketts. Not only did the war make goods scarce and prices high, but the embargo imposed by the United States made it nearly impossible for Mainers to sell their products abroad. Later, Massachusetts' failure to protect the District from attacks by the British—coupled with England's occupation of eastern Maine in 1814—angered Mainers so much so that after the war, residents sought separation from Massachusetts, ultimately gaining statehood in 1820.

In 1793, ten years after the United States won independence from England in the Revolutionary War, France declared war on Great Britain. As a fledgling nation, the United States hoped to remain neutral during this clash of titans; however, ships from both France and England began harassing American ships, impressing desperately needed seamen into their navies to man the ships. By the turn of the 19th century, British warships were so frequently attacking American ships and impressing sailors into the Royal Navy that the United States was forced to take drastic measures. In December of 1807, the U.S. Congress passed the Embargo Act, a drastic measure to keep neutral American ships and crews safe from warring French and British vessels. This extremely unpopular embargo closed all U.S. ports, including those in Maine, and barred imports from Britain.[56] Maine's Secretary of State's website covering the War of 1812-1815 explains the immediate effects of the embargo on the District:

> "The Embargo and other trade restrictions profoundly affected Mainers, dependent as they were upon the sea for most manufactured goods coming into the District as well as the export of their principal products, lumber and fish. All sorts of goods became scarce and inflation rose to unprecedented levels."[57]

The embargo, which all Americans hoped would last a relatively short period

---
56. "The War of 1812-1815: America's 'Second War for Independence.' (1812-1815.)" Maine Secretary of State webpage. The War of 1812-1815.
57. IBID.

of time, dragged on for months and then years. Not surprisingly, the longer the embargo remained in place, the angrier Mainers and other residents along the Atlantic seaboard became. Smuggling, which was not uncommon in Maine, became more frequent, especially as the embargo was all but unenforceable:

> "Maine was the greatest offender. Ever since the close of the Revolutionary War, to avoid burdensome restrictions, many a cargo had been transferred from an American to an English bottom in Passamaquoddy Bay, or on the shores of Campobello or some other neutral island."[58]

Finally, the federal government passed the Enforcement Act of 1809 and sent troops and ships to enforce the nearly unenforceable embargo in Maine and Massachusetts. This action was highly unpopular, and some communities, such as Newburyport, Massachusetts, where the Little family held shipping interests, plotted rebellion. Douglas Hodgkin in "Dear Parent" explains what happened next:

> "When the Congress passed the Enforcement Act of January 1809 to make the Embargo more effective, Newburyporters and other New England towns considered preparation for revolution. They held protest meetings to resist the execution of the Enforcement Act. In an analogy to the preparations for the Revolution thirty-five years earlier, on 10 February 1809, the town [of Newburyport] appointed a twenty-man Committee of Safety and Correspondence, including Edward Little (to watch, protect and defend the Town)."[59]

On June 18, 1812, the U.S. Congress, finding the country could no longer remain neutral, declared war on England. Most bankers and merchants in Massachusetts (including Maine), because of their dependence on foreign markets and goods, "openly sided with Britain and refused to cooperate with the federal government."[60] President Madison responded to this defiance in 1813 by ordering "all federal garrisons in the District of Maine to withdraw to more loyal states of the Union."[61] While the withdrawal of troops would have been greeted with glee by smugglers,

---
58. Rowe, William H. "The Maritime History of Maine: Three Centuries of Ship Building & Seafaring." Gardiner, Me. The Harpswell Press. 1989. (Copyright W.W. Norton, 1948). P. 81.
59. DEARPARENT, p. 24.
60. "The War of 1812-1815: America's 'Second War for Independence.' (1812-1815.)" Maine Secretary of State webpage, The War of 1812-1815.
61. Woodard, Colin. "The Lobster Coast." New York, NY. Viking-Penguin. 2004. P. 151.

it also left Maine unable to repel attacks by British ships cruising Maine waters, waiting for opportunities and easy prey. After the withdrawal of troops to "more loyal states," William King, major general of one of the principal militia units in Maine, found the District suddenly defended only by "a few invalids ... who were retained on account of their indispositions."[62]

The withdrawal of U.S. troops from Maine precipitated several British invasions of defenseless coastal communities. Hard to believe, but just over three decades after the United States secured her independence from England, territory in Maine east of the Penobscot River fell to the British and was once again subsumed into the British Empire.[63] Settlements along the coast dropped like dominos to the British navy. "On September first 1814, both Castine and Belfast surrendered. Shortly thereafter Bangor and Hampden were occupied, then Eastport and others."[64]

Having successfully invaded eastern Maine, British warships turned their attention to the midcoast area. There, the English were less successful. A group of British marines landed on Southport Island but were beaten back by local militia.[65] (Although Maine was attacked and invaded by the British during the War of 1812, the District was only a side theater of the war.)

Despite desperate pleas for help, Massachusetts chose not to come to the defense of her residents in Maine. Instead, Mainers were left to their own devices or to the capricious mercy of the British.[66] Captain Barry issued the following threat to the residents of Hampden:

> "My business is to burn, sink and destroy. Your town is taken by storm, and by the rules of war, we ought both to lay your village in ashes, and put its inhabitants to the sword. But I will spare your lives, though I mean to burn your houses."[67]

In September of 1814, word arrived in Norway, where Ephraim Crockett, Jr. and his family were living, that British warships had been spotted off the coast of

---

62. Woodard, Colin. "The Lobster Coast." New York, NY. Viking-Penguin. 2004. P. 151.
63. "The War of 1812-1815: America's 'Second War for Independence.' (1812-1815.)" Maine Secretary of State webpage. The War of 1812-1815.
64. Woodard, Colin. "The Lobster Coast." New York, NY. Viking-Penguin. 2004. P. 151.
65. IBID.
66. "The War of 1812-1815: America's 'Second War for Independence.' (1812-1815.)" Maine Secretary of State webpage. The War of 1812-1815.
67. IBID. Fortunately, threats like Barry's were rarely carried out by the British, because England was loath to terrorize those who she hoped to become new citizens of British Canada.

Portland.[68] Believing that an attack on Portland was imminent, a call went out for help. Captain Bailey Bodwell, who had recently returned to Norway from fighting the British in Plattsburg, New York, was one of many officers in Maine who raised a company of men to march to the defense of Portland.[69] Since Massachusetts would not defend her territory from the British, local Maine militias would do it. Less than a week from the day (September 7, 1814) that Ephraim, Jr. and Josiah Hill quit-claimed Lot 45 back to Edward Little, Ephraim volunteered to join Captain Bodwell's Norway company in defense of Portland.

When Ephraim enlisted in mid-September 1814, he and his family were living on Lot 45 in Lee's Grant. Ephraim might have enlisted in Bodwell's company because he needed money to repurchase Lot 45 from Edward Little. However, it is just as likely that Ephraim, son of a Revolutionary War veteran, would have felt strongly about the country's continued independence from England. (In fact, Ephraim's brother David, who remained in Pejepscot, served as a Colonel in the War of 1812.)[70] Whatever his motivation, Ephraim, Jr. marched off to Portland with Captain Bodwell, leaving his pregnant wife Sally and their ten-month-old daughter Sarah behind.

Sally and Sarah were not completely abandoned in the backcountry of Lee's Grant, however. Revolutionary War veteran Daniel Knight and his wife were living on North Pond at the time,[71] and Crockett relation, Joshua Crockett, Jr., four years younger than Ephraim, owned Lot 43,[72] just up the road (to the north) from Ephraim and Sally. (See Lee's Grant lot map later in the chapter for orientation.)[73] In addition, two men, Nathaniel Young, Jr. and Isaac Bennett, had purchased Lot 44 in May of 1814,[74] which was the lot next door to the Crockett homestead. It

---

68. WHITMAN, p. 92.
69. WHITMAN, p. 91-92.
70. CANDAGE, p. 85.
71. OCROD, Book 8, Page 521.
72. OCROD, Book 8, Page 509. Joshua Crockett, Jr. purchased Lot 43, excepting 21 acres and 40 rods of "Bog Land," from Edward Little on October 13, 1812, two years prior to Ephraim's enlistment for the defense of Portland. Joshua Crockett, Jr. and his wife Martha (Pike) Crockett were married September 4, 1812. Martha gave birth to their first child, Mahalon, in September of 1815. The family, which swelled to nine children, owned most of Lot 43, until Mahalon sold the property in March of 1847 to Nathan Crockett and his older brother Ephraim Stanford Crockett. The sale occurred eighteen months after Mahalon's father's death (presumably, his mother was deceased, as well). OCROD Book 79, Page 59. See also LAPHAM, p. 484-486 for this Crockett family's genealogy.
73. Lot 43 was situated just north of where Pam and Errol Libby reside today.
74. LAPHAM, p. 23-24. Nathaniel Young, Jr. purchased the south half of Lot 44 from Edward Little on May 3, 1814. (Most of this half of Lot 44 is owned by two trusts, that of my late mother, the Rowena Palmer Trust; and that of my brother and his wife, the Wesley and Lori Wixson Family Trust.) Isaac Bennett purchased the north half on May 23, 1814. (This is the half where Revolutionary War veteran Daniel Knight would eventually settle and where Pam and Errol Libby reside today.) Whether Bennett, Young, or Joshua Crockett, Jr. were living on their land in September of 1814 when Ephraim Crockett

is likely that Young or Bennett (or both men), as well as Joshua Crockett, Jr., were working the land they purchased when Ephraim Crockett marched off to defend Portland.

Ephraim was not alone on the road, either. He enlisted in Bodwell's company with two of Joshua Crockett, Jr.'s younger brothers—Lewis, age nineteen, and Samuel, age twenty-one.[75] This fact—combined with the proximity of Ephraim Crockett, Jr.'s and Joshua Crockett, Sr's homesteads (three miles apart) reveal a close familial connection that existed between these extended Crockett relations.

Joshua, Jr., Lewis, and Samuel were sons of Joshua Crockett, Sr. and Sarah (Hamblin) Crockett. The elder Joshua Crockett was another Revolutionary War veteran who sought land in the backcountry after the war, and who was probably a first cousin to Ephraim Crockett, Jr.'s father.[76] The son of Lieutenant Joshua Crockett,[77] Joshua moved to Norway with his wife and four young sons around 1795.[78] By 1814, the boys had grown up and the family were old-timers in the area, having built a substantial homestead on the western side of Little Pennesseewassee Pond (where Shepherd's Farm Preserve now is located).[79] Crockett's Bridge over the causeway was named for this family of Crocketts.

Captain Bailey Bodwell's company consisted of forty-five privates (of which Ephraim, Lewis, and Samuel Crockett were three), four sergeants, four corporals, and two musicians. In Portland, the company joined up with Lieutenant Colonel W. Ryerson's regiment, where they awaited a potential British attack. The attack never materialized.[80] After ten days of waiting, Bodwell released the men, and most of them marched back to Norway. (On September 25, Bodwell formed a new, larger company of mostly Portland men, although some of the Norway recruits remained

---

marched off to defend Portland is not known, but probable.

75. "Records of the Massachusetts Volunteer Militia War of 1812-1815," p. 252. For the ages of Lewis and Samuel I used the genealogy information in LAPHAM, p. 484-485, confirmed by CANDAGE, p. 94-95.

76. CANDAGE, p. 11. Candage notes he was unable to accurately connect Joshua Crockett, Sr. to the family tree because histories of Gorham, from where Joshua was said to have hailed, do not jive with Candage's research. It seems clear to me, however, that Joshua Crockett, Sr. and Ephraim Crockett, Sr. were related. (See next footnote.)

77. Lieutenant Joshua Crockett, the father of Joshua Crockett, Sr. who moved to Norway, was most likely a son of Richard Crockett II and his wife Mary (Robinson) Crockett, as was Richard Crockett III, the father of Ephraim Crockett, Sr. In other words, Ephraim Crockett, Sr. (of Danville) was probably a first cousin of Joshua Crockett, Sr. of Norway.

78. WHITMAN, p. 43.

79. In my earlier history of the Crockett family (written in the 1970s), I surmised that Ephraim, Jr. might have been shown Lot 45 by his father's relation, Joshua Crockett, Sr., one of the town's old timers, who possibly extolled the virtues of the area. Now, I believe that although Ephraim might have known his father's relatives who were living in Norway, it was more likely that he was shown the lot by Edward Little. It was also possible that Little gave Ephraim a copy of Greenwood's lot map of Lee's Grant so that he could travel to the area at his convenience to appraise Lot 45.

80. U.S. Adjutant General Military Records, 1631-1976. "Records of the Massachusetts Volunteer Militia, War of 1812-1814."

with the Captain until that company was released November 5th.)[81] Ephraim Crockett, Jr. was paid for ten days of service, plus three days of marching.[82] Prior to returning home, Ephraim likely made a visit to his grandfather Richard Crockett (III), then seventy-nine, who lived in Cape Elizabeth.

The Treaty of Ghent, the peace treaty between the United States and Great Britain, was signed in Ghent (then part of the Netherlands), December 24, 1814, two months after Ephraim Crockett, Jr. returned to Norway. The treaty was ratified by Congress on February 17, 1815,[83] ending the hostilities. The treaty formally opened U.S. markets to trade once again, not only with England, but also with other foreign ports, such as the West Indies, which had been blocked during the embargo. Former schoolteacher David Noyes captures the moment peace was declared in his Norway history:

> "In 1814, I [had] left my school to make ball-cartridges for the soldiers when they marched to Portland, but now I left it rather early in the afternoon to help the boys, and even the men of all classes, make preparations for their evening rejoicing. Several of the larger houses were handsomely illuminated, and the delightful word, 'PEACE,' exhibited in many a window. The boys had a little homemade artillery-piece, and although gunpowder was very dear, there was a plenty furnished; crackers and squibs were also added to help along; and to cap the climax, uncle Nat Bennet happened to have a tar-barrel, with a few gallons of tar in it, which was sent for, mounted on a hand-sled, set on fire, and drawn through our beautiful street, amidst the popping of crackers and squibs, the roar of the boys' artillery, and the loud huzzas of boys of 'larger growth.' "[84]

"Like Brothers" – Ephraim Crockett, Jr. and Nathan Morse, Jr.

By late 1813, Ephraim Crockett, Jr. knew he was in a bind. It had become obvious to him that Josiah Hill was not going to be the partner he hoped for. Although Hill lived in Norway, he apparently was disinclined to homestead Lee's Grant, where Ephraim, Sally, and young Sarah were building their future. What was Ephraim to do? He needed someone to help him repurchase Lot 45. Equally important, Ephraim

---
81. IBID, p. 255-256.
82. U.S. Adjutant General Military Records, 1631-1976. "Records of the Massachusetts Volunteer Militia, War of 1812-1814."
83. NOYES, p. 109.
84. NOYES, p. 109-110.

needed a partner with whom to share the physical labor of land-clearing and homesteading. In addition, he needed a friend for his wife in the backcountry and playmates for their children. Although Daniel Knight's wife Sally resided in the greater neighborhood, she was Ephraim's mother's age. Second cousin Joshua Crockett, Jr., who owned Lot 43, was not yet married.[85] Where was Ephraim to turn?

As was usual with the Crocketts, Ephraim directed his attention to his first family. At some point, perhaps not long after he returned from his march to Portland (or on the way home), Ephraim persuaded his younger sister Mary and her husband Nathan Morse, Jr. to throw in with him and Sally in the second purchase of Lot 45. In early 1814, Nathan and Mary were living in Pejepscot, where they had resided since their wedding on February 10, 1809.[86] At the time of the proposal from their brother and brother-in-law, Nathan and Mary had three young children at home, and Mary was pregnant with their fourth.[87] A move to Norway would be a big undertaking.

Much like his wife and brother-in-law, Nathan Morse came from pioneer stock. He was the son of Nathan Morse, Sr., another veteran of the American Revolution. At the onset of hostilities with the British, the senior Morse was living in Dedham, Massachusetts, where he was a minuteman on the alarm list.[88] When the alarm was given that the British were coming on April 19, 1775, Nathan Morse, Sr. turned out for the battles of Concord and Lexington.[89] After the first skirmishes and after General Washington had formed his army, Morse served in the "Northern Department," where he marched to Bennington.[90] He was eventually promoted to sergeant.[91] After the war ended, Nathan Morse, Sr. relocated to the backcountry of Lewiston,[92] a new town formed by the Pejepscot Proprietors across the Androscoggin River from the settlement of Pejepscot. Nathan, Jr. was born in Lewiston to Sergeant Nathan Morse and his wife Sarah (Bacon) Morse in August of 1788.[93]

Nathan and Mary were young when they married, ages eighteen and nineteen, respectively. I am unclear exactly where they were living in Pejepscot when they were approached by their brother and brother-in-law in 1814, although the 1810

---

85. Joshua Crockett married Judith Pike on September 4, 1814. CANDAGE, p. 94.
86. Morse genealogy, NHS. Mary was eighteen (going on nineteen) and Nathan was twenty at the time of their marriage.
87. SETTLERS, p. 4 and Morse Genealogy, NHS.
88. SETTLERS, p. 4 and WHITMAN p. 474.
89. SETTLERS, p. 4.
90. SETTLERS, p. 4.
91. SETTLERS, p. 4.
92. SETTLERS, p. 4.
93. Morse genealogy, NHS.

U.S. Census for Pejepscot shows them in the general Wagg-Crockett neighborhood. There are no records indicating Nathan purchased any real estate in Pejepscot or even in Lewiston.[94] It is possible Nathan was a tenant farmer, managing a farm for an absentee landlord in exchange for a share of the produce. If so, a proposition to own his own property would have seemed very attractive.

Most Norway histories suggest that Nathan Morse and Ephraim Crockett moved to Norway in 1814-1815, implying that the two men came together. I believe this is incorrect. Obviously, Ephraim was in Norway in September of 1814 when he (and Josiah Hill) deeded Lot 45 back to Little. In addition, shortly thereafter, we know Ephraim joined Bodwell's company for Norway. Had Nathan been with Ephraim in September of 1814, he, too, would probably have joined the company. Just as likely, had Nathan been in Norway then, he would have already agreed to purchase Lot 45 with his brother-in-law; thus, there would have been no reason why Crockett and Morse could not have facilitated the transaction with Edward Little earlier than February of 1816.

I believe that Nathan arrived in Norway early in 1815, probably waiting to travel there until after the safe birth of his and Mary's fourth child, Judith, who was born in Danville in November of 1814.[95] Mary would have stayed in Pejepscot with the children (and her family) while Nathan traveled to assess Lot 45. Unfortunately, baby Judith only lived two years. As her place of death is not recorded (just the date), I suspect Judith died in Norway, which would mean that the entire Morse family was living on Lee's Grant by October of 1816. In fact, in 1816, Nathan Morse (like Ephraim Crockett) was taxed $.55 by the Town of Norway on property valued at $252. (Ephraim's property was valued at $250, and he also paid $.55.)[96] The couple's fifth child (also named Judith) was born December 24, 1817, in Norway.[97] By then, Nathan and Ephraim had already signed a mortgage to Edward Little for Lot 45.

The warmth of relations between the two men—Ephraim Crockett and Nathan Morse—cannot be overstated. (In a token of affection, Ephraim and Sally named

---

94. See CCROD. Nor are there real estate transactions for Nathan Morse, Sr. in Lewiston, either, which means Sergeant Morse might have tangled with rapacious land speculator and Pejepscot proprietor Josiah Little, who was reviled by many in the area. If so, Morse likely lost.
95. Morse Genealogy, NHS.
96. LAPHAM, p. 637. This tax was payable under an Act of Congress passed March 5, 1816 whereby "lands, lots, dwelling-houses, etc." were taxed at a rate of twenty-two cents per hundred dollars of valuation.
97. Morse Genealogy, NHS. This child was baptized "Judith Crockett Morse." Unlike her namesake, the first Judith (who died just before her second birthday), Judith Crockett Morse lived to be seventy-four years old.

their fifth child Nathan Morse Crockett.)[98] In describing the two men, Norway historian Charles F. Whitman characterizes their relationship as that of brothers:

> "Mr. Crockett & his wife had thirteen children and Mr. Morse and his wife, twelve. Both were men of stability, upright in their dealings with others, moral, industrious and frugal. These qualities descended to their posterity. They lived and died with the respect and confidence of all who knew them and for over forty years they had been the closest of friends and neighbors. In fact, each regarded the other as an affectionate brother."[99]

Each man would have helped the other build their respective homesteads. Nathan would have contributed to the final construction of Ephraim's post-and-beam house, situated on the north half of Lot 45. Ephraim, in turn, would have assisted in the house-raising for the Morse family on the southern half of the lot. Together, the two men would have cleared the fields, dug the rocks out of the ground, and built the sturdy stone walls that fenced in their properties. Those stone walls still stand today—two hundred years later.

Stone wall on Ephraim Crockett's land on Crockett's Ridge.
Possibly built together by Ephraim and his brother-in-law Nathan Morse.
(Jennifer Wixson photo)

---

98. Crockett Genealogy, NHS.
99. SETTLERS, p. 1.

Nathan Morse and Ephraim Crockett probably even built together the "cow lane" that runs between the two homesteads. The cow lane consists of two parallel stone walls set about forty-five feet apart, running perpendicular to the road in a westerly direction down to the lake. Livestock from early generations of our family[100] was driven down (or turned out into) the cow lane to graze their way down the hill to the grassy sward along the edge of Lake Pennesseewassee.[101]

By 1828 Ephraim and Nathan had their homesteads so much in hand that they decided to expand their acreage. This might have come about after a trip made by Edward Little to Norway in April of that year. Edward, who had gone through bankruptcy by this time, was permanently living in Danville. From there, he managed much of his father Josiah Little's Maine real estate, including lots and farms on Lee's Grant (which Edward had sold to his father to protect the real estate from attachment by his creditors). Edward, who was regularly pressed for money by his father to help pay for Edward's old debts, appears to have called upon Nathan Morse during his April trip. While there, Edward sold Ephraim's brother-in-law half of Lot 30—the half to the south of the Cross Road, which adjoined on the east both Crockett's and Morse's land. On June 10, 1828, Edward wrote to Josiah and in the letter enclosed "a deed to Nathan Morse of a small sale made to him when last at Norway…."[102] On July 16, 1828, however, in another letter to his father, Edward enclosed a deed to both Ephraim Crockett and Nathan Morse for the same land. He wrote:

> "I enclose a deed to Morse + Crocket of the same land you executed a deed of to Morse. It was to both so I cancel that deed + wish you to execute + return this I have between $200 + $300 on hand to send when opportunity offers and expect more to be added."[103]

---

100. My mother's cousin George "Jo Bill" Young told me the history of the cow lane in a conversation we had at his kitchen table on March 7, 2020. George, who learned the information from his father, said the cow lane led down to the lake where it was all open meadow. "The cows would be brought back and forth on the lane by a dog, after spending their day in the meadow eating, and drinking from the lake." Another cousin of my mother's, Norman Young, in a phone conversation in August of 2020, told me that the cow lane was not in use during his time on the farm. As a child and young adult Norman spent summers on Young's Turkey Farm (as the place was known then) in the 1940s and early '50s with his grandparents and cousins (my mother and her siblings). According to Norman, the cow lane was "all grown up (to shrubs and trees)," as it still is today. (JoBill's father George W. Young was a generation ahead of his nephew Norman Young and therefore was closer to the time when the cow lane was still in use.)
101. When Nathan Morse and Ephraim Crockett split Lot 45, the cow lane ended up with Ephraim. On June 30, 2009, my cousin Pam (Young) Williams and her husband Lloyd purchased this interesting piece of family land and history. It was a natural purchase since they own the land on the Morse side of the wall. (OCROD Book 4464, Page 99.)
102. DEARPARENT, p. 140.
103. DEARPARENT, p. 141.

In fact, Crockett and Morse paid $210 for the south half of Lot 30. No mortgage was given, which means the men paid cash, probably the "between $200 + $300" mentioned in Edward's letter to his father. Edward, who prepared the deeds for his father, dated the deed to Crockett and Morse April 28, 1828. Josiah Little signed the second deed to both men on July 18, 1828, and, at some point, returned the instrument to Edward in Danville. (See Appendix #5 for a copy of this deed, which was recorded at the Oxford County Registry of Deeds in Book 79, Page 177.) Edward probably took the deed to Ephraim Crockett and Nathan Morse the next time he visited the Norway area. Unlike today, when a deed for real estate is given only after the payment has been received, the 1826-1830 letters[104] exchanged between the Josiah Little in Newbury, Massachusetts and Edward Little in Danville reveal that it was not uncommon for land to be purchased and paid for before a deed was executed. Apparently, settlers such as Ephraim Crockett and Nathan Morse trusted Edward Little (or they had no choice but to trust him if they wanted the property).

Crockett and Morse's new acquisition contained 44 acres and 110 rods. They paid approximately $4.75 per acre, somewhat less than the $6 per acre the brothers-in-law paid for Lot 45 (and less than the $5-$7 per acre that Josiah Little typically charged for land in Maine). Edward appears to have had license from his father to set a per-acre price of what he felt the market would bear. Since Edward was regularly pressed for money by his father, he probably lowered the price to net some quick cash.[105]

The addition of half Lot 30 afforded both Ephraim Crockett and Nathan Morse some better-quality land to the east of their holdings to clear and cultivate. Compared to the excellent bottomland on the Androscoggin River that Ephraim's father, Ephraim Crockett, Sr., farmed in Danville, the land in Norway on Lot 45 farmed by Ephraim, Jr. and Morse was rock-strewn, hard-scrabble, hilly, and had multiple ledge outcroppings. While part of Lot 30 had a swamp with a brook running through it (and still does, as all of us who have hunted that land know), much of the property that abuts the Cross Road is flat with good soils and is still in farm production today. The Lee's Grant lot map (later in the chapter) shows what

---
104. These letters were published in Dr. Hodgkin's book, "Dear Parent."
105. In the 1826-1830 letters exchanged between father and son there are many times when Josiah Little pressed his son for money and/or encouraged Edward to press harder to collect monies due from tenants or land buyers. See previous chapter for a few examples from DEARPARENT that occurred around the time of the Crockett/Morse sale of land in which Edward responds to his father's pressure.

a natural addition to their holdings the southern half of Lot 30 was for Crockett and Morse.

Ephraim Crockett and Nathan Morse had so much trust and confidence in one another that they did not draw up deeds dividing their jointly-owned real estate until April 16, 1833[106]—nearly twenty years after they purchased Lot 45 and five years after they purchased part of Lot 30. On the ground, the two men had divided their land from the beginning—the stone walls attest to this fact—but the deeded split was not executed until 1833. This legal separation was probably made with an eye to the future. After all, their many children—more than twenty altogether—were growing up. In 1833, Nathan and Mary's eldest child, Joseph, would turn twenty-three[107] and Ephraim and Sally's eldest, Sarah, twenty.[108] The description of what Ephraim Crockett released out of Lot 45 to Nathan Morse is as follows:

> "… all that part of the home lot on which said Morse now lives, lying southerly of the following described line, viz. beginning at a green hemlock tree marked as a corner in the east end line of said lot, thence south seventy-six degrees west, to a stake near the pond, containing fifty-five acres more or less."[109]

Nathan Morse released the other half of Lot 45 to Ephraim Crockett. His deed reads:

> "…all that part of the old or homestead lot on which the said Crockett now lives, which lies northerly of the following described line, beginning at a green hemlock tree marked as a corner, in the middle of the lot line on the east end of the lot, thence south seventy-six degrees west, to a stake near the pond, containing fifty-five acres more or less."[110]

---

106. OCROD, Book 80, Page 62 and 63.
107. Morse Genealogy, NHS.
108. Crockett Genealogy, NHS.
109. OCROD, Book 80, Page 62. See Appendix #7 for a copy of this deed.
110. OCROD, Book 80, Page 63. See Appendix #8 for a copy of this deed.

Stone wall separating the adjoining properties of Ephraim Crockett and Nathan Morse on Lot 45. (Photo by Jennifer Wixson, 2020.)

Lot 30 was split up in a more interesting fashion. Ephraim Crockett took seven acres of land that adjoined Lot 45. This piece netted him a woodlot close to the house.[111] For his share, Nathan Morse took seventeen acres abutting his land, which bulged out to the north and east, the entire middle section of the brothers-in-laws' property on Lot 30. Morse's addition provided some excellent farmland along the Cross Road.[112] To even out the split, Ephraim was also allotted nine acres at the end of the Cross Road, which piece of land fronts two roads. The total landmass in their mutual deeds added up to thirty-three acres rather than the forty-four acres described in their deed from Josiah Little. This fact suggests that when the land was surveyed for the split, it was discovered that there were not forty-four acres to begin with.[113] This brings the per acre price to over $6 per acre, which was more in line with Josiah Little's land prices, although unintended by Edward Little at the time of sale.

---

111. This cut expanded to the east the field and woodlot owned in 2024 by William Quimby, as well as a small section of land on the east side of the road currently owned by my cousin Pam and her husband, Lloyd Williams.
112. The section of Morse's land along the Cross Road is owned in 2024 by Gerald Frechette.
113. In my deed research, I did not find that either Morse or Crockett had sold off land in Lot 30 before the split.

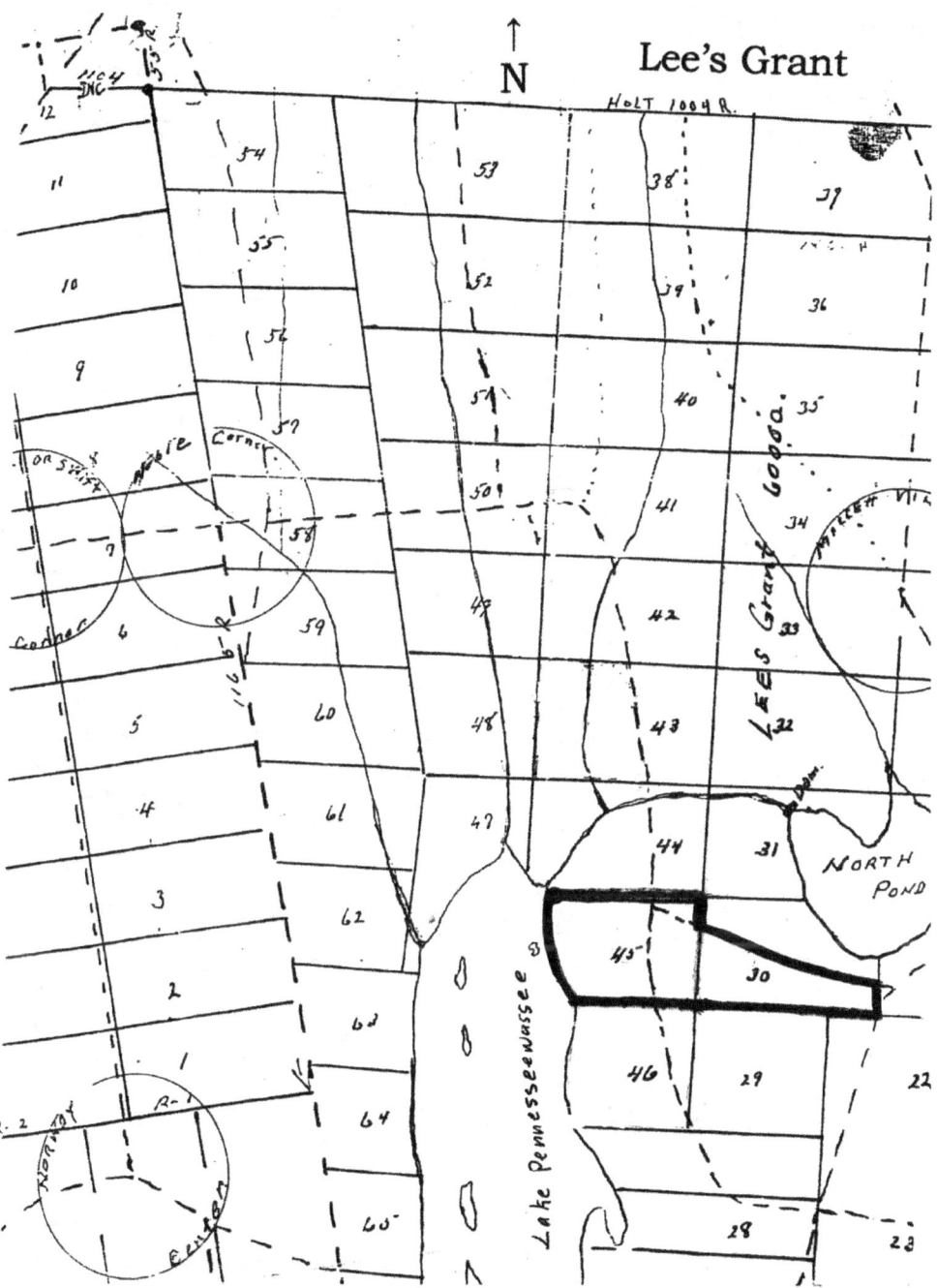

Lee's Grant map, Crockett and Morse holdings on Lot 45 and Lot 30 in 1828.
In 1828, Ephraim Crockett and Nathan Morse expanded their holdings to include half of Lot 30, the northern line of the property running along what is known today as the Cross Road.

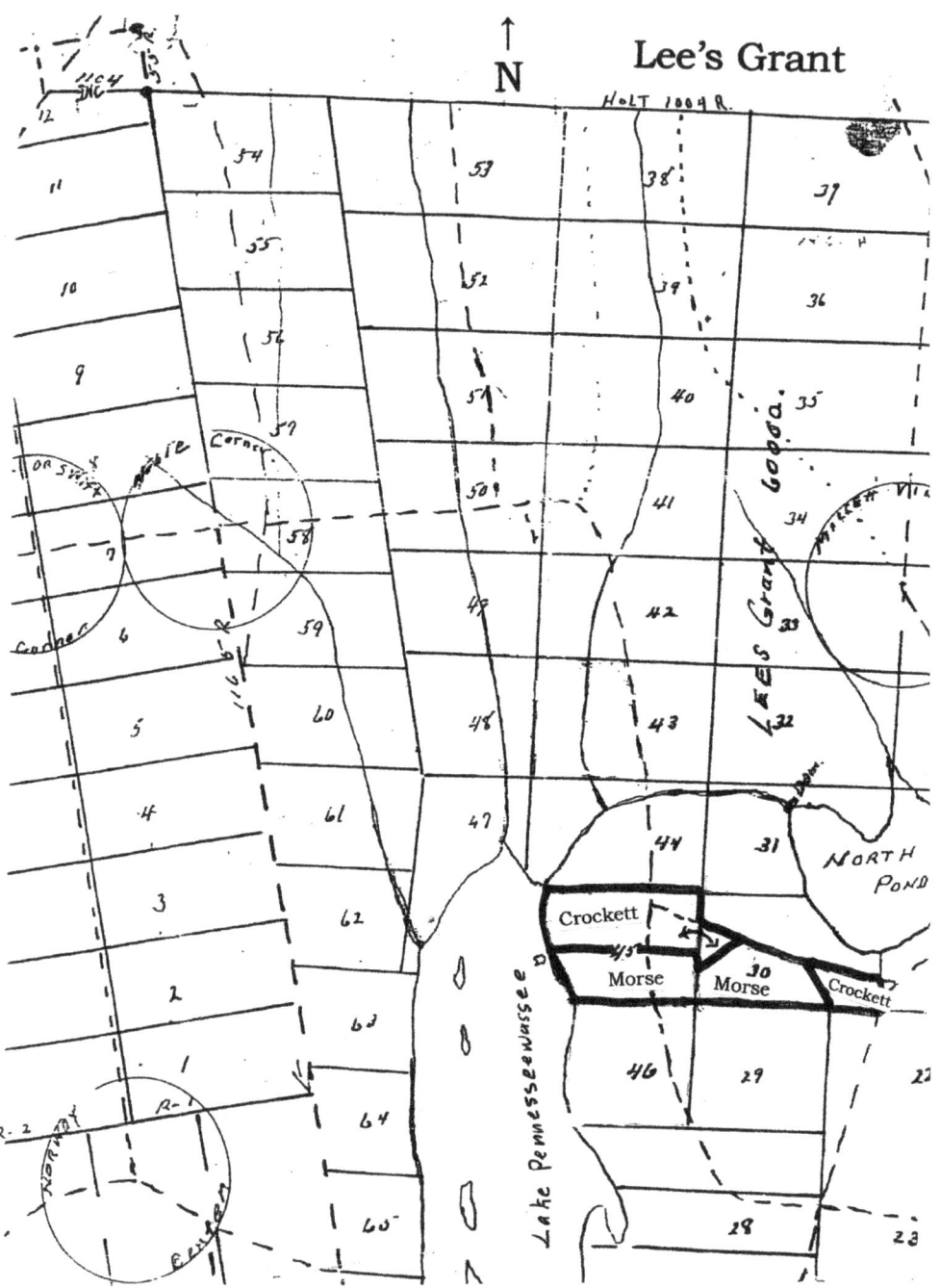

Lee's Grant map, Crockett and Morse split their joint property in 1833.
(NOTE: this hand-drawn lot division is not to scale.)

Iron pipe in the woods next to the Cross Road. This pipe marked the southeast corner of the Crockett-Morse line when the two men split the south half of Lot 30.
(Jennifer Wixson photo, 2020)

During my many years of research on the Crockett and Morse families, I have not been able to unearth a single photograph of Nathan Morse or even one of Mary (Crockett) Morse. Fortunately, historian Charles Whitman penned a detailed description of this wonderful couple, whose willingness to cast their lot with our ancestors Ephraim and Sally (Wentworth) Crockett played a significant role in our family history. Whitman writes:

"Mr. Morse had a light complexion and was of medium height and thickness. His wife was more slightly built, and of good form. She had dark eyes, full of spirit and swiftness and showed even in old age the beauty she must have had in youth."[114]

Ephraim and Sally's Family, and Life in Norway

Ephraim and Sally (Wentworth) Crockett raised thirteen children in Norway. Their children all lived to adulthood, although the second son and third child, Ephraim Stanford Crockett, had a narrow escape from the jaws of death. When he was about sixteen, Ephraim Stanford was saved from drowning by playmate Claudius Noyes, who lived across "the pond" (Lake Pennesseewassee) from the Crocketts. (Both families owned property that ran down to the lake.) Historian David Noyes, father of young Claudius, relates the story:

> "About 1833, on thanksgiving day, Ephraim S. Crockett, a son of Ephraim Crockett, who lives on the east side of the pond, nearly opposite the writer's farm, thinking to have a fine time skating on the ice, crossed the head of the pond to D. Noyes' [the author's home], and Claudius A. Noyes, then about twelve years of age, went with him to participate in the amusement of skating. They skated awhile, and growing more venturesome, went near the middle of the pond, when Crockett broke in, and could not get upon the ice again, as when he attempted to spring upon it, it would break, without assisting him from the water. In this dilemma, C.A. Noyes, although but a small boy, told him to hold upon the edge of the ice, and he would soon help him; he then skated quickly to the shore and took a long, slim pole from a fence, and going, within the length of the pole, to the other boy, he laid himself down on the ice, and reached him the small end, which he grasped tightly, and giving a smart spring, was pulled out of the water, and drawn to where the ice was strong enough to bear them. They had had skating enough for one thanksgiving."[115]

As mother of an extensive family, Sally's responsibilities were legion. In addition to her daily tasks, Sally was pregnant and/or nursing an infant for twenty-five years—a quarter of a century! Today, it is almost unfathomable to consider that—while nursing her babies and with multiple children at her knee—Sally kept the

---
114. SETTLERS, p. 4.
115. NOYES, p. 148-149.

house running and her husband and children fed, especially during the early years. Later, the older children would help the younger children and provide labor for the home and farm work. Female work consisted of household chores, such as cooking, sewing, weaving, and spinning. The boys would help their father (and uncle Nathan) in the fields and woods. Altogether, theirs was a large and busy family.

Some type of rough cabin was probably fashioned for the Crockett family before the post-and-beam house was built. Virgin timber was cut from the land, with hemlock the first choice for the sills due to its rot-resistant nature. Most of the house would have been built with pine and fir, thanks to its abundance in the area. Large diameter logs were hauled a short distance up the road to a sawmill located on the outlet to North Pond, owned and operated by William Foye.[116] The sawyer ran a mechanically-operated sash-type sawmill, which utilized a waterwheel to operate a straight saw blade that cut up and down (in a similar fashion as a pit saw worked by two men, one of whom would stand below the other in a pit while pushing and pulling a long saw up and down).[117] The up-and-down marks left on a board by a "pit" or "sash" saw are easily distinguishable from the curved marks left on boards by later circular saws. Following are photos of two boards from the shed of the old Crockett homestead, sawn decades apart, displaying the two types of saw marks. The first board came from a large tree that Ephraim Crockett would have hauled up to Foye's sawmill.

---

116. WHITMAN, p. 168. An "old settler's son," Foye purchased from Edward Little 61 ½ acres of the east end of Lot 41 on May 21, 1815 and proceeded to erect the sawmill on the stream that became known as "Foye Brook." Later, according to WHITMAN, Col. John Millett purchased this sawmill. NOYES, whose Norway history was published in 1852, says that Millett's mill "cuts from one hundred to one hundred and fifty thousand (board feet) annually." p. 179.

117. According to the website Ledyard Up-Down Sawmill (www.ledyardsawmill.org) sash-type sawmills operated about two hundred years in New England from 1630 onward. This low-tech operation consisted of "a wooden waterwheel with a crank connected by the 'pitman' arm to a wooden sash (frame) in which was mounted a straight saw blade…In 1800, essentially all sawmills were of the sash type, with the wooden building and structural components of the saw mechanism made locally by the millwright (except the steel saw blade, iron crank, and a few other parts)."

Straight up-and-down sash saw marks on board in the shed attached
to the old Crockett homestead.
(Photo by Jennifer Wixson, 2020.)

The type of saw that cut this board was identified in 2024 by Alan Ganong, a volunteer with Ledyard Up-Down Sawmill, a water-powered sawmill in Ledyard, Connecticut. In an email to the author Ganong writes:

"The board with the straight saw marks is from a sash, or up-down, sawmill. The marks are straight across the board and evenly spaced. The spacing shows the distance the log carriage moved the log on each stroke as the sawing advanced through the log. Sash sawmills were used through the colonial period and began to disappear in the mid-1800s (as circular sawmills became more common), although a few were still in operation into the early 20th century. (Marks from a two-man pitsaw are not as straight and the spacing is uneven)."[118]

According to Ganong, the second board (opposite page) was sawn much later:

---

118. Email from Alan Ganong to Jennifer Wixson, April 12, 2024.

"The other photo shows marks from a circular sawmill. Circular sawmills came into common use starting in about the 1840s-1850s, so this board would have been sawn decades after the original homestead date of 1814."[119]

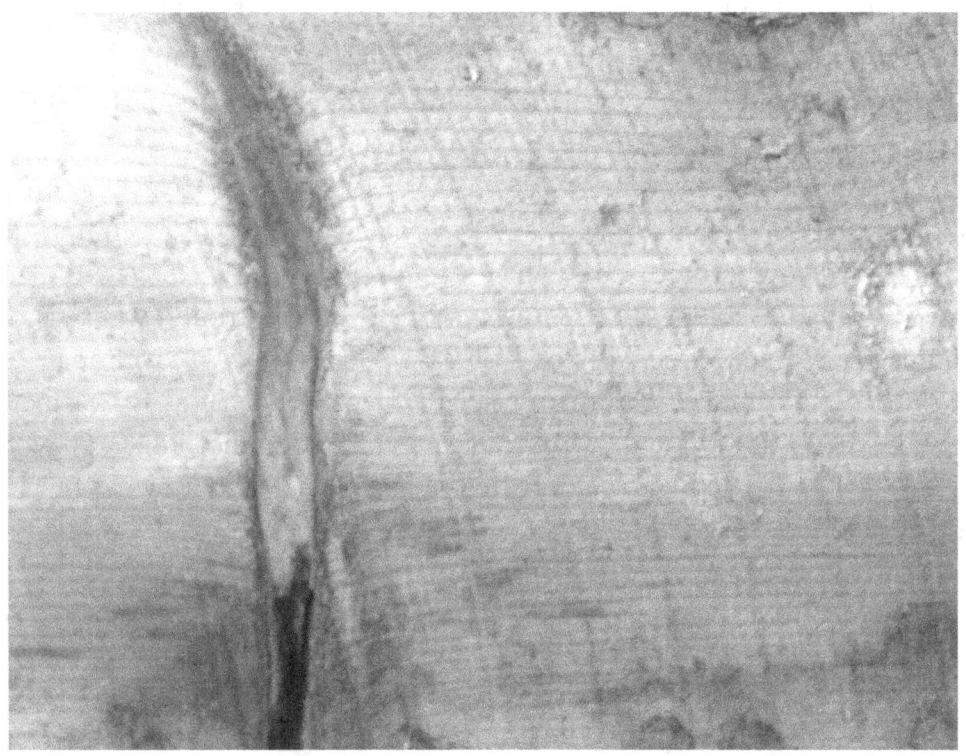

Circular saw marks on board in the shed attached to the old Crockett homestead.
This board was sawn decades later than the board shown in the prior photo
(probably at a different sawmill).
(Photo by Jennifer Wixson, 2020.)

When I lived with my grandmother in the 1970s and early '80s, she told me all that was left of the original Crockett house was the pantry.[120] Formerly a milk room until repurposed by my grandmother, the pantry (now gone) was only eight feet wide by seventeen-and-a-half feet long. I never saw evidence of a chimney (or a cut-out for a chimney) in the pantry, although the northwest corner of the later-built brick house did jut into the small room, and conceivably there could

---
119. IBID.
120. My grandmother was told this by her parents; she was not old enough to have seen the original house. But having renovated three post-and-beam houses since Winona shared this information with me, I am not sure I believe the milk room was part of the original house. I think it might have been a later addition. The attached shed, from which I took the photographs of the boards, was likely part of the original structure, however.

have been a chimney there. Many first-generation homes were constantly expanded without regard for beauty or consequence simply to meet the growing needs of the family. (With thirteen children, the Crockett family certainly needed more room over time!) These cobbled-together houses were usually replaced by so-called "second-generation" homes, which, like the elegant brick house built on the site in 1850 by Ephraim and his son William Robinson Crockett, were designed with an eye to style as well as utility.

The first order of business for Crockett and Morse was to clear land on which to build a home and plant crops. Land clearing was typically accomplished by burning down the old-growth trees. The burn not only provided space to plant but also ash for soil amendment. Indian corn was then planted around what was left of the stumps rather than in the neat rows or blocks like we plant corn today.

The early years on Lee's Grant must have been challenging for farmers like Ephraim Crockett and Nathan Morse. The year 1815, a harbinger of worse to come, was "cold and backward," according to historian David Noyes. On May 18, 1815, Noyes reported:

> "… a snow-storm commenced, and the next morning the snow was eighteen inches deep on an average. The funeral of Charles Stevens, the oldest son of Nathaniel Stevens, took place on [May] 19th, and people had hard work to get to the funeral with sleighs, on account of the snow; but the sun shining out warm, carried it off very suddenly."[121]

However bad the weather was in 1815, the cold did not hold a candle to the following year. The year 1816, known around the world as "the year without a summer," visited frost upon farmers in Norway every month of the year, and brought snow in June.[122] As a youth, I often heard my grandparents and great-grandparents refer to 1816 with a shudder, having been told of the cold weather calamity by their elders. In 1816, climate abnormalities caused by the volcanic eruption of Mount Tambora in Indonesia created a "volcanic winter," which lowered global temperatures by 0.72–1.3°F and created food shortages throughout the Northern Hemisphere.[123] In addition, settlers in Maine also suffered a drought in 1816, which later caused thousands of acres of land in western Maine to burn in what became known

---
121. NOYES, p. 113-114.
122. WHITMAN, p. 72.
123. "The Great Tambora Eruption in 1815 and Its Aftermath." Richard B. Stothers. *Science* magazine. Vol. 224, Issue 4654. June 15, 1984. Pp. 1191-1198.

as "the Great Fire."[124] Noyes, who was farming himself in 1816, recollects in his 1852 history the cold and its aftereffects from the year without a summer:

> "The spring was unusually cold and backward; there were snow squalls on the 7th, 8th, and 9th days of June, and on the 7th, plowed ground actually froze in many places…The crops in 1816 were very much injured by the cold and drought, and an early frost destroyed the corn. The writer this year planted the first corn on his new farm, on a piece of burnt ground by the side of the pond [Norway Lake]; and when the early frost came, the fog from the pond went over the corn, and saved it from injury in a great degree; and he probably had more sound corn than all north of the center of the town."[125]

In 1817, seed corn was worth "$3 or more per bushel," according to Noyes, who sold four bushes to Major Jonathan Cummings "to furnish the poor settlers in part, on his new settlement."[126] Due to Ephraim's location up on the ridge, his corn might have been spared the worst effects of the 1816 frost, even though he lived north of the center of town where the frost was worst. (Cold air sinks, which is why apple trees, to protect their blossoms, are now planted on hilltops, although in the early years, they were often planted next to a stone wall.) Nathan Morse, however, situated in a hollow below the Crocketts (but not as close to the lake as Noyes), most likely lost any corn he had planted. Fortunately, 1817 was an "abundant" harvest year, "perhaps never better," Noyes reports. "Although pressed by pinching want, people put a great deal of seed into the ground, and everything seemed to grow with great luxuriance."[127]

Although corn would have been the first crop planted by Ephraim and Nathan, as soon as more land was cleared, the two men would have expanded into the planting of wheat, rye, and oats.[128] Being somewhat late arrivals to the Norway area, they only had to haul their corn and grain into town for grinding. (Early settlers to Rust's Grant in the late 18th century had to cart their crops to Jackson's mill on Stony Brook in what is now South Paris.)[129] In the Village, Samuel Ames operated a gristmill situated on the outlet of Little Pennesseewassee Pond. As miller,

---

124. WHITMAN, p. 73.
125. NOYES, p. 113-115.
126. NOYES, p. 115-116. Major Cummings' settlement was a half township known as "Phillips Academy," now part of Greenwood. NOYES, p. 120.
127. NOYES, p. 116.
128. See 1850 Non-Population (Agricultural) Census for Norway.
129. WHITMAN, p. 62.

Ames would "take toll" for his labor, or appropriate "a certain quantity of the corn, wheat, and rye" from every lot ground.[130]

In 1818 and 1819, the idea of Maine gaining statehood was a hot topic. In 1819, voters in Norway, like in most towns in Maine, voted for independence from the thralldom of the Commonwealth of Massachusetts. We do not know how Ephraim Crockett or Nathan Morse voted; however, given that Ephraim marched to defend Portland because Massachusetts had abandoned Maine's defense during the War of 1812, I think we can surmise that both men voted for separation. On March 15, 1820, Maine's separation from Massachusetts went into effect under the Missouri Compromise and Maine was admitted into the Union as the 23rd state.

Gaining statehood probably had little effect on settlers' early lives. Life—and death—went on as usual. In the fall of 1823, a mysterious illness struck residents in northwest Norway. David Noyes writes that the sickness, "something like dysentery, accompanied with high fever … baffled the skill of the physicians in most cases," and killed thirteen people in one neighborhood.[131] Sadly, one of those who probably lost her life to this mysterious disease was Nathan and Mary Morse's thirteen-month-old daughter, Mary, who passed away on September 6, 1823. Death records kept by Mrs. Mercy A. Whitman note her death as caused by "lung fever."[132] The Crockett family was spared the worst, although we do not know if any of them—or others of the Morse family—were sickened.

Thanks to the reminiscences of Norway native Sebastian S. Smith, we have an excellent snapshot of the town amenities available to the Crockett and Morse families in 1825. Smith was born in Norway on February 1, 1819, making him the same age as Ephraim and Sally's fourth child Betsey Wentworth Crockett, who was born six days later.[133] Smith's recollection, "Norway Village in 1825," was first published by the *Lewiston Journal* in 1896 and later republished in its entirety by Whitman in his 1924 history.[134] According to Smith, the Village boasted thirty-five houses by 1825, as well as a sawmill, which operated on the opposite side of the stream from Samuel Ames' gristmill (and which Ames also ran for a short period). In addition, one could find in town several trading stores, a tavern, blacksmith services, a post

---

130. WHITMAN, p. 113. This information in Whitman's history comes from an 1896 *Lewiston Journal* article written by Sebastian S. Smith on Norway Village in 1825.
131. NOYES, p. 128.
132. LAPHAM, p. 558. See also NOYES, p. 194.
133. LAPHAM, p. 486. Betsey Wentworth (Crockett) Penley Chapman died January 26, 1876, twenty years before her contemporary Sebastian S. Smith penned "Norway Village in 1825."
134. See WHITMAN Chapter XX, p. 113-120.

office, a doctor, hat makers, a cobbler, dressmakers, harness and leather-makers,[135] a carding mill and a wool carder, a cabinet maker, a tannery, a wheelwright, who operated a second grist mill, a nail maker, and at least one religious meeting house. Also, cousin Lewis Crockett, who marched with Ephraim in Captain Bailey Bodwell's company for the defense of Portland, was a saddler in the Village[136] before later branching out into trade in Norway and Bryant's Pond.[137]

Smith also describes the first school he attended. The Village school operated two terms, although the "big boys" only attended during the winter term (likely because they would be helping in the field during the other term). The younger students were separated from the older kids by a wooden partition. Smith's oddest recollection about his early school years is of a certain teacher in the Village school, who had a singular way of disciplining her students. Smith writes:

> "My first teacher's name was Miss Allen. She punished her students in strange ways. She would often split the ends of sticks and put them on the children's noses. The longer the stick the more ashamed the scholars were. This reduced them to strict obedience."[138]

Smith concludes his reminiscences of Norway Village by observing how great the change had been from 1825 to 1896 when he penned his article. "The main thoroughfare has been crowded with new buildings," he writes, "new streets have been opened, and sections have been built up which then were covered with forest trees."[139]

Much like Norway Village, the Crockett neighborhood experienced an explosion of growth during the first few decades of the 19th century. New settlers arrived, as did a multitude of babies. The 1820 U.S. Census for Norway lists Ephraim and Sally Crockett with five children under the age of sixteen and Nathan and Mary Morse with six under that age. The Crocketts would add eight more children to the growing neighborhood over the next decade and the Morses six more children. Up the road, cousin Joshua Crockett, Jr. and his wife Martha also had a family of

---

135. According to the 1906 history, "Norway, Past *and* Present," the earliest harness store was started in 1801 by Benjamin Tucker. The store was still in the family more than a hundred years later when the history was written.
136. WHITMAN, p. 117.
137. LAPHAM, p. 485.
138. WHITMAN, p. 115.
139. WHITMAN, p. 120.

nine children (not all of them raised in the neighborhood, however, as Joshua, Jr. relocated his family down to Little Pennesseewassee Pond after his father died in 1844). Schools were quickly established. The Crockett, Morse, and other neighborhood children were educated at the corner schoolhouse, a one-mile walk from the Crockett homestead. (Today, the much-enlarged old schoolhouse across from the Heywood Club has been repurposed as a home.) The 1840 U.S. Census for Norway shows that girls, as well as boys, attended school, with the Crocketts chalking up eight scholars that year. Although there is no census data for Lee's Grant specifically (to my knowledge) since the grant had been folded into the town of Norway, the town's growth is illustrated by the following population data:

Growth of Population in Norway[140]
1790—448
1800—609
1810—1010
1820—1330
1837—1791

Parsing the numbers further, we can see the percentage of growth of Norway.

Census Year	Population	Percent Growth
1790[141]	448	35.9%
1800	609	65.8%
1810	1010	28.1%
1820	1294	32.4%
1830	1713	35.9%

Rather than growing up in a "wilderness," as did their parents in the backcountry of Pejepscot, the Crockett children came of age beside a well-traveled thoroughfare leading from Norway to Greenwood. According to Whitman, "One of the most traveled routes into Greenwood in those times from Norway Village, was through Lee's Grant, over what in later years and is now called Upton Ridge

---

140. This information was taken from a handwritten illustration in the front of one of my grandmother Winona Palmer's Norway history books. The book is now owned by Edward Staples, who allowed me to copy my grandmother's record and calculations, which I remembered from when I lived with her.
141. Norway was not incorporated until 1797. Until incorporation, Norway was part of the township called Rustfield, whose population in the 1790 census was 448. I am not sure from where my grandmother got her information.

[Upton Brothers Road] ...."[142] A traveler from the Village would have ridden up what is now Pleasant Street and then proceeded on the road around the pond (the original Crockett's Ridge Road) to the Upton Ridge road and from there into Greenwood. In fact, one of the regular travelers over this road was the post rider, Joshua Pool, a Revolutionary War veteran who first settled on Lee's Grant in 1797 (later, he relocated to Greenwood). In addition to delivering the mail, which came to Norway from Portland twice a week, Pool also delivered weather predictions in an almanac he created using "careful observance" of astronomical events. According to Whitman, Pool's almanac not only forecast the weather but also told of impending "disasters and calamities. [Pool's] advice and counsel were sought on every hand which he skillfully used for his own advantage."[143]

Not everyone took Pool's weather predictions as gospel, however. Whitman tells the story of a farmer in his dooryard, anxiously gauging whether or not it was going to rain that day, to whom Pool sagaciously advised he could proceed with his haying because the clouds would break up before noon and the sun would shine. Writes Whitman:

> "Thereupon [Pool] chirruped to his horse and rode off at a gallop. Soon missing something he had dropped, he turned and rode back to look for it, whereupon seeing the farmer he had accosted a short time before busily preparing for the hayfield, remarked: 'Ah, my friend, I see you have taken my advice and are getting ready to go into your field and cut down more grass.'
> 'Yes, by the Great George Washington, I am about to go into my hayfield,' retorted the farmer with some asperity, 'not to cut down more grass, but to get in what hay is bunched up, for I have noticed that when you predict fair weather, it generally rains.'"[144]

We know that growing up, the Crockett children spent a good deal of time with their grandparents in Danville because in adulthood, four of them—Sarah, Ephraim Stanford, Betsey, and Mary Amanda—married children of Captain John Penley, who lived next door to grandfather Ephraim Crockett, Sr. and grandmother Rebecca (Stanford) Crockett. There must have been prodigious intimacy between the Crockett and Penley families to account for the multiple marriages among them.

---
142. WHITMAN, p. 54.
143. WHITMAN, p. 54-55.
144. WHITMAN, p. 55. I like to think the smart farmer in Whitman's story of postman Pool could have been Ephraim Crockett or Nathan Morse.

Courtships would have been carried on by letter-writing, as well as via extended traveling visits, which were common in those days. In addition, the younger Crockett children often spent time with their older siblings after their Penley marriages. At their sibling's houses the unattached could more easily become acquainted with their in-law's brothers and sisters.[145] (John Penley had seventeen children with his two wives.)

By all accounts, the Crocketts were a happy, healthy, and loving family. Their emotional closeness as a family is substantiated by the fact that many of the grown children—once they had left the nest—elected to stay in the neighborhood near their parents. In fact, the four Crockett-Penleys purchased most of the lots around Ephraim, Jr.'s original purchase of Lot 45 and raised their own families on Lee's Grant. (In my youth, I affectionately described to outsiders the plentitude of family dwellings on Crockett's Ridge as "the Nest." Although hatching from different eggs in different generations, my second cousins and I all descended from the same line of chickens.)

The following list of Ephraim and Sally's children is taken from the Crockett genealogy compiled by the Norway, Maine Historical Society, with additional details provided by Charles Candage's Crockett genealogy. Since the next generation (covered in the following chapter) includes information on six of the thirteen Crockett children, I have provided additional information on the remaining seven children, who, for the most part, will pass from our story here:

1. Sarah Wentworth Crockett – born November 11, 1813, in Danville. Marries Charles Penley. Their life is covered in Chapter 3.
2. Samuel Wentworth Crockett – born January 15, 1815, in Norway. In 1838 or 1839, Samuel marries Nancy Twombly. They live in Norway before relocating to Sumner, where he is a farmer. After 1855, Samuel, Nancy, and their family go West to seek their fortune. She dies in 1857 in Prairie du Sac, Wisconsin. Samuel marries again at least once. Wisconsin must have agreed with Samuel because he dies in Eau Clair, Wisconsin, on August 17, 1909, at the age of 94—outliving all twelve of his siblings.[146]

---

145. Various Norway census data from 1850 onward show a good deal of shuffling around of family members, including children, among the Norway Crocketts and Penleys.
146. Find A Grave, 1600s-Current, Nancy Trombly Crockett and Samuel Wentworth Crockett, and Wisconsin, Marriage Index, 1820-1907, Samuel W. Crockett.

3. Ephraim Stanford Crockett – born July 20, 1817, in Norway. Marries Sally Dingley Penley. Their life is covered in Chapter 3.
4. Betsey Wentworth Crockett – born February 7, 1819, in Norway. Marries John Penley. Their life is covered in Chapter 3.
5. Nathan Morse Crockett – born September 18, 1821. Nathan marries Mary "Polly" D. Stowell of Paris (Maine) and begins his career as a farmer. Initially, he takes over the homestead from his father but later sells out to his brother William Robinson Crockett (our ancestor) and moves to Paris, where Nathan becomes a butcher.[147]
6. William Robinson Crockett (our ancestor) – born August 30, 1823, in Norway. Marries Lydia B. Stetson of Sumner. Their life is covered in Chapter 3.
7. David Bartlett Crockett – born July 27, 1825, in Norway. He marries Laura A. Swift. He is killed in a railway accident on the Grand Trunk Railroad in Gilead, Maine, on June 3, 1863.
8. James Sewall Crockett – born August 15, 1827, in Norway. He marries Salome Frank in Norway on December 8, 1850. We will meet James and Salome again in Chapter 3.
9. Joseph Francis "Frank" Crockett – born December 9, 1829, in Norway. We will visit with Frank and his wife Antoinette Stetson (a half-sister to William's wife Lydia Stetson) in the next chapter.
10. Hannah Jordan Crockett – born August 7, 1831, in Norway. Marries Thomas Hanford Richardson of Portland and Norway and remains in the Crockett's Ridge neighborhood. Their family's life is covered in Chapter 3.
11. Mary Amanda Crockett – born October 19, 1833, in Norway. Marries Isaiah Vickery Penley. Their life is covered in the next chapter.
12. Eliza Jane Crockett – born August 27, 1835, in Norway. Marries Joseph Little of Warren, New Hampshire, and goes to live with her husband's family in Warren.
13. Charles Alanson Crockett – born June 12, 1837, in Norway. Charles, like his older brother Samuel, goes West to seek his fortune. He settles in Indiana, where he marries Sarah B. League of Richmond. Eventually, Charles and Sarah make their home in Spring Grove. In 1865, Charles goes to work for the Panhandle railroad company. He becomes a veteran conductor for

---

147. 1870 U.S. Census, Paris, Maine.

the company and, from 1873 until 1891, conducts a passenger train that came to be known as "the Crockett accommodation train," running between Richmond and Indianapolis. In 1891, in a freak accident, Charles is thrown against a water tank and injured, forcing his retirement. For the next eight years, he suffers poor health and dies in 1899 from kidney failure.[148]

As one would assume about someone raising thirteen children, Ephraim did not become a rich man (in worldly goods, although one can certainly make a case that he was rich in what matters). The 1850 Non-Population (Agricultural) Census of Norway estimated the cash value of his farm in 1850 at $1,500, a modest amount compared to those of his neighbors, some of whose farms ranged from $2,000-$3,000. Indeed, in 1850 the estimated cash value of the farm owned by Charles Penley, Ephraim's son-in-law, was the same as his own—and Charles had only been in town five years![149] (Charles, who marries eldest Crockett child Sarah, is bankrolled by his wealthy father John Penley, as we will learn in the next chapter.) The agricultural census (see Appendix #9 for a copy of this 1850 census) notes Ephraim owned 60 acres of agricultural land and 20 acres of unimproved land. Given the rock-strewn, hilly nature of his farm, it is not surprising that sheep account for the majority of his livestock. In 1850, Ephraim was pasturing ten sheep. For comparison, Charles Penley had thirty-one sheep. Nathan Morse, who owned better crop land along the Cross Road, had none.

---

148. Information from Charles Crockett's obituary found at the Norway, Maine Historical Society.
149. NOYES, p. 155.

Colorized postcard, "A New England Road."
(The Hugh C. Leighton, Co. Manufacturers, Portland, ME. Printed in Frankfort, Germany.)

The Agricultural Census of 1850 also notes that Ephraim owned four oxen, five "milch" cows, a horse, and a pig. At the time the census was taken, Ephraim had 70 bushels of Indian corn on hand, 40 bushels of oats, and 13 bushels of rye.

In 1845, Sally came into some extra money when her father, Samuel Solley Wentworth of Danville, passed away. She and her sister Hannah sold their rights of inheritance to their father's real estate in Danville, including the right of reversion of the "Widdows Dower." Her son-in-law Charles Penley purchased their rights for $100.[150] (Charles dabbled in real estate, in addition to being a farmer and salesman.)[151] One hundred dollars was most likely the extent of Sally's inheritance from her father, since Samuel Solley Wentworth had another family by his second wife.

Conclusion to Chapter 2

On March 12, 1847, shortly after his fifty-ninth birthday, Ephraim Crockett, Jr. deeded his entire homestead—all the real estate Ephraim owned—to his third son (fifth child) Nathan Morse Crockett. This included the sections of Lots 45 and 30 that his brother-in-law Nathan Morse released to Ephraim when they split their property. Nathan Morse Crockett, who is noted in the deed as a "yeoman"

---

150. CCROD, Book 190, Page 49.
151. Per David Noyes, Charles Penley also engaged in trade, in addition to investing in real estate and farming. NOYES, p. 171-172.

(farmer), was to pay his father $500 for the real estate.[152] More important, however, Nathan promised in a separate conveyance deed to care for his parents for the rest of their natural lives. (See Appendix #10 & #11 for a copy of the warranty deed from Ephraim to his son, as well as Nathan's conveyance deed to his father.) If Nathan failed to provide for Ephraim and Sally as specified in this separate deed, the warranty deed on the property would be voided. What Nathan promised to provide his parents was comprehensively laid out in the conveyance deed and included:

> "… one good and comfortable room, suitable for a sitting or keeping room, together with all necessary furniture for the same, with one good and comfortable bedroom with good bed bedsteads, and all necessary bedding, at all times and all seasons of the year, together with good and sufficient fuel, well-prepared for the fire, with lights whenever necessary, likewise with good suitable wearing apparel both at home and abroad for all seasons, also with good and sufficient food, both in sickness and in health, of good and wholesome quality, well-cooked and prepared and in every way suitable for their condition and circumstances,[153] and provide for them the said Ephraim and Sarah all necessary medical attendance with good nurses in sickness, so long as they the said Ephraim and Sarah or either of them shall live, and then take care of and support the survivor in the same suitable manner, and whenever either shall decease, see that they are buried in a decent and proper manner …."[154]

For all intents and purposes, Nathan tacitly promised to care for his younger siblings, who were still in the home, in addition to his parents. The burden would have been daunting for anyone, let alone Nathan's new bride, who had to enter the well-established Crockett household. The agreement between Nathan and his father was executed less than two years after Nathan married Mary "Polly" Dennett Stowell of South Paris on January 16, 1845.[155] Polly gave birth to the couple's first child, Abby Anna Crockett, in January of 1849, presumably at the Crockett homestead.[156] In an unexpected turn of events, shortly after the birth of his and Polly's

---

152. OCROD, Book 79, Page 182. Warranty deed from Ephraim Crockett, Sr. to Nathan Morse Crockett.
153. This passage about food cooked "for their condition and circumstances" made more sense to me after I received a copy of the photograph of Ephraim and Sarah in their later years. (See photo at the end of this chapter.) Obviously, Sarah had lost all her teeth, probably not unusual for a woman without supplemental vitamins during her many pregnancies. Much of her calcium must have gone into her thirteen children. She would have needed food that did not require chewing, such as a healthy gruel or soup. That would have necessitated additional preparation from the cook in Nathan's family.
154. OCROD, Book 78/Page 363-364.
155. WENTWORTH, Vol. II, p. 303.
156. 1900 U.S. Federal Census, Norway, Maine. The 1900 Census gives the month and year of Polly's birth, although not

daughter, Nathan deeded the homestead—and all the burdens that went with it—to our ancestor William Robinson Crockett for $600.[157] Nathan then relocated his family to South Paris, where he worked as a butcher and lived out the remainder of his days.

William Robinson Crockett was twenty-five years old when he bought the Crockett homestead from his brother on April 2, 1849. He would be twenty-six that August and was not yet married. In addition to the care of his parents through their later years, he also assumed the care of at least three younger siblings. Despite William's youth, the transaction proved to be beneficial for the entire family. We will cover the colorful lives of William Robinson Crockett, his family, and the families of some of his siblings in the next chapter.

Ephraim Crockett, Jr. passed away November 12, 1856, at the age of sixty-eight. He was buried on a little knoll situated about 150' from the south side of the house, which small piece of ground served as the family cemetery for two generations. (In 1876, Ephraim and Sally's son Charles reinterred the remains of his parents in Norway Pine Grove Cemetery in South Parish, and relocated his father's headstone.)[158]

Sally outlived her husband by nearly twenty years. By all accounts, she remained a beloved and useful member of the family. In the 1860 and 1870 U.S. Censuses for Norway, Sally is listed as performing housework at the ages of sixty-five and seventy-five, respectively. Before her husband died, Ephraim had made an application for a Military Land Bounty for his service in the War of 1812 under the Script Warrant Act of 1855; however, he passed away before this application was approved. His widow followed up her husband's application and received on June 1, 1860, Ephraim's posthumous grant of 160 acres of land in Kansas. As was usual at the time, the land was immediately sold.[159] I have not yet unearthed the amount

---

the day. The Census also simply states she was born in Maine, without giving the town of her birth.
157. OCROD, Book 83, Page 346. The deed from Nathan to William Robinson was dated April 2, 1849. (See Appendix #12 for a copy of this deed.)
158. Information from Norway Pine Grove Cemetery records. The old cemetery at the Crockett homestead could be seen from the kitchen window of the brick house. My grandmother, like her mother, often sat in her rocker by the window and gazed out to this piece of ground, which in her day was still called "the cemetery" (even though most of the bodies had been removed). More on this in the next chapter.
159. National Archives, Script Warrant Act of 1855, Ephraim Crockett, Jr. Bounty-Land Warrant Application. Although there is no doubt Ephraim, Jr. met the qualifications for the land grant, I find the size of grant relative to his service—ten days of service plus three days of marching—painfully ironic compared to the lack of compensation given to his father, Ephraim Crockett, Sr., who served three tours of duty over two years in the American Revolution. Not only did Ephraim Sr. fail to net a land grant, but also he was forced to purchase the backcountry lot he settled and improved from the descendants of Tories. (Ephraim, Sr.'s eldest son, David, made the actual purchase, probably to spare his father the pain of knuckling under to Tories.)

that Sally received for the Kansas grant; however, any monies would have been a welcome addition to the household coffers.

Sally Bartlett (Wentworth) Crockett died May 6, 1875, at the age of seventy-nine. She was buried in the family cemetery on Crockett's Ridge next to her husband. The following year her and her husband's remains were relocated to Norway Pine Grove Cemetery. Later, a granite monument was set for the Crockett family and Sally's birth and death were recorded on that. Because there was only a year between her initial burial and reinterment, Sally probably did not have an original headstone. Ephraim's marble stone, however, was placed in the front row of the lot.

At the new cemetery, Ephraim's gravestone is located between that of his son James, who predeceased him by three years, and those of daughter Sarah and son-in-law Charles Penley and two of their children. The block of Crockett graves is situated in a grove of tall Norway pine trees. When one stands beneath the trees, facing the three rows of stones, it seems as though Ephraim still has his arms around his family, surrounded as he is by children and grandchildren. Upon Ephraim's original marble headstone is engraved the date of his death—November 12, 1856—and the simple phrase: "Gone but not forgotten."

By writing this history, I hope to ensure that Ephraim—and his beloved wife Sally—will long be remembered.

Ephraim Crockett, Jr. and Sally (Wentworth) Crockett

Ephraim and Sally (Wentworth) Crockett in their later years.
(Image is a photograph of a tintype in possession of Edward Staples of Norway.)[160]

---

160. Attached to this photograph is an explanatory note from Ed: "Ephraim Crockett Jr. and his wife Sally B. Wentworth Crockett. This picture is a photograph of a tin-type given to Mother by her Grandmother, Sarah Belle Penley Farnham. The tin-type was made from a black and white picture (the photographer could tell no more about it). Ephraim and Sally Crockett were Sarah Farnham's grandparents. – Edward Staples, 8/24/1978."

"Maine Logging Camp and Saw Mill near Norway, Me."
(Colorized Postcard No. 9422, Published by Robbins Brothers, Boston, MA and Germany.)

Chapter 3

THE CROCKETTS AND THE PENLEYS

Real Estate, Lumber, and Weddings

Three distinct factors color the history of the second generation of Crocketts in Norway (the eighth generation of Crocketts in the New World). The first was the immense amount of buying and selling of real estate that occurred on Lee's Grant. The second was the dramatic increase in the demand for lumber. And the third factor to affect the lives of second-generation Crocketts was the influx onto Lee's Grant of four adult children of John Penley of Danville, who married four of Ephraim and Sally's offspring.

Initially, the buying and selling of real estate resulted not only from a rush of people moving onto Lee's Grant but also from those who were born and raised in this later-settled section of Norway now seeking homes of their own. Like children playing musical chairs, the offspring of Ephraim and Sally (and their spouses) shifted around from lot to lot on Lee's Grant, attempting to find the property that best suited them. The available housing stock ran out long before the last Crockett child—Charles Alanson Crockett—reached the age of maturity (twenty-one) in 1858. As the population exploded in Norway, which it did throughout Maine during the early- to mid-nineteenth century until new land became available out West, the demand for lumber intensified. Standing timber, as well as boards and dimension lumber, became important commodities for the second generation.

The second generation in Norway was the high point for the Crocketts on Lee's Grant. By the time the eldest of the second generation, Sarah Wentworth Crockett, reached maturity, the wilderness was vanquished, and Norway was no longer a simple village but a flourishing town. From 1834 onward, the adult children of

Ephraim and Sally (Wentworth) Crockett began to consider matrimony. As mentioned, four of the Crocketts selected life partners from the family of Captain John Penley of Danville. Penley was a wealthy farmer, banker, and real estate investor, whose first farm (he owned many) abutted the homestead of their Crockett grandparents. After their marriages, the four Crockett/Penleys purchased real estate and raised their own families in the Crockett's Ridge neighborhood. Captain Penley invested liberally in Lee's Grant, his money going mostly to bankroll his children (and later, his grandchildren). Although none of our family are descended from Captain Penley—we are all descended from William Robinson Crockett and Lydia (Stetson) Crockett—the Penley family played a key role in setting up our futures.

With one exception,[1] the second generation on Crockett's Ridge was the last to bear the Crockett name there, in no large part thanks to the Penley family. In addition to marrying two Crockett daughters (and thus giving their offspring the surname "Penley"), the wealth that the younger Penleys inherited from Captain Penley liberated the four Crockett/Penley families from the rigors of farming. By the third generation, most of the Crockett/Penleys had chosen to leave the little world of Crockett's Ridge and seek their fortunes on the greater canvas of the expanding United States. (In fact, Warren Ephraim Crockett, son of Ephraim Stanford Crockett and Sarah Penley, became one of Teddy Roosevelt's "Rough Riders" and was with Roosevelt during the storming of San Juan Hill in 1898.)[2] The deaths of some of the second-generation Crockett/Penleys, and the exodus of others, left our ancestor William Robinson Crockett as the sole remaining Crockett residing on Crockett's Ridge. As we will see in the next chapter, the Crockett/Penleys acted as placeholders for some of the real estate that would later become incorporated into one family farm.

During this chapter, we will meet the second-generation Crocketts and their Penley spouses, as well as our ancestors William Robinson and Lydia (Stetson) Crockett. We will also get to know Hannah Jordan Crockett and her husband Thomas Hanford Richardson, who lived with their family in the greater Crockett's Ridge neighborhood.

---

1. The one exception was our ancestor, Emma Tuell Crockett, of the third generation.
2. 1915 Obituary of Warren E. Crockett. Unknown newspaper. Theodore Roosevelt also mentions Warren Crockett several times in accounts of the Rough Riders he wrote for several national publications. We will cover the lives of Warren and his siblings in the next chapter.

The Penley Family[3]

Since the Penleys play a pivotal role in the second generation, it is necessary (as well as interesting) to understand that family's rather romantic history. Captain John Penley and his father, Sergeant Joseph Penley, were individuals whose characters and personal stories were the stuff of legend, known by many Mainers outside their wide family circle.

Joseph Penley, the grandfather of the four Penleys who married the four Crocketts, had much in common with Ephraim Crockett, Sr. of Danville, the other grandfather to the second generation. Both men were early settlers onto the Pejepscot Claim and, although serving in different Maine companies, both fought as part of Col. Edmund Phinney's Massachusetts 31st Regiment of Foot during the early days of the American Revolution. Unlike Ephraim Crockett, Sr., who was born in Cape Elizabeth, Maine to a chairmaker of very modest means, Joseph was born to a relatively well-to-do family of long-time cloth and dye makers in Nailsworth, Gloucestershire, England. Joseph Penley's crossing to America from the Old Country in 1770 is steeped in romance. Most accounts claim that one day while walking down by the shore of the Thames River in London, admiring an impressive array of ships, the teenage youth, who was large for his age, was set upon by a press gang and taken aboard the man-of-war, *Rainbow*. When he reached America, unhappy with his impressment and the harsh treatment he had received aboard ship, Joseph Penley and a friend decided to desert the *Rainbow* in North Yarmouth (now part of Freeport). An account published in the *Lewiston Journal* in 1905 describes the two youths' escape:

> "Upon reaching North Yarmouth they were transferred to a smaller vessel of the size that could come nearer to the land, as wharves at that time were unknown. That night the boys seized the one boat on the vessel and rowing to the shore, disappeared into the forest. The officers of the vessel were obliged to swim ashore for their boat but no trace of the deserters could be found. To chase them thru the primeval forests of Maine would be useless and the hunt was soon given up."[4]

---

3. A note for family members, who know Richard Penley. Dick, who lives on former family land now known as Cathedral Island, has always said he is a descendant of the Paris Penleys, rather than the Norway Penleys. Although I have not traced his genealogy, I surmise that Dick would then be descended from Joseph Penley, who settled in Paris. This Joseph was the elder brother of Captain Penley (thus another son of Joseph Penley who came to America). I always thought it was ironic that Dick settled on what was known originally as "Penley Island."
4. "The First of the Auburn Penleys." Unnamed author. *Lewiston Journal*, Feb. 6, 1915.

Another account of Joseph Penley's arrival in America, based on information gleaned from his great-great-granddaughter Mrs. Harriet J. Ross, is much more prosaic and probably closer to the truth. Mrs. Ross suggests her ancestor, knowing there was no future in the family's cloth and dye business (thanks to the industrialization of cloth-making and dying), in 1770 willingly signed aboard a mast carrier, a ship specially outfitted to carry the King's pines for mast-making from Maine to England. Once reaching North Yarmouth, Joseph then jumped ship to make a new life for himself in America.[5] There was a "Sampson Penley" listed as an early settler of Falmouth,[6] prior to the 1690 destruction of that town and Fort Loyal by French and Indians during King William's War (also known as the Second Indian War), so it is possible Joseph had relations still living on the coast of Maine.

Regardless of which account is correct, it is certain that when hostilities broke out in 1775 between the Americans and the British, twenty-year-old Joseph volunteered to fight against the British. Like Ephraim Crockett, Sr., Joseph Penley signed up for several tours of duty during the Revolutionary War. Unlike Ephraim, Sr., he enlisted under an assumed name for all but the last tour. (According to several family biographers, Joseph Penley was afraid that if he was captured by the British under his real name, he might be shot or hanged as a deserter.)[7] Despite having turned against his home country during the Revolution, Joseph apparently remained on good terms with his family of origin back in England. After the war ended, he returned to Nailsworth to collect an inheritance from his grandmother, Rebecca (Pavy) Penley, and bring his youngest sister, Hannah, back to Freeport with him.[8] Joseph Penley died in Danville on June 4, 1844. Nearly eighty-eight at the time of his passing, Joseph lived long enough to have been personally known by the four Crocketts who married four of his many grandchildren.

John Penley, the eldest son of Joseph and Esther (Fogg) Johnson Penley[9] was born in 1782 near Strout's Point in North Yarmouth. Shortly after John's birth, Joseph Penley relocated his family to the Pejepscot Claim, where John grew up and lived out the remainder of his ninety-plus years. According to the history, "Study of

---

5. PENLEY, p. 2-4.
6. "The History of Portland from 1632 to 1864: With a Notice of Previous Settlements, Colonial Grants, and Changes of Government in Maine." William Willis. Portland: Bailey & Noyes, 1865. Second Edition. P. 306.
7. Penley family genealogy and notes, AHS.
8. PENLEY, p. 4.
9. Joseph Penley's first wife, Esther (Fogg) Johnson, was the widow of Joshua Johnson of North Yarmouth. According to Mrs. Harriett J. Ross, Johnson was killed during the Revolution. Esther relocated with Joseph to the Pejepscot claim where she died in 1796 after giving birth to their son James Penley. Joseph remarried Thankful Moody the following year (1797) and proceeded to father a total of sixteen children between his two wives. PENLEY, p. 3-7.

the Penley Family," archived by the Androscoggin Historical Society, John Penley, Sr. "had the unique distinction of living in the Town of Pejepscot, and later Danville during its entire municipal existence, and in Auburn six years after the annexation [of Danville by Auburn]"—without ever moving an inch.[10] There was no formal education in this frontier settlement during his childhood, but since John Penley's father could afford private instruction, John Penley was likely educated by Benning Wentworth, uncle of Sally (Wentworth) Crockett (later, the mother-in-law of four of Penley's children). Benning taught the Wentworths and other children of well-to-do parents in Pejepscot.[11]

By all accounts (and there are many of them), John Penley was just as remarkable as his father. A lifelong farmer, he was also a cattle dealer and drover, who made the second (some say first) of many cattle drives from Maine to Brighton, Massachusetts, to provide beef for the greater Boston market. John Penley could not swim—and there were not many bridges in those days—so when it came time to ford a river, he clutched the tail of the last animal in the herd and let the bovine pull him across the water.[12] John Penley became known throughout most of his life as "Captain Penley" after being chosen captain of the Danville Company (the local militia).[13] He was married twice[14] and fathered eighteen children (nearly one-quarter of whom married Crocketts) between his two wives. Captain Penley was involved in municipal affairs and was almost single-handedly responsible for getting the town of Danville annexed by the city of Auburn in 1867.[15] In addition, he was a well-known money-lender in the Danville area (as well as in Norway) and was one

---

10. PENLEY, p. 7.
11. PENLEY, p. 7.
12. The story of how John Penley forded rivers during his cattle drives is given in many histories of the Penley family. In addition, an account was included in an article that appeared in the newspaper, *Advertiser-Democrat*, which was an interview with John Penley's grandson, True Penley. "[True Penley] ... states that his grandfather could not swim, but by taking the last animal by the tail as it left the river bank he landed safely on the other shore." In the account, True Penley also says his grandfather was the first to drive the cattle from Maine to Brighton.
13. PENLEY, p. 7.
14. John Penley, Sr.'s first wife was Desire Dingley, daughter of William and Sarah "Sally" (Jordan) Dingley. William Dingley was a Revolutionary War soldier who settled in Pejepscot with the Crocketts and Waggs. After his first wife died, Penley married Julia Wagg, his late wife's niece. Julia was the daughter of Samuel Wagg (son of James Wagg, Jr. and Dorcas Strout) and Mary "Polly" Dingley (daughter of William Dingley and Sarah "Sally" Jordan). At the time of Penley's second marriage, Julia was his housekeeper and it is possible she was brought into the home prior to her aunt's death. According to Penley (and Crockett) descendant Edward Staples of Norway, Captain John was very fond of his second wife (who was thirty-one years his junior) and did a lot to please her. He built a new home for Julia, as well as the Penley Corner Church, a Freewill Baptist church, Julia's religious persuasion. Together the couple had five children. In a letter to the author dated April 3, 2022, Staples wrote: "[Julia's] family story of their wedding indicates friction. 'When they married all of his children came to the wedding in old work or play clothes.' Which could have indicated that the itinerant minister stopped at Capt. John's house, on his way to somewhere, just long enough to 'tie the knot' and keep Capt. John respectable."
15. ANDHIST, Chapter XXXIX.

of the founders of the Auburn Bank.¹⁶ John Penley was a self-made man. When he died in 1873, Captain Penley left a fortune of more than $100,000 (approximately $2.6 million in 2024 dollars)¹⁷ to his surviving children and grandchildren, many of whom he also supported during his lifetime. The "Study of the Penley Family," which includes information garnered from public records as well as from family members, sums up Captain Penley's character:

> "John Penley was a kind, indulgent man. He was just and honest in his dealings of whatever nature. He was liberal in aid to any worthy cause. He was a patient and kindly employer, and although of great energy and enterprise himself, he never sought more than an honest day's labor of those in his employ. His devotion to his family was proverbial, and he sought to assist his children in any manner their circumstances might require."¹⁸

John Penley, Sr.
(Photo courtesy of Ed Staples, Norway, Maine.)

---

16. ANDHIST, p. 642.
17. Conversion to today's dollars from the web page, CPI Inflation Calculator.
18. PENLEY, p. 8.

William Robinson Crockett and Lydia Stetson

Our ancestors William Robinson Crockett and his wife, Lydia Stetson, play a key role in the second generation. Born August 30, 1823 in Norway,[19] William was the sixth of Ephraim and Sally's thirteen children. His formative years seem unremarkable. William came into his own, however, when on April 2, 1848, he purchased the family homestead from his elder brother Nathan. His brother had only bought the property from their father the previous year but, out of the blue, elected to give it up.

Nathan, when he negotiated the deal with their father, had promised to care for Ephraim and Sally in their old age, and William, although only twenty-four, also assumed this responsibility. Their father, at sixty, was still active on the farm (in fact, the 1850 U.S. Agricultural Census lists Ephraim as the "Owner, Agent, or Manager of the Farm"),[20] so William likely found plenty of guidance—if not downright supervision—in that direction. (If this "guidance" had been an issue for Nathan, it was not so for William.) At the time of the property transfer, three (at least) of William's younger siblings were still at home with their parents: Mary Amanda, age fourteen; Eliza Jane, twelve; and Charles Alanson, eleven.[21] In the event of their father's death, William would be responsible for these three youngsters, as well as for the care of their mother in her final years. (Given the closeness of the Crockett family, however, one can assume his siblings would have offered to help.)

William was a bachelor when he arranged to buy his brother Nathan out, although he might have had an eye on a future bride. In 1844, William's brother Samuel, the eldest son of Ephraim and Sally, purchased some real estate at auction in Sumner (after having lived in Waterford and Norway) and not long afterward relocated his growing family to that town.[22] (There were Crocketts in Sumner at the time, but not close family members.) One of Samuel's neighbors in Sumner was Abel Stetson, Sr., a successful and well-regarded farmer with a bevy of daughters.[23] There is no doubt in my mind that William Robinson Crockett spent a good deal of time visiting his brother Samuel, both prior to and after assuming title to the family

---

19. CANDAGE, p. 179.
20. U.S., Selected Non-Population Schedules, 1850-1880. Schedule A, Productions in Agriculture, Norway, Maine. Ephraim Crockett.
21. See 1850 U.S. Census for Norway, Maine. It is possible one or two of the other older siblings were still "at home;" however, they were in other family dwellings by 1850.
22. See OCROD, Book 69, page 285.
23. See 1850 U.S. Census for Sumner, Maine. Samuel Crockett and Abel Stetson appear to be only a few houses apart.

homestead. Less than twenty miles separated the families, an easy day's journey by horseback via the well-traveled road through Greenwood and West Paris.[24] William probably began courting Abel's daughter, Lydia Stetson, before he made the deal with Nathan. It is doubtful he would have undertaken such a commitment without knowing whether his future wife was willing to join the family and assume her share of the burden.

William brought Lydia home to be mistress of the Crockett homestead in 1849. Lydia was nineteen when they wed, and William was twenty-six. Their wedding was held in West Sumner on November 11, 1849,[25] probably at her father's home. Reverend Manasseh Lawrence, an ordained Baptist minister and long-time pastor of the Sumner Baptist Church who preached in West Sumner on the fourth Sunday of the month, likely officiated the service.[26] (A decade after William and Lydia's marriage, the West Sumner Baptist Church was established, and the Sumner Baptist Church changed its name to the East Sumner Baptist Church.)[27]

Lydia was born in Sumner on February 27, 1830, to Abel Stetson, Sr. and his first wife, Hannah (Benson) Stetson. Her mother died when she was three, and her father remarried the following year. Lydia and the younger children of Abel and Hannah were raised by their stepmother Olive (Prince) Stetson. Abel and Olive added six more children to the family. (In 1864, one of Lydia's half-sisters, Antoinette, would marry Joseph Francis "Frank" Crockett, one of William's younger brothers.)[28]

Hezekiah Stetson, Lydia's paternal grandfather, originated from Plymouth, Massachusetts. After serving four tours of duty in the Revolutionary War, where he rose to the rank of corporal, he moved to Maine and became one of the founders of Sumner.[29] The May 24, 1797 voter list from West Butterfield (as Sumner was then known) included "Hezekiah Stutson" (as well as distant Crockett relations

---

24. The 1850 Agricultural Census for Ephraim Crockett shows the family had one horse. The horse was probably used for transportation purposes. Most of the work on the farm was likely done by the four working oxen.
25. CANDAGE, p. 179.
26. "Consolidated History of the Churches of the Oxford Baptist Association, State of Maine, and a Historical Sketch of the Association," p. 95. Deacon George G. Crockett. Bryant's Pond, Me.: A. M. Chase & Co., Printers, 1905. The Rev. Lawrence was pastor of the Sumner Baptist Church (later, East Sumner Baptist Church), from 1833 to 1858, p. 46. I have yet to unearth the actual marriage record of William Robinson Crockett and Lydia Stetson.
27. IBID, p. 95. Lydia's elder brother, Abel Stetson, Jr. was partly responsible for the establishment of the Baptist church in West Sumner.
28. NHS, Crockett genealogy.
29. U.S. Revolutionary War Pension and Bounty-Land Warrant Application Files, 1800-1900: Hezekiah Stetson. Hezekiah is also listed as having served in the Revolutionary War in Handy's "Centennial History of the town of Sumner" (SUMNER). See "Sumner's Soldiers," Appendix, p. XVII.

"Joseph Crocket, Levi Crocket, John Crocket, Joel Crocket, and John Crocket, Jr.").[30] In 1802, Hezekiah was elected one of the town's early selectmen.[31] (Later, from 1819–1826, his son Abel Stetson, Lydia's father, also served as a selectman.)[32] The Stetson family was well-regarded in Sumner. Charles Edward Handy, in his 1899 "Centennial history of the town of Sumner, 1798–1898," writes of them:

> "The Stetson family are known and respected as honest and upright Christian people, hard but willing workers in and for the church, generous and charitable to the needy, and beloved by all."

Due to the capriciousness of time, our family no longer has a photograph of William Robinson or Lydia Crockett. When I lived with my grandmother, pictures of these second-generation ancestors hung in the upstairs hall landing outside my bedroom door. I admired William considerably, knowing that he had built the brick house, which over the years I came to love almost as much as my grandmother did. I also admired Lydia, especially after learning that when she joined the family, she willingly agreed to care for her in-laws for the rest of their lives (and for her husband's younger siblings, in the event of their father's death). Ephraim Crockett, Jr. lived only six years after William and Lydia were married, so William would soon be able to do as he pleased with the farm. By contrast, Sally, Lydia's mother-in-law, lived for more than a quarter of a century! Lydia must have been a remarkable woman to be able to reside harmoniously with her mother-in-law—in her mother-in-law's house—for twenty-five years.

When I first moved in with my grandmother, the twin photographs of William and Lydia Crockett greeted me with a smile every evening when I went to bed. Years later, when I switched rooms to the north bedroom (from the south), their smiling faces greeted me when I arose. (The fact that both William and Lydia smiled for a studio portrait, which was unusual during the 19th century, says something about their characters.) Seeing my second-generation ancestors as often as I did, I recollect their likenesses. When his studio portrait was taken, William appeared to have been in his late thirties or early forties. Lydia, I estimate, was mid-to-late thirties when her portrait was taken. William Robinson was a tall, well-built man with brown

---

30. SUMNER, p. 91. These Crocketts were probably descendants of Joshua Crockett, the fifth child and third son of Thomas and Ann Crockett of Kittery.
31. SUMNER, Appendix, p. XXIII.
32. SUMNER, Appendix p. XXIII and XXIV.

hair and (probably) brown eyes. Lydia was a short, high-waisted woman, with smiling dark eyes and a glorious head of very dark curls, of which in my twenties I was quite envious. The open, good-natured expressions on both their faces made me believe William and Lydia were happy in their marriage, content with the path of life they walked together. I know now the path they trod was not easy. Three of their children died in infancy: Samuel, and later, twins William and Samuel.[33] (The names of these three lost babies suggest a particular closeness between William and his elder brother Samuel, for whom they were likely named.) The couple also lost their married daughter Josephine and cared for Josephine's orphaned child, Ada Gerry.

Charles F. Whitman, who, as a young teacher at School District No. 8, boarded around with neighborhood families, knew the entire Crockett family well. Of William and Lydia, Whitman remarks in his Norway history:

> "Wm. R. Crockett was a native of Norway. He married Lydia B. Stetson of Sumner, a woman respected and liked by all who knew her. They lived on the old homestead and faithfully cared for his parents in their old age. Mr. Crockett was a prosperous farmer and a good citizen."[34]

Respected. Well-liked. Good citizen. Faithful. With adjectives like these from a historical chronicler who personally knew them, we do not need photographs to "see" William and Lydia (Stetson) Crockett.

Weaving Together the Story of the Second Generation in Norway

Our story of the second generation opens in 1834 when Charles D. Penley, the sixth child and fourth son of Captain John Penley, and his first wife, Desire Dingley,[35] made his entrance into Norway by purchasing the south half of Lot 44 in Lee's Grant. Charles was twenty-one when he bought fifty-two acres of land from Amos Noble, which, although not mentioned in the deed, probably had some type of small dwelling upon it.[36] Lot 44 abutted to the north the real estate of his

---

33. CANDAGE, p. 180.
34. WHITMAN, p. 253.
35. Penley Family Records, Androscoggin Historical Society. Charles was born April 28, 1813 on the Pejepscot Claim.
36. This deed is not recorded; however, it is noted in the conveyance deed from Charles Penley to Amos Noble executed on Nov. 9, 1835 and recorded at OCROD Book 48, page 164. In this deed Charles conveys back to Amos the south half of Lot

soon-to-be in-laws, the Crocketts, who lived on the north half of Lot 45. (The Revolutionary War soldier Daniel Knight lived on the north half of Lot 44, although he did not own the property at the time.)[37] When he purchased the south half of Lot 44, Charles was likely engaged to Sarah Wentworth Crockett, the eldest child of Ephraim and Sally. (See following genealogy chart, "Crockett-Penley Marriages in the 2nd Norway Generation.")

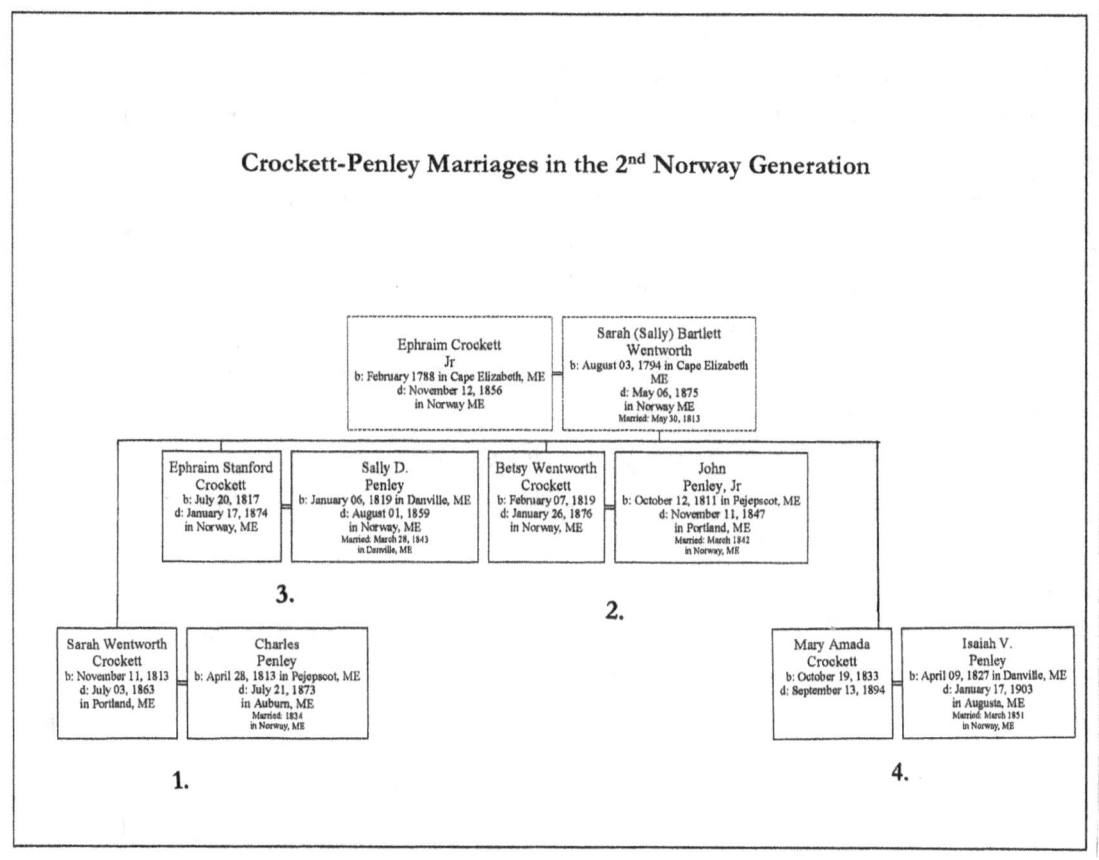

Genealogy Chart - Crockett-Penley Marriages in the 2nd Norway Generation.

44, which he previously purchased from Noble in 1834. The deed says Noble is living there, which suggests to me that one of the earlier owners had built a home on the property.

37. In 1838 Daniel's son William Knight purchased for $250 the north half of Lot 44 (minus nine acres on the lake previously purchased by James Crockett) from Ichabod Bartlett. The deed describes the real estate as being "the same lot upon which Daniel Knight now lives." OCROD, Book 96, page 460. According to Norway historian Lapham, Daniel Knight lived until at least 1850, when he was 90. LAPHAM, p. 542.

Sarah was the only child of the Crocketts born on the Pejepscot Claim. (The rest of the Crockett children were born in Norway.) She and Charles Penley were married November 8, 1834. We do not know if they were married in Norway or Danville;[38] however, there's little doubt that Charles and Sarah intended to make a permanent home in the Crockett neighborhood. Three months prior to their marriage, on August 20, 1834, Charles also bought Lot 46 in Lee's Grant from land speculator Josiah Little (who helped bail his son Edward out of debt by purchasing Lee's Grant from him). Lot 46 was situated due south from where Nathan and Mary (Crockett) Morse (Sarah's aunt and uncle) resided with their family on the south half of Lot 45.[39] It is certain Charles intended to build a new home on Lot 46. Less certain is whether he ever did.[40]

Charles paid $300 for the seventy acres on Lot 46, which, at $4.29 per acre, was a remarkable price from Josiah Little, who almost always sold raw land—regardless of its location and condition—for $7 per acre. This suggests the deal was arranged by Edward Little, who by 1834 was handling much of his father's Maine affairs. There would have been a close connection between the Little and Penley families. Edward Little, as well as Captain Penley and his father Joseph, were leading lights of Danville. Edward, constantly pressed for money by his father, probably gave Charles Penley a good price on Lot 46 so he could send immediate funds to his father back in Massachusetts.

About a year after Charles and Sarah's marriage, Charles conveyed the south half of Lot 44 back to Amos Noble,[41] possibly moving to another property he had purchased on Lee's Grant, the proposed home on Lot 46 not having been built. On June 27, 1837, Charles purchased for $400 the property known as "The Tongue" (so-named for the property's unique shape).[42] The Tongue, a nice parcel with a house on it, abutted the western side of North Pond. The property included parts of Lot 31, 32, and 33. In 1838 and 1839, Charles, who seemed to have had plenty of

---

38. Most Penley family trees on Ancestry.com say they were married in Danville; however, the information is not supported by a marriage record. CANDAGE says the marriage could have occurred either in Danville or Norway.
39. OCROD, Book 42, page 484.
40. OCROD, Book 53, page 54. In this deed of May 26, 1837, Charles sells lot 46 to Ezra Beals, reserving for himself one acre as a building lot for a house to be built within one year of the sale. In 1843 Ezra sells Lot 46 to John Beals. The deed description makes no mention of or cut-out for John Penley's 1-acre house lot, which implies that house was not built. See Book 68, page 200.
41. OCROD, Book 48, page 164. Charles signed the deed to Noble November 9, 1835.
42. OCROD, Book 51, page 442. Charles purchased from John Gurney "The Tongue ... with buildings thereon."

money to invest in real estate, also bought land on Lots 28[43] and 51.[44] Notably included in the purchase of Lot 28 was the six-acre island situated off the west side of Lot 45 (that is, off the land of Ephraim Crockett and Nathan Morse). Decades later, this six-acre parcel came to be known as Penley Island, which, although bought and sold several times, was eventually returned to the family.[45] The Lee's Grant lot map on the following page highlights some of Charles Penley's real estate purchases and their proximity to his in-laws.

---

43. See OCROD Book 58, page 302. Three months after buying this lot Charles sold most of the property, except one acre (probably a house lot) that he sold on the same day to someone else. Book 58, page 301 and Book 67, page 566.
44. See OCROD Book 60, pages 18 and 19.
45. When I was a kid, I often played on this lovely, peaceful island, which was covered by tall white pines. We could easily swim to the island from a family camp on the mainland. Sometimes, when the lake was low, we could walk across the short causeway, which was strewn with dead stumps and debris from the nearby trees. In the 1970s my grandmother Winona Palmer and her sister-in-law Florence Young renamed the parcel "Cathedral Pines Island" and developed the property, running a road out to it. Winona and Florence sold camp lots and as a result, none of the island remains in the family today (although Dick Penley, whom the author believes is a descendant of Joseph Penley, still owns two lots on the island).

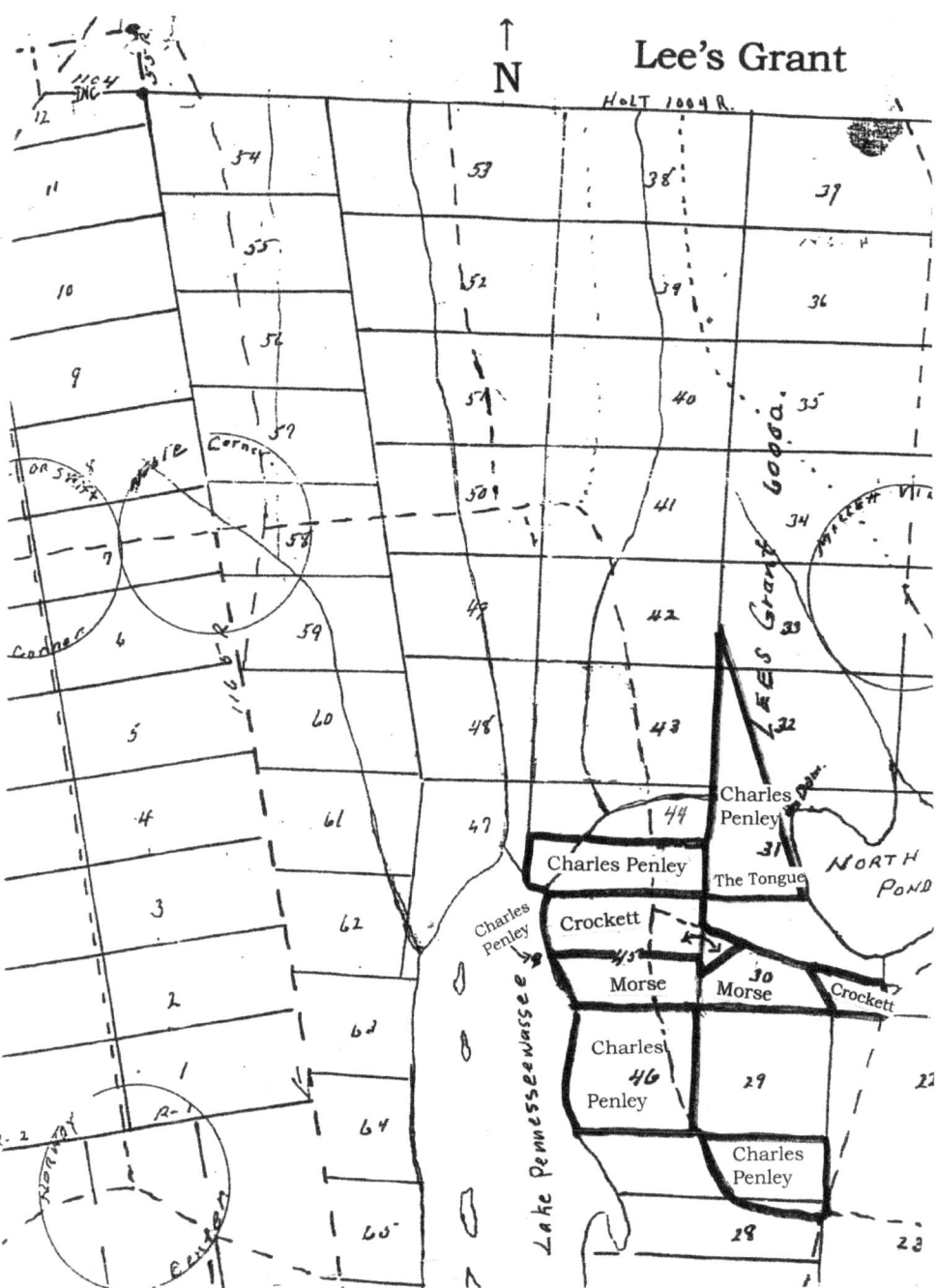

Lee's Grant lot map showing some of Charles Penley's real estate purchases.

Land records at the Oxford County Registry of Deeds reveal that Charles Penley was something of a real estate speculator. During the decade between 1834 and 1844, Charles executed more than twenty deeds, mortgages, and other types of real estate conveyances, all but one on Lee's Grant and many of them (including "The Tongue") in the greater Crockett's Ridge neighborhood. Two of his first twenty sales were properties he purchased and then resold to brothers-in-law, Samuel Wentworth Crockett[46] and Ephraim Stanford Crockett,[47] making a modest profit on each of them. Charles, who is listed in various deeds as "yeoman"[48] (farmer) and "trader[49] (salesman), also loaned money at interest,[50] probably getting some—if not all—of his starting capital from his father, Captain John Penley. Charles was also the person to whom his in-laws, Ephraim and Sally Crockett, turned when disposing of inherited real estate.[51] Altogether, these tidbits of information suggest that Charles was a man who was friendly and outgoing, probably good-natured, and trusted by the family.

In the meantime, other members of the second generation were growing up and taking part in Maine affairs. In 1839, long-simmering hostilities about the exact location of the border between Maine and Canada flared up. An international incident between Great Britain and the state of Maine resulted, which incident—originally known as "the Madawaska War,"[52] but later denoted the "Aroostook War"—was eventually settled by diplomatic efforts, however, not before local militia were called up.[53] Twenty-two-year-old Ephraim Stanford Crockett, Ephraim and Sally's second son (the youth who fell through the ice while skating one winter

---

46. OCROD, Book 53, page 402. On Nov. 24, 1837, Charles sold to his brother-in-law Samuel Crockett the piece of real estate on North Pond in Lee's Grant known as "The Tongue." Charles purchased the property on June 27, 1837, for $400 (see OCROD Book 41, page 442) and sold it to Samuel a few months later, on November 24, 1837 for $450.
47. OCROD, Book 62, page 96. On April 15, 1841, Charles sold to Ephraim Stanford Crockett the north half of Lot 58. Charles purchased this property for $675 in 1840 (see OCROD Book 60, page 19) and sold it to Ephraim Stanford in 1840 for $875.
48. See OCROD, Book 58, page 301.
49. See OCROD, Book 60, page 19. A "trader" in those days was a traveling salesman, not a real estate speculator. Charles is also noted as a trader in David Noyes' list of "many individuals who have engaged in trade...." NOYES, p. 171-172.
50. See OCROD, Book 51, page 443 for an example of Charles Penley loaning money at interest.
51. See CCROD, Book 190, page 49. In this deed dated February 26, 1845, Charles buys up his mother-in-law's inherited interest in her late father, Samuel Solley Wentworth's real estate.
52. NORWAY40s, p. 400. Madawaska was probably the site of the first boundary incident, hence the original moniker.
53. "The Maine Frontier and the Northeastern Boundary Controversy." Thomas Le Duc. *The American Historical Review* Vol. 53, No. 1. October, 1947. Pp. 30–41.

on Lake Pennesseewassee) was one of more than forty Norway men who volunteered to go and fight the British once again.[54] Historian William B. Lapham sets the scene:

> "The language of the treaty describing the line between Maine and New Brunswick was ambiguous and indefinite, and quite a broad strip of land was claimed by both sides and was called the disputed territory. The land agent of the State in the early part of 1839, reported that lumbermen in considerable numbers were stripping the timber, which constituted their chief value, from these disputed lands. The sheriff of Penobscot County upon whom the duty devolved, Aroostook County not then having been formed, with a posse of about two hundred men, went forward to drive the trespassers out. They retired before him, but arming themselves, they returned, captured the land agent, and [Sheriff] Strickland finding things worse than he expected, hastened back to Augusta and laid the matter before the Governor and Council."[55]

By this time the value of lumber had made itself known, not just in Norway, but in the entire state, and the stealing of standing timber by British lumbermen was especially egregious. Hard feelings toward the British likely still existed in the bosoms of Crocketts, whose Danville patriarch grandfather Ephraim Crockett, Sr. had fought the British in the Revolution, and father Ephraim, Jr. had gone to fight them in the War of 1812. In February and March of 1839, Maine Governor John Fairfield put out calls for fighting Maine men, and Ephraim Stanford Crockett volunteered. He joined a Norway company led by Captain Amos F. Noyes, which company was made up of forty-four privates (of which Ephraim Stanford was one); three commissioned officers, including Captain Noyes; eight non-commissioned officers; and one musician. The company organized and marched to Augusta, reaching the Capital on March 6th, where they "went into camp."[56] Dr. Osgood N. Bradbury writes of Captain Noyes and the Madawaska incident in his article No. 147, Third Paper, published March 1893 in the *Oxford County, Advertiser*:

> "At the time of the Madawaska War, Capt. Noyes, Lieut. Alva Hobbs and Ensign Washington French were detailed as officers to march to Augusta, where Historian Noyes says, they gained bloodless laurels with the rest of the officers and soldiers in that campaign, and received the praise, from the soldiers under their

---
54. LAPHAM, p. 242.
55. LAPHAM, p. 241.
56. LAPHAM, p. 241-242.

command, of being strict in discipline but attentive to the wants and comforts of those under their command. After the war Capt. Noyes was promoted to Lieutenant Colonel, and later he resigned his commission."[57]

In addition to calling up Maine militias, Governor Fairfield also sent a message to Washington pleading for national help with the "boundary trouble."[58] Congress approved an appropriation of ten million dollars, an amazing sum in those days, which signified how seriously the fledgling nation took the insult. President Martin Van Buren was also authorized to call for 50,000 men to serve for up to six months if the boundary dispute could not be settled by diplomatic means.[59] No less a personage than the famous lawyer Daniel Webster, then U.S. Secretary of State, was tasked with finding a diplomatic resolution to the fracas before it turned into an all-out war.

Cartoon published during the 1839 Maine-New Brunswick boundary dispute between the United States and Great Britain.
Queen Victoria is shown in pink with her "dog," the Duke of Wellington. Opposing Queen Victoria is U.S. President Van Buren on his "bull," shown with the head of Maine Governor Fairfield. The ox is being pulled by Henry Wise, a congressman from Virginia.[60]

---

57. NORWAY40s, p. 400.
58. The "Boundary Trouble" was another Maine nickname for the Aroostook War. LAPHAM, p.241. The Maine-New Brunswick boundary dispute was also satirically known as the Pork-and-Bean War.
59. LAPHAM, p. 241-242.
60. Unknown artist. The cartoon is at the Library of Congress, Washington, D.C. (file no. LC-USZ62-84451). Identification

It appears that while some of the Maine militias called up did march north to bolster the line against Canadian militias, the Norway militia remained in Augusta. The militiamen under Captain Noyes were each paid for twenty-eight days of service (March 3-March 28, 1839). Ephraim Stanford was paid for 110 miles of travel—the exact round-trip mileage from Norway to Augusta—so we know the company remained in Augusta. (Captain Noyes, who lived a bit further out of town, was paid for 120 miles.)[61] Once the President's order went out for Federal troops, all the Maine militias were sent home and disbanded. No shots were fired during the Aroostook War and no blood was spilled, except by two Canadian militiamen who tangled with black bears.[62] Using a successful propaganda campaign, Daniel Webster eventually negotiated a compromise with British diplomat Baron Ashburton. (The compromise was favorable to the U.S., which is why Maine protrudes so far north of the rest of our nation's boundary line with Canada.) In 1842, the Webster-Ashburton Treaty was signed, setting the international boundary between Maine and New Brunswick, where it remains today.[63]

On March 28th, Ephraim Stanford Crockett returned home, no doubt to a hero's welcome, after three days of marching from Augusta. He was then the oldest of the second generation still living at the Crockett homestead. Sarah and Charles Penley and their family had a home of their own on one of Charles' properties, and eldest son Samuel and his wife Nancy (Twombly) Crockett were then living on a farm he and his father-in-law had bought in Waterford.[64]

In mid-April of 1839, shortly after having returned from his expedition, Ephraim Stanford, possibly with money in his pocket from his enlistment (he received a total of $11.59 for his twenty-eight days of service),[65] purchased the Tongue from brother Samuel, who before moving his family to Waterford with his in-laws had bought the parcel from Charles Penley.[66] On April 16, 1839, Ephraim Stanford

---
of the characters was via Encyclopedia Britannica, "Aroostook War."
61. "Muster and pay roll for Amos F. Noyes' Company of Infantry, 1839, Aroostook War." Document courtesy of the Maine State Library.
62. "The Maine Frontier and the Northeastern Boundary Controversy." Thomas Le Duc. *The American Historical Review* Vol. 53, No. 1. October, 1947. Pp. 30–41.
63. IBID.
64. Samuel and Nancy were married in Norway October 18, 1838. CANDAGE, p. 177. Prior to their marriage, on April 11, 1838 Samuel and his father-in-law to be William Twombly, a "Gentleman from Norway," purchased together a farm in Waterford. OCROD Book 54, page 362.
65. "The Muster and pay roll for Amos F. Noyes' Company" shows that Ephraim Stanford Crockett, who appears to have been sick during some of his service (as was Captain Noyes and another private) earned the following: $7.29 pay for services (at a rate of $9.50 per month); $1.28 travel pay (at a rate of 23¢ per twenty miles); $1.10 for travel subsistence; and $1.92 for his clothing allowance for a total of $11.59.
66. Samuel Crockett purchased the Tongue from his brother-in-law Charles Penley for $450 on November 24, 1837. See

gave his older brother $450 for the house and fifty acres, borrowing $200 from Aaron Wilkins to make the purchase and giving Wilkins a mortgage upon the property.[67] Ephraim Stanford Crockett was a few months shy of twenty-two when he bought his first home, and there's every reason to believe he became attached to this property, as we will see later.

Ephraim Stanford probably did not live at the Tongue for long, however. When the U.S. census for Norway was taken in the summer of 1840, he appears to have been at his father's house. Samuel, his wife Nancy, and their year-old daughter Sarah Maria were once again living in Norway, probably in their former home at the Tongue. Samuel might have had a falling out with his father-in-law, to whom, in November of 1839, he sold his undivided half interest in their joint Waterford properties (and with whom he and his family had likely been living).[68] Ephraim Stanford was probably helping his older brother out of a tight situation, even though that meant he had to move back to the home farm with his parents and ten younger siblings.[69]

Because Charles Penley bought and sold so many properties, it is difficult to say precisely where he and Sarah were living in 1840. The census taker for the Lee's Grant area of Norway (and Greenwood), William Reed, visited Charles and his family directly after visiting Samuel Crockett.[70] To me, that suggests Charles was living in the greater Crockett's Ridge neighborhood, possibly even temporarily with Samuel at the Tongue. The Penleys had three children at the time: Esther, age five; Ephraim Crockett Penley, three-and-a-half; and Francina, one. (It is interesting to note the first boy in the third generation was named after grandfather Ephraim Crockett and the first girl, Samuel's daughter Sarah Maria, named after her grandmother Sarah.)

On August 1, 1840, Charles sold the six-acre island to William Beal, Jr. for $79, retaining for himself the ash swamp on the eastern side closest to his father-in-law's land.[71] (Charles was probably harvesting and selling ash—or dimension lumber sawn from the ash—for framing timbers utilized in the building of houses and barns.) The sale was likely to raise some quick cash. Eighteen days after selling

---

OCROD Book 53, page 402.
67. See OCROD Book 50, page 416 and Book 58, page 49.
68. OCROD, Book 57, page 269. There is a possibility that William Twombly was Nancy's brother, not her father; however, he is titled "Gentleman" in various deeds and thus I have assumed he was older.
69. See 1840 U.S. Census for Norway, Maine.
70. See 1840 U.S. Census for Norway and Greenwood, Maine.
71. OCROD, Book 64, page 249.

part of the island, Charles purchased the north half of Lot 58 from Evi Needham for $700. Needham's homestead, a house and forty acres, was situated on the new road to Greenwood. The new Greenwood Road was built in 1823[72] and connected the road around the northeastern section of the lake (now, Round the Pond Road) with the old road to Waterford (now part of the Greenwood Road). Penley's new homestead was still just a few miles from his in-laws. Charles, who was described as a "Trader" in the instruments between himself and Needham, paid the farmer only $25 down, giving Needham a mortgage for the balance of $675,[73] which was quite a good trade indeed.

Whether Charles relocated his family to the Needham place or whether he just saw the property as a good investment opportunity (which it turned out to be) we do not know. In February of 1841, Ephraim Stanford, after selling the Tongue back to Samuel,[74] purchased the Needham homestead from Charles. On April 15, 1841, Ephraim Stanford paid his brother-in-law $875 for the homestead, netting Charles Penley a neat $175 profit for the eight months he owned the property.[75]

Having branched out on his own, twenty-four-year-old Ephraim Stanford Crockett continued to invest in real estate. On April 29, 1841, he purchased the south side of Lot 51 from Bela Noyes for $200,[76] and in the fall of that year, he paid David Wilkins $13 for four acres on Lot 50.[77] He also purchased twenty-five acres from Evi Needham situated on the south part of Lot 57, which abutted his new farm and was no doubt originally part of Needham's farm.[78] Where did Ephraim Stanford get the money to invest in so much property all at once? To answer this question, we need look no further than the original source of Charles Penley's investment money—Captain John Penley.

On November 1st Ephraim Stanford sold most of his real estate to John Penley of Danville, including his homestead farm on the Greenwood Road. Captain Penley paid $900 for the real estate that young Crockett owned on Lots 57, 58, and Lot 50. John Penley, Sr. also purchased approximately twenty-five acres on Lot 51 from him, leaving Ephraim Stanford about thirty acres on that lot in his own

---

72. WHITMAN, p. 167. Whitman writes of the various settlements of Norway in this section.
73. See OXROD Book 60, page 18 and 19.
74. OXROD, Book 70, page 202. On Feb. 4, 1841, Ephraim Stanford Crockett sold the Tongue back to brother Samuel for $250, plus Samuel agreed to take up his younger brother's $200 note to Aaron Wilkins.
75. OCROD, Book 62, page 96.
76. OCROD Book 62, page 97.
77. OCROD, Book 62, page 429.
78. See OCROD, Book 62, page 96. Ephraim Stanford paid Evi Needham $100 for these 25 acres.

name.[79] This sizeable real estate transfer likely occurred because there was an engagement (or an "understanding") between Ephraim Stanford Crockett and twenty-two-year-old Sarah "Sally" Dingley Penley, the ninth child and third daughter of Captain Penley and his first wife Desire (Dingley) Penley.[80] (See genealogy chart, "Crockett-Penley Marriages in the 2nd Norway Generation" earlier in the chapter.) While the couple would not marry for three more years—not until 1844—Captain Penley probably wanted to see what the young man would make of himself before he gave his daughter away. Ephraim Stanford would have managed the farm as if it were his own, no doubt with plenty of free advice from his father-in-law to be. John Penley, Sr. was a prudent and judicious man. Not only did he bankroll his sons, but also his sons-in-law, thus setting up his daughters for successful marriages.

While Ephraim Stanford was working hard at the former Needham farm to prove himself, another Penley joined the Crockett family. On March 29, 1842, eight years after the arrival of Charles Penley in Norway, his older brother John Penley, Jr.[81] married Betsey Wentworth Crockett, the fourth child and second daughter of Ephraim and Sally. (See "Crockett-Penley Marriages" genealogy chart.)

John, Jr. was a well-known and successful man in Danville. He was voted a selectman in 1837, 1839-40, and 1842.[82] John, Jr.'s first wife, Mary Dyer (Jordan) Penley, died October 31, 1841, possibly after a prolonged illness.[83] According to Crockett historian Charles Candage, John and Betsey's wedding took place in Norway,[84] only five months after Mary Penley's death and a scant (and somewhat scandalous) two months after the birth of John and Betsey's first child. Their daughter was born January 23, 1842. She was named Mary Dyer Penley for John's first wife, which suggests the blessings of a dying woman who entrusted the care of her husband to another woman.[85] John and Betsey remained in Danville for several years, with little Mary and his two sons by his late wife, James Jordan Penley, age four

---

79. OCROD, Book 62, page 428.
80. Penley genealogy, AHS.
81. Only eighteen months separated the two brothers, John, Jr. and Charles Penley. The elder, John, Jr., was born on the Pejepscot Claim, October 12, 1811. CANDAGE, p. 178.
82. ANDHIST, Chapter XXXIX. While it is conceivable the John Penley mentioned here is Captain Penley, it is more likely to be John, Jr. given the dates. In addition, had it been Captain Penley who ran and was elected selectman there is no reason he would not have continued as a selectman into the future, while his son relocated to Norway not long after the last term ended.
83. Maine Death Records, 1761-1922. John and Mary's wedding was officiated by Edward Little, showing the close relations between these two important Danville families. Maine Marriage Index, 1761-1921.
84. CANDAGE, p. 178. Maine Marriage Index, 1670-1921 suggests there might have been a second wedding ceremony, possibly a religious one, in Danville in 1845.
85. CANDAGE, p. 178.

and John, Jr. (actually, John Penley III), two-and-a-half.[86] On April 26, 1844, son Charles Sewell Penley was born in Danville to John and Betsey,[87] rounding out the household to six, with four children aged six and under.

Meanwhile, back in Norway, Ephraim Stanford finally secured his Penley bride. He and Sally Penley were married in Norway on March 28, 1844.[88] Sally was twenty-five when she became mistress of his home, and Ephraim Stanford was twenty-six. He had been working to improve his situation (and impress his father-in-law) for three years—no short period of time, but certainly less than the seven years (plus seven) that Jacob worked for Rachel in the story from the Hebrew Bible.

Locket tintypes of Ephraim Stanford Crockett and Sally (Penley) Crockett.[89]
(Photo courtesy of Susan Allen Morgan.)

In the summer of 1844, Samuel Crockett, the eldest son of Ephraim and Sally, appears to have become restless again. Apparently, neither the Waterford farm nor the Tongue property satisfied him. On August 20, 1844, Samuel sold the Tongue— the property he had bought, sold, and bought again from Ephraim Stanford—to

---

86. According to Maine Birth Records, 1715-1922, James Jordan Penley was born April 8, 1838 in Danville and his younger brother, John, Jr. (John Penley III) was born October 8, 1839.
87. CANDAGE, p. 178.
88. CANDAGE, p. 177.
89. These locket tintypes were passed down through the line of Ephraim and Sally's daughter, Hannah Jordan (Crockett) Richardson, and were purported to be of our original Norway ancestors. But given that the tintype process was not invented until 1850 when Ephraim and Sally would have been sixty-two and fifty-six, respectively, the couple shown here logically must be Ephraim Stanford Crockett and his wife, Sarah "Sally" Dingley (Penley) Crockett. They were Hannah (Crockett) Richardson's brother and sister-in-law. Over the years, the younger couple was often confused with the Norway patriarch and matriarch, as both couples shared the same name—Ephraim and Sally Crockett.

Captain Penley for $600.[90] Samuel used the money to buy at a public auction in Sumner a house and 120 acres located near the home of Abel Stetson. Samuel was the highest bidder, paying $305 for the property; however, the real estate was also subject to a mortgage (given by the former owner) of $1250, the balance of which Samuel agreed to pay. Samuel relocated his family to Sumner in 1844. A decade later, he and his wandering family would move to Wisconsin,[91] but not before his younger brother William had wooed and won his future bride by visiting Samuel in Sumner.

It is unclear to me why John Penley, Sr. bought the Tongue property from Samuel. Did Penley have another daughter or a son he wanted to settle in Norway? Was he simply trying to help Samuel out? (By this time, there was obviously a very close connection between the Crocketts and the Penleys.) Or was Penley merely looking for a good investment? (In addition to his many real estate investments in the Danville area, Captain Penley bought and sold real estate in Oxford County.)[92] We do not know Captain Penley's motivation, nor do we know who was installed to manage this farm in the Crockett's Ridge neighborhood. An informed guess would be that Charles and Sarah (Crockett) Penley and their family took up residence on the Tongue when Samuel left for Sumner. After reviewing three decades of Penley real estate transactions, it seems there was a concerted effort to buy up the available properties in the greater neighborhood of Ephraim and Sally Crockett and to keep these properties in the family.

Further cementing the theory of "keeping it all in the family," on August 9, 1845, Charles repurchased the south half of Lot 44, the homestead to the north of his in-laws (and the first real estate purchase he made upon his entrance to Norway back in 1834). This parcel abutted the Tongue on the east, although a significant drop in elevation on Lot 44 (and a swamp in the middle) made it more convenient to access the two houses going around by road. Charles paid Israel Pike $500 for the real estate, but it was evident he had no intention of taking immediate possession because, in the deed, he gave Pike the "right to the produce raised on said farm the present season." Charles also agreed to take over Israel's mortgage to Luther

---

90. OCROD, Book 70, Page 203. Date on the deed from Samuel Crockett to John Penley of Danville is August 20, 1844.
91. Samuel's infant daughter Augusta Crockett died September 9, 1856 in Prairie du Sac, Wisconsin. (Find-A-Grave, Augusta Crockett.) Wife Nancy died the following year on January 23, 1857. (Wisconsin death records.) Samuel married twice more (Wisconsin marriage records) and lived to the ripe old age of 94. He died in Eau Claire on August 17, 1909. (Wisconsin death records.)
92. For some of John Penley, Sr.'s Oxford County real estate investments see OCROD Book 64, page 71; Book 73, page 183; Book 99, page 334; and Book 101, page 136.

Pike in the amount of $279.50.[93] Nine months after Charles brought the south half of Lot 44 back into the family, he sold it to his older brother John, Jr. for much what he had paid for it. (Charles appears to have had no qualms in making money off his brothers-in-law, but not so his brother.) John paid Charles $500 for the fifty-two-acre farm and took over the $150 remaining on the mortgage to Luther Pike.[94] (Both Penley brothers are described as "yeomen" in this deed, which signals that at that time, they considered themselves farmers.) With this latest real estate transaction, the third Crockett-Penley family—John, Jr., Betsey (Crockett) Penley, and their children—joined the Crockett's Ridge neighborhood.

To help readers follow along with these real estate purchases, I have updated the Lee's Grant lot map to 1846 (see following). Since I do not know for sure if the Charles Penley family was on the Tongue, I marked Charles and Captain Penley together with a question mark. Likewise, I have jointly marked the real estate Captain Penley bought from Ephraim Stanford to identify the homestead farm of his son-in-law and his daughter Sarah (or "Sally," as she was known). Completing the map are Uncle Nathan and Aunt Mary (Crockett) Morse, who in 1846 still owned the south half of Lot 45, which Nathan had purchased in 1815 with his brother-in-law Ephraim Crockett, Jr.

---

93. See OCROD Book 74, page 99.
94. OCROD, Book 74, page 100.

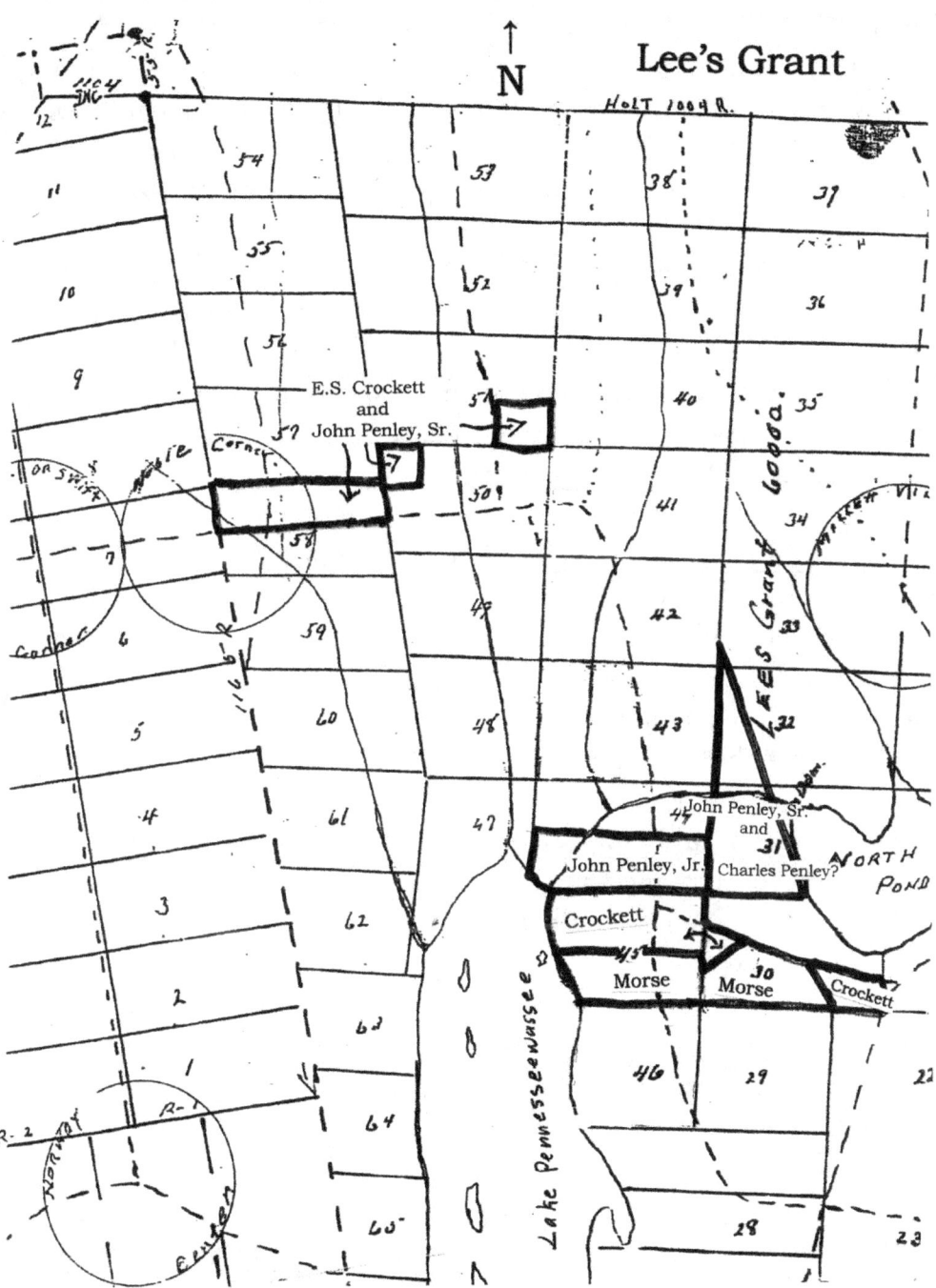

1846 Lee's Grant lot map showing the location of the Crocketts, Penleys, and Nathan and Mary (Crockett) Morse.

By the summer of 1847, Ephraim and Sally Crockett had eleven grandchildren living nearby, including two newborn babies. On May 17, 1847, Betsey (Crockett) Penley gave birth in Norway to her third child (John's fifth child), which they named Rufus L. Penley.[95] (Family records and census information suggest that after John and Betsey relocated to Norway in 1845,[96] John's sons by his first marriage— young James Jordan and John III—remained in Danville with Mary Penley's family,[97] possibly at their late mother's request.) Five weeks after Betsey gave birth, Sally (Penley) Crockett presented her husband Ephraim Stanford with their third child, Josiah Penley.[98] One can imagine how pleased Ephraim and Sally must have been having all their grandchildren, except Samuel and Nancy's children, living in the neighborhood. Following is a list, taken from Charles Candage's Crockett genealogy, of the Crockett-Penley grandchildren in Norway in 1847:

<u>The children of Charles and Sarah (Crockett) Penley</u>
Esther Penley – age twelve
Ephraim Crockett Penley – ten-and-a-half
Francina Penley – eight
Nathan Penley – five-and-a-half
Rufus C. Penley – three-and-a-half

<u>The children of Ephraim Stanford and Sally (Penley) Crockett</u>
John Freeland Crockett – age four
Abbie Jane Crockett – one-and-a-half
Josiah Penley Crockett – a newborn

<u>The children of John, Jr. and Betsey (Crockett) Penley</u>
Mary Dyer Penley – age five-and-a-half
Charles Sewell Penley – three
Rufus L. Penley – a newborn

These were halcyon days on Crockett's Ridge. The futures of the second

---

95. CANDAGE, p. 178.
96. NOYES, p. 155 lists John Penley (Jr.) as one of the new immigrants to Norway in 1845.
97. Unfortunately, I cannot remember the family record in which I read this information about John, Jr. and Mary (Jordan) Penley's two sons remaining in Danville; however, they do not show up in any Norway census data.
98. CANDAGE, p. 178. Josiah Penley Crockett was born June 22, 1847.

generation were shaping up nicely. Having the third generation to build a future for must have been a powerful motivating force.

On March 9, 1847, Ephraim Stanford Crockett and his younger brother Nathan purchased the part of Lot 43 situated on the west side of the road, approximately fifty acres. The brothers bought the property—probably a woodlot—from second-cousin Mahalon Crockett for $425.[99] (Mahalon's father, Joshua Crockett, died in 1845.)[100] The woodlot, which was located just up the road from the Crockett homestead, was conveniently situated near Colonel Millett's home and sawmill on the outlet of North Pond. According to Norway historian David Noyes, Millett's sawmill was cutting from 100,000-150,000 board feet annually by 1847.[101] There is little doubt that Nathan was preparing for his settled future on Crockett's Ridge. Only a few days after completing this purchase, Ephraim Crockett formally deeded his home place to Nathan. On March 12, 1847, Ephraim sold all the real estate he owned on both Lots 45 and 30 to his son for $500. Nathan also signed a separate deed of conveyance promising to care for his parents in their declining years.[102]

As the Crockett/Penley families expanded, so too had Maine's horizons. In 1844, there was an exciting proposal to connect, via railway, the cities of Portland and Montreal, Canada. The short-line railroad would provide Montreal with a winter port that rarely froze over, unlike the St. Lawrence River. For Mainers, the railroad would offer an alternative mode of travel to numerous station-stops in Maine, New Hampshire, Vermont, and Montreal other than by cumbersome stagecoach or horse-and-buggy. In addition, the proposed railroad would carry freight, such as lumber and livestock, which news was welcomed enthusiastically by the state's farmers, lumbermen, manufacturers, and businessmen.

The idea for the railway was the brainstorm of John A. Poor, a Bangor lawyer, who in the 1840s became concerned about the decline of Maine's economy.[103] Poor, fascinated with railways since his youth, knew he needed to convince the people of Maine that his idea had merit, as well as the Montreal Board of Trade, which board Boston was also wooing for the same purpose. To that end, Poor took in February of 1845 a rather daring sleigh ride from Bangor to Montreal during a blizzard.

---

99. OCROD, Book 79, page 59.
100. WHITMAN, p. 151.
101. NOYES, p. 179.
102. OCROD, Book 78, page 363 and Book 79, page 182.
103. "J.A. Poor and the Portland-Montreal Connection." Candace Kanes. Maine Historical Society via the Maine Memory Network.

Whether the Board of Trade was convinced by Poor's intrepidity or his ideas or both—he won the day, and the Board agreed to the Portland-Montreal railway.[104]

Poor successfully enticed rich men from the Portland area to back his project, as well as men from other well-heeled towns, such as Paris Hill. On February 10, 1845, the Atlantic and St. Lawrence Railroad was chartered in Maine, and construction on the railroad started in Portland on Independence Day, 1846. That same year Poor started the Portland Company, a foundry, which manufactured the cars and locomotives for the railroad. The rail route through Maine was to begin at the dockyard in Portland and run north, stopping at (among other stations) Danville, Lewiston, Oxford, Paris, and Bethel before continuing into New Hampshire, Vermont, and ultimately to Montreal. One can only imagine the enthusiasm of the younger generation of Crocketts and Penleys upon hearing the news that the Atlantic and St. Lawrence Railroad was coming to Paris—only five miles away.[105]

May of 1847 saw an exciting addition to the greater Crockett's Ridge neighborhood when wealthy Portland businessman Joshua Richardson settled his unmarried son Thomas Hanford Richardson on the Preble Farm.[106] Richardson purchased this landmark homestead, which formerly belonged to Jacob Tubbs (the only Lee's Grant settler to have bought his acreage freehold from Francis Lightfoot Lee) on May 27, 1847. (The original house where Thomas Hanford Richardson and his family lived was probably located at the sharp turn on what is today the Ralph Richardson Road.[107] The house was destroyed by fire in 1881.)[108] Joshua Rich-

---

104. IBID. Later, Poor wrote an eight-page account of that remarkable February journey to Montreal, which included this segment about passing through Dixville notch:
"Bragg soon was ready to carry me through 'The Notch' to Colebrook. Two young men volunteered to go ahead & broke the path & as they approached the Notch they started out other horses & riders so that we had 4 horses and 5 men to put us through this wonderful chasm or pass. This stupendous curiosity of which no adequate description has ever been given seemed more sublime than ever. The perpendicular Walls rising on either side for some 1000 feet hang in frightful mosses over head & was and the narrow path not more than 30 or 40 feet wide was filled with the drifted snow Where our path lay it was a sloping drift at an angle of 45 degrees & no sign of footsteps anywhere. We dug a track for the horses & carried our baggage sleigh through by hand. The Wind howled fearfully through the chasam & the drifting snow darkened the air which at the depth of the gorge always looks seems somber and blackened. In less than two hours we made our way through the notch tho one drift as we approached the western Entrance seemed to completely bar all approach." "John Poor account of trip to Montreal, 1845." Maine Historical Society via the Maine Memory Network.
105. "The Grand Trunk in New England." Jeff Holt. Railfare Enterprises, Limited. 1986. Construction started in Paris (Maine) in March of 1850 and was completed through to Bethel by March 1851.
106. NOYES, p. 134. Noyes notes that Joshua Richardson settled Thomas Hanford's younger brother William on another farm nearby. This was probably the former homestead of Luther Pike that Joshua purchased on November 1, 1850 for $2400. See OCROD, Book 90, page 299.
107. Map of Pennesseewassee Pond, 1858. Old Town Map Custom Print. Taken from the original Map of Oxford County, Maine, 1858 by H.F. Walling.
108. WHITMAN, p. 190. Whitman notes that several other buildings on the property were destroyed by the fire, which must have been a blazing inferno.

ardson gave $1850 for the 150-acre homestead (minus one acre that had been cut out for the No. 8 schoolhouse).[109] It is possible that the Portland magnate, familiar with the planned railway route, bought this large block of real estate with an eye to future lucrative opportunities in the Norway-Paris area.

Joshua Richardson was a self-made man. Much like Captain John Penley, he not only bankrolled his children and grandchildren but also, over the course of the next fifteen years, bought and sold real estate on Lee's Grant.[110] Unlike the Penley patriarch who grew up in Pejepscot and was tutored by Benning Wentworth, Joshua Richardson was born in Salem, Massachusetts, where he received a formal education. When he was a young man, Richardson traveled throughout Europe and even lived two years in France.[111] Joshua relocated to Portland in 1801 and joined his brother Nathaniel in trade on Richardson's wharf. According to North American Family Histories, Joshua was "many years in the West India trade" (probably buying coffee, molasses, sugar, and fruit grown by enslaved Africans), which trade would have ended with President Jefferson's embargo of 1807. He was a shipbroker and banker [112] and later the Treasurer of Portland manufacturing.[113] When the 1850 census for Portland was taken, the real estate in which Joshua Richardson and his family were living and which he owned (probably a block of buildings) was valued at $20,000 (about $900,000 in 2024 dollars).[114]

---

109. OCROD, Book 77, page 216.
110. Joshua Richardson bought and sold real estate on Lee's Grant from 1847 to his death in 1862. See OCROD Richardson, Joshua for the more than twenty deeds/mortgages/convenances, etc. he signed.
111. North American, Family Histories, 1500-2000. Capt. Joshua Richardson #5740.
112. The information that Joshua Richardson was a ship broker and banker came from his son's death record. See Maine Death Records, Thomas Hanford Richardson.
113. North American, Family Histories, 1500-2000. Capt. Joshua Richardson #5740.
114. Calculation from web page CPI Inflation Calculator.

Portland businessman Joshua Richardson.[115]

Thomas Hanford Richardson was twenty-six when his father purchased the Preble Farm (as the original Tubbs homestead was then known). Thomas, or "T.H." as he was sometimes called, was the eldest son and third child of Joshua and Ann (Hanford) Jones Richardson.[116] Unmarried, and apparently able to please himself, T.H. wasted no time seeking a wife to join him in his new home.

Hannah Jordan Crockett was the eldest unmarried Crockett daughter at home when Thomas Hanford arrived in Norway. She was still young—only sixteen—but from all accounts, she was beautiful and vivacious, so it is not surprising Thomas Hanford Richardson became captivated with her. Susan (Allen) Morgan, a Canadian cousin with whom I became connected via Ancestry.com, generously shared with me photographs and information about Hannah's life. (Susan, a direct descendant of Hannah's, was raised by Hannah's granddaughter Bertha Allen.) Susan identified the studio portrait of Hannah as a young woman (following), which our family possesses, and which was tucked away at the Crockett homestead along with other photos of unidentified Crocketts.

---

115. This photo of Joshua Richardson is taken from North American, Family histories, 1500-2000. Ancestry.com. P. 662.
116. North American, Family Histories, 1500-2000. Capt. Joshua Richardson #5740.

Hannah Jordan Crockett
(Studio portrait in the possession of Joyce Palmer, Norway, Maine.)[117]

By the summer of 1847, the future of the Crockett family seemed bright. Three Crockett-Penleys lived and farmed in their parent's neighborhood, having nearly a dozen grandchildren between them. Hannah had a new admirer from an extremely suitable and wealthy family. (Indeed, Joshua Richardson's fortune exceeded even Captain Penley's.) Nathan was working with his father on the Crockett homestead, which Ephraim had already signed over to the young man. William Robinson was visiting brother Samuel in Stetson, where William was courting neighbor Lydia Stetson. What happened next could hardly have been foreseen by anyone.

Death of John Penley, Jr. and Upheaval in the Family

In the fall of 1847, thirty-six-year-old John Penley, Jr. died unexpectedly, rending this tightly-knit family web. He died suddenly on November 7th in Westbrook (later, part of Portland), possibly after being run over by a horse-drawn streetcar.[118]

---

117. Although the mutton sleeves on Hannah's dress are commonly associated with the 1890s, poufy sleeves were also popular beginning in the 1830s thanks to England's Queen Victoria, who wore and popularized the style.
118. No cause of death is listed on the death record for John Penley, Jr. Edward Staples of Norway, who is a Penley-Crockett descendant, told the author in a letter dated April 3, 2022, that he heard John Penley, Jr. was run-over by a horse-drawn streetcar. "This may have been confusion of the story-teller's part," he wrote. "For Captain John's brother was killed when a streetcar ran over him May 12, 1865." Staples referred the author to an article telling of Joseph Penley's death, which says that the deaf man died (in Paris, Maine, his hometown) after being crushed by a train engine. "[Joseph Penley] was walking on the track above the station, in that city [Paris], when an engine used in making up trains, ran over him, crushing his left leg & arm completely. He was taken to the Sailor's Home, but the physicians summoned, found it would be impossible to

John, Jr. left behind his bereft wife Betsey; the couple's three children (including baby Rufus, only six months old); his many siblings and in-laws; the two sons by his first wife; and his father and namesake, John Penley, Sr., who must have been devastated. (John, Jr.'s mother was already deceased.) The abrupt death of John, Jr. was a shocking turn of events for the entire Crockett-Penley clan and appears to have changed the life trajectory of several family members.

John Penley, Jr. was buried in the Penley Corner Cemetery in Danville, near his father's house. John, Jr., only thirty-six, did not have a will. Betsey was appointed administratrix of his estate, and at a Probate Court session on March 6, 1848, she was given authority to auction off her husband's real estate, the south half of Lot 44. Once again, Captain Penley came to the rescue. He was the high bidder (paying only $65.66, plus agreeing to assume the mortgage) at a public auction held on April 28, 1849. John Penley, Sr. also provided for his daughter-in-law and grandchildren. In the instrument filed with the registry officially documenting the real estate transfer to him by Betsey, she writes: "... and I also [sign off on the property] for a valuable consideration to me paid by said John Penley, the receipt of which I hereby acknowledge."[119]

The death of John Penley, Jr. in 1847 had a domino effect on the lives of the Crocketts on Lee's Grant. By the spring of 1848, the futures of the second generation, which had appeared settled only six months earlier, were now in a state of flux.

Less than five months after John, Jr.'s death on April 2, 1848, Nathan turned over the Crockett homestead and all the responsibilities that went with it to younger brother William Robinson Crockett.[120] (See Appendix #12 for a copy of this deed.) Nathan and Polly moved to Paris Village, into a home belonging to Polly's family. (In 1853, this quarter-acre lot with buildings on it was deeded to Polly for $50 by Rufus Stowell.)[121] Nathan eschewed farming altogether and became a butcher.[122]

---

do more than alleviate his distress." "A Sad Accident." *The Oxford Democrat*, May 19, 1865. Death info for John Penley, Jr. from CANDAGE, p. 178. Penley family records also say John Penley, Jr. died in Portland (Westbrook). Maine Death Records 1761-1922 say he died in Danville, so possibly he lived for a while after he was injured. There is also a possibility that John, Jr. died from a heart attack.
119. OCROD, Book 81, pages 519-521.
120. On April 2, 1848 Nathan Crockett sold William Robinson the Crockett homestead for $600. OCROD, Book 83, page 346.
121. OCROD, Book 95, page 548. Rufus Stowell mentions in this quit-claim deed that he inherited this real estate from his late mother, Polly B. Stowell. My guess is that Rufus and Polly (Stowell) Crockett were siblings.
122. CANDAGE, p. 179.

Later, when Nathan sold his half-interest in Lot 43 to brother Ephraim Stanford on July 20, 1849, he no longer owned any real estate on Lee's Grant.[123]

On March 12, 1849, Hannah Jordan Crockett married Thomas Hanford Richardson and became mistress of his extensive household.[124] She was only seventeen when the couple wed, although she would be eighteen that August. I cannot help but think that Hannah was motivated to marry at such a young age in order to offer a home to her widowed sister. The 1850 census for Norway reveals that Betsey Penley and her daughter Mary Dyer Penley were living with Thomas Hanford and Hannah (Crockett) Richardson, and the couple's seven-month-old son, Albert. (John and Betsey's son Charles Sewell Penley, age three when the census was taken, was with his grandparents at the Crockett homestead. I have been unable to locate what happened to baby Rufus, although he was undoubtedly alive because he lived to be seventy-eight.[125]) The Richardson dwelling, which in 1850 was valued at $2500, must have been quite large (or the property included other houses) because there was also room for two of Hannah's older brothers, James Sewell Crockett and Joseph Francis "Frank" Crockett, neither of whom were yet married. James was twenty-two, and Frank was twenty. Both young men were listed as farmers in the 1850 census and likely worked on the Richardson estate.

With Betsey and the children residing with other family members, Captain Penley settled his nephew Joseph G. Penley (the son of his younger brother Joseph and wife Lovinia Penley)[126] on John, Jr.'s farm. In the 1850 census for Norway, Joseph G., twenty-eight, is shown there and listed as a farmer. With Joseph on the south half of Lot 44 (next to the Crockett homestead) is his wife Sarah, twenty-eight, and their daughter Isadore, age two. Charles F. Penley, sixteen, who might have been Joseph's younger brother, was living with them and listed as a farmer. While the family at the Crockett homestead would have considered it a positive move that Captain Penley kept the land in the greater family, it must have been difficult not to have Betsey and the children next door. (I know from personal experience—my late mother's house being located across the road from John and Betsey's home—that almost daily visits to the Crockett homestead would have occurred prior to John, Jr.'s death, because this is what still occurs today.)

In 1849, brothers-in-law Charles Penley and Ephraim Stanford Crockett

---

123. OCROD, Book 85, Page 47.
124. CANDAGE, p. 180.
125. CANDAGE, p. 178.
126. Penley genealogy, AHS. See also WHITMAN, pages 486 and 487.

swapped homesteads.[127] On December 18, 1849, Captain Penley sold the Tongue (which he owned and where I believe Charles and his family were living) to Ephraim Stanford.[128] Charles moved over to his father's other house on Lot 58, the property that Charles had originally purchased from Evi Needham and which Charles had earlier sold to Ephraim Stanford. The house swap would have been beneficial for both families. Charles, the trader, would have benefitted from a house situated on the new road to Greenwood and near two settlements, one at Noble's Corner and one at Swift's Corner (formerly, "Upper Corner"), where there were stores, a tavern, and blacksmith. Ephraim Stanford, whose wife Sally was probably suffering from consumption (tuberculosis), benefited by having his family closer to receive support from his parents and the children's grandparents. Also, the Tongue was the first property Ephraim Stanford had ever purchased, and I believe this remote property, nestled up against North Pond, was a place he had always loved.

When the 1850 census was taken, Ephraim Stanford and Sally (Penley) Crockett were living at the Tongue with their four children: John F., five; Abbie Jane, four; Josiah, three; and Minerva, one.[129] (Warren, the Rough Rider, and two other children had not yet been born.) Ephraim Stanford was listed as a farmer with a real estate value of $1200. He was thirty-three, and Sarah was thirty-one.

In 1850, Charles' real estate on the new Greenwood Road (actually, his father's property) was valued at $1500. Charles was thirty-seven when the 1850 census was taken, and Sarah was thirty-six. At the time, he and Sarah had six children: Ephraim Crockett Penley, thirteen; Francina, eleven; Nathan, eight; Rufus, five; Adrianne, two; and eleven-month-old Sarah. Sadly, little Sarah passed away a few months after the census was taken, on October 16, 1850.[130]

Since John Penley, Jr.'s death, the family residing at the Crockett homestead had altered considerably, too. Five adults, including the four elder Crockett children—who had all been living at home in 1847—moved out. Gone now were Nathan and his wife Polly; James; Frank; and Hannah Jordan Crockett. William Robinson Crockett (our ancestor) was now the eldest of the second generation at home and the owner of the property. When the 1850 census was taken, William was

---

127. A mortgage deed from William Paine to Joseph Penley dated September 22, 1852 shows that Charles Penley was an abutter to this one-acre parcel Joseph purchased on Lot 58. This is how I determined where Charles Penley was living and why I believed he and Ephraim Stanford must have swapped homes (both of which at the time were owned by John Penley, Sr.) See OCROD, Book 94, page 286.
128. See OCROD, Book 82, page 477 and Book 86, page 38.
129. 1850 U.S. Census, Norway, Maine. Crockett, Ephraim Stanford.
130. CANDAGE, p. 177.

twenty-six, and his new bride Lydia (Stetson) was twenty. His father, Ephraim, was sixty-two, and his mother, Sarah ("Sally"), fifty-five. The farm was valued at $1500. Still living at home were William's younger siblings Mary Amanda, sixteen; Eliza Jane, fourteen; and Charles Alanson, thirteen. As mentioned, Betsey and John Penley's son, Charles Sewell, was also living at the Crockett homestead in 1850.

In the two-and-a-half years since John Penley, Jr.'s tragic death, the families on Crockett's Ridge moved around like players in the child's game of musical chairs. Following is the Lee's Grant lot map of the neighborhood updated to 1850.

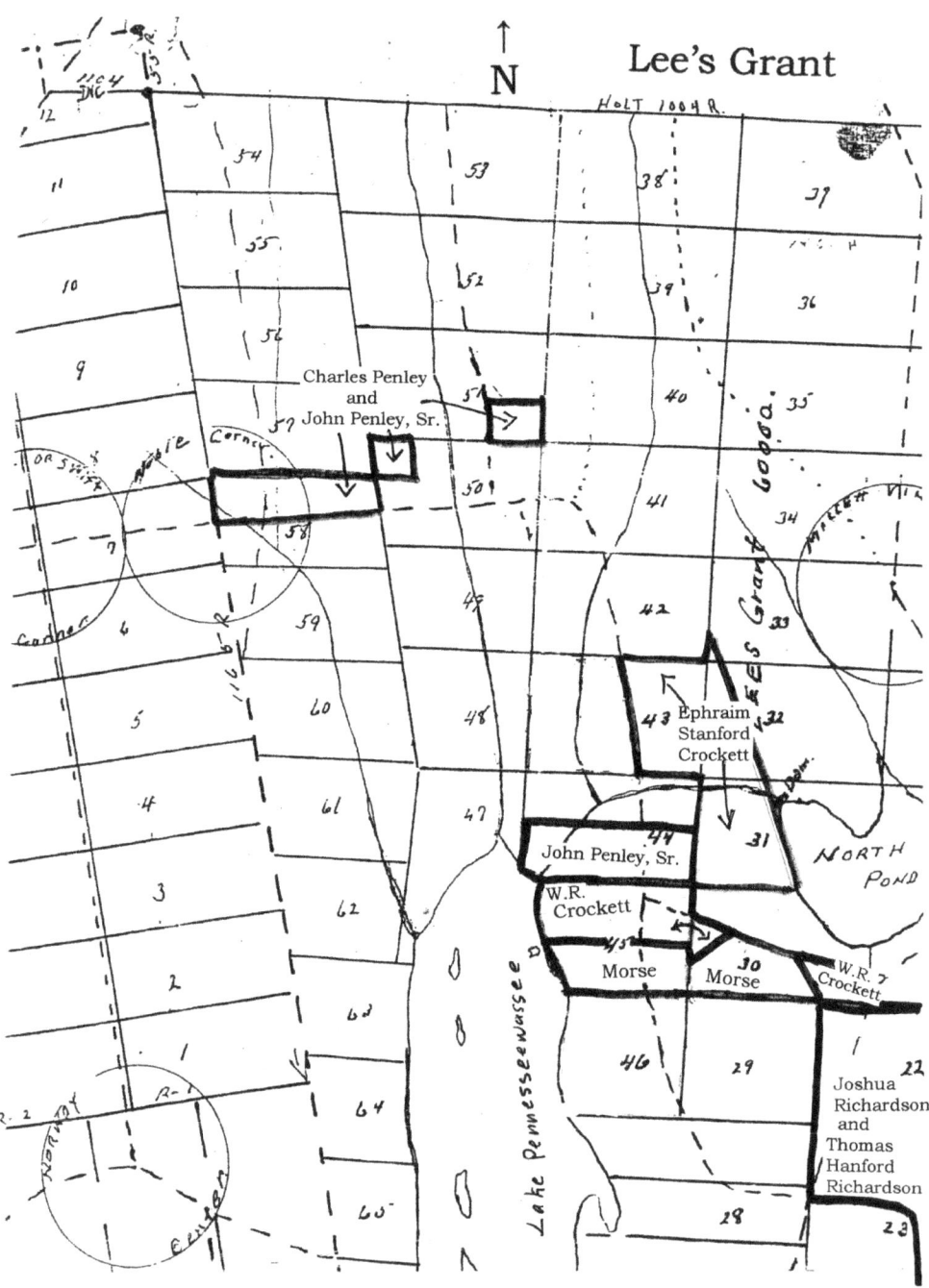

Lee's Grant lot map updated to 1850.

In 1845, John, Jr. and Betsey (Crockett) Penley had intended to settle permanently on the south half of Lot 44, next to her parents. By 1850, however, John was dead, and Betsey and the children had moved into the homes of other family members.

Despite his short tenure on Lot 44, the place continued to be called "the John Penley farm" for at least a generation. Via various other tragic twists and turns that we will follow in the next chapter, most of the fifty-two acres on this lot have remained in our family.[131] The cellar hole for the house where John and Betsey (Crockett) Penley lived with their three children lies across the road from my late mother's house. I never fail to think of the couple—and what a blow John, Jr.'s death must have been to everyone—when I walk past and glance over the stone wall to the cellar hole, inhabited now only by trees, chipmunks, and field mice.

The cellar hole from the home of John and Betsey (Crockett) Penley, on the south half of Lot 44. Today this property is owned by the author's brother Wesley Wixson and his wife Lori in their family trust. (Photo by Jennifer Wixson.)

---

131. The trust set up by my late mother, Rowena Palmer, owns twenty-five acres on the south half of Lot 44, on the west side of the road (plus nine more acres from Lot 43 that came into the family later). The trust belonging to my brother Wesley Wixson and his wife Lori owns twenty-two acres on the south half of Lot 44, on the east side of the road (where the cellar hole is).

William Robinson Crockett and His Father Build the Brick House

The 1849 exodus of adults from the Crockett homestead might have been hastened by another event in addition to John, Jr.'s death. William Robinson Crockett and his father were planning to build a new house.

Just prior to William's marriage to Lydia in November of 1849, he and Ephraim mortgaged the entire Crockett real estate, which consisted of the house, barn, and land on Lot 45 and pasture and woodland on Lot 30. On August 18, 1849, Ephraim and William borrowed $250 from Aaron Wilkins, a local man known for drawing up deeds and loaning money. (Wilkins also served as Justice of the Peace.)[132] In addition to the mortgage, William and his father gave Wilkins a note-of-hand. The two Crocketts agreed to pay Wilkins the $250 on demand, plus interest,[133] still a common way of doing business at the time.

The borrowed money was used to build the handsome brick house that still stands today. I believe the second-generation home that replaced most of the early frame house was built over the original cellar hole. The new home was designed to be large enough—and last long enough—to provide not only for Ephraim and Sally and their children still at home, but also for William and Lydia and their family and for generations to come (which the house has done). My grandmother Winona told me—and everyone else to whom she proudly showed off her house—that the brick home was built in 1850. The fact that she knew the exact year the house was built reveals the family pride in this second-generation home. It must have been a remarkable feat to live in the old remnant of the house (and attached shed and barn) while the new house was being built. To keep the Crockett family housed during this awkward transition would have necessitated a downsizing of people living at home.

The classic brick house, which boasts a granite foundation and granite lintels over the windows and doors, sits on a rise above the road. When it was new, it was the only brick house on Lee's Grant—and I believe it still is the only one today. The formal entryway (probably only used for weddings and funerals) was situated in the wide, east-facing front of the cape-style section of the house, with window lights on either side of the door. The narrower south side was elongated by a brick ell, which seamlessly connects the main brick house to what remained of the

---

132. LAPHAM, p. 624.
133. OCROD, Book 82, page 327.

original post-and-beam section. The brick ell (now the kitchen), opened to the west into the old kitchen, from which one accessed the attached shed, barn, office, and back house. On the east, the brick ell opened into the living room, from which one accessed the north bedrooms and parlor. Six tall windows on the south side provide the brick house with plenty of sunlight, assisted by two small window lights set over the doors. In William's day, the cape section of the brick house probably had four large rooms downstairs: two bedrooms, a living room, and the parlor. A connecting hallway led from the living room to the front entryway, where the stairs to the second floor are located. Upstairs is a large landing with built-in drawers and bookshelves, three bedrooms, and several large walk-in closets, suggesting the first Crocketts felt squeezed for space in the original house. The brick house built by William Robinson Crockett is owned today (in 2024) by my aunt Joyce Palmer, who lives there with her grandson Jonathan Palmer. The interior of the house has been modified over time to meet the needs of later generations, including the addition of two bathrooms (although the two-window outhouse off the back of the shed, which I enjoyed using as a child, remained until 2020). Recently, Jonathan has done significant restoration work to the sheds, attached barn, and old kitchen.

Second-generation brick house built in 1850 by William Robinson Crockett and his father. Photo circa 1925, about 75 years after the house was built. The original post-and-beam section begins at the left chimney.

The old Crockett homestead; photo circa 1980,
about 130 thirty years after William Robinson Crockett built the brick house. The restored 1929 Nash belonged to the author's grandmother, Winona (Young) Palmer.
(Family photos in the possession of the author.)

2021 restoration work at the old Crockett homestead.
In 2021, Jonathan Palmer (my cousin Jim's son), who lives with his grandmother Joyce Palmer in the old Crockett homestead, did some major restoration work to the frame and foundation of the old kitchen and sheds/barn. These outbuildings were attached to the original frame house, replaced by the brick house built by William Robinson Crockett in 1850. Jon, a seventh-generation descendant of Ephraim Crockett, Jr., said his goal is to keep the place standing for another 200 years. In the photo below, Jon is operating the excavator. The image also shows the original detached Crockett barn in the background.
(Photos by Jennifer Wixson, 2021.)

The new brick house was not only spacious and gracious but also served as a clear demarcation line between the first and second generations. While the old place belonged to Ephraim and Sally and their children, the new house belonged to William Robinson Crockett and his descendants. William's brothers James and Frank, who were then living with sister Hannah, would have known that there was no going back home. Likewise, the young Crocketts still residing at home—Mary Amanda, Eliza Jane, and Charles Alanson—would have known that eventually they would need to find homes of their own. This demarcation line became even more apparent when, on September 14, 1850, Lydia gave birth to her and William's first child, Abel Stetson Crockett.[134] The third generation—and heir apparent—had been born.

The 1850 agricultural census for Norway, which was taken on July 22nd while the brick house was being built, shows Ephraim and William managed sixty acres of improved land and twenty acres of unimproved land.[135] The cash value of the farm was $1500. That the farming practices were still old-school can be seen by the fact that the value of farm implements and machinery on hand was only $50. The bulk of the heavy labor on the farm—plowing, planting, hauling out firewood, and transporting logs up the road to the sawmill—was performed by oxen. The Crockett farm had four working oxen in 1850, likely two trained teams. Oxen would also have been used to ferry produce to market and bring bricks back from town to build the new house. With five "milch" cows on hand in 1850, another valuable commodity taken to market would have been butter. In addition to the cows, the Crocketts owned one horse (for transportation), ten sheep, and one swine, bringing the total value of their livestock to $270. The family had on hand 13 bushels of rye, 70 bushels of Indian corn, and 40 bushels of oats. The oats and rye had probably just been harvested; the Indian corn would have been what was left of the prior fall's crop.

By contrast, in 1850, the Preble farm, which Thomas Hanford Richardson managed (and which his father Joshua owned), was valued at $2500 and had 150 acres of improved land and 40 acres of unimproved land. Four second-generation Crocketts contributed to the success of the Richardson farm that year, including James and Frank Crockett, who worked as farm laborers. Mistress of the house, Hannah, and her widowed sister Betsey Penley, would have tended the six milk cows and

---

134. CANDAGE, p. 179.
135. U.S. Selected Census, Non-Population Schedule, Agriculture, 1850-1880, Norway, Maine. Ephraim Crockett.

made butter and cheese. When the agricultural census was taken, the value of the Richardson farm implements and machinery was $150, triple that of the Crockett homestead. In addition to the cows, the Richardson's livestock included two oxen (one team), sixteen "other cattle" (probably young stock or beef animals), and eight pigs. Crops on hand included two bushels of wheat, 111 bushels of Indian corn, and 179 bushels of oats.[136]

In November of 1850, Joshua Richardson also purchased the Latham farm, which real estate lay fallow in the 1850 agricultural census and which in fact had once belonged to the original 250-acre parcel purchased by Jacob Tubbs from Frances Lightfoot Lee. (Tubbs cut the farm out for his son Samuel.) Richardson paid Woodward Latham $500 for this modest, 50-acre property, where Latham had formerly lived with his mother. Six months later, on May 1, 1851, Joshua sold the farm to James Crockett, providing the young man (his daughter-in-law's brother) with a permanent home. The Portland businessman conveyed the Latham farm to James for $650, taking a mortgage on the entire amount.[137] (Unfortunately, James did not have the money to buy the place outright, and Latham obviously did not want to hold a note, which is why Richardson, acting as a banker, was able to make $150 on the deal.) James, who was not quite twenty-three, had married Salome Frank of Norway on December 8, 1850.[138] Salome gave birth to the couple's first child, Rose Emma Crockett, on January 3, 1852, adding another Crockett grandchild to the greater Crockett's Ridge neighborhood.[139]

A Walk to the Big Hill Field

When writing a history such as this, one tends to focus on facts compiled from dry and dusty birth and marriage records, real estate transactions, and obituaries. It is challenging to step back from the thousands of minute details and see our ancestors as flesh and blood individuals who lived and loved and whose lives and genes combined to make us the people we are. Although we have never known most of these ancestors, our lives overlap in inexplicable ways.

Once one summer day while walking up the small rise to get to the field and

---

136. U.S. Selected Census, Non-Population Schedule, Agriculture, 1850-1880, Norway, Maine. Thomas H. Richardson.
137. See OCROD, Book 87, page 437 and Book 90, page 254.
138. CANDAGE, p. 180. James was married one day before his twenty-third birthday. His bride, Salome Frank, was approximately eighteen.
139. CANDAGE, p. 180.

big hill behind the old Crockett homestead (my grandmother's house), I had the tingling sensation that I was not alone. Before I could glance back over my shoulder to see who might be there, Time twisted and I was suddenly overtaken by a group of laughing, happy young people from several generations past. Four or five Crockett fledglings were traipsing out to the very same sweet-scented hayfield where I was headed. The boys wore trousers held up with old-fashioned suspenders, the kind with the leather ends; and the girls were attired in full, flowing skirts and white blouses. They were a lively, talkative bunch, and I strained to hear what they were saying (as though their conversation affected me, too). But their words were lost in the rustling sounds of the wind in the trees and tall grass. I felt as though I had inadvertently stepped into a revolving loop of Crockett history, as though we were all on the same carousel at the fair, only on different horses. The carousel twirled round faster and faster until we blurred together as one. I held my breath, trying to hang onto the moment as long as I could. But nearly as suddenly as these transcendental beings had gained on me, they swept past me (or through me) and disappeared down over the rise, leaving me alone.

I never again experienced such a temporal inversion at the old Crockett homestead, although when I was at the house by myself, I often felt the presence of "others." Years later, while rummaging through some old studio portraits of unidentified 19th century Crocketts, one photograph jumped out at me (see following photo). I felt as though I had seen the young woman before in the flesh, but how was that possible? With an electrical jolt of recognition, I realized she was one of my companions from that Delphian day. It was then that I learned life offers us extraordinary opportunities to know our antecedents other than by sifting through dry and dusty marriage and birth records, real estate transactions, and obituaries.

One of my mysterious friends from a summer long, long ago.[140]
(Studio portrait of unidentified Crockett daughter, now in the possession of
Joyce Palmer, Norway, Maine.)

Overlapping Generations

Most of us were born into smaller families than our ancestors, with the generations neatly separated by a space of twenty or twenty-five years. (With Millennials delaying childbirth into their thirties, the number of children will be even less and the generations spaced even further apart.) But in the 19th century, when labor was needed in the field and on the farm, the overlapping of generations was common. In 1834, when Ephraim and Sally's eldest child Sarah married Charles Penley, their eleventh child, Mary Amanda, was only a year old. Sally, who was forty-one at the time, would go on to give birth to two more children, even as her daughter began presenting her and Ephraim with grandchildren.

In 1851, seventeen years after Sarah and Charles were married, the one-year-old

---

140. My best guess is that this is a studio portrait of Lydia "Frances" Crockett, the youngest child of William and Lydia (Stetson) Crockett.

child at their wedding, Mary Amanda Crockett, wed Isaiah Vickery Penley, Charles' younger brother. (See genealogy chart, "Crockett-Penley Marriages in the 2nd Norway Generation" earlier in the chapter.) Isaiah Vickery was the thirteenth child and eighth son of Captain Penley and Desire (Dingley) Penley. The fourth Crockett-Penley wedding took place in Norway on March 18, 1851.[141] Isaiah, who was fourteen years younger than Charles, was twenty-four when the couple wed. Mary was only seventeen and a half. Her youthful age suggests Mary might have been keen to remove from her parent's home, now, in fact, her brother William's domain. After this fourth (and final) Crockett/Penley marriage, the newlyweds resided in Danville, probably on one of Captain Penley's properties.[142]

In the meantime, Joshua Richardson continued to expand his holdings on Lee's Grant. On November 1, 1852, Richardson purchased Lot 46 from Edwin Stetson of Norway[143] (maybe a relation of William's wife Lydia, although not a sibling). Lot 46, situated below Uncle Nathan and Aunt Mary Morse, was one of the first properties Charles Penley had bought when he came to town nearly twenty years earlier. At one point, Charles had wanted to build a house on Lot 46, although he never did. Someone else did build a home there because "including buildings thereon" was in the language of the deed for which Joshua Richardson paid $700. He conveyed the real estate to his son Thomas Hanford for $600 on the same day he bought it. T.H. paid his father $100 and gave him a mortgage for the balance.[144]

There are many reasons why Joshua Richardson might have purchased Lot 46. He could have considered the place an investment opportunity and a way to expand his farm land. It is also possible Richardson wanted to secure his son's family a home in the Crockett neighborhood in the event he decided to sell the more expensive (and extensive) Preble farm, where T.H. and Hannah were living. Finally, Richardson, a shrewd businessman, might have seen Lot 46 as nothing more than a rental property, a way of providing his son with alternative income if T.H. failed as a farmer. Thomas Hanford, who grew up in the city of Portland, does not appear to have had much agricultural experience, which might be why his father secured James Crockett on the farm next door.

---

141. CANDAGE, p. 181 and Penley genealogy, AHS.
142. According to Isaiah Penley's obituary published in the *Oxford County Advertiser*, Jan. 30, 1903, Isaiah (and presumably his family) resided in Auburn until "close to the time of the Civil War, when he moved [to Norway] and carried on a farm." The family spent some time in Bethel, as we will see later in this chapter.
143. OCROD, Book 96, page 179.
144. OCROD, Book 124, page 475.

Another Death in the Second Norway Generation and More Family Losses

If Richardson had hoped James would teach his son Thomas Hanford to farm, he was disappointed. Tragically, on December 9, 1853, James Sewall Crockett passed away,[145] leaving his pregnant wife and one-year-old daughter Rose Emma behind.[146] We have no information about the cause of James' death, but given his young age—only twenty-six years and four months—and his hazardous occupation as a farmer, my best guess (as a farmer myself) is that he died by accident. James was buried with his little niece Sarah (Charles and Sarah Penley's fourteen-month-old daughter) in what became the Crockett family cemetery, situated on a knoll of land at the Crockett homestead that could be seen from the kitchen window (where his parents would later be buried). Five months after James' death, fatherless little Mary Jane Crockett was born to the widowed Salome Crockett.[147]

James' passing, just six years after the death of John Penley, Jr., was another blow to the interconnected web of Crockett and Penley families in the greater Crockett's Ridge neighborhood. One can only imagine the grief and anger felt by the older generation, wondering why they lived on and their children were being cut down like grass in the field.

Brother Ephraim Stanford Crockett acted as James' administrator, and on April 18, 1854, he was granted authority by the Probate Court to auction his brother's real estate, that farm so recently acquired. The auction was held on May 29, 1854. Eldest brother Samuel Crockett stepped up to purchase the former Latham farm for $700, covering the mortgage to Richardson.[148] A year later, on May 15, 1855, Samuel sold the property to his brother-in-law Thomas Hanford Richardson for $725, accepting a mortgage on the entire property.[149] Only two days after this real estate transaction Joshua Richardson swooped in and bought up his son's mortgage (and the personal note of hand given by T.H. to Samuel).[150] Thus this 50-acre parcel, which Joshua Richardson had sold to James only four years earlier, was rejoined to Richardson's extensive farm that T.H. managed.

The family losses continued to mount during the 1850s. On June 20, 1853,

---

145. CANDAGE, p. 180.
146. Rose Emma Crockett was born in Norway to James Sewell and Salome (Frank) Crockett on January 3, 1852. CANDAGE, p. 180.
147. Mary Jane Crockett was born in Norway on May 6, 1854. CANDAGE, p. 180.
148. OCROD, Book 104, page 119.
149. OCROD, Book 103, page 324 and Book 105/192.
150. OCROD, Book 104, page 166.

Lydia's father passed away. Abel Stetson, one of the founders of Sumner, was sixty-eight when he died. After her father's death, Lydia inherited a one-twelfth share of her father's real and personal estate. On December 2, 1856, she conveyed this one-twelfth share to her brother Hezekiah for $200, receiving from him a mortgage of $207.37 that came with very favorable terms (for him). Hezekiah would pay one-half of the mortgage in three years and the other half in twelve years, with interest paid annually.[151]

Three years after the death of Abel Stetson, on November 12, 1856, Ephraim, Jr.—the patriarch of the Crockett family and first settler on Crockett's Ridge—joined his son James and granddaughter Sarah in the little family cemetery next to the house. Ephraim was sixty-eight and eight months when he passed.[152] He departed the world knowing his family and homestead were in the capable hands of his son, William Robinson Crockett, and William's wife, Lydia. Ephraim's widow Sally, then sixty-two, outlived him by more than twenty years, continuing to be a productive member of the Crockett household.

Crocketts and Penleys in the Civil War

As the 1850s marched forward, the United States moved closer to Civil War. Maine's history was forever linked to the question of slavery when the state joined the union as part of the Missouri Compromise in 1820. Maine was only allowed to become a free state separate from Massachusetts if Missouri could be admitted to the union as a slave state. Eight months of "protracted negotiations" had been necessary to effect this compromise, partly because of "abolitionist Maine congressmen, who fervently opposed the spread of slavery anywhere—so much so that they were willing to torpedo the entire Maine statehood movement, just to keep slavery from spreading."[153]

Although there had been enslaved people in the homes of wealthy Mainers during the 17th and 18th centuries (mostly those with ties to the shipping industry and sugar plantations in the Caribbean), the abhorrent practice was outlawed by Massachusetts in 1783. During the 19th century, the state was a hotbed of abolitionist sentiment, producing leaders in the anti-slavery movement. In 1837, newspaper

---

151. OCROD, Book 112, page 197 and Book 113, page 111.
152. CANDAGE, p. 85.
153. "Maine's statehood is irrevocably tied to the defining issue of its time: Slavery." Emily Burnham. *Bangor Daily News*. February 15, 2020.

editor Elijah Parish Lovejoy, who hailed from Albion, Maine, was killed by a violent, pro-slavery mob in Alton, Illinois—part of the infamous Little Egypt—for his abolitionist writings. And, in 1851, while living in Brunswick, Harriet Beecher Stowe penned her classic novel, "Uncle Tom's Cabin," which dramatically shifted the northern white population's perception of the plight of the enslaved in the United States.

In 1854, the Kansas-Nebraska Act was passed by Congress, which repealed the Missouri Compromise. The Act also created two new territories, each given the right to decide the slavery question by "popular sovereignty." (Had the Missouri Compromise not been repealed, both territories would have come in as "free" states because they were both above the 36°30' parallel.)[154] The Act gave residents of Kansas and Nebraska the right to vote whether they wanted to allow the practice of slavery. This act sparked a land rush to the territories by both pro- and anti-slavery factions—one-cause political pioneers.[155] The Kansas-Nebraska Act, which was hoped to tamp down calls for civil war, instead inflamed the issue, and a new political party—the Republicans (the party of Abraham Lincoln)—was formed. One of those who abandoned the Democratic party for the new Republican party was Paris, Maine's Hannibal Hamlin, a staunch abolitionist.[156]

The late Father Don McAllister, a noted Norway historian in his retirement, collected data about the town's involvement in the Civil War. Father Don (as he was locally known) summarized for one of the town's annual reports Norway's participation in the war effort:

> "When the Confederate States of America fired on Fort Sumter on April 12, 1861, Norway was a prosperous and growing town of 1,982 inhabitants. Norway sent down to the war more than a third of its adult male population. Maine furnished thirty-two regiments for the war and the commanding officer for three of the regiments came from Norway. There were five Lieutenants, and ten Captains from Norway, with a total of 44 different commissions in all.
>
> "Norway had one Brigadier-General, two brevet Brigadier Generals, one brevet Major General, three Colonels, one Chaplain, one Assistant Surgeon and one Regimental Quartermaster. No citizen of Norway enlisted either in the Cav-

---

154. *"Franklin Pierce. The American Presidents Series."* (Kindle ed.) Michael F. Holt. Henry Holt and Company, LLC, 2010. Pp. 53–54, 72–73.
155. "The Wealthy Activist Who Helped Turn 'Bleeding Kansas' Free." Robert Sutton. *Smithsonian* magazine. August 16, 2017.
156. "The Life and Times of Hannibal Hamlin by his Grandson Charles Eugene Hamlin." Charles Eugene Hamlin. Cambridge, Massachusetts: Riverside Press, 1899.

alry or Light Artillery. All but two enlisted in the Infantry. These two enlisted in Heavy Artillery."[157]

Norway historian Charles F. Whitman is also effusive when recounting the town's war effort and the valor of her soldiers during the Rebellion. The specific details he provides about the various companies and their service has been especially helpful in piecing together the role of the Crockett and Penley families in the Civil War.

All three sons of Charles and Sarah Penley enlisted during the first year of the war: Ephraim Crockett Penley, Nathan Penley, and Rufus Crockett Penley. When the 5th Maine infantry regiment was mustered in Portland on June 24, 1861—two months after the firing upon and capture of Fort Sumter—Ephraim and Rufus Penley were two of the six "three-year men" (men who volunteered for a three-year stint) from Norway who joined the 5th Maine in Company I.[158] Ephraim, the eldest of the brothers, was twenty-four; Rufus, the youngest, was only seventeen.[159] The 5th Maine was equipped with Springfield muskets and bayonets and saw some of the worst fighting of the war:

> "During its three years of severe service, [the 5th Maine] was engaged in eleven pitched battles and eight skirmishes, prior to its participation in the terrible campaign of the Wilderness under Grant. Its list of battles includes First Bull Run, West Point, Gaines' Mill, Charles City Cross-Roads, Crampton's Gap, Antietam, Fredericksburg, Salem Heights, Gettysburg, Rappahannock Station, Wilderness, Spotsylvania Court House and Cold Harbor. In the battle of Gaines' Mill the 5th lost 10 killed, 69 wounded and 16 missing."[160]

Miraculously, Ephraim Penley survived his three years of service with the 5th Maine. Rufus, however, perished at White Oak Church, Virginia, on December 28, 1862. He died from a disease incurred in camp, only three weeks shy of his eighteenth birthday.[161] Rufus's embalmed body (undertakers and embalmers followed the Union army) was shipped via rail back to Maine for burial. Sarah and Charles,

---

157. Research and data by Donald L. McAllister. Published in the "Annual Report of the Municipal Officers of the Town of Norway, Maine For the Fiscal Year Ending December 31, 1964." My thanks to the Norway, Maine Historical Society who made this information (and the photo of the three Civil War soldiers from Norway) available on their website, Norway, Maine Historical Society. Norway in the Civil War. "Our Soldiers."
158. WHITMAN, p. 99.
159. CANDAGE, p. 176-177.
160. "The Union army; a history of military affairs in the loyal states, 1861-65 -- records of the regiments in the Union army -- cyclopedia of battles -- memoirs of commanders and soldiers. Vol.1." Madison, Wis: Federal Pub. Co., 1908.)
161. CANDAGE, p. 177.

who were living in Portland at the time of their son's death, most likely traveled with the coffin after it was transferred in Portland to the Atlantic and St. Lawrence railroad up to the station at Paris. From there, the sad procession would have made its way to the Crockett family cemetery, where Rufus was buried with his grandfather, baby sister Sarah, and uncle James.

In the fall of 1861 (prior to Rufus' death), Nathan Penley followed his two brothers into military service. He volunteered for the company that Norway resident Captain Amos F. Noyes was putting together—the very same Noyes under whom his uncle Ephraim Stanford Crockett served during the Aroostook War. Harry Rust, grandson of Captain Henry Rust, who settled Rustfield (Norway),[162] also joined this company, serving as Lieut. Colonel. Noyes planned to have his company join the 13th Maine infantry regiment; however, when the men were ready to be mustered in, the 13th Maine was full, and the Norway men were admitted into the 14th Maine as Company G.

Captain Noyes, who eventually was forced to resign due to sickness and injury, kept a diary in which he recorded daily incidents, including the death or wounding of his soldiers. According to Dr. Osgood N. Bradbury, who later penned accounts for the *Oxford County Advertiser*, Noyes kept his diary in his pocket and updated it daily. Dr. Bradbury had Captain Noyes' diaries before him when he wrote the following account about the early days of Noyes' company with the 14th Maine:

> "On Feb. 5, 1862, the Reg. went to Boston by rail. On Feb. 8th at six o'clock in the morning they left Boston in the sailing vessel North America for Ship Island at the mouth of the Mississippi River.
>
> "On the 18th at nine o'clock in the evening while off the coast of Carolina, Jesse Prince of Oxford (Pri. Co. G, 14th Reg.) died of lung fever. He was buried at sea at eight o'clock the next morning.
>
> "On Feb. 28th they were in sight of Tortugas Islands, and on March 9th landed at Ship Island. A journey of twenty-nine days from Boston. The North America was a slow vessel in those days.
>
> "On March 18th Lieut. Noyes was on duty on the ship Idaho and accidentally fell through the hatchway and broke two ribs on the left side. This injury gave him much trouble and with other physical ailments resulted in his resignation later.
>
> "April 11, Silas T. Crowell (Pri. G 14) of Oxford died at six o'clock in the morning of congestion of stomach. George E. Needham (Pri. G 14) of Norway

---

162. WHITMAN, p. 499.

died at three o'clock in the afternoon of the same day. Both buried on the Island.

"April 16, Charles H. French (Pri. G 14) of Oxford died at two o'clock in the morning of diphtheria. He was buried on the Island. His friends later brought the body home to Oxford."[163]

In his Norway history, Whitman summarizes the action of the 14th Maine, to which Nathan Penley belonged:

"The regiment served in Gen. [Benjamin] F. Butler's Department of the Gulf. The Norway company was in the severe battle of Baton Rouge, La., where the Union Army gained a great victory. Lieut. Noyes had previously resigned on account of an injury received. In 1864, the 14th Maine Regiment participated in the battles of the Opequon and Cedar Creek. Its losses from casualties in battle and disease were very great. Company G. had the greatest number of men from Norway of any that went from the town to the war, and the largest number of deaths."[164]

The list of local men who died during their tenure with the 14th Maine is long. Nathan Penley, however, was not one of them. He survived his three-year tour of duty. After such an ordeal, however, Nathan must have returned to Norway a much different man than when he left in 1861.

---

163. *Oxford County, Advertiser*. Dr. Osgood Bradbury, No. 147, Third Paper. Also, see NORWAY40s, p. 400-401.
164. WHITMAN, p. 100.

The Crocketts and the Penleys

Three Civil War Soldiers from Norway.
Then 2nd Lieutenant Harry Rust (left), grandson of Norway founder Captain Henry Rust; Captain George Beal (middle), who was later promoted to General; and 1st Lieutenant Jonathan Blake. (Photo courtesy of Norway, Maine Historical Society.)

The 23rd Maine regiment of "nine-month men" was formed in Portland in 1862. Charles Sewell Penley, son of John, Jr. and Betsey (Crockett) Penley, was mustered into the 23rd Maine on September 29th, three months before his cousin Rufus' death. He was only eighteen at the time of his enlistment. Compared to his cousins, however, Charles Sewell had an easy time with the 23rd Maine. Whitman writes of his regiment:

> "The regiment was in no battle and was stationed to guard the fords of the Potomac between Washington and Harper's Ferry. The 23rd Regiment started for home to be mustered out late in June, 1863, while General Lee's army was invading Pennsylvania. When it reached Philadelphia, the city authorities tried to get it to stay there till the Rebel Army should be driven back across the Potomac or captured, but this was refused and it kept on to Maine and was mustered out July 15th. This action of refusing to stop in Philadelphia was deeply regretted afterwards, because all through the war that city had furnished free entertainment for all Union soldiers passing through the city."[165]

---

165. WHITMAN, P. 101-103. Philadelphia residents and shopkeepers also offered soldiers free meals and beverages, haircuts, and baths.

Charles Sewell Penley survived his nine-month enlistment. He mustered out on July 15, 1863.[166] The following spring, on April 27, 1864 (the day after his twentieth birthday), Charles reenlisted, joining Company H of the Maine State Guards. This was a very short-term assignment, and he was discharged on July 9, 1864. Charles Sewell Penley was one of the few of the third generation Crockett-Penleys who settled on Crockett's Ridge. We will learn more about him in the next two chapters.

The only second-generation Crockett to see active duty during the Civil War was Joseph Francis "Frank" Crockett. Frank was a farmer who, along with brother James and sister Betsey, had lived with Thomas Hanford and Hannah Richardson in 1850. Frank was the second to youngest son of Ephraim and Sally. When he was thirty-two, Frank joined the 25th Maine Regiment, Volunteer Infantry, Company D.[167] Frank was mustered in on the same date as his nephew Charles Sewall, September 29, 1862. Like the 23rd Maine, the 25th Maine served in defense of Washington and was called up for nine-months service. The regiment had no engagements, although twenty soldiers died of disease. Frank, who rose to the rank of Sergeant, survived, although he became disabled, probably from a serious illness or accident he incurred in camp. On July 10, 1862, Frank was mustered out[168] and formally discharged from the service for disability on February 24, 1863.[169] He returned to Norway and married on May 16, 1864, Antoinette Stetson, Lydia's half-sister from Sumner. The couple was married in Paris and made their home in Norway Village.[170]

As the war dragged on and the army became desperate for fresh troops to replace the fallen and wounded, some of the older males from the second generation became vulnerable to the new draft. The Enrollment Act of 1863 required every male between the age of twenty and forty-five to register whether they wanted to leave their farms and go to war or not. (According to Whitman, eighteen or twenty Norway men fled to Canada to escape the draft.)[171] As a result of their ages, Nathan Morse Crockett (the butcher) age forty-two; William Robinson Crockett, forty; Thomas Hanford Richardson, forty-two; Isaiah Vickery Penley, thirty-six;

---

166. U.S. Civil War Soldier Records and Profiles, 1861-1865. Penley, Charles Sewell.
167. CANDAGE, p. 180.
168. Maine State Archives, Maine Civil War Units, 25th Regiment, Maine Volunteer Infantry.
169. Maine U.S. Veterans Cemetery Records, 1676-1918. Crockett, Frank.
170. CANDAGE, p. 180.
171. WHITMAN, p. 103. The Norway historian says many of these draft-dodgers regretted their actions later in life.

and cousin Edwin A. Morse (son of Nathan and Mary Crockett Morse) forty-three; were required to register.

When called up, many older men either served a short-term enlistment in-state or paid a bounty to another man (usually around $300) to serve in their stead. In 1864, Isaiah Vickery Penley, Mary Amanda Crockett's husband, served sixty days as a private in Cobb's Company, Maine Militia State Guards.[172] Cobb's Company was in service at Fort McClary, Kittery, from April 27th to July 9, 1864.[173] T.H., William Robinson, and Edwin A. Morse all registered for the draft in 1863. None show a service record, so they likely were not called up. Although the Richardson family could have afforded to send a substitute, I suspect it was unnecessary or it would have been noted. By contrast, William Robinson Crockett would not have had $300 to pay the bounty for a replacement soldier.[174] Crockett genealogist Charles Candage reports that William's older brother Nathan was a veteran of the Civil War; however, I have been unable to find a military service record for him.[175]

In total, Norway sent 248 men to fight the Rebellion.[176] The Civil War did not just take a toll in lives lost, wounded, or shortened, however. The war was an incredibly expensive undertaking. As President Lincoln called for men (and more men), towns like Norway were required to raise money (and more money) to pay the bounty necessary to attract fresh recruits or tempt soldiers to re-enlist who had already mustered out. As the years wore on—and the deaths and disabilities piled up—the bounties needed to be increased. In addition, towns raised money via taxation to provide for the families of the soldiers while the men were away from their farms, and for those whose soldier never returned. The town also raised money for hospitals and other war-related charities. Whitman recounts the total financial burden picked up by Norway residents through taxation during the Civil War:

> "Norway paid in bounties during the war, $22,066.42. —The citizens of the town contributed for the U.S. Sanitary and U.S. Christian Commissions and Hospitals, besides private contributions, $2,475. The town furnished aid to 117 families of 322 persons, $4,197.75."[177]

---

172. U.S. Civil War Soldiers, 1861-1865. Isaiah Vickery Penley.
173. WHITMAN, p. 106.
174. U.S. Civil War Draft Registration Records, Maine, 1863-1865. Thomas Hanford Richardson, William Robinson Crockett, Edwin A. Morse.
175. CANDAGE, p. 179.
176. WHITMAN, p. 156.
177. WHITMAN, p. 156.

Concluding Synopses – Crocketts and Penleys

Having now traveled thirty years with the second generation of Crocketts and Penleys, we have begun to overlap with the lives of their children. Some of the younger members of the second generation we will meet again in Chapter 4; most we will not. Likewise, only a few of the third-generation cousins will appear in the next chapter. Chapter 4 is dedicated to the children of William Robinson and Lydia (Stetson) Crockett, especially our ancestor Emma Tuell Crockett. As a result, we will conclude this chapter with synopses of the lives of the second generation of Norway Crocketts and Penleys.

Captain John Penley, Sr., the father of the four Penleys who married four Crocketts, passed away in Auburn (formerly Danville) on January 10, 1873, at the age of ninety. He was buried in the Penley Corner Cemetery with his son and namesake, next to the church he helped build, although never attended.[178] Prior to his death Captain Penley made financial arrangements for his children and grandchildren. Those of his descendants who outlived him were named as beneficiaries in his extensive will. As mentioned at the beginning of this chapter, Captain Penley's wealth—more than $100,000 when he died—materially affected the disposition of the Crockett-Penley families on Crockett's Ridge.

Charles and Sarah Penley, who had been living at the former Needham farm his father owned on the Greenwood Road, relocated to Portland before 1860. In the census for 1860, Charles is listed as a "provisions dealer," and the family is living in Ward 9. With Charles and Sarah in Portland was their youngest child, thirteen-year-old daughter, Adrianne, and a young man named Samuel Dewll (sic).

Sarah (Crockett) Penley would never return to Norway to live. She died in Portland on July 3, 1863, just six months after her son Rufus' death in the war. She was only forty-nine. Sarah's body was brought back to join those of her two deceased children and her father and brother in the Crockett family cemetery next to the brick house.

By 1870, Charles had relocated to the city of Auburn (West Danville)[179] near

---

178. Penley family records and genealogy, AHS. According to Ed Staples, Penley Corner Church is a Freewill Baptist Church. John Penley's first wife was a Congregationalist and it is likely that he was a well. Penley's second wife, however, was a Baptist. Penley built the church for his second wife, although not being of the same religious bent he never attended. (Conversation between Ed Staples and Jennifer Wixson, March 26, 2022, Norway, Maine Historical Society.)

179. According to the Penley genealogy by Father Robert Penley, "Charles returned to West Danville after his wife died but was returned to Norway to be buried next to his wife in the old cemetery near William Crockett's." From, "Penley family in England and America, ca. 1377-1958 : being principally an account of the ancestry and descendents [sic] of Joseph Penly of

where his father and many of his siblings resided. Living with Charles in 1870 was a thirty-one-year-old housekeeper, Ellen Taylor, and her thirteen-year-old son William, who is listed as a farm laborer. Charles—once a Norway real estate speculator—had no real estate transactions in that town after 1855. In 1870, the value of Charles' real estate in Auburn was a paltry $600.[180] When Captain Penley died in 1873, he left Charles the eighty-acre farm on the Greenwood Road, which had become known as the Charles Penley farm (although Charles' son Nathan had been living and farming there since returning from the war). When John Penley, Sr.'s estate was settled, Charles also received a share of the residue of his father's estate. Although we do not know the total value of Captain Penley's residue, it was probably a substantial sum.[181]

Charles did not live long enough to enjoy his inheritance. He followed his father to the grave only six months after Captain Penley passed. Charles died suddenly on Monday, July 21, 1873, of apoplexy (a stroke), having taken sick only the night before.[182] He was sixty-one. Charles was buried in the Crockett family cemetery with Sarah, their little daughter Sarah, and their son Rufus.

By devise of Captain Penley's will, Charles' surviving children inherited the property where Nathan lived and farmed. Nathan agreed to sell out to his brother-in-law Henry B. Cotton (sister Esther's husband), the administrator of Charles' estate.[183] On July 23, 1873, Cotton paid Nathan Penley $600 for his interest in the property, including the current year's hay crop[184] On March 1, 1875, Esther, Ephraim, Francina, and Adrianna—the other four of Charles' living children—sold all of Charles' inherited real estate to Daniel Bennett for $1500.[185] The five Penleys from the third generation would also inherit Charles' share of the residue of their grandfather's estate. When the estate was settled, Esther was living in New Hampshire; Ephraim Crockett Penley in Mississippi; Francina in Norway; Adrianna in Massachusetts; and Nathan in Bethel. None of them would ever again reside in the Crockett's Ridge neighborhood.

In 1859, many years before his death, Captain Penley sold to his daughter, Sarah "Sally" Dingley (Penley) Crockett, wife of Ephraim Stanford Crockett, the

---

Danville, Maine (1756-1844)." The Rev. Robert Penley. Alexandria, Canada: R. Penley, 1958. P. 41.
180. U. S. Census, 1860, Auburn, Maine. Charles Penley.
181. Maine Wills and Probate Records, 1584-1999. John Penley.
182. Charles Penley's Obituary, *The Oxford Democrat*, July 29, 1873, p. 2.
183. See Maine Wills and Probate Records 1584-1999. Charles D. Penley.
184. OCROD, Book 164, pages 244 and 175.
185. OCROD, Book 169, page 441.

south half of Lot 44. The purchase price was $700, and, as was usual with Captain Penley and family members that he wanted to bankroll, he accepted a mortgage for the entire amount. (John Penley, Sr. had previously sold the property to his grandson Joseph; however, Joseph decided to move elsewhere, so the property reverted to Captain Penley.) When she purchased the property, it is not likely Sally intended to move up the hill to the home of her late brother, John, Jr. Rather, Sally knew she was dying and wanted to ensure that her children had a farm of their own. Indeed, Sally (Penley) Crockett died on August 1, 1859, five months after becoming the owner of the John Penley farm. She passed away from tuberculosis,[186] a drawn-out and terrible disease, nearly eradicated after the discovery of antibiotics in 1928 (although making an unfortunate comeback today, thanks to antibiotic-resistant strains of TB).[187] Sally was buried on the little knoll at the Crockett homestead with her father-in-law and the others in the family cemetery.[188]

Sally (Penley) Crockett had given birth to nine children in fourteen years. All the children were minors when she was taken from them.[189] Whitman notes that her eldest daughter, Abbie Jane, who was thirteen when her mother died, took over much of the household responsibilities after Sally's passing. (My guess is that Abbie Jane also had the bulk of the chores prior to her mother's death too, although other female members of the extended family would have helped.) Whitman writes of Sally and Abbie Jane in his Norway history: "The mother had died six years before and the oldest daughter, a very capable girl, was head of the household."[190] —offering an inside peek at what sounds like a woebegone family.

When Captain Penley died in 1873, he willed to Sally's children the $700 mortgage she had given him for the south half of Lot 44. (Basically, he gave them the property.) In addition, Captain Penley also left the nine siblings $300 in cash to split between them.[191] On November 8, 1873, the property was auctioned off and John Freeland Crockett, the second son, purchased it for $333 to keep the place in the family.[192]

In the instrument regarding the auction of the south half of Lot 44 (recorded at

---

186. U.S. Federal Census Mortality Schedules, 1850-1885, Sarah D. Crockett.
187. According to the CDC, in 2018 TB was the leading infectious disease killer with 1.5 million deaths per year. This sad statistic would be surpassed by SARS COV 2 in 2020-2022.
188. CANDAGE, p. 176.
189. CANDAGE, p. 177-178.
190. WHITMAN, p. 253.
191. Maine Wills and Probate Records, 1584-1999. John Penley.
192. OCROD, Book 169, page 9-10.

the Oxford County Registry of Deeds in 1873), it is noted that Ephraim Stanford Crockett, the children's father, was then living at his wife's property. Most likely, he was ill or infirm and was being cared for there by some of his older children, who had moved up the hill. Ephraim Stanford Crockett passed away on January 17, 1874, at the age of fifty-six.[193] He left two minor children behind, Warren Ephraim Crockett, age sixteen, and Oscar Rufus Crockett, age fifteen.

After Ephraim Stanford's death, his second son, Josiah Penley Crockett, acted as guardian to the two minor youths. On October 20, 1875, Josiah sold Warren's and Oscar's share of their late father's estate, the Tongue property, to Albert Farnham.[194] Farnham, who was then married to their cousin Sarah Belle Penley (daughter of Isaiah Vickery and Mary Amanda Crockett Penley),[195] paid $300 at auction for Warren and Oscar's share. Albert also bought out the other seven siblings for $700.[196] We will meet Albert and Sarah (Penley) Farnham in the next chapter, where most of Ephraim Stanford and Sarah (Penley) Crockett's children will also appear.

According to Crockett genealogist Charles Candage, Betsey Wentworth (Crockett) Penley, widow of John Penley, Jr., married again almost a quarter of a century after her first husband passed. Candage says Betsey Penley married Albion P. Chapman of Bethel on October 11, 1871.[197] The marriage did not last long, nor did Betsy remain in Bethel. She died in Norway (probably at one of her siblings' homes) on January 26, 1876, a week shy of her fifty-seventh birthday. She is buried in the Penley Corner Cemetery in Auburn with her first husband, John, Jr.[198]

In his will, Captain Penley left the sum of $1000 to be equally divided between John, Jr.'s children.[199] Assuming this included the two children by John, Jr.'s first wife, Mary Dyer (if they survived), the money would have been split five ways, amounting to $200 per child (including obviously the three children John, Jr. had with Betsey Crockett). I have no doubt that John Penley, Sr. provided for these fatherless children during his lifetime, as well. Although I have no information about what happened to John, Jr.'s two eldest children, his children with Betsey lived long lives.

---

193. CANDAGE, p. 178.
194. OCROD, Book 169, page 570.
195. Sarah Belle Penley was Albert Farnham's second wife. He was previously married to her older sister Laura Aramantha Penley, who passed away in 1869. CANDAGE, p. 181.
196. OCROD, Book 173, page 7. The seven eldest children of Ephraim Stanford Crockett accepted a mortgage from Farnham for the entire $700.
197. CANDAGE, p. 178.
198. CANDAGE, p. 178.
199. Maine Wills and Probate Records, 1584-1999. John Penley.

Mary Dyer Penley, who had been named for her father's first wife, married Norway resident William Churchill in 1861, whom she met at her aunt and uncle's house (the home of Hannah and T.H. Richardson, to which she and her mother relocated after her father's death). Churchill, who was twenty-three when the 1860 census was taken, was listed as a farm laborer on the Richardson estate. Mary Dyer Penley was seventeen.[200] Sadly, William Churchill died in 1873, leaving Mary with two young children. She was married a second time to James Hibbard Aldrich, with whom she had one child, but from whom she was later divorced. Mary Dyer (Penley) Churchill Aldrich died in 1930 at the age of eighty-eight. She is buried with her first husband in Norway Pine Grove Cemetery.[201]

As mentioned, Civil War veteran Charles Sewell Penley, the second child of John and Betsey, remained in Norway. He and his first wife, Sarah Elizabeth Frost, lived on Crockett's Ridge for a time in her house, the former home of Revolutionary War veteran Daniel Knight (on the north half of Lot 44, where Pam and Errol Libby reside today). Charles Sewell, a farmer, became a colorful character in town, and we will learn more about him in the next two chapters.

Rufus L. Penley, the third child of John and Betsey, who was just six months old when his father died, moved out West where he married his first wife. He returned to Maine prior to 1870, where he was married again. Rufus died in 1926 at the age of eighty-eight.[202]

After their 1851 marriage, Mary Amanda (Crockett) and Isaiah Vickery Penley made their home in Danville before relocating to Bethel prior to 1860.[203] In Bethel, thirty-two-year-old Isaiah Vickery fell into financial difficulty. On January 2, 1860, the Deputy Sheriff held a public auction of Isaiah Vickery's farm to pay a judgment received against him by a man named Newton Swift, also of Bethel. Swift bought the property at auction for $76, although per order of the writ of execution, the family was allowed to continue to live there, and Isaiah Vickery was given one year to redeem his homestead for what was owed Swift.[204] Only two days before the right of redemption would expire, on January 2, 1861, Captain Penley stepped in

---

200. CANDAGE, p. 178. See also 1860 U.S. Census, Norway, Maine. Thomas H. Richardson.
201. The information that Mary Dyer Penley was buried with her first husband came from Stuart Goodwin, Trustee of Norway Pine Grove Cemetery. He told the author in an email that Mary has a gravestone in Section 1 of NPGC. Charles Candage writes in his Crockett history that Mary was buried with her Penley parents and grandparents in the Penley Corner Cemetery in Danville. I am not sure which is accurate, however, not having checked for a stone in Danville and having found one in Norway, I believe it is likely Mary was buried in Norway. CANDAGE, p. 178.
202. CANDAGE, p. 178.
203. U.S. Census, 1860, Bethel, Maine. Isaiah Vickery Penley.
204. OCROD, Book 122, Pages 436 and 437.

and paid the amount due to Swift, $78.41 ($76 plus interest), thereby rescuing his son's family from eviction and from losing a valuable farm.[205]

Possibly considering this particular son would be safer settled in life next to his fiscally-responsible in-laws, John Penley, Sr. relocated Isaiah Vickery and family to Crockett's Ridge. On April 19, 1861, Captain Penley purchased from Nathan Morse (then seventy-three) Morse's entire estate, including the house and all the land on Lots 45 and Lot 30, which Nathan had purchased with Ephraim Crockett. John Penley, Sr. also bought the six-acre island once owned by his son Charles, and which Nathan Morse had acquired. (The island, which became known as "Penley Island" was likely named for Captain Penley, not for his son Charles.) Penley paid $1600 for the entire Nathan and Mary (Crockett) Morse estate. (Two of the Morse sons, who had initially farmed with their father, by 1860 had prosperous properties of their own.) Nathan and Mary (Crockett) Morse moved to the town of Paris, where they lived until their deaths.

Isaiah Vickery and Mary Amanda (Crockett) Penley, and their family, settled into her aunt and uncle's longtime home, next door to where she grew up. The couple then had four young children: Laura Aramantha, age nine; Sewell Thomas, seven; Sarah Belle, four; and Channing Robert, one. On March 27, 1862, Mary Amanda gave birth to their fifth child, True Davis Penley.[206] Grandmother Sally Crockett was still active and likely came down and helped her daughter Mary with the birth. The family appears to have been happy living on Crockett's Ridge. Regrettably, two of Isaiah and Mary's sons perished in April of 1864, probably from the same disease. Childhood deaths were all too common in the 19th century. Early Norway death records show many children dying from "canker rash" (a form of scarlet fever), dysentery (an infection of the intestinal tract caused by bacteria), and whooping cough. Channing Robert Penley, who was four, died on the first of April. His older brother Sewell Thomas died on April 14, 1864, at the age of ten.[207] It is likely these two boys were buried in the Crockett family cemetery with their grandfather and other family members. Two years after the boys' deaths, a daughter, Harriet Jane Penley, was born to Isaiah and Mary on September 18, 1866.[208]

Upon John Penley, Sr.'s death in 1873, Isaiah Vickery inherited a share of the

---

205. OCROD, Book 124, Page 129. John Penley purchased this farm from Isaiah Vickery (Book 124, page 17), and shortly thereafter sold it to W.F. Brown for $940. Book 128/Pg.310.
206. CANDAGE, p. 181.
207. Norway, Maine death records, April 1864.
208. CANDAGE, p. 181.

residue of his father's estate. More germane to our story, Captain Penley willed to Isaiah the former Morse homestead (and Penley island), where the family had been living for twelve years.[209] Thanks to Captain Penley, and the twists and turns of fate that we will cover in the next chapter, this homestead has remained in our extended family since Nathan and Mary (Crockett) Morse first settled in Norway around 1815.

Hannah Jordan Crockett, who married Thomas Hanford Richardson, lived one of the most challenging—yet interesting—lives of the second generation. Although from the standpoint of money and social status, hers was the "best" marriage of the family—T.H. being the son of wealthy Portland businessman Joshua Richardson— the marriage was not a happy one. Hannah's husband was financially unsteady and possibly an alcoholic and/or opium user, and she had this to deal with on top of the burden of running a large household. The couple had five children born on the Richardson estate: Albert, George Hanford, Thomas Putnam, Julia Ann, and Edwina Maud Richardson.[210]

After residing in what was his father's house for nearly a decade, on March 18, 1857, Thomas Hanford legally purchased the property from Joshua Richardson. T.H. was to pay his father $5000, the entire amount in a mortgage (the real estate increased in value because it also now included the Latham farm, formerly owned by the late James Crockett). The interest on the mortgage was to be paid annually.[211] T.H. did not make his promised payments, although his father appears to have taken no notice. Joshua Richardson passed away on November 4, 1862. Less than eight months later, T.H.'s uncle Nathaniel P. Richardson, Joshua's brother and the executor of his estate, "peaceably and openly entered upon and [took] possession of the premises…for conditions broken and for purposes of foreclosure."[212] Hannah, T.H., and their family might have relocated to the house at Lot 46, next to Isaiah Vickery and Mary Amanda Penley. Joshua had given part of Lot 46 to his grandson, Albert Richardson, before his death (when Albert was thirteen),[213] and the other part had been purchased by T.H. But when Richardson's extensive estate was settled, the family who had moved out, returned once again to the grander property

---

209. Maine Wills and Probate Records, 1584-1999. John Penley.
210. CANDAGE, p. 180.
211. OCROD, Book 125, page 178.
212. OCROD, Book 132, page 177. Nathaniel P. Richardson took possession of the Richardson farm on August 21, 1863.
213. OCROD, Book 124, page 476. Joshua Richardson had sold Lot 46 to T.H.; however, he apparently took it back because his son failed to pay the mortgage.

to live. Although I have not seen a copy of Joshua Richardson's will (nor can I find a disposition of the will recorded at the Oxford County Registry of Deeds), later deeds recorded at the registry explain that the Portland magnate devised to Thomas Hanford Richardson the use of the Preble farm for his lifetime.[214]

By 1870, Hannah Richardson began investing in real estate in Norway. I am not sure whether this was because her husband's credit was ruined (and she was investing on his behalf) or whether by then she was thinking of leaving him and was looking for a home for herself and her children. On March 4, 1870, Hannah purchased from William H. Carpenter of Boston, a one-acre lot "with buildings thereon" situated next to the Universalist Society on the corner of Main and Pleasant streets. She paid $2700 for the real estate, giving Carpenter a mortgage for $2000.[215] A year later, Hannah refinanced this property with Norway Savings Bank (T.H. had to sign off on his dower rights), which suggests that whatever Hannah was doing, her credit was good (and that her husband agreed with what she was doing).[216] Because in later years Hannah supported herself as a dress-maker,[217] I suspect she might have used the house as a shop at first. Hannah, T.H., and the Richardson children will appear in the next chapter, and so for the time being, we will leave them in 1870, a transitional year for this family.

No longer a carefree young girl, Hannah Jordan (Crockett) Richardson.
Married with five children and heavy responsibilities, she appears careworn in this locket photo.
(Photo courtesy of Susan Allen Morgan.)

---

214. Although I have found no record in the registry about the disposition of Joshua Richardson's will and his Norway real estate, in a later deed from Albert Richardson's siblings (the children of T.H. and Hannah) it is mentioned that their father had the use of the property during his lifetime. See OCROD Book 203, page 420. See also Book 211, page 332, where Thomas deeds this same place to Albert for $200 on March 16, 1881.
215. OCROD, Book 156, page 246 and Book 155, page 159.
216. OCROD, Book 160, page 165.
217. 1870 U.S. Census for Auburn, Maine. Hannah Richardson.

By the close of the Civil War, our ancestors William Robinson and Lydia (Stetson) Crockett had a family of three children: Abel Stetson, Josephine Bonaparte, and Emma Tuell Crockett. William's mother Sally was still alive and performing household chores for the family. At least two more children would be born at the Crockett homestead: Henrietta and Lydia Frances, or "Frances" as she was known. As previously mentioned, the couple lost in infancy a son, Samuel, and a set of twins, William and Samuel; however, we do not know their birth and death dates. Following is a list of William and Lydia's family from Candage's Crockett genealogy. All the children were born in Norway.

Abel Stetson Crockett – born September 14, 1850.
Josephine Bonaparte Crockett – born February 23, 1854.
Emma Tuell Crockett – born December 15, 1858.
Henrietta Crockett – born February 2, 1868.
Lydia Frances Crockett – born April 9, 1874.
William – unknown.
Twins, William and Samuel – unknown.

As U.S. Lieutenant General Ulysses S. Grant tightened the noose around Robert E. Lee and the Army of Northern Virginia at Petersburg, raising the hopes of the north that the Civil War would soon be over, William Robinson Crockett began adding to his real estate holdings. Over the next fifteen years, William purchased four more parcels of land to add to what he had purchased from his father, all but one of those properties a woodlot. Altogether, William added just over one hundred acres of land. Two of the four properties he purchased during this period remain in the family today (albeit in different family trusts).

On September 12, 1864, William Robinson Crockett, and William Knight (son of Revolutionary War soldier Daniel Knight, who lived next door on the north half of Lot 44), purchased the southwest corner of Lot 40. The two men paid John Millett, owner of the sawmill, $370.82 for this twenty-six-acre woodlot off the Needham Road[218] (another old road to Greenwood from Norway).

Five months after this purchase, on February 24, 1865, William Robinson Crockett and Henry B. Cotton, husband of William's niece Esther Penley (Sarah

---

218. OCROD, Book 135, page 205.

The Crocketts and the Penleys

and Charles' daughter),[219] gave John Davis $190 for ten acres in the northwest section of Lot 41.[220] This second, smaller woodlot abutted Lot 40. Both parcels in Lot 40 and Lot 41 were conveniently situated close to the sawmill, which was located on the outlet to North Pond. (We will revisit this woodlot in Chapter 5.) Some of the wood was probably also cut for firewood. The following year Henry Cotton sold his share of the ten-acre woodlot to William Robinson Crockett for $75.[221]

On December 15, 1866, William purchased the entire north half of Lot 41, except for the ten acres he already owned. He paid Joseph Morse $210 for what appears to have been twenty-four acres, giving William Robinson Crockett a total of thirty-four acres in the northern half of Lot 41.[222] William gave Harriet Millett a $200 mortgage on the twenty-six-acre parcel.[223] Combining everything, William now owned (or co-owned) sixty acres of standing timber off the Needham Road. In April of 1869, William sold his older brother Ephraim Stanford a half-interest in the twenty-four-acre parcel. The two brothers, who lived next door to each other and appear to have been close, worked these woodlots together for the next five years. Access to the woodlots was via a right-of-way off the Needham Road (as it still is today). After Ephraim Stanford Crockett's death in 1874, William's nephews and nieces sold William back their father's undivided half interest in Lot 41 for just $1.00.[224] Today, the entire thirty-four acres on Lot 41—still a woodlot—is owned by my cousin Byron Young in his family's trust. The twenty-six-acre woodlot on Lot 40 has gone out of the family.

---

219. Esther A.W. Penley was the eldest daughter of Charles and Sarah (Crockett) Penley. She married Henry B. Cotton on November 17, 1863.
220. See OCROD, Book 137, page 254; Book 132, page 276; and Book 136, page 202.
221. OCROD, Book 145, page 52. This real estate transaction was signed April 14, 1866.
222. OCROD, Book 146, page 109.
223. OCROD, Book 143, page 294.
224. See OCROD, Book 154, page 156 and Book 176, page 489.

Logging right-of-way off the Needham Road, Norway, Maine.
The use of this right-of-way is still in the family, as is the land to the right, formerly part of Lot 41 in Lee's Grant.
(Photo by Jennifer Wixson, 2021)

Closer to home, William Robinson Crockett purchased on August 10, 1868, nine acres and ten rods of land situated behind neighbor William Knight's homestead on the north half of Lot 44 (behind where Pam and Errol Libby reside today). William Robinson harvested hay and sedge from these nine-plus acres abutting Lake Pennesseewassee. The parcel, mostly wetlands, curls up around the head of the lake where Foye Brook (as the stream was then known) enters. William Robinson Crockett paid James Bennett $200 for the nine acres.[225] This small but interesting tract—now mostly protected wetlands and a haven for birds and wildlife—is part of our late mother's trust.

Continuing with his land-buying spree, on March 13, 1871, William Robinson Crockett and Calvin Richardson bought thirty-one acres on the east end of Lot 61. The two men paid Joseph Sanderson of Bethel $350 for the parcel, another woodlot, situated at the upper west side of Lake Pennesseewassee.[226] Crockett and

---

225. OCROD, Book 159, page 131. James' father Isaac Bennet originally purchased for $318 the entire north half of Lot 44 from Edward Little on May 23, 1814.
226. OCROD, Book 161, page 240.

Richardson might have worked the woodlot together for a time or each taken a certain value of the timber. But in December of 1877, Richardson sold William Robinson his share for only $75.[227] (1877 was the year after thousands of acres of forestland had been defoliated by tent caterpillars, which could account for the price drop.) This tract of land remained in our family until 2012,[228] serving as a woodlot throughout most of the twentieth century.

Colorized postcard, "Crockett's Bridge, Lake Pennesseewassee, Norway, ME." (No. 817, The Hugh C. Leighton Co., Manufacturers, Portland, ME Printed in Frankfort, Germany.)

Osgood N. Bradbury, in his folksy collection of writings published as "Norway in the Forties," takes the reader (among other places) on a trip around Norway Lake. As he winds along, the Bradbury points out the Crockett homestead and the nearby sawmill. Osgood writes:

> "Now if the reader please we will take a tramp over Crockett's bridge[229] and so beyond to two miles or more until we come to four corners where a school house stands. Here we turn square to the left, and keep on up past several farm houses, among them the Wm. Crockett brick house, up and down numbers of short hills, until among the trees, a mile or more beyond the brick house, we pass over a small stream tumbling over the rocks rather nosily to the left. This is the brook

---
227. OCROD, Book 179, page 110.
228. This thirty-one-acre parcel was inherited by my mother's cousin Norman Young, and was sold by him and his daughter Cindy Spagnuola on January 13, 2012. OCROD, Book 4806, page 251.
229. Crockett's Bridge was named for Joshua Crockett, an extended Crockett relation.

that carries the waters of North Pond into the Pennesseewassee and just above the little bridge where we cross, in the olden times, a saw mill stood, which converted the logs of that broken region into lumber for house building."[230]

Trees reflected in the Mill Pond at the site of the former North Pond Dam.
(Photo by Jennifer Wixson, 2021.)

---

230. NORWAY40s, p. 289.

Remnant of North Pond Dam where Col. Millett's sawmill (formerly belonging to William Foye) was located.
(Photo by Jennifer Wixson, 2021.)

Life in Norway did not stand still while William Robinson Crockett and his various logging partners were cutting, hauling, and selling wood and lumber. On June 3, 1867, at a special town meeting "to ascertain the will of the people concerning the sale of intoxicating liquors," Norway voted in favor of prohibition. The vote was 64 in favor and 21 opposed.[231] We do not know how William voted or even if he left the farm to go into town to vote. That fall, the Norway Savings Bank was robbed, the thief making off with "Notes, bonds, and papers belonging to the bank, and also some belonging to the town…and a small quantity of cash."[232] The bank robber did not enjoy his loot for long, for in March of 1867, Truman F. Young, "sometimes called Dr. Young," was tried and convicted of the robbery and sentenced to nine years in the Maine State Prison.[233] One can only imagine the exciting conversation and speculation about the bank robbery that occurred at the Crockett dinner table during the six months that Young was on the lam. Just prior

---

231. LAPHAM, p. 148.
232. LAPHAM, p. 149.
233. LAPHAM, p. 149.

to Young's capture, on February 2, 1868, Lydia gave birth to the couple's fourth (living) child and their third daughter, Henrietta or "Etta" Crockett.[234]

When the next U.S. census was taken in the summer of 1870, William, forty-six, was listed as a farmer, with a homestead valued at $2000 and personal property worth $325. His only son Abel, nineteen, was then working on the farm with his father. Lydia, forty, was the main housekeeper in the Crockett household; however, she had plenty of help. Aiding Lydia with the housework was eldest daughter Josephine, sixteen; my great-great-grandmother, Emma Tuell, eleven; and the seventy-five-year-old matriarch of the family, Sally (Wentworth) Crockett. Baby Etta was two when the 1870 census was taken.

In the fall of 1870, the Crocketts would have experienced tremors from an earthquake centered in the Province of Quebec, Canada. Norway historian Lapham described the event as "a heavy shock of earthquake," which was felt in Norway on October 20, 1870, at "eleven and a half o'clock."[235] The magnitude 5.9 quake occurred in the Charlevoix seismic zone in Quebec, an active zone during the second half of the 19th century. (A decade earlier, on October 17, 1860, there had been a magnitude 6.0 quake in the same zone, and several tremors occurred there after 1870.)[236]

On April 9, 1874, Lydia gave birth to her and William's last child and fourth daughter, Lydia Frances Crockett.[237] The baby was named for her mother and her uncle Joseph Francis "Frank" Crockett. Frank, who was disabled during the war, had married Lydia's half-sister Antoinette. No doubt the couple, who lived in town, were frequent guests at William and Lydia's home and dinner table. Although the baby's given name was Lydia, she was known as Frances for the rest of her life, much as her uncle Frank, whose given name was Joseph, was also known by his middle name.

On October 16, 1873, Josephine Bonaparte Crockett, the eldest daughter of William and Lydia, married Joseph W. Gerry.[238] He was the son of John F. Gerry and his first wife, Sarah. Joseph's father was a stonemason from Ireland who appears to

---

234. CANDAGE, p. 179.
235. LAPHAM, p. 152.
236. Webpage, The Northeast States Emergency Consortium. "Maine Earthquakes."
237. CANDAGE, p. 179.
238. In her February 1877 filing for divorce from Joseph W. Gerry, Josephine states that the couple was married in Mechanic Falls on October 16, 1873. The ceremony was performed by the Rev. Jonas Thompson, "a minister of the gospels." Maine State Archives. Maine Supreme Judicial Court records, March term, 1877, Book 17, Page 118.

have been brought over with other Irishmen to work in a granite quarry in Woodstock.[239] By 1860, however, John Gerry had left the mine and purchased a farm in North Norway, upon which his son Joseph worked. It is possible Josephine initially went to live with her husband's family on their farm after the couple's marriage, although we do not know that for sure.

A year after Josephine's marriage, on October 24, 1874, the Norway Grange (Number 45) was organized. Charter members, who met at the local schoolhouse, included (among others) William Robinson Crockett, his cousin Edwin A. Morse, and Ansel Dinsmore, the husband of William's cousin Judith Morse. (Edwin and Judith were children of Nathan and Mary Crockett Morse.) Other charter members were J.T. Crockett, William Knight, and Calvin Richardson.[240] According to historian Lapham, William Robinson Crockett served as the initial Assistant Steward for two years and was also one of the Gatekeepers.[241]

In 1875, the matriarch of the Crockett family in Norway—Sarah "Sally" Bartlett (Wentworth) Crockett—passed away at the age of eighty. Sally died on May 6, 1875.[242] She was buried in the family cemetery upon the knoll with her husband, Ephraim, her son James, and other Crockett and Penley family members who had predeceased her. Over a twenty-four-year span—from 1813 to 1837—Sally had given birth to thirteen children, all of whom lived to adulthood. At the time of her death, she had sixty-three grandchildren and five great-grandchildren living. Throughout Sally's long life and housekeeping career, she remained a much-loved and well-valued member of her extended family.

Helping to balance the family's loss, William and Lydia Crockett welcomed their first grandchild in 1875. Sometime that year, Ada L. Gerry was born to daughter Josephine and her husband Joseph W. Gerry. (I have yet to find a birth record.)

The year 1876 in Norway would have been made memorable for the family on Crockett's Ridge by two unconnected events. First, in June, an explosion of tent caterpillars ushered in a season of devastation for woodland owners such as William Robinson and his partners. According to Norway historian Whitman: "The Tent caterpillar made its appearance in June. Thousands of acres of forest trees

---

239. 1850 and 1860 U.S. Census, Woodstock and Greenwood, Maine. John F. Gerry. See also Ralph M. Bacon's 1970 "Historical Sketch of Woodstock, Maine, 1808 to 1840-1850," in which he notes that about 50 men worked in the granite mill, which was located just south of town. Historical sketch courtesy of the web page, Bacon Family Genealogy, Stephens Mills. (www.stephensmills.net).
240. LAPHAM, p. 216-217.
241. LAPHAM, p. 217.
242. CANDAGE, p. 85.

were stripped of their foliage."²⁴³ Second, in July of 1876, the first steamer was launched upon Lake Pennesseewassee.²⁴⁴ While the pleasure boat would no doubt have attracted the enthusiastic interest of the entire Crockett family, one wonders how much pleasure William Robinson would have had cruising the lake and seeing firsthand the damage done to his trees lining the shore by the invasion of tent caterpillars.

Colorized postcard, "Boat Landing, Lake Pennesseewassee, Norway, Me." (No. 816, The Hugh C. Leighton Co., Manufacturers, Portland, ME. Printed in Frankfort, Germany.)

In February of 1877, William and Lydia's eldest daughter Josephine filed for divorce from Joseph Gerry, her husband of less than four years. According to Josephine's February 17, 1877 petition to the Maine Supreme Judicial Court—which petition was considered at the March term, 1877, in Oxford County—on February 26, 1875, Joseph had deserted her and their daughter, Ada, who was now two years old.²⁴⁵ (Apparently, Joseph took off for Lynn, Massachusetts, probably before Ada was born.) In her filing, Josephine stated that her husband had not been providing support for either her or Ada since he left. As a result, it is most likely Josephine and her daughter had returned to her parent's home. In her filing, Josephine also requested that she be awarded full custody of the couple's only child. Her plea was heard; witnesses verified Josephine's story; and on April 24, 1877, a certificate of

---

243. WHITMAN, p. 189.
244. LAPHAM, p. 157.
245. Maine State Archives. Records of the Maine Supreme Judicial Court, March term, 1877, Oxford County. Book 17, Page 118.

divorce was issued. Josephine was once again a free woman, and she was given full custody of Ada.

Six months after her divorce, Josephine (Crockett) Gerry remarried. She wed Anson Joseph Millett of Norway on October 14, 1878.[246] The couple was married in West Paris by the Rev. Andrew Hill at his parsonage.[247] Anson was the son of Israel Dwight Millett and Anna (Emery) Millett and the grandson of Norway Millettville pioneer, Israel Millett. Whether a coincidence or just the result of living in a small world, Anson's younger brother Justus Millett married Emma J. Gerry, younger sister of Josephine's first husband Joseph, and thus Ada's aunt. It is unclear to me whether Ada, who was then around three years old, went to live with her mother and step-father on the Millett family farm or whether she continued to reside with her grandparents, with whom she and her mother had been living.

Sadly, Josephine's newly-found happiness did not last long. She passed away on November 21, 1879, leaving behind her husband, Anson, and four-year-old Ada. Josephine was only twenty-five years old when she died.[248] I have yet to uncover the cause of Josephine's death; however, given her age and the fact that she had recently remarried, she probably died as the result of childbirth. If young Ada had gone to live with her mother and step-father, she returned to the home of her grandparents William and Lydia Crockett after her mother's death.[249]

Sometime in 1875 or 1876, Abel Stetson Crockett married Mrs. Josephine P. Knight of Minot.[250] It appears that after his marriage, Abel decided to quit farming with his father and strike out on his own. He possibly calculated that since his father was yet only in his mid-fifties, it would be many years yet before he, as the only son, would be able to take over the Crockett homestead. By 1880, Abel and Josephine were living in Pownal, where Abel farmed, and Josephine was a housekeeper. (The couple never had children.)[251] The 1880 Non-Population Census (Schedule 2, Agriculture) for 1880 for Pownal shows twenty-nine-year-old Abel as a tenant farmer, who managed the property of an absentee owner for a share of the produce (usually one-half). Abel's farm included thirty acres of tillable land; fifty-seven acres in permanent meadows or pastures; fifteen acres of woodland; and twenty-five acres

---

246. CANDAGE, p. 179.
247. NORWAY40S, p. 288.
248. CANDAGE, p. 179.
249. U.S. Census, Norway, Maine. 1880. William Robinson Crockett.
250. CANDAGE, p. 179. Candage has both a marriage for Abel and Josephine in November of 1875 in Mechanics Falls, and marriage intentions filed October 16, 1876 in Minot (from Minot Vital Records).
251. CANDAGE, p. 179.

of other unimproved land, including old fields and immature stands of trees. The farm was valued at $1200, a modest value compared to other farms in the area, worth between $1800 and $2500. Abel's farm implements were valued at only $25 and his livestock $75. The estimated value of all Abel's 1879 farm production sold, consumed, or on hand was only $110. That amount was probably his half of the production, which was still meager compared to two neighboring farmers whose production estimates were $404 and $593.

With Abel managing a farm in Pownal, William was left to farm alone on Crockett's Ridge. At fifty-six, William was the only man in a household of five women. Lydia, age fifty, was keeping house by herself, as Emma, now twenty-one, had gone to work for B.F. Spinney & Co., the recently-established shoe factory in Norway Village. Etta, twelve, was at school, but daughter Frances, six, and granddaughter Ada, five, had not yet begun their education.[252] (There was no kindergarten in those days.)

The 1880 Non-Population Census for Agriculture shows William's farm, including fences and buildings, was valued at a modest $1500. William had twenty-one acres of tillable land (including fallow grass and cropland in rotation); thirty-seven acres of permanent meadows, pastures, and orchards; and fifty acres of woodland that he managed. It appears that William Robinson Crockett farmed much the same as his father had; the value of the farm implements—only $40—did not change from the Agricultural Census taken in 1850, just after William purchased the farm from Ephraim.

Although not as imposing as the farm owned by his brother-in-law Thomas Hanford Richardson, William's homestead provided the family with a comfortable living. In addition, the property was debt-free, and nearly sixty years of continuous operation had worked the bugs out. According to the 1880 Agricultural Census for Norway, William owned one working team of oxen, three milk cows and two other cows (probably young stock), and two beef cattle. He also had at least one sheep, a pig, and twenty chickens. The total value of all livestock was $237, substantial compared to the $75 owned by Abel in Pownal. Regarding 1879 production, William sold one hundred gallons of milk (or sent it to the butter or cheese factory). One hundred pounds of butter was made at the farm and one hundred pounds of cheese, most likely by Lydia and the girls. The chickens, also cared for by the womenfolk, produced seventy-five dozen eggs in 1879. In addition, William sold one clipped

---

252. 1880 U.S. Census for Norway, Maine.

fleece and had one lamb drop and sold one lamb living. For crops, he planted one and a quarter-acre of Indian corn, which produced fifty bushels; one acre of oats, thirty bushels; and one acre of wheat, eleven bushels. A staple of the Crockett diet would have been dry beans, especially during the winter months, and William produced two bushels of beans[253] in 1879. Potatoes were another major crop with which farm families were fed. William planted one acre of the spuds and harvested one hundred bushels, meaning he had plenty of extra to sell. During the nineteenth century, apples were an essential part of everyone's diet, providing necessary vitamin C during the winter months. Much like potatoes, apples were put into cold storage and kept as long as possible. Cider was made to last the whole winter through. Lydia and the girls would also have made and dried apple rings for cooking and snacking. By 1879, William had planted one acre of the farm to apple trees, with ten trees bearing eight bushels of fruit that year. Finally, William cut ten cords of wood in 1879, valued at $25. All ten cords likely went to heating the Crockett homestead and keeping the wood cookstove going. My cousin George Young told me in January of 2022 that when he was young, he and his father and brother cut eight cords of wood for the Crockett homestead (then, Young's Turkey Farm), and another eight cords of wood for where they lived in the old Nathan Morse homestead.

In 1881, second daughter Emma Tuell Crockett married George P. Young, an older man from New Hampshire who also worked for B.F. Spinney & Co. When they wed, she was only twenty-two and George was a decade older. (We will cover their story in the next chapter.)

Less than a year after Emma's wedding, the close-knit family of William Robinson Crockett was sundered by the unexpected death of matriarch Lydia (Stetson) Crockett. Mother Lydia fell ill and later died on January 5, 1882. She was only fifty-one years of age.[254] Although I have not yet unearthed the cause of Lydia's death, it appears to have been from a contagious disease because less than three weeks later, William, too, passed away (on January 23rd). A week after his wife's death, knowing he was gravely ill—and that he had under his care three minors: Henrietta, "Etta," not quite fourteen; Lydia Frances, "Frances," seven; and granddaughter Ada Gerry, six or seven—William Robinson executed a will[255] to provide for them. Wil-

---

253. Two bushels of dry beans would have been enough to bake 150 pots of beans, utilizing two cups of dry beans per batch.
254. CANDAGE, p. 179.
255. Maine Wills and Probate Records, 1584-1999. Volume 19, page 467. Crockett, William Robinson. The will was executed January 12, 1888. Probate date October 12, 1882, Oxford, Maine. Extracts of the will of William Robinson Crockett were recorded at the Oxford County Registry of Deeds on April 26, 1882. Book 185, page 91.

liam appears to have struck a deal with Emma to take care of her younger sisters in exchange for the bulk of his and Lydia's estate. The Crockett homestead, which normally would have gone to son Abel Stetson Crockett—who was a farmer like his father and grandfather before him —now went to Emma to house and maintain her, her younger sisters, and niece. Emma's husband, George P. Young, was not mentioned as a beneficiary in the will; however, he and Emma were appointed co-executors of her father's estate.

By way of a consolation prize for Abel, William left his son $200. Abel, who was then thirty-one, took the money and, with his wife, Josephine, moved (by way of Eau Claire, Wisconsin) to Duluth, Minnesota, where he began a new and much different life. Over the next few years, Abel worked as a hostler, a porter for Twin City Packing Company, and a driver for Armour Package Company.[256] Abel likely relocated out west because he did not want to stay in Maine to see what his sister and new brother-in-law, a shoe shop worker and new to town, did with the farm that for thirty years he had expected to inherit.

William also left his granddaughter Ada $200. As executors, Emma and George P. Young were to put Ada's $200 at interest until she reached the age of eighteen or was married, at which time she was to be paid the entire sum. Sadly, little Ada died only four years after her grandparents and thus would not have collected the $200. (Most likely Ada's father Joseph Gerry, who had abandoned Ada and Josephine, as next of kin to Ada, inherited the money, if it was paid, which would have made William roll over in his grave.) Sometime after her grandparent's death, Ada went to Massachusetts to live with her father and his second family. She died there of diphtheria on April 13, 1886, at the age of eleven.[257]

The remainder of William Robinson Crockett's estate—real and personal—was divided into two sections. Emma was to inherit one half, which included half of the

---

256. The Wisconsin State Census for 1885 shows A.S. Crockett in Eau Claire with an unnamed female, most likely his wife Josephine. The 1889 Duluth, Minnesota, directory lists Abel S. Crockett as a hostler working for H.C. Kendall, with a residence at 1205 Piedmont Avenue. The 1890-90 Duluth directory lists Abel as a porter with Twin City Packing Co (same address as before); and the 1893 city directory has Abel as a driver for Armour Package Co., at 1205 W. Michigan, which suggests a street name change rather than a change of abode.

257. According to Massachusetts Death Records, 1841-1915, Ada died in Lynn, although her father and his second family lived in Watertown. (I am grateful to Stuart Goodwin of Norway for finding Ada's death record.) Joseph Gerry, after abandoning his wife Josephine and daughter Ada, began a new life in Massachusetts, where on September 23, 1880, he married Elizabeth B. Greenhaigh in Watertown (Massachusetts Marriage Records), which appears to have been a financially astute marriage. By the time of Joseph Gerry's death in 1932 he was known as the "U.S. Wallpaper Dean," per the obituary published in *The Boston Globe*. Archives, *The Boston Globe*, Monday July 25, 1932, Page 11. According to Find-a-Grave, Joseph is buried in the Common Street Cemetery, in Watertown in lot 190, the same lot in which Ada was buried in 1886. Most likely his second family is there with him as well.

house, woodlots, livestock, tools, home furnishings, cash, and savings. The other half was to be equally divided between William's three living daughter's—Etta, Frances, *and* Emma, which settlement netted Emma two-thirds of her father's estate, leaving her sisters a claim on the estate of one-sixth each. William included the following instructions with the residue to be split between his daughters, writing:

> "...and my executors hereinafter so named [Emma and George P. Young] shall have full power to manage the said real and personal estate for the benefit and use of the said Emma T. Young, Henrietta Crockett and Frances Crockett, as the said executors may judge proper in the premises until the said Frances Crockett is twenty-one years of age, is married, or dies, when what remains of said personal and real estate shall be equally divided between the said daughters still alive."[258]

This language in William's will gave Emma and her new husband great license to manage the farm and other properties as they saw fit. The story of their lives—and that of Etta, Frances, Abel, and other extended family members from the third generation in Norway—is told in Chapter 4.

Following is an updated Lee's Grant lot map showing William Robinson Crockett's real estate holdings at the time of his death in 1882. As one can see from the map, by 1882 William was already surrounded by the third generation. In 1875, William's brother-in-law Isaiah Vickery Penley (Mary Amanda's husband) deeded the Nathan Morse homestead to his son-in-law, Albert P. Farnham,[259] (although Isaiah and Mary remained living there). Albert, who married two of Isaiah and Mary's daughters, Laura and Sarah (Laura died in 1869), also purchased the Tongue property from Ephraim Stanford Crockett's children.[260] In 1880, Abbie Jane (Crockett) Tubbs, William's niece and the girl who ran the Ephraim Stanford Crockett household after her mother's death, bought out her siblings' share of Lot 44,[261] the former John Penley farm. William's nephew Albert Richardson now owned Lot 46, and although Albert's father Thomas Hanford Richardson still owned the former Preble/Tubbs farm on Lot 22, Albert ran the day-to-day operations there. None of Charles and Sarah Penley's surviving children remained in the neighborhood.

---

258. Maine Wills and Probate Records, 1584-1999. Volume 19, page 467. Crockett, William Robinson. Probate date October 12, 1882, Oxford, Maine. Extracts of the will of William Robinson Crockett were recorded at the Oxford County Registry of Deeds on April 26, 1882. Book 185, page 91.
259. OCROD, Book 174, page 367.
260. OCROD, Book 173, page 7.
261. OCROD, Book 196, page 13.

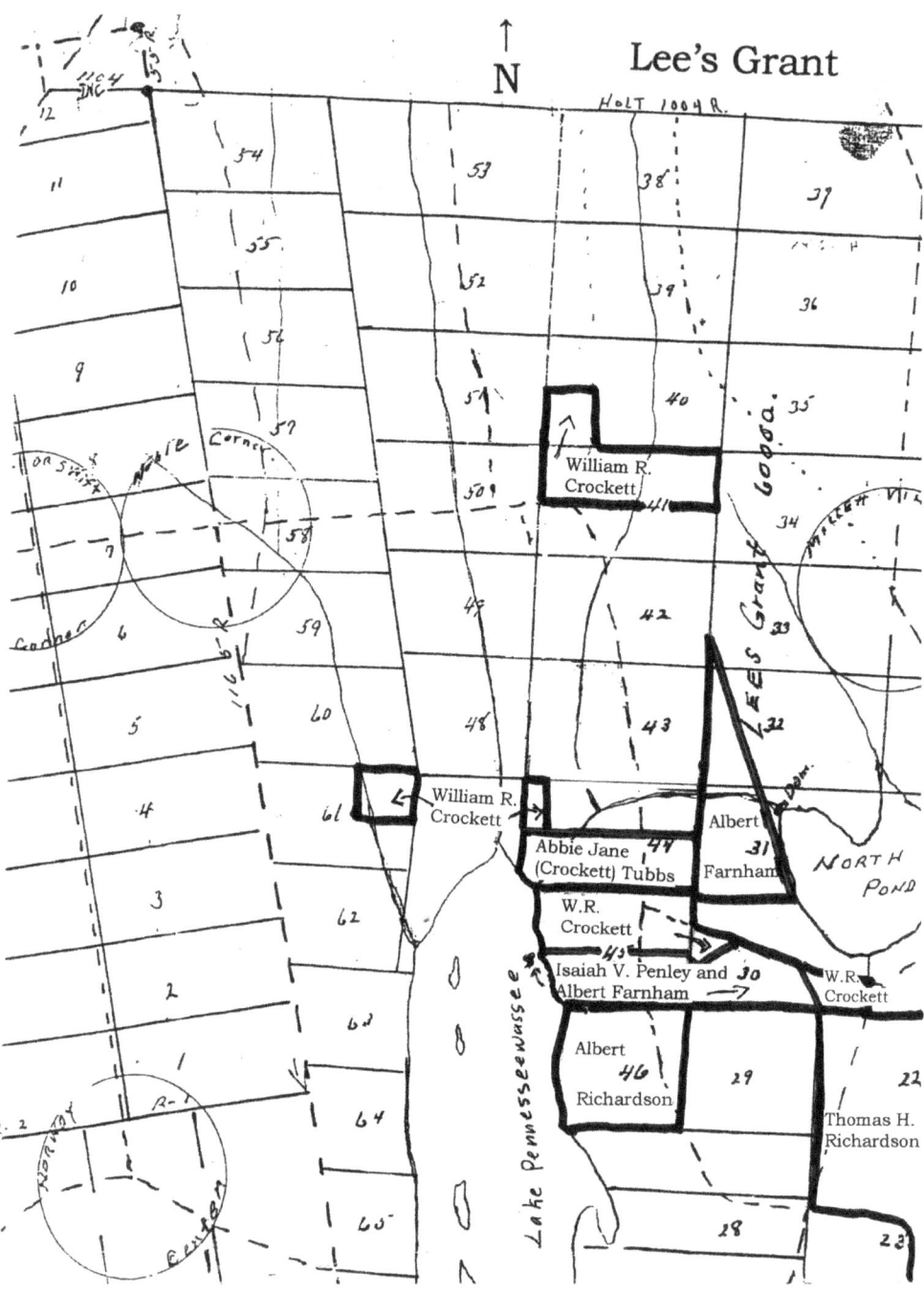

Lee's Grant Lot Map updated to 1882, the year of William Robinson Crockett's death.

The Move to Norway Pine Grove Cemetery

Unlike those family members who predeceased them, William and Lydia were not buried in the little family cemetery upon the knoll next to the house. Rather, the couple was buried in a new private cemetery, Norway Pine Grove Cemetery, which was situated downtown. By the time of their deaths—1882—most of those family members who had been buried at the Crockett homestead had already been reinterred in the new cemetery.

Ephraim Stanford Crockett precipitated the family's move to change the burial site. On August 16, 1873—most likely when he was ill and knew he was dying—fifty-five-year-old Ephraim Stanford purchased Lot 51 in Range 3, Section 3 of the newly-established Norway Pine Grove Cemetery. He paid $25 for the burial plot, which contained twelve gravesites.[262] By now, it had become obvious that there would not be enough space in the family cemetery at the Crockett homestead to bury him and Sarah, as well as their large brood of children. Before he died, Ephraim Stanford likely had the body of his wife Sarah "Sally" (Penley) Crockett, who had predeceased him by fifteen years, removed from the family cemetery and reinterred in his burial plot at Norway Pine Grove. After Ephraim Stanford's death on January 17, 1874,[263] he was buried in Lot 51 with his wife.

Ephraim Stanford and Sally's eldest son, John Freeland Crockett, who was much beloved by his eight younger siblings, was the first to join his parents in Lot 51. He died April 25, 1875,[264] in Richmond, Indiana, at the age of thirty-one, while working on the railroad. His body was shipped back East and interred at Norway Pine Grove. Altogether, four of Ephraim and Sally's nine children are buried with their parents: Oscar (who passed in 1884), Josiah (in 1881), Abbie Jane (in 1929), and John.[265] Later, they were joined by Ephraim Stanford and Sally's granddaughter Inez (Tubbs) Tabor Wiltsie (Abbie Jane's daughter), and her second husband, Clarence Wiltsie. Clarence died in 1945, and Inez passed away in 1962.[266]

---

262. Record of deed to Ephraim Stanford Crockett from John Whitman for Norway Pine Grove Cemetery Lot 51, Range 3, Section 3. NPG Record Book 1, Page 56. Stuart W. Goodwin, Trustee of Norway Pine Grove told the author in a March 2021 email that this lot contained twelve, rather than the usual, six gravesites. I have noticed that how we live in life is often reflected in how we remain in death, and unlike his siblings, who later selected lots in the very front of the cemetery, Ephraim Stanford Crockett selected a plot closer to the rear of the cemetery. This plot was very reminiscent of his homestead lot, which (situated as it was on North Pond) was more isolated than the homes of his siblings, who all lived on the main road.
263. CANDAGE, p. 177.
264. CANDAGE, p. 177.
265. Death dates from CANDAGE, p. 177-178.
266. CANDAGE, p. 177.

We do not know who was responsible for adding the lovely stone arch bearing John Crockett's name. Most likely, the arch and granite stones that define this little cemetery within a cemetery were added by John's younger siblings (with money from John's estate) after his death.

Burial plot of Ephraim Stanford and Sally (Penley) Crockett and family at Norway Pine Grove Cemetery.
(Photo from Find-A-Grave, John F. Crockett.)

According to Stuart W. Goodwin, President of the Board of Trustees of Norway Pine Grove Cemetery Association, the private cemetery was formed in 1860 "by citizens of the Town of Norway, to be managed by a Board of Directors elected each year at annual meeting of stockholders."[267] (New rules and regulations adopted by the cemetery Trustees on May 22, 2018, give the purpose for the cemetery as: "…a peaceful & beautiful area that serves as a reverent symbol of the citizens respect for the deceased.")[268] An association was formed in 1860, and land was purchased for the new cemetery. (A tug-of-war between Norway and Paris over some acreage between their two towns inadvertently landed the cemetery, which was founded by Norway residents, in the town of Paris.)[269] The cemetery was "situated in a

---
267. Email from Stuart W. Goodwin to Jennifer Wixson, March 29, 2021.
268. Norway Pine Grove Cemetery Corporation Rules & Regulations to Be Adopted May 22, 2018. Article One – General. 1. PURPOSE.
269. "*A Town's Memorial, Norway Pine Grove* - A Talk Before the Norway, Maine Historical Society" given by Larry Glatz, March 20, 2002. Text made available on the Norway, Maine Historical Society website. Interesting Places. "Pine Grove Cemetery." Ironically, the first person to be buried in the newly-established Norway Pine Grove Cemetery, a burial place for Norway residents, resided prior to her death in Paris (Maine). (Information gleaned from a conversation between the author and Stuart Goodwin.)

beautiful grove of Norway Pines and overlooking the meandering river valley."[270] Norway Pine Grove Cemetery became popular with descendants of early settlers like the Crocketts, who were struggling with the issue of where to bury their dead. In the mid- to late-1800s, second- and third-generation descendants discovered that the family cemetery was too crowded already. Where would the children and grandchildren be buried? In addition, burial at what was now a cousin's or even a sibling's residence was inconvenient, and possibly led to an uncomfortable intrusion. And who could guarantee that the original homestead with the family cemetery would not pass out of the family altogether? These were questions and issues with which descendants wrestled.

Norway Pine Grove Cemetery offered families easy access to their loved ones, as well as privacy, order, and charm. The well-maintained and methodically laid out cemetery on the main street connecting Norway and Paris provided the perfect resting spot for those of Norway's days gone by, as well as for the area's growing population. No longer would extended family members have to make awkward calls at the old homestead to bury their dead or visit loved ones, a common practice in Victorian times. Also, there was comfort in knowing there was room for those left behind when their time had come.

As a private cemetery, Norway Pine Grove was not town-maintained. The sale of burial plots covered expenses. These plots of land were sold in sections of six or twelve gravesites, and families took the opportunity offered by the new cemetery to secure large sections for themselves. In the 1930s, cemeteries in Maine began offering perpetual care bonds to help with the increasing costs of maintenance of the state's cemeteries. Perpetual care was seen, not as a money-making proposition, but rather as a way of making sure cemeteries had enough funds to maintain the family plots.[271] Finding that the sale of lots did not cover the expenses of maintaining a cemetery the size of Norway Pine Grove, trustees began selling perpetual care bonds to help cover the increasing costs. These bonds offered family members the additional peace of mind knowing that there would be money invested to care for the gravesites of their loved ones—and later, themselves—even if the family moved from the area.[272]

---

270. IBID.
271. Email from Stuart Goodwin to Jennifer Wixson, June 28, 2021: "Today if you purchase a plot in any cemetery 30% of purchase price is supposed to go to a separate PC [perpetual care] account, that is to remain the purchaser's money for perpetuity, not part of Cemeteries operating account."
272. Conversation between Stuart W. Goodwin, and Jennifer Wixson, March 2021.

Two years after Ephraim Stanford Crockett purchased his lot—and a year after matriarch Sally (Wentworth) Crockett died—Charles Alanson Crockett, the youngest son of Ephraim, Jr. and Sally, bought Lot 15 in Range 1, Section 1 in Norway Pine Grove. On July 22, 1876, Charles paid $25 for the six-grave plot situated in the cemetery to the left as one entered through the magnificent Victorian archway.[273] (The archway was replaced by concrete pillars in the 1960s.)[274] This would have been a prime burial plot since it is in the very front of the cemetery.

Original Victorian archway entrance to Norway Pine Grove Cemetery.
(Colorized postcard courtesy of the Norway, Maine Historical Society.)

Although William owned the Crockett homestead at the time, thirty-nine-year-old Charles—no doubt with the consent of his six surviving siblings (including William)—took upon himself the task of relocating their parents from the family cemetery to Norway Pine Grove. Charles also reinterred his brother James Sewell Crockett, who had predeceased their parents and with whom they were buried. In addition, Josephine (William and Lydia's daughter) who died in 1879, was buried in Norway Pine Grove with her grandparents. Josephine's grave is situated behind

---

273. Record of deed to Charles A. Crockett from Jonathan Blake for Norway Pine Grove Cemetery Lot 15, Range 1, Section 1. NPG Record Book 1, Page 82.
274. MEMORIESTIES, p. 194.

those of Ephraim and Sally Crockett, although Sally's grave has no individual marker. (Sally's name *is* listed on the Crockett family monument, which was placed in the plot in the 20th century.)

Last to be removed from the family cemetery at the Crockett homestead were the four members of Charles Penley's family: Charles, his wife Sarah (Crockett) Penley, their little daughter Sarah, who died in 1850 at fourteen months of age, and son Rufus, who died in the Civil War. On July 11, 1876, the heirs of Charles Penley purchased Lot 15 in Range 1, Section 1 in Norway Pine Grove.[275] The three deceased Penleys were reinterred in the lot adjacent to the Ephraim Crockett lot. Today, Charles Penley—the first Penley of the four in his family to marry into the Crocketts—remains as close to his in-laws in death as he had been in life since he first appeared in Norway in 1834. In these adjoining lots lie the remains of two soldiers; one who volunteered in the War of 1812 (Ephraim Crockett, Jr.) and one who fought and died in the Civil War (Ephraim's grandson, Rufus Crockett Penley).

When Lydia (Stetson) and William Robinson Crockett passed away in January of 1882, George P. Young—their son-in-law and co-executor of William's estate—purchased Lot 34 in Range 1, Section 1 for them. George paid the typical $25 fee for the six-grave burial plot situated directly behind Lot 15, where Ephraim and Sally were buried.[276] Rather than face the lane that went with their lot, however, the stones were turned around so that they, too, could be read from the road. As these stones are immediately behind the stones of Ephraim and his son James Crockett, it appears to the eye that they are all one unit. Thus, William and Lydia lie at rest with his parents and other family members, just as they would have done had they all been buried in the family cemetery at the homestead on Crockett's Ridge.

Other family members also purchased plots in Norway Pine Grove near their parents. Hannah (Crockett) Richardson purchased Lot 16 in Range 1, Section 1, which is the plot to the left (facing the cemetery) of Ephraim and Sally. Hannah appears to have bought the plot the December after the death of her and T.H.'s son, George Hanford Richardson, in 1877. She paid the usual $25 for the six-grave site on December 22, 1877.[277] Also, in 1886, Frank Crockett's wife Antoinette (Stetson)

---

275. Record of deed to the heirs of Charles Penley from Jonathan Blake for Norway Pine Grove Cemetery Lot 14, Range 1, Section 1. NPG Record Book 1, Page 125. The heirs paid $25 for this lot of six gravesites.
276. Record of deed to George P. Young from Jonathan Blake for Norway Pine Grove Cemetery Lot 34, Range 1, Section 1. NPG Record Book 1, Page 139.
277. Record of deed to Mrs. Hannah Richardson from Jonathan Blake for Norway Pine Grove Cemetery Lot 16, Range 1, Section 1. NPG Record Book 1, Page 96. We will cover George Hanford Richardson's death in the next chapter.

Crockett (Lydia's half-sister), after the death of her and Frank's daughter Clara, purchased the plot adjacent to Hannah's and next to where Ephraim and Sally Crockett were buried. She bought for $25 Lot 17 in Range 1, Section 1 on August 17, 1886.[278]

Both Frank and Antoinette, who remained in Norway after his service in the Civil War, outlived their only child by nearly two decades. Antoinette passed away on February 11, 1903 and Frank died the following year, on June 20, 1904.[279] Maine, U.S. Veterans Cemetery Records, 1676-1918, show that Frank originally had an upright stone with a G.A.R. (Grand Army of the Republic) marker for his service in Company D of the 25th Maine. In 2021, the stone (and marker) was found to be missing and was replaced (at no charge) with an upright marble stone provided by the U.S. Department of Veteran Affairs. (My thanks to Stuart Goodwin of Norway Pine Grove Cemetery for helping with the stone replacement.) All the Crockett and Penley lots have perpetual care bonds.[280]

Today, cars whiz past Norway Pine Grove Cemetery on Route 26, the drivers and passengers oblivious of those who lie peacefully on the other side of the fence. Inside the gates of the cemetery serenity reigns, and history lives in the writing upon the chiseled stones. In his collection of writings, "Norway in the Forties," Dr. Osgood N. Bradbury tells of Jonathan Whitehouse, the long-time sexton of Norway Pine Grove Cemetery. Whitehouse oversaw the burials and dug the graves for his friends and neighbors, as well as for his wife. Of this faithful cemetery steward Bradbury writes:

> "Wandering in Pine Grove Cemetery one day last summer, I discovered the old Grave Digger [Whitehouse] busy at his wonted employment, whistling quietly to himself, or humming snatches of some familiar tune, while he wielded his pick and spade and slowly built the house for the final resting place of some fellow traveler, who had at last ended his wandering and come home to rest and sleep. Seating myself on a neighboring grave, I quietly and patiently listened while the singing and the work went on. As he leaned upon his spade to rest his aged limbs, I remarked that he was engaged in a lonesome and unpleasant business, digging graves for his neighbors and friends.
>
> "'Lonesome,' repeated he, and he looked up and laughed in his quiet way,

---

278. Record of deed to Mrs. F. Crockett from Jonathan Blake for Lot 17, Range 1, Section 1. Norway Pine Grove Record Book 1. Clara died on July 9, 1986.
279. CANDAGE, p. 180.
280. This information was provided by Stuart Goodwin of Norway Pine Grove. For those family lots without perpetual care, bonds were purchased by the author in 2021.

'Why sir, in the street of yonder village I know but a few of the people I meet, while here, I know them nearly everyone. There they are strangers, or if known to me, it is in many cases only by name, while here I meet the dear friends of my youth, my neighbors and companions of my younger days. Why, pray, should I be lonesome here? As I walk these paths, gather in the grass of June or the autumn leaves, my old friends whose graves I have made and whose silent forms I have helped lay away hereabouts, come at my call, one by one, and I see them as of old and talk with them of the thoughtless times when our years were few; and they cheer my heart, and I am happy as I think that soon, quite soon, perhaps someone will kindly help me away to sleep among them.' "[281]

Despite the removal of most of the bodies in the old cemetery at the Crockett homestead, the knoll of land upon which the family cemetery once stood was treated as sacred ground well into the twentieth century. My grandmother Winona told me she believed the cemetery still contained the remains of some family members. It seems probable that this cemetery might be the final resting place for some Crockett and Penley children who died before the move to Norway Pine Grove. William and Lydia (Stetson) Crockett lost three infants—Samuel and twins William and Samuel—who do not appear to have been reinterred with their parents. In addition, according to Penley-Crockett descendant Ed Staples,[282] the final resting place for the two young sons of Mary (Crockett) Penley and Isaiah Vickery Penley, who passed away in Norway in April of 1864, is unknown. As there are no graves for the boys in Penley Corner Cemetery in Danville (Auburn), where their parents and grandparents are buried,[283] it is most likely Channing Robert Penley (age four) and Sewell Thomas Penley (age ten) were buried in the Crockett family cemetery, where they remain to this day.

In her later years, my grandmother Winona would often sit in her rocking chair by the kitchen window and gaze out at the knoll where her ancestors were once buried. When I was present with her, this often led to an interesting discussion of the ancestors, including how most of them had been removed to Norway Pine Grove. Every Memorial Day, Winona placed red geraniums[284] on the graves of her

---

281. "*A Town's Memorial, Norway Pine Grove - A Talk Before the Norway, Maine Historical Society*" by Larry Glatz, March 20, 2002. Norway, Maine Historical Society website. Interesting Places. "Pine Grove Cemetery."
282. One Saturday in June of 2021, while both of us were at the Norway, Maine Historical Society, Ed Staples and I had a conversation about the location of the remains of these Penley youngsters. He had searched Penley Corner Cemetery for the graves of Channing and Sewell Penley and not found them there and asked me if I thought the boys might have been buried in the cemetery at the Crockett homestead. After checking my information on Isaiah and Mary Penley, and the dates of their sons' deaths, Ed and I concluded that the children were buried on Crockett's Ridge, where they likely remain.
283. John Penley, Sr. could certainly have afforded the gravestones.
284. One Memorial Day, on a visit to the grave of Hezekiah Stetson (Lydia's grandfather and my 5th great-grandfather) in

parents, grandparents, and Crockett ancestors, and faithfully watered the plants throughout the summer. The serenity of the cemetery offered her an opportunity to joyfully remember her late family members and recollect her family history with pride. After Winona's death, my mother Rowena Palmer, her sister Paula (Palmer) Johnson, and sister-in-law Joyce (Nelson) Palmer continued the tradition of placing red geraniums on the family graves. Today, I carry on this joy-filled duty, visiting with my mother, grandmother, and others I have loved and lost. I also pay my respects to the Crocketts and Penleys, whose history I have come to know and whom I have come to admire and love. My future hope is that when I am gone, someone will come along to carry on—to plant and water the geraniums—and to keep the memories alive.

Adjoining gravestones of William Robinson Crockett and Lydia (Stetson) Crockett.
(Photo by Jennifer Wixson, May 2024.)

Sumner, I found red geraniums planted in front of Stetson headstones. I have since come to believe that Lydia brought the tradition of red geraniums into our family when she married William Robinson Crockett. My grandmother loved red geraniums because the flowers matched the brick house that William and Ephraim built (where Lydia lived after she and William were married). Winona often had potted geraniums in black pots and kettles around the homestead, as well as at the cemetery.

Original gravestone of Ephraim Crockett, Jr.
This stone was placed first at the Crockett family cemetery at the homestead on Crockett's Ridge and then removed in 1876 when Charles reinterred his parents and brother James in Lot 15 in Range 1, Section 1 at Norway Pine Grove Cemetery. During a bad windstorm in the spring of 2024, Ephraim's stone was blown over and separated from the base. The marble gravestone has since been repaired.
(Photo by Jennifer Wixson, May 2021.)

Emma Tuell (Crockett) Young Harding
(Photo courtesy of Yvette Young.)

Chapter 4

EMMA TUELL (CROCKETT) YOUNG HARDING – LAST CROCKETT STANDING

The Last of the Crocketts on the Ridge and the Age of Industrialization

For the first time in our family history we have a female Crockett—Emma Tuell Crockett—as the lead ancestor in our story. Emma (my great-great grandmother) was the second daughter and third child of William Robinson and Lydia (Stetson) Crockett. She was a member of the third generation of Crocketts in Norway (the ninth in the New World). When her parents died unexpectedly in January of 1882, Emma inherited most of the Crockett homestead. She and her new husband George P. Young also shouldered the responsibility of raising her two younger sisters. Emma was the last owner of the Crockett homestead ever to bear the surname of Crockett (and even then, not when she owned the property). Emma was the ancestor who single-handedly tripled the size of the property, adding two other family farms to form what would become in the next generation Young's Turkey Farm (my great-grandparent's place).[1]

Emma was born at the Crockett homestead on December 15, 1858.[2] When she came into the world her brother Abel was eight and sister Josephine was four. By the time of Emma's birth, her father had complete control of the farm. (Her grandfather, Ephraim Crockett, passed away two years before Emma was born). Sally (Wentworth) Crockett, Emma's grandmother, played an important and active role in the family until her death in the summer of 1875, when Emma was sixteen.

In the last chapter the fortunes of the Crocketts and Penleys were affected by the settlement of Maine and the increasing demand for lumber as a result of the

---
1. Emma also purchased two Norway Village houses, which were passed down in the family as rental properties.
2. CANDAGE, p. 179.

population explosion. By contrast, Emma's life was shaped by the advancement of industrialization in the 19th century. The move to mechanization cleaved family life that formerly revolved around the farm as cleanly as a disk harrow rolls up soft spring sod. The Industrial Revolution emptied farms in the United States, England, and Europe, remolding the offspring of farmers into factory and mill workers. As a young woman, Emma worked in a shoe factory, where she met her first husband. But despite the march of progress into the 20th century, Emma Tuell (Crockett) Young Harding never lost her love for—nor let go of—the farm on which she was born.

A Cocoon of Security

A cocoon of security surrounded Emma in the spring of 1874 when she was fifteen. Her grandmother, Sally, was still alive, as were both of her parents. Although death had touched Emma's extended family—her uncle Ephraim Stanford Crockett had died that January, leaving her cousins next door without a living parent—she had not yet experienced loss in her immediate family. (Three siblings who perished as infants died when Emma was young, possibly all before she was born.) At fifteen, and with a grandmother still living, Emma naturally would have assumed (if she thought about it at all) that her parents would live for another twenty or thirty years, especially as her mother had just given birth to baby Frances in April of 1874. That spring Emma's younger sister Henrietta, was six. Her older sister Josephine, twenty, was probably no longer living at home, having married the prior fall.

Contributing to the warmth of the cocoon around Emma, a phalanx of Crockett and Penley family members surrounded her. To the south residing on the former Nathan Morse homestead were her aunt and uncle, Mary Amanda (Crockett) and Isaiah Vickery Penley. With them lived their married daughter Sarah Belle and Sarah's husband Albert P. Farnham.[3] Also at the former Morse homestead was Emma's younger cousin True Davis Penley, age eleven.

To the north of Emma, owning both the John Penley farm and the property at the Tongue, lived eight of Emma's cousins, the tightly-knit family of Ephraim Stanford Crockett. These young-adult Crocketts—whom going forward I will distinguish as the "Crockett heirs" (Abbie Jane, Josiah, Ella, Sarah Alamanza or "Allie,"

---

3. CANDAGE, p. 181.

Edgar, Louisa, Warren, and Oscar)—ranged in age from twenty-eight to sixteen. The Crockett heirs were in possession of a modest fortune inherited from their deceased parents, as well as from their grandfather, Captain John Penley. Eldest brother, John Freeland Crockett (who had his own home) worked for the railroad and contributed to the support of this large family, as did Abbie Jane and Ella, who were employed as local schoolteachers.

On the following page I have updated our Lee's Grant map to reflect ownership of the various family farms and woodlots to 1874, when Emma was fifteen. I have taken the liberty of moving Ephraim Stanford Crockett, father of the Crockett heirs—who did not die until January of 1875—off the scene a bit early. He was ill before he passed and it is likely his eldest daughter Abbie Jane was already in charge of the household. By 1874, when our story begins, none of the Charles Penley family remained in the area. Emma's uncle Thomas Hanford Richardson and some of her Richardson cousins were still in the neighborhood, although by this time the relationship between aunt Hannah (Crockett) Richardson and her husband was strained to the breaking point. (In fact, Hannah had probably already left her son with T.H., and taken their daughters Julia, seventeen, and Edwina Maud, nine, with her to a new house in Norway Village.)

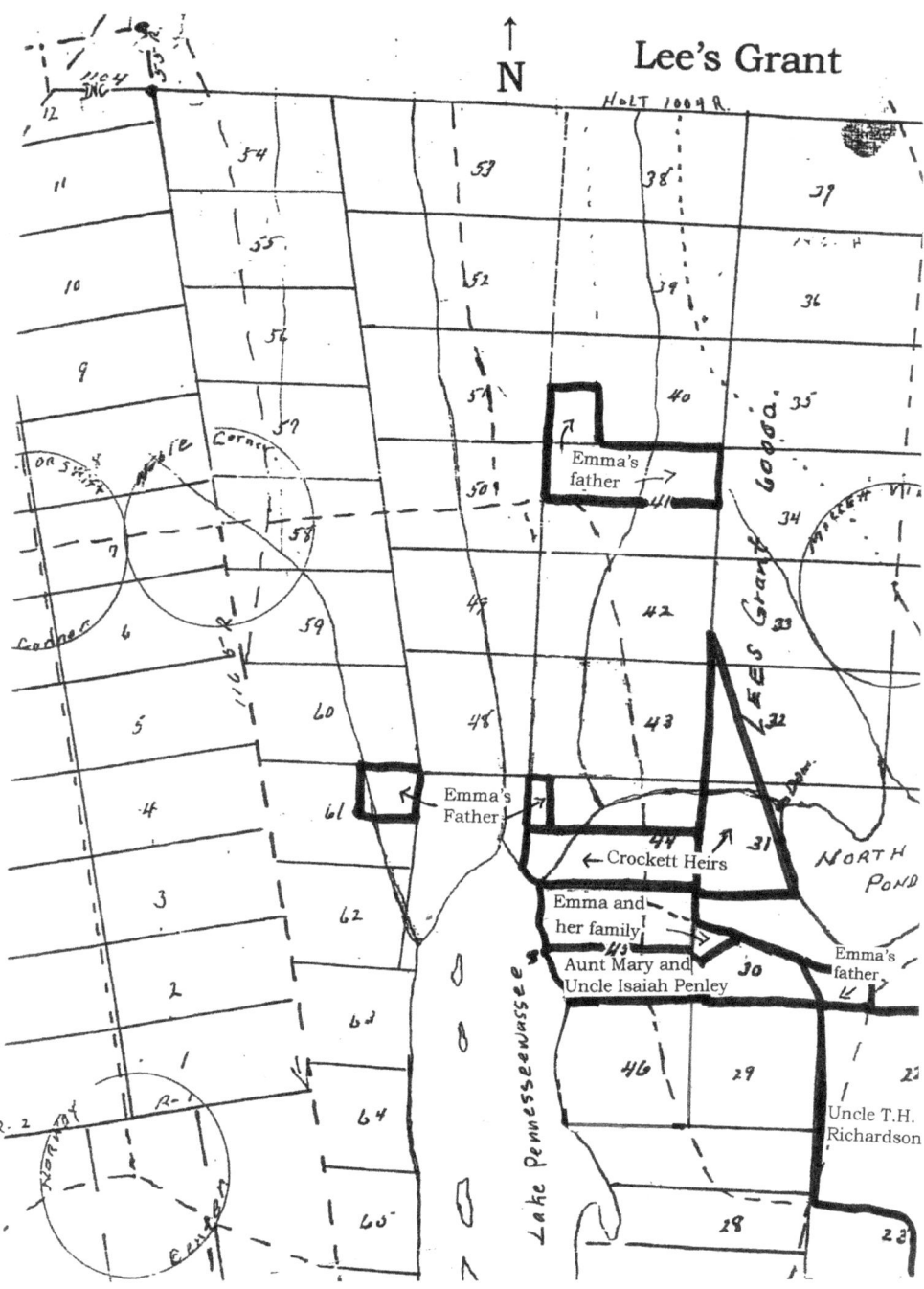

Lee's Grant map updated to 1874 when Emma Crockett was fifteen, showing the cocoon of family surrounding her.

When considering who might have been among the teenage Emma's closest confidantes, one must consider proximity between the parties, life circumstances, and family history. Future events in Emma's life reveal a well-trod trail (probably emotionally as well as physically) from the Crockett homestead to the (former) John Penley farm up the road, where a large cohort of Emma's cousins—the Crockett heirs—lived without parental supervision. Next to her older sister Josephine (who was no longer at home), Emma was likely most influenced by and closest with the Crockett heirs, particularly Abbie Jane, with whom Emma (as well as her brother Abel) had a lifelong-friendship.[4]

Born five days—and thirteen years—apart, Abbie Jane and Emma lived next door to each for most of Emma's life to the spring of 1874. With a bevy of independent female cousins living so close at hand, especially those free from the watchful eye of a mother or maiden aunt, it is easy to deduce that Emma made regular, if not daily, visits to their house. Having once been young myself, I know the powerful attraction of a houseful of independent-minded young women who are free to do what they please. At the home of her cousins Emma would have found companionship, friendship, understanding, encouragement, information, and a shoulder to cry upon.

In 1874, with elder brother John Freeland away working on the railroad, Abbie Jane was almost certainly in charge. (Abbie Jane was the "very capable girl" who Norway historian and teacher Whitman describes as the head of the household after her mother's death.) She was working as a teacher in the Norway schools, although it is possible she had taken off the last term to care for their ailing father. (In 1870, when Abbie Jane and Ella were both teaching school, the household duties were assumed by Sarah, nineteen, and Louisa, sixteen.)[5] Abbie Jane seems to have been a motherly, industrious young woman, an excellent role model for young Emma. She was certified as a schoolteacher in 1866 by the School Committee in Gilead (about thirty miles to the northwest) where she probably taught for a short period of time before returning to teach in Norway.[6] Like many of the third generation Crocketts, Abbie Jane was well-educated. Since neither the 1850 nor 1860 census for Norway show her as "at school" (which could have been an omission of the census taker) Abbie Jane might have been educated at home by her father

---

4. In the 1920 U.S. Census for Norway, Abel Crockett is living as a lodger in his cousin Abbie Jane's house on Main Street.
5. 1870 U.S. Census for Norway. Ephraim Stanford Crockett.
6. The 1870 U.S. Census for Norway shows Abbie Jane living at home as working as a teacher.

or even by grandmother Sally (Wentworth) Crockett, the Wentworths having a history of teaching. The letter from the school committee at Gilead certifying Abbie Jane's qualifications gives us insight into the breadth of the twenty-year-old's understanding and capabilities:

> "To whom it may concern. This certifies that we have this day examined the Bearer, Abbie J. Crockett, in Orthography, Reading, Writing, Arithmetic, Geography & English Grammar and find her competent to teach the same; and being fully satisfied that she possesses a good moral character, and the essential qualifications for the government and instruction of Children and Youth, she is hereby authorized to teach in the schools of this town."[7]

When our story opens in the spring of 1874, Abbie Jane was engaged to marry Charles Newell Tubbs, the great-grandson of Jacob Tubbs, the first settler on Lee's Grant (the only settler to purchase his lot freehold from Francis Lightfoot Lee). Abbie Jane and Charles were first cousins once removed, connected through the Wentworth family (with a skipped generation). Charles was the son of James Tubbs and Hannah Jordan Wentworth, who was Sally (Wentworth) Crockett's half-sister. The following genealogy chart shows their relationship:

Samuel Solley Wentworth (great-grandfather to Emma and Abbie Jane)

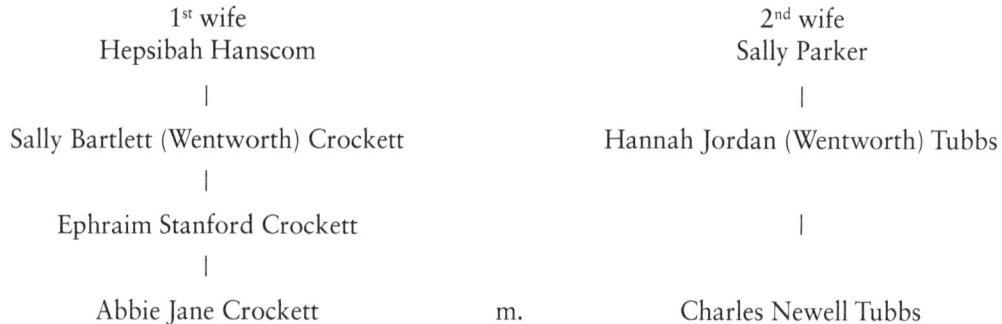

James Tubbs, Charles' father (the husband of Hannah Jordan Wentworth), was the son of Angiers Tubbs and grandson of early Lee's Grant settler Jacob Tubbs.[8]

---

7. 1866 Letter from the School Committee of Gilead, Maine, certifying Abbie Jane Crockett as a qualified teacher. The letter (which is in the public domain) found on the website, "Heirlooms Reunited."
8. LAPHAM, p. 610. At the time of her niece Abbie's marriage, Hannah Jordan (Crockett) Richardson, who was probably named for her mother's half-sister Hannah Jordan Wentworth, was living with her family on the original Jacob Tubbs property, owned by her husband Thomas Hanford Richardson. Although our history to date has been focused on the Crockett

According to Norway historian Whitman, James was "born in a log house on a lot running down into the lake from the Noble school house, which lot his father cleared and sold."[9] At some point, James removed his family, including Charles, from Norway to Gorham, New Hampshire, where he and Charles worked as purveyors of groceries and meats.[10] In 1873—probably after learning that a new shoe factory, B.F. Spinney & Co., was being built in Norway—the father and son returned to the Village, where they built a store, and eventually two homes, on the corner of Main and Lynn streets, only a stone's throw from the new factory, which was situated on the opposite end of Lynn Street.[11] It is possible that Abbie Jane and Charles became reacquainted when he revisited the neighborhood of his youth, or perhaps they met again when she patronized the shop in Norway Village.

Abbie Jane Crockett and Charles Newell Tubbs were married on June 24, 1874. Emma was fifteen when her twenty-eight-year-old cousin married a man nearly a decade older. Seven years after Abbie Jane's wedding Emma would also marry a man at least a decade older than herself.

Abbie Jane and Charles made their home with his parents in Norway, probably initially in or near the building in which the family store was located until the other houses were built. Although the shop's customers would naturally include Village residents, the grocery and variety store also served the factory workers who flooded into town after the arrival of B.F. Spinney and Company.

As Emma was growing up, she was also likely influenced by her Richardson cousins (the children of Hannah and Thomas Hanford Richardson), probably Julia in particular. Julia, who was born in 1857, was just six months older than Emma. Julia and her younger sister Edwina Maud (six years younger than Emma) were "fine" young ladies, having been sent away to a finishing school in Coaticook, Quebec, Canada. According to a descendant of Edwina, Susan Allen Morgan, the finishing school was at a French convent. Susan says at finishing school the sisters

---

family, the Wentworth family remained in the picture to some degree. In fact, Foster Wentworth, half-brother of matriarch Sally (Wentworth) Crockett (and a full brother of Hannah Jordan Wentworth) came to Norway in 1842 and resided for a while in North Norway and Greenwood. WHITMAN, p. 634. Foster was apparently a pauper most of his life. In 1880, while living in Greenwood, he is listed in the U.S. Federal Census Schedule of Defective, Delinquent, and Dependent Classes.
9. WHITMAN, p. 522. The school house referred to here is the house across the road from where the Heywood Club is today, the same school that the Crocketts would have attended. Noble is the name of the hill on the ridge south of the Heywood Club, where at one point the Noble family lived.
10. WHITMAN, p. 522. See also p. 308, where Whitman writes in 1924 that Charles' son James Tubbs "has a large grocery and meat trade in his father's store, corner of Main and Lynn Streets. The store was built and the business established about 50 years ago." The author also referred to the Norway Village Map from the Atlas of Oxford County, Maine, published by Caldwell & Halfpenny in 1880.
11. WHITMAN, p. 522 and p. 308.

learned "tatting, music, French and Refinement." (While at boarding school Edwina also met her future husband, Canadian William Henry Allen.)[12] Given the physical distance that separated the three young ladies, Emma was probably not emotionally close with her female Richardson cousins; however, their lives showcased the "better life" to which young Emma Crockett might have aspired.

Julia Ann and Edwina Maud Richardson, studio portrait.
Julia Ann (left) and Edwina Maud were daughters of Hannah Jordan (Crockett) and Thomas Hanford Richardson. Circa late 1870s.
(Photo courtesy of Susan Allen Morgan.)

Julia's finishing school polish paid off when she made a very advantageous marriage. On June 1, 1875, when Emma was sixteen, Julia married Chester Horne of Norway.[13] He was twenty-five and Julia was seventeen. Chester was the eldest son

---
12. Information from Susan Allen Morgan in an exchange of emails and messages with the author.
13. CANDAGE, p. 180.

of John L. Horne, then one of the most influential men in town. John Horne owned the prosperous local tannery. He also served on various boards and committees in Norway. Of the elder Horne, Whitman wrote in 1924: "For nearly half a century [John L. Horne] was one of the leading business men and citizens of the town and village..."[14]

Originally from New Hampshire, John Horne was apprenticed as a young man to a tanner in Berwick, Maine, from whom he learned the craft. In 1852, when he was about twenty-eight, Horne bought out Norway tanner Mark P. Smith and proceeded over the years to enlarge and modernize the business.[15] In 1854, Horne installed the first steam engine in Norway at his tannery.[16] Later, he ran a spur from the railroad directly to the tannery (and the shoe factory). By 1885, when Horne turned his business over to the Norway Tanning Company (with his son Harry L. Horne serving as Treasurer), the tannery was doing $500,000 in sales (about $3.2 million in 2024)[17] and employed 150 workers with a monthly payroll of $4800 ($155,000 in 2024).[18]

Tannery of John L. Horne and Horne's Main Street, Norway, residence.[19]
Lithographs by George H. Walker and Co., Boston.[20]

---

14. WHITMAN, p. 445.
15. WHITMAN, P. 445.
16. LAPHAM, p. 400.
17. CPI Inflation Calculator.
18. LAPHAM, p. 399, and CPI Inflation Calculator.
19. The John L. Horne home became an Old Ladies' Home in 1903. At least eight female inmates were accommodated within the first two years. Unfortunately, a suspicious fire and lack of funding put the charitable home out of business in 1905. The Horne home reverted to a private residence until the late 1950s, when it became the original Stephens Memorial Hospital building. The house was demolished later during an expansion of the hospital. "News from Bygone Days," researched by Ed Staples, trustee of the Norway, Maine Historical Society. *Norway Museum & Historical Society newsletter*, November 2022, pp. 3-4.
20. The images of John L. Hornes home and tannery were taken from LAPHAM, p. 533 and p. 398 respectively, and are in the public domain.

Prior to her marriage, Julia and her younger sister Edwina Maud were probably living with their mother (when not at school in Quebec) on a small homestead that Hannah (Crockett) Richardson had purchased just outside Norway Village. Hannah, who appears to have left Thomas Hanford permanently by 1873, bought a house and sixty-seven acres from Nathan W. Millett in September of that year.[21]

Chester Horne was working at his father's business when the couple was married. (By 1880, Chester was overseeing the tannery.)[22] After their marriage, the newlyweds resided with Hannah (and Edwina Maud), although there was certainly plenty of room in John Horne's estate on Main Street. In May of 1876, Hannah sold the farm to her son-in-law for $1. (Chester Horne also picked up Hannah's mortgage to Millett.) Since she had left her husband's home, Hannah was probably hoping to reside permanently under the protection of her son-in-law and eldest daughter. (Unfortunately for Hannah, that was not to be.)

John L. Horne proved prescient (or just downright shrewd) when he selected a tannery in Norway to purchase. The process of leather-making required high-tannin bark obtained from oak and hemlock trees, which the Norway area had in abundance. The tannins extracted from the ground bark helped break down the protein in the cow hides, turning them into leather, an important commodity in the 19th century. Tom Murphy, in his piece, "The Clark Tannery in 19th Century Amesbury," explains the value of this important commodity:

> "In the 19th Century, leather was a necessity that filled a unique niche. Rugged and flexible, it was used in shoes and boots for soles and uppers, tack for horses for transportation and work, and belts to run machinery in steam and water mills. A tannery would appear early in the life of any town. In the eighteenth century tanneries were small-scale, local operations, perhaps part-time work for a farmer, but as the country grew the demand for leather grew, and in the nineteenth century larger operations appeared."[23]

A shoe factory was a natural companion company for a tannery, and by the early 1870s John L. Horne and other leading men in Norway made overtures to B.F. Spinney & Co., a Lynn, Massachusetts shoe company, to see if Spinney would be interested in opening a factory in town. These overtures were favorably received

---

21. See OCROD, Book 166, Page 520. Hannah paid Millett $100 for the property, plus gave him a bond for $800 with 10% interest.
22. U.S. Census, Norway, Maine, 1880. Chester W. Horne.
23. "The Clark Tannery in 19th Century Amesbury." Tom Murphy. ACM (Amesbury Carriage Museum) website.

by B.F. Spinney and Horne was instrumental in bringing the factory to Norway.[24] When in the summer of 1875 (two years after the new factory opened in Norway) sixteen-year-old Emma attended her cousin Julia's wedding to Chester Horne, she could not have dreamed how pivotal a role the shoe factory would play in her life.

B.F. Spinney & Co.

"Bottoming Room in Factory of B.F. Spinney & Company, Lynn, Mass."
(The Miriam and Ira D. Wallach Division of Art, Prints and Photographs: Picture Collection, The New York Public Library.)[25]

Three years prior to Julia's wedding, when Emma was thirteen (and probably completely unaware of important Norway history in the making), a meeting was held at Beals Hotel in Norway between the town's leading men, including John L. Horne, and representatives from B.F. Spinney & Co. The shoe manufacturer was looking to expand its operation beyond its factory in Lynn, Massachusetts. Worried that potential labor issues in Lynn could sideline its operation, the company management thought it wise to relocate the new factory to a place where labor issues

---
24. LAPHAM, p. 393 and p. 163-164.
25. "Bottoming Room In Factory Of B. F. Spinney & Co., Lynn, Mass." The Miriam and Ira D. Wallach Division of Art, Prints and Photographs: Picture Collection, The New York Public Library. New York Public Library Digital Collections. Accessed May 4, 2021. Print in the public domain.

(strikes and the organization of a union) were less likely to occur.[26] In addition, easy access to leather provided by Horne's tannery was also a positive factor. In October of 1872, the committee met with B.F. Spinney to entice the company to open a new shoe factory in Norway near the tannery, on what was known as the Tucker lot.[27]

After the meeting at Beals Hotel, B.F. Spinney himself penned on October 21, 1872, a letter to Freeland Howe, a Norway insurance company owner and businessman also instrumental in bringing the shoe factory to town. The letter, which is dated from Lynn, informed Howe that Spinney was sending up to Norway two of his associates, G.W. Spinney and Allen Stony, to further evaluate the situation. Spinney continued:

> "I have requested them to visit your town with a view to making it their place of residence should they feel that it is the place for the successful prosecution of business in our line and that they can make themselves contented there.
>
> "We desire to treat your proposition with the respect which your kindness and courtesy demand and shall be able to make some definite reply to the citizens of Norway soon after the return of these gentlemen."[28]

The men returned a good report, and on November 9, 1872, at a special Town Meeting, citizens of Norway voted to raise a sum of money—not to exceed $10,000[29]—to "aid with the establishment of a shoe factory in Norway Village." At the same time the town also voted to exempt the proposed shoe factory from taxation for a period of ten years.[30] Six days later, on November 15, 1872, an agreement was formally completed and the necessary paperwork signed. In his Norway history, William B. Lapham describes the agreement, which was meant to be mutually beneficial (although from modern eyes appears weighted toward the manufacturer), as the deal would bring jobs and investment money into the town of Norway:

> "In substance ... the town was bound by the contract to erect a building forty feet wide and one hundred feet long and four stories high, furnished with a sixty horse-power boiler, and a fifteen horse-power engine, an elevator, piping, etc.,

---

26. LAPHAM, p. 395-396.
27. LAPHAM, p. 153. John L. Horne was one of the members of the committee negotiating with B.F. Spinney & Co. to bring the shoe factory to Norway.
28. Letter from B.F. Spinney to Freeland Howe, Esquire. October 21, 1872. Copy of the letter courtesy of Stuart Goodwin.
29. $10,000 is about $256,000 in 2024 dollars. CPI Inflation Calculator.
30. LAPHAM, 154-155.

and to complete the building and have it ready for occupancy, on or before the first day of May, 1873, to bear the expense of keeping the building insured, and at the expiration of ten years, B.F. Spinney and Company should have the privilege of buying the building at an appraised value. B.F. Spinney & Company, on their part, agreed to put in machinery for the manufacture of shoes, and give the business a fair trial, and if successful, to occupy the building for this purpose, for ten years, and to pay to the town an annual rent of ten dollars, and keep the building in repair."[31]

Stuart Goodwin, a local historian and grandson of the Stuart Goodwin who took over the Norway insurance company founded by Freeland Howe in the 1860s, has given talks on the history of the shoe factory. He likes to highlight the fact that B.F. Spinney & Co. did not own the factory building. Instead, the town floated bonds ($25 each) in the aggregate of $10,000, with coupons paying 7% interest semi-annually.[32] The bonds paid for the erection of the building, the boiler to heat it, and the piping. In public talks that he gives about the bonds and the building of the shoe factory, Goodwin notes that regular individuals purchased the bonds, not just well-heeled businessmen. (In fact, one of the initial purchasers of the shoe shop bonds was Emma's cousin, John F. Crockett.)[33] In a letter to the author Goodwin further explained this unique arrangement:

"The buildings were never owned by the shoe manufacturers, but leased for little or nothing by a local volunteer board who held stocks funded by local citizens. In those days you did not go to government agency to fund development, but went to the community to sell shares in order to provide jobs for your friends and neighbors and grow the town… [It is] amazing that farmers, shopkeepers, etc., were able to put up $25 or $50 cash in 1870 to build [the shoe factory] in hopes 'they would come'."[34]

Initial bids from builders to erect the factory were rejected by the committee tasked with bringing the shoe factory to town, but on December 10, 1872, Moses Houghton (who was one of two members of the committee to bid on the project)

---

31. LAPHAM, p. 393.
32. LAPHAM, p. 394.
33. Norway Shoe Shop Company ledger, p. 52. John purchased one share of original stock, #47, for $25. Information courtesy of Stuart Goodwin.
34. Email from Stuart Goodwin to the author June 16, 2021. Stuart's father Robert W. Goodwin was the last President of the volunteer board (that began with Freeland Howe and later included Stuart's grandfather, also Stuart Goodwin) that managed the shoe corporation building and negotiated leases with shoe manufacturers. Stuart adds: "We are still benefiting from the 1872 decision, as New Balance came to Norway in the 1970s as a result of the area having experienced shoe workers."

was awarded the contract.[35] Amazingly, Houghton built the factory—four stories high and the length of a football field—in a little over four months, during a Maine winter! On May 3, 1873, the committee voted to accept Houghton's completed building with only a few changes to be made, for which he was paid extra.[36] The new building was turned over to B.F. Spinney for an annual rent of $10 for ten years, and the shoe company quickly expanded half its operation to Norway from Lynn, Massachusetts.

Historian Lapham, who is effusive in his praises for B.F. Spinney & Co., writes of the effect the shoe factory had on Norway:

> "The establishment of the shoe factory here very soon had a marked effect upon the business of the village and town, and more than realized the hopes and expectations of those who had been foremost in bringing it about. There was a marked increase in population, rents soon became scarce, new streets were laid out, and new building enterprises projected, and the Village, always enterprising and thrifty, entered upon an era of growth and prosperity unknown before."[37]

Stuart Goodwin says "Norway did not become a real town until the [arrival of] the shoe factory…The whole state and nation was changing from an agrarian economy to manufacturing, so it was very forward-looking to keep local youths in the community."[38]

As soon as the factory was built, young people from the surrounding farms (females as well as males) poured into town to fill the hundreds of factory jobs. In addition, shoe workers from other factory towns in Massachusetts—Marlborough, Brockton, North Brookfield, Haverhill, and Lynn—began gravitating to Norway in search of better jobs and working conditions. One of those who came to Norway from out-of-state in 1873 when the shoe factory opened was Emma Crockett's future husband, George P. Young, then twenty-eight-years-old.

---

35. Ansel Dinsmore, a house builder and carpenter (and husband to Nathan Morse's daughter Judith), who was another member of the committee to bring a shoe factory to Norway, also bid on the project; however, his and other bids were initially rejected before Houghton's bid was finally accepted.
36. LAPHAM, 394.
37. LAPHAM, p. 394.
38. Email from Stuart Goodwin to the author June 24, 2024.

Employees at the newly-open B.F. Spinney shoe factory in Norway, Maine, summer 1873. George P. Young, Emma's future husband, is third from right, standing in a wheelbarrow. (Photo a gift from Stuart Goodwin to the author.)[39]

With many years of experience working as a shoe cutter in Massachusetts,[40] George P. (as my grandmother used to speak of her grandfather to distinguish him from her brother, George W. Young) would have been a welcome addition to the new B.F. Spinney factory. When the handsome shoe cutter arrived in Norway in the summer of 1873, Emma was just fourteen-years-old. Eight years later Emma Tuell Crockett and George P. Young would be married.[41]

---

39. The Norway, Maine Historical Society has a copy of this same photo with George P. Young identified. While not in good condition, the NHS photograph helped the author positively identify her great-great grandfather.
40. 1865 census for Middleton, MA. George P. Young. At the time, George P. was nineteen years old (according to the census) and listed as living with a family named Perkins, probably as a boarder. He was employed as a shoe cutter.
41. Maine Marriage Records, Emma Crockett. Also, NHS, Crockett genealogy. MMR says the couple was married in Norway; however, the NHS reports they were married in Paris.

George P. Young

George P. Young circa 1880.
(Photo courtesy of Norway, Maine Historical Society.)[42]

Little has been known in our family about my great-great grandfather, George P. Young. His tragic early death in 1890 at age forty-five (his gravestone and obituary say he was forty-one) account for the main reason few of us knew his story—because our parents and grandparents did not know his story. George and Emma's only child, William F. Young, (my great-grandfather), was six-years-old when his father died, and so naturally his knowledge of his father's history was limited. In addition, the way in which George died—a self-inflicted gunshot wound—although explained as accidental in great detail in his obituary, was a half-step from suicide, scandalous in the late-19th and early-20th centuries. Indeed, my grandmother Winona, when discussing her grandfather with me, often spoke *sotto voce*, as if she was worried someone other than me might be listening (or care)—and that was eighty years after his death!

George P. Young was born in Mont Vernon, New Hampshire on February 17, 1845[43] to John C. Young of Gilmanton, N.H. and Harriet A. Vittum[44] of Sandwich. The couple, who were married in Amherst, New Hampshire on September 24, 1843, remained in that area (Mont Vernon was formerly a part of Amherst) at least

---

42. Head shot of George P. Young taken from photo on p. 196. George is back row, far left
43. After close perusal of early census, marriage, and military records, I believe George was born in 1845 (rather than 1849, per his obituary). George likely presented himself as a younger man when he arrived in Norway.
44. The official New Hampshire marriage record for George's parents lists his mother's name as Harriet C. Reed/Read, but I have concluded that Harriet Read/Reed and Harriet Vittum are one and the same woman, and that she was the daughter of William and Elkina (Clough) Vittum of Sandwich. Why George's mother, who I believe was from a well-established Sandwich family, was residing in Mont Vernon and possibly using a different name when she married John Young of Gilmanton is a mystery to me. If she was indeed the Harriet from Sandwich, she would have been about fifteen years old (which could explain the mystery) when she and John wed on September 24, 1843.

until after George's birth. By the time George was five-years-old (and probably before), the family had relocated back to John Young's hometown of Gilmanton, where George's grandparents Dudley and Sally (Jacobs) Young resided.[45] George appears to have split his youth between the hometowns of his parents—Gilmanton and Sandwich, N.H.

The Youngs were long-time Gilmanton residents.[46] George's grandfather Dudley Young, Jr. was born in Gilmanton,[47] as was probably his father, whose given name according to public records was, oddly enough (considering that his son was a junior), not "Dudley," but "Joseph."[48] Thanks to the superfluity of Dudley and Joseph Youngs in Gilmanton (from which the towns of Belmont and Gilford later split), I have been unable to conclusively determine the particular Young line from which George descended.[49] (Basically, I cannot with confidence identify Dudley Young's parents.)

Various public documents reveal that Dudley Young was a man possessed of a large family, but small financial means.[50] He was a farmer and carpenter, who, for most of his married life dwelt on twenty-five acres of land on Young's Pond in

---

45. 1850 U.S. Census, Gilmanton, N.H. Young, John C.
46. See U.S. Census data for Dudley and Joseph Young, Gilmanton, New Hampshire. For example, the 1830 census shows that there were two Dudley Youngs and three Joseph Youngs residing in Gilmanton.
47. The fact that Dudley Young was born in Gilmanton came from his death record. See N.H. Death and Burial Records, 1654-1949. Gilmanton, Dudley Young.
48. See N.H. Death Records, 1650-1969. Gilmanton, Dudley Young. Dudley Young died June 21, 1863 in Gilmanton. In the death record his father's given name is Joseph. See also N.H. Marriage Records, 1637-1947. Gilmanton, Dudley Young. In this record Dudley is denoted as a "Jr." He was married to Sally Jacobs in Barnstead, N.H. in 1808. One possible explanation for why Dudley, Jr. and his father Joseph had different first names could be that Dudley, Jr. might have been christened "Joseph Dudley Young, Jr.," but was known by his middle name with the junior designation to distinguish him from his father and other Joseph Youngs in Gilmanton. The reverse is equally true, however. "Joseph" could have been Dudley Joseph Young, and he was known by "Joseph" to distinguish him from the other Dudley Youngs in Gilmanton.
49. One of George's ancestors in Gilmanton might have been the Joseph Young, who, among other settlers, on June 4, 1789, petitioned the New Hampshire legislature to move the General Court (the citizen legislature) closer to the center of the state, rather than its then location in the southern part of the state, as that was too far for them to travel. (New Hampshire, U.S. Government petitions, 1700-1826. Box 25: Feb. 1788-June 1789.) It is worth mentioning that a "Dudley Young" was also one of the signers of the petition, possibly an uncle or other relation of our Dudley (who was only one-year-old at the time). Concord, the exact center of the Granite State, was eventually selected as the permanent site of the state legislature. Another Joseph Young of Gilmanton (possibly that same petitioner) was a long-time selectman and later a representative to the New Hampshire General Court. ("The History of Gilmanton, New Hampshire to 1875." William Badger. Phillip M. Zea, editor. Published by the New Hampshire Historical Society, 1976. Pgs. 32 and 34.) This Joseph Young was also a ruling elder in the Freewill Baptist Church and founder of the 3rd Freewill Baptist Church of Gilmanton, later, Belmont. ("The History of Gilmanton," p. 38.) The first Dudley Young arrived in Gilmanton in 1766, when he purchased Lot 13 in the 2nd range, settling on that lot in 1768. ("The History of Gilmanton from the First Settlement to the Present Time." Daniel Lancaster. Printed by Alfred Prescott. Gilmanton. 1845. P. 75 and 79.) This Dudley Young was chosen as one of three selectmen during Gilmanton's annual Town Meeting held March 9, 1769. ("The History of Gilmanton from the First Settlement to the Present Time," p. 79-80.)
50. I gleaned this information from records at the Stafford County Registry of Deeds and from the will of Dudley Young, Jr.

Gilmanton. He seems to have received much aid from his two eldest sons Aaron and John—especially Aaron—during his seventy-five years of life.

On August 25, 1834, a writ of execution was issued for Dudley Young, Jr. for $27.22 in damages recovered against him by Nicholas Durrell. Added to the $27.22 was $4.29 for the cost of the suit, 17¢ for the writ, and $12.02 in fees to collect Durrell's damages (a total of $43.70).[51] At the time of the writ, Dudley and Sally and their family (including at least four of their numerous children) appear to have been living in a barn on approximately twenty-five acres.[52] Three appraisers reviewed the property to see if they could satisfy the $43.70 balance due. The appraisers carved out an eight-acre chunk to cover the amount Dudley Young owed Durrell. In January of 1835, eldest son Aaron paid $100 to secure both parcels (the eight acres and the mortgaged property from which it was split) and deed them back to his father.[53] In 1840, John C. Young, (then only about eighteen) would also redeem this same property from creditors.[54]

Eventually, Dudley's fortunes improved and in 1851 he purchased for $1500 what was then known as the John Ring farm on the Province Road in Gilmanton,[55] probably not far from where he had previously been living in the barn. Dudley mortgaged the entire property to Thomas Durrell,[56] a wealthy neighbor (and possible relation to Dudley's former creditor). On April 25, 1853, the mortgage was assigned to son Aaron. A note in the margin of the mortgage reveals that Aaron Young satisfied the $1500 mortgage and the property was transferred to him by Thomas Durrell via quit claim deed on May 25, 1855.[57] The fact that anyone was willing to lend Dudley Young, Jr. money considering his history of debt suggests that he was either a well-liked man or that it was generally known his eldest son would cover his debts—or both.

Indeed, the fortunes in the Young Family in Gilmanton seem to have hinged upon George's successful uncle, Aaron B. Young, whose financial success in manufacturing likely influenced his nephew's career. According to census data, Aaron B. Young (brother of George's father John) moved to Lowell, Massachusetts by

---

51. Belknap County Registry of Deeds, Book 15/Page 32-33.
52. Belknap County Registry of Deeds, Book 15/Page 25-26.
53. Belknap County Registry of Deeds, Book 15/Page 25-26. Aaron purchased the property from John Watson, a machinist, who purchased it from Durrell.
54. Belknap County Registry of Deeds, Book 40/Page 537.
55. Belknap County Registry of Deeds, Book 18/Page 61. Dudley purchased the property from David M. Clough.
56. Belknap County Registry of Deeds, Book 18/Page 63. Mortgage dated August 14, 1851.
57. See note in margin of deed in Book 18/Page 63, Belknap County Registry of Deeds.

at least age twenty-five, where he became a manufacturer, probably of cloth or clothing.[58] In 1858 Aaron was initiated into the Masons, the fraternal organization that traces its roots back to the guilds of stone masons. Aaron joined the venerable Pentucket Lodge.[59] In 1860, when Aaron relocated his family back to Gilmanton (perhaps to help his brother care for their parents) the census shows him with a real estate value of $2000 (the John Ring farm) and a very high personal estate valued at $3000, which leads me to believe that total included manufacturing equipment and machinery and/or Aaron's business.[60]

George's father, John C. Young, was a machinist, who might have worked on some of his brother's equipment. In 1850, the U.S. census for Gilmanton reports John employed as a machinist on "miscellaneous machinery."[61] In addition, John could have been employed by the Gilmanton Iron Works or could also have worked for the newly-established shoe factory in town.

George was the eldest of four children born to Harriet (Vittum) and John C. Young. The four children were (in order of their birth): George, Charles, Eddie, and Emma.[62] Between George and his younger brother Charles was a seven-year gap. Charles was born in Gilmanton on May 10, 1852.[63] The next son, Mark Edward (known as "Eddie" throughout his life), was born in 1858,[64] making him about thirteen years younger than George. The youngest in the family was only daughter Emma, born in their mother's hometown of Sandwich in 1860 (after the census was taken).[65] Emma was fifteen years younger than George.

George appears to have been close to his younger siblings, assuming the elder child's role as protector and advisor. Sadly, all but one of his brothers, as well as his sister Emma, predeceased him. Emma died at age ten of "dropsy" (heart failure) on January 29, 1870,[66] just two weeks shy of George's twenty-fifth birthday. Charles died of consumption (tuberculosis) on August 22, 1888.[67] He was thirty-six. (George was then forty-three.) The only sibling to outlive George was Eddie,

---

58. 1840 U.S. Census, Lowell, Massachusetts. Aaron B. Young.
59. Massachusetts Mason Membership Cards, 1733-1990. Aaron B. Young.
60. 1860 U.S. Census, Gilmanton, New Hampshire. Aaron Bartlett Young.
61. 1850 U.S. Census, Gilmanton, New Hampshire. Young, John C.
62. George Young's sister and his second wife shared the same given name: "Emma."
63. The information about Charles' birth date came from his death record, Massachusetts Death Records 1841-1915. Young, Charles A. Charles, who was a shoe shop worker in Haverhill, died of consumption at the age of thirty-six.
64. Eddie's birth year comes from various U.S. Censuses. I am unclear whether he was born in Gilmanton or Sandwich.
65. Emma Young's birth year comes from her death record, New Hampshire, Death and Disinterment Records, 1754-1947. Young, Emma E.
66. New Hampshire Death and Disinterment Records, 1784-1947. Emma C. Young.
67. Massachusetts Death Records, 1841-1915. Charles A. Young. Haverhill.

who was mentioned (although not named) in George's obituary.⁶⁸ I have wondered if the loss of George's first family contributed to George's depression and possible suicide (if indeed the gunshot wound that killed him was not accidental). George's own passing in 1890 occurred just eighteen months after Charles' death.

George grew up with one foot in Gilmanton and another in Sandwich. These two communities were well-established and in step with the changing times of the mid-nineteenth century. Although Gilmanton was primarily a farming community, there was already a shoe factory and an iron works in that town. As an agricultural community, Sandwich was at the crossroads of New Hampshire commerce. George's letters later in life reveal him to have received a good education from his tenure in these two communities. Gilmanton Academy, which he likely attended (for at least a year or two) was one of the first three secondary schools chartered in New Hampshire.⁶⁹ During George's life, that town even boasted a seminary for the training of ministers.⁷⁰

In 1855, when George was ten, his maternal grandfather, William Vittum of Sandwich, passed away.⁷¹ After Vittum's death, John and Harriet Young and their family relocated to Sandwich. By 1860, George's grandmother, Elkina (Clough) Vittum, had moved to Middleton, Massachusetts to live with her son Joseph Wentworth Vittum (Harriet's younger brother and George's uncle), whose life would also be a role model for George.⁷² When the 1860 census was taken, John and Harriet and their family were living in a dwelling inhabited by seventy-year-old Stephen Vittum (possibly Harriet's uncle or even her grandfather).⁷³ According to the census, John Young and Stephen Vittum were both farmers. John was accorded the lion's share of the value of the real estate in the census, $1200, to Stephen's $500.

---

68. Emma died in Gilmanton in 1870 at age ten, and Charles A. died in Haverhill, Massachusetts in 1888, a year and a half before George's death in 1890. According to my research, only Mark Edward, "Eddie," outlived George, and then perhaps only by one year. The only hint of his death I have is a gravestone in Los Angeles, California, for a Mark E. Young, who died there February 15, 1891. Find-a-Grave, Mark E. Young.
69. Gilmanton Academy was incorporated by the New Hampshire legislature in 1794. "History of Merrimack and Belknap Counties, New Hampshire." D. Hamilton Hurd, editor. Philadelphia: J.W. Lewis & Co., 1885. Joseph Young, possibly an ancestor of George P. Young's, was one of the signers of a report to appropriate the school right and subscribe £500 for the establishment of the academy. Report dated April 19, 1792. "The History of Gilmanton from the First Settlement to the Present Time," pages 148 and 153.
70. "The History of Gilmanton from the First Settlement to the Present Time," pps. 169-179. Groundbreaking for the seminary was April 23, 1839. The Seminary was opened for students in 1840.
71. According to Find-A-Grave Index, 1600s-current, Harriet's father William Vittum of Sandwich died August 18, 1855.
72. 1860 U.S. Census, Middleton, Massachusetts. Vittum, Joseph Wentworth.
73. A quick perusal of Vittum deeds in Sandwich during this time revealed that it was not uncommon for a property to be left to two offspring as tenants-in-common at the father's death. I elected not take the time, however, to research either the entire Vittum family tree or their deed history in Sandwich. More no doubt can be learned about Harriet's family.

The census also lists John with a personal estate worth $400, which might have been Harriet's share (or her mother's share) of the personal property on the farm.[74]

John and Harriet could have intended to remain permanently in Sandwich. If so, their plans changed when John's father, Dudley Young, Jr., died of lung fever on June 21, 1862[75] at the age of seventy-five.[76] At that point the family, including probably seventeen-year-old George, returned to Gilmanton to live. It appears that George's uncle Aaron, who was then in Gilmanton, wanted to return to his manufacturing career in Lowell.[77] John was now needed to care for their widowed mother Sally, as well as to manage the John Ring farm.

Dudley Young's last will and testament gives us insight into the character of George's grandfather:

> "In the name of God, Amen.
>
> "I, Dudley Young of Gilmanton in the County of Belknap and the State of New Hampshire, being weak in body, but of sound and perfect memory, blessed be Almighty God for the same, do make and publish this my last will and testament in manner and form that is to say.
>
> "First ~ I give and bequeath unto my beloved wife Sally Young, the income of one third part of my farm after it is carried on, including the crops and hay, and one third part of all the buildings if occupied by herself during her natural life. Also, I give unto my said wife all of my household furniture and one cow and one calf for her benefit.
>
> "Also, I devise and bequeath to my son John C. Young all my homestead farm situated in said Gilmanton by his the said John C. Young giving to his mother Sally Young one third the income from said farm during her natural life. Also I give to my son John C. Young my horse and oxen, it being the only horse and oxen I own."[78]

Dudley Young, Jr. was not a rich man. In 1860 his real estate[79] was valued at only $250 and his personal estate at $100. By contrast, his neighbor, Thomas

---

74. 1860 U.S. Census, Sandwich, N.H. Young, John C. and Vittum, Stephen, dwelling number 678.
75. Year of death from the gravestone of Dudley Young, Jr., Smith Meeting House Cemetery, Gilmanton, New Hampshire. N.H. Death Records, 1650-1969, report Dudley Young, Jr. died on June 21, 1863 (not 1862); however, as his will was probated the prior day on June 20, 1863, I believe the gravestone is correct.
76. Death records and Dudley Young, Jr.'s gravestone disagree on the year of his death; however, his stone says he was seventy-five-years-old.
77. See 1865 Massachusetts State Census, Lowell. Aaron B. Young.
78. New Hampshire Wills and Probate Records, 1643-1982. Dudley Young, Gilmanton. Belknap County probate date June 20, 18
79. This would be the twenty-five acres on Young's Pond, where Dudley previously resided in a barn.

Durrell, who helped Dudley purchase the John Ring farm, had property valued at $16,000, with a personal estate worth $5000. Another of Dudley's neighbors, John F. Nelson, had real estate valued at $4000 and a personal estate valued at $1200.[80] In addition to deeding his homestead to John (upon which Aaron held the mortgage) and one-third the income to his widow, Dudley also bequeathed to his other surviving children—Mary (Young) Johnson, Aaron B. Young, Clarry (Young) Sawyer,[81] Abigail (Young) Weare, Harriet (Young) Davis, Charles H. Young, and Lewis A. Young—the sum of $5 each. The residue of Dudley's estate was left to John, who, as executor, was charged with paying the modest legacies to his siblings within six months of their father's death.[82]

In 1863, after his grandfather's estate was settled, eighteen-year-old George stood on the cusp of adulthood. The Civil War had already been raging for two years, and tens of thousands of young New England farm boys had enlisted in the Union army to do battle with Confederate soldiers at places such as Bull Run and Antietam. Many of these young men, like Emma Crockett's cousin Rufus Crockett Penley, would not return from the war. On March 3, 1863, Congress passed the conscription act, "An Act for enrolling and calling out the national Forces and for other Purposes." The Act called for all able-bodied men between the age of twenty and forty-five to serve in the army (with some exceptions), or pay a substitute $300 to serve for him. (The new draft was necessary to backfill the loss of troops from disease and battle, after calls for 500,000 men in 1862 and an original call of 75,000 men in 1861 were not enough.) Since George would not be twenty until 1865—the year the Civil War ended—he was able to avoid the draft. If he had wanted to volunteer to serve, however, George could have done so, like thousands of younger men (including Rufus Penley) had done before him.

But George also had the life examples of five close male relatives, none of whom appear to have been soldiers, upon which to fashion his own. He could become a farmer, like his father and both grandfathers before him, and help feed the troops. Or George could go to work in the booming manufacturing business, many of whose employees were employed making boots, clothing, and tents for Union soldiers. In manufacturing, George had the examples of his two uncles—Aaron Young and Joseph Wentworth Vittum—to draw upon.

---

80. 1860 U.S. Census, Gilmanton, New Hampshire.
81. Clarry was left one calf valued at $5. The other six siblings were left $5 in cash.
82. New Hampshire Wills and Probate Records, 1643-1982. Dudley Young. Probate date June 20, 1863, Belknap, N.H.

Of his two uncles, George was probably personally closest to Joseph Vittum, who was only about ten years his senior.[83] (By contrast, Uncle Aaron Young was thirty years older than George.) In 1860, Joseph lived in Middleton, Massachusetts with his wife Martha (Rennard) Young, and their first-born son William. George's grandmother Elkina Vittum, then fifty-two, also lived with her son and his family. That year, Joseph worked as a shoe cutter,[84] probably for a shoe manufacturer situated on Essex Street in neighboring Haverhill, where he later would set up his own shoe manufacturing business.[85] Uncle Joseph was an entrepreneur, with an interesting career path that led him from shoe manufacturing to leather dealing and ultimately to banking. His venture into the shoe industry is the career path that George would follow.

By 1865, when George was twenty, he relocated to Middleton, where he went to work as a shoe cutter.[86] By then, Uncle Joseph had moved to Haverhill, where he owned a restaurant in Hammond's Block on Merrimack Street. Although a restaurant-owner engaged in feeding the hundreds of Haverhill shoe factory workers, Joseph was also still in the boot and shoe business. The 1865 Massachusetts Census lists Joseph's occupation as manufacturer. Between 1865 and 1867 Joseph started a shoe manufacturing business. He might even have enticed his nephew George to leave New Hampshire and come to work for him. By 1867, J. W. Vittum was listed in the Massachusetts Register as a boot and shoe manufacturer in Haverhill, where (among other Massachusetts cities) the shoe industry was bursting forth. The 1869 Haverhill City Directory also lists George's uncle as a shoe manufacturer with a business situated at 148 Merrimack Street. (In 1869, Joseph and George's grandmother Elkina Vittum both also had houses on Howe Street.)

In 1865, perhaps because there was not enough room at his uncle's house with a growing family (which included what appears to be a seventeen-year-old servant), George boarded in Middleton with a family named Perkins. As mentioned, he was employed as a shoe cutter, either in his uncle's shoe shop or at a larger factory in the Washington Street Shoe District, which eventually eclipsed Essex Street (where

---

83. Massachusetts marriage records, 1840-1915, for Joseph Wentworth Vittum and Martha M. Rennard indicate that he was born in 1834. His Mason membership card and other records, however, say that Joseph was born in 1838. Most likely the earlier date is correct.
84. 1860 U.S. Census, Middleton, MA. Joseph W. Vittum.
85. Haverhill, Massachusetts City Directory, 1867. Joseph W. Vittum. This is the first year in which Joseph is listed as a shoe manufacturer. See also the 1867 Massachusetts Register, p. 151, in which J.W. Vittum is listed as a company under "Boot and Shoe Manufacturers."
86. Massachusetts State Census, 1865, Haverhill. George P. Young.

Uncle Joseph operated) as the epicenter of shoe manufacturing in Haverhill.[87] In 1865, when he turned twenty, George enrolled in the Massachusetts Reserve Militia No. 106 (under Captain Henry N. Hunt), in order to satisfy the conscription requirements passed by Congress.[88] (There is no evidence that this reserve militia was ever called up to fight during George's tenure.)

By 1868, Uncle Joseph had expanded his business so much so that he opened an office in Boston. J. W. Vittum is listed as a "Boot and Shoe Wholesaler" at 48 Hanover Street in the Boston City Directory. The 1869 Boston City Directory also noted that Joseph's home was still in Haverhill, even though his company had an office on Hanover Street.[89]

In the meantime, George began keeping the company of Middleton native Martha "Mattie" Wilkins Fuller. She was one of twin daughters born November 21, 1845 to Abijah Fuller and Abigail (Weston) Fuller.[90] Mattie was raised by her stepmother, Sarah Blake. Her mother Abigail passed away July 7, 1846, less than eight months after giving birth to the twins. Mary Ward Fuller, Mattie's twin, lived just two months longer than her mother.[91] Mattie's father Abijah Fuller was a farmer in Middleton. In 1870, Abijah farmed 76 acres of land, 36 acres improved for planting or haying, and 40 acres of woodland. His farm was valued at $3300, with a modest amount of farm implements valued at $200, and stock value of $550.[92]

In 1865, twenty-year-old Mattie was still living at home with her father, stepmother, and younger siblings. According to the 1865 Massachusetts state census for Middleton, Mattie was employed as a shoe stitcher. Mattie could have done her stitching work at the farm, since women were still being paid for shoe and boot piecework at the time. (A decade later, in 1875, there were still 222 women from Haverhill paid to do work on shoes and boots at home.)[93] As a younger woman just starting out, however, it is more likely Mattie went to work in Haverhill, where capitalists were taking over the shoe industry and setting up "manufactories" or shoe shops. The invention of the Blake-McKay Stitching Machine revolutionized

---

87. Webpage, Essex National Heritage Area. "Washington Street Shoe District."
88. The 1865 militia record lists George as nineteen. He would be twenty in February.
89. See also the Massachusetts Register 1869, p. 412, J. W. Vittum.
90. North American Family histories, 1500-2000. Genealogy of some descendants of Thomas Fuller of Woburn. P. 73.
91. Mary Ward Fuller died on September 19, 1846. North American Family histories, 1500-2000. Genealogy of some descendants of Thomas Fuller of Woburn, p. 73.
92. 1870 U.S. Census, Non-population schedule; Agriculture. Middleton, MA. Abijah Fuller.
93. The Massachusetts State Census for 1875 (vol. ii, p. 825). For the year ending May 1, 1875, there were 222 women in Haverhill who earned wages for piecemeal work on shoes and boots at their homes. Total wages paid in Haverhill that year was $20,207, with the average annual wage for a woman worker $89.80+.

the shoe industry.[94] In Massachusetts, the transition from home (and farm) to factory worker occurred about a decade prior to the transition experienced by Norway in 1873, when B.F. Spinney & Co. brought the first shoe shop to that town. The transition to factory work brought an end to what was known as the Domestic Stage of shoe-making:

> "But it was generally the manufacturer who put the [sewing] machines into his central shop, or the man with some capital and genius for machinery, who bought or leased the 'wax thread' and 'dry thread' machines and set them up either in a stitching shop or in a central shop where space was hired. Men and young women followed the machines, leaving the older people to 'side up' and bind shoes by hand at home. Thus a new stage of organization had come in the boot and shoe industry, bringing to an end not only the third phase but the main life of the Domestic Stage, where the 'putting out' system had prevailed and the entrepreneur had worked in his central shop while the domestic workers labored in their 'ten-footers'."[95]

George P. Young and Martha W. Fuller were married on July 6, 1868, in Pittsfield, New Hampshire, about ten miles from George's hometown of Gilmanton. The couple was married by Congregational clergyman Reverend S.Z. Ferris, probably at his home. In the New Hampshire marriage record George is listed as a shoe manufacturer. (He might have been running his uncle's shop in Haverhill, while Joseph Vittum worked at his office in Boston.) No occupation is given for Mattie.[96]

The year 1870 seems to have been an emotional roller coaster for George. His ten-year-old sister Emma died on January 29, 1870 and it appears that George left Mattie in Middleton for a time and returned to Gilmanton to be with his recently widowed father and two younger brothers, Charles, now eighteen, and Eddie, just twelve. (George's mother, Harriet, had previously passed away on March 20, 1867 from an "internal rupture.")[97] The 1870 U.S. Census for Gilmanton, which was taken in Lower Gilmanton on June 1st, shows that George was then living and working on the farm with his father, John C. Young. By the end of June, however, when the census in Middleton was enumerated, George was back home in

---

94. Webpage, CTW Photography. Shoe Blog. "Blake-McKay Stitching Machine." The shoe industry was revolutionized again in 1883 by Jan Ernst Matzeliger's invention of the shoe lasting machine. See also the webpage National Inventors Hall of Fame. "Jan Ernst Matzeliger."
95. "The Organization of the Boot and Shoe Industry in Massachusetts Before 1875," p. 256. Blanche E. Hazard. *The Quarterly Journal of Economics*, Feb., 1913, Vol. 27, No. 2 (Feb., 1913), pp. 236-262 Published by: Oxford University Press.
96. New Hampshire Marriage and Divorce Records, 1659-1947. Pittsfield, N.H. George P. Young and Mattie W. Foller [sic].
97. New Hampshire Death Records 1650-1969. Gilmanton, N.H. Harriet Young.

Massachusetts with his wife. (Either that, or Mattie, when the census taker visited, claimed George still resided there.) The Middleton census reported George "works in a factory" and that Mattie was "keeping house."⁹⁸ His appearance in both censuses—working both on the farm and in the factory—suggests that George might have been torn between his love for farming and shoe manufacturing. Perhaps that is why in 1873, when B. F. Spinney & Co. opened a new shoe shop in Norway, Maine—a small agricultural community not unlike Gilmanton—George P. Young decided to relocate there.

B.F. Spinney employees of the cutting room, 1880.
(Photo courtesy of the Norway, Maine Historical Society.)⁹⁹

Mattie accompanied George to Maine in the summer of 1873. She cohabitated with her husband for approximately six months. By February of 1874, however, Mattie had left George and returned to Middleton, Massachusetts, where she appears to have resumed her old life prior to her marriage.¹⁰⁰ Mattie filed for divorce

---

98. 1870 U.S. Census, Middleton, MA. George P. Young.
99. This photo of shoe cutters was taken on the library steps, according to Sue Denison of the Norway, Maine Historical Society. The author is grateful to Sue for finding this and other B.F. Spinney photos.
100. The information about Mattie accompanying George to Maine, and then leaving him, came from the record of George's divorce from Mattie, which was granted by the Maine Supreme Judicial Court in January of 1881 at Androscoggin County. See Maine SJC Volume 18, Page 361. In that record George noted how long Mattie had been absent as a wife, leading one to conclude that she did spend time with him initially in Norway.

in Massachusetts in April of 1877 on grounds of desertion (even though it appears from the later Maine divorce record that she abandoned her husband).[101] Her divorce was made absolute by the Supreme Judicial Court of Massachusetts in November 1877, at which time Mattie was given "leave to resume her maiden name" of Fuller,[102] which she did.[103] (Mattie eventually remarried, but not until 1883.)[104] In the meantime, George remained in Norway, living a bachelor's life.

Summary of the divorce record of Martha W. Young and George P. Young.
The divorce was made absolute in November 1877 by the Massachusetts Supreme Judicial Court.
The original record detailing the particulars of the divorce has been lost.
(Summary courtesy of Elizabeth C. Bouvier, archivist, Massachusetts Judiciary Archives.)

Emma and George

Among those who also went to work at the new shoe factory in Norway Village was Emma's cousin Josiah Penley Crockett, one of the Crockett heirs. Whether or not the two men—George and Josiah—worked together in the cutting room at B. F. Spinney & Co., they certainly would have known each other. Both men were about

---

101. We do not have the complete Massachusetts divorce record (the archivist who helped me stated that the record was lost), so we do not know the particulars. According to the archivist, it is possible that George might have been "already involved with another [woman]" in Maine, and that's why Mattie's divorce on grounds of desertion was granted. Unless the original Massachusetts divorce record is located, we will never know for certain. (Information from December 16, 2021 email between Elizabeth C. Bouvier, archivist for the Massachusetts judiciary, and Jennifer Wixson.)
102. MA SJC divorce record for Martha W. Young and George P. Young. (See copy of record #516 attached.)
103. Massachusetts Marriage Records, 1840-1915. Martha W. Fuller and Gilman A. Kimball. March 8, 1883. Middleton, MA.
104. Massachusetts Marriage Records, 1840-1915. Martha W. Fuller. According to this 1883 marriage record, Mattie, 37, married Gilman A. Kimball, 45, who was supervisor of a mill in Middleton at the time. (This mill was probably the one at which Mattie had previously been working). The record lists her occupation as "at home." This was a second marriage for both.

the same age; both were single; both lived in downtown Norway near one another; and both were members of the Independent Order of Odd Fellows (IOOF),[105] a benevolent organization like the Masons. Josiah, who came from a good family and had real estate investments in town, would have taken note of George P. Young, who was not only a member of the IOOF, but also a charter member of Wildey Encampment No. 21. (An Encampment was a higher order of the IOOF, composed of Third Degree members in good standing, whose mission in furthering the work of the Odd Fellows was specifically to "impart Faith, Hope and Charity.")[106]

The Wildey Encampment of the IOOF was instituted on November 19, 1874.[107] In May of 1875, George P. Young received an official certificate welcoming him into the Independent Order of Odd Fellows, Wildey Encampment No. 21.[108] The Wildey Odd Fellows met on a regular basis, probably at least twice a month. (In 1903-1904, the Wildey Encampment No. 21 met on the second and fourth Friday of each month at the Masonic Block on Cottage Street.)[109] According to Norway historian Lapham, George P. Young also at one point served in the principal office of Scribe.[110] As Scribe, which was an elected position, George's job would have been to record the minutes of the meetings, handle the necessary paperwork, and send and receive communications.[111]

It is not a stretch of the imagination to envision that in 1878 or 1879 twenty-year-old Emma Crockett met her future husband at the dinner table of her independent female cousins—Ella, Allie, and Louisa Crockett—presided over by their elder brother Josiah. The Crockett heirs were then living in Norway Village in their late brother John's house, following his 1875 death in a railway accident in

---

105. We know that Josiah P. Crockett was a member of the IOOF because he mentions his life insurance policy from that organization in his 1881 will.
106. Webpage, Independent Order of Odd Fellows. "Encampment."
107. LAPHAM, p. 215. One had to be fairly comfortable financially to join the Odd Fellows. IOOF members paid dues, which funds were used for benevolent purposes. Lapham notes that: "Up to January 1st, 1886, this encampment had paid for sick and funeral benefits, four hundred and fifty dollars, and had funds on hand amounting to nine hundred dollars. At the time, its membership amounted to seventy."
108. Information from IOOF certificate found in George P. Young's trunk, currently in the possession of his great-grandson, George W. Young of Norway. See Appendix #14 for a copy of George P. Young's IOOF certificate.
109. Norway Register, 1903-1904.
110. LAPHAM, p. 215.
111. Webpage, Grand Lodge of Illinois, IOOF. "Structure of Odd Fellowship."

Indiana.[112] Although Emma was employed by B. F. Spinney & Co. in 1880,[113] the work areas of men and women were segregated, and thus she likely would not have met her future husband without the aid of friendly intermediaries.

After the death of their father Ephraim Stanford Crockett in 1874—followed by the death of brother John in 1875—the Crockett heirs moved into Norway Village to be near sister Abbie Jane, whose husband Charles Tubbs operated a grocery store with his family near the shoe factory. (Although Josiah owned a house of his own in the Village,[114] he lived with his sisters and his house was kept as an investment property.) The house of their late brother John, where the young people lived, was situated on the corner of Danforth and Main Streets, next to local physician Dr. Osgood Bradbury, who was also the first Chief Patriarch (the highest officer) of the Wiley Encampment of the IOOF.[115] (In his book, *Norway in the Forties*, Dr. Bradbury would later call George Young a "good friend.")[116] In 1880, Josiah Crockett, as head of the household, was then thirty-one, and employed by B.F. Spinney & Co.[117] Three of the girls with whom Emma spent much of her youth—Ella (now twenty-nine), Allie (twenty-seven), and Louisa (twenty-three)—ran a millinery shop together.[118] The young ladies rented space for their shop from their neighbor up Main Street to the west, insurance company owner Freeland Howe,

---

112. Although John was mortally injured in the railroad accident, he survived long enough to make a will, leaving everything he owned to his eight younger siblings to share and share alike. The will was dated April 25, 1875, the day of John's death. Although John could almost assuredly read and write (two of his sisters were schoolteachers), he signed the will with a mark, suggesting he was physically unable to sign his name when the will was drawn up. John left an estate valued at more than $8000, much of it inherited from his parents, Ephraim S. and Sally (Penley) Crockett, and his grandfather, Captain John Penley. (Maine Wills and Probate Records, 1584-1999; John F. Crockett.) The three young ladies—Ella, Allie, and Louisa—purchased John's house from their siblings (including Josiah) on June 16, 1879, although Josiah appears to still have resided with them, possibly as "protector." OCROD, Book 179, Page 499.
113. 1880 U.S. Census, Norway, Maine. Emma Crockett.
114. On November 28, 1877, Josiah purchased a lot in Norway Village from Aroline A. Sargent for $1700. Presumably, because of the cost of the property, there was a house situated on the lot as well, although it is not mentioned in the deed. OCROD, Book 178/Page 452. The following year, on May 18, 1878, Josiah also purchased a lot in Norway Village from Jonathan Blake. (Book 180/Page 240.) Even though the purchase price was only $175, there might have been a house on this lot as well because it appears as though he also took over a prior mortgage. See Book 195/Page 246.
115. WHITMAN, p. 170.
116. NORWAYFORTIES, p. 317. The paragraph in which George P. Young is mentioned is about James and Martha Crockett. Dr. Bradbury, as he is writing, remembers George as he travels Crockett's Ridge in his mind and adds a compliment to his deceased comrade. The paragraph reads: "[James and Martha] first went to housekeeping on his father's farm where their first child was born. From there they went to Crockett Ridge, so called, a short distance beyond, or north of the Wm. Crockett farm, where our good friend, Geo. P. Young, so suddenly went out of this life a short time since."
117. 1880 U.S. Census, Norway, Maine. Josiah Crockett.
118. According to Allie's obituary, which was published in *The Oxford County Advertiser*, November 7, 1924, the three sisters that kept shop together—Ella, Allie, and Louisa Crockett—were remembered long after they moved from the area to live with their brother Warren in Marietta, Georgia. The obituary stated that their millinery shop was located at the present location of Goodwin's Insurance Agency.

who had moved his fire insurance business to Norway from Sumner in 1865.[119] Youngest brother Oscar Rufus Crockett, twenty-one, was studying at college in Texas, although his permanent residence was with his sisters in Norway. Two other Crockett heirs, brothers, Warren and Edgar Little Crockett, lived in Marion, Indiana, where they were employed by a railroad company (despite brother John's deadly railway accident).[120]

When Emma Tuell Crockett went to work for B.F. Spinney & Co. she was twenty or twenty-one. It is not likely she commuted the eight miles (four miles each way) to work every day, especially in winter. She would not have walked that distance, and if Emma had ridden horseback (again, not likely) or driven a carriage, the daily stable charges for the steed would have eaten up what little money she earned as a female worker in the shoe factory. During the work week, Emma must have either rented a room or stayed at the home of her Crockett cousins.[121] Either way, Emma would have been a regular guest (or boarder) at the home of the Crockett heirs. Some slight match-making schemes might have unfolded as George P. Young was welcomed to share a meal with the young people. (Ella, Allie, and Louisa, who lived together for the rest of their lives, were committed spinsters.) In 1880 (if not before) George also boarded in Norway Village. He resided with a family named Keene, whose house appears to have been near the Tubbs store and the dwelling of Abbie Jane (Crockett) and her husband Charles Tubbs.

The 1880 census for Norway lists George P. Young's occupation as shoe cutter. The enumerator noted that George had been unemployed for four months when the census was taken on June 8th, which leads one to wonder if the factory was shut down for a period. George gave the census-taker a marital status as "single," although there was a checkbox for a divorced person. George also dropped five years from his age.[122] (In June of 1880, when the census was taken, George would have been thirty-five; however, he is listed in the census as thirty.) Why George misstated his age is not known, but certainly an eight-year difference between him and Emma would be more acceptable to her parents than thirteen. In addition, a man who was only fifteen when the Civil War ended need not explain his absence from

---

119. Email from Stuart Goodwin to Jennifer Wixson regarding the history of Goodwin's Insurance Agency, June 15, 2021.
120. 1880 U.S. Census, Marion, Indiana. Warren and Edgar Crockett. Edgar was a brakeman and Warren worked as a conductor.
121. The 1880 U.S. Census for Norway lists Emma as living with her parents on the Crockett homestead, although she likely boarded with her Crockett cousins downtown when the shoe factory was operational.
122. George P. Young certainly is not the first person who has dropped years from his age!

military service to an extended family of Crocketts who had lost one member to the war and had many other members (including Rufus Penley and John F. Crockett)[123] who proudly served.

As the relationship between Emma Crockett and George Young deepened, it would have become necessary at some point for him to disclose to her (and to her family) his prior marriage. (Until that time, the Crocketts might have assumed George was single.) That this information shook Emma—and/or her parents—is suggested by the fact that, although his first marriage was legally dissolved in 1877 by the Supreme Judicial Court of Massachusetts, George was moved to file for a divorce in Maine before he and Emma were married. This he did on December 14, 1880,[124] the day before Emma's twenty-first birthday. Although at age twenty-one Emma was now free to walk out her father's door and marry whom she pleased, it is not likely she would have wanted to marry without her parent's blessing. Thus, it was important to ensure that George's prior marriage was legally ended.

Divorce was still extremely rare in the 19th century in the United States. In 1880, only 0.4 of every 1,000 American marriages ended in divorce.[125] Marrying a divorced man, as Emma would be, would normally have been considered scandalous. Compared to the scandals that engulfed the extended Crockett family in the years prior to Emma's engagement, however, her marriage to George could hardly have risen to the level of mildly shocking.

Family Scandals Come to the Aid of Emma

The first family scandal was caused by Emma's uncle Isaiah Vickery Penley, who with aunt Mary Amanda (Crockett) Penley, dwelt in the farm below the Crockett homestead. Captain John Penley had relocated Isaiah's family there after rescuing his son from debt in Bethel. In his will, Captain Penley left the former Morse homestead (and the small island off the mainland) to Isaiah and bequeathed him other money (as he did all of his children and grandchildren). But the elder Penley's death in 1873 meant that there was nobody to rescue Isaiah from financial distress if he mismanaged his affairs. (Isaiah might have been something of a gambler, although

---

123. According to the U. S. Civil War Soldier Records and Profiles, 1861-1865, John F. Crockett enlisted from Portland (Maine) as a private on April 6, 1865 at the age of twenty-one. He was mustered-out (discharged) on September 25, 1865. John was about six months older than George P. Young.
124. Records of the Maine Supreme Judicial Court, Volume 18, Page 361-362.
125. "How the divorce rate has changed over the last 150 years." Frank Olito. Insider.com. January 30, 2019.

I have found no confirmed proof.) Barely a year after his father was buried, Isaiah was in financial trouble again. He had failed to pay a debt in the amount of $70, and the creditor took him to court. What made the affair particularly ugly was the fact that the plaintiff was Isaiah's nephew (Emma's cousin), Nathan Penley. Thirty-three-year-old Nathan was the second-born son of Charles and Sarah (Crockett) Penley. The fallout between the two family members must have made for some distressing dinner table conversation up at the Crockett homestead and in the other Penley-Crockett homes in the neighborhood.

In April of 1874, Nathan recovered judgment against his uncle Isaiah, who was ordered by the Supreme Judicial Court, sitting in Auburn, to pay him the $70, plus interest and fees. Whether Isaiah did not have the ready money or whether he was just stiff-necked, we will never know. But—court order or not—Isaiah did not pay up. On March 11, 1876 (two years after the judgment against Isaiah) the Deputy Sheriff of Oxford County was ordered by the court to seize "goods and chattels" from Isaiah Penley in the amount of $85.45, to satisfy the debt (including mounting interest and fees). If the Deputy Sheriff could not recover the $85.45, he was ordered to lock up Isaiah Vickery Penley until the debt was satisfied.

Three appraisers were appointed to assess the value of Isaiah's real estate to satisfy the judgment. One of the appraisers was Edwin A. Morse, son of Nathan and Mary (Crockett) Morse. Edwin was not only Isaiah's neighbor, but also first-cousin to his wife, Mary. Having grown up on the property, which included the five-acre island, Edwin was all too familiar with its boundaries and value. The three appraisers valued Isaiah's life interest in the estate to be $106.64, which was the amount of the execution, fees and charges (including appraisers' fees of $3.76). The property was seized to satisfy the debt, and made over to Nathan Penley.[126] Rather than lose his homestead farm, however, Isaiah, on September 5, 1876, sold the property to his son-in-law, Albert Farnham. (Albert and Sarah were living at the farm with her parents at the time.) Farnham, a well-regarded carpenter and Civil War veteran paid $500 cash for the real estate.[127] The ready money finally brought an end to what might be considered boorish familial infighting. Isaiah Penley settled his debt to his nephew (and associated charges), and managed to keep the place in the family.

But this sad affair of welching on a relative was as nothing compared to the

---

126. OCROD, Book 175, p.136-138.
127. OCROD, Book 174, Page 367.

sordid scandal that rocked the extended Crockett family the following year. This second scandal exposed the disharmony and debauchery in the Richardson family.

On March 6, 1877, Emma's cousin George Hanford Richardson, second-born son of Hannah Jordan Crockett and Thomas Hanford Richardson, was found nearly drowned and bleeding from his ear after a tumble into Steep Falls in Norway. Hannah, who had already left her husband, had recently deeded her place on the outskirts of Norway Village to her son-in-law Chester Horne. After the injured man was discovered, the twenty-five-year-old was taken to his brother-in-law's house. George lived only a short while before expiring, his grieving mother no doubt by his side.

The circumstances of George's death were mysterious from the beginning. Many in the Norway-Paris area firmly believed the young man was murdered;[128] hit over the head and/or pushed into the falls. Others thought George's tumble into Steep Falls was accidental or intentional, caused by his dependence upon drugs and alcohol. In the 19th century, patent medicines commonly prescribed by physicians utilized an alcohol base (up to 16%) and were often laced with opiates. Physicians were unfamiliar with the addictive nature of opiates and as a result "many doctors advocated the use of cocaine and other drugs."[129] As with oxycontin addiction in the 21st century, it is probable that George's drug dependence originally stemmed from physician-prescribed opiates.

---

128. CANDAGE, p. 180.
129. Webpage, Digital Public Library of America. Patent Medicine, 1860-1920. "Quack Cures & Self-Remedies."

Postcard, "Steep Falls, Norway, ME."
George Richardson fell or was pushed into Steep Falls in 1877.
(Postcard published by Miss M. [Minnie] F. Libby, Norway, Maine.)[130]

An inquest was held into the cause of George's death. This public proceeding garnered the Richardson family and their relations on Crockett's Ridge unseemly and unwanted publicity during a time of great grief. George Richardson's death, and his opium use, became a topic of much speculative gossip. Historian William Lapham describes the incident:

---

130. Minnie Libby (1863-1945) was a noted photographer and artist with a studio in Norway. Although she wore pants and affected masculine mannerisms, Libby was nevertheless respected for her fine portrait photography and artwork. Knowing how much my grandmother Winona admired Miss Libby's work, I gave her one of the artist's framed photographs for her birthday one year when I lived at the old Crockett homestead. See Harry Walker's write-up on Miss Libby on the Norway, Maine Historical Society website. Interesting People. "Miss Libby."

"George Richardson was found near the piano-key manufactory, at the Falls, his clothing soiled and blood discharging from his right ear. He was taken to the residence of Mr. C.W. Horne [his brother-in-law] and physicians summoned, but he died in a few minutes. An inquest was held. He was addicted to drinking, and it was thought by some that he might have fallen from the walk(way). His stomach contained quite a quantity of opium, as shown by the analysis of its contents, and there were other circumstances which could not be accounted for on the theory of death from an accidental fall. The coroner's jury were a long time in investigating the case, and then were unable to arrive at any satisfactory conclusion."[131]

The mystery of George Richardson's death—whether accidental or not—was never solved. Hannah, however, appears to have blamed her husband Thomas Hanford Richardson for their son's demise. (Thomas himself might have been addicted to opiates and alcohol, which is why Hannah had left him in the first place.) Any hope of reconciliation between Hannah and her husband evaporated after George's death. Instead, Hannah, who had been living a quiet and respectable life with her daughter Julia and son-in-law Chester Horne, threw off all concern for the Richardson name. She left the protection of her son-in-law, and—in a move that must have been exceedingly shocking and distressing for the entire family—took up residence with her cousin Benning Wentworth.[132]

Benning was the son of William Wentworth, a brother to Emma's grandmother Sally (Wentworth) Crockett. William had followed his uncle Benning Wentworth to Ohio (even though his father had remained in Danville). His son, named for uncle Benning, was born in Ohio in 1826.[133] Hannah's cousin Benning grew up in that state where, prior to the Civil War, he lived in Cincinnati and worked as a carpenter.[134] On July 30, 1861, Benning Wentworth enlisted in the 1st Illinois Light Artillery, Company C, and was mustered-in on December 31st.[135] During his nearly two years with the 1st Illinois Light Artillery, Benning was involved in some of the most dramatic engagements of the Civil War, including the Battle of Fredericktown, the capture of Fort Donelson, the Battle of Shiloh, Grant's Central

---
131. LAPHAM, p. 158.
132. See "The Wentworth Genealogy" (WENTWORTH), p. 304 and p. 634 for Hannah and Benning's family connection.
133. Information from U.S. Civil War Soldier Records and Profiles, 1861-1865. Benning Wentworth.
134. U.S. National Homes for Disabled Volunteer Soldiers, 1866-1938. Benning Wentworth.
135. U.S. Civil War Soldier Records and Profiles, 1861-1865. Benning Wentworth.

Mississippi Campaign, and much more.[136] He was mustered-out of the Union army on March 13, 1863, for injury and illness he suffered during the preceding winter.[137]

Benning, who was thirty-seven when he was discharged, was apparently unable to work after his time with the 1st Illinois. He lived on a small pension of $15 month, and from 1871-1877, was housed rent-free in a home for disabled soldiers in Dayton, Ohio.[138] For some reason, Benning was actuated to leave the rest home and move to Maine, where he found solace in the company of his cousin Hannah. Having grown up in the Midwest, Benning was not likely to have been personally acquainted with much of his family in Maine, including Hannah. Possibly their relationship blossomed via the U.S. Postal Service. One can envision a disabled soldier with time on his hands corresponding with a sympathetic female cousin, who herself might have been looking for a shoulder to cry upon.

On January 2, 1879, Hannah and Benning purchased a house together on School Street in Auburn. They likely were living together and renting the home prior to the purchase. The house was owned by Benning's brother Stephen Wentworth, who apparently was sympathetic and supportive of the relationship between his brother and cousin. Benning and Hannah paid Stephen $2300 for the residence.[139] They were not young star-crossed lovers when they made the purchase together (and a case could be made that they were not lovers at all). In 1879, Hannah was forty-seven and Benning was fifty-three. But the fact that Benning was an invalid, of whom Hannah might have been taking care, probably did not affect the light in which Hannah's family—especially her husband and children—regarded their cohabitation.

Six weeks after formally buying the house together on School Street, Benning Wentworth passed away. He apparently knew death was approaching because on February 14, 1879 (St. Valentine's Day), Benning made out a will. He left everything to Hannah, except for $1 each—an obvious thumbing of his nose—to his brothers Samuel and William. [140] (The $1 could also have been a lawyerly device to avoid later court cases where Samuel and/or William might have claimed that the dead

---

136. Webpage, National Park Service. The Civil War. Battle Unit Details. "Union Illinois Volunteers. 1st Regiment, Illinois Light Artillery."
137. U.S. Civil War Soldier Records and Profiles, 1861-1865. Benning Wentworth, and see also U.S. National Homes for Disabled Volunteer Soldiers, 1866-1938. Benning Wentworth.
138. U.S. National Homes for Disabled Volunteer Soldiers, 1866-1938. Benning Wentworth.
139. ACROD, Book 97, Page 124. Hannah mortgaged the property for $1500 the same day to a man named Jesse Davis of Lisbon. See ACROD, Book 96, Page 231.
140. Maine Wills and Probate Records, 1584-1999. Benning Wentworth.

man had some wish different than the actual stated one. We can guess that the brothers might have objected to Benning living with his married cousin and leaving Benning's share of the house to her.) Benning died two days later, on February 16, 1879.[141] In a further affront to *her* family, Hannah, as executrix of his estate, arranged for Benning's burial in Norway Pine Grove Cemetery. He was laid to rest in the plot next to that in which her parents (his aunt and uncle) Ephraim and Sally (Wentworth) Crockett had been reinterred just three years earlier. Hannah had purchased lot No. 16, in the 1st Range, Section 1, in 1877 following her son George's death.[142] Benning's placement in this highly visible front-row plot near George signaled to the world that Hannah's regard for him was more like that of a spouse than a cousin.

Without question, this indignity was too much for Hannah's husband to bear. Thomas Richardson finally petitioned for divorce in 1879. He told the judge sitting for the Supreme Judicial Court, Western District, that Hannah had left him in 1873; that he had tried to get her back for many years; that he had sent money for her support during this time; and that he had always been a true and faithful husband. Hannah was summoned to provide her side of the story, which summons she ignored. After weighing the evidence (one-sided though it was) the judge granted Thomas Richardson a divorce in December of 1879.[143] Hannah was now free to take up with whom she pleased, which she did with a second marriage to a man named Harris shortly thereafter.[144]

Since Hannah is no longer germane to our story in this generation, we will leave her in Auburn in 1879 prior to her second marriage. (Hannah's life is worth a book by itself!) The front-row resting spot in Norway Pine Grove Cemetery in which Benning was buried, also, ironically, became in 1896 the final resting spot for Thomas Hanford Richardson. Hannah joined them after her death in 1901.[145] Today, the six-person plot is only occupied by the four whose lives were engulfed in scandal and tragedy: George Richardson, Benning Wentworth, Thomas Hanford Richardson, and Hannah (Crockett) Richardson Harris. A casual observer reading

---

141. Maine Veteran Cemetery Records, 1676-1918. Benning Wentworth.
142. Norway Pine Grove Cemetery Record Book 1, Page 96. Hannah Richardson paid $25 for this six-person cemetery plot. In 2021, the author purchased perpetual care for this burial lot.
143. Records of the Maine Supreme Judicial Court, Docket No. 306, Volume 18, Page 419.
144. Finding herself in financial straits, Hannah married circa 1880 a man named Oscar A. Harris, about whom little is known. She divorced him in 1881. See Maine Divorce Records, 1798-1891. Hannah Harris, Plaintiff. Records of the Maine Supreme Judicial Court, Docket No. 171, Volume 23, Page 234.
145. Norway Pine Grove Cemetery Records. See Record Book 1, Page 96.

headstones in the cemetery today would have no inkling of the drama of their intertwined lives.[146]

Hannah Jordan (Crockett) Richardson Harris, circa 1895–1900
(Photo courtesy of Susan Allen Morgan.)

Considering these other family scandals, the fact that in 1880 Emma Crockett wanted to marry a divorced man must have seemed inconsequential by comparison. It need only be ensured that George P. Young was indeed legally divorced.

Taking a page out of Thomas Richardson's divorce from Hannah, George P. Young, on December 14, 1880, filed for a divorce from his first wife Mattie on grounds of abandonment (the same grounds with which she charged him in 1877). George noted in his filing that he and his former wife Martha "Mattie" W. Young (formerly, Martha W. Fuller) had not lived together since February of 1874; that he had tried to ascertain her whereabouts since then and failed; and that their marriage had already been set aside by the Supreme Judicial Court of Massachusetts. In the filing, George also gave his address as Auburn; however, if so, that was of a very recent date since in June when the census was taken, he resided in Norway. (The temporary move to Auburn[147] could have been to have the divorce heard in

---

146. In a little bit of further whitewashing, Hannah is buried next to her former husband, not Benning. The children inscribed "Mother" on her stone, and "Father" on Thomas Hanford Richardson's, making it seem (in death, anyway) as though the couple was happily married.
147. My research revealed that there was a possibility George's father, John C. Young, was living in the Lewiston-Auburn

Androscoggin County rather than Oxford County, where there might be unwanted publicity.) George's deposition of facts was sworn before Charles F. Whitman, who was then a practicing attorney and Justice of the Peace in Norway.[148] (Whitman later penned the 1924 classic, "A History of Norway, Maine.") Whitman, who was about the same age as George Young, might have shepherded him through the divorce process, although George had attorneys from Androscoggin County making his case for him. Charles Whitman was related to Emma Crockett by marriage,[149] and the families had always been close.[150]

George's divorce from Mattie was granted by the Maine Supreme Judicial Court in January of 1881.[151] He and Emma wasted no time. The couple was married April 3, 1881. The Crockett genealogy at the Norway, Maine Historical Society says Emma and George were married in Paris; however, Maine Marriage Records list Norway as the venue. Whichever town, given the fact that George was a divorced man, the marriage was likely not a church wedding, but rather was performed by a Justice of the Peace (maybe even Charles Whitman) or a minister in his home office.

Possible photo of Emma Tuell (Crockett) Young in her bridal veil.
This image was found taped to the inside of George P. Young's trunk. If it is indeed Emma, it is the only image the family has of Emma as a young woman.
(Photo courtesy of George W. Young, who is in possession of his great-grandfather's trunk.)

---

area at that time. See Lewiston City Directory for 1883, in which John C. Young is listed (without an occupation given, suggesting he was older) as residing on Spring Street. If that is George's father, he might have been living in Auburn in 1880 and his son just utilized his address.
148. Records of the Maine Supreme Judicial Court, Volume 18, Page 361-362.
149. Charles F. Whitman's wife was Mary A. Dinsmore, daughter of Ansel and Judith (Morse) Dinsmore. Judith, as the daughter of Nathan Morse and Mary Crockett, was great-aunt to Emma Crockett.
150. When I saw Charles Whitman's name on George P. Young's divorce papers, I became convinced that this man and Emma's future husband were one and the same person. Unless there had been a friendship and/or family connection of some sort between Whitman and Young, there would have been no reason why a Justice of the Peace from Norway would have taken a deposition from a man who supposedly resided in Auburn.
151. Records of the Maine Supreme Judicial Court, Volume 18, Page 361-362.

Life of the Newlyweds in Norway Village

The newlyweds probably started their life in a rental home in Norway Village, maybe even the house belonging to cousin Josiah. Not only was this house close to Emma's cousins, it was also within easy walking distance of the shoe shop where both George and Josiah were employed. One can almost visualize the two men walking arm and arm to work.

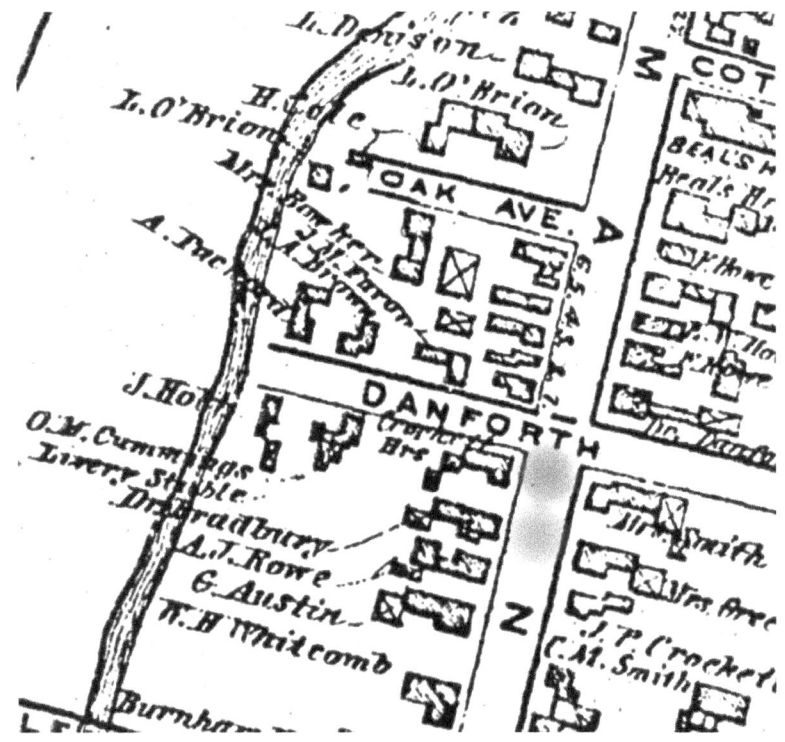

Close-up of an 1880 Norway Village map showing Danforth and Main Streets. The "Crockett heirs" (left of upper gray circle) inherited their home from their late elder brother John F. Crockett (killed in a railroad accident). Their house was next to the home of Dr. Osgood N. Bradbury (lower gray circle), a local physician, author of "Norway in the Forties," and friend of George Young's. Opposite (and just below) Bradbury's house was the rental property belonging to Josiah Crockett (who lived with his sisters). Josiah's house is possibly where Emma (Crockett) and George P. Young began their married career.
(Map courtesy of Norway, Maine Historical Society.)

Shockingly, on May 22, 1881—only six weeks after Emma and George were married—cousin Josiah Penley Crockett passed away. He was one month shy of his thirty-fourth birthday.[152] Josiah died in Marion, Indiana, where he was probably visiting his brothers Edgar and Warren, who worked for the railroad in that city. I have been unable to locate a death record for Josiah to determine whether his death was caused by accident or illness. Either way, Josiah knew he was dying. He made out a will the day before he passed, noting in that document that he was "of sound mind, but feeble in body." Josiah signed the will in the presence of his sister-in-law Lizzie (Allison) Crockett (Edgar's wife), and a man named James W. Harper.[153]

Sister Allie (the middle of the three sisters) was Executrix of brother Josiah's will. With a few exceptions Josiah left everything to his seven remaining siblings (as his brother John had done before him), including his real estate and investments. Notably, Josiah bequeathed Ella, Allie, and Louisa $1000 (over and above other proceeds from the will), to be paid from his $1500 Odd Fellows Relief Association life insurance policy. Josiah left his youngest brother Oscar his silver watch. To Edgar, he gave his gold chain, and to Warren he willed his three gold rings. (Abbie Jane seems to have received short shrift and is not mentioned specifically in the will, although she is one of the seven heirs.)[154] Josiah was buried with his parents, Ephraim Stanford Crockett and Sally (Penley) Crockett, and brother John, in Norway Pine Grove Cemetery.

Josiah's death left his three unmarried sisters—Ella, Allie, and Louisa—financially secure, yet without a male protector. Although sister Abbie Jane and her husband lived nearby, Charles Tubbs was probably not a candidate for a stand-in brother. The couple was having marital issues and the family had probably already heard about Charles' cruelty to Abbie Jane. Crockett heirs Edgar and Warren resided in Indiana, and youngest sibling, Oscar, was at school in Texas. (If Oscar came home for a while after Josiah's death, he did not remain in Norway.) As a result, George P. Young might have stepped forward to help fill the role of male adviser in the lives of the three spinsters.

Emma and George would still have been in mourning for Josiah, when, less than eight months later, Emma's mother was taken ill. Lydia (Stetson) Crockett passed away at the Crockett homestead on January 5, 1882 at the age of fifty-one. Emma had just turned twenty-three when her mother died. The cocoon of security that surrounded her eight years prior in the spring of 1874, had burst. Since then,

---

152. CANDAGE, p. 178.
153. Last will and testament, Josiah P. Crockett. Maine Wills and Probate Records, 1584-1999. Volume 19, page 462.
154. Last will and testament, Josiah P. Crockett. Maine Wills and Probate Records, 1584-1999. Volume 19, page 462.

Emma had lost her grandmother, her mother, uncle Ephraim Stanford Crockett, and cousins George Richardson and John and Josiah Crockett. Now, her father, William Robinson Crockett, was also gravely ill.

A Tipping Point for the Crockett Homestead

January 1882 was a tipping point for the future of the Crockett homestead. In 1880, Emma's older brother Abel, then thirty-one, was living with his wife Josephine (Knight) in Pownal (Maine).[155] Abel was a tenant farmer, renting someone else's land, probably awaiting the time when he could join his father at the Crockett homestead, as William had done with his father before him. But William not only had the Crockett homestead to consider, he also had to think about the welfare of his two minor daughters, Henrietta, "Etta," thirteen, and Lydia "Frances," seven. (William Robinson Crockett was also responsible for his granddaughter Ada Gerry, who was then living with the family.) When her parents had taken ill, Emma had likely moved home to care for everyone. She and her husband would have been an obvious choice as guardian of her minor siblings. In addition, William might also have considered the fact that, although his son-in-law was a shoe shop worker, George P. Young had grown up on a farm and his grandfathers had also been farmers.

One can almost imagine the touching scene of Emma and George summoned to the bedside of her dying father and charged with the care of Henrietta and Frances, as well as the Crockett homestead. On January 12, 1882, a week after his wife's death, William Robinson Crockett published his last will and testament, leaving the farm, including his real estate holdings and personal property, to Emma and her sisters. (See Appendix #13 for a copy of William Robinson Crockett's last will and testament.) To George and Emma, as co-executors of his estate, William consigned the care of Etta and Frances. He gave George and Emma complete control over his estate, writing, "…my executors hereinafter named shall have full power to manage the said real and personal estate for the benefit and use of the said Emma T. Young, Henrietta Crockett and Frances Crockett, as the said Executors may judge proper in the premises until the said Frances Crockett is twenty-one years of age, is married, or dies, when what remains of said real and personal estate shall be equally

---

155. 1880 U.S. Census, Pownal, Maine. Crockett, Abel and Josephine.

divided between my said daughters still alive."[156] Eleven days later William Robinson Crockett was dead, and Emma and her siblings were orphans.

George handled the burial arrangements, purchasing Lot 34 in Range 1, Section 1 in Norway Pine Grove Cemetery for his deceased in-laws. George paid the standard $25 fee for the six-grave burial plot, which was situated directly behind Lot 15, where Emma's grandparents, Ephraim. and Sally (Wentworth) Crockett were buried.[157] William's funeral would have been held in the parlor of the Crockett homestead, after which his corpse (and Lydia's) would have been stored in the family's ice house or taken by wagon (or sleigh) to Norway Pine Grove Cemetery for storage in a "receiving" vault until the ground thawed in the spring.

Emma's brother Abel was left $200 by his father, a poor consolation prize for one who must have expected to inherit the Crockett homestead. Abel took the money and with his wife Josephine moved (by way of Eau Claire, Wisconsin) to Duluth, Minnesota, where he began a new and much different life. Over the next few years Abel worked as a hostler, a porter for Twin City Packing Company, and a driver for Armour Package Company.[158]

Fair View Farm

One wonders how George P. Young must have felt to have been handed the reins of the Crockett homestead in his mid-thirties. Although his name was never on any of the real estate deeds, William's will, combined with George's male sex, would have accorded him most of the privileges of ownership and necessarily the responsibilities that accompanied that privilege.

Influenced in his youth by the lives of longtime gentlemen farmers in Gilmanton and Sandwich, New Hampshire, George's passion to become a gentleman farmer seems to have burst forth after the deaths of Emma's parents. Over the next nine years George transformed the Crockett homestead into Fair View Farm. (The act of naming one's farm became common in the latter part of the 19th century.)

---

156. Maine Wills and Probate Records, 1584-1999. William Robinson Crockett. Probated October 12, 1882. Oxford, Maine.
157. Record of deed to George P. Young from Jonathan Blake for Norway Pine Grove Cemetery Lot 34, Range 1, Section 1. NPG Record Book 1, Page 139.
158. The Wisconsin State Census for 1885 shows A.S. Crockett in Eau Claire with an unnamed female, most likely his wife Josephine. The 1889 Duluth, Minnesota directory lists Abel S. Crockett as a hostler working for H.C. Kendall, with a residence at 1205 Piedmont Avenue. The 1889-90 Duluth directory lists Abel as a porter with Twin City Packing Co (same address as before); and the 1893 city directory has Abel as a driver for Armour Package Co., at 1205 W. Michigan, which suggests a street name change rather than a change of abode.

George began raising standardbred horses, registered Jersey cattle, and Ohio Improved Chester pigs. Fair View also boasted purebred Plymouth Rock fowl and trotting-bred stallions "for service."

 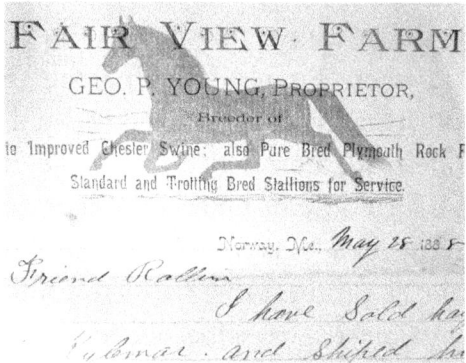

Envelope and letterhead from Fair View Farm, Geo. P. Young, Proprietor.[159]
(Photos by Jennifer Wixson. Letter and envelope courtesy of George W. Young.)

George's improvements and additions to stock, however, cost money. After the Civil War, few gentlemen farmers remained in New England who could pay the bills simply from farming alone. As a result, George continued to work at B.F. Spinney & Co. while Emma ran the household and cared for the chickens and milk cows, with her younger sisters to help her. George hired a hand to help on the farm, but the hand had to be paid, as well.[160] Twice a day and in all seasons (unless forced to stay overnight in Norway due to inclement weather), George commuted the four miles to and from the shoe factory. (In his obituary the burden of commuting and paying livery fees on his steed is described as a way to "exercise the different young horses he kept on his farm.") At one point, George had been the supervisor of the cutting room;[161] however, after taking over the farm, he appears to have given up this additional responsibility, and one assumes the extra pay that accompanied it.

On August 18, 1883, Emma sold to neighbor William Knight her father's one-half undivided interest in the southwest corner of Lot 40 (see map in beginning of chapter), one of the parcels off the Needham Road.[162] Knight and Emma's father

---

159. This letter, now in the possession of my cousin George W. Young, was penned May 28, 1888, by George P. Young. The letter was to Rollin Stetson, Emma's cousin, and son of Abel Stetson and Adeline (Howe) Stetson.
160. The fact that George had a hired hand at the farm came from the article about his death, "Fatal Accident," published in a local newspaper.
161. This information came from George's obituary.
162. OCROD, Book 204, Page 392.

had purchased this woodlot to work together in 1864. Knight paid $325 for his late partner's share. This money gave George additional capital to use on the farm.

On January 24, 1884, Emma's cousin Oscar Rufus Crockett passed away in San Antonio, Texas. (A 1901 death notice for his sister Allie says Oscar died in Florida.) Oscar, the youngest of the Crockett heirs, was only twenty-six years old when he died, just one year older than Emma. Oscar was a fledgling writer and some of his work had been published in *The Cherokee Advance*, a small newspaper in Canton, Georgia, a community of about six hundred souls.[163] Canton was located about twenty miles from Marietta, a "noted summer and winter resort,"[164] which Oscar might have visited for his health. On March 6, 1884, *The Cherokee Advance* published a notice of his death:

> "We are pained to learn of the death of Oscar R. Crockett in San Antonio, Texas, last November.[165] He was well known to many of our readers and respected by them as an upright and honerable [sic] young man. Among us he made many warm and faithful friends who will hear of his death with profound sadness."[166]

An Heir Is Born

Good news finally arrived in the extended family in the spring of 1884. On May 14, 1884, Emma gave birth to her and George's first (and only living) child, William Foss Young. (The Crockett genealogy at the Norway, Maine Historical Society notes that the couple lost a child, but does not give a date.) "Willie," as the newcomer was known in childhood,[167] was likely named for his grandfather, William Robinson Crockett of Norway (with a possible nod to his great-grandfather,

---

163. *The Cherokee Advance*, published on Fridays, was only four, 24"X36" pages. Rowell's American Newspaper Directory, 1887, p. 126. Printer's Ink Publishing Company. George Presbury Rowell, Editor. Rowell noted the community had a population of about six hundred.
164. Rowell's American Newspaper Directory. Printer's Ink Publishing Company, 1887, p. 131. George Presbury Rowell, Editor.
165. Oscar passed away in January of 1884, not November of 1883.
166. *The Cherokee Advance*, March 6, 1884, p. 2. *The Cherokee Advance* included with Oscar's death notice an extract from his obituary in *The Oxford County Advertiser*: "Mr. Crockett was a young man of very active mind, of ready scholarship and ability as a writer, and of a cheerful temperament; a general favorite both in his native place and at school, where he was familiarly spoken of as 'Oscar' by the entire school of two hundred scholars. His natural vivacity and quickness of perception gave promise of much future usefulness, if his life had been spared. He was a young man of thoroughly moral character, and though never having made any outward profession of religion, yet a schoolmate speaks of receiving letters from him breathing a tender thoughtfulness on the subject."
167. This information came from the probate record of the will of George P. Young, in which the deceased's minor child is listed as "Willie F. Young."

George's grandfather, William Vittum of Sandwich). The origin of Willie's middle name "Foss" is a mystery.[168] With two aunts, Henrietta, now sixteen, and Frances, ten, to fuss over the new baby, as well as a doting mother—"Mamie,"[169] as Emma came to be known—we can be sure that the child was spoiled.

During the holiday season of 1884, the celebration continued when Emma's cousin Sarah (Penley) Farnham (Isaiah and Mary Amanda Crockett Penley's daughter) and her husband Albert P. Farnham, threw open their new house for a neighborhood Christmas party. Farnham, a prosperous former carpenter who had been wounded in the Civil War,[170] had purchased the Tongue property from the Crockett heirs, and, the dwelling having burned years earlier, had built a new home on the land for his family. The Youngs would have bundled themselves into their sled or walked down to join the party, which Norway historian and lawyer Charles F. Whitman attended. Whitman wrote about the gathering for *The Oxford County Advertiser* in "Christmas Eve in School District No. 8," published January 2, 1885. The article captures the camaraderie and festive spirit of the evening:

> "…we arrived there in due time, found a goodly company already assembled, and were allowed a peep at the huge Christmas tree, loaded with gifts for the crowd. The neighborhood was well represented. After a time our ears were gladdened by the call, 'supper is ready.' Our end of the table was well represented there being Messrs D.P.M. and your humble servant, 'good feeders all.' When we looked at the table groaning under its weight of eatables, pork & beans, white and brown bread, golden butter, pastry, and cake of all kinds, frosted and unfrosted doughnuts, tea and coffee, etc., etc., we sighed and regretted our foolishness in having eaten a dinner. You ought to have seen us go for the frosted custard pie… Everything comes to an end, including our appetites. The Christmas gifts were distributed, 'making glad the hearts of many.' We then go in for the rollicking, frolicking games of chase the squirrel,[171] hunt the thimble,[172] Jacob and Ruth,

---

168. Because Foss is a Scandinavian last name and there were many Norwegian families who settled in Oxford County, it is possible this was a compliment to a local friend. Had Bill Young's birth been a decade later, I would have suspected his middle name was a nod to Samuel Walter Foss, the beloved New Hampshire poet and author of "The House by the Side of the Road," a framed print of which hung in the Crockett homestead when I lived with my grandmother.
169. I gleaned this information from my mother's cousin Norman Young, who was given (probably by his grandmother Addie Young, Bill Young's wife) "6 silver spoons with 'Y' on them … a piece of Mamie's." I also recollect that my grandmother herself once or twice mentioned that Emma (Crockett) Young was called "Mamie" by her son and his wife, although (much as one would expect) Winona referred to her grandmother as "Grammie Harding."
170. This information came from the newspaper article, "Christmas Eve in School District No. 8, etc." penned by Charles F. Whitman, published by *The Oxford County Advertiser*, January 2, 1885, p. 3.
171. "Chase the squirrel" was a "play party" reel for a minimum of three couples during which the male dancer must (after other parts of the dance are completed) chase his female partner down through the center aisle and around the back of other dancers until he catches and kisses her. Webpage, Bluegrassmessengers.com. Bluegrass and Lyrics. "Chase the Squirrel."
172. "Hunt the thimble" was a popular 19th century parlor game in which a thimble was hidden in the parlor or other room

throwing the handkerchief,[173] etc. ... The 'most unkind cut of all' was when the ladies (bless their hearts) tried to induce us to eat a second supper, that was the 'feather that broke the camel's back,' for there is a limit to human endurance. We unanimously voted it the best time of the season & departed for our respective homes contented and happy."

Thanks to Charles Whitman and his articles for the *Advertiser*, we know more about the lives of those on Crockett's Ridge during the mid-1880s than any other period in our history to date. Whitman, who once taught at the local schoolhouse, probably still lived in the neighborhood (although not still boarding around). He might have been Supervisor of Schools at the time, one of the many hats he wore throughout his life.[174] Whitman's stories lift the veil of history that separates the living from the dead, enabling us not only to learn more about our family, but also to feel as though we ourselves are present at their gatherings. On February 20, 1885, Whitman published an account of the birthday celebration held for Emma's younger cousin True Penley. The party was held about a month prior to the young man's actual birthday[175] at his father's home (which was owned by Isaiah Vickery Penley's son-in-law Albert Farnham). Whitman writes:

> "On Friday evening a goodly company of us, 'with buxom dames and maidens fair,' assembled at an early hour at the house of I.V. Penley to celebrate the birthday of his son, True. We went there for a jolly good time and were not disappointed. One venerable friend, E.M., was present as a spectator. He seemed to enjoy himself in watching us 'trip the light fantastic, toe through the maze dance,'[176] regretting no doubt, that he had neglected learning that important art

where the party was held. Guests would later be asked to find the thimble, with a cash prize or bragging rights going to the winner. The only rule of the game was that the thimble could not be hidden inside or under anything, but must be hidden "in plain sight." YouTube, History Bytes: "Hunt the Thimble, a parlor game from the 19th century."
173. Another popular Victorian parlor game in which a player sitting in the center of a circle throws his folded handkerchief to one of those sitting around him (often, someone of whom he is enamored). She throws the handkerchief to others in the circle and he must attempt to reclaim it from one of them. This information came from a footnote in "The Selected Works of Margaret Oliphant." Part VI, Volume 24. Footnote #24, p. 379.
174. In his Norway history, Whitman mentions himself in Chapter XXXIV, "Norway Lawyers." He writes: "Charles F. Whitman was born in Buckfield, February 6, 1848. He married M. Addie Dinsmore [Judith Morse and Ansel Dinsmore's daughter] of Norway. Fitted for college at Hebron Academy and Bates Latin School Lewiston; taught school, read law in office of Sullivan C. Andrews; admitted to practice in 1868. Settled first at Mechanic Falls in 1869. Removed to Buckfield in 1871. Settled in Norway in 1873. School Supervisor, Trial Justice, first Judge of the Norway Municipal Court, 10 years, Clerk of the Courts for 20 years, memorial speaker, originator of Norway Public Library and Municipal Court. Story and local history writer; one of the authors of the Buckfield History and author of this work.
175. True Penley's birthday was March 27th. It was possibly celebrated early because of the weather and the stage of the moon, i.e. a full moon (for traveling at night).
176. "Trip the light fantastic" and "buxom dames and ladies fair" are probably references to John Milton's 1645 poem, "L'Allegro." "Buxom dames" is self-explanatory. "Trip the light fantastic" means to dance lightly or nimbly on one's feet to music. "Clichés: Over 1500 Phrases Explored and Explained." Betty Kirkpatrick and Elizabeth McLaren Kirkpatrick. "Light

in his younger days. Isaiah is good on racket, but thinks he is too old[177] to dance; his 'better half' [Emma's aunt, Mary Amanda Crockett Penley] is always in for a good time."[178]

One can also glean important clues in Whitman's stories, such as the fact that George Young might have been musically-inclined. In "A Birthday Jollification in School District No. 8," Whitman also comments: "As was said before, we had a goodly company, and a jolly one too. We did not have Young's Orchestra, but we did have [local fiddle player] Mellie[179] [Dunham]…"[180] The designation "Young's Orchestra" was probably Whitman's tongue-in-cheek way of describing the George P. Young family, which would have included George, Emma, and her younger sisters Henrietta and Frances Crockett (who appear to have missed this party).[181] The family might have regularly sung together, accompanied by Emma on the piano. (Emma's piano was a fixture in the parlor of the old Crockett homestead when I lived with my grandmother.)[182] George Young himself might have played the violin or other musical instrument.

On July 4, 1885, the Youngs would have been part of those from the Crockett's Ridge neighborhood who celebrated Independence Day "in goodly numbers on the shore of our beautiful Pennesseewassee Lake." Emma was likely one of the "ladies of our circle" who arranged the event, of which Whitman recounts in his story, "Social Circle Picnic in School District No. 8:"[183]

---

fantastic," p. 115. New York: Macmillan, 1999.
177. Isaiah Vickery Penley was just shy of his 58th birthday during this party for his son. His wife Mary Amanda (Crockett) was 51, and obviously still young at heart.
178. "A Birthday Jollification in School District No. 8, by 'One of Them'." Published in *The Oxford County Advertiser*, February 20, 1885, page 3.
179. Mellie Dunham, who played the violin for local dances, such as this party at Isaiah V. Penley's home, later became famous nationally after playing for Henry Ford at his home in Dearborn, Michigan. ("Melody Three." *Time* magazine, December 21, 1925.) Dunham was also a noted Norway snowshoe maker, who fashioned the snowshoes for the artic expedition of Commodore Robert Peary. ("Mellie Dunham making snowshoes, ca. 1925." *Maine Memory Network*, Maine Historical Society.) Mellie was married to Emma (Richardson) Dunham. "Gram" (as she was known) was not related to T.H. Richardson, but rather was the daughter of Calvin Richardson and his wife Calista Churchill. Calvin was a descendent of the Richardsons of Richardson Hollow in Greenwood. When playing for local dances, Gram usually accompanied Mellie on the piano. The couple was still fondly recollected by old-timers in the 1970s and early 1980s when I lived with my grandmother at the Crockett homestead.
180. "A Birthday Jollification in School District No. 8" was published in *The Oxford County Advertiser* on February 20, 1885, p. 3.
181. It is striking (to me, anyway) that Charles Whitman, in his history of Norway, makes little mention of George Young, a man he knew well. Whitman notes only that George was Emma's first husband and records his death date and nothing further. (By contrast, Dr. Osgood Bradbury mentions George and his death in one of his articles, calling him a "good friend.") To me this suggests that Whitman either wanted to spare the family pain by not mentioning George (and the unusual circumstances of his death) or that his opinion of George had diminished by the time of Young's passing.
182. After Winona's death, my mother Rowena Palmer moved the piano up to her house, where the tradition of singing around the piano continued with her grandchildren. The piano remains in my late mother's house today.
183. "Social Circle Picnic in School District No. 8" was published in *The Oxford County Advertiser*, July 10, 1885, p. 3.

"We had no table. Mother Earth however furnished us with a good solid foundation, the cloths were soon spread on the grass, and were soon covered with eatables. In the mean time the materials were collected and prepared for a fish chowder…Our company was composed of comely matrons, fat widows, and lads and lassies too. Not being able to procure a bill of fare, the outside world will forever remain in ignorance of the variety of courses. Of course we had something to drink. Start not, Maine law man, the services of Sheriff Bassett will not be required; it was only coffee, lemonade and Adam's ale[184]—not the three X.[185] In memory of the occasion we fired a salute. Then followed the reading of the Declaration of Independence, followed by the singing of patriotic songs, waking up the beautiful echoes which reverberated from shore to shore.

Such songs have power to quiet
The restless power of care
And come like the benediction
That follows after prayer."[186]

The Purchase of the John Penley Farm and the Shoe Factory Is Threatened with Closure

The summer of the 4th of July party on the lakeshore, George and Emma made a real estate purchase that would dramatically affect their future lives (as well as the lives of their descendants). On June 24, 1885, they purchased the John Penley farm from Emma's cousin Abbie Jane (Crockett) Tubbs.[187] (See Appendix #15 for a copy of this deed.) Why the couple, already burdened with the care and maintenance of the Crockett homestead (then, Fair View Farm) would want to go into debt to increase their real estate holdings is unclear. Perhaps George felt that he needed additional land for the expansion of Fair View Farm (he might have needed more pasture for his horses) or maybe Emma's fond memories of her time with her cousins next door precipitated the purchase. Abbie Jane might also have approached the couple, espying an opportunity to sell the place, yet keep it in the family.

Emma and George agreed to pay Abbie Jane (who had bought out her younger brothers and sisters) $700 for the John Penley farm, with Emma's cousin taking a mortgage for the entire amount. The mortgage, to be paid in the amount of $100

---
184. Water.
185. "XXX" was a label used to denote that something was poisonous.
186. A stanza from the poem, "The Day Is Done," by Maine poet Henry Wadsworth Longfellow.
187. OCROD, Book 209, Page 351.

per year (beginning in 1886) for seven years at 6% interest, was not just placed upon the John Penley farm, however. Emma and George also mortgaged the Crockett homestead![188] Because the mortgage was for the entire $700 with no money down, Abbie Jane, who appears to have been a shrewd businesswoman, must have insisted that it also include the higher-value property. This meant that if George did not make the annual payment, Abbie Jane would have the right to foreclose on their family home—the original Crockett homestead. That her cousin had the power to foreclose on her home (if the payments were not made) likely never occurred to Emma, but certainly both George and Abbie Jane would have understood the ramifications of the deal.

About a month after George and Emma mortgaged their home, B.F. Spinney & Co., threatened to pull its operation out of town and return all business to Lynn, Massachusetts. The company, which was playing hardball with its employees, blamed the impending closure of the Maine shoe shop upon "threatened interference by labor organizations with the business at Norway."[189] (Ironically, it had been similar labor organizing issues at the Lynn factory that precipitated the building of the Norway shoe shop in the first place.) Hundreds of B.F. Spinney employees, including George Young, might lose their jobs. This news would have thrown the Young household into anxiety and distress, especially George, who was sole provider for a bevy of dependents: Emma, Henrietta (now seventeen), Frances (eleven), and baby Willie. Regular income, a staple that the family had taken for granted and depended upon, might evaporate.

The closing of the shoe factory in Norway would also wreak financial havoc on the small community. The town would be unable to replace that volume of jobs nor was it possible to cushion the collateral damage from the job losses. Local businesses, rental properties, groceries, and service providers would all be devastated. A Town Meeting was called to deliberate the situation, and in a Resolve voted upon August 1, 1885, citizens begged the company to give Norway a hearing to see if something could be done to rescue the shoe factory:

> "We, the citizens of the town of Norway here assembled, learn with regret that B.F. Spinney & Co., Shoe Manufacturers, contemplate moving their business from this town, in consequence of a Lasters' Union being formed, thereby con-

---

188. OCROD, Book 206, Page 265.
189. LAPHAM, p. 395.

trolling prices of work to such an extent as to destroy all advantages gained by manufacturing shoes here in Norway, therefore be it

"*Resolved*, that we tender to B.F. Spinney & Co. our thanks for the many acts of kindness, and laborious exertions by himself, and others connected with the firm, in doing what was intended to make a success of shoe manufacturing in the town. While regretting exceedingly the movement of forming any organization, having in view the object of dictation, we, the citizens and property holders, would respectfully request (if not now too late) that we may be allowed a hearing, in this matter, to see if some arrangement cannot be made, satisfactory to all parties whereby the business can be continued to run as successfully and harmoniously as for the last twelve years..."[190]

Committee members appointed by the town signed the Resolve to rescue the shoe factory and included John L. Horne, Ansel Dinsmore, and Freeland Howe, who had been on the committee to lure B.F. Spinney & Co. to Norway in 1872. A week after the resolution was sent, on August 7, 1885, B. F. Spinney himself responded to the communication:

"We thank the people of your town for the kind spirit of the resolution and assure you that our wish is to keep in mind the interests of the town so far as we can do so without definite injury to ourselves. The present situation of affairs is serious. Without doubt the labor question will assume formidable proportions during the next year or two and how to meet the issue most wisely is now our most important thought. We located a portion of our business in Norway solely with the object of protection. The writer has always assumed and still believes that the business of the firm would have been more profitable conducted in Lynn under one organization, than separated as it has been. The sense of safety however has been the controlling motive in keeping us with you. That element being eliminated our best judgment leads us to believe that remaining in Norway simply accumulates difficulties at no corresponding increase of economy in the management of our business. The writer will be glad to confer with your Committee as suggested in your vote at any convenient season."[191]

The committee met with representatives of the firm, which ultimately proposed a unique solution—move the entire business to Norway! B.F. Spinney would close the Lynn factory and set up altogether in Norway, *if* the town would provide the

---
190. LAPHAM, p. 395.
191. LAPHAM, p. 395-396.

shoe manufacturer "another building of sufficient capacity to accommodate it."[192] The citizens of Norway "in a large and enthusiastic meeting" decided "without a dissenting voice" to build a huge new factory building, "two hundred by sixty feet in size, and three stories high."[193] The building was to be leased to B.F. Spinney & Co. for 5% of the building cost per year. The company also agree to pay the insurance premiums and keep the building in good repair. (The initial lease was for a period of five years.)

The relief in the Young household upon learning that B.F. Spinney & Co. was not closing, but rather going to relocate its entire operation to Norway, must have been tremendous. George was not going to lose his job! When in November a horse race between True Penley, Dastine Turner, and another young man was proposed, George might even have felt comfortable enough to wager a small bet on Emma's cousin. (If so, George lost his bet, because True lost the race.)[194]

On January 2, 1886, the Norway Shoe Shop Company, with John L. Horne as the company's President, began issuing $25 stock shares for the new building.[195] According to historian Lapham, "The business men of Norway subscribed liberally, and very soon the building was assured."[196] By November 1886, the building was so far along that the machinery was moved in. The new building was called the "Big Shop" to distinguish it from the "Little Shop," the original building leased to B.F. Spinney & Co.

---

192. LAPHAM, p. 396.
193. LAPHAM, p. 396.
194. "After running their horses the whole length of the plains, Turner licked out the other fellow and the Norway chap." *Oxford Democrat*, Nov. 10, 1885. The "Norway chap" was True Penley.
195. LAPHAM, p. 396. See also the copy of the first two Norway Shoe Shop Company stock shares issued January 2, 1886. Company Treasurer was H.D. Smith, who along with Horne signed the stock certificates.
196. LAPHAM, p. 396.

First two shares of the Norway Shoe Shop Company stock issued
January 2, 1886, to E.G. Allen.
Mr. Allen purchased two shares—$25 each—for $50.
(Photo courtesy of Stuart Goodwin.)

Colorized postcard, "B.F. Spinney & Co., Shoe Factory, Norway, Me."
(Pub. by Frank Kimball, Norway, Me. Printed in Germany.)

Norway's Centennial

The year 1886 also marked the Centennial of the town of Norway's settlement. On September 8th residents celebrated the "glorious occasion" with the firing of cannons and ringing of the bells. Emma would have hustled the family together early that morning because George was one of the three-member committee in charge of the huge procession.[197] The parade began in Norway Village at nine o'clock and was so large (nearly a mile and a half long, according to Lapham) that it necessitated five streets to line up before proceeding down a thronged Main Street, after which the procession circled throughout the town. George P. Young, in I.O.O.F. Encampment regalia, also participated in the procession (see George's photo opposite). Many local businesses, including B.F. Spinney & Co., prepared floats for the parade; however, the "biggest display was made by Mr. C.B. Cummings, who exhibited six teams, representing the various kinds of business in which he is engaged—saw-mill, 'pancake' or ground leather factory, flour, feed, and boxes."[198] Norway businesses and homes—including probably the home of Emma's cousins, Ella, Allie and Louisa Crockett—were awash with red, white and blue buntings, streamers and flags; some were even decorated with Japanese lanterns.[199] Emma and George (and family) might have attended the literary exercises held at Ordway Grove, and most certainly would have attended the dinner at the Norway Concert Hall, an "immense affair" where the "tables were bountifully spread and the great multitude ate and were satisfied."[200] At the dinner George would have been pleased to hear—in the Original Ode composed by Mrs. Elliot Smith (sung to the tune of "Old Hundredth," the Doxology in many Christian churches)[201]—that that a "trotting park" on "our eastern bound" was mentioned as one of the town's highlights.[202]

---

197. LAPHAM, p. 444. The other two members of the Centennial Procession Committee were William C. Cole and W.H. Tracy.
198. LAPHAM, p. 409.
199. LAPHAM, p. 407.
200. LAPHAM, p. 427.
201. Taking its name from Psalm 100, "Old Hundredth" or *All People that on Earth do Dwell*, is probably the best-known Christian hymn in the world. In most hymnals, the tune is attributed to the French composer Louis Bourgeois, around 1552. The tune is also used for the Common (Christian) Doxology, "Praise God, From Whom All Blessings Flow."
202. LAPHAM, p. 432.

Emma Tuell (Crockett) Young Harding – Last Crockett Standing

George P. Young in his International Order of Odd Fellows Encampment regalia.[203]
The crossed shepherd's hooks on his cuffs and sash represent an Encampment member's duty to watch their flock, and protect and defend them. This photo might have been taken on September 8, 1886, during the town of Norway's Centennial Celebration.
(Family photo, courtesy of Yvette Young.)

---

203. The sash and cuffs—with the shepherd's hooks—clearly indicate that George is an Encampment member, and not a member of the uniformed branch of IOOF, the Patriarch's Militant. Had George moved up to become a Patriarch Militant, he would have been wearing a complete uniform, which insignia would have been that of a crossed shepherd's hook and sword. The fact that George is wearing a sword is confusing, though, since only Patriarch Militant members carried them. Possibly, when this photo was taken, George was in the process of moving up to Patriarch's Militant and had only received his sword, not his uniform.

In 1887, a celebration of another sort occurred when Emma's sister, eighteen-year-old Henrietta "Etta" Crockett, married Frank G. Hobbs, a shoe worker from Massachusetts. Hobbs, who was about twenty-two when the couple was married, was likely employed by B.F. Spinney & Co. prior to relocating with his new bride to Portsmouth. New Hampshire had a booming shoe industry that nearly rivaled that of neighboring Massachusetts. By 1879, the "total value of boots, shoes, harness and finished leather [in New Hampshire] was $10,226,000," which was said to have been the value of the entire hay and grain crop in New Hampshire for the same year.[204]

Whether Etta, who had inherited one-sixth of the Crockett homestead from her father (as well as one-sixth of his personal property) received any money when she left the family nest, is not known. Her claim to the estate could not legally be effected until the youngest, Frances, then thirteen, reached the age of twenty-one. Nor was Etta likely to force her sister to sell real estate that was currently in use. As co-executor of his father-in-law's estate, however, George Young must have been acutely aware of the financial claim upon Fair View Farm that both Etta and Frances possessed.

That March a permanent addition to the Crockett's Ridge neighborhood occurred when Emma's cousin Charles Sewell Penley and his wife Lizzie (Frost) Penley [205] moved into the Knight place (the property to the north of the John Penley farm). Charles Sewell, a teamster in 1880, was something of a character in Norway, according to stories later published by Charles Whitman. It is possible that prior to this purchase Lizzie and Charles were renting the John Penley farm (where he had grown up) from George and Emma. Although built around the same time as the John Penley house, the Knight place was a larger and better farm. (When my mother was growing up this homestead was known as the Burgess Orre farm—the Bobbie Orrie farm in my day—currently owned by Pam and Errol Libby.) Charles and Lizzie had no children of their own, and, as Charles was known to be a friendly, affable fellow, he probably frequently visited the George Young family, as well as

---

204. "Shoe Industry in New Hampshire." W.B. Grover. *Yankee* magazine, November 8, 2018.
205. Charles wife Sarah Elizabeth "Lizzie" Frost purchased the property from William Knight's widow Sarah, for $1000. Lizzie mortgaged the entire amount to Sarah, which mortgage would be considered paid in full if Lizzie cared for the older woman at the homestead for the rest of her natural days. See OCROD Book 210, Page 217, and Book 214, Page 217. Charles Sewell Penley was the only surviving son (his brother Rufus having perished in the Civil War) of Betsey (Crockett) Penley and John Penley, Jr.

his uncle Isaiah and aunt Mary (Crockett) Penley further down the hill on the former Nathan Morse property.

The only letters of George P. Young's that the family has are dated from this period of his life. The two letters, penned by George in 1888, were written to Emma's cousin Rollin Stetson. Rollin was the son of Abel Stetson (Lydia Stetson Crockett's brother, who was named for their father) and Adeline (Howe) Stetson.[206] When the letters were written, twenty-year-old Rollin was still living with his parents on Elm Ridge Farm in West Sumner. George, who was forty-three, appears to have been a mentor to the youth, perhaps in the same way he had mentored his two younger brothers. His letters contain a certain amount of masculine bawdiness that would have been appreciated by Rollin, but probably precluded them from being read aloud around the dinner table. (Emma naturally would have written her own letters to her Stetson relatives, which would be shared at the dinner table.) On May 28, 1888, George wrote:

"Friend Rollin

I have sold half of Kylemar[207] [one of his studs] and shipped him to Day to So. Abbington, Mass. to be given some track work to fit him for the Fall races. How is the old Mare? Buttoned up yet?[208]

The Heifer has begun her Hellish career sucking again but she is so good a cow that Em says she won't sell her. She is agoing to try her a week to see how much she will make.

Redemption [George's standardbred trotter] has had quite a bad leg on him but it is getting all right now. He has got to take all of the work now Kylemar is gone. How is all of the Girls down to Buckfield?

Hopeing to hear from you soon. I am yours Truly

G. P. Young"

Rollin appears to have returned a quick reply to George's letter. Shortly thereafter George followed the younger man's note up with another missive of his own,

---

206. The letters were probably returned to Emma after George's death. She must have packed them away in her husband's trunk with his wallet, Odd Fellow's hat, and other items, thus the letters survived the unfortunate purge of family correspondence stored at the Crockett homestead that occurred after my grandmother's death.
207. The name "Kylemar" identifies the ancestry of George's standardbred. In the Maine Colt Stakes held in Lewiston in April of 1889, E.C. Douglas entered a bay horse, Ned D., "Sire Kylemar by Prescott; dam Lady Redwood by Redwood." This horse was a foal in 1888 and thus not the trotter mentioned in George P. Young's letter. "Maine Colt Stakes – List of the Youngsters which will Trot at Lewiston." *Portland Daily Press*, April 17, 1889.
208. "Bred yet?"

this one almost exclusively about horses (revealing, perhaps, the extent to which horse breeding and harness racing had taken over his life). On June 6, 1888, George wrote the following (to which I have added some punctuation and explanatory notes for clarity):

> "Friend Rollin
>   Yours received. Am glad the old Mare can keep her tail down.[209] Hope it will stay that way.
>   You did not say whether Stet's Mare had Folded or not.[210]
>   You may tell Porlin if he will Put them both you will let him have them for $40.[211] I find the rest [of the horse breeders] are takeing of[f] 5 whare they get 2 good ones from the same place and want to beat somebody else. Get them if you can away from Barrett if you have got the pr. $35.[212]
>   Perhaps Em will be induced to take $40 for the Heifer when you come down. I don't know. She is a good one.
>   You had aught to of Bought her last Fall. How is Gust? Is he agoing to Put his Mare?
>   Run down when you get your work done.
>   Give my regards to all the Girls.[213]
>
> Yours Truly,
> G.P. Young"

In May of 1887, Abbie Jane, in a move that probably did not surprise Emma (or anyone else in the family), sued her husband of fourteen years, Charles N. Tubbs, for divorce. Abbie Jane sought relief from her marriage on the grounds of "cruel and abusive behavior," claiming Charles "frequently struck her, knocked her down and dragged her about the house by the hair." His treatment of her had continued for "a series of years until it has seriously impaired her health." In addition, Abbie Jane declared that Charles "had neglected to provide her with reasonable maintenance" despite having "sufficient ability to do so," being worth between $30,000-$40,000. She asked the Supreme Judicial Court for the custody of the couple's four minor children,

---

209. This turn of phrase probably signifies that the mare was successfully bred.
210. Foaled.
211. To "put a mare" is to breed the horse, i.e. "put a mare in foal." George might be suggesting that he would let Porlin breed his two mares to George's horse for $40 in stud fees. (Rollin appears to have one of George's studs at the farm.)
212. George seems to suggest that, since other horse breeders are giving a $5 discount, he could also take $35, if Rollin could get the price.
213. Rollin Stetson apparently did like "the girls." He was married four times. His first wife Addie died of typhoid fever; his second wife, Elva, died of Pluritis (inflammation of the plurea in the lungs); and his third wife, Belle, died of TB. His fourth wife, Ursula, outlived Rollin.

child support, and $10,000 in alimony. Charles made a counter-offer to Abbie Jane's proposal, and the divorce dragged on for sixteen months until the sparring couple, with the aid of the Court and various lawyers, finally negotiated a settlement. In that settlement, three of the four children (Inez, age twelve; Idonia, six; and Oscar, two) were to live with their mother, eldest son James, eight, was to live with his father (although both parents had the right to see all their children); all children must continue to reside in Norway; and Charles was to pay Abbie Jane a lump sum of $4200 in lieu of alimony (at which time she would release her dower rights on his properties).[214]

Abbie Jane's divorce became absolute on September 11, 1888.[215] She moved into her own home on Main Street, taking three of her four children with her.[216] No mention of child support is made in the final settlement, so Abbie was probably financially responsible for the children under her care (as Charles was for son James). The regular $100 per year plus interest paid to Abbie Jane by George P. Young (for the purchase of the John Penley farm) would now be more important to this single mother than ever before. By the fall of 1888, George was supposed to have made his third of the seven $100 payments to Abbie Jane. Whether he made that payment or not remains to be seen.

Compounding Troubles for George

On August 22, 1888, George's younger brother Charles passed away in Haverhill, Massachusetts, where Charles had lived many years.[217] Like George, Charles was a shoe cutter. (His death certificate lists him as a "laborer," but he likely labored in a shoe shop.) The cause of Charles' death was the lingering infectious disease consumption (tuberculosis), which disease was common in shoe shops in the 19th century.[218] Charles was only thirty-six (seven years younger than George), when he passed away. He was the second of George's three younger siblings to die, and his death must have hit George hard.

---

214. Abbie J. Tubbs v. C.N. Tubbs. Maine Superior Judicial Court, Oxford County. Docket #201, Court SJC, Vol. 22, Page 93. Information about the ages of the Tubbs children came from CANDAGE, p. 177-178.
215. IBID.
216. OCROD, Book 221, Page 223.
217. Massachusetts Death Records, 1841-1915. Charles A. Young.
218. Jan Ernst Matzlieger, who invented the lasting machine, began working in a shoe shop in 1877 at age twenty-five. Twelve years later, like many other shoe shop workers (including George Young's brother Charles), he died of tuberculosis at age thirty-seven. Webpage, Lemelson-MIT. Jan Matzlieger. "Lasting Machine." Because a worker was able to use Matzlieger's lasting machine standing up, he was able to breathe better. This offered some relief to consumptive workers until the advent of antibiotics in the 20th century.

On February 4, 1889—two weeks before his forty-fourth birthday—George mortgaged the John Penley farm for $520 to the Stanley Dry Plate Co. of Lewiston. This mortgage accompanied a personal promissory note George gave the company owners, issued the same day and for the same amount of money. No interest was to be paid on the loan (that line was crossed out in the form mortgage document) and no specific repayment date or schedule was noted, although the mortgage does seem to suggest that payment would be due in one year's time. (The promissory note, given to the company's owners, would have included the payment date.)

A mortgage to the Stanley Dry Plate Co. of Lewiston suggests that George was friends with or had a professional relationship with (maybe through the IOOF or Knights of Pythias) Francis E. and Freelan O. Stanley, the owners of the company. These ingenious twins from Kingfield, Maine, invented the factory production of dry-plate photographic printing materials. The successful duo (who later invented the steam-powered automobile known as the "Stanley Steamer"), had a photographic studio in Lewison at the time of the mortgage. Taking studio portraits was a sideline for the brothers, however; the bulk of the Stanley fortune came from national sales of their dry-plate printing materials. When George P. Young approached them for a loan, the twins would have been very wealthy. (In fact, the Stanleys relocated to Watertown, Massachusetts the following year to be closer to larger markets, before eventually selling their business to Eastman Kodak.)[219]

Freelan O. Stanley, circa. 1910.
(Photo in the public domain.)

Francis E. Stanley, circa 1882.
(Photo in the public domain.)

---

219. Webpage, Virtual Steam Car Museum. "Stanley Dry Plate Co." In addition, some of my information on the Stanley twins was provided by my husband Stanley Luce, who is a huge fan of the brothers and their accomplishments and who has taken me to tour the Stanley museum in Kingfield several times.

The loan from the Stanley Dry Plate Co. to George P. Young was extremely unusual. Although the Stanley brothers individually bought, sold, and loaned money on real estate in Oxford County,[220] (and most likely Androscoggin County, as well) there is only one mortgage from 1875-1898 in the Oxford County Registry of Deeds that bears the grantee's name of Stanley Dry Plate Co. (In fact, it is the only document of any kind bearing the name of Stanley Dry Plate Co., meaning the twins neither bought, sold, nor loaned money in their company's name *on any other property* in Oxford County.) When he heard this information, my husband, Stanley Luce, who is a long-time devotee of the Stanley brothers and familiar with their personal histories and generous natures, suggested that one of the twins, upon hearing George's story of financial woe (perhaps one day when George visited the Lewiston studio) simply put his hand in the till or wrote a company check to help his friend. (The Stanleys and George P. Young were about the same age, the twins having been born June 1, 1849 in Kingfield.) My husband believes that it was George P. Young, rather than one of the Stanleys, who insisted upon granting a mortgage upon his property as collateral for the personal loan. If this is indeed the case it would explain the unusual nature of the mortgage, in which no interest was charged and no specific due date is noted.

The mortgage to Stanley Dry Plate Co. was the second one placed upon the John Penley farm, which was the only real estate George owned. (The first mortgage was to Abbie Jane herself.) No mention is made in the deed of the prior mortgage, which—if the mortgage was at the insistence of George—would have been an understandable omission. (In other words, if the Stanleys had been willing to accept George's personal note-of-hand without a mortgage, they would not have cared whether the property was encumbered or not.) Even though her name was on the original deed from Abbie Jane, Emma was not a grantor in the mortgage, although she did release her dower rights.[221]

This unconventional transaction and the way in which it occurred signals that, by 1889, George P. Young was in financial distress (something of which his thirty-year-old wife might have been completely unaware). If George failed to make his annual payment to Abbie Jane, she would have had the right to foreclose upon his family's home, the old Crockett homestead, as well as the former John Penley farm. (Although whether Abbie Jane would have proceeded with foreclosure, we cannot know.) That George approached the Stanley twins for a loan rather than a local

---

220. See OCROD for particulars of these many purchases, sales, and mortgages.
221. OCROD, Bk. 215, Page 551.

bank—or his well-heeled uncle Joseph W. Vittum in Massachusetts—implies that he wanted to keep his financial situation private. He might have been embarrassed to ask his family for a loan, especially if he had led them to believe he was doing well in Norway.

In 1889, George's grandmother Elkina Vittum was eighty-three, and lived with her son Joseph in his Haverhill home.[222] Uncle Joseph was still engaged in the shoe manufacturing business, and was also a leather dealer. His business was located on Main Street in Haverhill. (Joseph Vittum probably also still had his Boston office.) In 1889, Uncle Joseph was certainly wealthy enough to extend a small loan to his nephew. (In fact, Joseph W. Vittum later became president of the Pentucket Savings Bank,[223] and probably had something to do with the bank's establishment in 1891.)[224] Instead of turning to his uncle, however, George decided to seek financial aid from the Stanley twins. (It is possible that George did ask his uncle for a loan and was turned down. The prior mortgage on the John Penley farm likely precluded a bank from loaning money upon the property.)

On March 5, 1889, Frank Harriman Hobbs, Emma's nephew, was born to Henrietta (Crockett) and Frank G. Hobbs.[225] The baby was born in Portsmouth, N.H., where his father was employed as a shoe shop worker. This boy was first cousin to Emma's son Willie, and one can imagine the tender letters and photographs that flew back and forth between Norway and Portsmouth via the U.S. Postal Service. Again, the birth of this child would have been a subtle reminder to George that Etta (and Frances) had a claim upon the Crockett homestead.

That July, rather than celebrate Independence Day with a neighborhood picnic down at the lake, George Young, in concert with his harness racing associates, decided to hold a horse trot at the fairgrounds between Norway and Paris. The Oxford County Trotting Horse-Breeders' Association, of which George was Secretary, planned a splendid day, which included a baseball tournament beginning at 9 a.m. (with a $75 purse), with the horse races to follow at 1 p.m. The colorful poster for the grand event, which was plastered around the surrounding towns, also proclaimed "Good Music Will Be In Attendance!"

---

222. Haverhill, Massachusetts, City Directory, 1887. The Vittums lived on Washington Street.
223. Haverhill, Massachusetts, City Directory, 1917. Joseph W. Vittum was likely president of the bank before this date, and might even have had a hand in its establishment in 1891.
224. Pentucket Bank, webpage. "About Us."
225. CANDAGE, p. 179.

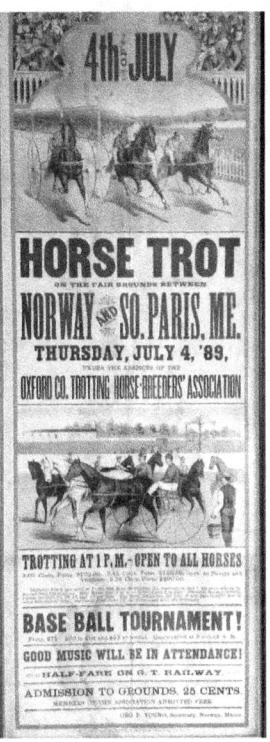

Colorful poster announcing the 4th of July Horse Trot, 1889.
This framed poster still hangs in the kitchen of the old Crockett homestead.
(Photo by Jennifer Wixson. Poster courtesy of Joyce Palmer.)

Close-up of the bottom of the poster with more details, including the
name of Geo. P. Young, Secretary.
(Photo by Jennifer Wixson. Poster courtesy of Joyce Palmer)

As secretary of the horse-breeders' association, George collected the entry nominations and fees. Although pacers could be entered in one of the heats, the races were primarily for trotters. Horses were classed into races by the speed at which they completed the mile. The purse for the slowest horses (3.00 class) was $100, and the fastest (2.35 class) was $200. Unfortunately, we have no record of what horse (if any) George P. Young entered, although it is possible he raced his bay stallion, "Redemption." The races also offered an opportunity for horse enthusiasts such as George to buy and sell standardbreds and/or studs services. Betting on the horse races, although not mentioned on the poster, also likely occurred.

In 1889, Emma experienced the loss of an important emotional support system when her female cousins, the Crockett heirs—Ella, Allie, and Louisa—moved to Georgia.[226] The three ladies, now forty, thirty-nine, and thirty-five, respectively—relocated under the protection of their brother Warren Ephraim Crockett. Warren orchestrated the move to Georgia, quitting his job on the railroad in Indiana, where he had lived with brother Edgar and his family.

Emma's cousins settled in Marietta, Georgia, a stop on the Western and Atlantic Railroad. The city had a population of 2,327 (in 1887) and was "an agricultural and stock raising region," as well as a noted resort community.[227] (Oscar Crockett, their late brother, might have visited Marietta for his health prior to his death.) The move south was an odd choice for a bachelor Northerner and three spinster ladies; however, Warren had received an appointment as a revenue officer there. In his government job he was charged with "suppressing illicit distillers or moonshiners…"[228] With Warren's income—and their pooled financial resources—the Crockett heirs lived a genteel life (the ladies became known for serving afternoon tea). They lived in a beautiful home, known as "Gray Gables," which was situated on Cherokee Street.[229]

---

226. The death notice for Miss Allie (Sarah) Crockett, which appeared in *The Oxford County Advertiser*, November 7, 1924, notes that she and her sisters relocated to Georgia with Warren in 1889.
227. Rowell's American Newspaper Directory. Printer's Ink Publishing Company, 1887, p. 131. George Presbury Rowell, Editor.
228. 1915 obituary of Warren E. Crockett. This obituary was probably published in *The Oxford County Advertiser*, and is attached to Warren's genealogy at the Norway, Maine Historical Society.
229. Information from the Facebook page, Old Marietta, (O.M.), which on September 14, 2020, published a post about Gray Gables and Warren E. Crockett, including his service as one of Teddy Roosevelt's "Rough Riders."

Gray Gables, the Marietta, Georgia home of Warren, Ella, Allie and Louisa Crockett.[230] (The photo, which is in the public domain, is from the GA Galileo Project, courtesy of Old Marietta [O.M.] Facebook page.)

Abbie Jane must have felt the loss of her siblings even more than Emma. Had she desired to relocate to Georgia with them, she was prevented from doing so by the terms of her divorce, which required her to reside in Norway until her children reached the age of maturity. Their mutual loss would have brought Emma and Abbie Jane even closer together. Letter-writing (and sharing) would now be an important way for the women to keep in touch.[231] Thanks to Charles Whitman, we know that Warren Crockett himself regularly corresponded with his friends back in Norway. Whitman, who obviously was one of the friends who received Warren's letters, penned a story in 1901 for *The Oxford County Advertiser* in which he details how Warren (as a revenue officer) shut down a notorious moonshiner by locating the secret room in which the renegade's still was kept.[232]

On November 26, 1889, there was a terrible fire in Lynn, Massachusetts, during

---

230. Gray Gables is located at 200 Cherokee Street in Marietta. Today the house is the home of United Community Bank in Marietta. In a Facebook message to the Old Marietta (O.M.) Facebook page May 4, 2024, the site manager told me that the photos I have used in this book (the Gray Gables home and later clipping of Warren E. Crockett in his Rough Riders uniform), were in the public domain. She had taken them from the GA Galileo Project.
231. Although we have none of Emma's letters to Allie, Ella, and Louisa—nor theirs to her—we do know that someone(s) in the Crockett household was an inveterate letter-writer. When I lived with my grandmother, the built-in drawers in the upstairs halls, and some of the cabinets, were stuffed with thousands of letters penned mostly in the 19th century. I used to occasionally pull a letter out of the drawer and peruse it, although not being familiar with my ancestors at the time I did not comprehend half of what was written.
232. "Jim Hulsey's Secret Room." *The Oxford County Advertiser*, February 8, 1901, p. 3 (probably written by Charles F. Whitman).

which eighty-seven shoe factories (and other businesses) were destroyed. In addition to the buildings that were lost, the fire obliterated the incomes of six thousand shoe workers. One of the blocks of buildings that burned was owned by B.F. Spinney. This edifice housed several smaller shoe manufacturers, including one of Spinney's smaller shoe businesses, Faunce & Spinney.[233]

"Lynn Conflagration No. 2, view from high rock during the progress of the fire, November 26th 1889."
(Library of Congress photo, in the public domain.)[234]

On February 18, 1890, an update regarding the destroyed Lynn shoe businesses appeared in the trade journal, *Shoe and Leather Reporter*, to which George P. Young, as a longtime shoe worker and former shoe shop supervisor, might have subscribed. The article claimed that the great fire "will not, eventually, it is believed, hurt the business of the city" because many of the shoe manufacturers had already relocated their business to the outskirts of the city and were operational again. In addition, the article noted that several shoe companies formerly situated in the downtown area, such as G.W. Herrick & Co. and Davis Shoe Co., had already been rebuilt and were near to reopening. In regard to B.F. Spinney's holdings in

---

233. *Shoe and Leather Reporter*, February 18, 1890, p. 333.
234. Library of Congress Prints and Photographs Division Washington, D.C. 20540. Reproduction number LC-USZ62-529 (b&w film copy neg.)

Lynn, however, the writer was more circumspect, suggesting that, although B.F. Spinney Co.'s operations were currently in Norway, Spinney might do something grand in Lynn:

> "B.F. Spinney is as yet undecided just what he will make of his land on Union and Almont Streets. When it is occupied doubtless commodious factories will be provided for Faunce & Spinney, A.P. Legro & Co., and the Consolidated Adjustable Shoe Company. B.F. Spinney & Co. now do all their manufacturing in factories in Norway, Me., having an office at No. 2 High street, Boston."[235]

To a disinterested reader, the paragraph would seem innocuous. To an interested reader, such as George Young, the information that Spinney was undecided as to what he would do with his real estate in Lynn would have been a reminder of the precariousness of employment in the shoe industry. If B.F. Spinney decided to rebuild his block in Lynn, what was to stop him from moving all of his business back to that city when his five-year lease on the "Big Shop" was up in 1891? George would have known that Spinney, who regularly took advantage of labor when deciding where to locate his businesses, might have decided to capitalize on the thousands of unemployed shoe workers in Lynn. With workers desperate for jobs, labor prices would remain low and workers would be less likely to agitate for a labor union or better pay and working conditions.

George turned forty-five on February 18, 1890 (the same day the update on the Lynn fire was published). He was a man in the prime of his life. A stranger assessing George P. Young's life from the outside would have thought he had it all: a pretty young wife and five-year-old son; a good job; and a handsome farm. George was well-liked and active in the community, belonging to (in addition to his position as secretary for the Oxford County Trotting Horse-Breeders' Association) the Pennesseewassee Lodge; the Knights of Pythias; the Norway Lodge, I.O.O.F and the Wildey Encampment, I.O.O.F. What George thought of himself at mid-life, we cannot know.

On February 25, 1890, *The Oxford County Democrat* published several articles and editorials that would have been of interest to George. The first was an editorial on how farmers were unfairly taxed, because their real estate was visible to the eye. (By contrast, personal property, such as watches, carriages, and even musical

---
235. *Shoe and Leather Reporter*. February 18, 1890, p. 333.

instruments, which were also considered personal property, could be hidden from the assessor's view.)[236] In the same vein was an editorial admonishing local officials to collect personal property taxes to lessen the burden on those who paid the lion's share of taxes. Another item of interest in the issue, Vol. 57, No. 8, was an article (and accompanying advertisement) for an upcoming auction—"the first combination sale[237] of horses at public auction ever held in the state of Maine." The sale, which certainly would have caught George's eye as a buyer and seller of horseflesh, was organized by auctioneer A.T. Maxim, and was to be held at Cummings' stables in Norway, March 26-27. *The Oxford County Democrat* also dedicated in its February 25th issue one-half page to a collection of foreclosure notices and notices of creditor meetings. Included with these were several insolvency notices against named individuals published by the Sheriff of Oxford County.[238] The specter of the local Sheriff seizing one's property and dispossessing a man's family would have been enough to chill the heart of any honorable debtor.

Three days later, on February 28, 1890, George walked into his stable office (a small wooden outbuilding attached to the barn and house) and shot himself. A local newspaper article, "Fatal Accident," published March 7, 1890, gives a detailed account of the incident:

> "Geo. P. Young was fatally shot by the accidental discharge of a shot gun last Friday morning.
>
> "Mr. Young resided on his farm some 3 ½ miles out of the village and worked in the cutting room of B.F. Spinney & Co.'s factory in the village and he drove to and from the shop each day, thus giving exercise to the different young horses he kept on his farm. This morning as it was 'soft travelling'[239] [Mr. Young] was to come to the village with a young colt to get it shod and it was necessary to change some parts of the harness he was using, and for this purpose Mr. Young left the kitchen and went into the stable office to get a bridle that he wanted. On the pins [hooks] on which this bridle was lay the fatal gun wrapped in a cloth case. In tak-

---

236. As a former Selectman in the small town of Troy, Maine, I can attest that this tug-of-war between real estate tax and personal property tax continues today. While all towns and cities in Maine are legally required to collect personal property taxes, many do not, resulting in an increased burden on those paying real estate taxes. Because personal property taxes are not universally collected in Maine, opportunistic businessmen often play one town off against another. In fact, when I was on the Board of Selectman a central Maine garbage company headquartered in Troy threatened to pull out of Troy and move its business up the road to Thorndike (which did not collect personal property taxes) if Troy Selectmen levied taxes against any of its dumpsters. As a result, a majority of the Selectmen elected to overlook the dumpsters when calculating personal property taxes (I was not one of them) and the business remained in Troy.
237. A sale of different types of horses: carriage, riding and work horses, and possibly even race horses.
238. *The Oxford County Democrat*, February 25, 1890.
239. 'Soft travelling' meant that the roads were not frozen and would thus not damage the hoofs of an unshod horse.

ing down the bridle the muzzle of the gun slipped from the pins and the hammer caught in such a manner as to discharge the gun, the contents striking Mr. Young on the left side, just below the heart and inflicting a fatal wound.

"Physicians were immediately called who did everything possible for the unfortunate man. There were no hopes of his recovery. He was able to talk for an hour or more after the accident and to explain how it occurred.

"It seems that the gun had been loaded by Mr. Young some weeks before for the purpose of shooting a dog that belonged to him, but somehow he disliked to kill the dog and his hired man didn't want to do it and finally the dog was disposed of by being given away to a neighbor and the loaded gun forgotten."[240]

Although George's death was regarded publicly as accidental, most of the family, including two of his three grandchildren (my grandmother Winona Young Palmer and her brother Willard "Bud" Young) were told by their parents that George committed suicide.[241] Painful as it is to contemplate a man destroying himself because he was in financial trouble, the evidence remains that George P. Young was in debt and struggling financially. He also had his life insured for $11, 680[242] (over $400,000 in 2024 dollars). By the time of his death, George, who likely purchased his first life insurance policy at the insistence of his father-in-law William Robinson Crockett prior to George's marriage to Emma, owned a total of five policies with the following companies:

Knights of Pythias Relief – $4290
Maine Benefits – $3000
Maine State Relief, I.O.O.F. – $1500
Odd Fellows' Graded Relief of Maine – $1890
Mutual Benefit, Newark, N.J. – $1000

Since George's death was considered accidental, the life insurance policies were paid. The generous amount of the proceeds would have been cold comfort to his grieving widow and fatherless son, though. One can imagine how Emma must have

---

240. "Fatal Accident," newspaper article published March 7, 1890, either in *The Oxford County Advertiser* or *Norway Advertiser*. The family has a copy of this article, as well as the Norway, Maine Historical Society, but it does not indicate the publisher. The publication date was determined by the information given in the article.
241. The information that Bud believed his grandfather's death was a suicide came from Bud's son, Norman Young. (Questionnaire completed by Norman Young for Jennifer Wixson, 2021.) When I lived with my grandmother, Winona told me that George killed himself.
242. The newspaper in the article "Fatal Accident" in which these policies were individually listed made a mistake in totaling the policies, giving a grand total of $10,080, rather than $11,680.

felt clinging to her husband as he lay dying.[243] At the house with Emma when the "accident" occurred would have been her fifteen-year-old sister, Frances; the couple's five-year-old son, Willie; and the hired hand, who probably carried George into the house and then went for the doctors. (It must have been a quick ride that fetched more than one doctor from Norway Village in an hour!) George lived long enough to tell his tale to the physicians, then expired. Many whispered words of love and reassurance must have passed between the dying man and his wife prior to the arrival of help.

George's funeral was held the Sunday after his death at the Crockett homestead, probably in the parlor. The doors into the hall and connecting sitting room would have been thrown open to accommodate the large number of mourners. In addition to family and friends, the funeral was attended by the members of the local Odd Fellow lodges and Knights of Pythias.[244] The service was officiated by the celebrated Universalist minister, the Rev. Caroline E. Angell,[245] pastor of the First Universalist Church of Norway and Paris.[246] Interment was at Norway Pine Grove Cemetery. George was laid to rest in the same plot he had purchased for his in-laws just eight years earlier. George was part of the Crockett family for only nine years, yet his surname has continued on Crockett's Ridge in Norway for four generations (as of this writing).

Condolences poured in to the young widow, including resolves from the Odd Fellows. A condition of membership to the I.O.O.F. was a belief in a Supreme Being (which George necessarily would have attested to when joining). This belief in God and His Providence can been seen in the Resolve passed by the Norway Lodge I.O.O.F. after George's death:

---

243. My grandmother told me that George was carried to the large oak table—the same serviceable piece of furniture upon which she had been born—where he was more easily attended. With all the leaves in the table (which still remains in the kitchen of the Crockett homestead), it would have been large enough to hold him. Most likely the women would have placed sheets, blankets, and pillows upon the table prior to George being moved upon it. Having sat at the table countless times, I know that it is just the right height for a doctor (or anyone) to work upon an injured person (hence why the table was used during childbirth, because it was higher than most beds).
244. "Fatal Accident," local newspaper article about George's death published March 7, 1890.
245. Caroline E. Angell was born in Smithfield, Rhode Island, June 28, 1842. She was educated at St. Lawrence University, Canton, New York, and ordained in Kittery soon after her college graduation in 1876. She came to Norway in 1884, where she succeeded Rev. Washington W. Hooper. According to Norway historian William B. Lapham, Rev. Angell was "a gifted pulpit orator, and has ever been popular where she has had settlements, and ranks among the ablest of the ministers of her denomination in the State." LAPHAM, p. 185.
246. The First Universalist Church of Norway has a celebrated history. The church, of which my mother, grandmother, great-grandmother, and great-great grandmother Emma were members, was not only the first Universalist church in Norway, it was also the first Universalist church in the state of Maine.

"WHEREAS, By the dispensation of a just and all wise Providence, another member of our Order has been called from life to the great beyond, be it therefore

Resolved, That while the members of Norway Lodge I.O.O.F. acknowledge the hand of an overruling Power, we express our heartfelt sympathy to the widow of our departed and recommend her to the loving care of our Heavenly Father who draws his children to Himself by the golden links of love in a union that shall be consummated in a glorious eternity.

Resolved, That in the death of our late Brother young, our Order loses a worthy member, and we extend to his family our love and sympathy, and assure them that we share their loss.

Resolved, That a copy of these Resolutions be read in open lodge and spread on the records, and a copy be presented to the widow of the late Brother.
J.W. Crommett, A.L.F. Pike, A.S. Kimball
Committee for Resolutions Norway Lodge I.O.O.F.
Presented and adopted, April 29, 1890.
T.L. Webb, Secretary"

Emma placed her copy of the Resolve in George's leather travel trunk, in which he also kept his I.O.O.F. hat and membership book. She also tucked in her late husband's wallet and other miscellaneous items, including books and papers. The trunk was then closed and latched, and moved up into the open chamber at the old Crockett homestead. After my uncle Kurt Palmer's death, the trunk and various other photos and memorabilia related to George P. Young were given by my aunt Joyce Palmer to George's great-grandson, George W. Young.

Leather trunk belonging to George P. Young, and a look inside the trunk.
Attached to the upper inside is George's I.O.O.F. manual and what we believe to be a photo of Emma (Crockett) Young as a bride.
(Photos by Jennifer Wixson. George's trunk courtesy of George W. Young.)

Life After George

After her husband's death, Emma Tuell (Crockett) Young was left with a heavy yoke resting upon her slim shoulders. In addition to settling her late husband's estate, she was now solely responsible for the couple's son Willie, her sister Frances, Fair View Farm, and other real estate (including the John Penley farm). Her parents were both deceased, as was Emma's older sister Josephine. Emma's brother Abel still lived in Duluth, Minnesota, where he worked as a Teamster,[247] and sister Etta resided in Portsmouth with her family. To make matters worse, Emma had recently lost a major female support system when Ella, Allie, and Louisa Crockett moved to Georgia. Fortunately, Emma did have aunt Mary (Crockett) and Isaiah Vickery Penley next door, as well as her cousin Charles Sewell Penley and his wife, Sarah, who lived up the road. Uncle Frank Crockett and his wife Antoinette (a half-sister to Emma's mother), lived in Norway Village and most certainly would have been there to help Emma, as would have been other extended family members and local businessmen.

In fact, the prominence of those who stepped forward to aid the young widow after George P. Young's death speaks to the esteem in which he was held by the greater community. George left no will, and so Emma formally requested that Norway attorney Henry M. Bearce (likely at his encouragement) be appointed as administrator of her husband's estate.[248] Bearce was not just a run-of-the-mill local lawyer. He was also treasurer of Norway Savings Bank and a representative to the Maine House of Representatives.[249] The three men who acted as appraisers of George's estate were also prominent businessmen and (probably not coincidentally) had a connection to the Crockett family. Herman L. Horne was the son of tannery owner John L. Horne[250] (and thus brother-in-law to Emma's cousin Julia Richardson Horne); Edwin A. Morse was son of Nathan Morse and Mary (Crockett) Morse (a first cousin to Emma's father);[251] and Ansel Dinsmore was the husband of Judith Morse (Edwin A. Morse's sister).[252]

The appraisers valued George's estate—real as well as personal—at $913. George's most valuable asset was his bay standardbred stallion "Redemption" (an

---

247. Duluth, MN city directories, 1890-1892.
248. Maine Wills and Probate Records. George P. Young, March 1890, Oxford County, Maine.
249. LAPHAM, p. 331.
250. LAPHAM, p. 533.
251. LAPHAM, p. 558.
252. LAPHAM, p. 558.

ironic name considering George's manner of death), which was valued at $300. George's next most valuable asset was one-half of the John Penley farm, which the appraisers set at $200 (meaning the farm's total worth was only $400). Other items of value in George's estate include one full-blooded Jersey cow, "Jessica," ($70); a two-year-old full-blooded Jersey heifer ($25—possibly the one mentioned in his letters to Rollin Stetson); a buggy wagon ($60); three sleighs ($52); three sets of harnesses ($30); and six meters of 6-inch boards ($36).

George's debts amounted to $1,061.99. This figure did not include any debts of honor (such as gambling debts), if he had any. Debts of honor ended with a person's life and thus the administrator of a deceased's estate was not bound to pay them. Most prominent of George's debts was $500 due to Abbie Jane Tubbs (the balance due on the John Penley farm). The amount due to Abbie Jane reveals that George did not use any of the $520 he borrowed from the Stanley brothers to make his third $100 installment (the 1889 payment) on the John Penley farm. Before he died, however, George had paid back some of the Stanley's money. Probate records show that the balance on George's note to the Stanley twins had been reduced from $520 to $201.12. Other debts included $41.38 to C.B. Cummings (likely for stable charges for George's horse), and similar debts to local merchants. In addition, George left a variety of personal debts, which indicates he was in the habit of borrowing sums of money from friends and/or co-workers at the shoe factory. These loans included $75 borrowed from a person named H.L. Libby; $25 from George C. Noseworthy; and $10 from F.I. Elliott. These loans would have been repaid by Administrator Bearce.

Altogether, George's debts exceeded his net worth by $148.99. This meant that, even if he had liquidated everything he owned, he would not have been able to pay off his debts. With the proceeds of his life insurance, however, Emma (or, Bearce for her) was able to discharge her husband's debts without liquidating any assets—leaving Emma $10,618 from George's life insurance (about $364,500 in 2024 dollars) with which to provide for herself and the couple's son. On May 16, 1891, the $500 balance due to Abbie Jane was finally paid.[253] The mortgage she and George gave Abbie Jane on both the John Penley farm and the Crockett homestead was fully discharged. The mortgage to Stanley Plate Co. was never discharged. Because this note was listed on George's schedule of debts, however, we can assume the

---

253. See discharge notice on the mortgage to Abbie Jane, OCROD, Book 206, Page 265.

balance of the loan was paid by Henry Bearce. This lack of a legal discharge (something Bearce, as a banker and attorney would not have overlooked) is the strongest indication that the mortgage to Stanley Dry Plate Co. was George Young's idea. In fact, had the Stanley brothers been satisfied with George's hand-written promissory note, they might not even have known about the mortgage upon the John Penley farm that he had granted them.

Prior to the settlement of her husband's estate, Emma and her family suffered another shock when Etta's husband, Frank G. Hobbs, died of acute meningitis in Portsmouth. Frank's death occurred on June 21, 1890, just three months after the death of George P. Young. He was only twenty-five. Frank left behind his widow Henrietta (Crockett) Hobbs, twenty-two, and baby Frank, only fifteen-months. Both Emma and Etta were now widows with young children. One would have assumed after Frank's death that Etta would return to the Crockett homestead with her baby, where she and her sisters could support one another in their woe. Because the 1890 census for Maine is lost, however, we do not know whether Etta and baby Frank came back to Norway. (If Etta did return, she elected not to make a permanent home in Norway because by 1900 she had relocated to Haverhill, Massachusetts, where she was the forelady of a stitcher room.)[254]

Although Emma was left in an excellent financial shape thanks to George's life insurance, her emotional and mental state after his suicide would have been fragile. One can only imagine the nightmares evoked by her husband's ghastly death.

That August the first lake carnival was held on Pennesseewassee—something the family would have enjoyed prior to George's death. Local people gathered by the hundreds to celebrate and have fun. According to a newspaper account of the carnival written by H. H. Hosmer, there was even a band on board the steamship Pennesseewassee, which musical ship made a continuous tour of the lake. The steamer carried flaming beacons and, when the ship set off around the lake at night, the beacons combined with the glow of "hundreds of flaming torches on floats made a wonderful display."[255] Needless to say, the joy experienced by the revelers

---

254. 1900 U.S. Census for Haverhill, Massachusetts. Etta Hobbs, Haverhill Ward 3. Etta's son Frank, who would have been around eight, is not listed with his mother in Haverhill, nor is he shown with his aunt Emma. I have yet to locate the 1900 census for Frank's paternal grandmother Susan (Buzzell) Hobbs Shatwell, to see if he was staying with her. Susan had recently married her second husband and was likely living with him in Ipswich, Massachusetts.
255. "Hosmer's Lake History—Some Facts Gleaned in Thirty Years Around Lake Pennesseewassee." Article by H.H. Hosmer. Published in the *Advertiser-Democrat* August 28, 1936, p. 1. (Copy of the article courtesy of the Norway, Maine Historical Society.)

would have been as dust and ashes to Emma and her family, who would not have felt there was much to celebrate that day.

Once the initial shock of her husband's death receded, Emma would have been faced with many life questions and key decisions to make. Should Fair View Farm be carried on? Even with a hired hand, it seems unlikely Emma would have been able to (or would have wanted to) keep her husband's race horses. Redemption would have been sold, as well as some of George's other breeding stock, such as his registered Jerseys. At some point Emma would need to supplant George's regular shoe shop income, too. Should she return to work at the shoe shop herself? Or should she seek out other income-producing investments using the proceeds from George's life insurance? In making these decisions it is likely Emma had help from her uncle Frank, as well as from Henry Bearce, administrator of George's estate. (She certainly would not have turned to uncle Isaish Penley for financial advice!)

For two years—the full period of mourning for a Victorian-era widow[256]—Emma appears not to have made any major life decisions. When the period of mourning ended, however, Emma took her first small step into real estate investing, which income-producing avenue had worked well for her cousins, the Crockett heirs. On February 29, 1892, Emma lent $40 at 6% interest to a man named Clarence Merrill. The promissory note was secured by a mortgage on Merrill's real estate, which was situated on the road from Norway Village to the lake. The loan was to be repaid in a year's time, and registry of deeds records indicate that it was paid, netting Emma $2.40 in investment income.[257] This small success appears to have encouraged the young widow.

On May 7, 1892, Emma ventured a much larger investment, lending $800 to Joseph Long at 5% interest. Long's personal note was secured by a mortgage on his property on Pleasant Street in Norway Village. Although the mortgage says the $800 is to be repaid in one year, it also states that the interest should be continued to be paid annually until the balance is paid off. In addition, the right to foreclose on the mortgage in one year is crossed out, suggesting that Emma was aware this was not a short-term investment, but rather a long-term one that would produce $40 in income per year.[258] Henry Bearce, the administrator of George's estate, witnessed the deed, and probably brought the investment to Emma in the first place.

---

256. Webpage, Victorian Mourning Etiquette.
257. OCROD, Book 222, Page 465.
258. OCROD, Book 222, Page 541.

The year Emma's son turned ten, she began to consider moving from the farm into Norway Village. Although Emma appears to have been determined from the beginning to keep Fair View Farm for Willie upon his majority, she personally might have felt inclined to remove from the site of the tragedy. How hard it must have been for the young widow to go out into the office in which her husband destroyed himself in order get a harness for the horse! In the Village, Emma could easily visit Abbie Jane, as well as Frank and Antoinette. She would not need to keep a horse at all (or cows or chickens), but rather she could walk to the shops to purchase groceries and other supplies. Perhaps even more important to the young widow, she could regularly attend church in the Village, too.

Another factor in Emma's decision to move into Norway was that the corner school, District No. 8, only went to eighth grade. In the Village, however, Willie could attend the high school. The former Norway Liberal Institute had been purchased in 1865 by the town, and Norway High School was established in its place. Dr. Osgood N. Bradbury, a family friend, was a popular teacher at the high school and served on the school committee. A notable (former) teacher at the high school was the celebrated Norway author, C.A. Stephens, who published popular stories in the national magazine, *A Youth's Companion*.[259]

Emma made the final decision to leave Crockett's Ridge in 1894. Once the move from farm to village was complete, Emma never again returned to live at the Crockett homestead (although she did later live at the former Nathan Morse farm).

In the summer of 1894, Emma purchased two properties on Beal Street. The parcels were situated next to each other. One of the lots had a dwelling on it[260] (probably a rental property, given its location near the shoe factory) and the second had either lesser-value home on it or was an empty lot, upon which Emma later built a rental property.[261] Beal Street, which parallels Main Street, was within easy walking distance to the high school, and a stone's throw from B.F. Spinney & Co. where both George and Emma had once worked (and where she probably still had friends). On July 17, 1894, Emma purchased the first parcel from Francis A. Danforth, paying $2300 from George's life insurance proceeds for the lot and house.[262] Six days later, on July 23, 1894, papers were passed on the second parcel, which

---

259. WHITMAN, p. 143.
260. Although the deed description was that of a lot, the price of the property--$2300—indicates that it had a dwelling built upon it sometime after the original deed description was inked.
261. The price of this property indicates it might have been a vacant lot. If so, Emma had a house built on it.
262. OCROD, Book 239, Page 189.

Emma also bought from Francis A. Danforth. She paid $1000 cash for the second property.[263] Even after spending $3300 of her late husband's life insurance money, Emma would still have had $5000 or $6000 remaining. Emma now had two properties on Beal Street—one in which to live and a rental property that would provide her regular income.

No one in the family alive today knows who lived at the Crockett homestead when Emma and Willie relocated to Norway Village. Other interesting questions arise, too. Did Emma's sister Frances, who owned one-sixth of her father's real and personal estate, remain behind at the house? Or did she move into the Village with Emma? Frances was twenty in 1894, and it is conceivable that she and a hired man remained at the homestead to care for the place (with funds supplied by Emma). Or, did Abel Crockett, Emma's older brother, return from out west and live at the farm for several years? In 1893, Abel was living in Duluth, Minnesota, working as a driver for Amour Packing Co.[264] By 1896—and probably before—Abel, whose first love had always been farming, was back in Norway. Maine. (In 1896, Abel was divorced from his wife Josephine, who was then living in Portland. He lived in Norway.)[265] We do not know exactly where in Norway Abel resided when he returned home, but it seems reasonable—especially considering that Emma moved into the Village around the same time—that Abel came back to the Crockett homestead. If so, Frances might have remained with her brother, shouldering the household duties that previously she had shared with Emma.

In the fall of 1894 Emma lost another member of her dwindling female support system, when her aunt Mary Amanda (Crockett) Penley, uncle Isaiah's wife, passed away on September 13, 1894. Until she moved into Norway Village, Emma had lived next door to her aunt Mary her entire life. Mary, who was only sixty, died of a tumor. Her death was attended by Dr. Bial Francisco Bradbury,[266] son of family friend Dr. Osgood N. Bradbury.[267] Mary was buried in the Penley Corner Cemetery in Auburn (formerly Danville), where her father-in-law Captain Penley and many of his children and their spouses were buried, including Mary's older sister Sarah (Crockett) and husband John Penley, Jr.

The following fall, on October 5, 1895, a Sunday School fair was held at the

---

263. OCROD, Book 239, Page 190.
264. 1893 Duluth City Directory.
265. CANDAGE, p. 178.
266. Norway, Maine death record. Mary A. Penley, September 18, 1894.
267. WHITMAN, p. 363.

District No. 8 schoolhouse, with proceeds used for the religious instruction that occurred there. Mary and Isaiah Penley's granddaughters, Ella and Edith Farnham, were among those who helped raise money for their Sunday School. A barge from town brought young people from Norway Village to the northeast edge of the lake, where they disembarked and hiked the short distance up to the corner school. Popcorn balls, ice cream, and candy were sold, and a "very interesting" short program (probably musical selections) was performed.[268] Although there were no more Crocketts with children on Crockett's Ridge, the descendants of Ephraim and Sally (Wentworth) Crockett, bearing other surnames, were embedded in the greater neighborhood. It seems likely that eleven-year-old Willie, as owner-in-waiting of Fair View Farm, would have attended the fair, too.

Five years had now passed since the death of George P. Young. Emma spent her days running her household and caring for the couple's son. She also managed the investment properties she had purchased with George's life insurance money.

When I lived with my grandmother Winona (Young) Palmer in the 1970s, I visited (with Winona) on several occasions the two Beal Street houses Emma purchased in 1894. Both properties were rental units then, managed by my grandmother. Each of these houses had two units, one up and one down (four in total). In Emma's day, she and Willie would have resided in one house (using the extra rooms for guests), and rented out the other two-unit complex. Residential housing in the Village was in high demand thanks to the shoe factory, and these two rentals would have provided Emma with a nice income. The balance of George's life insurance proceeds, about $5000, was probably kept in an interest-bearing account at a local bank, no doubt earmarked for Willie upon his majority.

---

268. From, *The Oxford County Advertiser*, October 18, 1895, p. 1. The author of this piece, although not noted in the newspaper, was probably Norway historian Charles F. Whitman.

Fatherless Willie Young with bicycle at his mother's Beal Street home in Norway Village. (Family photo, courtesy of Yvette Young.)

While living in the Village, Emma switched from the First Universalist Church to the First Baptist Church, even though the Universalist Church was still under the care of the Rev. Caroline E. Angell, the celebrated minister who had performed George Young's funeral service. Whether Emma became disenchanted with Rev. Angell or whether the Universalist services simply failed to meet her needs (or perhaps conform to her altered religious beliefs), we do not know. At the Norway Baptist Church, however, Emma certainly would have found a more intense type of religious experience, one that included uplifting hymns that the musically-inclined Emma found appealing. Serving as pastor of the Norway church was a newly-ordained Baptist minister, the Rev. John Aberdeen Harding. Rev. Harding was a bachelor, whom Emma apparently found appealing, as well. By the spring of 1896, he and Emma had fallen in love, and planned to marry. Their mutual love and affection not only healed and sustained Emma, but also gave her a new vocation—the minister's wife.

John Aberdeen Harding

In many ways, John Harding was the opposite of George Young. He was reserved, steady, and deeply-religious. John was also nine years Emma's junior. My grandmother, who remembered Reverend Harding well (Winona was twenty-one when her step-grandfather died), described John as a kind, thoughtful man. Winona told me that John Harding was much loved by the family, including his stepson, Willie (soon to be known as "Bill"), who was twelve when his mother remarried.

The Rev. John A. Harding
(Family photo, courtesy of Yvette Young.)

John was born in Liverpool, Nova Scotia (Canada) on December 9, 1867, to John B. and Catherine (Wright) Harding.[269] His parents were both natives of Nova

---
269. CANDAGE, p. 178 and Nova Scotia, Canada, Births, 1840-1917. John A. Harding.

Scotia, but shortly after John's birth the family sailed for Boston, landing in that city on March 18, 1869.[270] Twelve days before his twenty-first birthday John petitioned to become a U.S. citizen. At the time of his petition (November 27, 1888) John was working as an electrotyper, someone who produced metal plates for newspaper printing.[271] His U.S. citizenship was granted by judges of the U.S. Circuit Court sitting in Boston.

Sometime after his naturalization, John Harding experienced a call to ministry. Although Baptist ministers of the time could preach without an advanced degree in Divinity, formal coursework and/or suitable church experience would have been preferred. Whether or not John had any high school education, we do not know. But in 1893, he was accepted at Hebron Academy, an historic preparatory school located in the quaint village of Hebron, Maine, only eight miles from Norway. Hebron Academy was chartered in 1804 by Revolutionary War veterans who had received the promised grants of land for their services. Unlike a regular high school, students at Hebron studied there until they felt prepared for college.[272] While at Hebron Academy, John came under the benevolent wing of the Rev. A.R. Crane, D.D. (Doctorate of Divinity), a Baptist clergyman who taught at the academy and held a pastorate in Hebron. When in 1895 John felt as though he was sufficiently schooled (or, more likely, when Dr. Crane felt he was sufficiently schooled) the Baptist clergyman was instrumental in finding him employment in the ministry. Dr. Crane appears to have brought together this young man and members of the Norway Baptist Church.

Less than a decade earlier, in 1884, the Norway Baptist Church had been "in the process of extinction," having only nine members.[273] In 1889, however, a new Baptist church was built on Cottage Street in the Village. Norway historian Charles Whitman was one of the many prominent citizens who, although not members of the Baptist Society, nevertheless "generously assisted in erecting the pretty little meeting-house."[274] This new church was initially supplied by the Baptist pastor from South Paris, but after a while attendance increased and in 1895 the church congregation decided to seek a pastor of their own. Upon the recommendation

---

270. Massachusetts, U.S., State and Federal Naturalization Records, 1798-1950. John A. Harding, 1888.
271. Massachusetts, U.S., State and Federal Naturalization Records, 1798-1950. John A. Harding, 1888. See also, "History of Electrotype Making." *Electrotyping and stereotyping*. Harris B. Hatch and Alexander A. Stewart. Chicago: United Typothetae of America, 1918.
272. Information from Hebron Academy's website and other publications.
273. WHITMAN, p. 131.
274. WHITMAN, p. 131.

of Dr. Crane, John Harding filled the pulpit as a possible candidate, probably for many months. In the spring of 1896, the church was pleased enough with John's gifts to formally "call" him as their minister.

John's ordination certificate from the Norway Baptist Church (see Appendix #16) discloses what happened next. On April 16, 1896, a select council of twenty Baptist ministers and deacons, headed by the Rev. Dr. Crane (the council even included a minister from Boston),[275] met in Norway to "consider the propriety of ordaining to the gospel ministry Mr. John A. Harding, the pastor-elect of the church."[276] The inquiry into John's fitness for the ministry began at four o'clock, after a prayer offered by the Rev. G.S. Chase of Mechanic Falls. John read a prepared statement about his Christian experience, after which he was questioned by the august members of the council. He next stated his views of Christian doctrine, and was questioned some more. John was then asked to leave the meeting and the council discussed his fitness for the ministry. A vote was taken and it was decided that the council was "satisfied with the candidate's views on Christian doctrine so far as given." The council then voted to ordain, "with the express understanding that Bro' Harding pursue a course of further study in preparation for the work of preaching the gospel." (Apparently, the council approved of John's studies to date, but thought he could benefit from additional religious instruction.) Once the council's decision was made, John was brought back into the fold to hear the news—and the ordination ceremony proceeded. After his ordination, the Rev. Harding was welcomed into the "community" and given the sacred "hand of fellowship" by his mentor, the Rev. A.R. Crane, D.D., of Hebron.[277]

Emma might have been present at the ordination (although not during the council's discussion). The couple was married seven months later, on November 24, 1896. (Marriage intentions were filed on November 18th.) Emma was three-weeks shy of her thirty-eighth birthday when they wed. John was almost twenty-nine. (Both John and Emma were born in December.) Their marriage ceremony was held at the church in Norway and was officiated by John's mentor, the Rev. Dr. Crane.[278] From the day of her second wedding forward, Emma (Crockett) Young Harding threw her heart and soul into her new career as the minister's wife.

---
275. The Boston minister mentioned in the record of John's was the Rev. B.R. Harris, who might have been pastor of the church John Harding attended prior to moving to Norway.
276. Record of the ordination of the Rev. John A. Harding, Norway Baptist Church, April 16, 1896.
277. Record of the ordination of the Rev. John A. Harding, Norway Baptist Church, April 16, 1896.
278. Maine Marriage Records, 1713-1922. John A. Harding and Emma Young.

John continued as pastor of the Norway Baptist church until the following year. In 1897, the charge placed upon him by his ordination council to pursue "a course of further study in preparation for the work of preaching the gospel" led him to apply to Newton Theological Institute. [279] This Baptist divinity school in Newton Centre, Massachusetts, founded in 1825, offered a three-year program of graduate courses focusing on Christian evangelism. If John's call to ministry was to spread the "Good News" about Jesus Christ—and it appears that it was—the calling would have been enriched and deepened at Newton Theological Institute.

"The Newton Theological Institute."
(Print courtesy of Yale Divinity Library, Special Collections.)

In the fall of 1898, John, Emma, and young Bill relocated to Massachusetts so that John could attend divinity school. In December, in addition to his full-time studies, John took over the pastorate of the North Easton Baptist Church.[280] Although Emma certainly was financially able to support the family while her husband was in school, it seems that John was initially either too proud to depend

---

279. In 1965 Newton Theological Institute merged with Andover Theological Seminary to become the venerable Andover Newton Theological Seminary. In 2016, the seminary gave up its campus and courses were moved to Yale Divinity School. (Info from January 25, 2021 email from Joan R. Duffy, Senior Archives Assistant, Special Collections, Yale Divinity Library to Jennifer Wixson.)
280. "Andover Newton Theological School—General Catalogue of The Newton Theological Institution 1826-1943." Edited by Richard Donald Pierce. Newton Centre: The Newton Theological Institution, 1943. P. 207.

upon his wife's money (the proceeds from her first husband's death) or felt his evangelical calling too strongly to stay away from the pulpit (or both). The North Easton pastorate likely came with a parsonage, too, where the family lived.

Commuting by rail was common during the late 19th century and as there was a station stop in North Easton John probably commuted by train into school each day. In June of the following year, however, John vacated his pastorate to have more time to focus on his studies. (He might have been falling behind.) He did not accept a position in another church until after he was graduated from Newton Theological Institute.

Warren E. Crockett in the Spanish American War

In the summer of 1898, just when Emma and John were in the process of relocating to Massachusetts, the Spanish American War broke out. Emma's cousin Warren E. Crockett, who had moved to Marietta, Georgia with his three spinster sisters, was selected to join one of Assistant Secretary of the Navy Theodore Roosevelt's "Rough Riders." Apparently, Warren's successful work as a revenue agent chasing after moonshiners so impressed Roosevelt that when "he had ten applications to one he could take, Warren E. Crockett was accepted."[281] After the charge up San Juan Hill on July 1st, Warren wrote home to Norway (either to his sister Abbie Jane or his friend Norway historian Charles Whitman) from the camp of Troop D, Rough Riders:

> "When they commenced firing on us we lay down on the ground and listened to the bullets singing and whistling about us for a minute or two. Then came the command to 'left flank,' and we were up and at them in a hurry. They fought with great bravery and only retreated when we were at close quarters. They were armed with the Mauser rifles & used smokeless powder, which made them very hard to locate.[282] They also had machine guns which used smokeless powder too. In our advance we were exposed to a heavy cross fire of both rifles and machine guns, and from the way the bullets ripped and tore the foliage around us, it seemed impossible to advance against such a withering fire. Our Troop D had six hundred. I do not see how any escaped. In the whole regiment there were about thirty wounded and eight killed. I do not mean to boast but will say to you that

---
281. Obituary, Warren E. Crockett. 1915. The obituary was clipped to Warren's genealogy sheet at the Norway, Maine Historical Society. Newspaper and date unidentified.
282. Smokeless powder for guns was invented by Hudson Maxim, an American inventor, born in Sangerville, Maine.

I was in front during the whole fight, and had some close shaves, but did not get a scratch."[283]

Emma would have proudly read about her cousin's exploits in the Norway newspaper. She might even have received other particulars about Warren's war experiences in letters from her cousins Ella, Allie, and Louisa in Marietta, where their brother Warren became something of a local hero. Sometime after Teddy Roosevelt was elected President in 1901, Warren, in the company of Georgia Senator Alexander Clay, visited the President at the White House. Warren did not expect Roosevelt to remember him out of his hundreds of Rough Riders, however, the President recognized him immediately, greeting Warren with a cheerful, "Hello, Crockett!"[284] When the President went to Roswell, Georgia in 1905 to visit the childhood home of his mother, Warren—mounted on horseback and wearing the old uniform—acted as Roosevelt's escort.

Warren E. Crockett escorts President Roosevelt during his trip to Roswell, Georgia, 1905.
Clipping from *The Atlanta Journal*, October 22, 1905.
(GA Galileo Project, courtesy of Old Marietta [O.M.] Facebook page.)

---

283. "Warren E. Crockett's Letter Home When He Was A Rough Rider With Teddy Roosevelt." *The Oxford County Advertiser*, July 22, 1898, p. 5.
284. Obituary, Warren E. Crockett. 1915.

Family Updates and Leasing the Crockett Homestead

On March 2, 1899, Emma's uncle Isaiah Vickery Penley and his son True sold the former Nathan Morse farm to Howard A. Knightly, the husband of Edith Farnham (Isaiah's granddaughter). After aunt Mary passed away, Isaiah, being in poor health, had been admitted to Togus, the veteran's hospital in Augusta. True did not want the property, and so it was sold to Edith and her husband. Knightly paid only $500 for the farmstead, which included the house, barn, and outbuildings, as well as approximately eighty acres of land and the six-acre island. In addition, Edith and her husband also kept the carpet, dining table and chairs, and hay.[285] Emma, in Massachusetts, would have been glad to hear that the place—the other half of Lot 45 purchased in 1814 by Nathan Morse with her grandfather Ephraim Crockett—remained in the family.

On April 9, 1899, Emma's sister Lydia "Frances" Crockett turned twenty-one. Frances' twenty-first birthday was the day that William Robinson Crockett specified in his will when his real and personal estate should be divided between his then-living daughters.[286] All three of William's daughters mentioned in his will—Emma, Etta, and Frances—were still alive. The real estate formerly belonging to William, which should then have been sold, included the homestead farm, a woodlot on the Needham Road, the nine-acre parcel of grassland next to Lake Pennesseewassee, and another forty-acre woodlot. Regardless of the directive in her father's will, Emma did not sell any of her father's real estate. It is possible that her sisters wanted her to keep everything in the family. It is also possible that Emma did not know her father's directive because George settled William Robinson Crockett's estate, although there is some evidence that Frances received a sum of money (likely from George's life insurance money) in lieu of her inheritance. By 1900, Frances had left Norway. Where she went initially, we do not know; however, Frances emigrated to Canada in 1906. In 1911, she was living in London City, Ontario, where she worked as a dress-maker. Frances owned her own home in London, which indicates that she had received some capital from Emma, enough anyway to purchase a house.[287] It appears less clear, however, that sister Etta received her share of their fa-

---
285. OCROD, Book 257, Page 501.
286. Maine Wills and Probate Records, 1584-1999. William Robinson Crockett. Probated October 12, 1882. Oxford, Maine.
287. 1911 Census of London, Canada. Francis Crockett. Much like her sister Emma, Frances, who then also listed her religion as "Baptist," took in boarders (also Baptists), a forty-five-year-old widow with two children

ther's estate at the same time. In 1900, Etta was living in Haverhill, Massachusetts, where she worked as the forelady of a stitching room. She resided in a boarding home with three other shoe shop workers. Etta's son, Frank, who was eleven in 1900, was not with his mother. [288] Her financial condition suggests that Etta had not received any of her inheritance and indeed, there is every indication that she never did. (We will cover this small family drama in the next chapter.)

In 1900, although John was still attending Newton Theological Institute, the family returned home to Norway (most likely after school ended in May). The Hardings were at their Beal Street house when the U.S. census was taken in Norway Village on June 13th. John was then thirty-two and Emma forty-one. John's occupation was listed as clergyman. Although he did not have a pastorate at the time, he likely worked locally as an itinerant Baptist preacher.

The shoe factory was running full force when the family returned and aunt Antoinette Crockett was then one of its employees. She and uncle Frank would have been regular visitors at the Harding house. Frank and Antoinette rented a home on nearby Danforth Street, although Frank, who worked out as a farmer, was not always at home.[289] Another change that had occurred since Emma had left, was the removal to Waterville of Abbie Jane and her two youngest children. This relocation could only have occurred with her ex-husband's approval, since the terms of Abbie Jane's divorce required her to remain in Norway until her youngest child was eighteen. The move to Waterville was done to further the education of Abbie Jane's children, Idonia and Oscar Tubbs, both of whom appear to have been great scholars (understandable considering their mother was a teacher). In the summer of 1900, Abbie Jane and her children lived on Mudd Street in Waterville, where she rented a home. Although Charles N. Tubbs (Abbie Jane's ex-husband) was still alive, she told the census taker she was a widow.[290] Idonia, then eighteen, was prepared to enter Coburn Classical Institute (a college prep school) that fall, and Oscar (named for his mother's deceased younger brother, Oscar Rufus Crockett) would be a sophomore at Waterville High School. Both Idonia and Oscar would go on to graduate from the renowned Colby College in Waterville, where the 1909 yearbook, *The Colby Oracle*, described Oscar as "one of the brightest scholars of his class." The

---

288. 1900 U.S. Census, Haverhill, Massachusetts. Etta Hobbs.
289. 1900 U.S. Census, Norway, Maine. Antoinette Crockett.
290. 1900 U.S. Census, Waterville, Maine. Abbie J. Tubbs.

same yearbook wrote of Idonia—who graduated in 1909: "Her recitations are the despair of her classmates and the joy of the Profs."[291]

In 1900, after Frances had left home, Emma appears to have plotted the future course of the Crockett homestead. With her younger sister gone, the house, which might have been kept for Frances per their father's directive, could now be leased, along with the rest of the farm. If brother Abel had been at home with Frances, he, too, had left by 1900. Abel remained in Norway, though, working as a farm laborer for a man named John Rhodes.[292] Emma chose to lease the Crockett homestead to twenty-seven-year-old Fred Noble,[293] son of friends in the neighborhood. Her son Bill, interestingly enough, was listed as a boarder in the Noble household in the 1900 census. Although Bill is also listed on the Beal Street census with his mother and stepfather that year, the census taken at the Noble house (by a different enumerator) suggests that the fifteen-year-old wanted to learn how to farm. Bill (or his mother for him) aspired to take over Fair View Farm, following in his late father's footsteps.

During the summer of the family's return from Massachusetts, Emma also dealt with the non-payment of the mortgage given her by Joseph Long in May 1892. This $800 loan had been Emma's second foray into real estate investing. Long was supposed to have been making principal payments, as well as regular interest payments of 5%, but the principal payments were never made. (Long might even have stopped his interest payments after Emma moved to Massachusetts.) Emma, perhaps feeling that a good Christian woman should not foreclose on someone, assigned the note to Hattie Harmon for $885.75.[294] Ms. Harmon apparently did not feel the same trepidation because she foreclosed on Long on October 27, 1900,[295] taking over what was likely a very valuable property on Pleasant Street.

Purchase of the Original Nathan Morse Farm

One of the most significant financial transaction Emma ever made (as far as our

---

291. *The Colby Oracle*, 1909, p. 72 and p. 90. Oscar seems to have had a chip on his shoulder about his father Charles Tubbs (perhaps because of Tubbs' treatment of his wife). While at Colby Oscar dropped his last name and used his mother's maiden name of Crockett.
292. 1900 U.S. Census, Norway, Maine. Abel S. Crockett. The location of the farm upon which Abel was working is unknown, although census data indicates it was not in Norway Village, which was a different enumerator.
293. 1900 U.S. Census, Norway, Maine. Fred H. Noble.
294. OCROD, Book 245, Page 423.
295. OCROD, Book 265, Page 122.

family goes) also occurred in 1900. On Christmas eve, Emma purchased the former Nathan Morse farm (see Appendix #17 for a copy of this deed), which her uncle Isaiah and cousin True Penley had recently sold to Howard Knightly. Emma paid Knightly $800 for the entire property,[296] the amount she had recently received from Ms. Harmon. Knightly made a quick $300 on the deal, and likely purchased a better farm elsewhere. Notably, Emma did not add her second husband's name to the deed. The original money for this purchase had come from the proceeds of George P. Young's life insurance. William F. Young, as George and Emma's only child, was now heir to a grand estate that included the John Penley farm; the Nathan Morse homestead; Penley Island; and two-thirds of the Crockett homestead and woodlots. Following is an updated Lee's Grant lot map showing the real estate Emma owned on Crockett's Ridge by the end of 1900. Now, much of the real estate owned by prior generations of Crocketts and Penleys was consolidated into one branch of the family.

---

296. OCROD, Book 266, Page 201.

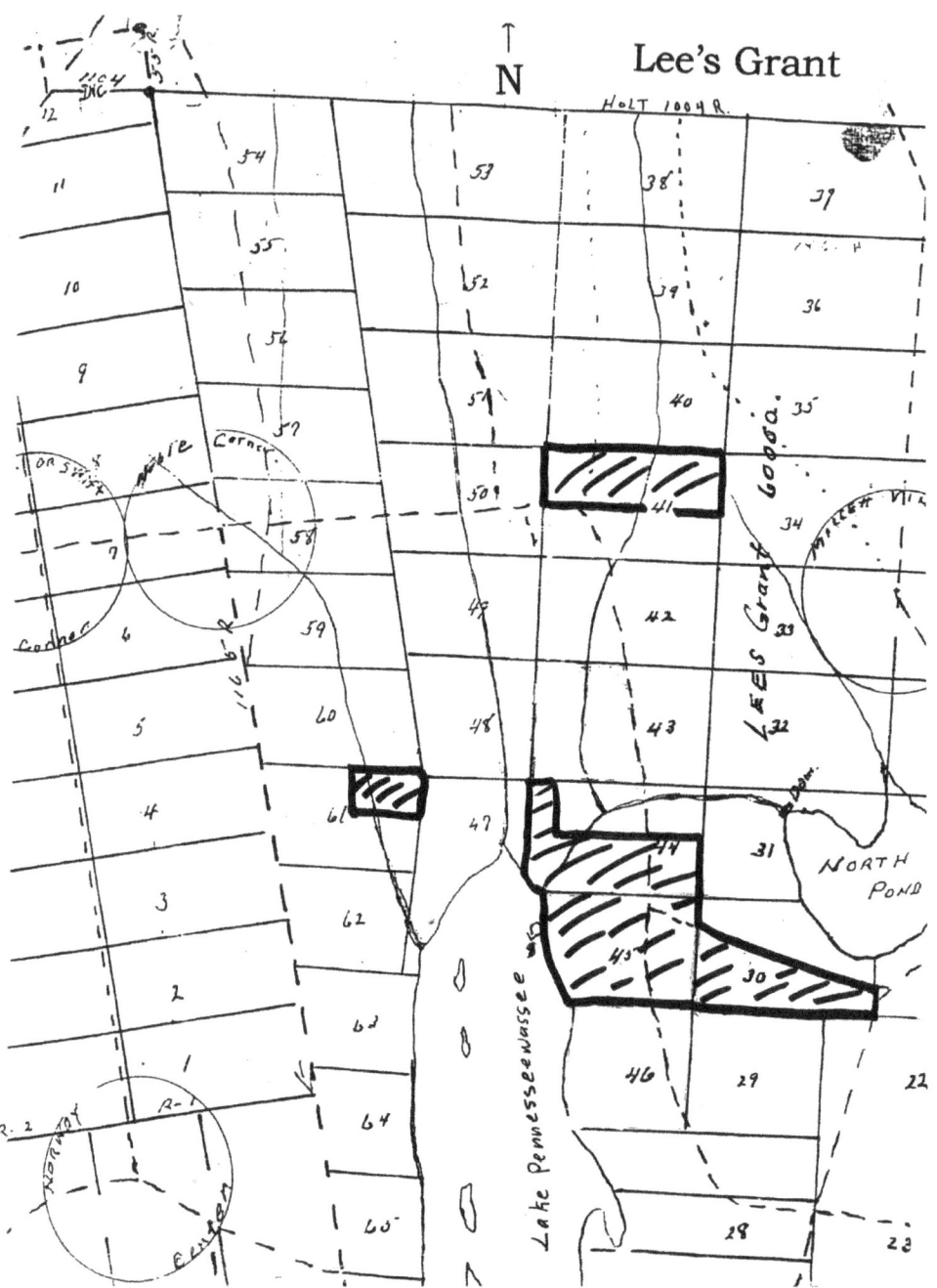

Lee's Grant lot map updated to 1900.
Emma (Crockett) Young Harding's holdings are the shaded areas. I have not separated out Henrietta's and Frances' share of their late father's estate since Emma managed it all.

The Call to Evangelism and Spreading the Good News

The Hardings continued to reside on Beal Street until John Harding was officially graduated from Newton Theological Institute in May of 1901.[297] Because the third year of a three-year divinity degree is not in the classroom, but typically consists of two, six-month periods of pastoral care appointments, the family did not need to reside in Massachusetts. It seems most likely John completed his pastoral care in Norway or a surrounding town. After his graduation in May, John and Emma left Norway. The Beal Street home was likely kept for Bill, who was still in high school (although it appears he also spent some time up at the farm, too). Uncle Frank and aunt Antoinette would have kept an eye on the seventeen-year-old youth. Emma's second Beal Street house remained a rental property, and her real estate on Crockett's Ridge probably remained leased until she felt that Bill was old enough to take over the management of everything.

Beginning in September of 1901, John and Emma embarked upon a spiritual journey that would lead the couple to at least ten different Baptist churches in New England over the next twenty-seven years.[298] While John's large number of pastorates might make it appear as though Rev. Harding had difficulty holding employment, his calling in ministry was not pastoral, but rather evangelical in nature, with a focus on missionary work. His desire would have been to move from church to church, town to town, spreading the "Good News" and helping congregations increase their missionary outreach.

From September 1901 to June 1902, John served as assistant pastor of the venerable First Parish Church of Charleston (Boston), Massachusetts. Founded in 1632, the First Parish Church was one of six churches responsible for the creation of Harvard University.[299] In the summer of 1902, John and Emma moved from the city to the country, when he was called to become the pastor of the First Baptist Church of Warner, New Hampshire. He served this church from June 1902 to February 1904.

---

297. "Directory of Norway and Paris, 1900-1901." Merrill and Webber Printers and Bookbinders, Auburn, Maine. John A. Harding, Baptist clergyman, is listed on p. 25 in the directory as residing at 45 Beal Street.
298. All information about John A. Harding's education and church appointments from "Andover Newton Theological School—General Catalogue of The Newton Theological Institution 1826-1943." Edited by Richard Donald Pierce. Newton Centre: The Newton Theological Institution, 1943. John Aberdeen Harding, p. 207.
299. Webpage, First Church of Charleston. "Our History."

First Baptist Church of Warner, New Hampshire.
Where the Rev. John A. Harding served as pastor from June 1902 to February 1904.
(Photo courtesy of Andover Newton Theological School, Franklin Trask Library.)

In March of 1904, John and Emma returned to Maine, where he accepted the position of pastor of a Baptist church in Brewer. While serving as a clergyman in Brewer, John performed the wedding ceremony for his stepson, Bill. On August 4, 1904, William F. Young was married to Louise Adalade "Addie" Chaplin of Gorham. The wedding took place in Gorham, at the home of the bride's father, Willis Chaplin, a local blacksmith. Bill and Addie (my great-grandparents) were both only twenty-years-old when they were married.[300] (One wonders if Bill married young because he was basically alone in the world. More on Bill and Addie in Chapter 5.) The newlyweds resided at the old Crockett homestead, where Bill had moved prior to their wedding.[301] From this time forward the management of Fair View Farm—and the other real estate on Crockett's Ridge belonging to his mother—was in Bill's hands. John and Emma remained in Brewer for nearly four years. In 1905, Emma became a grandmother when Addie gave birth on August 9th to George Willis Young, named for both his grandfathers.[302]

In February of 1908, John and Emma returned to Massachusetts, where John

---
300. Info from CANDAGE, p. 179, and the family Bible.
301. The Norway Register, 1903-1904. William F. Young is listed at RFD 1 in Norway. Information courtesy of Charles Longley, Norway, Maine Historical Society.
302. CANDAGE, p. 179, and family records.

accepted a pastorate at the First Baptist Church of Franklin.[303] John and Emma resided in Franklin for more than three years. Rev. Harding served as pastor of the First Baptist Church of Franklin until July of 1911. While in Franklin, Emma's only granddaughter (my grandmother), Winona Young, was born on February 2, 1908.[304]

Both John and Emma were well-loved by the Franklin congregation. During his time with them John "helped them move forward to become a self-supporting church." When in July of 1911 Rev. Harding announced that he had accepted a call to the First Baptist Church of Tiverton, Rhode Island, the church responded with regret. A Resolution of gratitude and farewell was adopted by the First Baptist Church of Franklin on July 27, 1911. The Resolution, which was presented to John prior to his departure, included a summary of his accomplishments. This summary reveals Rev. Harding's passion for missionary work, as well as a love of music, which both he and Emma shared:

> "Whereas, he has rendered loyal and efficient service among us, helping us to move steadily forward and become a more self-supporting church, and
>
> Whereas, under his leadership we have more than doubled our contributions for missions, and,
>
> He has been instrumental in greatly improving the character and tone of the singing, and
>
> Whereas, he has been a leader in helping to start an Italian Mission in our town, and
>
> Whereas, by the introduction of Daily Bible and special music, the weekly prayer meetings have been helpful and the attendance well maintained, and
>
> Whereas, This church wishes to express its earnest and sincere appreciation of his loyalty and fidelity that have been characteristic of his ministry among us,
>
> Therefore, be it Resolved, That it is with sincere regret that we accept his resignation as tendered, realizing that in so doing we are losing a faithful pastor and friend, and a man who has ever held before us the highest ideals of Christian living."[305]

The Resolution from the First Baptist Church of Franklin also contained a

---

303. Webpage, Franklin, Massachusetts. "Community Profile." The town, situated south of Boston, was formerly known as Exeter, but in 1778 changed its name to honor Dr. Benjamin Franklin. The American statesman and inventor had responded with a gift to the town of 116 books, which in 1790 became the first free public library in the United States.
304. CANDAGE, p. 179, and family records.
305. Resolution adopted July 27, 1911 by the First Baptist Church of Franklin, Massachusetts, accepting with regret the Rev. John A. Harding's resignation. The original Resolution is stored with other Crocket family memorabilia at the old Crockett homestead, currently in the possession of my aunt Joyce Palmer.

section about Emma. From these two paragraphs we gain insight into the role Emma assumed as minister's wife, as well as her gifts for ministry:

> "Resolved, That we also express our sincere and hearty appreciation of the earnest and faithful work done by our preacher's wife.
>
> Her many quiet deeds of kindness made of love and the spirit of helpfulness, especially where illness and sorrow have come, will be long remembered."[306]

Emma's gift of providing solace to individuals during times of suffering arose from the great crisis of her first husband's death. The Resolution from the First Baptist Church of Franklin concluded with a prayer that "God's richest blessing may attend them both in their next field of labor, and that the Harvest may be great."[307] From the Resolution and its conclusion we can see that Emma and John labored side-by-side as partners in the ministry.

Grandchildren and a New Barn for Fair View Farm

In the summer of 1911, Emma (if not both she and John) returned to Maine to visit her son and his growing family. It was during this visit to Crockett's Ridge that the three-generation photo was taken of Emma holding her granddaughter Winona, with her daughter-in-law Addie and Addie's mother, Luella (Batchelder) Chaplin standing behind her. Although Emma was only fifty-two at the time the portrait was taken, the rigors of her work as minister's wife and the couple's transient lifestyle had aged her considerably.

---

306. Resolution adopted July 27, 1911 by the First Baptist Church of Franklin, Massachusetts, accepting with regret the Rev. John A. Harding's resignation.
307. Resolution adopted July 27, 1911 by the First Baptist Church of Franklin, Massachusetts, accepting with regret the Rev. John A. Harding's resignation.

Three generations: Emma (Crockett) Young Harding seated and holding Winona Young; Adalade "Addie" (Chaplin) Young (rear left)[308] and Addie's mother Luella (Batchelder) Chaplin (right). (Family photo, a copy of which hangs in the home of the author's late mother, Rowena Palmer.)

During her visit home, Emma's son must have approached her about building a new barn, adding onto Fair View Farm. Although there was a good-sized barn in back of the house (the original Crockett barn), as well as attached sheds, Bill wanted to build a 105' by 45' modern barn opposite the house, on the other side of the front yard. Emma, who still had a sizable amount of money left from George's life insurance, advanced her son around $6000 and the barn was built in 1912.[309]

From August 1911 to June of 1914, John served as minister of the Baptist

---

308. I first took notice of this photo in 1978 (when I lived with my grandmother Winona) and was shocked to see the swastika belt buckle worn by my great-grandmother Addie. Winona then explained to me that prior to Hitler's appropriation of the swastika during World War II, the ancient Eastern religious symbol was widely seen in the Western world as a symbol of good luck. According to Winona, her mother got the belt buckle (and perhaps the belt) via a promotion by Swastika Flour, whose slogan was, "The Lucky Flour." For more information on the swastika's use prior to Hitler see webpage, The Society Pages, Sociological Images. "The Swastika before World War II."
309. Information on the size and cost of the new barn came from an *Oxford County Advertiser* article published in 1931 after the barn was destroyed by fire.

church in Tiverton, Rhode Island. While in Tiverton Emma's third (and last) grandchild, Willard Harding Young, was born on August 12, 1912.[310] In 1913, Emma would have received a copy of the charming photograph of her and George's three grandchildren.

Emma's grandchildren circa 1913.
George Willis Young (back left); Winona Young (back right) and Willard Harding Young (front).
(Family photo, courtesy of Yvette Young.)

In the summer of 1914, the couple once again relocated to Maine, perhaps to be closer to Bill and Addie and their family. In July, Rev. Harding answered a call to ministry from the First Baptist Church of Madison (Maine). He served as pastor of the church in Madison for two years.

In August of 1916, John once again assumed the pastorage of the First Baptist Church of Franklin, Massachusetts, where he and Emma had been so well loved. John and Emma remained in Franklin twenty-seven months. Following his second tenure with Franklin, John accepted three more pastorates in Massachusetts and Rhode Island in quick succession. He served Baptist churches in Lonsdale,

---

310. CANDAGE, p. 179, and Maine Birth Records, 1912. W.F. Young and L.A. Young. Some family members believe Willard's "Bud's" birthday was August 9th not 12th.

Rhode Island (January 1919-June 1921); Pascoag, Rhode Island (July 1921-January 1923); and Avon, Massachusetts (February 1923 to approximately 1926).

Death of John Harding and Emma's Financial Difficulty

In 1926, when John was only fifty-nine, he appears to have fallen ill. (I have not yet found a later photograph of the Rev. Harding to see how he, like Emma, had aged over the years.) It is possible the clergyman was simply exhausted by the frenetic pace he had maintained since his graduation from Newton Theological Institute. It is also possible that John, who came into contact with hundreds of people, contracted tuberculosis, still a serious disease in the early twentieth century prior to the development of antibiotics in 1949.

On July 14, 1926, short on funds since her husband was not employed, Emma borrowed $1400 against one of her properties on Beal Street in Norway. (The remains of George Young's life insurance proceeds had been depleted by the building of the new barn at Fair View Farm.) The loan was at 6% interest. Due to national banking regulations of the time, the mortgage was payable in one year and was not renewable. If after a year Emma wanted to renew the mortgage, she needed to secure a new loan from the bank.[311]

Not long after Emma received the $1400, she and John moved back to Norway, into her Beal Street home.[312] She might have been hoping to nurse her husband back to health that summer. By 1929, however, John was a patient at the New England Baptist Hospital (now a teaching hospital affiliated with the New England School of Medicine and Tufts University Medical School).[313] The treatment John received at "The Baptist" did not alleviate his condition. By September of 1929, John was home in Norway, where he passed away on September 3, 1929.[314] The Reverend John Aberdeen Harding was only sixty-one when he died. John's funeral was held at the Norway Baptist Church, the site of his ordination twenty-eight years earlier.

---

311. OCROD, Book 382, Page 130.
312. Emma's obituary states that she returned to Norway about nine years before her death in 1937. When the mortgage to Norway National Bank was executed on July 14, 1926, Emma was still living in as Avon, Massachusetts. The original newspaper clipping of Emma's obituary is pinned in the family Bible (currently in the possession of Joyce Palmer). A copy is attached to her and George Young's genealogy page at the Norway, Maine Historical Society.
313. This information is thanks to a post card the family has addressed to the Rev. John A. Harding and directed to the New England Baptist Hospital. (Postcard in the Crockett Family History Collection now in the possession of Joyce Palmer.)
314. CANDAGE, p. 179.

He was interred at Norway Pine Grove Cemetery in the plot purchased by George P. Young for Emma's parents, and in which Emma's first husband was also buried.

Extended Family Summaries and Emma's Final Years

Several of Emma's relatives rented (or lived rent-free) in one of her Beal Street houses over the years, including her uncle Frank and aunt Antoinette Crockett. In fact, the couple was living on Beal Street when Antoinette passed away February 11, 1903, at the age of sixty-three.[315] Her husband, uncle Joseph Francis "Frank" Crockett died (probably in the same Beal Street home) the following year, on June 20, 1904. Frank and Antoinette were also interred in Norway Pine Grove Cemetery, in the lot next to that of his parent's, which lot Antoinette had purchased in 1886 after the death of the couple's young daughter Clara.

Emma's cousins, the Crockett heirs, remained in Marietta, Georgia for the rest of their natural lives. Minerva "Ella" Crockett, the oldest of the three spinster ladies known for hosting afternoon tea at their home, Gray Gables, died of pneumonia on February 21, 1901, at the age of fifty-two.[316] Louisa Frances Crockett, the youngest of the three, passed away in May of 1910 at the age of fifty-four.[317] Middle sister Sarah Alamanza "Allie" Crockett outlived Louisa by fourteen years. She died of apoplexy (a stroke) on October 29, 1924.[318] Prior to their deaths Ella and Louisa had joined the Episcopal church, but the Rev. J.H. Patton, pastor of the Marietta Presbyterian Church—rather than an Episcopal priest—performed Allie's funeral service, suggesting that by the time of her death Allie had changed churches. The three sisters who had remained together in life, however, also stayed together in death. Allie was laid to rest with her sisters in the St. James Episcopal Cemetery in Marietta, Georgia.[319] Their brother Warren Ephraim Crockett, with whom they moved to Marietta and under whose protection the three ladies resided, died February 7, 1915. Thanks to his time as a "Rough Rider" with Theodore Roosevelt, Warren was buried in Arlington National Cemetery with full military honors.[320] Today, at

---

315. Maine Death Records, 1761-1922. Norway, 1903. Antoynett Crockett.
316. Obituary of M. Ella Crockett, *Norway Advertiser*, March 1, 1901.
317. Fulton and Campbell Counties, Georgia, Cemetery Records, 1857-1933. St. James Episcopal Cemetery, Louisa F. Crockett.
318. Funeral notice, Miss Allie S. Crockett. *The Atlanta Constitution*, October 30, 1924. Also, obituary notice of Miss Allie (Sarah) Crockett, published in *The Oxford County Advertiser*, November 7, 1924, p. 1.
319. Fulton and Campbell Counties, Georgia, Cemetery Records, 1857-1933. St. James Episcopal Cemetery. Allie S., Louisa F., and M. Ella Crockett.
320. Obituary of Warren E. Crockett published in a local Norway paper in February 1915. My thanks to the Norway, Maine

Christmastime, a balsam wreath from Warren's home state of Maine is placed upon his headstone at Arlington, courtesy of the Wreaths Across America Project.

Wreaths at Arlington National Cemetery, 2005.
(Photo courtesy of Wreaths Across America.)[321]

After her children Idonia and Oscar both graduated from Colby College, Abbie Jane returned home to Norway. By 1916, Abbie Jane owned a boarding house at 75 Main Street, where she is listed in a local directory as "housekeeper."[322] In 1920, Emma's brother Abel Crockett was the sole boarder at her house.[323] That year, Abbie Jane and Abel were both seventy years of age. Abbie Jane (Crockett) Tubbs died November 25, 1929, at the age of eighty-three. She was buried in the same plot as her parents, Ephraim Stanford Crockett and Sally (Penley) Crockett, and several of her siblings, including Abbie Jane's beloved brothers John, Josiah, and Oscar Crockett.[324]

Emma's only brother, Abel Stetson Crockett never remarried after his divorce from Josephine. In 1916-1917, prior to moving in with Abbie Jane he worked as a farmer on RFD 1 in Norway.[325] (Unfortunately, it is not possible to discern exactly where Abel resided.) Over the years Abel was a frequent guest of his nephew

---

Historical Society for providing me with a copy of Warren's obituary.
321. Webpage, Wreaths Across America. "Our Story." Used with permission from Wreaths Across America.
322. "Directory of Central Oxford County Maine. 1916-1917." Published by Merrill & Webber, Co., 99 Main St., Auburn, Maine. See also 1920 U.S. Census, Norway, Maine. Abbie J. Tubbs.
323. 1920 U.S. Census, Norway, Maine. Abbie J. Tubbs and Abel Crockett.
324. CANDAGE, p. 177, and records from Norway Pine Grove Cemetery.
325. "Directory of Central Oxford County Maine. 1916-1917." Published by Merrill & Webber, Co., 99 Main St., Auburn, Maine.

Bill at the old Crockett homestead, the farm he had once expected to inherit. My late mother Rowena Palmer often recounted stories about "Uncle Abe" that she and her siblings (and cousin Norman) were told as children by their parents and grandfather. Abel passed away on March 9, 1922 of lobar pneumonia[326] at age seventy-one[327] While cataloging old Crockett family photos in 2021, I came across a lovely miniature portrait of Emma and a man who resembled her. I believe the man is her brother Abel, and the photo was taken a year or two before his death. (Emma would have been in her sixties.) Abel Stetson Crockett was buried in Emma's plot, next to their parents, in Norway Pine Grove Cemetery.[328]

(Probably) Abel Stetson Crockett and his sister Emma (Crockett) Young Harding.
Portrait circa 1920.
(Family photo, courtesy of Joyce Palmer.)

Lydia "Frances" Crockett, the youngest offspring born to William Robinson and Lydia (Stetson) Crockett, remained in Canada, where she became a citizen of

---

326. Lobar pneumonia, one of the three types of pneumonia, occurs when one lobe of the lung is particularly affected. The disease is typically caused by the bacteria streptococcus. Information from the Mayo Clinic webpage, "Pneumonia."
327. Maine Death Records, 1761-1922. Abel S. Crockett.
328. Abel was buried in the plot purchased by George P. Young for William Robinson and Lydia (Stetson) Crockett. His headstone is facing the road, while those of Emma and her husbands—George and the Rev. John Harding—in the same plot are facing the opposite direction, toward the lane in back.

that country. On July 9, 1913, the spinster dressmaker married Canadian William James Felker, a carpenter from Toronto. The marriage took place in London (Canada) where Frances was living at the time. She was thirty-seven and the bridegroom was forty-three.[329]

William Felker and his bride, Lydia "Frances" (Crockett) Felker.
(Family photo, courtesy of Joyce Palmer.)

After the wedding, the couple resided in Toronto. In 1921, William's work as a carpenter earned him $1800 a year, a comfortable living for them both. That year they rented a five-room brick row house for $40 per month.[330] William and Frances never had children. Throughout her life Frances remained fond of her nephew Bill, who was only ten years her junior and with whom she was raised at the Crockett homestead. She wrote the family regularly and sent annual Christmas cards, as well as photos of herself and husband.

From everything we know, the couple led a very happy life. William Felker died on New Year's Day, 1952. Frances passed away just four-and-a-half months later, on May 16, 1952. William was eighty-two when he died and Frances was

---
329. Ontario, Canada, Marriages, 1826-1938. Francie Lydia Crockett.
330. 1921 Census of Canada. William J. Felker.

seventy-eight. They were interred at Prospect Cemetery in Toronto.[331] Frances was the only one of William Robinson and Lydia (Stetson) Crockett's five offspring not buried with her parents in Norway Pine Grove Cemetery. Although Frances never signed a release to her rights of one-sixth of their father's estate, those rights were extinguished at her death since she died without issue.

By 1920, Emma's other sister Etta had returned to Norway from Haverhill, Massachusetts, where she had been forewoman of the stitching room. When the census was taken in 1920, Etta was working at the Norway shoe shop. Etta, then fifty-one, rented a house on Main Street, where she lived by herself.[332] Her only child, Frank H. Hobbs, then thirty, was married to an Irishwoman, Mary Gertrude Montague.[333] They lived in Lynn, Massachusetts, where Frank worked as a shoe cutter.[334] Henrietta "Etta" (Crockett) Hobbs died June 3, 1925, at the age of fifty-seven. She was interred at Norway Pine Grove Cemetery with her parents and siblings. Like her sister Frances, Etta never released her rights to her one-sixth inheritance of their father's estate. At her death, those rights passed to her son Frank.

Frank H. Hobbs divorced his first wife, and, on October 12, 1923, married his second wife, Mary Louise Hunter, of Lynn.[335] After their marriage, the couple made their home in Norway. Frank was proprietor of a billiard parlor in town, which he managed (and later owned). By 1930, he and Mary, were living in a rented home on Main Street (probably the same house in which his late mother had resided) with three of their five children born to date.[336]

Emma was very fond of her nephew Frank, who was an outgoing, cheery man. In her later years she even spent the winters with Frank and Mary (and their growing family) in their Main Street home. After John's death, money being scarce, Emma turned her Beal Street home into a second rental property. During the summers Emma lived—not at the farm with Bill and Addie and their family—but at the home of her late uncle Isaiah Penley (the former Nathan Morse farm),[337] which she had purchased in 1900 from Howard Knightly. When cold weather and snow set

---

331. Find A Grave, William J. Felker and Francis Lydia Crockett.
332. 1920 U.S. Census, Norway, Maine. Etta H. Hobbs.
333. New Hampshire Marriage Records Index, 1637-1947. Frank Harrison Hobbs.
334. 1920 U.S. Census, Lynn, Massachusetts. Frank H. Hobbs.
335. Maine Marriage Index, 1892-1996. Frank H. Hobbs.
336. 1930 U.S. Census, Frank H. Hobbs.
337. This information came from my grandmother Winona Palmer. Apparently, Emma kept the Nathan Morse place as sort of a dower house for herself. She preferred that to living with her son and his family at the Crockett homestead, where frankly there probably was not much room for her. In the winter, Winona said—and Emma's obituary confirmed—she preferred to move back to her Beal Street house to be closer to shops and the Baptist church.

in, Emma migrated back to Frank's house.[338] In the Village Emma could be closer to the shops, and to the Baptist Church, which she still regularly attended. Emma, who had moved many times in her life with John, apparently was unfazed relocating from country to town. She followed this pattern for the rest of her life.

Emma Tuell (Crockett) Young Harding lived to meet three of her great-grandchildren: Rowena and Kurt Palmer, and Norman Young. My mother, Rowena Mae Palmer—daughter of Winona Young and William Palmer—was Emma's first great-grandchild. In 1933, my grandmother Winona with my mother and Elizabeth (Palmer) Smith, (Winona's sister-in-law), visited her parents Bill and Addie Young at the old Crockett homestead (then Young's Turkey Farm), where Winona was raised. Emma came up from her summer place down the hill (the former Nathan Morse place) to meet baby Rowena.

Emma (Crockett) Young Harding holding her great-granddaughter, Rowena Mae Palmer. The younger woman is Elizabeth (Palmer) Smith, the baby's aunt. The photo was taken in 1933 at the old Crockett homestead, then Young's Turkey Farm.
(Photo currently in the possession of the author.)

---

338. Obituary, Emma T. Harding, 1937. Published in a local newspaper. Courtesy of Norway, Maine Historical Society.

Emma's final years were not without challenges. She was no stranger to adversity, however, and Emma's strong religious faith helped her overcome difficulties. The stock market crashed in 1929, ushering in the Great Depression. By 1931, Emma still had not paid off the $1400 she had borrowed when John fell ill. The 1926 mortgage to Norway National Bank was supposed to have been repaid in one year unless a new mortgage was reissued, which it was not. On July 21, 1931, Norway National Bank, perhaps not wanting to foreclose against a well-known local widow, assigned Emma's mortgage to Casco Mercantile Trust Company.[339]

On December 18, 1935, three days after Emma's seventy-seventh birthday, Casco Mercantile Trust Company foreclosed on her Beal Street property. All of the residue from her first husband's life insurance money had been spent (and apparently her second husband had no life insurance), leaving Emma with little in the way of a safety net. It is also probable that, given the financial crisis of the time, Emma had difficulty collecting rents, too. One can only imagine Emma's mortification when she read the foreclosure notice against her in the local newspaper. Banking law required the notice to be published for three consecutive weeks, and so the foreclose notice against Emma Harding was published in the *Advertiser-Democrat* on December 27, 1935; January 3, 1936; and January 10, 1936.[340]

Regardless of the foreclosure, Emma did not lose the Beal Street property. It took her nearly a year, but, somehow, she managed to raise enough money to pay off Casco Mercantile. Rather than sell any of her extensive real estate (which probably was not possible because of the hard times), Emma either borrowed from family or friends or might have sold some of her more valuable personal possessions. On December 23, 1936, a year after the first foreclosure notice was published, Casco Mercantile was paid in full and the bank discharged Emma's mortgage. Six days later, on December 29, 1936, Emma—her credit worthiness apparently still recognized locally—borrowed $450 from South Paris Savings Bank against the same Beal Street property. The terms of the mortgage from South Paris Savings Bank were very liberal. Emma was only required to pay $10 a month, plus 6% interest (also payable monthly). She also promised to pay the taxes on the real estate and keep the property in good repair.

Emma did not live to make many payments to South Paris Savings Bank. She

---
339. OCROD, Book 403, Page 5.
340. OCROD, Book 409, Page 189-190. The foreclose statement says that Emma was living in Avon, Massachusetts because that was where she had been living at the time the original mortgage was executed.

died in the new year, on January 25, 1937. Emma's obituary, which details her final days, was published in the local paper, (probably the same newspaper in which the foreclosure notices had appeared the prior year). Her obituary read:

> "After a few hours of critical illness with heart trouble, Mrs. Emma Tuell Harding, seventy-eight, passed away suddenly early Monday morning, Jan. 25, at the home of her nephew, Frank H. Hobbs, Main St., where she was spending the winter.
> The deceased was born at Norway on Crockett Ridge, Dec. 15, 1858, the daughter of William and Lydia Stetson Crockett.
> Most of her early life was at the old Crockett homestead, one of the first to be cleared in town. She married George A. Young,[341] he died in 1891, and some years after she was married to Rev. John A. Harding, then pastor of Norway Baptist Church. They resided in Massachusetts and Rhode Island, but returned to Norway nine years ago. Her husband passed away about a year later.
> Mrs. Harding has passed the summers on Crockett Ridge and been in the home of her nephew in the village during winters.
> She was a member of the Baptist Church and an honorary member of the Heywood Club.
> Surviving her are her son, William F. Young, of Norway; three grandchildren, George W. Young, Mrs. Winona Palmer and Willard H. Young, all of Norway; four great-grandchildren and a nephew, Frank H. Hobbs. Also one sister, Mrs. Frances Crockett Felker of Toronto, Canada."[342]

Emma's funeral was held at a local funeral home and was officiated by the Rev. G. Howard Newton, pastor of the Norway Baptist Church. One of the bearers of her casket was Fred H. Nobel,[343] a prominent organizer of the Farmers' Union of Norway, who as a young man had leased the Crockett homestead from Emma (and with whom the teenage Bill had boarded).[344] Emma Tuell (Crockett) Young Harding was laid to rest in Norway Pine Grove Cemetery between the graves of her two husbands, George P. Young and John A. Harding.

---

341. This is likely a mistake or a typo. George's middle name began with "P." John Harding's middle name (as noted) began with "A," however.
342. Obituary of Mrs. Emma T. Harding, 1937. Courtesy of the Norway, Maine Historical Society.
343. IBID.
344. WHITMAN, p. 479.

Emma's Importance in Our Family History

It is hard to overemphasize the importance of Emma's life in our family history. Her ability to rise above her grief after George's suicide—to take care of her sisters, to keep the household and the homestead together—bespeak a remarkable courage and faith. Had it not been for Emma's desire to keep the Crockett homestead in the family, the place might have been sold out long ago. Certainly, the property would not have been as large as it was during her father's time, thanks to Emma's addition of the John Penley farm and former Nathan Morse homestead. It was Emma's dream to preserve the Crockett-Penley family's heritage and homesteads for her son (and his descendants). George's life insurance money made this ambition possible.

After George's death Emma was able to find consolation and love in the arms of her second husband, the Rev. John Harding. For more than a quarter-century Emma filled the vital role of minister's wife, faithfully accompanying her husband from state to state as John worked to "increase the harvest." Her labor in the ministry was less obvious than his, but when the couple moved on, Emma left in her wake "many quiet deeds of kindness made of love." On Crockett's Ridge, she left us all a legacy of Crockett and Penley lands and houses.

L. Adalade Chaplin and William Foss Young
(Family photo, courtesy of Yvette Young)

Chapter 5

BILL AND ADDIE (CHAPLIN) YOUNG

A Bride for Bill

The opening line of Jane Austen's famous novel "Pride & Prejudice" also serves as a suitable beginning for the final chapter in our Crockett family history: "It is a truth universally acknowledged, that a single man in possession of a good fortune, must be in want of a wife."

In 1903, Bill Young, then only nineteen years of age, was in want of a wife. He had moved from Norway Village up to Crockett's Ridge to take over the old homestead, and there he lived without the blessings of family.[1] His mother, Emma (Crockett) Young Harding, and stepfather John Harding were then residing in Warner, New Hampshire, where Rev. Harding was pastor of the Baptist church. An only child, Bill would one day inherit more than 300 acres of Crockett-Penley family real estate, as well as his mother's two houses on Beal Street in Norway. The good things of life with which young Bill was provided would not feel providential without someone to share them with, however. Thus, as with Austen's character Mr. Bingley in "Pride and Prejudice," Providence soon supplied Bill with a wife.

In June of 1903, Adalade L. Chaplin,[2] then twenty, the daughter of Willis B. and Luella (Batchelder) Chaplin of North Gorham, was graduated from the Western State Normal and Training School.[3] After graduation, Addie (as she was known)

---
1. The Norway Register, 1903-1904. Information courtesy of Charles Longley, Norway, Maine Historical Society.
2. My great-grandmother, known most of the time as "Addie" (or "Grammie") utilized many different renditions of her name throughout her life. Her birth record lists her as "Louisa Adalade Woodsum," but prior to her marriage she legally changed her family name to "Chaplin" (her natural father's name—more on this later in the chapter). She was graduated from Western State Normal and Training School as "Adalade L. Chaplin;" however, her marriage license (issued not long after Addie's graduation), gives her name as "Louise Adalade Chaplin." After she was married, she became usually "L. Adalade Young" or simply, "Addie."
3. Adalade L. Chaplin was graduated from Western State Normal and Training School in Gorham on June 19, 1903. There were thirty-two students in her graduating class. Western State Normal and Training School, "Western State Normal and

was hired to teach in the Norway schools by Superintendent Charles P. Barnes. During her first year of teaching, Addie met Bill Young, and the couple fell in love. When he shortly proposed marriage, she accepted.[4] Addie finished out the school year, but she never taught again.

Adalade L. Chaplin's graduation photo from Western State Normal and Training School, 1903. Addie is the young lady in the center.
(Family photo, in the author's possession.)

Bill and Addie were married in "a very pretty home wedding" on the evening of August 4, 1904, at her father's house in North Gorham. Bill's stepfather, the Rev. John Harding, performed the ceremony. The bridal couple entered the room to the music of the wedding march played on the piano by a friend of the bride's, preceded by a young ring bearer. The two mothers—Emma (Crockett) Young Harding and Luella (Batchelder) Chaplin—acted as witnesses. Guests were served refreshments

---

Training School at Gorham Maine 1902-1903" (1902). Course Catalogs. 92. My thanks to Jill Piekut Roy, Special Collections Librarian, USM Libraries, for providing me this information.
4. The information that Bill and Addie met when she was a teacher in the Norway schools (1903-1904) working under Superintendent Charles P. Barnes comes from a newspaper write-up about the couple's 50th anniversary. The clipping is in the family's possession. Unfortunately, the date and newspaper are not identified. The write-up, which announced an Open House to celebrate Bill and Addie's 50th anniversary, was most likely printed in one of the local papers at the end of July or beginning of August 1954.

following the ceremony, and "Many beautiful presents were received and best wishes are extended to the happy couple by a large number of friends."[5]

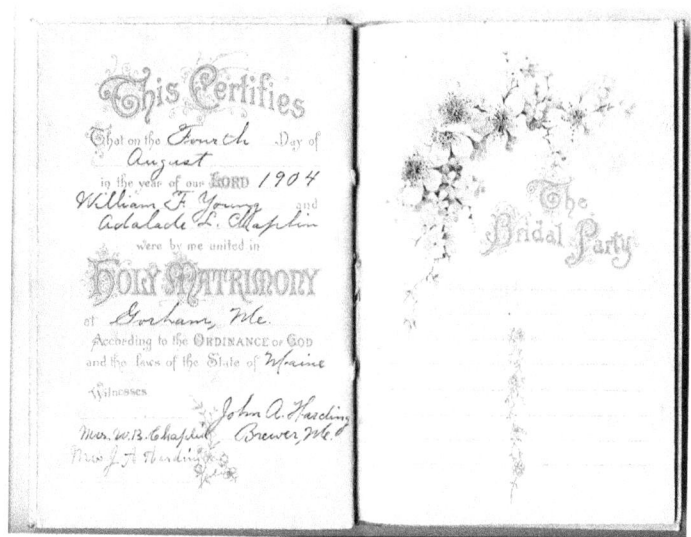

Addie in her wedding dress and the wedding book of Addie (Chaplin) and Bill Young.
(Family photo of Addie in her wedding dress in the author's possession.
Photo of wedding book courtesy of Yvette Young.)

Bill and Addie Young (my great-grandparents) were married just over fifty years. They lived out their days on Crockett's Ridge, in the old Crockett family homestead, where they raised three children and several grandchildren (including my mother). Many of us older descendants of Bill and Addie fondly remember them, as well as the homestead, which they turned into Young's Turkey Farm. Few of us know the complete story of this fascinating couple, however. If Providence brought them together, grit and hard work kept them together. Since we have covered Bill's family history in the prior chapters, we will begin our final chapter with a review of Addie's rather irregular family history.

---

5. From Bill and Addie's wedding announcement, pinned to an old family Bible.

Luella Batchelder and Willis B. Chaplin

One might consider the history of Addie's parents—Willis B. Chaplin and Luella Batchelder—a true love story, had the story not been so unseemly. Willis and Luella were both descended from well-known and respected families in Naples (Maine) in the Edes Falls neighborhood. There must have been a powerful bond forged between the two young people to risk the scandal of a long-term extramarital affair, which produced two children out of wedlock (Addie and her younger brother Harry Chaplin). Willis and Luella's affair lasted nearly a decade from 1882 to 1892, when—after Willis' wife divorced him—the couple was finally free to marry.

Willis Benjamin Chaplin was born in Naples on April 9, 1856 to Washington and Joanna (Stuart) Chaplin.[6] Washington Chaplin was a bulwark of the Naples community. A prosperous farmer, Washington was active in town affairs, where he served as a selectman for a period.[7] Washington's grandfather (Willis' great-grandfather), John Chaplin, was a Revolutionary War soldier from Rowley, Massachusetts, who in 1775 accompanied Benedict Arnold on his march through the wilderness of Maine in a failed attempt to capture Quebec from the British. Fortuitously, John Chaplin survived the trek and the battle,[8] and returned to Massachusetts in time to fight at the Battle of Bunker Hill. After the war (which included at least one other

---

6. Joanna was the daughter of Joseph Stuart and Nancy (Lombard) Stuart. The Stuarts were descended from the large group of Ulster Scots who immigrated to New England from Ireland in 1718-1720. Joanna's great-grandfather, Captain Wentworth Stuart, was a veteran of the French and Indian wars and an officer during the American Revolution, participating in the siege of Boston. See "Early Settlers of Harrison, Maine with an Historical Sketch of the Settlement, Progress and Present Condition of the Town." Rev. G.T. Ridlon. Kilby & Woodbury Printers: Skowhegan, Maine, 1877. Pps. 111-113.
7. CHAPLIN, p. 55.
8. John Chaplin survived the battle because he was on guard duty back at camp when the rest of the troops attempted to scale the walls of Quebec City. Chaplin's declaration as part of his pension application, which includes a description of his time on the Arnold expedition, makes for vivid reading:
As told to the Special District Court of the United States, Portland, Maine, August 31, 1832: "... [in 1775] he entered as a volunteer in the Company commanded by Capt. Ward in Col. Arnold's Regt. to go to Canada & Quebec & marched to Newbury Port & took passage from there by water to the Kennebec River to Hallowell and went on said expedition under Col. Arnold through the wilderness up to Quebec—That he served under Capt. Ward till the first of January 1776 when Genl. Montgomery was killed and Capt. Ward with many of the troops were taken prisoners. That he was doing duty as sentry and guard when the others were scaling the walls and that he and several others escaped from being taken. That he then served under Capt. Bailey till May when he went to remove some men from before Quebec back into the Country and before he returned, the house containing his equipment, clothes and six days allowance was burnt with its contents and he was left destitute. Capt. Bailey and his company retreated toward Montreal while he was after the sick and & has never seen him since. That he begged his way to the river Sorel & there got a discharge for himself & James Welch on the same piece of paper, and as Welch was a foreigner he gave him their discharge. That he proceeded to Crown Point & Ticonderoga & made the best of his way home, barefooted & ragged, and got back to Rowley about the last of May." Copies of documents from the pension file of John Chaplin, National Archives, Washington, D.C. See CHAPLIN, pps. 99-100.

enlistment), John Chaplin removed to Maine where he was one of the founders of Bridgton.[9]

Willis Chaplin's mother, Joanna (Stuart) Chaplin, the daughter of Joseph Stuart and Nancy (Lombard) Stuart, was a descendant of a family of Ulster Scots who came to Maine from Ireland between 1718-1720. Her grandfather, Joseph Stuart, served in the Revolutionary War under his father, Captain Wentworth Stuart, who was also a veteran of the French & Indian War (1754-1763). A Representative from Gorham to the General Court of Massachusetts in 1773 and 1774, Captain Wentworth Stuart participated in the siege of Boston with his "company of patriots" under Col. Edmund Phinney's 31st regiment.[10] Captain Wentworth Stuart's Revolutionary War career was cut short, however, after he contracted smallpox at Small Point (near Boston), where he died April 17, 1776.[11]

Luella Batchelder (Addie's mother) and Luella's twin brother Llewellyn, were born in Naples June 1, 1864, to Abner Batchelder and Mary (York) Batchelder. Abner Batchelder was born in Eaton, New Hampshire in 1825, and moved to Maine prior to 1847 when he married Naples native, Mary York.[12] Mary was the daughter of Samuel York, and the great-granddaughter of Nathaniel Folsom York (Luella's great-great grandfather) of Middlesex, Massachusetts. Nathaniel York served in both the Revolutionary War[13] and the War of 1812.[14] Abner and Mary (York) Batchelder settled in Naples (her hometown), where they had a modest farm of 70 acres. In 1880, Abner's farm was valued at $800 and his livestock—ten cows, two pigs, and fifteen chickens—was valued at $150. That year Abner's major product was butter (300 pounds in 1880) and his main field crop was one-half acre of Indian corn, which produced 50 bushels of corn.[15]

Willis' and Luella's fathers—Washington Chaplin and Abner Batchelder—were both farmers, each having a homestead situated on the road leading to that part of Naples known as Edes Falls.[16] Addie's parents, therefore grew up in proximity,

---

9. CHAPLIN, p. 14-15.
10. Ephraim Crockett, Sr., father of Ephraim, Jr. who settled Crockett's Ridge in Norway, also served in Col. Phinney's regiment from Cape Elizabeth.
11. "History of Gorham, Maine," p. 779-780. Hugh D. McClellan. Compiled and edited by his daughter, Katharine B. Lewis. Portland: Smith & Sale, Printers. 1903.
12. According to information in a framed Batchelder family register (a copy of which is in the author's possession), Abner Batchelder and Mary T. York were married March 5, 1847 in Windham. From the same family register we learn that Mary was born October 16, 1828 in Naples.
13. Massachusetts Soldiers and Sailors in the Revolutionary War, Vol. 17, p. 1009. Nathaniel F. York
14. U.S. Pension Roll, 1835. Nathaniel F. York.
15. U.S. Selected Federal Census Non-Population Schedules (Agriculture), 1850-1880. Abner Batchelder.
16. Information from a replica map of the Town of Naples, Maine from the "Atlas of Cumberland County, Maine, 1871."

although since Willis was eight years Luella's senior, Willis and Luella would not have attended school together.

As a young man, Willis Chaplin was handsome and outgoing. He reportedly attended a private school in Waterford for a while,[17] graduated from Naples High School, and went on to Bridgton Academy. After his education was complete, Willis taught in the district schools in winter and worked on his father's farm in summer.[18] On November 13, 1880, when Willis was twenty-four, he married a sixteen-year-old girl, Etta Iola Libby.[19] Etta was an orphan from Minot, then living in the town of Harrison with a family named Strout (possibly some relation to the girl).[20] Willis and Etta were married by a Justice of the Peace,[21] rather than by a minister, suggesting—given Etta's age and Willis' life history—the marriage was a shotgun wedding to protect the reputation of one or both parties.[22] During the early years of his marriage to Etta, Willis became romantically involved with Luella, then only seventeen. (Willis was twenty-six.) Luella and Willis' affair resulted in Luella's pregnancy, and in 1882, the unmarried pregnant woman was sent to Boston to live with her uncle Charles S. Woodsum, who resided at 5 Hingham Street. (Woodsum was brother-in-law to Luella's mother, Mary. His wife Susan York Woodsum had died the prior year in 1881.)[23] Luella gave birth in Boston to a baby girl on January 22, 1883.[24] Uncle Charles Woodsum allowed Luella to put his family name on the birth record

---

Atlas of Cumberland County published by F.W. Beers & Co.
17. CHAPLIN, p. 7.
18. CHAPLIN, p. 7. Some of the information taken from Willis' obituary, a copy of which from an unidentified newspaper is pinned in a family Bible.
19. The date of marriage of Willis Chaplin and Etta Iola Libby came from the court records of their divorce. Maine Supreme Judicial Court records, Divorce of Etta Iola Libby and Willis B. Chaplin. February 1891, Oxford County, Maine. Case No. 254.
20. U.S. Census, Harrison, Maine. 1880. Etta Iola Libby. (See also Benjamin Strout.) Etta's father, Isaac Libby, died in February of 1870 of consumption when she was about six. (U.S. Federal Mortality Schedules, 1850-1885. Minot, Maine. Isaac Libby.) Etta's mother Nellie (Ford) Libby went to work in a cotton mill in Lewiston. (1870 U.S. Census, Lewiston, Maine. Nellie Libby.) She died in 1875 when Etta was about nine. (Maine Tombstone Inscriptions, Surname Index, 1718-2014. Nellie and Isaac Libby.) Etta's second husband was Perley Strout.
21. Maine Supreme Judicial Court records, Divorce of Etta Iola Libby and Willis B. Chaplin. February 1891, Oxford County, Maine. Case No. 254.
22. If Etta was pregnant when she and Willis were married (and I suspect she was), the pregnancy did not result in a live birth.
23. Massachusetts Death Record, 1841-1915. Susan J. York Woodsum. Susan died June 4, 1881. After her death, her and Charles' daughter Jennie Woodsum went to live with her uncle Paul York and his wife in Naples. (Information from a direct descendant of Jennie Woodsum's via Ancestry.com.) Charles Woodsum died in Boston in 1898 at the age of sixty-eight. (Massachusetts Death Records, 1841-1915. Charles Woodsum.)
24. Information from Addie's Boston Hospital Birth Record, a copy of which was provided to me by my uncle Robert B. Johnson. Certain family members will remember that Addie always celebrated her birthday in April, rather in January. Nobody alive today knows why Addie did that, though. It is possible that Addie was unaware of her true birth date and/or that her mother, Luella, out of romantic flight of fancy, elected to use the month of April (rather than January) since that was the month Addie was conceived.

as the child's father. This child was Addie[25] Louisa Woodsum, the natural daughter of Luella Batchelder and Willis Chaplin. On August 10th of the same year, Willis' wife Etta gave birth in Naples to her and Willis' first child, Elroy Willis Chaplin.[26] (Addie was thus Willis' first child, albeit illegitimate.)

Over the course of the next seven years, Willis' wife Etta gave birth to three more children, only one other of whom survived. Sidney Wiatt Chapin was born July 31, 1885, and twins Myrtie and Bertie Chaplin were born June 26, 1887. (The twins died three days later, on January 29, 1887.)[27] In 1885, Charles Woodsum, Luella's uncle with whom she and Addie had been living, removed from Boston back to Naples,[28] where his and Susan's daughter Jennie Woodsum resided with her uncle Paul York and wife Georgianna (Hill) York.[29] Woodsum's return to Maine might have triggered the renewal of relations between Luella and Willis Chaplin, resulting in a second illegitimate child, Harry Chaplin.

According to older family members, Addie used to tell people that Harry Chaplin, born in 1888, was her half-brother. This seems to have been the story that her mother fabricated in Addie's childhood (Addie was five when Harry was born), when Charles Woodsum was still considered by the world to have been Addie's father. It appears that Addie continued the story into adulthood, although she likely knew that Harry was her full brother. [30] Regrettably, I have not been able to find Harry Chaplin's birth record. Other documents indicate Harry was born March 3, 1888.[31] In the disposition of Luella's property after her death, Harry and Addie are termed her "natural children," so we know Luella was Harry's mother. (Willis' wife Etta could not possibly have been Harry's mother, because she was pregnant with the twins when Harry was conceived.) This information (and other information shared with me by my grandmother) has led me to conclude that both Addie and Harry were the natural children of Luella Batchelder and Willis Chaplin.[32]

---

25. Luella had an older sister, Adelaide Batchelder, who died at the age of eight in 1864, the year Luella was born. She appears to have named her daughter after her deceased sister.
26. World War I Draft Registration Cards, 1917-1918. Elroy Willie Chaplin.
27. CHAPLIN, p, 83-84.
28. Boston City Directory, 1885, p. 1174. The directory lists Charles Woodsum, but says he has "removed to Naples, Me."
29. This information came from a direct descendant of Jennie Woodsum's via Ancestry.com.
30. About three months prior to her marriage to Bill Young, Addie went to court to legally change her last name from Woodsum to Chaplin. According to my uncle Robert Johnson, who researched Addie, her name change occurred May 17, 1904 in Cumberland County Probate Court. This leads me to suspect that Luella told her daughter that Willis was her father, not Charles Woodsum, prior to her wedding.
31. Veterans Administration Master Index, 1917-1940 and from the Social Security Death Index, 1935-2014 Harry Chaplin.
32. Many pieces of information have convinced me that Willis was Addie's father. First and foremost is the proximity of Willis to Luella when she was a teenager, and his penchant for young girls. Second is their on-going relationship, which resulted in the birth of another illegitimate child, Harry Chaplin, whom Addie always identified as her half-brother (although

Apparently, after Luella's uncle Charles Woodsum returned to Maine in 1885, Willis, while still married to Etta, set Luella and Addie up in a house of their own in the Andover-Lawrence area of Massachusetts. He frequented the home regularly or resided there for a period. My uncle Robert Johnson (husband of Paula Palmer, Addie's granddaughter), told me that in Addie's later years he and she used to have personal conversations about her life and childhood. During at least one of the conversations (which were quaintly carried on in the old horse barn attached to the Crockett homestead), Addie told Robert that she was born in Boston and later lived in a city north of Boston (he recollected Andover, but it could have been Lawrence, he said), until she was eight or nine.[33] When Harry was born in 1888,[34] Addie, at age five, was old enough to understand that she and Harry shared the same mother. Indeed, both Louisa Adelaide Chaplin and Harry Elmer Chaplin are listed as Willis' adopted children in the Chaplin genealogy (after his legitimate children).[35] No mother or father for either Addie or Harry is given in that genealogy, although Luella is noted as Willis' second wife.

It is probable that—given Willis' affair with Luella (and perhaps his fondness for teenage girls)—he was forced to "retire" from teaching. Willis, who was now supporting two households—one in Maine and one in Massachusetts—might also have realized that he could make more money as a blacksmith than he could from teaching (even though at one point he was supervisor of schools).[36] On July 8, 1885, Willis purchased the local blacksmith's shop in Edes Falls, and, with the help of a loan from his younger brother Joseph, set up in that trade.[37] Willis' uncle Joshua B.

---

she likely knew that she and Harry had the same set of parents). While no birth record has been found for Harry, in the disposition of Luella's property after her death he and Addie are termed her "natural children." Third is information in the divorce record of Etta Iola Libby (Willis' first wife) and Willis Chaplin, which insinuates that he was unfaithful to his wife (i.e. that he continued to carry on his affair with Luella). Also, the fact that Addie went to court and changed her last name to "Chaplin" from "Woodsum" shortly before her marriage, suggests that prior to her wedding Luella told her the truth. (W.B. Chaplin is listed as Addie's father on her marriage record.) And last, but probably most important, are modern DNA test results that show that I have genetic matches with other Chaplin descendants, which I would not have had if Addie had not been Willis' daughter. These matches include (in 2022) four connections with other descendants of John and Margaret (Chaplin) Chaplin, and one with a descendant of Washington and Joanna (Stewart/Stuart) Chaplin. (Indeed, I have more DNA connections to Chaplins than to Wixson/Wixon descendants.)

33. Emails between Robert Bruce Johnson and Jennifer Wixson, February 2022.
34. Harry's birth date, March 3, 1888, means that Willis' wife Etta was pregnant with the twins when he was conceived in June of 1887.
35. CHAPLIN, p. 83-84.
36. The information that Willis was once a supervisor of schools came from his obituary, which is pinned inside a family Bible.
37. CCROD, Book 520, page 457. Willis paid John Robinson of Naples the strange sum of $3.25 for the shop and land upon which it set. Willis borrowed $135 from his brother Joseph S. Chaplin, probably to purchase the tools of the blacksmith trade. He gave Joseph a mortgage on the shop, land, and tools for that amount on July 8, 1885. In an unusual move, the section where Willis' wife Etta would sign off on her dower rights in the mortgage is crossed out, suggesting that Joseph might

Stuart (his mother's brother) was a blacksmith in Norway, and he likely learned the trade (or took a liking to it) from his uncle.[38] Although Willis occasionally engaged in other money-making activities, he worked as a blacksmith for the rest of his life.

Willis B. Chaplin and horse.
(Family photo in the author's possession.)

Needless to say, Willis' propensity to stray outside his marriage vows became too much for his long-suffering wife Etta. On January 19, 1891, she filed for a divorce from Willis, stating that "regardless of his marriage vows, [he] has been guilty of extreme cruelty to her, has contracted gross and confirmed habits of intoxication, has been guilty of cruel and abusive treatment of her - and being of sufficient ability has grossly and wantonly and crudely injured [her] and neglected to provide suitable maintenance for her."[39] When she filed for divorce, Etta was living in Paris (Maine). She stated in her divorce petition that her husband was then living

---

have had some empathy for his brother's wife. If Willis failed to make his payments, Joseph might not be able to foreclose because Etta would still have rights to the property. CCROD, Book 521, page 81.
38. WHITMAN, p. 516. Willis' great-grandfather John Chaplin (the Revolutionary War soldier) was also a blacksmith. (CHAPLIN, p. 14.)
39. Records of the Maine Supreme Judicial Court, Oxford County, February 1891. Divorce of Etta (Libby) Chaplin and Willis B. Chaplin. Case No. 254.

in Lawrence, Massachusetts. Willis appears to have taken his legitimate children, Elroy, age seven, and Sidney, five, with him when he relocated to Lawrence to be with Luella and his second family. In the divorce filing, Etta did not ask for custody of the couple's two sons. Nor were the boys, who for the rest of their childhood remained with their father, mentioned in the divorce petition. Etta was abandoned or fled the marriage; either way, she would have had little money. Her divorce from Willis was granted on February 19, 1891, and she was given the right to assume her maiden-name of Libby.[40] Etta remarried twice and had two more children with her third husband, James A. Turple.[41] It does not appear that she had any kind of relationship with her and Willis' sons Elroy and Sidney, either as children or after they were grown. Both men listed their stepmother Luella as their mother on their marriage licenses.[42]

Following the departure of Etta from the scene,[43] Willis created a new life for himself with Luella and the four children from his two families. He relocated to Gorham, where some genealogies suggest Harry was born (although this seems unlikely), and where the Stuart family (Willis' mother's people) originated in Maine. On March 10, 1892, Willis and Luella were finally married, in Standish.[44] It is probable that the wedding took place at the home of Abner and Mary Batchelder, Luella's parents, who had relocated to that town from Naples. (One does not have to wonder why the Batchelders, long-time Naples residents, relocated to Standish, considering that their unwed daughter had borne two illegitimate children with a married man.) At the time of Willis and Luella's marriage, Addie was nine; Elroy was eight-and-a-half; Sidney was five-and-a-half; and Harry was four. From that moment forward, they all became one family unit. The family's neighbors in North

---

40. IBID.
41. On January 9, 1893, Etta married Perley Strout in Minot. (Maine Marriage Index, 1670-1921. Etta Libby and Cyrus Perley Strout.) Her third marriage, to James A. Turple, was in Mechanic Falls on April 23, 1903. (Maine Marriage Records, 1713-1922.) Etta Strout and James Turple. Etta and James had two children, Marjorie (born around 1903) and Maurice (born around 1904). Etta was thirty-eight when she gave birth to Marjorie and forty when she gave birth to Maurice. Etta's husband James appears to have predeceased her (no census data is available for him after 1920). In 1930, Etta, then sixty-five, was living in Portland with and working as a servant for Theresa and Alice Brown, seventy-nine and seventy-six, respectively. (1930 U.S. Census, Portland, Maine. Iola Turple, Theresa Brown, and Alice Brown.) I have yet to find a death record for Etta Iola (Libby) Chaplin Strout Turple. Sadly, it does not appear that Etta had contact with her children by Willis, who were brought up by Luella.
42. Elroy W. Chaplin married Mary A. Libby (who had the same maiden name as his mother, Etta Iola Libby, but was no relation as far as I can determine) in Westbrook on March 2, 1914. (Maine Marriage Records, 1713-1922. Elroy W. Chaplin.) Sidney W. Chaplin married Ella A. Miller in Westbrook on December 23, 1914. (Maine Marriage Records, 1713-1922. Sidney W. Chaplin.)
43. Willis was likely trying to provoke Etta to divorce him for several years, since she—not he—was the one who had grounds for divorce.
44. Family records and Maine Marriage Records, 1817-1922. Willis B. Chaplin and Luella Batchelder.

Gorham (the section of town in which they lived) might not even have known that the children were not all Luella's. She stepped into the shoes lately filled by Etta, and raised the other woman's sons as her own.

Willis and Luella (Batchelder) Chaplin.
(Family photo, courtesy of Yvette Young.)

In May of 1892, shortly after his marriage to Luella, Willis sold his blacksmith shop and land in Edes Falls.[45] (He kept his blacksmith tools, however, with which implements he was still making his living.) The following May, Willis purchased three acres and buildings in North Gorham. Willis paid an undisclosed amount to Apphia D. Davis ($1 and other valuable considerations)[46] and mortgaged the same property to Francis A. Mabury for $600, promising to pay a total of $650 at 6% interest, payable in six years.[47] In North Gorham, Willis expanded his blacksmith

---

45. Willis sold the shop and land to Edward Ayers of Naples for $75. CCROD, Book 590, page 323. Luella, then Willis' legal wife, signed off on her dower rights to the property.
46. CCROD, Book 610, page 49.
47. CCROD, Book 592, page 410.

trade into the carriage-making business.⁴⁸ Willis and Luella raised the four children at this home in North Gorham, and it was from here that Addie and Bill Young's "very pretty home wedding" took place in 1904.

Bill and Addie Young – The Early Years

After their wedding on August 4, 1904, Bill and Addie made their home at Fair View Farm (as Bill's father, George P. Young had named the Crockett homestead). Although the farm and house had been rented out to Fred Noble for a short while around 1900, Bill had taken possession of the place prior to his marriage. Addie rearranged the house to suit herself, as would any young bride. A cheerful, upbeat woman, Addie "always had a smile on her face and a twinkle in her eye," and her decorating style reflected her personality.⁴⁹ She hung photographs of her family on the walls, as well as popular prints, especially those containing the aphorisms that she loved. (Many of Addie's favorite pithy sayings were passed down to her descendants. I can still hear my mother chide me with one of her grandmother's aphorisms while washing dishes: "It's a poor dishwasher that can't wipe off a little dirt!")⁵⁰ Some of the "many beautiful presents" that the couple received for their wedding were showcased in a built-in cupboard in the parlor, which boasted a door with window lights. Some older Crockett items were moved up into the large open chamber for storage, including (eventually) two sets of chairs and a framed print of St. Cecilia (patron saint of singers and musicians) playing the piano for three cherub angels.⁵¹ (The popular 1891 print by Gustav Naujok might have been given to Bill's mother Emma for consolation after the death of her husband George Young, who appears to have loved music.) Her mother-in-law's piano, however, Addie left in the parlor, as well as the framed photographs of the original ancestors, Ephraim and Sally (Wentworth) Crockett.

Addie seemed to fit right in at the old Crockett homestead. During the first year of Bill and Addie's marriage a series of photos reveals a woman who felt entirely

---

48. Westbrook, Maine City Directory, 1904. Willis Chaplin, p. 185. (Willis is listed in the Gorham section of this directory.)
49. Email from Paula (Palmer) Johnson (Addie's granddaughter, who grew up on the farm) to Jennifer Wixson, January 16, 2022.
50. Addie also kept newspaper clippings with aphorisms in her Fannie Farmer cookbook, which I loved to browse through when I lived with my grandmother, who had inherited the book from her mother.
51. My mother Rowena Palmer rescued the print of St. Cecilia from the open chamber at the Crockett homestead. The print hung over Mom's mantle for many years. Following Mother's death, however, the large religious print of St. Cecilia has been taken down and returned to storage.

comfortable at her new home (one might even say Addie was a natural). The three images (following), pasted upon a cardboard backing and strung together with pink velvet ribbons, hung in my grandmother's bedroom (formerly, Bill and Addie's bedroom) when I lived with her. The series was most likely a gift from Addie to her husband, perhaps for Bill's twenty-first birthday on May 14, 1905. The three photographs feature what my great-grandfather loved best: his wife, his team of horses, his cows, his dogs, and his family homestead (perhaps not in that order).

Addie with Bill's team of horses.

Addie with the family dog on the granite steps of the old Crockett homestead.

Bill's cows in the cow lane, headed down to pasture.
(Photo series on this and the prior page in the author's possession.)

Also in 1905, Bill gave Addie her first pair of turkeys. The birds, an unusual gift for a city girl, were perhaps more pets than poultry. Apparently, Addie had a fondness for turkeys. "They say that one must be crazy to like turkeys," she told a newspaperman forty-five years later, "and I guess I am for I have always been crazy about them."[52]

After settling in on the farm, the first order of business (as with most newlyweds in the early 20th century) was to start a family. Despite her awkward beginning in life as an only child of an unwed mother, Addie, from the time of Harry's birth in 1888, had grown up with siblings. Bill, however, was an only child who had been left at times by his mother with various friends and family members. The couple wanted multiple children.

A year after Bill and Addie were married, their first son was born. George Willis Young arrived on August 9, 1905. He was delivered by Dr. Bial F. Bradbury, son of Dr. Osgood Bradbury, a friend of Bill's father.[53] Named for his two grandfathers (George P. Young and Willis B. Chaplin), George Willis Young was Emma's first grandchild (and the first step-grandchild for her husband John Harding), as well as the first grandchild for Luella and Willis Chaplin. George, the great-great grandson of Ephraim and Sally Crockett, was the fourth generation born at the old Crockett

---

52. "45 YEARS WITH TURKEYS IS A LONG TIME," by Ralph H. Whittum, Agricultural Editor. 1950 newspaper article about Addie and her turkeys. This article was pasted into the scrapbook Addie kept on Young's Turkey Farm and the family.
53. Maine Birth Records, 1621-1922. Infant "Young," born 9 August 1905 to William F. and Adelaide (Chaplin) Young.

homestead. The greater Young-Harding and Chaplin-Batchelder families rejoiced along with the happy couple at George's birth.

William F. Young carves a piece of wood in the kitchen of the old Crockett homestead, accompanied by his son, George Willis Young.[54]
(Photo courtesy of Yvette Young.)

Bill and Addie's second child and only daughter, Winona Young, was born on February 2, 1908. (I used to tease my grandmother about being born on Groundhog's Day, which certainly made her birthday easy to remember.) Like her brother George, Winona was delivered by Dr. Bial F. Bradbury, on the kitchen table, as she told me.[55] (The height of the oak table would have made the doctor's job easier, but perhaps not the mother's.) The couple's third and last child, Willard Harding Young, was born August 12, 1912. He was delivered at the homestead by Dr. F.N.

---

54. The chair to Bill's left (holding the basin) is one of a set that Addie eventually consigned to the open chamber. This set was rescued and redone in the 1970s as a gift for my grandmother Winona Palmer by her adult children. After Winona's death my mother inherited the set of chairs, which, since her passing, now belongs to my brother Wesley Wixson.
55. Maine Birth Record, 1621-1922. Winona Young.

Barker[56] of Norway, who for at one point served as President of the Oxford County Medical Association.[57]

George Willis and Winona Young
(Photo courtesy of Yvette Young.)

Willard Harding Young
(Photo courtesy of Yvette Young.)

During the early years, Bill turned his attention to farming. His dream was to raise registered Jerseys at Fair View Farm, once his father's dream. (Bill apparently did not share his father's penchant for raising race horses.) Because of George P. Young's untimely death, Bill did not grow up on the farm; therefore, he had a lot to learn. No doubt Bill had absorbed some agricultural information while boarding with Fred Noble, and from his classes at Norway High School. Still, there was nothing like hands-on learning.

Bill was fortunate to have some of his mother's family still living in the neighborhood to help him farm. Living up the road was his mother's cousin, Charles Sewell Penley, who was sixty when Bill and Addie were married. Charles was a small-scale farmer and familiar figure at the annual Oxford County Fair, where he

---

56. Maine Birth Record, 1621-1922. Infant "Young," born 9 August 1905 to William F. and L. Adelaich [sic] (Chaplin) Young. Dr. Bial Bradbury, who had delivered George and Winona, was still in practice when Willard was born, however, it is possible that he was then serving as U.S. Surgeon at the Soldier's Home at Togus (Augusta). See WHITMAN, p. 233.

57. *Journal of Medicine and Science*, December 1897 issue, p. 16. Published in Portland, Maine by the Maine Academy of Medicine and Science.

served as marshal of the cattle department.[58] Probably more helpful to Bill, however, was Albert Farnham, the son-in-law of Isaiah Vickery Penley. Farnham and his wife Sarah Belle (Penley) Farnham (Emma's cousin)—who previously dwelt in the Nathan Morse homestead (now owned by Bill's mother)—then lived down on the "The Tongue" property where Farnham had built a new house (after Ephrain Stanford Crockett's old place burned). Farnham was generally thought to be "one of the best farmers in Norway."[59] In a 1918 newspaper article about him entitled "Prosperous Farmer – Albert P. Farnham," the unidentified author says working with Farnham was better than an Ag college education. The author describes Farnham's success with his dairy and poultry operations; praises wife Sarah's prudence and saving abilities; and concludes: "Many young farmers and their wives might take a course of instruction from [the Farnhams], which would be worth more than a year at the Agricultural College."[60]

Albert and Sarah (Penley) Farnham and family.
(Photo courtesy of Ed Staples, Norway, Maine.)

Other family members and friends of the family also served as mentors for Bill.

---

58. Obituary of Charles S. Penley. *The Oxford County Advertiser*, April 2, 1920. Although Charles Sewell Penley, a veteran of the Civil War, entered Togus Soldier's Home in 1914, the obituary notes that he spent "considerable time at Norway on furloughs."
59. "Prosperous Farmer – Albert P. Farnham." *The Oxford County Advertiser*, July 5, 1918, p. 1. This interesting piece on Farnham was likely penned by Norway historian Charles Whitman.
60. "Prosperous Farmer – Albert P. Farnham." *The Oxford County Advertiser*, July 5, 1918, p. 1.

In 1913, Fred Noble returned to the Crockett's Ridge neighborhood, taking over his father-in-law Elhanan B. Tubb's[61] farm (at the top of Noble's Hill).[62] No doubt Bill's former mentor was once again available for agricultural assistance whenever he needed it. Probably just as important a resource for Bill was his uncle Abel Crockett. Abel was fifty-three and still farming in Norway when Bill resumed possession of the old Crockett homestead in 1903.[63] From stories about "Uncle Abe" passed down in our family (including some told to me by my grandmother), we know that Abel Crockett often visited his nephew and his wife. While at the home of his youth, Abel would have been able to share with Bill valuable information about the farm, woodlots, and homestead. This information Abel learned from his father, William Robinson Crockett, and would have included valuable knowledge that not even his sister Emma could possibly have known.

Finally, Bill did not depend completely on family and friends for his agricultural education, either. In the early years he was well-enough off to hire full-time farm workers, who lodged with the family. In 1910, Bill employed a fifty-nine-year-old farmhand named William Mesene.[64] After Mesene moved on (possibly to another world), Bill hired William A. Pool, age forty-nine, as a farmhand.[65]

During his early years on Crockett's Ridge, Bill overcame the typical challenges presented to farmers, including pests and inclement weather. In 1906, the browntail moth (*Euproctis chrysorrhoea*), an invasive species from Europe, made its appearance in Norway.[66] The browntail moth, accidentally introduced to the United States in the late 19th century, infested certain hardwood and fruit trees.[67] Hordes of browntail moth caterpillars nesting in these species of trees caused branch dieback and, in the worst case, destroyed the tree completely by consuming its green foliage. The pests also raised havoc with human populations living nearby the affected trees. Microscopic hairs shed by the caterpillars are hollow and contain a poison

---

61. Fred Noble was married to Elhanan's daughter Christina Bird Tubbs. WHITMAN, p. 522.
62. This property was formerly Lot 26 in Lee's Grant. OCROD Book 324, p. 62 mortgage; Book 322, p. 472 deed. See also Book 24, p. 299 for a description of the property.
63. In 1900, Abel Crockett lived and worked in Norway as a farm laborer for a Canadian named John Rhodes. (1900 U.S. Census for Norway, Maine. Abel Crockett.) By 1910, however, Abel had retired, and was boarding with his cousin Abbie Jane (Crockett) Tubbs in Norway Village. (1910 U.S. Census for Norway, Maine. Abel Crockett.)
64. 1910 U.S. Census for Norway, Maine. William Mesene. (See also William F. Young.)
65. 1920 U.S. Census for Norway, Maine. William A. Pool. (See also William F. Young.)
66. WHITMAN, p. 267. This horrible creature has made its reappearance in Maine in recent years. We battled the browntail moth here on our farm in Troy from 2020-2023. I still have a pest management plan (PMP) in place that currently addresses checking for and destroying browntail moth nests late winter-early spring.
67. "The browntail moth, *Euproctis chrysorrhoea* (L.). A report on the life history and habits of the imported browntail moth, together with a description of the remedies best suited for destroying it." Charles H. Fernald & Archie H. Kirkland. Boston: Wright & Potter Printing Co., 1903.

that irritates the skin and lungs, causing respiratory distress and nasty rashes similar to those from poison ivy.[68] Farmers like Bill would have read about the march of the browntail moth from Massachusetts to Maine in agricultural newspapers, and would have been encouraged to eliminate any caterpillar nests in winter before the caterpillars emerged and destroyed his valuable hardwood and apple trees. (Fortunately, it seems as though the abatement measures taken were successful since the browntail moth infestation in Norway is not mentioned in Whitman's annal's for 1907, as it was in 1906.)

In 1907, Bill's homestead was hit by a late-season snow and ice storm. That storm took down many Norway-area trees and fences. After the snow was plowed around the house and farm, Bill no doubt took his horse team and sled out to gather wood from the downed trees. That spring after the surprise storm, his fence-fixing detail would have been larger than usual.

Norway, Maine postcard, "Storm of '07." (Family photo)

Bill Young with team and sled in winter. (Family photo)

The New Barn

In 1912, the year the couple's third child was born, Bill decided to increase his dairy operation. Because he had little capital of his own, Bill turned to his mother for financial assistance. Emma and her husband were then living in Tiverton, Rhode Island, where John was pastor of the Baptist church. So that her son did not have to borrow money from a bank, Emma gave Bill $6000, which appears to have been the remaining money from his father's life insurance policies. With that money, Bill dug into the hillside and placed an enormous granite foundation for the barn to

---

68. "Browntail Moth: History, Background, Conditions in ME." Bulletin from the Maine Forest Service, Division of Agriculture, Conservation and Forestry, February 2018.

the south of the house. Then he commenced to build the wooden structure. When completed, the barn was 105' long and 45' wide. The interior of the barn was finished with "hard pine" and the floorboards were matched lumber.[69] The new barn was "thoroughly equipped for a dairy business" and was considered a "model of efficiency and convenience."[70] A new "Fair View Jersey Farm" sign was tacked onto the north-facing front of the barn, and Bill increased his herd of registered Jerseys. (For nearly a century, Jerseys were the preferred breed by dairy farmers because of the milk's high butterfat content. Until the advent of the popularity of low-fat milk later in the twentieth century—when the volume of milk not its butterfat content was most prized—farmers were paid more money for Jersey milk.)[71]

Fair View Jersey Farm - new barn, circa 1920.
(Family photo, courtesy of Joyce Palmer.)

---

69. The hard pine referred to in the newspaper article about Bill's barn was probably pitch pine, *Pinus rigida*. This hard species was often used in lumber and construction. It was then also readily available in Oxford County. See "Pines" pdf published by Maine.gov.
70. Information about the new barn came from the newspaper article, "Barn Burned at W.F. Young's," published in 1931 by the *Oxford Advertiser*. (The date of the article, which appears to have been published on page 1, is missing.)
71. Interjection here is from the author's own experience, having been born on a Jersey farm in 1956, and worked on a dairy farm in 1974 that had by that time switched to Holsteins. When the preference for low-fat milk occurred, farmers were no longer paid extra for their butterfat, and thus most dairymen in New England switched to Holstein cows, which breed gave much larger volumes of milk than Jerseys.

Addie and the Heywood Club

While Bill was building up his dairy business, Addie directed her energy to raising their three children and to fitting into the tightly-woven fabric of Crockett Ridge society. A woman with an active mind, a sunny disposition, and a willingness to help others generally has no trouble finding friends, and Addie soon became popular in the neighborhood. Not long after her arrival in Norway, Addie became part of a group of local women who in 1903 had started a literary society initially called "the Benevolent Literary Club." The group's purpose was not only to expand the women's literary horizons, but also "to promote sociability and good fellowship among our neighbors and to give a helping hand in any good cause."[72] The first elected officers of the Club were: Addie Thurston, President; Mrs. A.W. Thomas, Vice President; Mrs. Sarah Morse, Secretary; and Mrs. Fannie Dinsmore, Treasurer. The ladies gathered at each other's houses to listen to readings by members and to work on a patchwork quilt for the Old Ladies Home.[73] The group gained in popularity and the Club invited the ladies from Millettville to join them. (The Crockett's Ridge neighborhood was then known as District No. 8, after the corner school.)

On April 26, 1904, the Club voted to join the Women's Federation of Clubs after attending a meeting at the home of the popular North Norway author C.A. Stephens, whose wife acted as hostess. As a result of the association with the national club, the Crockett's Ridge ladies voted to rename their club, the "Heywood Club," in honor of the 16th century English poet and playwright John Heywood.

Addie officially joined the Heywood Club in the fall of 1904, after her marriage to Bill. On September 20, 1904, the club met at Mrs. Albert Richardson's home. (Albert was the son of Thomas Hanford and Hannah Jordan Crockett Richardson.) "Mrs. W. F. Young" not only was admitted into membership that day, but also was one of the speakers. Addie read from one of the published lectures by John L. Stoddard, an American writer popular for his travelogs.[74] Addie might have read from Stoddard's Volume 1, which contained his lectures on Norway, Switzerland, Athens, and Venice. About the country of Norway, Stoddard writes:

---

72. "History of the Heywood Club," by Rowena Palmer (the author's mother), March 16, 1994. (This was a talk that Rowena gave to the Heywood Club members.) History courtesy of the Heywood Club.
73. "Heywood Club Lights of Love," posted to the *Advertiser Democrat* online happenings board by Barbara Townsend on October 28, 2021. See also, "History of the Heywood Club," by Rowena Palmer, March 16, 1994.
74. Information from the Heywood Club minutes of the meeting of Sept. 20, 1904. Minutes and other Heywood Club records preserved by the Norway, Maine Historical Society.

"There have been few experiences in my life more joyful and exhilarating than my arrival in Christiania [now Oslo]. It was six o'clock in the morning when our steamer glided up its noble harbor. The sky was cloudless; the water of the deepest blue; a few white sails rose here and there, like seagulls, from the waves. The forest-covered islands, emerald to the water's edge, seemed gems upon the bosom of the bay. Beyond, were mountains glistening in an atmosphere, the like of which for clearness I had never seen: while the first breath of that crisp, aromatic air (a most delicious blending of the odors of mountains, sea, and forest) can never be forgotten."[75]

Membership in the Heywood Club soon swelled so much so that meetings became too crowded at individual homes. The ladies decided they needed to build a clubhouse. On April 10, 1907, Horace G. Dinsmore (no doubt prodded by his wife, Fannie Towne Dinsmore, the Club's first treasurer) donated a 37' by 100' plot of land from his home farm for a new clubhouse. The plot was centrally located across the road from the District No. 8 schoolhouse. Rather than deed the property to the Heywood Club, Dinsmore deeded it to twenty-one of the (all female) members, including his wife, three Richardson ladies, Ellen Millett, Addie Thurston, two female Tubbs, and Adalaide Young.[76] The only deed restriction Dinsmore placed upon the property was that whenever the Heywood Club was dissolved (or ceased to exist) the land would revert to whomever owned his original homestead farm.[77] The men in the neighborhood donated their labor to build the clubhouse, and the ladies raised the necessary funds. Fannie Dinsmore collected $150 in donations, and the remaining $135.91 for building supplies was raised by suppers and dances that were held every two weeks at different member's homes.[78] On July 10, 1907, the Heywood Club was formally dedicated, accompanied by a big supper and a talk given by Judge Charles P. Barnes of Houlton (formerly a Norway attorney).[79]

---

75. "John L. Stoddard Lectures." Volume 1. Boston: Balch Brothers Co., 1897. Ebook made available by Project Gutenberg.
76. Although Emma (Crockett) Harding Young was not living in Norway at the time, she became an honorary member of the Heywood Club. Emma, as did many others no longer residing in the neighborhood, likely contributed money for the building of the clubhouse.
77. OCROD, Book 298, page 104. The twenty-one members to whom the land was deeded were: Evis Allen, Eleanor Buck, Algie Crooker, Fannie Dinsmore, Georgie Fogg, Inez Freeman, Addie Hill, Emma Hull, Rose Judkins, Ellen Millett, Emogene Lovejoy, Calista Richardson, Eva Richardson, Louisa Richardson, Addie Thurston, Lydia Titcomb, Hattie Tubbs, Tena Tubbs, Ella Thomas, Adalaide Young, and Emma Dunham. On November 10, 1964, Henry Kudson, Jr. and Liesolette Knudson, then owners of the Dinsmore homestead, relinquished their claims to the Heywood Club real estate, voiding the reversion clause in the original Dinsmore deed. OCROD, Book 621, page 458.
78. "History of the Heywood Club," by Rowena Palmer, March 16, 1994.
79. IBID.

The Heywood Club and some of the attendees at the dedication of the new clubhouse July 10, 1907.
(Photos courtesy of the Heywood Club.)

Not long after the new clubhouse was built, the Heywood Club began to change from a literary society into a dynamic neighborhood support group. (The building boasted a kitchen and a hall big enough to feed 75–100 people.) The Club's motto became "neighbors helping neighbors." Local families in need were provided with financial support from the club's treasury, as well as physical, emotional, and spiritual support from members. Dances were held to raise money for scholarships (and for fun), and annual fundraising dinner parties were held at the clubhouse on holidays such as Christmas and Patriots' Day. The hall was also available to rent for weddings and family reunions. Many local funerals were held at the Heywood Club, and our family is particularly grateful to the ladies of the club for providing the food for our mother's funeral.[80] (I am now a regular member of the Heywood Club and my sister Cheryl Wixson and aunt Paula Johnson are honorary members.)

---

80. According to my parent's wedding announcement, the Heywood Club also provided the food for my mother's wedding.

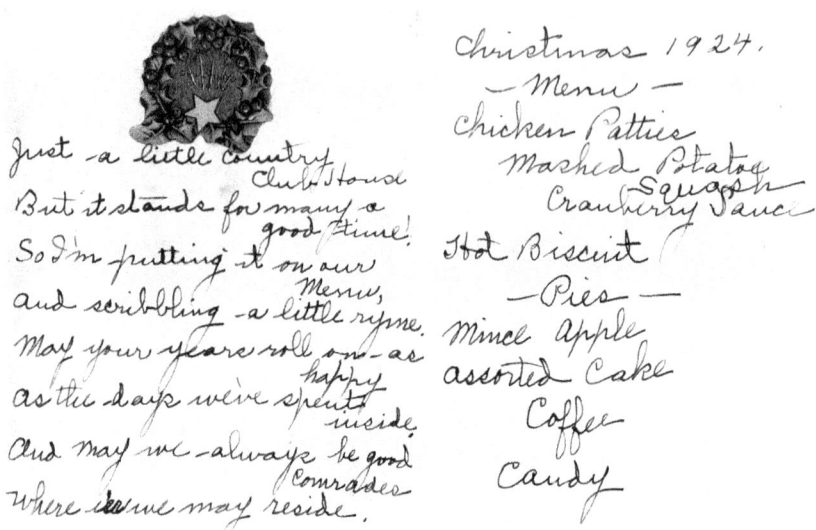

Poetic invitation to the Heywood Club's 1924 Christmas party and a copy of the menu.
(Jennifer Wixson photo. Invitation courtesy of the Heywood Club.)

Family Life

Meanwhile, Bill and Addie's children were growing up fast. The youngsters, when they were old enough, attended the District No. 8 school across from the Heywood Club, walking the mile twice a day, as their ancestors had walked before them. All three children—George, Winona, and young Willard (known as "Bud")—helped out at home by doing chores around the house and farm. They lugged firewood to keep Addie's cookstove going; emptied chamber pots; turned the cows out and brought them in; gathered eggs from the flock of chickens their mother added to the livestock menagerie; and pumped water from the well out back to lug to the house and hens.

Bill and Addie (Chaplin) Young

Doing chores on the farm circa 1917.
Left to right: Bud, Winona, unknown person (possibly the hired hand), George, Bill and Addie.
(Family photo, currently in the author's possession.)

Addie and her chickens (and German shepherd) circa 1920.
(Family photo, in the author's possession.)

The Youngs kept up via letters with the ever-changing lives of their friends and family, too. On May 25, 1913, Bill's cousin Frank Harriman Hobbs (son of Etta Crockett and Frank Hobbs) married Mary Montague in Epping, New Hampshire. At the time, Frank and his mother were both employed by a shoe manufacturer in Haverhill, Massachusetts. Frank was a shoe cutter and Aunt Etta was a stitcher.[81]

On July 9, 1913, Aunt Frances (Lydia Frances Crockett), who had moved to Canada after 1900, married William James Felker in Middlesex, Ontario, Canada.[82] Aunt Frances was fond of her nephew Bill (and later, his family), with whom she kept in regular contact via cards and letters, which sometimes included photographs. (No doubt letters and photos of the family were sent to Aunt Frances in Canada, too.)

---

81. New Hampshire Marriage Records, 1659-1947. Frank Harriman Hobbs.
82. Ontario, Canada, Marriages, 1826-1938. William James Felker and Francis [sic] Lydia Crockett.

"Aunt Frances." Lydia Frances (Crockett) Felker.
(Family photo, courtesy of Joyce Palmer.)

In 1914, John Harding received an appointment to the Baptist Church in Madison, Maine, and he and Emma relocated once again back to the Pine Tree State. But John and Emma only stayed in Maine two years, before he accepted a variety of pastorates in Massachusetts and Rhode Island, taking the couple away from their grandchildren for a decade.

In North Gorham, Addie's father's health was failing. Willis Chaplin was no longer able to keep up his physically-demanding blacksmith work and carriage trade. In 1913, Willis sold his property in Gorham,[83] and with their children grown and gone, he and Luella moved out to a home on Peaks Island,[84] then known as "the Coney Island of Maine."[85] Willis became a fruit seller and dealer on the wharf in Portland. He commuted daily from the island by steamboat to his storefront at 60 Portland Pier,[86] and eventually turned the business into a restaurant.[87] In 1917,

---

83. CCROD, Book 933, page 358. Willis sold his North Gorham property to Mary E. Knight on May 15, 1913. (Price undisclosed.)
84. CCROD, Book 927, page 180. Willis purchased this Peaks Island lot on February 5, 1914 from Maude M. Foss. (Price undisclosed.)
85. Webpage, Peaks Island Historical Society. "About." According to the website, during the summer season thousands of visitors a day descended on the island, carried there by twelve different steamboat lines.
86. Portland, Maine, City Directory, 1914, p. 378.
87. Information from the obituary of Willis B. Chaplin, pinned to a family Bible.

Willis and Harry (Addie's brother), an electrician at S.D. Warren Paper Company in Westbrook,[88] purchased three lots (and cottages) on Peaks Island.

With their Peaks Island purchase of three cottages, Willis and Harry were likely trying to tap into the lucrative tourism business. (Willis' restaurant and fruit business also catered to tourists.) Thousands of summer visitors flocked daily out to the resort island from the Portland wharf, traveling by the many steamboats that covered the route.[89] Willis sold his other house on Peaks Island,[90] and he and Luella moved into one of the cottages.

Over the years, there would have been occasional visits from family and friends to Bill and Addie's place on Crockett's Ridge. Mostly, however, connections were kept alive by letters, which often included photographs of the Young's growing family.

The Young family, circa 1922 or 1923.
Left to right: Bill, Willard "Bud," George (behind Bud), Addie, and Winona.
Bill and Addie's pride in their homestead is revealed in the set-up of this pastoral photograph. The iron kettle hanging from the tripod contains flowers; roses are in bloom behind the family; and a garden containing pole beans can be seen in the background.
(Family photo, in the author's possession.)

---

88. U.S. Census, Westbrook, Maine, 1910 and 1920. Harry E. Chaplin.
89. Webpage, Peaks Island Historical Society. "About."
90. CCROD, Book 988, page 428. Willis sold his first Peaks Island property on May 3, 1917, to Hjalmar E. Peterson for an undisclosed amount.

There were losses in the greater family, too, especially Addie's (as would have been expected, since she had a larger family than Bill). Addie's grandfather Abner Batchelder died in Standish in 1908.[91] After his death, Abner's widow Mary (York) Batchelder moved in with her daughter Luella, and son-in-law Willis Chaplin. Grandmother Batchelder lived in North Gorham with Willis and Luella, until they relocated to Peaks Island,[92] at which time she returned to her hometown of Naples, where Mary Batchelder died on May 21, 1915.[93] Two years later, on October 17, 1917, Grandfather Chaplin (Willis' father, Washington Chaplin) died at age eighty-nine in Conway, New Hampshire,[94] where he had been living with one of his daughters. (Washington's wife, Joanna Stuart Chaplin, passed away in 1905.)[95] Also in 1917, Luella's brother, Grinlief Batchelder, a widower, died in Westbrook.[96] Luella, as one of Grinlief's four living siblings, inherited one-quarter of his estate. In addition to sharing in Grinlief's personal property and savings, Luella and her three siblings—Luella's twin brother Llewellyn Batchelder, Charles Durham Batchelder, and Annah (Batchelder) Annis—divided their brother's real estate investments. For her share, Luella took Grinlief's home at 106 Haskell Street in Westbrook,[97] where she and Willis relocated by 1918.

After they moved to Westbrook, Luella and Willis kept the three cottages on Peaks Island, but they no longer made that resort community their permanent residence. Thanks to the advent of the family automobile, which enabled vacationers to explore other idyllic spots in Maine, tourism on Peaks Island had declined so much that Willis was no longer able to earn a living from his fruit and restaurant businesses. Instead, he fell back into his old trade of blacksmithing. Although sixty-two and with a bad heart (Willis once had a "fainting fit and cut his head considerably")[98] he hired on at Messen's blacksmith shop on Union Street, about a mile from their house. On February 10, 1919,[99] Willis was found dead at the shop by

---

91. Information from a framed Batchelder genealogical register in our family's possession.
92. 1910 U.S. Census for Gorham, Maine. Mary Roddie. (See also Willis B. Chaplin.) The surname "Roddie" was likely a census-takers error since if eighty-year-old Mary had remarried after her husband Abner Batchelder died in 1908, she likely would have been living with her new husband.
93. Information from Batchelder genealogical register.
94. New Hampshire Death and Disinterment Records, 1754-1947. Washington Chaplin. Washington and his wife Joanna (Stuart) Chaplin were both buried in Riverside Cemetery, Cornish, Maine.
95. Find A Grave Index, 1600s-current. Joanna Chaplin. Riverside Cemetery, Cornish, Maine.
96. Maine Death Records, 1761-1922. Grinlief Batchelder.
97. CCROD, Book 1008, page, 181. See also the other real estate divisions between the siblings: CCROD Book 991, page 136; Book 996, page 94; and Book 1008, page 178.
98. Obituary of Willis B. Chaplin, pinned to a family Bible.
99. Maine Death Records, 1761-1922. Willis B. Chaplin.

a fellow worker, who "looked around and saw his body lying in the corner of the shop."[100] Dr. George I. Gaer of Portland, who officially reported his death, declared that Willis died of natural causes, "probably heart disease."[101]

Willis' death was an unexpected blow that shocked his family. Although some, like his wife, knew he suffered from poor health, none were prepared to learn that Willis—who always appeared to be a hale and hearty man—would only outlive his father by sixteen months. Bill, Addie and their three children attended the funeral of her father, which was held at Willis and Luella's home on Haskell Street. Also attending was Addie's brother Harry and his wife; Addie's two half-brothers Sidney and Elroy and their families; and friends and neighbors of the blacksmith. After his death Willis B. Chaplin's past transgressions were forgotten and his sins forgiven. (As it should be for all of us.) Willis' obituary painted the picture of a man much-loved by his family and community:

> "He was loved and respected by all those associated with him. He was a man of unselfish motives, and took a great interest in his home affairs. His kind and gentle manner endeared him to all."[102]

Luella inherited the Peaks Island real estate from her husband (she owned the Haskell Street house), as well as Willis' personal property. In 1922, Luella sold the three Peaks Island lots (and cottages)[103] and purchased in 1924 a new house on the island closer to the downtown area.[104] During most of the year she resided at her home on Haskell Street, and summered on Peaks Island. We can guess that Luella's visits (via train) to her daughter's home in Norway became more frequent after her husband's death.

---

100. Information from newspaper notice, "Blacksmith Drops Dead, Union St. Shop," pinned in a family Bible.
101. Maine Death Records, 1761-1922. Willis B. Chaplin.
102. Obituary of Willis B. Chaplin, pinned in a family Bible.
103. CCROD, Book 1108, page 389.
104. CCROD, Book 1173, page 433.

Luella (Batchelder) Chaplin in later years.
(Family photo, in the author's possession.)

In another blow to the Chaplin family, Addie's half-brother Elroy Chaplin (Willis' son by his first wife Etta) died on December 14, 1925.[105] Elroy, forty-two, outlived *his* father by less than seven years. (I have not been able to locate a death record for Elroy, so we do not know the cause of death.) At the time of his passing Elroy had been working at a foundry, casting metal for ships.[106] One can imagine how Addie received this distressing news, since her half-brother Elroy was only eight months younger than she was. (When Willis' two families were joined, Addie and Elroy would have gone to school together, possibly even in the same grade.) Elroy left behind a wife and four children ranging in age from five to ten. He was buried with his father in Woodlawn Cemetery in Westbrook.[107]

Bill's side of the family lost Charles Sewell Penley (Emma's cousin) on March 25, 1920. Charles died at the age of seventy-five at the Soldier's Hospital at Togus. Charles had been living in the Soldier's Home off and on for many years, although he appears to have been at his home on Crockett's Ridge when he suffered a stroke. Charles was taken to Togus Hospital, where he died two days later.[108] In 1916, less

---

105. Find A Grave, 1600-current. Elroy W. Chaplin. Westbrook, Maine.
106. Westbrook City Directories, 1921, 1923, and 1924. Elroy Chaplin.
107. Find A Grave, 1600-current. Elroy W. Chaplin. Westbrook, Maine.
108. Maine Death Records, 1761-1922. Charles Sewell Penley's death certificate says he had only been at Togus this time

than four years prior to his death, Charles, a Civil War veteran, had married (for the third time) a thirty-year-old widow by the name of Laura McLellan. Penley's estate was heavily mortgaged at the time of his death, but Laura, after paying off the debts, was able to salvage something for herself when she sold the property to Dennis Pike in 1922.[109] After more than a hundred years, the ownership of the north half of Lot 44 was sold to a family without a connection to the original Lee's Grant neighborhood.

By 1922, Bill's aunt Etta (Crockett) Hobbs and his cousin Frank Hobbs returned to Norway. Etta had taken a job at Norway Shoe Company (as the shoe shop was then known) and Frank was a shoe cutter.[110] Frank had divorced his first wife, and on October 12, 1923, he married Mary Louise Hunter from Lynn, Massachusetts.[111] The couple was married in Maine and made their home in Norway. By 1930, Frank had given up the shoe shop and was running a billiard parlor in downtown Norway.[112] He and Mary had five children (two of whom, Bob and Emma Hobbs, I knew in their later years).

According to family stories (and a plethora of photographs) the Hobbs and their children became regular visitors of the Youngs at the farm on Crockett's Ridge. In fact, the visits became so regular over the years that Addie was known to occasionally grumble that "those Hobbs are always around."[113] Addie did not know (but would discover after Bill's death) that Frank Hobbs had inherited his mother's one-sixth interest in the estate of his grandfather, William Robinson Crockett (the original Crockett homestead and the woodlots William had added to the property).

---

for two days, leading me to conclude that he was taken there from his farm following the stroke.
109. OCROD, Book 360, Page 550.
110. "Directory of Oxford County Maine," published by Portland Directory Co, Fred L. Tower, prop; 199 Federal St., Portland.
111. Maine Marriage Index, 1892-1996. Frank Harriman Hobbs.
112. 1930 U.S. Census, Norway, Maine. Frank H. Hobbs. Reportedly, gambling occurred at the billiard hall, which did not endear Frank to some members of the family, although it appears not to have bothered his aunt Emma (Bill's mother), despite her strong religious beliefs, since she wintered with Frank and his family in later years.
113. This information came to me from my grandmother Winona Palmer.

A visit from the Hobbs family, circa 1932.
Back row, l to r: Addie Young, Bill Palmer (husband of Winona Young, perhaps taking the photo),[114] Frank Hobbs, and Bill Young. Front row, l to r: four of the Hobbs children: Bob, Emma, Fred, and Irene. (Missing is Louise Hobbs, the oldest child.)
(Family photo, currently in the author's possession.)

Henrietta (Crockett) Hobbs passed away June 3, 1925.[115] She was buried with her parents (William and Lydia Crockett) and grandparents (Ephraim and Sally Crockett) in Norway Pine Grove Cemetery. Etta was predeceased by her and Emma's older brother Abel Stetson, who died in Norway on March 9, 1922, at the age of seventy-one.[116] He, too, was buried with their parents and grandparents. Uncle Abel, who had received $200 cash upon the death of their father, never had a legal interest in the old Crockett homestead.

Mellie and "Gram" Dunham

Meanwhile, in the Crockett's Ridge neighborhood, Mellie Dunham, master snowshoe maker (he supplied snowshoes for Commodore Robert E. Peary's Arctic Expedition) was becoming one of the most popular men in Maine. A talented self-taught fiddle player, Mellie had played for years for all the local dances. Sometimes the dances were held at the Heywood Club and sometimes in Mellie's

---
114. Bill Palmer was the author's grandfather. He was from Whitneyville, Maine.
115. CANDAGE, p. 179.
116. CANDAGE, p. 179.

cavernous post-and-beam barn. Like everyone else in the neighborhood, Bill and Addie attended these dances.

Neighborhood Christmas dance held in Mellie Dunham's barn.
Mellie and Emma "Gram" Dunham are in the center; Addie Young is behind Gram's left shoulder.
Bill is likely standing near his wife; however, his face is not pictured.
(Heywood Club photo, courtesy of the Norway, Maine Historical Society.)

Mellie Dunham became a national celebrity in 1925. That year, when Mellie was seventy-two, he received an invitation from Henry Ford (who loved fiddle music) to play at a dance at Ford's home in Dearborn, Michigan. Mellie let Ford's letter languish unopened for several days (he thought it was a request for snowshoes), before answering. Initially, Dunham declined the invitation. After some prodding and encouraging (no doubt by family and friends), Mellie and his wife Emma (known as "Gram" by everyone) agreed to go to Dearborn.

The couple received a huge send-off for their trip to Michigan. Schools were closed, and the Governor even came to Norway to see them off. Bill, Addie, and the family would have gone into Norway Village to attend the spectacular send-off parade for Mellie and Gram, who were popular in the Crockett's Ridge neighborhood. A police escort took the couple to the train station in Paris, where Ford had sent a Pullman car for them. The national press became obsessed with Mellie and Gram, and even though other fiddler players attended Ford's dance party on December 11, 1925, Mellie Dunham stole the show, receiving most of the publicity. Mellie played several tunes for the guests—songs he often played at the neighborhood dances held at the Heywood Club—including *Speed the Plow* and *Old Zip Coon*.[117]

Newspaper photo of Mellie Dunham playing for Henry Ford and
"'Mellie' Dunham's Fiddlin' Dance Tunes" songbook.
(Mellie and Henry Ford by Underwood & Underwood. Unknown publication. "Fiddlin' Dance Tunes" published in 1926 by Carl Fischer, Inc., New York.
Both items currently in the author's possession.)

Mellie shrewdly decided to capitalize on his fifteen-minutes of fame. After playing for Ford, Mellie and Gram immediately signed up for a vaudeville tour around the United States. The tour reportedly earned them $20,000 (about $357,000 in 2024 dollars).[118] On December 21, 1925, Gram wrote a letter from the Lenox Hotel in Boston to Addie Thurston in Norway (one of the Heywood Club's founding members). In the letter Gram describes getting ready for the opening of the vaudeville tour:

---

117. Considered racist and offensive today, *Old Zip Coon* was a black-faced minstrel show song in the 19th century. The tune is the same as *Turkey in the Straw*, which likely post-dated *Old Zip Coon*. The most popular sheet music sold for the song has a caricature of a black man on its cover. Information from webpage, Ferris State University. Jim Crow question. "Which came first? Old Zip Coon or Turkey in the Straw?"
118. CPI Inflation Calculator.

"Mell and I are fine and having lots of fun and have made good. Melli starts to morrow but we have been rehursing ever since Wednesday and we have lots of fun just like we was at the club house. The[re] is to be a barn scene and 6 couples of old dancers and six young ones. The young people are of the best families in Boston. Their will be 12 couples in all on the stage. We have been rehursing twise a day. We have not started for the theater the last two nights until 11 o'clock so have to get a little nap in the day time… Mellie has had another lamb skin lined coat given him since he has been here from one of the big stors here. They sayed to be no charg and no string attached. It is a little bigger than the other one and a nicer one. Now when I go ice fishing I can have his other one."[119]

Mellie and Emma "Gram" Dunham on the road.
(Heywood Club photo, courtesy of the Norway, Maine Historical Society.)

Mellie Dunham songbooks and sheet music also became hot-ticket items. The fiddler craze eventually died down a few years after it started, and Mellie and Gram returned to Norway, where he went back to making snowshoes and playing for the local dances. Prior to Mellie's death in 1951, however, he and Gram lost their home to fire. After the fire it was discovered that the couple was broke and had no fire insurance. To help them out, the Heywood Club hosted a big dance in Mellie's barn (which survived the fire), charging an admission fee of $1 to see and hear Mellie play. The club also sold refreshments. From the fundraiser the Heywood Club "got a sizable sum of money which was given to Mellie and Gram for furnishings

---

119. Letter from Emma "Gram" Dunham to Mrs. Addie Thurston, December 20, 1925. Heywood Club collection, courtesy of NHS.

for their new home."[120] A bright light went out in the neighborhood when Mellie Dunham died September 28, 1931, at the age of seventy-eight.[121] My grandmother Winona, who attended many Heywood Club dances where Mellie and Gram (who played the piano) provided the music, shared many fond memories of those days from her youth with me. Mellie and Gram Dunham are still remembered today as icons of the Crockett's Ridge neighborhood.

Mellie Dunham in later years.
(Heywood Club photo, courtesy of the Norway, Maine Historical Society.)

The Ford connection to Norway did not die with Mellie Dunham, however. The automobile magnate—and indeed, other auto company officials in Detroit—had become enamored with the lifestyle of the simple folk on Crockett's Ridge. According to my grandmother, some of the auto executives long kept in touch with families in the neighborhood.

Death of Bill's Stepfather and Emma Returns to Crockett's Ridge

By 1928, Bill's stepfather's health was failing. The Rev. John Harding's twenty-five-year career hopping from church to church, from Rhode Island to Massachusetts to Maine, took a heavy toll on him. By the spring of 1929, John was

---

120. "History of the Heywood Club," by Rowena Palmer, March 16, 1994.
121. Information about Mellie and Gram Dunham came from the New England Historical Society's Webpage; Arts and Leisure. "Mellie Dunham, Maine Snowshoe Maker, Takes a Meteoric Ride to Stardom on the Vaudeville Circuit."

admitted to the New England Baptist Hospital in Roxbury, Massachusetts for rest and recovery. The treatment was unsuccessful, however, and John returned to Norway, where he died September 3, 1929. He was buried next to George P. Young, Bill's father, in Norway Pine Grove Cemetery.

Emma's finances had been strained by John's illness. In 1926, to help provide for the couple (and perhaps pay John's medical bills), she had mortgaged one of her Beal Street properties for $1400. (See prior chapter.) Unfortunately, Emma failed to make her scheduled payments. Busy with his own life up on the farm, Bill probably never knew of his mother's worsening financial situation.

Emma was able to borrow enough money to rescue her property, but to pay back those loans she needed more income. She likely was forced to rent out both of her Beal Street houses, including the one in which she had been living. Sometime after John's death Emma moved up to Crockett's Ridge to live at the old Nathan Morse farm, where her aunt Mary (Crockett) and uncle Isaiah Vickery Penley had raised their family, and which she had purchased with her first husband's life insurance money in 1900. In winter, Emma, who preferred to be in town, resided with her nephew Frank Hobbs and his wife Mary (and their family) in Norway Village. Her seasonal residence with Frank forged an even closer connection between the Young and Hobbs families.

The New Barn Burns

In 1931, an event occurred that would completely alter the lives of the Youngs on Crockett's Ridge. That year, after the haying season was done and the new barn was stocked with 65 tons of hay for the winter, a fire started in the barn cellar. Probably a spark from a tractor driven by Bill and Addie's son Willard, "Bud," then nineteen, accidentally caused the blaze.[122] The fire was discovered in the evening around six o'clock, then "burning furiously."[123] By the time the fire department arrived from

---

122. This information came from Bud's son, Norman, who was told it by his father. Norman informed me in a questionnaire I sent him in 2021 that "my father started [the] barn fire with [a] tractor." In a follow-up phone call between the two of us, Norman allowed that he was not sure about the details because "Nobody talked about it." A tractor sparking a fire would not have been unusual in 1931, according to my husband Stanley Luce. He noted that old tractors had manual sparking mechanisms. In addition, John Deeres and Fordsons had two fuel tanks: gasoline and kerosene. Due to its lower combustion level, the old tractors were started with gasoline. Once the engine was heated up, however, the farmer would switch to kerosene, which was a cheaper fuel to run. Stanley explained that often during the switch from gasoline to kerosene the old tractors would spark, sending flames shooting out the exhaust. In fact, Stanley was with his grandfather on an old Fordson tractor once which did just that, starting a tractor fire.

123. All information about the loss of the new barn came from a front-page *Norway Advertiser* article, "Barn Burned at

Norway Village "only a shell of the barn was still standing." Bill, Addie, and the family; the hired hand; and neighbors had formed a bucket brigade carrying water from the well (located behind the house) to the barn, but the old hand-dug well could not provide anywhere near enough water. They were able to save a nearby garage; however. The fire department also sprayed a chemical flame-retardant upon the old Crockett homestead to save the eighty-one-year-old brick house from the inferno.

The losses were devastating. In addition to the new barn, which was destroyed, Bill lost ten head of cattle, including four heifers and a pair of steers, all blue-ribbon winners. Also incinerated was a prize bull, "Oxford Ferry Boy," owned by David Moulton of Portland. (Bill had probably been renting the bull to breed his heifers.) Fortunately, Bill was able to save his team of horses, and neighbors rescued ten of Bill's prized Jersey herd. Even the family dogs participated in the rescue; the German shepherds kept the terrified cows and horses from running back into the blaze. There were no personal injuries, except to the couple's youngest son Bud, whose hands had been badly burned in his efforts to put out the blaze.

Addie and two of the family's German shepherds.
During the barn fire the dogs kept the terrified livestock from rushing back into the blazing barn.
(Family photo, courtesy of Joyce Palmer.)

W.F. Young's." The article date is 1931, but the month and day are cut off. Because the barn was full of hay, however, it was after haying season had ended.

The *Norway Advertiser* estimated the Young's total loss to be $20,000 (about $411,000 in 2024).[124] Reportedly, Bill and Addie had $3,000 or less in fire insurance. With the remainder of his father's life insurance money used up to build the new barn, there was nothing left for Bill to draw upon. Bill's mother, dealing with her own financial difficulties, was unable to help, either. Probably after Bill reimbursed David Moulton for the loss of "Oxford Ferry Boy," there was not much left of the fire insurance money. His desire to resurrect his father's dream of Fair View Farm had literally gone up in smoke. Bill, now forty-seven, and Addie, forty-eight, would need to start over—during the Depression—the greatest economic calamity to hit the United States.

Young's Turkey Farm Rises From the Ashes

What arose like a phoenix from the ashes of the barn fire was a new vision for the old Crockett homestead—Young's Turkey Farm. As previously mentioned, Addie, who always loved turkeys, had been given a pair of turkey hens by her husband during the first year of their marriage. Those turkeys had not survived. Addie tried again, but lost her next batch of turkeys, too. After a few years, however, Addie began to raise her turkeys in confinement for at least the first three or four months of their lives. All those birds survived, and by the time of the barn's blaze Addie had been successfully raising turkeys on a small scale for more than two decades.[125] A resourceful woman, whose education at Western State Normal and Training School had included algebra, physics, botany, zoology, and book-keeping,[126] Addie believed she could create a market for turkey meat, and not just at Thanksgiving time, either. She conceived of a plan to expand her turkey flock, eventually replacing the farm's lost income from milk with the sale of turkey meat. To do this, though, Addie would need not only to increase the scale of her production, but also increase the public's demand for turkey meat.

According to a 1950 newspaper article that featured Addie and her turkey business, Bill initially was not interested in her new business venture, "… so the building up of the business rested solely on the shoulders of his wife." Addie not only

---

124. CPI Inflation Calculator.
125. "45 YEARS WITH TURKEYS IS A LONG TIME." Ralph H. Whittum, Agricultural Editor. 1950 newspaper article about Addie and her turkeys. Unknown publication. Clipping pasted by Addie into her Young's Turkey Farm scrapbook.
126. Western State Normal and Training School, "Western State Normal and Training School at Gorham Maine Catalog 1901-1902" (1901) Course Catalogs. 91.

took care of the birds, but also kept the records, and—perhaps more importantly—handled the sales and marketing. (Bill, in those early years, remained focused on slowly rebuilding his Jersey herd, going back to using the old Crockett barn.)

Addie's was a bold plan, and it worked. The first year Young's Turkey Farm was officially in business Addie dressed and sold ninety turkeys. "I was quite thrilled with that record," she told a reporter, twenty years later.[127] She slowly continued to expand her turkey flock, purchasing chicks and raising them in confinement as she had learned to do. As Young's Turkey Farm's business grew, Bill became more and more interested in the operation. He built his wife a small village of turkey houses on the hill behind the brick house, each equipped with feeders, waterers, and oil heaters to keep the young turkey poults warm. Bill eventually came to like the turkeys as much as Addie did, although the two continued to keep separate books for their farming operations.[128]

Addie was not just a businesswoman, but also a mother, and by 1932, she was a grandmother. Not all the chicks she raised at the farm had wings. Over the next decade, as Addie was building up the turkey business, her children and grandchildren became woven into the fabric of Young's Turkey Farm. The next generation helped replace the loss of the two matriarchs—Emma and Luella.

Luella (Batchelder) Chaplin passed away in Westbrook on April 23, 1934, after an illness of several weeks. She was sixty-nine. Luella appears to have died intestate, because in a deed dated October 9, 1934, Addie sold her brother Harry Chaplin "my one-half interest" in their mother's Haskell Street home as "heir at law"[129] (i.e. as one of Luella's "natural children"). Luella's stepson, Sidney Chaplin, then living in Springfield, Massachusetts, is mentioned in Luella's obituary as one of her two sons;[130] however, Sidney—who was not related to Luella and had never been officially adopted by her—did not inherit any of his stepmother's personal or real estate. Before her death, Luella had sold her Peak's Island home,[131] a fortuitous move since Harry and Addie might have had trouble disposing of this asset during the height of the Depression. The money Addie inherited from her mother was a much-needed infusion into the expansion of Young's Turkey Farm.

---

127. "45 YEARS WITH TURKEYS IS A LONG TIME." Ralph H. Whittum, Agricultural Editor. 1950 newspaper article about Addie and her turkeys.
128. IBID.
129. CCROD, Book 1451, page 499.
130. Obituary of Luella (Batchelder) Chaplin pinned inside a family Bible.
131. CCROD, Book 1333, page 159.

On January 25, 1937, Bill's mother Emma (Crockett) Young Harding passed away unexpectedly. She had been staying at the home of her nephew Frank in Norway Village, where Emma preferred to spend the winter.[132] In 1935, Casco Mercantile Trust Company had foreclosed on the Beal Street home in which she formerly wintered, and, although Emma had paid off her mortgage a month prior to her death, she never went back to her Beal Street house.[133] Upon Emma's death, her son Bill Young inherited Emma's significant real estate holdings on Crockett's Ridge and in North Norway (see Lee's Grant lot map following), as well as her two properties downtown. The Beal Street houses both became rental properties, which would provide the farm with enough money to pay the real estate taxes. Bill had now joined the ranks of farmers everywhere who found themselves "land poor"—short on cash, but long on real estate—during the Great Depression.

---

132. Obituary of Emma (Crockett) Young Harding pinned inside a family Bible.
133. Emma discharged her mortgage to Casco Mercantile Trust on December 23, 1936, one month before her death. See OCROD, Book 412, page 582.

Bill and Addie (Chaplin) Young

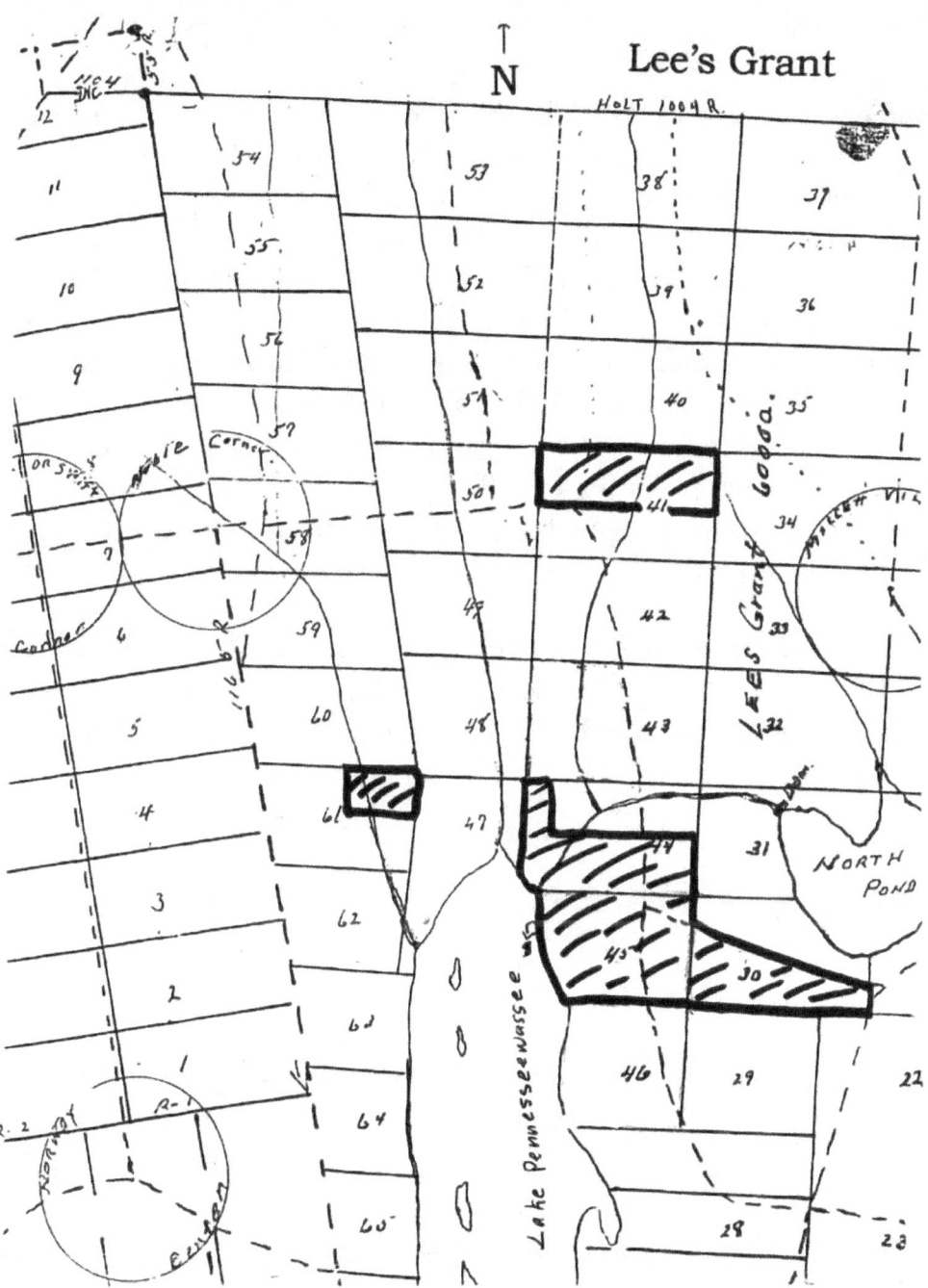

Lee's Grant lot map showing the property Bill Young inherited from his mother in 1937. (Frank Hobbs, Bill's cousin, was entitled to a 1/6th share of their grandfather's homestead and land.)

George, Winona, and Bud

Bill and Addie's eldest son George stayed on the farm to help his parents with the turkey business. George remained single until 1944, when he married Florence A. Andrews, of Auburn, a teacher in the local schools. Like her mother-in-law, Florence also graduated from Gorham Normal School.[134] After George and Florence were married, they continued to reside with his parents, until a case of scarlet fever in the homestead made it unsafe for the pregnant Florence to remain there. It was then that George and Florence moved down to the old Morse farm,[135] where Emma had spent most of her final days (when not wintering in Norway Village). George continued to work at Young's Turkey Farm, and the couple raised their three children—Byron, George Willard ("Jo Bill"), and Pamela Young—at the companion farm to the old Crockett homestead, which homestead had been in the greater family since it was settled in 1814 by Nathan Morse and his wife Mary (Crockett) Morse.

Bud, the younger son of Bill and Addie, eventually moved away from Crockett's Ridge. He attended Bates College in Lewiston for two years, studying business.[136] After graduation Bud went to work in an office in Lewiston. On New Year's Day 1933, Bud married Lillian Hilden, a shoe shop worker from West Paris.

---

134. 1944 newspaper wedding announcement, Young-Andrews. Copy of the clipping courtesy of the Norway, Maine Historical Society.
135. This information came from the author's grandmother, Winona Palmer.
136. This information came from the author's aunt, Paula (Palmer) Johnson via email February 3, 2022.

Willard "Bud" Young and his new bride, Lillian (Hilden) Young.
(Photo courtesy of W. Norman Young.)

Bud and Lillian's son Willard Norman Young (known as "Norman" to the family) was born in 1934. Norman would grow up spending his summers and school vacations at Young's Turkey Farm. In addition, Bud and Norman also returned to the farm every year to help with the Thanksgiving turkey harvest.[137]

Bill and Addie's only daughter, Winona, graduated from Norway High School in 1925 at the age of seventeen. (To give you an idea of Winona's character, my grandmother told me that prior to graduating from high school she used to swim across the head of the lake in summer to earn money cleaning house for a woman who lived in a stone house on the Greenwood Road.)[138] After graduation, Winona lived at home and taught in a local one-room school for a year. She entered the University of Maine at Orono in 1926 when she was eighteen. In her first year at Orono, Winona, a good country girl, joined the women's rifle club, where—in what

---
137. This information was told to me by Bud's son, Norman Young.
138. This is information my grandmother Winona told me when I lived with her in the seventies and eighties.

was a strange twist of fate—she met my other grandmother-to-be, Hope Craig, from Presque Isle. The two women did not become fast friends, but they were intimate enough for each to pass on (in later years) interesting stories about the other to a granddaughter who asked a lot of questions.

Winona Young, Norway High School graduation photo 1925; and UMO Women's Rifle Club members 1926-27, including Winona Young and Hope Craig.[139]
In the rifle team photo, the author's paternal grandmother Hope Craig is in the front row, 2nd from right. Winona Palmer (her maternal grandmother) is behind Hope to the right."
(Family photos in the author's possession.)

For some reason, possibly financial, Winona did not then complete her bachelor's degree.[140] She returned to Norway where she resumed teaching. Prior to 1932 (the year after the barn burned), Winona met and married William Palmer (my grandfather), a traveling salesman who hailed from Whitneyville. According to Winona, her parents were opposed to the wedding, and as a result, on April 8,

---

139. This is a partial photo of the entire 1926-1927 Women's Rifle Club. The photo appeared in the 1927 *Prism*, the UMO yearbook. (The author also has a copy of the photo.) In another strange twist of fate, my great-uncle Charles Wesley Wixson, (backrow right) for whom my brother Wes is named, was the Assistant Coach of the Women's Rifle Club. A few years later Wesley (as he was known) would become Hope's brother-in-law. Obviously, none of the three—Winona Young, Hope Craig, and Wesley Wixson—knew when this photograph was taken how their lives would become intertwined. Hope married Wesley's brother Eldwin Wixson, and had my father, Eldwin, Jr. Winona and her husband William Palmer had my mother, Rowena Palmer. My parents, Eldwin and Rowena, were married in 1955. My grandmothers did not need to be introduced to one another at the wedding.
140. In later years, Winona went back to school, earning her Bachelor of Science in Education degree at UMO in 1959. Following that, Winona earned a Master's degree in Education at UMO, after which she became Supervisor of Elementary Education in the Norway area schools. (Winona's bachelor's degree is currently in the author's possession.)

1932, she and Bill ran off to Portland to get married.[141] She was twenty-four and he was twenty-eight.

Winona (Young) and Bill Palmer on their honeymoon, at Forget-Me-Not train station in Maine. (Family photo in the author's possession.)

The Grandchildren at Young's Turkey Farm

Although their first child was born in Whitneyville, Bill and Winona eventually made their home in Norway Village. Back then, married women were allowed to teach, but pregnant women were not. My grandmother told me that in the early days of their marriage both she and Bill worked for a local drugstore. The couple had three children: Rowena, (my mother), born in 1932; Kurt, born in 1934; and Paula, born in 1935. Regrettably, my grandfather was an alcoholic, and my grandmother—who loved her husband deeply—was forced to choose between providing for their three children or his drinking. (Sadly, there were few treatment

---

141. Marriage certificate of William H. Palmer and Winona Young. The couple was married by the Rev. Ralph Stoody. Witnesses were: Francea A. Riel, Eugene D. Warren, Frank C. Dow, Richard W. Davis, possibly friends of my grandparents.

options for addicts in those days.) Winona applied to her mother for help, and Addie allowed her (and the kids) to move back to the farm, but only after Winona promised she would never see Bill again.[142] (To my knowledge, Winona never did.) She and Bill were divorced March 15, 1940.[143] My grandmother went back to teaching school, and Rowena, Kurt and Paula were raised at Young's Turkey Farm under the wing of their grandparents.

Bill and Addie's grandchildren, part of the fabric of Young's Turkey Farm.
Left to right: Paula Palmer, Kurt Palmer, Rowena Palmer, and Norman Young.
(Family photo, courtesy of the Rowena Palmer Trust.)

The three Palmer kids loved growing up on the farm, especially when their cousin Norman Young came to stay. According to Norman, a summer's day on the farm would see the kids arise at 7 a.m. He and Kurt would help water the turkeys, after which they came in for breakfast. Then there were more chores, a break for lunch, then haying, finding and bringing the cows into milk, and supper. After supper Norman and Kurt (and maybe Rowena and Paula) played some baseball, and then the boys would "sit the hay" (watch that no damp hay became hot and

---
142. This information my grandmother told me during the years that I lived with her.
143. Decree of Divorce, Winona Young Palmer vs. William H. Palmer. Oxford, Superior Court. March Term, 1940. No. 127.

spontaneously combusted). When asked what else he remembered about his summers on the farm, Norman replied: "My grandmother's biscuits were the best!!"[144]

Paula (Palmer) Johnson recollects that her grandmother Addie "was the woman I would like someday to be compared to. She was respected in the poultry association, in her town, and in the business world, be it the bank, town, or major [turkey] buyers." According to Paula, everyone loved Addie, who always had a smile on her face and a twinkle in her eye. ("Makes you wonder now what she was up to," Paula says.) Her grandfather Bill, on the other hand, "loved us [kids] but hated to show his feelings," Paula remembers. "When he said be home by 10:00 o'clock we sure were home by ten. He could be fun-loving and loved to play jokes on us. We had to work but he always kept an eye on us and would interject ideas to make [the work] more fun and challenging. He taught us many things in life."[145]

Norman Young, and Paula, Kurt and Rowena Palmer.

Paula Palmer and Norman Young (with guns) and Kurt Palmer, kneeling, with Charlie the dog.

(Family photos, courtesy of the Rowena Palmer Trust.)

---

144. Information from Norman Young from the Questionnaire sent him by the author and completed and returned in 2021. My mother told me growing up that her least favorite chore was emptying bed pans. Regrettably, she passed away before I began my new Crockett history, and so I could not have Mom respond to my Questionnaire.
145. Email from Paula (Palmer) Johnson to the author, January 16, 2022.

Expanding the Turkey Business

In 1937, the year Bill's mother died, he and Addie made a big expansion in the turkey business. Bill built a large grower house for his wife, one that Addie designed, and possibly the first of its kind in Maine. The wooden grower house was 75' long and featured a wide-plank porch where the turkeys could take in the fresh air and sunshine, even while confined. Wire surrounding the porch protected the turkeys from predators, and the floor of the house was also fashioned of wire for sanitation and protection purposes. By November of 1937, Addie would harvest 1,100 turkeys, and had plans to raise 2,000 birds in 1938.[146]

Addie's new turkey grower house, 1937.
(Family photo, courtesy of Joyce Palmer.)

---

146. "Norway Woman Raises Turkeys By 'Off the Ground' Method." *Portland Press Herald*, November 23, 1937.

1937 Portland Press Herald photo and caption about Addie's new grower house.
(Clipping from Addie's Young's Turkey Farm scrapbook, currently in
the possession of Joyce Palmer.)

The major pitfall to raising so many birds in confinement was the temperament of the turkeys themselves. The birds, not the brightest of fowl, were easily spooked. One day a child (likely one of Addie's grandchildren) decided to feed a number of birds on the porch. He tossed handfuls of green grass in through the wire, terrifying the turkeys, which were not used to any intrusion into their pen. The birds rushed back into the house where they piled up in a corner. By the time Bill and Addie noticed the incident, twelve of the turkeys had been smothered.[147]

As their business expanded, Bill and Addie joined the fledgling Maine State Turkey Growers Association. Addie, who was particularly interested in enlarging the market for turkey meat, was one of the first members who favored inspecting, grading, and tagging Maine-raised birds. Addie saw that this was being done with other agricultural products in the state as a way of promoting a quality Maine product, and she wanted turkey growers to have the same advantages. As a result, in 1937 the Maine Department of Agriculture began a tagging and inspection program for turkeys through the state's division of marketing. Tags were sold to growers for 2¢ each, with one-half of the money raised to go toward paying for the cost of the tags, and the other half dedicated to a fund for advertising Maine turkeys.[148]

Not all turkey growers saw the same benefit to their business as Addie did. She understood that the tag was an "implied guarantee of quality" to the consumer. In 1937, only 2,400 turkeys were inspected and tagged. By 1938, however, that number had more than doubled, and the numbers continued to climb as the years progressed.[149] Addie was one of the turkey tag's most ardent supporters and for the next decade she made sure her customers knew that they were getting a quality product when they purchased their bird from Young's Turkey Farm.

---

147. "We Are Ready No Matter When Thanksgiving Comes." *Lewiston Daily Sun*, August 19, 1939. Addie pasted this clipping in her Young's Turkey Farm scrapbook, currently in the possession of Joyce Palmer.
148. "Tags First Turkey with Maine Branding Insignia." 1937 newspaper clipping pasted in Addie's Young's Turkey Farm scrapbook.
149. "Maine Turkeys Tagged Blue, White & Red." *Lewiston Daily Sun*, November 22, 1938. Clipping Addie pasted in her Young's Turkey Farm scrapbook.

Young's Turkey Farm newspaper ad touting the state turkey tag.
(Ad from Young's Turkey Farm scrapbook.)

In 1939, thanks to the passage of the Rural Electrification Act of 1936—part of President Franklin D. Roosevelt's "New Deal" for Americans—electricity came to Crockett's Ridge. On January 9, 1939, Bill Young granted Central Maine Power (CMP) an easement across his property along the Crockett Ridge Road so that the power company could string a line of ten poles.[150] Soon, electric lights replaced oil lamps and candles in the old homestead (shed and barn), and likely an electric radio replaced the battery-operated radio that Bill had owned since at least 1930.[151] During the next decade Addie was often heard to expound upon the benefits of electricity: "Cheapest hired hand we ever had!" she would declare.[152]

That year President Roosevelt also created an unnecessary imbroglio for his administration and the turkey business by changing the date of Thanksgiving. The President decided that in 1939 the holiday would be celebrated on the third Thursday of November, rather than the traditional fourth Thursday of that month. Roosevelt had caved to pressure from the National Retail Dry Goods Association, which group of retailers appealed to him for the change to extend the Christmas shopping season by one week. This move to change the traditional Thanksgiving

---
150. OCROD, Book 424, page 109.
151. 1930 U.S. Census, Norway, Maine. According to the census, Bill had one of the few radios in the neighborhood.
152. This story was told us kids by our mother, Rowena Palmer, who grew up with her grandparents at the old Crockett homestead.

Day—which had been celebrated on the last Thursday of November since President Lincoln proclaimed the holiday in 1863 (with only two exceptions)[153]—simply for commercial reasons, not only angered the public, but also caused unnecessary confusion throughout the country:

> "At the time, [Roosevelt's] 1939 proclamation only applied directly to the District of Columbia and federal employees. While governors usually followed the president's lead with state proclamations for the same day, on this year, twenty-three of the 48 states observed Thanksgiving Day on November 23rd; twenty-three celebrated on November 30th; and Texas and Colorado declared both dates to be holidays. Football coaches scrambled to reschedule games set for November 30th; families didn't know when to have their holiday meals; calendars were inaccurate in half the country; and people weren't sure when to start their Christmas shopping."[154]

Where many consumers saw confusion—and other turkey growers saw chaos—Addie recognized an opportunity. She made sure that the newspapers knew Young's Turkey Farm would be ready no matter what date Maine Governor Lewis O. Barrows selected for Thanksgiving. (Maine ultimately stuck with the traditional date, the last Thursday of November.) Addie also ensured that a photo of her grandson Kurt accompanied the article, which ended up being more about Young's Turkey Farm than it was about the date change for Thanksgiving. (Congress ultimately passed legislation that pronounced Thanksgiving officially to be celebrated on the fourth Thursday of November.)[155]

---

153. In 1865, President Andrew Johnson proclaimed the first Thursday of November as Thanksgiving, and in 1969 President Ulysses S. Grant selected the third Thursday. LOC.gov webpage. Wise Guide. "When Is Thanksgiving Again?"
154. IBID.
155. IBID.

"We Are Ready Whenever Thanksgiving Comes"

A Grandson of the Young's brandishes the ax, but "Mr. Turk" is not disturbed. Turkeys are not slaughtered that way now.

Young's Poultry Farm at Norway Has 2400 Birds—Incubating Poults Now

"Make Thanksgiving November 23 or 30th, as you like, we are ready now!" That was the answer that came from Young's Turkey Farm in Norway, as to the proper time for the "Great National Turkey Day."

"We now have 2400 birds on the farm this year and expect to round out the number to 3000 before we stop the electric incubator."

Talk about changing times in agriculture or livestock. Folks really in the business don't seem to follow the old traditions at all. Here it is the middle of August and these folks still hatching and incubating turkeys.

The writer remembers meeting Mrs. Young on Lisbon street a cold day last Winter, long after the Christmas holidays. She had brought some birds to the local market then. I questioned her about her mother and she said, "We are going to have birds to sell every week in the year," and evidently they have brought that program about.

Just after the hurricane last September their place was a sorry looking sight; some piles of boards were nearby ready to erect new buildings. These were blown in every direction. The Young's went right out among the birds in the midst of the storm and kept them from going into a panic. They didn't lose many birds.

About a great a loss as they ever had at one time was caused by a little child. It had thrown handfuls of grass into the pens and frightened the birds. Unseen to anyone he kept this up and when they looked over the birds again 12 were dead, rushed inside the house in a mass and were smothered. The child didn't mean any harm.

It is not many years since the Young's tried their first venture with 50 poults; it was successful and they have kept on being successful. It's not just haphazard. There is a lot of work to it but more than all else, careful planning.

August 19, 1939 *Lewiston Daily Sun* article and photo of Kurt Palmer with axe and turkey.[156] (Article pasted by Addie into her Young's Turkey Farm scrapbook.)

---

156. "We Are Ready No Matter When Thanksgiving Comes." *Lewiston Daily Sun*, August 19, 1939. Note that the caption reads: "Turkeys are not slaughtered that way [with an axe] now." Young's Turkey Farm, like other poultry producers, had switched to the sticking method of killing birds, which does not make for such a cute photo.

Around 1940, the addition of two large incubators at the farm (about 8' by 8'),[157] in which hundreds of eggs could be hatched at a time, boosted Young's Turkey Farm into large-scale, year-round meat production. Given the finicky nature of hatching chicks, nobody but Bill or Addie tended the incubators, turning the eggs on average five to seven times a day, and maintaining the correct temperature and moisture.[158] The Youngs hatched eggs from their own turkeys, raising classic Bourbon Red and Black Diamond breeds. Addie also traded or purchased White Holland eggs from other Maine turkey growers to hatch and raise.[159]

Addie holding one of her Black Diamond turkeys.
(Family photo, courtesy of Paula and Robert Johnson.)

---

157. The estimated size of the incubators came from my aunt Paula (Palmer) Johnson, who was raised at the farm.
158. Information about the incubators from my aunt Paula (Palmer) Johnson, who was raised at the farm with my mother and uncle Kurt Palmer. Email from Paula (Palmer) Johnson to Jennifer Wixson, January 16, 2022.
159. Information about turkey eggs and breeds from my aunt Paula (Palmer) Johnson in an email to the author dated February 4, 2022. Also, the three breeds raised by the Youngs were mentioned in the newspaper article, "Every Day Is Turkey Day At the Young Turkey Farm At Norway."

Bill and Addie (Chaplin) Young

The author's mother Rowena Palmer with some turkey chicks newly-hatched in the incubator.
Published in the *Portland Press Herald* circa 1945.
(Clipping from the Young's Turkey Farm scrapbook.)

Bill (center, holding pole) and Addie (right) moving a flock of White Hollands with the help of
their son George Young (far left) and grandson, Kurt Palmer (center).
(Family photo, courtesy of Paula and Robert Johnson.)

The new incubators enabled Young's Turkey Farm to sell thousands of birds year-round, not just at Thanksgiving. Such a growth spurt can be particularly challenging. As any farmer (including myself) will tell you, it is often harder to find a market for your product than it is to raise the product. But rather than view increasing the year-round market for turkey meat as a problem, Addie saw it as a challenge to tackle and overcome.

Addie's Sales and Marketing Genius

Although Addie never took a course in marketing, my great-grandmother seemed to know exactly how to net publicity. Addie built up relationships with writers and photographers at the local paper, the *Norway Advertiser*, as well as at the state-wide newspapers, *The Portland Press Herald* and *The Lewiston Daily Sun*. Young's Turkey Farm was regularly featured in Maine newspapers prior to Thanksgiving, plus special features and/or turkey photos ran at other times of the year, keeping the name of the farm fresh. As the reader has likely noticed, Addie shrewdly ensured that some of her cute grandchildren were around when photographers visited the farm. Naturally, news and layout editors could not resist the compelling images of the kids with the turkeys that their photographers provided them. What might otherwise have been a small news item buried in the newspaper, often turned into a well-placed feature photo about Young's Turkey Farm.

Newspaper photo, "Day's Getting Near, Feller."
Featuring a White Holland turkey on the chopping block between my mother Rowena Palmer (left) and her younger sister Paula (right). Rowena is looking at a calendar, while Paula deplores the turkey's impending demise as Thanksgiving fast approaches.
(Clipping from Young's Turkey Farm scrapbook.)

Other Young's Turkey Farm photographs—usually posed—were sensational in nature, such as the one published in 1942 that featured 2000-2500 birds blocking the Crockett Ridge Road. Since the farm's turkeys were raised in confinement (foxes would have had a field day with that number of birds), the fowl must have been let loose just for the sake of the photograph, certainly an arresting picture.

Newspaper photo, "It's Crowded Here—Right Now." Turkeys blocking the Crockett Ridge Road, September 4, 1942.
The old Crockett homestead is shown in the background.
(Clipping from Young's Turkey Farm scrapbook.)

All the free publicity Addie netted helped her enlarge the year-round market for turkey meat, something the writer of the article, "Every Day Is Turkey Day At the Young Turkey Farm At Norway," took pains to highlight:

> "Perhaps the most notable thing is that [Mrs. Young] has secured for the product a good market. It is often easy to grow something but quite another thing to sell it profitably... Mrs. Young early showed people how to use turkey meat advantageously, not only for Thanksgiving Day, but any and every day. Sales are continuous through the whole year."[160]

---

160. Newspaper clipping from Young's Turkey Farm scrapbook kept by Addie, currently in the possession of Joyce Palmer.

Every Day Is Turkey Day At the Young Turkey Farm At Norway

The ladies take off the feathers, including the pin feathers. Mrs. Young, wearing the "checkered apron." The little girl standing in the chair is more of an ornament than a help, very likely.

When the writer thinks back to the time when Mrs. William F. Young started the Young Poultry Farm at North Norway he sees the progress that has been made.

Perhaps the most noticeable thing is that she has secured for the product a good market. It is often easy to grow something but quite another thing to sell it profitably. The first year they had about 50 birds and this year about 2500 have been reared; about a thousand were sold as young poults with plenty older ones on their happy way to tables for Thanksgiving. Of the number already shipped 22 went to Detroit, Mich., where they will adorn the tables of automobile officials of General Motors.

Mrs. Young early showed people how to use turkey meat advantageously, not only for Thanksgiving Day but for any and every day. Sales are continuous through the whole year.

This farm was once the headquarters of a fine herd of Jersey cattle. The writer remembers taking a picture of the herd bull as he was on his leisurely way back to the barn walking alone and unattached. He accommodatingly stopped when his picture was taken. The writer can say he felt relieved when Farmer Bill came up and took the bull in charge.

Mr. Young is the chief of the poultry department; the two sons, George and Willard have the work well divided between them each having his own department. They do the killing and the feathering is done by Mrs. Young and her helpers.

We rather expect to see a mechanical picker installed at this farm, a sort of robot, with fingers padded with rubber, and suction in the fingers that take off the feathers, pin feathers and all, after the birds have been given a semi-scald bath.

The varieties now kept are, Black Diamonds, White Hollands and Bourbon Reds.

Newspaper article featuring Young's Turkey Farm, likely published in the *Norway Advertiser* around 1939 or 1940.
Note: the "little girl on the chair" is my aunt Paula Palmer.
(Clipping from Young's Turkey Farm scrapbook.)

In this article the reporter notes that Addie was shipping twenty-two turkeys to Detroit, "where they will adorn the tables of automobile officials at General Motors." Addie had even tapped into the market of those who fell in love with the neighborhood when fiddler Mellie Dunham introduced the world to his friends on Crockett's Ridge!

Prior to the stock market crash of 1929, summer visitors had discovered the Oxford Hills, thanks to the beauties of Lake Pennesseewassee and the ubiquity of the family automobile that led to road touring trips (hence the moniker, "tourists"). As the country began to pull itself out of the grips of the Depression, visitors returned to Norway. Some summer people had purchased lots and built individual camps on the lake, but most tourists stayed at summer camps, such as Shepard's Camps, situated on the east side of Norway Lake, off the Crockett Ridge Road. Shepard's started as a large family home, but gradually added individual camps on the shore of Lake Pennesseewassee for additional income. One large camp was built nearby in which employees lived, and there was a hall where guests were served their meals family-style.[161] There were also boarding houses in Norway Village where tourists could stay, and dine out at one of the many local restaurants. Always looking for ways to increase her market, Addie began knocking on doors, and soon turkey cropped up on the menus of summer camps and restaurants in the greater Norway area, and even at the Oxford County Fair. The Youngs and other local farmers sold milk, eggs, butter, and fresh fruits and vegetables to the summer people with camps on Lake Pennesseewassee.[162] Addie believed she could market turkey meat to individual camp owners, too. To facilitate these year-round sales, Bill and his son George made deliveries in a new farm truck, emblazoned with Young's Turkey Farm's logo and slogan—"Direct from the farm to you!"

---

161. Information from Paula (Palmer) Johnson via emails to Jennifer Wixson February 4th and 7th, 2022. The author's mother, Rowena Palmer, waited tables at Shepard's Camps when she was young. Her sister Paula waited tables for Mildred and Don McAllister's camps, a smaller outfit on the same camp road as Shepard's.

162. Information from the Norway, Maine Historical Society webpage, Interesting Places. "Norway as a Summer Resort." This page is a reprint of an article that appeared in the *Norway Advertiser* July 31, 1908.

Bill and Addie (Chaplin) Young

Winona (Young) Palmer and an unidentified youth (possibly son Kurt) standing in front of Bill's new farm truck.
(Family photo, courtesy of Joyce Palmer.)

Sales to summer residents did not end when the visitors went home, either. Once it became known that Young's Turkey Farm had shipped dressed birds to Michigan for the Thanksgiving tables of automobile executives from Ford and General Motors, some of the summer people, who had discovered how juicy and tasty Addie's turkeys were, stopped into the farm before departing for the season and placed their holiday orders. In 1944, Young's Turkey Farm shipped 45 turkeys to summer visitors residing in New York, Massachusetts, and New Jersey. Although the farm raised more than 2000 turkeys in 1944, thanks to a national shortage of birds—and Addie's marketing skill—the farm did not have enough turkey to meet local demand. Many Norway area residents had to go without their usual bird on the table, which painful fact reminded people to order their turkey earlier next year (especially when they saw the Young's Turkey Farm truck go by). When asked in November of 1944 about the shortage of turkeys, Bill Young told a reporter he had been "besieged by buyers for the last few days and could sell 1000 birds just by stepping to the telephone."[163]

---

163. November 1944 newspaper article, "35 Summer Guests Get Holiday Turkeys." Addie pasted this clipping in her Young's Turkey Farm scrapbook, currently in the possession of Joyce Palmer.

35 Summer Guests Get Holiday Turkeys

Norway, Nov. 20—Thirty-five residents of Massachusetts, New York and New Jersey are sure of receiving their Thanksgiving turkeys.

Summer residents of this area, they noted the 2,000-bird flock of William Young of Norway and placed their orders early and the birds were shipped today.

This made them more fortunate than residents of the Norway-South Paris area who had failed to place their orders early. For there just were no turkeys on the retail market and Young, after dressing 650 to fill Thanksgiving orders and shipping a few to Portland hotels, was not selling any more, preferring to keep the rest for breeding. He declared he has been besieged by buyers for the last few days and could sell 1,000 birds just by stepping to the telephone.

1944 newspaper clipping from Young's Turkey Farm scrapbook.

Addie did not just rely on free publicity and word-of-mouth from local (and summer) people to expand the year-round market for turkey meat. She also believed in advertising. Addie judiciously spread her advertising dollars around between the newspapers that frequently featured the farm. The ads, which ran year-round, were attractive and generally carried a message that spoke directly to the consumer. Addie's ads not only triggered additional business, but also often served as a reminder to newspaper editors that it might be time to send a photographer out to Young's Turkey Farm.

A selection of Young's Turkey Farm ads from Addie's scrapbook.
(The author, who formerly raised Scottish Highland cattle, especially enjoys the
"Eat turkey, save beef" ad.)

Finally, Addie also made sure local people knew which of their favorite stores carried Young's Turkey Farm birds for sale. She printed up posters for shopkeepers and restauranters to place in their windows, alerting customers and passers-by that turkeys were available inside.

Shop window poster for Young's Turkey Farm.
(Poster courtesy of Joyce Palmer.)

Bill and His Other Livestock

Bill spent more and more time with the turkeys as the years passed, but he did not completely give up on his other livestock. He still kept a few dairy cows, which he loved and which had once been the mainstay of the farm, but were no longer.

Bill Young with some of his cows.
(Photo courtesy of Yvette Young.)

One of Bill Young's cows with her new calf.
(Family photo, courtesy of Joyce Palmer.)

In the late 1930s, Bill also went to raising pigs in the barn cellar. The high granite foundation of the barn that burned, once the site of his hopes and dreams, made the perfect pen for hogs. The pigs had plenty of room and they could "root around" in the ground to their heart's content. A newspaper article in the *Norway Advertiser* entitled, "Norway Farmer Grows Yellow Corn for His Herd of 17 Good Pigs," glowingly described Bill's feed corn:

> "An acre or more [of corn] was grown this summer and came to full maturity, some of the handsomest corn this writer has seen this year. The pigs won't get all the corn, as Mrs. Young's turkeys will have to have some…
>
> "This corn we started to tell you about is a fine lot; the ears are all well filled out, way to the tip; the cobs are small, just the way it should be. The yield will run way over a hundred bushels to the acres.
>
> "Mr. Young [also] had a good piece of sweet corn, four or five acres, that turned out well in rather a backward year."[164]

Photo from *Norway Advertiser* article on Bill Young's yellow corn for his pigs.
(Newspaper article and photo in possession of the author.)

---

164. The author has a clipping of this newspaper article that was saved by Addie; however, it is not dated nor is the author's name given. From the content, I believe it was published in the local paper, the *Norway Advertiser*. Accompanying the piece is the photograph of Bill with his seventeen pigs in the barn cellar.

Probably the most valuable livestock Bill kept, however, was his team of horses. Rescued from the barn fire that destroyed his livelihood, the horse team was repurposed for turkey farm chores, such as the spreading of turkey manure on the fields. In addition, Bill used his team to harvest wood, plow and harrow, and to move lumber and supplies around when building grower houses.

Bill and his team of horses in front of the old Crockett homestead.
(Family photo, courtesy of Joyce Palmer.)

Although his team was not as cute as his grandchildren, Bill found them one day featured in a local newspaper. A reporter had seen the horses in harness, stopped by the farm, and snapped a photo. Bill, who likely was used to visits from reporters, good-naturedly answered a few questions about what such a big team of horses did on a turkey farm.

Newspaper clipping about Bill's team from Young's Turkey Farm scrapbook. (Courtesy of Joyce Palmer.)

The team was eventually replaced by the new farm truck, of course, but the horses were never sold. According to my grandmother, her father kept the pair until each horse ended its natural life. Last to die was Bill's horse Charity, for whom the pasture in which the horse spent her final years was named. (This pasture is currently a woodlot owned by my brother Wes Wixson in his family trust.) It was in Charity's Pasture that the old workhorse spent her final peaceful days.

Overdue Taxes and Black Growth Timber

The capital necessary to increase the turkey business—money to build the grower houses, to buy the two large incubators, to raise and buy the turkey feed, and to advertise—put a strain on the family's finances. After Bill's mother died, the rent from her two houses on Beal Street was supposed to have been set aside to pay the real estate tax on the two farms (the old Crockett and Morse homesteads) and various woodlots, as well as on the rentals. But either properties were not rented for several years or the rent was not paid (or was not enough), because by 1940 Bill had fallen behind on his taxes. In the fall of 1941, the Town of Norway placed tax liens amounting to $333.62 on the homestead farm, the woodlots, and on one of the Beal Street houses.[165] The town added further tax liens in 1942,[166] 1943,[167] and 1944.[168] Finally, in 1945, in a move that would clear the liens and net him additional income (and some top-notch lumber), Bill sold some timber from his Needham Road lot. On July 25, 1945, Bill sold to Walter F. Cullinan of Norway, "All of the standing black growth [evergreens][169] on a certain tract or parcel of land situated in that part of Norway, called the 'Lee Grant,' in the county of Oxford and State of Maine, being the northerly part of Lot numbered forty-one (41)..."[170] This woodlot had been purchased in two installments in 1866 by Bill's grandfather, William Robinson Crockett.[171] The thirty-four acres, which William Crockett had occasionally worked with his ox team (and Bill with his draft horses), was once part of a larger wooded parcel formerly owned by John Millett, an early mill owner and sawyer. Bill was very particular in his deed to Cullinan, which included the following caveats:

> "It is understood between the Grantor and the said Grantee in this deed that the said Grantee shall have one year from the date of this deed to enter, cut and remove the said standing black growth.
> "It is understood between the Grantor and the Grantee in this deed that the said Grantee shall saw out for the said Grantor five or six hundred feet of hemlock plank and like amount of boards, from the said standing black growth, and is a part of the consideration for this deed.
> "Excepting and reserving from this conveyance the two hemlock trees now standing in front of the camp located on this lot."[172]

---

165. OCROD Book 452, pages 161-163.
166. OCROD, Book 454, pages 263-265; and page 244.
167. OCROD, Book 461, pages 96-98; page 100; page 109; and page 198.
168. OCROD, Book 466, pages 162-165.
169. I am indebted to historian James Phinney Baxter for providing me with the definition of "black growth." In a footnote to *The Trelawny Papers* ("Documentary History of the State of Maine," Volume 3, p. 11) Baxter explains where the "Black Pointe" River (now the Nonesuch River) got its name: "So called on account of the forests of evergreens, or *black growth*, [emphasis Baxter's] which covered this point."
170. OCROD, Book 472, page 322.
171. OCROD, Book 145, page 52 and Book 146, page 109.
172. OCROD, Book 472, page 322.

On July 25, 1945, because of the timber sale to Cullinan, Bill was able to discharge all his real estate tax liens, which amounted to a total of $1,262.87[173] (about $22,000 in 2024 dollars).[174] In addition, he most likely used the hemlock planking and boards to build Addie's turkey grower houses.

The Maine State Turkey Growers Association and Civic Duties

Bill and Addie were active members of the Maine State Turkey Growers Association. As mentioned, Addie had been an early supporter of the Maine turkey tag to help promote the sale of quality state birds. The practice of tagging turkeys fell by the wayside during World War II, but in 1947 Addie and others worked hard to resurrect it.[175] In November of 1947 she wrote an editorial calling for a return of the State of Maine turkey tag, calling the tag "your guarantee of a Grade A Fancy bird." Addie noted in her op-ed that immature turkeys were being dumped on the market because of the high price of grain. Thanks to Reciprocal Trade Treaties, she said, U.S. growers could not compete on price with Canadian turkey growers, who were paying only $2 to $3 per bag of grain to feed their birds while Americans were paying $5 to $5.50. "Are we going to be driven out?" Addie implored in the piece.[176] Her efforts not only helped resurrect the Maine state turkey tag, but also raised consumer awareness about the importance of buying a state bird.

---

173. OCROD, Book 470, pages 375 and 471 (a corrected version of the tax liens discharge).
174. CPI Inflation Calculator.
175. "State of Maine Blue, White and Red Labels—Resuming Pre-War Use of Labels." Newspaper article published November 14, 1947, and pasted into Addie's Young's Turkey Farm scrapbook. The article noted that about 30,000 of the 50,000 Maine turkeys raised that year could be marketed using the Grade A tag.
176. "Musings of a Turkey Grower, As Told by Mrs. Adalade Young of Norway." Unknown newspaper. Published November 14, 1947. Clipping was pasted into the Young's Turkey Farm scrapbook.

MUSINGS OF A TURKEY GROWER

As Told by Mrs Adalade Young of Norway

NE, FRIDAY, NOVEMBER 14, 1947

Long, long ago when our first American settlers came to this country, history tells us that their first Thanksgiving was a feast of "Venison and Wild Turkey," with "Thanks to God" for their blessings.

They were delighted with the wild turkey which the "Old Pilgrim got with his rifle," this bird was small, blue, dry, and often tough. Since turkeys were first domesticated there has been a great change for the better. Through all these years breeders have developed a fa different type of turkey. One that is fine flavored, tender, juicy, larger size and quick to mature, by modern methods of turkey raising. Proper care, cleanliness, and proper feed (which has all the necessary vitamins) are as important to the baby turkey today as to our own babies. Is it any wonder we are producing a better bird than our ancestors?

As Thanksgiving time draws around for another year, you will be thinking about a turkey once more. You will want the best you can get for your dollars, and we are concious of these dollars today, with the high cost of everything. We learned during the war years that we could not produce near enough in the east, it was our western states that practically supplied our markets; consequently the western price ruled our markets; we can not grow a turkey as cheaply as they can, but we have to complete with them. Many states have done much to advertise their turkeys, through their Turkey Associations. Maine has done very little.

If we talked as much about our turkeys as Vermont has, we would be eating more of our own birds in our own state.

We learned during the war, that when the government ruled our small business, we might be the loser. Today, we have poultryless Thursdays, with the country full of poultry; turkeys coming in from Canada, through our Reciprocal Trade Treaties; turkeys that are fed $2.00 and $3.00 a bag grain and we on $5.00 to $5.50 a bag grain. Are we going to be driven out? If Mr Luckman would listen to just one poultry grower, any one of them would tell him " a chicken in the pot" eats no wheat. What are we saving them for? This year as never before, you will see many birds that are not mature; sick of buying $5.00 grain and poultryless Thursdays, so they dumped them on the market. That is why some of the growers have asked for a "State of Maine Tag" again. Maine has done a lot on the potatoes, blueberries, etc, and we could with our State of Maine Tags for our turkeys. That is your guarantee of a Grade A Fancy bird. We have the right climate here in Maine, good growers and a lot of State of Maine birds going on the market for Thanksgiving.

"Musings of a Turkey Grower," op-ed piece written by Addie Young in 1947.
Later pasted into her Young's Turkey Farm scrapbook.
(Courtesy of Joyce Palmer.)

As early as 1940, Bill and Addie began to host the Maine State Turkey Growers Association meetings at their Crockett's Ridge farm. In 1940 a poll was taken at the meeting at Young's Turkey Farm to discover how many turkeys would be ready for Thanksgiving. (1940 was one of the years during which the date of Thanksgiving was in flux.) It was during that meeting when Association members—and the public—learned about the unique grower house Addie had designed and Bill had built.[177]

Over the next fifteen years the Youngs continued to host Turkey Grower Association meetings at their farm on a regular basis. The meetings were not only educational in nature, but also offered an opportunity for more publicity for the farm. Press releases were sent to the newspapers, which occasionally sent out a photographer and sometimes even a reporter. During one such meeting on Crockett's Ridge Addie was voted as the Association's representative to the National

---

177. "Turkey Meeting Day at Young's Farm at Norway for Census." 1940 newspaper article pasted by Addie into her Young's Turkey Farm scrapbook.

Turkey Federation, the national advocate for the turkey industry.[178] The National Turkey Federation initiated the practice of presenting the President of the United States—beginning with Harry Truman—with a turkey for Thanksgiving. One wonders whether there was a Norway, Maine woman with a twinkle in her eye behind this marketing stroke of genius! (Turkeys from the National Turkey Federation graced the President's table at Thanksgiving until George H.W. Bush began pardoning the fowl.)

In addition to belonging to the Maine State Turkey Growers' Association, Bill and Addie were members of the Norway Grange (The National Grange of the Order of Patrons of Husbandry). Bill also belonged to the Norway Farm Bureau, and served on the town of Norway's Budget Committee. In 1948, Bill decided to run for Norway selectman. By that time Bill was so well-known and respected in Norway that he was easily elected to the three-year term.[179]

NORWAY
BOARD OF SELECTMEN
In session with Allen L. Wilcox, *Town Manager*
Pictured: William F. Young, Hervey L. Wiley, Archie G. Goodwin, Allen L. Wilcox, *Manager*, Franklyn A. Towne, and Leroy C. Luce, *Chairman*.

Norway Board of Selectman 1948.
(Bill Young is far left.) Photo published in the Norway Town Report, 1948.
(Courtesy of the Norway, Maine Historical Society.)[180]

---

178. "Turkey Meeting Day at Young's Farm at Norway for Census."
179. Information from Bill's obituary, as well as from the Norway, Maine Historical Society.
180. My thanks to Sue Denison of the Norway, Maine Historical Society for providing this photo, as well as the information about the years Bill Young served as Selectman.

Despite running a full-time business (and raising her grandchildren), Addie remained a faithful and active member of the Heywood Club. In addition to attending meetings on a regular basis, she also served as President of the club at one time.[181] Plus, whenever the club held dinners, Addie was always one of the many neighborhood ladies who baked for the meal. On April 19, 1951, the Heywood Club held its 45th Annual Patriots' Day Dinner and the *Portland Press Herald* sent out veteran photographer Jack Quinn to write a feature on the club the day in advance. Quinn snapped a photograph of the Heywood Club and proceeded up the road to Young's Turkey Farm, where he had often been before and where he knew he could find the oldest working member of the club—Addie Young. Quinn caught Addie in the act of putting one of two custard pies she was baking for the Patriots' Day Dinner into the oven, with a large pot of baked beans cooking atop the woodstove. According to the caption that accompanied the photographs, Addie had baked two custard pies for the Heywood Club's Annual Patriots' Day Dinner for " 'Don't know how many years.'"[182]

Top of *Portland Press Herald* article showing Addie preparing for the Heywood Club's Annual Patriots' Day Dinner, April 19, 1951.
(Clipping from Young's Turkey Farm scrapbook.)

---

181. The information that Addie Young served as President of the Heywood Club came from the envelope of a letter directed to "Mrs. Adelaide Young, President Heywood Club, Norway." The letter was from The Phoenix Insurance Company of Hartford, CT, and contained the property insurance policy for the Heywood Club. The letter was postmarked July 1913. The policy expired August 3, 1916. (Heywood Club records, NHS.)
182. "Plenty Cookin' On Crockett Ridge At Norway For Heywood Club's Annual Patriots' Day Dinner." *Portland Press Herald*, April 19, 1951. (Clipping pasted into Addie's Young's Turkey Farm scrapbook.)

Portland Press Herald photographer Jack Quinn was a regular visitor to the farm. Two years prior to the 45th anniversary of the Heywood Club's Patriots' Day dinner, Bill and Addie celebrated their 45th wedding anniversary. Children and grandchildren gathered on Saturday, August 13, 1949, at Young's Turkey Farm to celebrate with the couple. (The couple's actual anniversary was August 4th.) Jack Quinn came out to photograph the Youngs for his newspaper, netting the turkey farm more valuable publicity. (When I saw all the Jack Quinn photos in Addie's scrapbook, I started to suspect that the photographer liked to eat, and knew where he could get a good meal!) The caption accompanying their anniversary photo noted that Bill and Addie were selling 500 pounds of dressed turkeys a week that summer. *Five hundred pounds a week!*

Bill and Addie on their 45th wedding anniversary.
Photograph by Jack Quinn for the *Portland Press Herald*.
(Newspaper clipping from Young's Turkey Farm scrapbook.)

In 1949—thanks to the publicity and Addie's advertising campaign—turkey sales exceeded expectations. Bill and Addie ended the year with a nice little nest egg. Now, what to do with that money?

A New Well – Finally!

Bill and Addie's first thought for their nest egg was to put the money toward their retirement. (Agricultural workers were then ineligible to participate in the new Social Security program.)[183] After all, Bill was sixty-five and Addie was sixty-six. Bill also thought he might like to buy a new tractor. The couple's nest egg survived the winter's dreaming, but in the spring of 1950, the money was channeled toward a more practical and important purpose—drilling a new well.

The proposed new artesian well would replace the homestead's original hand-dug surface well, which was only eleven-feet deep.[184] Since the latter part of the 1940s, the farm had been experiencing summer dry spells, including times when the well went dry. (Lack of water had been one of the contributing factors of destruction of the new barn back in 1931.) During the prior two summers (1948 and 1949), Bill and his crew had been forced to make two, ten-mile round trips per day with the truck, hauling twenty-two barrels of water each trip. The water was needed for domestic use and to water the thousands of turkeys. It was amazing that the farm had carried on as long as it did with the old well. The couple decided it was way past time to address the farm's water situation (or lack thereof), and in the spring of 1950 Bill and Addie hired a local well-drilling company. The well drillers went to work as soon as ground conditions permitted.[185]

---

183. Agricultural workers, as well as hotel and laundry, and state and federal employees, could not participate in Social Security until 1954. "In Pursuit of Equity." Alice Kessler-Harris. New York, New York: Oxford University Press, 2001. P. 150.
184. This was the original well on the property, likely dug by Ephraim Crockett, Jr. between 1812-1814.
185. All information about the new well came from the article, "They Got Water!" written by Harry A. Packard for the *American Agriculturist* newspaper, and published May 20, 1950.

Dilling the new well at Young's Turkey Farm, Spring 1950.
Note the snow piled up against the foundation of the house.
(Family photo, courtesy of Joyce Palmer.)

The new well would cost the Youngs $6 per foot to drill. There was no guarantee that water would ever be struck, either. If not, Bill and Addie would spend their nest egg on a hole in the ground. The well-drilling crew worked for three straight weeks, boarding with the family during the week and going home on weekends. By the end of the third week, the drillers had gone down 170-feet through bedrock, and still no water. When the workers dispersed for the weekend, Bill and Addie were understandably discouraged. So far, they had spent over $1000 with nothing to show for it. The couple's dilemma was chronicled in an article by Harry A. Packard,[186] "They Got Water!" published May 20, 1950 in the *American Agriculturalist* newspaper:

> "'We will go 30 feet more and that's the end' [Addie said]. 'If 170 feet has not produced water, then doubtless 200 feet will not. Bill and I have $1,200 in the bank, which will pay for 30 feet more drilling. Then we quit!'
> 'That was the worst weekend I ever spent,' Mr. Young says. 'Mother couldn't eat the Sunday dinner she had prepared. I couldn't go fox hunting, being Sunday,

---

186. Norway native Harry Packard was a well-known journalist, photographer, and freelance writer. Norway Museum & Historical Society newsletter, June 2024.

and that day it began to spit snow, even though it was early spring. I would almost have sold the farm, turkeys and all, for the amount of the well bill.'

Monday the drillers showed up at noon in a blinding snow. 'Sap snow,' the farmers called it. Farmer Young wondered if he wasn't a sap, too!

At the dinner table ... Mr. Young showed [the well drillers] some catalogs he had gotten at the village store. There was one of the 50 gallon tank for water storage under pressure, and another of the jet pump ... and still another with pictures of the hot water unit, etc.

Mrs. Young had dreamed about all these things. The water outfit and the well would cost $2,000. Mrs. Young had said, 'I know that I am 67, but if I can have just one year on this farm with all the water I want and not be obliged to measure it by the cupful (and stint at that), then I'll rest in peace the rest of my days.'

One of the drillers said (he wasn't cheerful about it either): 'It does not look like we would find water even at 200 feet, but my boss told me confidentially that if we do not find water at 200 feet, where you say we must stop, then to drill a day and a half more going to 225 feet—the last 25 feet on the house because of the pluck you folks have shown!'

'Pluck and courage or anything else,' answered Mrs. Young. 'I haven't any of these things left. An old farm couple ready to die, and putting $1,200 into a hole in the ground!'

As the group ate, the drilling machine, which had been put into operation just as the dinner call sounded, kept pounding away. During the midday meal the drill went down through another foot of ledge rock.

Suddenly, there was a different sound in the drilling operation outside the kitchen window: The drill dropped through the ledge rock, evidently into a split in the eternal rock foundation. An old and experienced well driller sensed what that might mean. He leaped from the table and the overturned chair went smashing on the floor. There was no excusing himself and he left the kitchen door wide open when he raced through. The Youngs followed.

One-hundred-seventy-one feet! A rift of crevice in the ledge. Water! They couldn't pump it dry... [The water flowed] 30 gallons per minute. More water than turkeys can drink, water for a bathroom, a tank of hot water—water for everything!"

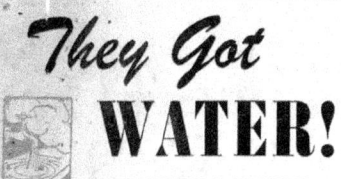

They Got WATER!

By HARRY A. PACKARD

CITY FOLKS with convenient water taps about the house seldom give a second thought to what farmers frequently go through to obtain water for domestic purposes.

In Norway, Maine, Mr. and Mrs. William Young live on the ancestral acres of Mr. Young's great-grandfather, the old "Bill" Crocket place five or six miles from the village. Pioneer Crocket had a land grant and thereon more than a century ago built one of the first frame houses in the town, using birch bark for insulation between the outside boarding and the shingled sides of his home. A water vein which came close to the surface supplied their small needs for water.

In the hundred year old brick house which now marks the site, a surface well (so-called because it was only 11 feet deep) supplied a moderate amount of water. However, farmer Young felt the pinch a few years ago when fire broke out in his barn and he lost the entire structure with a number of valuable Jersey cattle because of the lack of water.

From dairying the couple went into turkey-raising in a small way. In this venture they felt the increasing lack of water.

While the flock was small, the pinch was not too great, but when the flock increased from 500 turkeys a year to their present endeavor of 3,000 strutting gobblers, the water situation became acute.

The famous dry seasons in the past four years climaxed the woes of the Youngs. They even hauled water two years prior to that. Imagine two ten-mile trips a day with the truck to haul 22 barrels of water for the needs of the turkeys and for domestic purposes.

Bill says that camels and elephants may be heavy drinkers but these animals cannot hold a candle to 3,000 turkeys! "Water, water everywhere" didn't apply to the Young farm. The only water on the place was what they hauled in, for the well had become as dry as a bone. Bill says the hotter the summer days and the drier the weather, "the more those blamed gobblers panted for water."

Bill Young is 66 and Mrs. Young about the same age. The doctor says she will not raise turkeys many years more, but Mrs. Young says she will raise them as long as she lives! Bill says, or rather did say, "Mother'll raise turkeys only as long as I can haul water."

At Christmas time the pair salted away a few dollars from their 1949 turkey raising. Bill said, "We'll this for old age since we [don't] have any social security." But Mrs. Young said, "Let's drill an artesian well!"

Neighbors were astounded. A couple traveling fast along towards three score and ten, and an artesian well could cost as much as $2,000!

Theirs did!

The drillers began at the Young farm as soon as spring conditions made it possible. They drilled three weeks! Drillers get $6 per foot for drilling, and there is no assurance they will be able to get water. They started the drilling at the ledge bottom of the old 11 foot well.

The first day they went down ten feet—ten feet through solid ledge rock. Nate Noble said that it was the bed rock over which the glacier passed, but that was too long ago for anyone to give it even a second thought.

In due course of time the drill worked down 100 feet. The Youngs had sunk $600 in the hole in the ground.

The drill went 150 feet—always through solid rock. Plunk, plunk, plunk! Not a drop of water. Not even a promise of water, but a drilling bill of $900! If you had hauled water to turkeys six years, 22 barrels a day; if you needed a new truck to haul new water to the new turkeys hatching out for the 1950 Pilgrims' feast, otherwise known as Thanksgiving, the situation could be something to cause one to ponder seriously. "Money does not grow on trees up here," Bill declares.

Did someone say 150 feet down through the ledge rock? Well it was 170 feet through the ledge rock when the drillers went home one Friday night. Multiply that by $6 per foot and you will see where the Youngs stood.

Mrs. Young was more discouraged than was her husband. When the drillers left for the weekend, Mrs. Young took stock of the situation.

"We will go 30 feet more and that's the end. If 170 feet has not produced water, then 200 feet doubtless will not. Bill and I have $1,200 in the bank, which will pay for 30 feet more drilling. Then we quit!"

"That was the worst weekend I ever spent," Mr. Young says. "Mother couldn't eat the Sunday dinner she had prepared. I couldn't go fox hunting, being Sunday, and at dusk that day it began to spit snow, even though it was early spring. I would almost have sold the farm, turkeys and all, for the amount of the well bill!"

Monday the drillers showed up at noon in a blinding snow squall. "Sap snow," the farmers called it. Farmer Young wondered if he wasn't a sap, too!" *(Continued on Page)*

Mr. and Mrs. William Young and their son George (in the water hole) are glad they "stuck to their guns."

Page one of the *American Agriculturalist* story by Harry Packard, May 20, 1950. (Newspaper from Addie's Young's Turkey Farm scrapbook, currently in the possession of Joyce Palmer.)

Open House at Young's Turkey Farm

Since the farm now had plenty of water, Bill and Addie decided to throw the doors open more often. They began to host summertime Open Houses, usually around the couple's anniversary in August. Initially, the Open Houses were a way of thanking their friends and neighbors, especially those who helped out during Thanksgiving. Most of the extended Young family —including in-laws (and in-laws to be, such as the author's father) pitched in to feed and entertain the guests.

Open House, Young's Turkey Farm, 1954.
Back row (l to r): Bill and Addie Young; Eldwin "Windy" Wixson, Jr. (the author's father); Richard Bean; Andres Heath; Dean Thurston; Florence Young; Willard "Bud" Young; and Kermit Allard. Front row (left to right): Unknown woman; Paula Palmer; Tessa Thibodeau; Mrs. Frost; Winona Palmer; Barbara Conant; Rowena Palmer (the author's mother);
George Young; and Norm McAllister.
(Family photo, a copy of which is in the author's possession.)

Bill and Addie (Chaplin) Young

Willard "Bud" Young carves up a turkey under the supervision of his mother Addie. (Family photo, courtesy of Norman Young.)

But the Thanksgiving holiday always remained the big draw. On Sunday, November 19, 1950, Bill and Addie welcomed hundreds to their pre-Thanksgiving Open House. (More than 150 signed the guest book, and Addie estimated that only half the attendees signed.) Customers were invited to take a tour of the turkey pens, where they could pick out their holiday bird, just like choosing a Christmas tree at a tree farm today. While they waited for their bird to be prepared, guests stepped into the old kitchen,[187] where my mother Rowena and aunt Paula Palmer greeted them and served free hot turkey sandwiches prepared by cook Addie Frost of South Paris. Bud Young and his sister Winona took charge of the cellar "which means hanging up the freshly drawn bird and picking out the right bird as the orders [were] called out."[188] Bill and Addie's grandsons Norman Young and Kurt Palmer did the killing, assisted by Jack Frost and Gene Bickford, youths from the

---

187. During renovations done at the homestead in 2021 by Jonathan Palmer, it was discovered that the old kitchen was part of the original Ephraim Crockett house built around 1814. Jonathan is the 8th generation to farm and reside at the Crockett homestead.
188. Article about Young's Turkey Farm 1950 Open House written by Mrs. Beryl Daniels, correspondent for the *Lewiston Daily Sun*, published November 21, 1950. Clipping pasted by Addie into her Young's Turkey Farm scrapbook.

agricultural course at the high school. Neighbors Stanley Thurston, Bob Orre, and Ethelyn Millet did the drawing of the turkeys, and Florence Young (George's wife), Ava Rogers and Mary Larson did the pin-feathering.[189] An article about the Open House published November 21, 1950 and written by *Lewiston Daily Sun* Norway correspondent Mrs. Beryl Daniels noted that the Youngs had sold over 1300 dressed turkeys in the two weeks prior to their Open House. A photo of Addie in the cellar with drawn turkeys highlighted the fact that she had also sold to the Bangor State Hospital fifty birds weighing a total of 1400 pounds.[190]

Lewiston Daily Sun article about the 1950 Open House and Addie's sale of 50 turkeys to Bangor State Hospital.
(Clipping pasted by Addie into her scrapbook.)

---

189. Most of this information came from an article about Young's Turkey Farm 1950 Open House written by Mrs. Beryl Daniels, correspondent for the *Lewiston Daily Sun*, published November 21, 1950. (Clipping pasted by Addie into her Young's Turkey Farm scrapbook.) Other information about the Open Houses at Young's Turkey Farm came from my aunt Paula (Palmer) Johnson in an email dated February 8, 2022, and from my own recollections of what my grandmother Winona told me. Prior to her death in 1993, my grandmother gave me a large collection of silver-plate that had been purchased specifically for the turkey farm's Open Houses, which I treasured for decades. I have since passed the silverplate along to a younger family member in the Willard Young line.

190. Article about Young's Turkey Farm 1950 Open House written by Mrs. Beryl Daniels, correspondent for the *Lewiston Daily Sun*, published November 21, 1950. Clipping pasted by Addie into her Young's Turkey Farm scrapbook.

The End of Young's Turkey Farm and the Birth of Young's Cottage Lots

By 1954, however, the health of both Bill and Addie had declined. They were now seventy and seventy-one, respectively. As a result, the couple was forced to reduce the number of turkeys raised. In August of 1954, Bill and Addie welcomed friends from all over Maine to the farm for what would be their last Open House, held on their 50th wedding anniversary. The *Norway Advertiser* wrote a feature article on the couple, which included how they met; the tragedy of the barn that burned; and the success of the turkey business that arose from the ashes.

August 1954 newspaper article and photo from the *Norway Advertiser*.
(Article from Young's Turkey Farm scrapbook.)

"Direct from the Farm to You"

YOUNG'S TURKEY FARM
NORWAY, MAINE

Young's Turkey Farm stationery.
(Courtesy Rowena Palmer Trust.)

Bill and Addie (Chaplin) Young

A TRUE LOVE MATCH: Postcard Addie Young sent to her husband "Billy" while visiting her ailing mother in North Gorham, March 19, 1912.
(Postcard courtesy of Karen Caddle, Brighton Colorado. In June 2024, Karen tracked the author down via Ancestry to return this postcard to the family.)

Bill Young died at his family's homestead on February 17, 1955. He was seventy years old. There was not enough room in the old part of Norway Pine Grove Cemetery to bury Bill with his mother and father (and all the Crockett ancestors), and so Addie purchased a plot in the new section of the cemetery for him and their family. Addie also purchased perpetual care for this plot on April 11, 1955 for $275.[191]

Bill missed meeting his first great-grandchild by two weeks. My sister Cheryl Ann Wixson was born in Lewiston, Maine on March 1, 1955, about two weeks after Bill's death. Addie, who was proud of her family, was thrilled to welcome their great-granddaughter to the farm, which addition helped make up for the loss of her husband.

Four Generations: Addie holding her great-granddaughter Cheryl Wixson, summer 1955. Behind her is our mother Rowena, and grandmother Winona.
(Family photo, currently in the author's possession.)

William F. Young left his entire estate—his real estate and personal property—to "my beloved wife, L. Adalade Young, to her and her heirs and assigns forever."[192] During his lifetime, Bill never sold an acre of the land his Crockett ancestors had acquired over the prior 143 years, and which he had inherited from his mother, Emma (Crockett) Young Harding, in 1937.

Addie and the couple's eldest son George struggled to carry on the turkey

---

191. Records from Norway Pine Grove Cemetery Association. Page 157. Perpetual care agreement No. 499.
192. OCROD, Book 523, page 281.

business for a year after Bill's death. In 1956, however, (the year I was born), the last of the turkeys were sold. The era of Young's Turkey Farm had ended.

To provide for her retirement, as well as for the continuation of the family farm, Addie decided to develop some of the thousand-plus feet of lakefront property that came with Ephraim Crockett's and Nathan Morse's purchase of Lot 45 in Lee's Grant in 1814. Addie hired civil engineer E.W. Cummings to draw up a survey plan. Cummings produced the plan, "Young's Cottage Lots," on June 2, 1956. A second plan, which included three more lots to the north of Penley Island, was produced on June 6, 1959, by C.B. Davis, C.E. Between the summer of 1956 and 1960, Addie sold more than a dozen camp lots on Norway Lake to nine buyers, all but one from out-of-state.[193] She also built a road down to the water,[194] and granted rights of way to CMP so the camps could have electricity. A prime west-facing lot (Lot 5) was kept for the family's use, and it was here that Addie's son George built a log cabin. Lot 5, where most of us kids learned to swim, is still in the family today, as well as Lot 2, which my mother and brother Wes Wixson brought back into the family in the 1990s. Another prime lot (Lot 12) was gifted to son Bud, as well as some other land next to (and behind) the lot. (Penley Island—renamed "Cathedral Pines Island" after the tall pines that dominated the six acres—was developed in the 1970s by my grandmother Winona and her sister-in-law Florence Young, George's widow.)

---

193. Hamilton and Alice Cornwall, of Paris, Maine (OCROD, Book 578, page 365 and page 485), were the only in-state residents to purchase lakefront property. See OCROD Grantor Book 28, 1956-1960.
194. The original camp road was on the south end of the old Nathan Morse farm property; however, later the road was relocated between the Crockett homestead and what was known as the John Penley farm. (The old road had a pretty steep hill.)

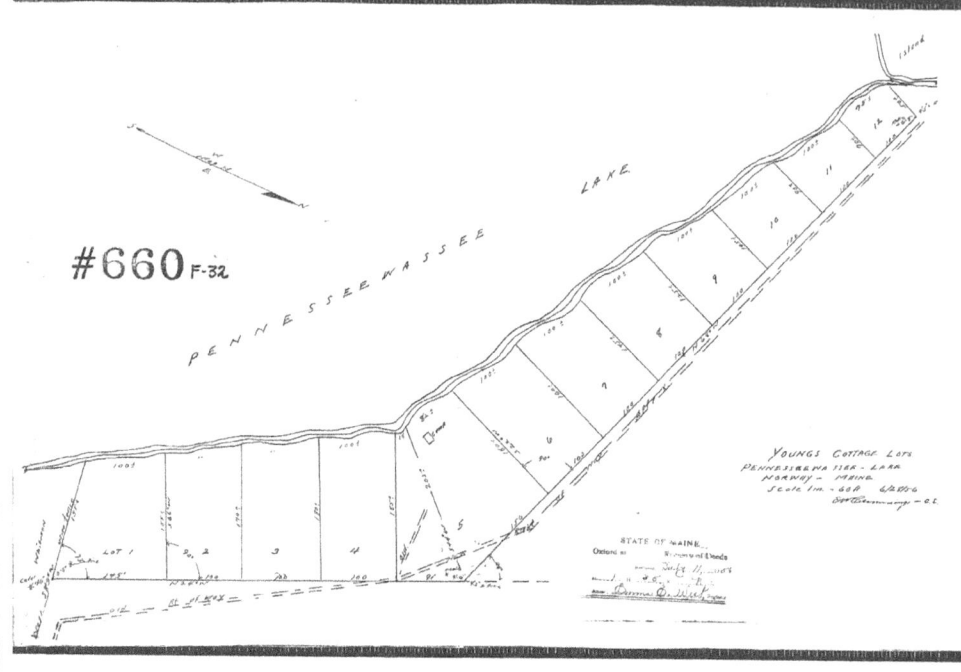

Original Plan of Young's Cottage Lots prepared by E.W. Cummings, C.E., June 2, 1956.
(Oxford County Registry of Deeds, Plan #660, recorded July 11, 1956.)

It was during the development of the Norway Lake waterfront that Addie discovered that Frank H. Hobbs, the son of Etta (Crockett) and Frank G. Hobbs, was a partial owner of the property. According to the will of Bill's and Frank's grandfather William Robinson Crockett, Frank owned a one-sixth share of the old Crockett homestead, as well as the several woodlots William had acquired during his lifetime. Addie made Frank an offer (less than $500, according to the deed) and bought him out on August 18, 1959.[195] This warranty deed, in which Frank sold to L. Adalade Young "any and all real estate title to which may have vested in my Mother, Henrietta Crockett Hobbs, now deceased, under the will of William R. Crockett," closed the door to any future Hobbs' claims, and brought the Crockett homestead entirely into the Young family.

My great-grandmother outlived her husband by eight and a half years. During Addie's final days she loved receiving visits from family and friends. Addie remained at the homestead, where she lived with my grandmother Winona, who by this time,

---

195. OCROD, Book 578, page 457.

had been promoted to Supervisor of Elementary Education in the Norway area schools. Despite her advancing age and worsening health, Addie was still cheerful and fun to be around. My cousin Pamela (Young) Williams told me that as a young girl she used to fake sickness so she could skip school and spend the day up at the farm cooking with her grandmother.[196] In addition to summer visits, I loved spending Thanksgiving, Christmas, and special occasions with the extended families on Crockett's Ridge. Once the turkeys were gone, Addie was free to roam for the first time in decades, too. I recollect several occasions when Addie accompanied my grandmother to Winslow where our family lived on a dairy farm. The duo motored over several times to celebrate Christmas and birthdays with us great-grandkids.

The author's sister Cheryl Wixson presents a cake to Addie for her 77th birthday in April 1960.
This party was held at the farm in Norway.
(Family photo currently in the author's possession.)

---

196. Pam, the daughter of George and Florence Young, is my mother's cousin. Pam and her brothers Byron and George ("Jo Bill"), grew up at the old Nathan Morse homestead. Since Pam and I and my sister Cheryl are separated by two years or less in age, we were raised more like first cousins.

Addie with five of her great-grandchildren.
Left to right: Cheryl Wixson, Deborah and Mark Johnson (in Addie's lap), William Wixson, and Jennifer Wixson (the author). Family photo circa 1961, taken either Thanksgiving or Christmas at the farm in Norway.
(Family photo in the author's possession.)

Addie had always loved flowers and plants, which in her later years became another delight of her life. After Young's Turkey Farm closed, Addie was able to concentrate more on gardening. She and my grandmother began raising and selling flowers at the farm. Summer people, who used to stop in for a turkey, now dropped by to purchase (or be gifted) gladiolus, pansies, and petunias. The killing room, a one-room building attached to the shed, which boasted a concrete floor and lots of windows, became the plant shop. Here, Addie and Winona repotted pansies that they purchased from larger greenhouses, and potted up geraniums. Addie also loved the succulent, Hens and Chickens[197] (*Sempervivum*), many varieties of which she planted atop the granite foundation of the barn that burned. She also planted a variety of perennials and annuals around the foundation of the brick house. Beautiful peonies decorated the east-facing front door of the Crockett homestead, bookended by lilac bushes. In addition, there were always potted geraniums scattered around the yard and atop the granite foundation. Altogether, in spring, summer and fall, the farm was a gorgeous sight to behold. Addie's love of plants and

---

197. The actual name for these is "Hens and Chicks;" however, our family always called them "Hens and Chickens," which usage likely began with Addie. *Hens & Chickens* is the title of the author's first published novel.

flowers has carried down through the generations, too, many of us descendants having learned to appreciate them, thanks to her green thumb.

Addie and her granddaughter Paula (Palmer) Johnson in Addie's garden of gladiolus.
This garden was situated across the road from the house.
(Photo courtesy of Norman Young.)

Adalade (Chaplin) Young passed away at the old Crockett homestead on October 20, 1963. She was eighty years old, and had lived a long, loving and caring life. Addie was buried with her husband in Norway Pine Grove Cemetery. Every Memorial Day I remember and celebrate her and Bill by placing colorful geraniums (one of my great-grandmother's favorite flowers) upon their graves. I like to think of Addie and Bill together in Heaven, enjoying each other's company, as they did for half a century at the old Crockett homestead, Fair View Jersey Farm, and Young's Turkey Farm.

Bill and Addie enjoying a happy moment together.
(Family photo, courtesy of Yvette Young.)

Conclusion to Our History of the Crockett Family of Crockett's Ridge

Addie left a clear and concise will, explaining how she wanted the extensive family property to be divided between the couple's three children after her death.[198] (See Appendix #18 for an abstract of her will.) George, the eldest son who had helped his parents on the farm, inherited most of what had been the old Nathan Morse homestead on the south half of Lot 45 in Lee's Grant (called the "Penley farm" in the deeds after Isaiah Vickery Penley). My grandmother Winona, who cared for Addie in her mother's final years, received the old Crockett homestead and the land that went with it on the north half of Lot 45 in Lee's Grant. Winona also inherited the Abbie Jane Tubbs farm (the original John Penley farm) and the nine acres of lakefront adjacent to this farm on the north. Willard, "Bud," inherited Young's Cottage Lot #12 on Lake Pennesseewassee, some land around this lot, and the thirty-acre woodlot on the northwest side of the lake. In addition, George and Winona inherited together the six-acre Penley Island; the Crockett-Morse land on Lot 30 in Lee's Grant; and the two rental properties on Beal Street in Norway Village. In her will, Addie requested that my grandmother manage the rental properties and pay her brother George one-half of the income after expenses to help maintain his place. Winona was to keep the other half of the rental income to help maintain the old Crockett homestead. Addie, always an excellent business woman, concluded her will with these remarks:

---

198. OCROD, Book 587, page 437.

"I have tried to treat all my children fairly during my lifetime and under the provisions of this will. If any of my said children object to the allowance of this will or present a bill against the estate the bequest and/or devise made to said child herein is revoked and shall be inoperative and the bequest and/or devise herein made to said child shall become a part of the residue of this will."[199]

We have now covered over two hundred years of Crockett family history, from 1812 when Ephraim Crockett, Jr. first purchased Lot 45 on Lee's Grant to the spring of 2024, when I conclude this final page about Bill and Addie Young. Most of our time has been pleasurably spent on Crockett's Ridge in Norway. I have written this history for the descendants of Bill and Addie (more than fifty of us alive today) so that they may know of the hard work and sacrifices of their Crockett and Young ancestors.

Today, much of the real estate passed on by Addie in 1963 remains in the family, albeit several different branches of us. (See Lee's Grant lot map following.) The Crockett-Penley-Young real estate on Crockett's Ridge that we love and preserve today, came to us through the toil, the suffering, and the personal tragedies of our ancestors. Let us remember Ephraim Crockett, Jr., whose love for Lot 45 in Lee's Grant led our family to Norway and whose wife, Sally (Wentworth) Crockett, gave birth to thirteen children (twelve at the homestead on Crockett's Ridge), all of whom lived to adulthood; and William Robinson Crockett, who built the brick house in 1850, where his wife Lydia (Stetson) Crockett came as a young bride to live with and help care for her mother-in-law and her husband's young siblings; and Emma Tuell (Crockett) Young Harding, who carried on after her parents died and after her first husband, George P. Young, committed suicide, and who bought up the acres of her Crockett-Penley relations; and William F. Young, who lost his dream of Fair View Farm when the new barn he built went up in flames, and his wife, Adalade (Chaplin) Young, who helped resurrect that dream with Young's Turkey Farm.

May we cherish the land as our ancestors did, remembering their courage and fortitude when times get tough in our own lives (which it will). Finally, when our time has come to join our ancestors, let us rest easy knowing that if nothing else, the land—and the memories—will continue.

---

199. See OCROD, Book 587, page 437.

Aerial view of Young's Turkey Farm circa 1950s.
(Photo courtesy of Cindy Spagnuola.)

Bill and Addie (Chaplin) Young

Lee's Grant map, updated to 2024.
Black area represents the Crockett-Young real estate still in the extended family's possession as of 2024.
(NOTE: hand-drawing is not to scale.)

Acknowledgements

Many people contributed to the success of this book. My thanks go first to the historians, archivists and genealogists who helped me on this five-year journey (which frankly my husband thought would never end.)

In Norway, Sue Denison, curator at the Norway, Maine Historical Society, was instrumental in helping me gather up important pieces of our family's history. If Sue did not have the exact information I was looking for, she pointed me in the right direction. She also showered me with relevant photographs and maps, all of which make the book much more interesting. Fellow NHS curator Charles Longley also provided me with Crockett and Young family facts and tidbits. On the days I visited the historical society in person Charles always seemed to find what I needed, with just a few quick steps. I am also grateful to NHS trustee, friend, and relation Edward Staples, a Penley and Crockett descendant, who not only shared with me family information and photographs, but also personal stories passed down through his line, which put flesh on the bones of my history.

Also in Norway, Barbara Townsend generously allowed me access to important Heywood Club documents, records, and photos that were stored at her home. In addition, Barbara was able to answer my questions about families in the neighborhood, confirming my recollections of what my grandmother Winona told me in 1978-79. Stuart Goodwin, Trustee of Norway Pine Grove Cemetery, deserves special mention for giving me access to the cemetery records of our ancestors (and their families), which contain valuable historical information. Stuart also sent me the paperwork to formally request the U.S. Department of Veterans Affairs to replace the missing gravestone for Civil War soldier Frank Crockett (which Veterans Affairs did) and had the NPG sexton install the stone when it arrived. In addition, Stuart turned out to be a repository of facts about B.F. Spinney & Co. and the Norway Shoe Company. Our branch of the family is particularly grateful to Stuart for the 1873 photograph he gave me of our ancestor George P. Young (with other employees) in front of the "Little Shop" the year the shoe shop opened. The framed photo now hangs in our late mother's study.

My especial gratitude to Jill Piekut Roy, Special Collections Librarian, USM Libraries, who provided me with information about Western State Normal and

Training School at Gorham, Maine, from which Addie (Chaplin) Young was graduated. Thanks also to Dr. Douglas Hodgkin, Secretary of the Androscoggin Historical Society, whose books on Edward Little and the history of Lewiston (including information on the Pejepscot Proprietors) helped me lay the foundation for the history of the Crockett and Morse families in Pejepscot and Lewiston. In addition, Dr. Hodgkin's personal insight into the character of Edward Little, casually shared with me one afternoon at the Androscoggin Historical Society, enabled me to figure out why Ephraim Crockett, Jr. was able to secure Lot 45 in Lee's Grant in Norway, even after Ephraim deeded the lot back to Little. (Unlike his father Josiah, Edward Little was a pretty decent guy!) Joan R. Duffy, Senior Archive Assistant, Special Collections, Yale Divinity School, sent me with information about Newton Theological Seminary, as well as the print of the school, which the Rev. John A. Harding attended. She also forwarded me a list of Rev. Harding's church placements so that I was able to follow the careers of the evangelist and his wife Emma Tuell (Crockett) Young Harding. My thanks also to Anne Onion of the Gilmanton (N.H.) Land Trust, who provided me with maps of Gilmanton and also helped me correct an error that I had regarding the location of Young's Pond in that town.

As one might expect, family members played a key role in this history. My aunt Joyce Palmer gave me carte blanche to all the old Crockett and Young family photos and papers stored at the farm, which she now owns. Every time I thought I was done with the materials, I ended up on Joyce's doorstep looking for more. I am also grateful for the renovation work done at the Crockett homestead by Joyce's grandson Jonathan Palmer (my cousin Jim's son), who lives with Joyce and whose goal is to keep the place standing for another 200 years. You go, Jon! My aunt Paula (Palmer) Johnson provided me with personal information and stories about growing up at Young's Turkey Farm, and faithfully answered my questionnaires. Paula's husband, my uncle Robert B. Johnson, was responsible for the genealogies found in this book, which nobody but another genealogist can know how complicated and arduous that work was! I would also like to thank my uncle for his support, encouragement, information, and guidance, especially as it relates to my great-grandmother Adalade (Chaplin) Young. I am so glad that Robert was around years ago to have those very personal conversations with Addie so we could all understand her history better.

Another important family member who helped me on this journey was Norman

Acknowledgements

Young, my mother's cousin, who sadly passed away before my book was completed. Norman, who spent summers and vacations at the farm with his three cousins (becoming then the "Four Musketeers"), shared photographs, stories, and his take on growing up at Young's Turkey Farm. In addition, Norman answered my questionnaires, from which I learned interesting and important details (such as how the fire in the "new barn" started).

The Four Musketeers (left to right): Rowena Palmer, Norman Young, Paula (Palmer) Johnson, and Kurt Palmer. The cousins grew up together on Young's Turkey Farm.
(Photo courtesy of the Rowena Palmer Trust.)

Thanks also to cousin George Young, who with his wife Linda lives in the Nathan Morse homestead. George generously shared with me our ancestor George P. Young's personal items, many of which were stored in an old leather trunk, including photographs, papers, certificates, George's IOOF book and hat, and much more.

I met some interesting people on my journey, including a new cousin, Susan

Margaret (Allen) Morgan of Ontario, Canada. Sue is a descendant of Hannah Jordan (Crockett) Richardson (and thus also a descendant of Ephraim and Sally Wentworth Crockett). We "met" on Ancestry.com and soon began emailing each other stories and photographs. Sue helped me identify some studio portraits of Crockett women stored at the old Crockett homestead.

Another new friend the genealogical website yielded up was Karen Caddle of Brighton, Colorado. Karen has an interesting (and rewarding) hobby—she buys old postcards from yard sales and antique shops and returns them to the descendants of the correspondents. I am very grateful that Karen not only found the gorgeous postcard Addie Young sent her husband "Billy" in 1912, but also that Karen was able to track me down and ship me the postcard in time for it to be included in this book (see page 363), so the card could be enjoyed by the greater family.

On the technical side of the book production, I would like to thank my first editor John Goldfine of Swanville, whose light yet confident touch editing my prose always makes me appear a better writer than I am. Following his edits, my cousin Yvette Young (daughter of George W. and Linda Young) went through my chapters and footnotes with a fine-toothed comb, ferreting out mistakes, typos, confusing verbiage, and much more. Yvette also provided many of the photographs for the book, some of which she had scanned years earlier for her own genealogical work, another excellent resource for me. I am lucky to have had a family member involved so extensively in the project, and appreciate Yvette's on-going support and encouragement. The gorgeous book cover was done by Peter Harris of Peter Harris Creative, Spofford, N.H. That I love Peter's work can be seen by the fact that this book was the seventh cover Peter has created for me. I had to lure Peter out of semi-retirement to do the cover, and I am grateful he obliged. My thanks also to Clark Kenyon of Camp Pope Publishing for his outstanding job typesetting this book.

Finally, I would like to thank my husband Stanley Luce for his support and encouragement over the years. I couldn't have done this without you, de-ah.

Jennifer Wixson
Troy, Maine
April 19, 2024

Acknowledgements

Laundry hanging on the clothesline next to the old barn cellar at the Crockett homestead, Norway, Maine.
(Photo taken by the author in 1978 when she lived on Crockett's Ridge with her grandmother Winona Palmer.)

Appendix

List of Appendix Items

1. Mortgage given to Edward Little for Lot 45 in Lee's Grant by Ephraim Crockett, Jr. and Josiah Hill, Jr., December 26, 1812.   378
2. Quit claim deed from Ephraim Crockett, Jr. and Josiah Hill, Jr. transferring Lot 45 back to Edward Little, September 7, 1814.   379
3. Warranty deed from Edward Little for Lot 45 in Lee's Grant given to Ephraim Crockett, Jr. and Nathan Morse, Jr., signed on February 3, 1816 and backdated to September 7, 1814.   380
4. Mortgage given to Edward Little for Lot 45 in Lee's Grant by Ephraim Crockett, Jr. and Nathan Morse, Jr., December 26, 1815.   381
5. Warranty deed from Josiah Little for the south half of Lot 30 in Lee's Grant given to Ephraim Crockett, Jr. and Nathan Morse, Jr., April 28, 1828.   382
6. Service record of Captain John Wentworth in the French and Indian War and American Revolution. Information from: U.S., Sons of the American Revolution Membership Applications, 1889-1970. James Albert Wentworth.   383
7. Release deed from Ephraim Crockett to Nathan Morse, April 16, 1833.   384
8. Release deed from Nathan Morse to Ephraim Crockett, April 16, 1833.   385
9. U.S., Selected Federal Census Non-Population Schedules (Agriculture) 1850 for Ephraim Crockett, Jr. (Line 23.) Norway, Maine, July 15, 1850.   386
10. Warranty deed from Ephraim Crockett to son Nathan Crockett for his homestead farm on Lots 45 and 30 in Lee's Grant, March 12, 1847.   387
11. Deed of conveyance (p. 1) from Nathan Crockett to Ephraim Crockett promising to care for his parents in their old age or the property reverts to his father, March 12, 1847.   388
12. Warranty deed from Nathan Crockett to his brother William Robinson Crockett conveying the Crockett homestead and the responsibilities that went with it, April 2, 1848.   391
13. Last will and testament (p. 1) of William Robinson Crockett, January 12, 1882. Maine Wills & Probate Records, 1584-1999. Volume 19, Page 467.   392
14. George P. Young's Wildey Encampment membership certificate, IOOF, Norway, Maine, May 1, 1875.   394
15. Warranty deed from Abbie Jane Tubbs to George P. Young and Emma T. Young for the John Penley farm, June 24, 1885.   395
16. Ordination certificate (p. 1) for John A. Harding, Norway Baptist Church, April 16, 1896.   396
17. Warranty deed from Howard A. Knightly to Emma T. Harding for the Isaiah V. Penley farm, December 24, 1900.   398
18. Abstract of the will of L. Adalade Young, Nov. 22, 1963.   399

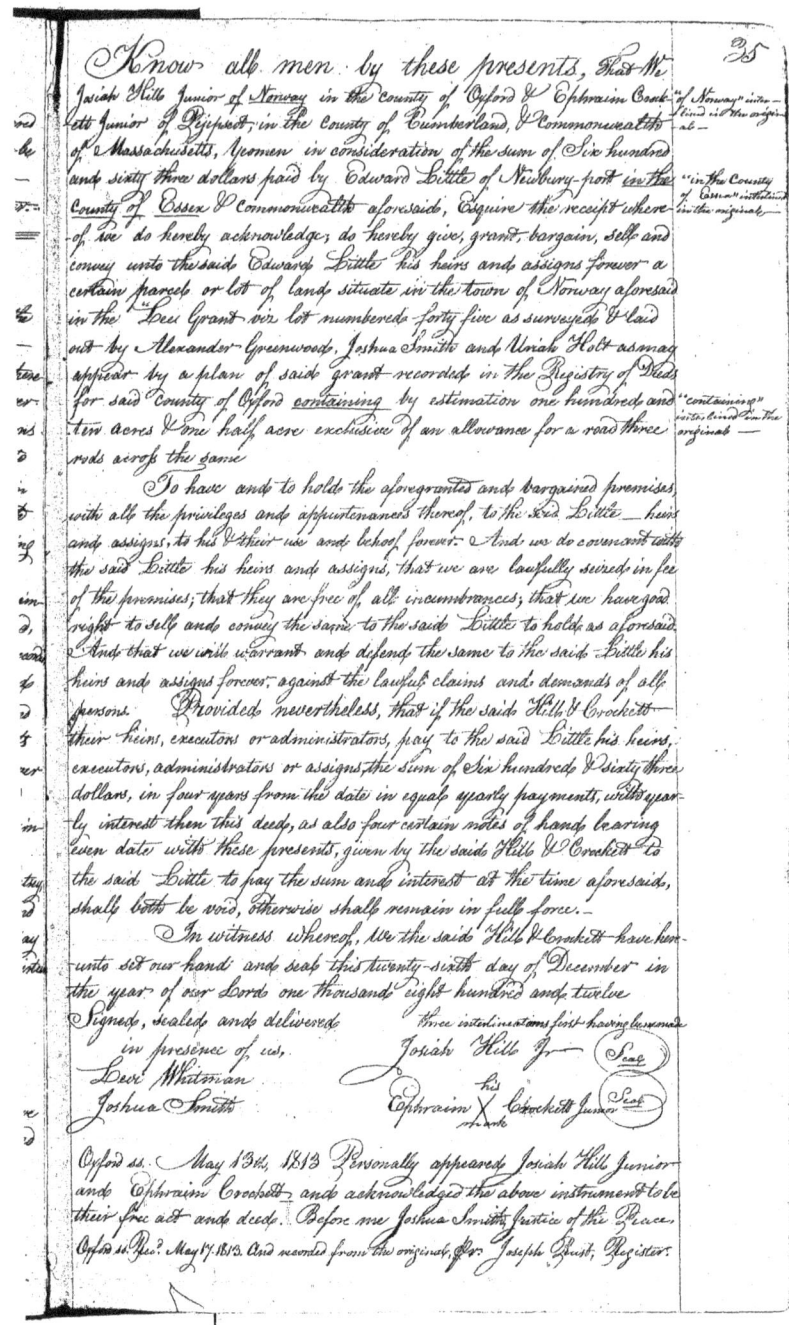

1. Mortgage given to Edward Little for Lot 45 in Lee's Grant by Ephraim Crockett, Jr. and Josiah Hill, Jr., December 26, 1812.
OCROD Book 9, Page 35.

Appendix

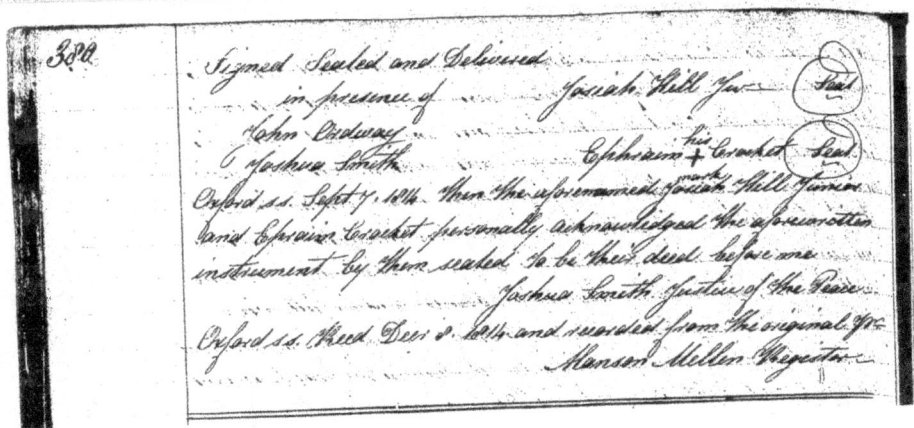

2. Quit claim deed from Ephraim Crockett, Jr. and Josiah Hill, Jr. transferring Lot 45 back to Edward Little, September 7, 1814.
OCROD, Book 10, Pages 379-380.

3. Warranty deed from Edward Little for Lot 45 in Lee's Grant given to Ephraim Crockett, Jr. and Nathan Morse, Jr., signed on February 3, 1816 and backdated to September 7, 1814. OCROD Book 13, Page 253.

Appendix

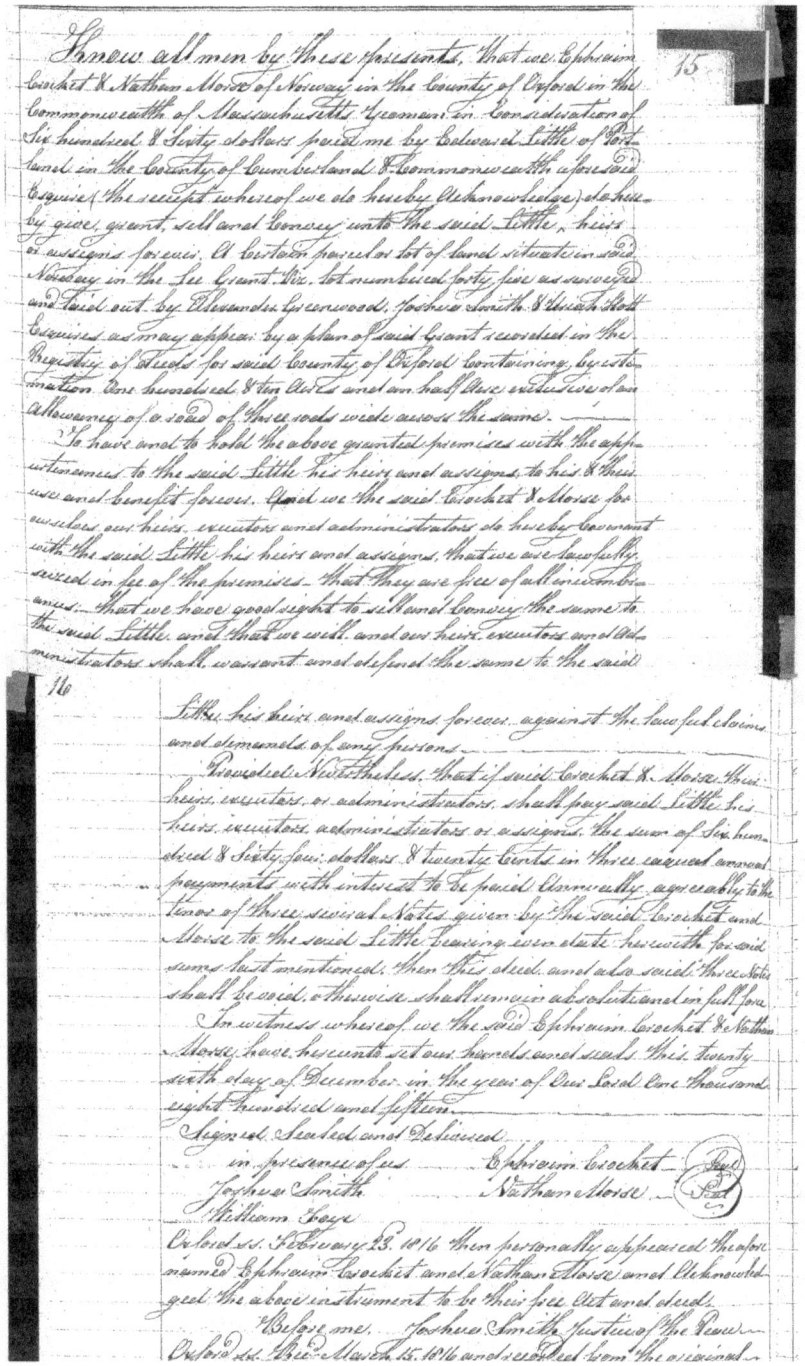

4. Mortgage given to Edward Little for Lot 45 in Lee's Grant by Ephraim Crockett, Jr. and Nathan Morse, Jr., December 26, 1815.
OCROD, Book 12, Page 15.

KNOW ALL MEN BY THESE PRESENTS, THAT I Josiah Little of Newbury in the county of Essex and Commonwealth of Massachusetts, Esquire, in consideration of the sum of two hundred and one dollars paid by Nathan Morse and Ephraim Crockett of Norway in the County of Oxford and State of Maine, yeomen, the receipt whereof do hereby acknowledge, do hereby give, grant, bargain, sell and convey unto the said Morse and Crockett their heirs and assigns forever, a certain tract or parcel of land situate in the Lee Grant so called in said Norway and is part of Lot numbered thirty, bounded, beginning at the most south westerly corner of said lot, thence running northerly on the end line of said lot to the new County road leading from the upper part of said Norway to Paris, across said Lee Grant; thence easterly on said road to the town road, running southerly by Nathaniel Bennett's to the village; thence on said last mentioned road, to the side line of said lot, thence westerly on said side line, to the bound begun at, containing by Joshua A. Smith's survey, forty four acres and one hundred and ten rods.

To Have and to Hold the aforegranted and bargained premises, with all the privileges and appurtenances thereof, to the said Morse & Crockett their heirs and assigns, to their use and behoof forever. And I do covenant with the said Morse & Crockett their heirs and assigns; that I am lawfully seized in fee of the premises; that they are free of all incumbrances; that I have good right to sell and convey the same to the said Morse and Crockett to hold as aforesaid: and that I and my heirs shall and will warrant and defend the same to the said Morse and Crockett their heirs and assigns forever, against the lawful claims and demands of all persons.

In Witness Whereof, I the said Josiah Little have hereunto set my hand and seal this twenty first day of April in the year of our Lord, one thousand eight hundred and twenty eight.

Signed, Sealed and Delivered,
In Presence of
Edward P. Little
Thomas Hale

Essex
OXFORD, SS. July 18th, 1828. Personally appeared Josiah Little and acknowledged the above instrument to be his free act and deed. Before me, Thomas Hale Justice of the Peace.
Received March 1, 1848, at 11 o'clock, and 30 m. A. M., and recorded from the original. By Stephen A. Hutchinson Register.

5. Warranty deed from Josiah Little for the south half of Lot 30 in Lee's Grant given to Ephraim Crockett, Jr. and Nathan Morse, Jr., April 28, 1828.
OCROD Book 79, Page 177.

6. Service record of Captain John Wentworth in the French and Indian War and American Revolution. Information from: U.S., Sons of the American Revolution Membership Applications, 1889-1970. James Albert Wentworth.

> 62.
>
> **KNOW ALL MEN BY THESE PRESENTS,** That I Ephraim Crockett of Norway, County of Oxford, State of Maine, yeoman, in consideration of one hundred dollars paid by Nathan Morse the receipt whereof I do hereby acknowledge, do hereby remise, release, bargain, sell and convey, and forever quit claim unto the said Nathan Morse his heirs and assigns forever, all right, title and interest in and to all that part of the home lot on which said Morse now lives, lying southerly of the following described line, viz: beginning at a green hemlock tree, marked as a corner, in the middle of the east end line of said lot, thence south seventy-six degrees west, to a stake near the pond, containing fifty-five acres more or less. Also one other parcel of land bounded as follows: beginning at the southeast corner of the aforesaid home lot, thence north seventy-seven and half degrees east by Wm Brown's land, fifty-six rods and twenty links, thence north seventeen degrees west to the county road, thence by the county road, north seventy degrees west, thirty rods, thence south seventeen east, thirty-nine rods, thence south seventy-seven and half degrees west, twenty-seven rods, to the east line of the home Lot, thence to the first mentioned bound, containing seventeen acres more or less.
>
> **To Have and to Hold** the same, together with all the privileges and appurtenances thereunto belonging, to him the said Nathan Morse his heirs and assigns, forever. And I do covenant with the said Nathan Morse his heirs and assigns, that I will warrant and forever defend the premises to him the said Nathan Morse his heirs and assigns forever, against the lawful claims and demands of all persons claiming by, through, or under me.
>
> **In Witness Whereof,** I the said Ephraim Crockett have hereunto set my hand and seal this sixteenth day of April in the year of our Lord, one thousand eight hundred and thirty-three.
>
> Signed, Sealed and Delivered in presence of
> Henry Rust
> Mary Rust
>   Ephraim Crockett (Seal)
>
> OXFORD, SS. Apr. 16. 1833 Personally appeared Ephraim Crockett and acknowledged the above instrument to be his free act and deed. BEFORE ME, Henry Rust, Justice of the Peace.
>
> Received March 2, 1848 at 11 o'clock, and 30 m. A. M., and recorded from the original. By Stephen D Hutchinson Register.

7. Release deed from Ephraim Crockett to Nathan Morse, April 16, 1833. OCROD Book 80, Page 62.

KNOW ALL MEN BY THESE PRESENTS, That I, Nathan Morse of Norway, County of Oxford, State of Maine, Yeoman, in consideration of one hundred dollars paid by Ephraim Crockett of said Norway, yeoman, the receipt whereof I do hereby acknowledge, do hereby remise, release, bargain, sell and convey, and forever quit claim unto the said Ephraim Crockett his heirs and assigns forever, all right, title and interest in and to all that part of the old or homestead lot on which the said Crockett now lives, which lies northerly of the following described line: beginning at a green hemlock tree marked as a corner in the middle of the lot line on the east end of the lot, thence south seventy six degrees west to a stake near the pond, containing fifty five acres more or less. Also one other parcel of land bounded as follows, beginning at a stake on the easterly end line above described, distant from the south east corner of said home lot thirty six rods and ten links, thence north seventy seven and half degrees east twenty seven rods, thence north seventeen degrees west thirty nine rods to the county road, thence by said road north seventy degrees west twenty six and half rods to said east line, thence by said easterly line to the first bound, containing seven acres more or less. Also one other parcel of land bounded as follows, beginning at a stake on the county road near a spotted post in the rail fence, thence south two degrees east forty six rods to William Brown's land, thence on Brown's land south seventy seven and half degrees west twenty four rods and twenty links, thence north seventeen degrees west to the county road, thence by said road to the first bound, containing nine acres more or less.

To Have and to Hold the same, together with all the privileges and appurtenances thereunto belonging, to him the said Ephraim Crockett his heirs and assigns, forever. And I do covenant with the said Ephraim Crockett his heirs and assigns, that I will warrant and forever defend the premises to him the said Ephraim Crockett his heirs and assigns forever, against the lawful claims and demands of all persons claiming by, through, or under me. In witness whereof, I the said Nathan Morse have hereunto set my hand and seal this sixteenth day of April in the year of our Lord, one thousand eight hundred and thirty three.

Signed, Sealed and Delivered
in presence of
Henry Rust
Mary Rust

Nathan Morse (Seal)

OXFORD, SS. Apr. 16, 1833. Personally appeared Nathan Morse and acknowledged the above instrument to be his free act and deed. BEFORE ME,
Henry Rust, Justice of the Peace.

Received March 7, 1848 at 11 o'clock, and 30 m. A. M., and recorded from the original. By Stephen D. Hutchinson, Register.

8. Release deed from Nathan Morse to Ephraim Crockett, April 16, 1833.
OCROD Book 80, Page 63.

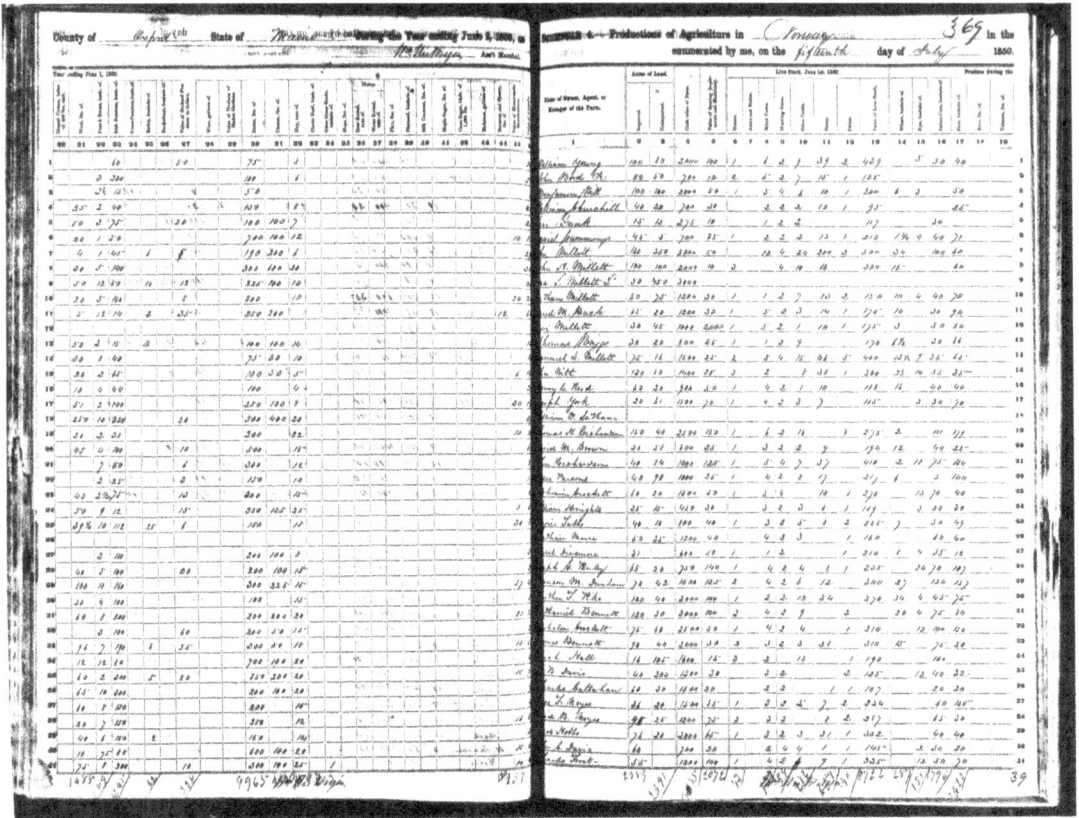

9. U.S., Selected Federal Census Non-Population Schedules (Agriculture) 1850 for Ephraim Crockett, Jr. (Line 23.) Norway, Maine, July 15, 1850.

182.

KNOW ALL MEN BY THESE PRESENTS, THAT

I Ephraim Crockett of Norway in the County of Oxford and State of Maine, Yeoman, in consideration of the sum of five hundred dollars paid by Nathan M. Crockett of the same Norway, Yeoman, the receipt whereof I do hereby acknowledge, do hereby give, grant, bargain, sell and convey unto the said Nathan M. Crockett his heirs and assigns forever, all the land which I now own in the said town of Norway by virtue of two deeds to me of said land, one of said deeds was given me and Nathan Mouse by Josiah Little of Newbury in the County of Essex and commonwealth of Massachusetts, on the twenty first day of April in the year of our Lord eighteen hundred and twenty eight, and acknowledged by said Little on the eighteenth day of July the same year, the other of said deeds was given to me by Nathan Mouse of said Norway, on the sixteenth day of April in the year of our Lord eighteen hundred and thirty three, and acknowledged the same day, meaning to convey to the said Nathan M. Crockett all the land included in said deeds of Little and Mouse to me, for a more particular description of the same reference is to be had to said deeds

To Have and to Hold the aforegranted and bargained premises, with all the privileges and appurtenances thereof, to the said Nathan M. Crockett his heirs and assigns, to their use and behoof forever.

And I do covenant with the said Nathan M. Crockett his heirs and assigns, that I am lawfully seized in fee of the premises; that they are free of all incumbrances; that I have good right to sell and convey the same to the said Nathan M. Crockett to hold as aforesaid: and that I and my heirs shall and will warrant and defend the same to the said Nathan M. Crockett his heirs and assigns forever, against the lawful claims and demands of all persons.

In Witness Whereof, the said Ephraim Crockett and Sarah B. Crockett wife of the said Ephraim Crockett, in testimony of her relinquishment of her right of Dower in the above described premises have hereunto set their hand and seal this Twelfth day of March in the year of our Lord, one thousand eight hundred and forty seven

Signed, Sealed and Delivered,
In Presence of

Asa Barton

Ephraim Crockett (Seal)
Sarah B. Crockett (Seal)

OXFORD SS., March 12th 1847 Personally appeared the above named Ephraim Crockett and acknowledged the above instrument to be his free act and deed. BEFORE ME,
Asa Barton Justice of the Peace.
Received March 7th 1848 at 11 o'clock and 30 m. A. M., and recorded from the original. By Stephen D. Hutchinson Register

10. Warranty deed from Ephraim Crockett to son Nathan Crockett for his homestead farm on Lots 45 and 30 in Lee's Grant, March 12, 1847.
OCROD Book 79, Page 182.

363.

Know all men by these presents, that I Nathan M. Crockett of Norway, in the County of Oxford and State of Maine, yeoman, for and in consideration of five hundred dollars, paid by Ephraim Crockett of the same Norway, yeoman, the receipt whereof I do hereby acknowledge have given, granted, bargained, sold and conveyed, and do hereby give, grant, bargain, sell and convey unto the said Ephraim Crockett and his heirs and assigns forever all the land I have this day purchased of the said Ephraim Crockett, according to his deed of warranty of this date, for a description of which in a more particular manner, reference thereunto is to be had.

To have and to hold the aforegranted premises, with all the privileges and appurtenances thereof, to the said Ephraim Crockett his heirs and assigns, to their use and behoof forever, and I do hereby, for me and my heirs, executors and administrators, covenant and engage, to and

11. Deed of conveyance (p. 1) from Nathan Crockett to Ephraim Crockett promising to care for his parents in their old age or the property reverts to his father, March 12, 1847. OCROD, Book 78, Pages 363-365.

with the said Ephraim Crockett his heirs and assigns, that I am lawfully seized in fee of the aforegranted premises, that they are free free from all incumbrances, that I have good right to sell and convey the same to the said Ephraim Crockett, and that I and my heirs executors and administrators shall and will warrant and defend the same premises to the said Ephraim Crockett his heirs and assigns forever against the lawful claims and demands of all persons.

Provided nevertheless, that if the said Nathan M Crockett his heirs, executors or administrators shall well and truly furnish to the said Ephraim Crockett, and to Sarah B Crockett wife of said Ephraim, from the date hereof, with one good and comfortable room, suitable for a sitting or keeping room, together with all necessary furniture for the same, with one good and comfortable bedroom, with good beds, bedsteads and all necessary bedding, at all times and seasons of the year, together with good and sufficient fuel, well prepared for the fires, with lights whenever necessary, likewise with good suitable wearing apparel, both at home and abroad for all seasons, also with good and sufficient food, both in sickness and health, of good and wholesome quality, well cooked and prepared, and in every way suitable for their condition and circumstances, and provide for them the said Ephraim and Sarah, all necessary medical attendance with good nurses in sickness, so long as they the said Ephraim and Sarah or either of them shall live, and then take care of and support the survivor, in the same suitable manner as is herein provided, and whenever either shall decease, see that they are buried in a decent and proper manner, then this deed shall be void otherwise shall remain in full force and virtue.

11. Deed of conveyance (p. 2) from Nathan Crockett to Ephraim Crockett, 1847.

365.

In witness whereof I the said Nathan M Crockett, have hereunto set my hand and seal this twelfth day of March, in the year of our Lord one thousand eight hundred and forty seven.
Signed, Sealed and Delivered
    in presence of   Nathan M Crockett (Seal)
Asa Barton,

Oxford ss. March 12, 1847. Personally appeared the above named Nathan M Crockett, and acknowledged the above instrument by him signed and sealed, to be his free act and deed.

Before me, Asa Barton, Justice of the Peace.
Rec'd March 7, 1848. at 11th 30m A.M. and recorded from the original. By Stephen D Hutchinson Register.

11. Deed of conveyance (p. 3) from Nathan Crockett to Ephraim Crockett, 1847.

Appendix

> 346.
>
> **KNOW ALL MEN BY THESE PRESENTS,** That I Nathan M Crockett of Norway, in the County of Oxford and State of Maine, yeoman,
>
> in consideration of the sum of six hundred dollars paid by William R Crockett of the same Norway, yeoman,
>
> the receipt whereof I do hereby acknowledge, do hereby give, grant, bargain, sell and convey unto the said William R Crockett his
>
> heirs and assigns forever,
>
> a certain parcel of land situated in Norway aforesaid, and is the same which was deeded to me the said Nathan M Crockett by Ephraim Crockett by his deed of warrantee, dated March twelfth, eighteen hundred and forty seven, and recorded in Oxford Records, Book seventy nine, Page one hundred and eighty two, reference to said deed being had for further particulars.
>
> **To Have and to Hold** the aforegranted and bargained premises, with all the privileges and appurtenances thereof to the said William R Crockett his heirs and assigns, to their use and behoof forever.
>
> And I do covenant with the said William R Crockett his heirs and assigns, that I am lawfully seized in fee of the premises; that they are free of all incumbrances; that I have good right to sell and convey the same to the said William R Crockett to hold as aforesaid: and that I and my heirs shall and will warrant and defend the same to the said William R Crockett heirs and assigns forever, against the lawful claims and demands of all persons.
>
> **In Witness Whereof,** I the said Nathan M Crockett and Polly R Crockett wife of the said Nathan M Crockett in testimony of her relinquishment of her right of Dower in the above described premises have hereunto set our hands and seal this second day of April in the year of our Lord, one thousand eight hundred and forty-nine.
>
> Signed, Sealed and Delivered,
> In presence of
> R. H. Goodenow
> G. P. Howell
>
> Nathan M Crockett (Seal)
> Mary D. Crockett (Seal)
>
> OXFORD, SS. April 2ᵈ 1849. Personally appeared the above named Nathan M Crockett and acknowledged the above instrument to be his free act and deed. Before me,
> R. H. Goodenow JUSTICE OF THE PEACE.
>
> Received April 10. 1849 at 10 o'clock, and 30 m. A. M., and recorded from the original. By Stephen D Hutchinson Register.

12. Warranty deed from Nathan Crockett to his brother William Robinson Crockett conveying the Crockett homestead and the responsibilities that went with it, April 2, 1848. OCROD Book 83, Page 346.

> Know all Men by these Presents
> That I William R. Crockett of
> Norway in the County of Oxford
> & State of Maine do make,
> publish & declare this my last
> Will & Testament in manner
> following to wit—
>
> First, I give & bequeath
> to my son Abel D. Crockett
> the sum of Two Hundred
> Dollars
>
> Second; I give & bequeath
> to my grandchild Ada R. Perry
> the sum of Two Hundred
> Dollars which sum shall be put
> at interest at the time of my decease
> by my Executors hereinafter named
> till my said grandchild shall
> have attained the age of Eighteen
> years or is married, when the
> same with the accumulated interest
> if any shall be paid over.
>
> Third: I give & bequeath to
> my daughter Emma V. Young
> one half the residue of my
> Estate both real & personal
>
> Fourth; All the residue of my
> estate both real & personal
> I give & bequeath to my daughters
> Emma V. Young, Henrietta Crockett
> and Frances Crockett

13. Last will and testament (p. 1) of William Robinson Crockett, January 12, 1882. Maine Wills & Probate Records, 1584-1999. Volume 19, Page 467.

and my executors hereinafter named shall have full power to manage the said real & personal estate for the benefit & use of the said Emma T. Young, Henrietta Crockett & Frances Crockett, as the said executors may judge proper in the premises till the said Frances Crockett is twenty one years of age, is married or dies, when what remains of said personal & real estate shall be equally divided between my said daughters then living — & I hereby appoint Emma T. Young and Wo. P. Young Executors of this my last will & testament, hereby revoking all former wills made by me.

In witness whereof I the said William R. Crockett have hereunto set my hand & seal this twelfth day of January A.D. 1882

W^m R Crockett

Signed sealed published and declared by the said William R Crockett to be his last will & testament in presence of us who at his request & in his presence & in the presence of each other have subscribed our names as witnesses thereto
G. H. Whitman
[illegible]

13. Last will and testament (p. 2) of William Robinson Crockett, January 12, 1882.

14. George P. Young's Wildey Encampment membership certificate, IOOF, Norway, Maine, May 1, 1875.
(Courtesy of George Young.)

Know all Men by these Presents, That I, Abbie J. Tubbs of Norway, County of Oxford and State of Maine, in consideration of the sum of Eleven hundred dollars paid by George P. Young and Emma T. Young both of said Norway, the receipt whereof I do hereby acknowledge, do hereby give, grant, bargain, sell and convey unto the said Geo. P. Young and Emma T. Young their Heirs and Assigns forever, a certain lot or parcel of land situated in said Norway together with the buildings thereon and described as follows: Being the same premises conveyed to Abbie J. Tubbs by deed of Josiah P. Crockett, et als, by deed recorded in Oxford Records Book 196, Page 13, to which reference is hereby had for a more particular description. Also one undivided eighth part of the John Penley farm deeded by him to Sarah D. Crockett by his deed recorded in Oxford Records Book 121, Page 506. Intending hereby to convey all my interest in said Penley farm.

To have and to hold the aforegranted and bargained premises, with all the privileges and appurtenances thereof, to the said Geo. P. and Emma T. Young their Heirs and Assigns, to their use and behoof forever. And I do covenant with the said Grantees their Heirs and Assigns, that I am lawfully seized in fee of the premises; that they are free of all incumbrances; that I have good right to sell and convey the same to the said Grantees to hold as aforesaid; and that I and my Heirs, shall and will warrant and defend the same to the said Grantees their Heirs and Assigns forever, against the lawful claims and demands of all persons.

In Witness Whereof, I the said Grantor and Charles W. Tubbs husband of the said Grantor in testimony of her relinquishment of his right of dower in the above-described premises, have hereunto set our hands and seals this twenty fourth day of June in the year of our Lord one thousand eight hundred and eighty five.

Signed, Sealed and Delivered in presence of
Victor A. Greenleaf
Geo. A. Wilson

Abbie J. Tubbs. Seal
Charles W. Tubbs. Seal

State of Maine.

Oxford, ss. June 24th 1885. Personally appeared the above-named Abbie J. Tubbs and acknowledged the above instrument to be her free act and deed.
Before me, Victor A. Greenleaf, Justice of the Peace.

Received Aug. 19th 1885, at 10 o'clock — A. M., and recorded from the original by
John F. Stanley, Register.

15. Warranty deed from Abbie Jane Tubbs to George P. Young and Emma T. Young for the John Penley farm, June 24, 1885.
OCROD, Book 209, Page 351.

1

A council duly called met with the Baptist church in Norway, Wednesday April 15th 1896 at two o'clock in the afternoon, to consider the propriety of ordaining to the gospel ministry Mr. John A. Harding the pastor-elect of the church. The council was composed of the following pastors and delegates: Hebron, Rev. A. R. Crane D.D. Rev. S. D. Richardson, Bro' Frank Glover; First Paris, Rev. M. A. Roberts, Dea. Carroll King; East Sumner, Rev. A. C. Murray, Bro' Alonzo Pomeroy; First Livermore, Rev. G. W. Colby; Mechanic Falls, Rev. G. S. Chase, Bro' S. U. Hawkes; South Paris, Rev. T. J. Ramsdell, Bro' Addison Tirrell, Bro' F. W. Bonney; Norway, Deacons N. W. Millett and Wm. Pratt. There were also present by invitation as members of the council Rev. B. R. Harris of Boston, Rev. A. T. Dunn D.D. of Waterville, Prof. W. A. Sargent of Hebron and Rev. G. M. Stilphen of Farmington.

The council was called to order by the clerk of the Norway church, Dea. N. W. Millett, who read the record of the action of the church in calling the council. Rev. A. R. Crane D.D. was chosen moderator and Rev. T. J. Ramsdell clerk. Voted to invite Rev. B. S. Rideout pastor of the Norway Congregational church to sit with the council.

The clerk stated that a telegram had been received from Rev. A. T. Dunn saying that he could not reach Norway till the arrival of the afternoon train. The council then voted to postpone the examination of the candidate till after the arrival of the afternoon train.

The council was called to order again at four o'clock. Prayer was offered by Rev. G. S. Chase. The roll of delegates was read by the clerk. The council listened to a statement by Bro' Harding of his Christian experience. After answering some questions asked by members of the council Bro'

16. Ordination certificate (p. 1) for John A. Harding, Norway Baptist Church, April 16, 1896. (Courtesy of Joyce Palmer.)

Appendix

2

Harding stated the facts in relation to his call to the ministry.

The candidate next proceeded to state his views of Christian doctrine. After questioning Bro'Harding at some length the council voted to be by itself. After discussion the council voted itself satisfied with the candidate's Christian experience and call to the ministry. The council voted to express itself satisfied with the candidate's views of Christian doctrine so far as given. The council voted to proceed to ordain the candidate with the express understanding that Bro'Harding pursue a course of further study in preparation for the work of preaching the gospel. Voted that the clerk furnish a copy of his record to the Zion's Advocate and to the Norway Advertiser. The following brethren were appointed a committee of arrangements for the ordination services: Bro'J.A.Harding,Bro'Frank Glover,Dea.N.W.Millett,Rev.T.J.Ramsdell. Voted to adjourn after carrying out the following program: Reading of Scriptures and Prayer, Rev.A.G.Murray.Sermon,Rev.B.R.Harris. Ordaining Prayer,Rev.G.W.Colby.Charge to the Candidate,Rev.A.T.Dunn D.D. Charge to the Church,Rev.G.S.Chase.Welcome to the Community,Rev.B.S. Rideout.Hand of Fellowship,Rev.A.R.Crane D.D.

T. J. Ramsdell, Clerk

"In compliance with the express understanding", I attended Newton Theo. Seminary and was graduated from the regular course. June, 1901.

A. R. Crane
Moderator

16. Ordination certificate (p. 2) for John A. Harding, Norway Baptist Church, April 16, 1896.

17. Warranty deed from Howard A. Knightly to Emma T. Harding for the Isaiah V. Penley farm, December 24, 1900.
OCROD Book 266, Page 201.

Appendix

ABSTRACT OF THE WILL OF

L. Adalade Young

State of Maine

Oxford, ss.   PROBATE COURT.

November 27, A.D. 19 63

Vol. 587 — 437

I, Paul L. Nevers, Register of the Probate Court for said County of Oxford, hereby certify that the last Will and Testament of L. Adalade Young late of Norway in said County, deceased, was proved, approved and allowed by the Judge of Probate for said County of Oxford at a Court held at Paris on the nineteenth day of November A.D. 19 63; and that the following is a true copy of so much of said Will as devises Real Estate in said County of Oxford aforesaid.

First— I give, bequeath and devise to my beloved son, George W. Young, the Penley Farm on which he lives in Norway, Maine, with the exception of the Penley Island, so-called, to him and his heirs and assigns forever.

Second— I give, bequeath and devise to my beloved son, George W. Young, the "Upper Lot", so-called, in said Norway, Maine, to him and his heirs and assigns forever.

Third— I give, bequeath and devise to my beloved daughter, Winona Y. Palmer, the home farm together with the contents, being the same on which she now lives, in said Norway, Maine, which is bounded on the north by the Berger Orre place, and on the south by the Penley farm, so-called, to her and her heirs and assigns forever.

Fourth— I give, bequeath and devise to my beloved daughter, Winona Y. Palmer, that small parcel of land in Norway, Maine, known in the family as the Abbie Jane Tubbs lot, to her and her heirs and assigns forever.

Fifth— I give and bequeath to my beloved son, Willard H. Young, the "Back Lot", so-called, and also Camp Lot #12 as shown on a plan recorded in the Oxford County Registry of Deeds, together with a right of way thereto, said property being in said Norway, Maine, to him and his heirs and assigns forever.

Seventh— I give, bequeath and devise to my beloved son, George W. Young and my beloved daughter, Winona Y. Palmer, the buildings and land owned by me situated on Beal Street in Norway Village, Norway, Maine. It is my desire that my beloved daughter, Winona Y. Palmer, during the time that she and my son own the property, be the one to collect the rents, pay the bills and divide the net profit with my said son.

Eighth— I give, bequeath and devise to my beloved son, George W. Young, and my beloved daughter, Winona Y. Palmer, Penley's Island, so-called, and Lot #5 as shown on a Plan recorded in Oxford County Registry of Deeds, said property being in Norway, Maine, and also the Morse and Crockett lot at the junction of the Millettville Road and the Cross road facing Thurstons, in said Norway, to them and their heirs and assigns forever.

Tenth— All the rest, residue and remainder of my estate, real, personal or mixed, wherever situated and however and whenever acquired, I give, bequeath and devise to my beloved children, George W. Young, Winona Y. Palmer and Willard H. Young, to them and their heirs and assigns forever, and I direct that they share and share alike therein.

Twelfth— I have tried to treat all my children fairly during my lifetime and under the provisions of this will. If any of my said children object to the allowance of this will or present a bill against the estate the bequest and/or devise made to said child herein is revoked and shall be inoperative and the bequest and/or devise herein made to said child shall become a part of the residue of this will.

Witness my hand and the Seal of the Probate Court for said County of Oxford, the day and year first above written.

Court SEAL   Paul L. Nevers, REGISTER.

Received November 27, 1963 at 11 A. 54 m. A.M. and recorded from the original.

18. Abstract of the will of L. Adalade Young, Nov. 22, 1963.
OCROD Book 587, Page 437.

Bibliography

Original Records

_____. Map of 18th Century Land Grants, Norway, Maine. Norway, Maine Historical Society.

_____. Record book belonging to an unidentified agent of Josiah Little (Pejepscot Proprietor). Danville files. Androscoggin Historical Society.

Androscoggin County Registry of Deeds. Deeds, mortgages, and other instruments as noted.

Androscoggin Historical Society. Original records as noted.

Belknap (N.H.) County Registry of Deeds. Deeds, mortgages, and other instruments as noted.

Bouvier, Elizabeth C., archivist. Massachusetts Judiciary. December 16, 2021, email between Elizabeth C. Bouvier and Jennifer Wixson about the divorce of George P. Young and Martha W. Young.

Boston (MA) Hospital Birth Records, 1864.

Canada Census. 1911 Census of London, Canada. Also, 1921 Census of Canada.

Cumberland County Registry of Deeds. Deeds, mortgages, and other instruments as noted.

Cummings, E. W. Original Plan of Young's Cottage Lots prepared by E.W. Cummings, C.E., June 2, 1956.

Duffy, Joan R., Senior Archives Assistant, Special Collections, Yale Divinity Library. Email between Joan R. Duffy and Jennifer Wixson, January 25, 2021, relating to the Rev. John A. Harding and Newton Theological Institute.

Dunham, Emma "Gram." Letter from Emma "Gram" Dunham to Mrs. Addie Thurston, December 20, 1925. Heywood Club collection. Courtesy of Norway, Maine Historical Society.

Elder, Janus Ganville. "A list of early settlers in the Pejepscot Claim (and the towns from which they came)." Edited by David C. Young. Androscoggin Historical Society.

First Baptist Church of Franklin, Massachusetts. "Resolution Adopted with Regret upon the Resignation of the Rev. John A. Harding, July 27, 1911." Crockett Family Memorabilia, Crockett Homestead. Courtesy of Joyce Palmer.

Fulton and Campbell Counties, Georgia, Cemetery Records, 1857-1933. St. James Episcopal Cemetery. Allie S., Louisa F., and M. Ella Crockett.

Ganong, Alan, Volunteer, Ledward Up-Down Sawmill, Ledyard, Connecticut. Email to Jennifer Wixson identifying saw marks on old Crockett boards, April 12, 2024.

Glatz, Larry. "A Town's Memorial – Norway Pine Grove." A Talk Before the Norway, Maine Historical Society given by Larry Glatz, March 20, 2002.

Gilead (Maine), School Committee of. 1866 Letter from the School Committee of Gilead, Maine, certifying Abbie Jane Crockett as a qualified teacher.

Goodwin, Stuart, Trustee, Norway Pine Grove Cemetery Association. Email exchanges between Stuart and Jennifer Wixson (dates as noted), as well as personal conversations with the author.

Greenwood, Alexander. Plan of Lee's Grant, executed around 1812 by Maine surveyor Alexander Greenwood, assisted by Norway residents Joshua Smith and Uriah Holt. In possession of the author; original from Oxford County Registry of Deeds.

Heywood Club. Meeting minutes, other information, and photos (as noted). (Courtesy of Norway, Maine Historical Society.)

Independent Order of Odd Fellows (IOOF). Membership certificate. George P. Young.

Johnson, Paula (Palmer). Replies from 2021 Questionnaire about Young and Palmer family history sent to her by the author and emails between Paula and Jennifer Wixson (as noted).

Johnson, Robert. Emails between Robert B. Johnson and Jennifer Wixson, February 2022 and other dates as noted.

Maine Death Records, 1761-1922. Individuals as noted.

Maine Marriage Records, 1713-1922. Couples as noted.

Maine State Archives. Maine Civil War Units, 25th Regiment, Maine Volunteer Infantry.

Maine State Archives. Maine Supreme Judicial Court records, March term, 1877, Book 17, Page 118. Gerry v. Gerry (divorce record).

Maine State Library. Muster and pay roll for Amos F. Noyes' Company of Infantry, 1839, Aroostook War.

Maine Superior Court records. Decree of Divorce, Winona Young Palmer vs. William H. Palmer. Oxford, Superior Court. March Term, 1940. No. 127.

Maine Supreme Judicial Court records. February 1891, Oxford County, Maine. Case No. 254. Divorce of Etta Iola Libby and Willis B. Chaplin.

Maine Supreme Judicial Court records. Volume 18, Page 361. Divorce of George P. and Martha W. Young.

Maine Supreme Judicial Court records. 1879. Docket No. 306, Volume 18, Page 419. Divorce of Thomas and Hannah Richardson.

Maine Supreme Judicial Court records. 1881. Docket No. 171, Volume 23, Page 234. Divorce of Hannah and Oscar Harris.

Bibliography

Maine Superior Judicial Court records. 1888. Docket No. 201. Vol. 22, Page 93. Divorce of Abbie Jane Tubbs and C.N. Tubbs.

Maine Tombstone Inscriptions, Surname Index, 1718-2014.

Maine U.S. Veterans Cemetery Records, 1676-1918. Crockett, Frank.

Maine Wills and Probate Records, 1584-1999. Individuals as noted.

Massachusetts Archives Maps and Plans #883. Plan Book 25, page 38. Plan of grant to Arthur Lee, 1785.

Massachusetts Archives. Resolve of the General Court of Massachusetts, Nov. 8, 1785 setting the boundaries of Lee's Grant in York County, Maine.

Massachusetts Archives. Records of the Massachusetts Volunteer Militia War of 1812-1815. (Volunteers as noted.)

Massachusetts Death Records 1841-1915.

Massachusetts Masons. Mason Membership Cards, 1733-1990.

Massachusetts Supreme Judicial Court record. Divorce of Martha W. Young and George P. Young. November 1877. Record #516.

Massachusetts, U.S., State and Federal Naturalization Records, 1798-1950. John A. Harding, 1888.

Massachusetts Vital Records.

Morgan, Susan Allen. Emails relating to and photos of Hannah Jordan (Crockett) Richardson and other Crockett family members exchanged with the author.

National Archives. Script Warrant Act of 1855, Ephraim Crockett, Jr. Bounty-Land Warrant Application.

New Hampshire Death and Burial Records, 1654-1949.

New Hampshire, Death and Disinterment Records, 1754-1947.

New Hampshire Death Records, 1650-1969.

New Hampshire Marriage Records, 1659-1947.

New Hampshire, U.S. Government petitions, 1700-1826. Petition from Gilmanton settlers, dated June 4, 1789, to move the General Court closer to the center of the state. Box 25: Feb. 1788-June 1789.

New Hampshire Vital Records.

New Hampshire Wills and Probate Records, 1643-1982.

Norway Baptist Church. Record of the ordination of the Rev. John A. Harding, Norway Baptist Church, April 16, 1896. Crockett Collection. Courtesy of Joyce Palmer.

Norway, Maine Historical Society. Original records as noted.

Norway (Maine) Lodge I.O.O.F. "Resolve Passed Upon the Death of George P. Young, April 29, 1890."

Norway Pine Grove Cemetery. Record books and Corporation Rules & Regulations. Original cemetery records as noted. (Courtesy of Stuart Goodwin.)

Norway, Maine. Vital records.

Norway Shoe Company Leger. P. 52. Copy of ledger page. (Courtesy of Stuart Goodwin.)

Norway Shoe Company stock issued January 2, 1886. First two shares. (Courtesy of Stuart Goodwin.)

Norway, Town of. "Annual Report of the Municipal Officers of the Town of Norway, Maine For the Fiscal Year Ending December 31, 1964."

Ontario, Canada, Marriages, 1826-1938.

Oxford County Registry of Deeds. Deeds, mortgages, and other instruments as noted.

Palmer, Rowena. "History of the Heywood Club." March 16, 1994.

Palmer, Winona. Family information and stories as told to the author from 1978-1993.

Pejepscot, Maine, Town of. "Order for payment to Ephraim Crockett for labor done on a bridge near James Waggs dated February 15, 1808." Pejepscot/Danville folder "Miscellaneous receipts and assessments." Androscoggin Historical Society.

Pejepscot, Maine, Town of. "Order for payment to David Crockett for labor done on a bridge near James Waggs dated February 13, 1808." Pejepscot/Danville folder "Miscellaneous receipts and assessments." Androscoggin Historical Society.

Pejepscot, Maine, Town of. Tax Assessments 1811. Pejepscot/Danville records of assessments and receipts. Androscoggin Historical Society.

Pejepscot, Maine, Town of. Authorization by Pejepscot Selectmen to reimburse Samuel S. Wentworth "for paying the interest on John Nevens order." Dated December 15, 1800. Pejepscot receipts folder, Androscoggin Historical Society.

Pejepscot, Maine, Town of. Authorization by Pejepscot Assessors Benning Wentworth and John Witham to reimburse Samuel S. Wentworth for paying the town's fine for "not being provided with military stors [sic] as the law dictates." February 11, 1809. Pejepscot receipts folder, Androscoggin Historical Society.

Phoenix Insurance Company. Letter from The Phoenix Insurance Co. of Hartford, CT. to Mrs. Adelaide Young, President Heywood Club, Norway, containing property insurance policy for the Heywood Club. July 1913. Heywood Club records. (Courtesy of Norway, Maine Historical Society.)

Social Security Death Index, 1935-2014.

Bibliography

Sons of the American Revolution. Membership Applications, 1889-1970. James Albert Wentworth.

Spinney, B.F. "Letter from B.F. Spinney to Freeland Howe, Esquire. October 21, 1872." (Courtesy of Stuart Goodwin.)

Stafford (N.H.) County Registry of Deeds. Deeds, mortgages, and other instruments as noted.

Staples, Edward. Various stories and Penley/Crockett family history shared with the author while researching at Norway, Maine Historical Society over the years.

Starbird, Charles. Genealogies of Danville, Maine families (Crockett, Wagg, Penley, Dingley, etc.) assembled by the historian. Androscoggin Historical Society.

U.S. Adjutant General Military Records, 1631-1976. Records of the Massachusetts Volunteer Militia, War of 1812-1814. Volunteers as noted.

U.S. Census Bureau. Census data from 1790-1970. Towns and families as noted.

U.S. Civil War Draft Registration Records, Maine, 1863-1865. Draftees as noted.

U.S. Civil War Soldier Records and Profiles, 1861-1865. Soldiers as noted.

U.S. Federal Census Mortality Schedules, 1850-1885. Crockett, Sarah D.

U.S. Selected Non-Population Schedules, 1850-1880. Schedule A, Productions in Agriculture. Towns, years, and individuals as noted.

U.S. National Homes for Disabled Volunteer Soldiers, 1866-1938, records of. Wentworth, Benning.

U.S. Revolutionary War Pension and Bounty-Land Warrant Application Files, 1800-1900. Soldiers as noted.

Veterans Administration Master Index, 1917-1940.

Wisconsin Death Records. Individuals as noted.

Wisconsin State Census. Individuals as noted.

World War I Draft Registration Cards, 1917-1918. Elroy Willis Chaplin.

Young, Addie. Scrapbook that Addie kept for decades into which she pasted articles about Young's Turkey Farm, the family on Crockett's Ridge, farm advertisements in local papers, the Heywood Club, and much more. Crockett Collection. (Courtesy of Joyce Palmer.)

Young Family Bible. (Courtesy of Joyce Palmer.)

Young, George P. "Letter to Rollin Stetson, May 28, 1888" and "Letter to Rollin Stetson, June 6, 1888." (Courtesy of George W. Young.)

Young, George W. Stories about Young family history shared with the author.

Young, Norman. Replies from 2021 Questionnaire about Young and Palmer family history sent to him by the author, also phone conversations between Norman and the author (as noted).

Young, William F. and Addie C. Wedding announcement. Pinned to a family Bible.

Family Histories and Genealogies (Published and Unpublished)

_____. "Study of the *Penley* Family." Typed family history by an unknown author who garnered his or her information from Mrs. Harriet J. Ross, the great-great granddaughter of Joseph Penley. Penley genealogy papers. Androscoggin Historical Society.

Batchelder. Family Genealogical Register for *Batchelder* family. Framed. In the possession of the author.

Candage, Charles Samuel. "*Crockett* Genealogy 1610-1988; Some Descendants of Thomas and Ann Crockett of Kittery Maine (with 1990 Addendum)." Rockland: Picton Press. Second Printing, with Addendum, July 2000.

Dingley, Edward Nelson. "The Life and Times of Nelson *Dingley*, Jr." Kalamazoo, Michigan: Ihling Bros. & Everard, 1902. Published by subscription.

Ellis, Milton and **Ellis,** Leola Chaplin, Compilers. "John *Chaplin* (1758-1837) of Rowley, Mass. and Bridgton, ME, His Ancestry and Descendants." Self-published. 1948.

French, Janie Preston Collup. "Notable Southern Families, Volume V: The *Crockett* family and connecting lines." Bristol, TN: The King Printing Co., 1928.

Hamlin, Charles Eugene. "The Life and Times of Hannibal *Hamlin* by his Grandson Charles Eugene Hamlin." Cambridge, Massachusetts: Riverside Press, 1899.

McCoy, Dr. Carol. "Descendants of Richard *Crockett*." Including Notes of Dr. David Crockett. Self-published, June 2007.

North American, Family Histories, 1500-2000. Published by Ancestry.com. Capt. Joshua *Richardson* #5740.

North American Family histories, 1500-2000. Published by Ancestry.com. "Genealogy of some descendants of Thomas *Fuller* of Woburn."

Norway, Maine Historical Society. Norway family genealogies, including *Crockett*, *Morse*, *Richardson*, *Penley*, and others as noted.

Penley, Rev. Robert. "*Penley* family in England and America, ca. 1377-1958 : being principally an account of the ancestry and descendents [sic] of Joseph Penly of Danville, Maine (1756-1844)." Alexandria, Canada: R. Penley, 1958.

Scott, Donna Hopkins, Compiler and Editor. "The *Crockett* Family of Maine." Provo, Utah: BYU Press, 1968.

Wentworth, John, LL.D. "The *Wentworth* Genealogy: English and American." In three volumes. Boston: Little, Brown and Company, 1878.

Bibliography

Magazines, Periodicals, Other Printed Materials and Websites

_____. Death notice of Oscar R. Crockett. *The Cherokee Advance*, March 6, 1884.

_____. Death Notice of Miss Allie (Sarah) Crockett. *The Oxford County Advertiser*, November 7, 1924.

_____. Funeral notice, Miss Allie S. Crockett. *The Atlanta Constitution*, October 30, 1924.

_____. Obituary of Luella (Batchelder) Chaplin. Unknown newspaper. Pinned in a family Bible.

_____. Obituary of Willis B. Chaplin. Unknown newspaper. Pinned in a family Bible.

_____. Obituary of M. Ella Crockett, *Norway Advertiser*, March 1, 1901.

_____. Obituary of Warren E. Crockett. Unknown date and newspaper. Crockett genealogy files, Norway, Maine Historical Society.

_____. Obituary of Joseph Gerry. *The Boston Globe*. Archives, *The Boston Globe*, Monday July 25, 1932.

_____. Obituary of Emma T. (Crockett) Harding. Unknown newspaper and date. Pinned in a family Bible.

_____. Obituary of Charles Penley. *The Oxford Democrat*, July 29, 1873, p. 2.

_____. Obituary of Charles S. Penley. *The Oxford County Advertiser*, April 2, 1920.

_____. Obituary of Isaiah V. Penley. *Oxford County Advertiser*, Jan. 30, 1903.

_____. Obituary of William F. Young. Unknown newspaper. 1955. Pinned in a family Bible.

_____. Wedding announcement. [George] Young-[Florence] Andrews. 1944. Unknown newspaper. Courtesy of Norway, Maine Historical Society.

_____. "The First of the Auburn Penleys." *Lewiston Journal*, Feb. 6, 1915.

_____. "A Sad Accident." *The Oxford Democrat*, May 19, 1865.

_____. "Melody Three." *Time* magazine, December 21, 1925.

_____. "Maine Colt Stakes – List of the Youngsters which will Trot at Lewiston." *Portland Daily Press*, April 17, 1889.

_____. "Norway Woman Raises Turkeys By 'Off the Ground' Method." *Portland Press Herald*, November 23, 1937. Clipping from Addie Young's scrapbook. Crockett Collection. (Courtesy of Joyce Palmer.)

_____. "Rough Rider Crockett Escorts Pres. Roosevelt." *Atlanta Journal*, October 22, 1905.

_____. "Barn Burned at W.F. Young's." *Oxford Advertiser*. 1931. Unknown day/month. Clipping in the possession of the author.

_____. "We Are Ready No Matter When Thanksgiving Comes." *Lewiston Daily Sun*, August 19, 1939. Clipping from Addie Young's scrapbook.

_____. "Maine Turkeys Tagged Blue, White & Red." *Lewiston Daily Sun*, November 22, 1938. Clipping from Addie Young's scrapbook.

_____. "State of Maine Blue, White and Red Labels—Resuming Pre-War Use of Labels." Unknown newspaper article published November 14, 1947. Clipping from Addie Young's scrapbook.

_____. "Plenty Cookin' On Crockett Ridge At Norway For Heywood Club's Annual Patriots' Day Dinner." *Portland Press Herald,* April 19, 1951. Clipping from Addie Young's scrapbook.

Amesbury Carriage Museum (ACM) website. "The Clark Tannery in 19th Century Amesbury." Tom Murphy.

Bacon, Ralph M. *"Historical Sketch of Woodstock, Maine, 1808 to 1840-1850."* 1970.

Bluegrassmessengers.com. Bluegrass and Lyrics, "Chase the Squirrel."

Boston (MA) City Directory, 1885.

Bradbury, Dr. Osgood. No. 147, Third Paper. *Oxford County, Advertiser*. Unknown date.

Burnham, Emily. "Maine's statehood is irrevocably tied to the defining issue of its time: Slavery." *Bangor Daily News*. February 15, 2020.

Chisholm, Hugh, ed. 1911. "Lee, Arthur." Encyclopædia Britannica (11th ed.). Cambridge University Press.

Colby College, Yearbook. *The Colby Oracle*, 1909.

Crockett, Warren E. "Warren E. Crockett's Letter Home When He Was A Rough Rider With Teddy Roosevelt." *The Oxford County Advertiser*, July 22, 1898.

CTW Photography website. Shoe Blog. "Blake-McKay Stitching Machine."

Daniels, Mrs. Beryl. Young's Turkey Farm Open House (1950) announcement written by Mrs. Beryl Daniels, correspondent for the *Lewiston Daily Sun*, published November 21, 1950.

Digital Public Library of America website. Patent Medicine, 1860-1920. "Quack Cures & Self-Remedies."

Duluth, Minnesota. City directories, 1889-1893.

Essex National Heritage Area website. Explore Haverhill. "Washington Street Shoe District."

Ferris State University website. Jim Crow question: "Which came first? Old Zip Coon or Turkey in the Straw?"

Find-A-Grave website. Gravesites and individuals as noted.

First Church of Charleston (MA) website. "Our History," First Church of Charleston.

Franklin, Massachusetts webpage. Franklin, Massachusetts. "Community Profile."

Bibliography

Grand Lodge of Illinois, Independent Order of Odd Fellows (IOOF) website. "Structure of Odd Fellowship."

Grover, W.B. "Shoe Industry in New Hampshire." *Yankee* magazine, November 8, 2018.

Hankins, Jean F. "Settling Oxford County: Maine's Revolutionary War Bounty Myth." *Maine History*. Vol. 2, No. 3. October 1, 2005.

Haverhill, Massachusetts City Directory, 1867; 1887; and 1917.

Hazard, Blanche E. "The Organization of the Boot and Shoe Industry in Massachusetts Before 1875." *The Quarterly Journal of Economics*, Feb., 1913, Vol. 27, No. 2. Published by: Oxford University Press.

Hebron Academy website.

History Bytes (YouTube). "Hunt the Thimble, a parlor game from the 19th century."

History of Massachusetts blog. "History of Lynn, MA."

Hosmer, H.H. "Hosmer's Lake History—Some Facts Gleaned in Thirty Years Around Lake Pennesseewassee." *Advertiser-Democrat*, August 28, 1936.

Independent Order of Odd Fellows (IOOF) website. "Encampment."

Kanes, Candace. "J.A. Poor and the Portland-Montreal Connection." Maine Memory Network. Maine Historical Society.

Le Duc, Thomas. "The Maine Frontier and the Northeastern Boundary Controversy." *The American Historical Review* Vol. 53, No. 1. October, 1947.

The **Ledyard** Up-down Sawmill website. "An operating water-powered 19th century sawmill" and "Identifying saw marks on boards."

Lemelson-MIT webpage. Jan Matzlieger. "Lasting Machine."

Lewiston (Maine) City Directory, 1883.

LOC.gov webpage. Wise Guide: "When Is Thanksgiving Again?"

LOC.gov webpage. Photo, print, drawing. "Lynn Conflagration No. 2."

Maine Academy of Medicine and Science. *Journal of Medicine and Science*, December 1897 issue.

Maine.gov. "Pines" pdf.

Maine Forest Service (Division of Agriculture, Conservation and Forestry). "Browntail Moth: History, Background, Conditions in ME." Bulletin from the Maine Forest Service. February 2018.

Maine Memory Net. "Mellie Dunham making snowshoes, ca. 1925." Maine Historical Society.

Maine Secretary of State website. The War of 1812-1815: America's "Second War for Independence." (1812-1815.)

Massachusetts Register 1869.

Merrill and Webber. "Directory of Norway and Paris, 1900-1901." Merrill and Webber Printers and Bookbinders, Auburn, Maine.

Merrill and Webber. "Directory of Central Oxford County Maine. 1916-1917." Published by Merrill & Webber, Co., 99 Main St., Auburn, Maine.

National Inventors Hall of Fame website. "Jan Ernst Matzeliger."

National Park Service website. The Civil War. Battle Unit Details. "Union Illinois Volunteers, 1st Regiment, Illinois Light Artillery."

New England Historical Society website. Arts and Leisure. "Mellie Dunham, Maine Snowshoe Maker, Takes a Meteoric Ride to Stardom on the Vaudeville Circuit."

Northeast States Emergency Consortium website. "Maine Earthquakes: History of Maine Earthquakes."

Norway (Maine) Historical Society website. Interesting Places, "Norway as a Summer Resort." (Reprint of an article that appeared in the *Norway Advertiser* July 31, 1908.)

Norway (Maine) Board of Trade. Stationery marketing flier for Norway. 1928. Author's personal copy given to her by Winona Palmer.

Norway Museum and Historical Society. "News from Bygone Days." Researched by Ed Staples, trustee of the Norway, Maine Historical Society. Newsletter, November 2022.

Norway (Maine) Register, 1903-1904.

Old Marietta, (O.M.), Georgia, Facebook page. Gray Gables, home of Warren E. Crockett, one of Teddy Roosevelt's "Rough Riders."

Olito, Frank. "How the divorce rate has changed over the last 150 years." Insider.com. January 30, 2019.

Packard, Harry A. "They Got Water!" *American Agriculturist* newspaper, May 20, 1950.

Peaks Island Historical Society website. "About."

Pentucket Bank website, "About Us."

Portland, Maine, City Directory, 1914.

Portland Directory Co. "Directory of Oxford County Maine." Fred L. Tower, prop; 199 Federal St., Portland, Maine.

Rabushka, Alvin. "The Colonial Roots of American Taxation, 1607-1700." *Policy Review*. August & September 2002 issue. Published by Hoover Institution, Stanford University.

Rowell, George Presbury, editor. "Rowell's American Newspaper Directory." Printer's Ink Publishing Company, 1887.

Offices of the **Shoe** and Leather Reporter. *Shoe and Leather Reporter*. February 18, 1890.

The **Society** Pages website. Sociological Images, "The Swastika before World War II."

Bibliography

Strothers, Richard B. "The Great Tambora Eruption in 1815 and Its Aftermath." *Science* magazine. Vol. 224, Issue 4654. June 15, 1984. Pp. 1191-1198.

Sutton, Robert. "The Wealthy Activist Who Helped Turn 'Bleeding Kansas' Free." *Smithsonian* magazine. August 16, 2017.

Townsend, Barbara. "Heywood Club Lights of Love." Posted to the *Advertiser Democrat* online happenings board by Barbara Townsend on October 28, 2021.

U.S. Congress, Biographical Dictionary of. LEE, Arthur (1740-1792).

U.S. Bureau of Labor website. CPI Inflation Calculator.

Virtual Steam Car Museum website. "Stanley Dry Plate Co."

Westbrook, Maine City Directory, 1904, 1921, 1923, and 1924.

Western State Normal and Training School. "Western State Normal and Training School at Gorham Maine 1902-1903" (1902). Course Catalogs. 92. (Courtesy of USM Libraries.)

Whitman, Charles F. "The Settlers of Crockett Ridge." Magazine article by C.F. Whitman, published in the *Lewiston Journal,* Illustrated Magazine Section. Unknown date. (Author's personal copy.)

Whitman, Charles F. "Christmas Eve in District No. 8, etc." *The Oxford County Advertiser*, January 2, 1885.

Whitman, Charles F. "A Birthday Jollification in School District No. 8, by 'One of Them'." *The Oxford County Advertiser*, February 20, 1885.

Whitman, Charles F. (probably). "Social Circle Picnic in School District No. 8." *The Oxford County Advertiser*, July 10, 1885.

Whitman, Charles F. (probably). "Jim Hulsey's Secret Room." *The Oxford County Advertiser*, February 8, 1901.

Whitman, Charles F. (probably). "Prosperous Farmer – Albert P. Farnham." *The Oxford County Advertiser*, July 5, 1918.

Whittum, Ralph H., Agricultural Editor. "45 YEARS WITH TURKEYS IS A LONG TIME." Unknown newspaper, 1950. Clipping from Addie Young's scrapbook.

Wreaths Across America website. "Our Story."

Wright, Walter. "Notes and Documents: Norway, Maine." *Norwegian-American Studies, Vol. XV.* University of Minnesota Press, 1949.

Young, Addie. "Musings of a Turkey Grower As Told by Mrs. Adalade Young of Norway." Op-Ed, Nov. 14, 1947. Unknown newspaper. Clipping from Addie Young's scrapbook.

Books

Badger, William. "The History of Gilmanton, New Hampshire to 1875." Phillip M. Zea, editor. Published by the New Hampshire Historical Society, 1976.

Baxter, James Phinney. "Documentary History of the State of Maine, Vol, III, Containing the Treelawny Papers." Portland: Hoyt, Fogg, and Donham, 1884.

Bradbury, Dr. Osgood N. "Norway in the Forties." A compilation of stories and newspaper articles written in the 19th century by Dr. Osgood N. Bradbury. Edited by Don L. McCallister. Norway: Twin Town Graphics, 1986.

Crockett, Deacon George B. "Consolidated History of the Churches of the Oxford Baptist Association, State of Maine, and a Historical Sketch of the Association." Bryant's Pond, Me.: A. M. Chase & Co., Printers, 1905.

Fernald, Charles H. & **Kirkland**, Archie H. "The browntail moth, *Euproctis chrysorrhoea* (L.). A report on the life history and habits of the imported browntail moth, together with a description of the remedies best suited for destroying it." Boston: Wright & Potter Printing Co., 1903.

Goold, Nathan. "History of Colonel Edmund Phinney's Thirty-first regiment of foot." Maine Society Sons of the American Revolution. Portland, Maine: Thurston Press, 1896.

Handy, Charles. "Centennial History of the town of Sumner, 1798-1898." West Sumner: Charles Handy, Jr., Publisher, 1899.

Hatch, Harris B. and **Stewart**, Alexander A. "History of Electrotype Making." *Electrotyping and stereotyping*. Chicago: United Typothetae of America, 1918.

Hodgkin, Douglas I. "Dear Parent: A Biography and Letters of Edward Little." Auburn: Androscoggin Historical Society, 2017.

Hodgkin, Douglas I. "Frontier to Industrial City: Lewiston Town Politics, 1768-1863." Topsham, Maine: Just Write Books, Topsham, 2008.

Holt, Jeff. "The Grand Trunk in New England." Railfare Enterprises, Limited. 1986.

Holt, Michael F. *Franklin Pierce*. The American Presidents Series." (Kindle ed.) Henry Holt and Company, LLC, 2010.

Hurd, D. Hamilton, editor. "History of Merrimack and Belknap Counties, New Hampshire." Philadelphia: J.W. Lewis & Co., 1885.

Kessler-Harris, Alice. "In Pursuit of Equity." New York, New York: Oxford University Press, 2001.

Kirkpatrick, Betty and **Kirkpatrick**, Elizabeth McLaren. "Clichés: Over 1500 Phrases Explored and Explained." New York: Macmillan, 1999.

Bibliography

Lancaster, David. "The History of Gilmanton from the First Settlement to the Present Time." Printed by Alfred Prescott. Gilmanton. 1845.

Lapham, William Berry. "The History of Norway, Maine – A reprinting of the 1886 edition on the occasion of the town's Bicentennial Year. Including a new foreword by Rev. Donald L. McAllister." Originally published 1886 by Brown Thurston & Co., Publishers, Portland, Maine 1886. Reprint 1986 by New England History Press in collaboration with the Norway, Maine Historical Society.

Little, George Thomas, A.M., Litt.D., Editor and Compiler. "Genealogical and Family History of the State of Maine." New York: Lewis Historical Publishing Company, 1909.

McAllister, Don A. "Bound By Memories Ties: A Pictorial History of Norway, Maine." Norway: Twin Town Graphics, 1988.

Merrill, Georgia Drew, Editor. "History of Androscoggin County, Maine, Illustrated." Boston: W.A. Fergusson & Co., 1891.

Nash, Gary B. 2008. "The Unknown American Revolution." New York: Viking Penguin. p. 114–115.

Noyes, David. "The History of Norway: Comprising a Minute Account of Its First Settlements, Town Officers, the Annual Expenditures of the Town, with Other Statistical Matters; Interspersed with Historical Sketches and Anecdote, and Occasional Remarks by the Author." Published by the Author, 1852.

Noyes, Sibyl; **Libby**, Charles Thornton; **Davis**, Water Goodwin. "Genealogical Dictionary of Maine and New Hampshire." Boston, Massachusetts: New England Historic Genealogical Society, 2012.

Pearson, Gardner W. "Massachusetts Volunteer Militia Called out by the Governor of Massachusetts to suppress a threatened invasion during the War of 1812-14." Published by Brig. Genl. Gardner W. Pearson, The Adjutant General of Massachusetts, 1913. Reprinted for Clearfield Company Inc. Baltimore, Maryland: Genealogical Publishing Co., Inc., 1993.

Pierce, Richard Donald, Editor. "Andover Newton Theological School—General Catalogue of The Newton Theological Institution 1826-1943." Newton Centre, The Newton Theological Institution, 1943.

Ridlon, Rev. G. T. "Early Settlers of Harrison, Maine with an Historical Sketch of the Settlement, Progress and Present Condition of the Town." Kilby & Woodbury Printers: Skowhegan, Maine, 1877.

Rowe, William H. "The Maritime History of Maine: Three Centuries of Ship Building & Seafaring." Gardiner, Me. The Harpswell Press. 1989. (Copyright W.W. Norton, 1948).

Stackpole, Everett S. "History of Durham, Maine." Lewiston, Maine: Press of the Lewiston Journal Co., 1899.

Stoddard, John L. "John L. Stoddard Lectures." Volume 1. Boston: Balch Brothers Co., 1897. Ebook made available by Project Gutenberg.

Taylor, Alan. "Liberty Men and Great Proprietors: The Revolutionary Settlement on the Maine Frontier, 1760-1820." Chapel Hill & London: The University of North Carolina Press, 1990.

U.S. Government. "The Union army; a history of military affairs in the loyal states, 1861-65 -- records of the regiments in the Union army -- cyclopedia of battles -- memoirs of commanders and soldiers. Vol.1." Madison, Wis: Federal Pub. Co., 1908.

Whitman, Charles F. "A History of Norway, Maine, from the Earliest Settlements to the Close of the Year 1922." Lewiston, Maine: Lewiston Journal Printshop and Bindery, 1924.

Woodard, Colin. "The Lobster Coast." New York, NY. Viking-Penguin. 2004.

Wright, Walter W. "Notes and Documents: Norway, Maine." *Norwegian-American Studies, Vol. XV.* University of Minnesota Press, 1949.

Family Recipes and Remedies

AUTHOR'S NOTE: This section on recipes and remedies is taken from my 1979 Crockett family history.

Introduction

Despite all the photos, the history books, the conversations with my grandmother Winona, I never really felt close to any of our ancestors ... until I opened up Grammie Young's cookbook. The old book was stuffed with faded newspaper clippings, addresses, patterns, and other irreplaceable memorabilia of days gone by. Most important, however, the cookbook was full of Addie (Chaplin) Young herself.

As I stared at a page somewhere in the middle of the jam-packed cookbook, I suddenly felt as though my great-grandmother were still alive; as if she had just stepped out of the kitchen, probably to collect a few turkey eggs for the lemon pie she was baking, and that she would be back at any moment. She was there, so close, I felt like a child stealing glimpses of a forbidden world; eavesdropping on people I would never get the chance to meet in the flesh, like her good friends Lydia Abbott, Una Jackson, and Addie Robinson. The ladies came alive in the cookbook, talking, laughing, exchanging recipes and local gossip. I felt as though I had stepped into another time, another world, all safely preserved in Addie's feminine handwriting, recipes and remedies interspersed with flyers for Pebeco toothpaste and a romantic *Gone with the Wind* cookbook.

As the days and years slipped away Addie added other keepsakes to her cookbook: a letter from Forest Gilbert of the Androscoggin Farmers Co-op inviting "the folks" to the annual supper meeting April 18, 1955. That Grammie Young went and enjoyed the supper was evident ... a cookie recipe was scribbled on the back of the invitation. Also tucked inside the cookbook were pamphlets for LUCKY flour and stationery from Hill View Inn in Chesuncook offering "an abundance of game in open season (and) fishing unsurpassed" for the tidy price of $1 per meal and $1 per night lodging. A program for the Star Theatre revealed that *Shanghai Express* with Clive Brook and Marlene Dietrich was playing on Mondays and Tuesdays. Did Addie and Bill attend, I wondered?

More meaningful to me than the memorabilia, however, was the cheerful and encouraging spirit of Addie evidenced by the poems she chose to clip from newspapers and magazines. I like to think my great-grandmother kept these poems close to her as she worked through her day, taking a moment now and again to glance at the open cookbook lying on the counter. The poem below, which Addie copied out by hand onto one of the pages of her cookbook, perfectly captures what I see as her positive spirit:

When the weather suits you not
try smiling,
When your coffee isn't hot
try smiling.
When your neighbors don't do right
and your relatives all fight
sure it's hard, but then you might
try smiling.
Doesn't change the thing of course,
just smiling.
But it cannot make it worse
just smiling.
And it seems to help your case
brighten up the gloomy place;
then it sort of rests your face
just smiling.

Addie's cookbook is a door to our ancestors' past, a way for us to share in their history. The recipes found inside her cookbook—some of them handed down for generations—also offer a way for our ancestors to share in our future.

Recipes

Green Tomato Mincemeat

This family recipe, always a favorite at Thanksgiving, came from Addie (Titcomb) Thurston Robinson, a close friend of Addie Young's. Mrs. Robinson (and her second husband Delmore Robinson) lived on the Thurston homestead with her son Stanley Thurston and his family. Today, the Thurston farm is owned by Rick Morse, Stanley and Lillian Thurston's grandson, and Addie Robinson's great-grandson. (The farm is on the old road to Millettville, now part of the Crockett Ridge Road.)

Chop 4 quarts green tomatoes, drain, cover with cold water and cook about 30 minutes (or until tender). Drain again. Add:

1 quart chopped apples
2 cups chopped suet (small pieces!)
1 cup apple cider vinegar
2 pounds brown sugar
1 pound raisins (chopped fine)
1 pound currants (chopped fine)
Salt to taste (approximately 1 teaspoon)

Cook all together, slowly. Simmer on gas stove or cook slowly on back of woodstove. (We used to make this on Winona's Atlantic end heater in her kitchen, just keeping the fire going. We would simmer the mix for 6-8 hours.) Add the following spices while simmering: 1 teaspoon each of cloves, cinnamon, allspice, and nutmeg. Simmer until the mixture is thick enough for pies.

Can green tomato mincemeat pie filling in pint jars for small pies and quart jars for 9"-10" pies. Follow canning instructions that come with your canner. (I use a pressure cooker.) Pie filling is best if used the year after it is made.

Welsh Rarebit

Melt 2 tablespoons butter in top part of double boiler and then break into the butter ½ pound of cheese.

Beat together 1 ½ cups of milk, 2 level tablespoons of flour, and 1 egg. Pour this mixture into the cheese/butter mix after that mix is thoroughly melted.

Just before the Welsh Rarebit seems ready to serve add a pinch of soda, a little salt, and cayenne pepper. Beat vigorously.

Serve hot over toast or Saltines.

Mother's Chocolate Cake
(NOTE: This would be Addie's mother, Luella Chaplin.)

1 cup sugar
1 ½ cups sifted flour
2-3 heaping teaspoons or 2 tablespoons cocoa
Little salt
Sift these ingredients all together, then add:
¼ cup shortening
1 cup sour milk* with 1 teaspoon soda dissolved in it
Beat well, then at last, add 1 well-beaten egg and beat again.
Bake in moderate oven.

To make sour milk, add 1 teaspoon vinegar to a cup of milk.

Frosting

Put whites of 2 eggs in double boiler (not beaten)
Add 5 tablespoons cold water
1 teaspoon cream of tartar
1 ½ cup sugar
Beat with egg beater over boiling water until the mixture will stand alone. Add flavoring (i.e. vanilla, almond, lemon) and cool and spread on cake. Add a little red sugar to make pink or a little chocolate if you wish. For smaller cake, use ½ amount as this will make a large amount

Graham Pudding

1 cup sweet milk
1 cup molasses
1 cup chopped raisins
2 cups Graham flour
1 teaspoon soda
Salt
Steam 3 hours – serve hot with sugar and cream or hard sauce.

Adalade Young's Recipe for Lemon Pie Filling

2 tablespoons cornstarch wet in a little cold water
Pour on it 2 cups of boiling water, add:
½ cup sugar
2 eggs and 1 cup of sugar beaten together
Rind and juice of 2 lemons
Will make 2 pies, with one or two crusts.

Winona's Lemon Sponge Pie Filling
(My grandmother, Winona Young Palmer)

1 cup sugar
Juice of 1 lemon
2 eggs beaten separately
2 tablespoons cornstarch
1 cup milk
Salt and a little piece of butter
Add last, beaten stiff egg whites (from one egg)
Bake in one crust

Grammie Young's Christmas Steamed Pudding
(Addie Young)

1 large cup sugar
½ cup molasses
1 large cup sour milk
1 cup seedless raisins
1 cup finely-chopped suet
½ cup currants
1 cup mixed (candied) fruits
½ cup candied pineapple
½ cup candied cherries (save back some to put on top in cans)
½ cup lemon and orange peels
½ cup nuts
1 heaping teaspoon soda
Salt
2 eggs beaten in last
Put in 4 mid-sized tin cans
Steam 3 hours

Hard Sauce

1 cup cream
1 cup milk
¼ pound butter
1 to 1½ cup sugar to taste
Bring to a boil and set off heat. (Boils over quickly)
Stir in 1 teaspoon vanilla.

Remedies

Addie's Constipation Resept

5 cents (worth) whole ginger
5 cents calomel
5 cents ginger root
5 cents Epsom salts

Mix together and let set 5 hours.

Directions for Deep Breathing
(from a newspaper clipping inside Addie's Cookbook)

Stand erect, throw shoulders back, let arms hang easily by sides. Hold head erect and draw all the air into your lungs that you possibly can. Let escape slowly when you have to.

> "You have bent all morning over the washboard or worked with the hot irons or found the cooking unusually tiresome and it seems to you as if every ounce of blood in your body has gone to your head or your feet.
> "If you are a deep breather, you can correct that tendency to either faintness or sluggishness by just a minute of naturally inhaling or exhaling."

Can You Honestly Judge?
by an anonymous philosopher
(from a newspaper clipping found inside Addie's Cookbook)

Pray don't find fault with the man who
limps or stumbles along the road,
unless you have worn the shoes he wears
or struggled beneath his load.
There may be tacks in his shoes that hurt,
though hidden from view;
or the burden he bears placed on your back
might cause you to stumble, too.

Don't sneer at the man who's down today,
unless you have felt the blow
that caused his fall, or felt the shame that
only the fallen know.
You may be strong, but still the blows that
were his, if dealt you
in the self-same way at the very same time
might cause you to stagger, too.

Don't be too harsh with the man who sins
or pelt him with words or stones,
unless you are sure, yes, doubly sure
that you have no sins of your own.

"Will the Real Crockett's Ridge Please Stand Up?"
By Jennifer Wixson

Nowadays, most people assume that Crockett's Ridge in Norway is that rise of ground on the Crockett Ridge Road that stretches along the height of land at the top of Noble's Hill down to the Heywood Club. This is incorrect. No Crockett ever settled there. Crockett's Ridge, for which the road was named, is the ridge of land rising above the northeastern edge of Lake Pennesseewassee behind the Ephraim and Sally (Wentworth) Crockett homestead settled in 1814. Today, the brick house (built by Ephraim and his son William Crockett in 1850 to replace the original wooden structure) is located on Round the Pond Road. (The house, the only brick home built on what was then known as Lee's Grant, is owned at this writing by my aunt Joyce Palmer.)

Charles F. Whitman, author of the 1924 Norway history, "A History of Norway, Maine," knew the Crockett family well. (As a young man, Whitman boarded around with various Crockett's Ridge neighborhood families when teaching at School House No. 8.) In his history Whitman writes of Ephraim and Sally Crockett:

> "They settled in Norway on the east side of the Great Pond. His name is perpetuated in the ridge of land where [Ephraim Crockett] lived."[1]

The confusion between the two heights of land evolved over time. Early 20th century photographers working for postcard manufacturers were partly to blame. Impressed by the view of Norway Lake presented at the top of Noble's Hill, these photographers simply assumed that—given the name of the road—the ridge must be Crockett's Ridge, and postcards were labeled such. Around the same time, the last of the Crocketts bearing the name disappeared (moved away or died) from the greater Crockett's Ridge neighborhood. While many Crockett females remained, including our ancestor Emma Tuell (Crockett) Young Harding, these women married and bore their husband's name. (Unlike other women who married into neighborhood families and removed to their husband's home, Emma remained on the old Crockett homestead. Her husband, George P. Young, new to the area, named

---

1. WHITMAN, p. 381.

the place Fair View Farm, and Emma and George's son William Young and his wife Addie later transitioned the place to Young's Turkey Farm.)

Once the Crockett name disappeared—and the family history was supplanted by that of later families (including the Youngs)—the section of the Crockett's Ridge Road that ran by the old homestead (which turns left at the Heywood Club) began to be known as "the road 'round the pond." U.S. mail in those days was delivered via R.F.D. (Rural Free Delivery) addresses, not by road names, but people still needed a way to describe how to get places, and hence the development of the new name for our section of road. So, the question, "How do I get to Greenwood from here?" would be answered by locals: "Turn left at the Heywood Club and take the road 'round the pond until you get to the Greenwood Road."

The final blow to the true Crockett's Ridge came with the formal adoption of road names during the implementation of the 9-1-1 Emergency System in Norway in the 1990s. With the adoption of 9-1-1, every road was officially named and every house numbered. My mother, Rowena Palmer, then assessor of the town of Norway, worked with the Postmaster to officially designate road names (which caused no little heartache and confusion). During that process, our section of the Crockett's Ridge Road officially became "Round the Pond Road." This severed the Crockett Ridge Road from the man—Ephraim Crockett—who had originally given his name to the travel way. When the transition occurred, I brought to my mother's attention that the change was a regrettable loss of family history. In return, Rowena pointed out to me that the history had been lost for nearly a century by common usage, including by our ancestors, some of whom even utilized "the 'road round the pond" when describing former Crockett property in deeds and wills.

At the same time the link was severed between the true Crockett's Ridge and the road name, the road formerly known as the "road to Millettville" became an extension of the new Crockett Ridge Road. (According to my mother, this was at the request of residents, who thought the old name sounded "hick;" however, I know some who still live on that road and consider it—in their hearts, anyway—as the Millettville Road.) This designation would be the final nail in the coffin for the true Crockett's Ridge, since anyone now driving the length of the Crockett Ridge Road would assume that the ridge in question *was* the height of land situated at the top of Noble's Hill. Without turning left at the Heywood Club to go around the head of the lake, one would never know that another ridge overlooking Lake Pennesseewassee exists.

Probably the Crockett Ridge Road will never return to run past the true Crockett's Ridge. But ... one never knows. Time has a funny way of changing things.

Crockett Genealogy
By Robert B. Johnson

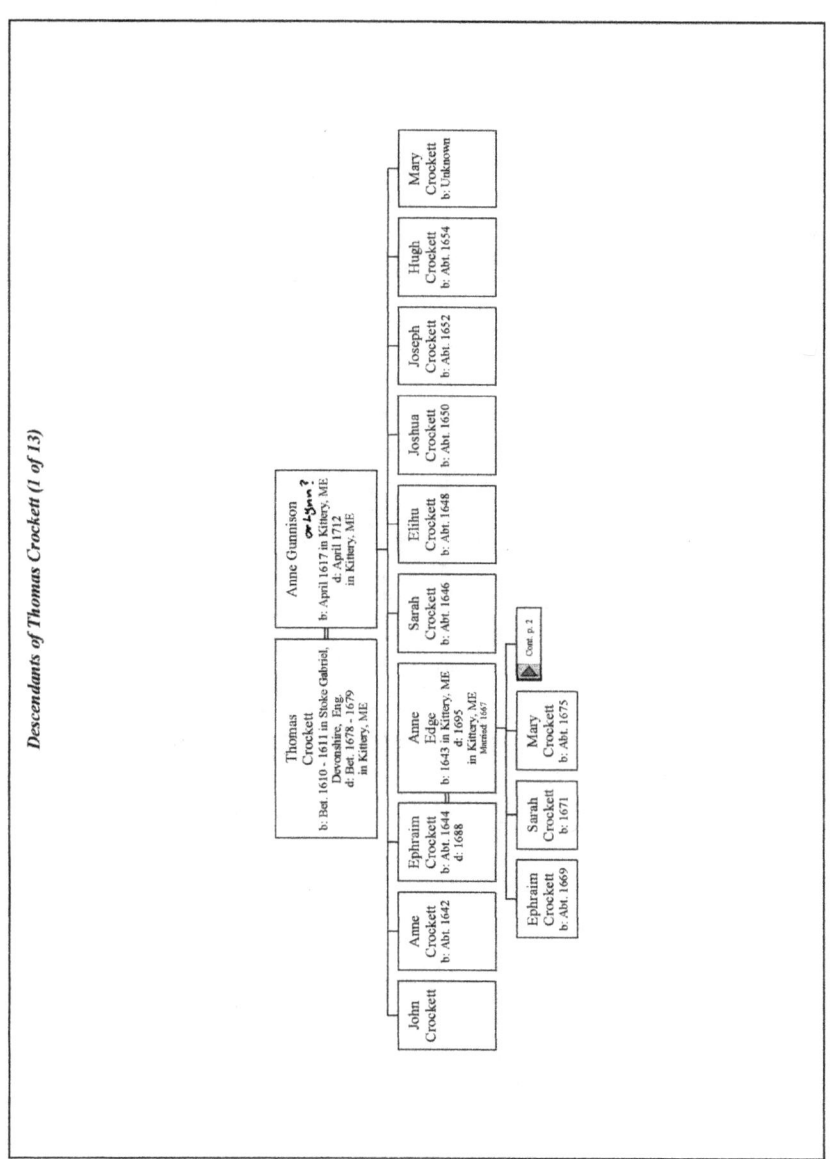

Descendants of Thomas Crockett – p. 1.
Our direct line from Thomas Crockett (1st Crockett in the New World, 1630) through Emma Tuell Crockett, including children, siblings, and spouses.

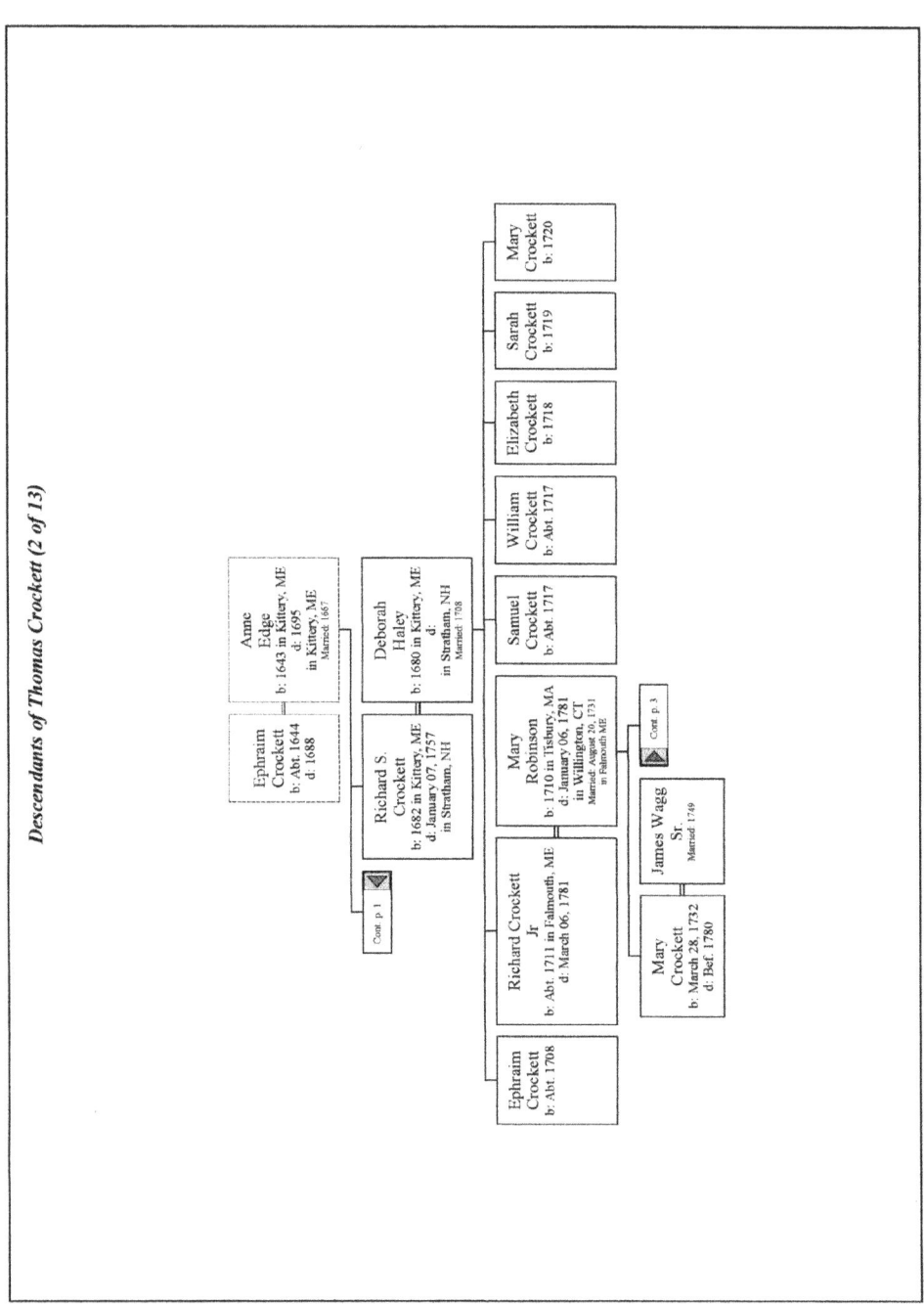

Descendants of Thomas Crockett – p. 2.

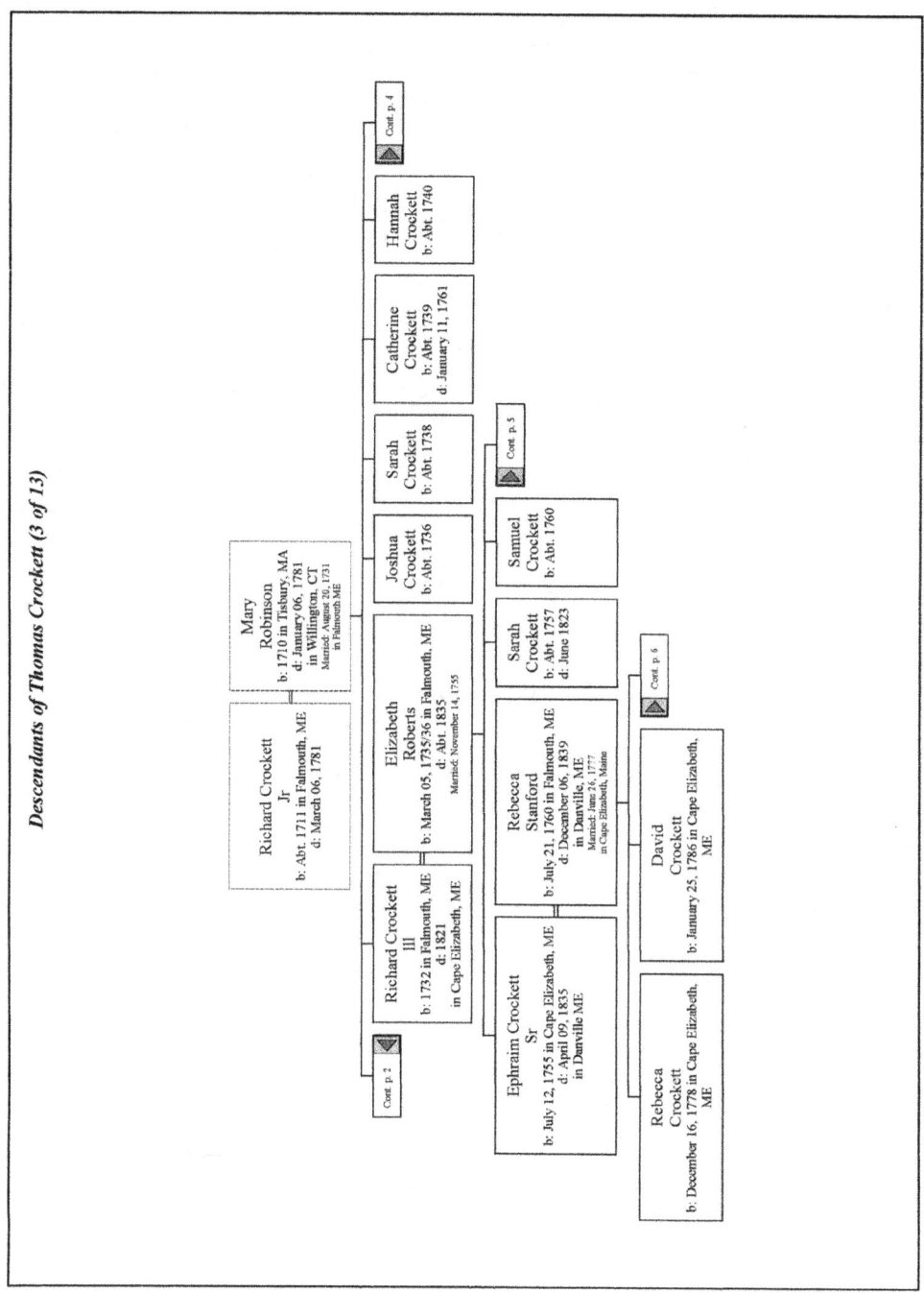

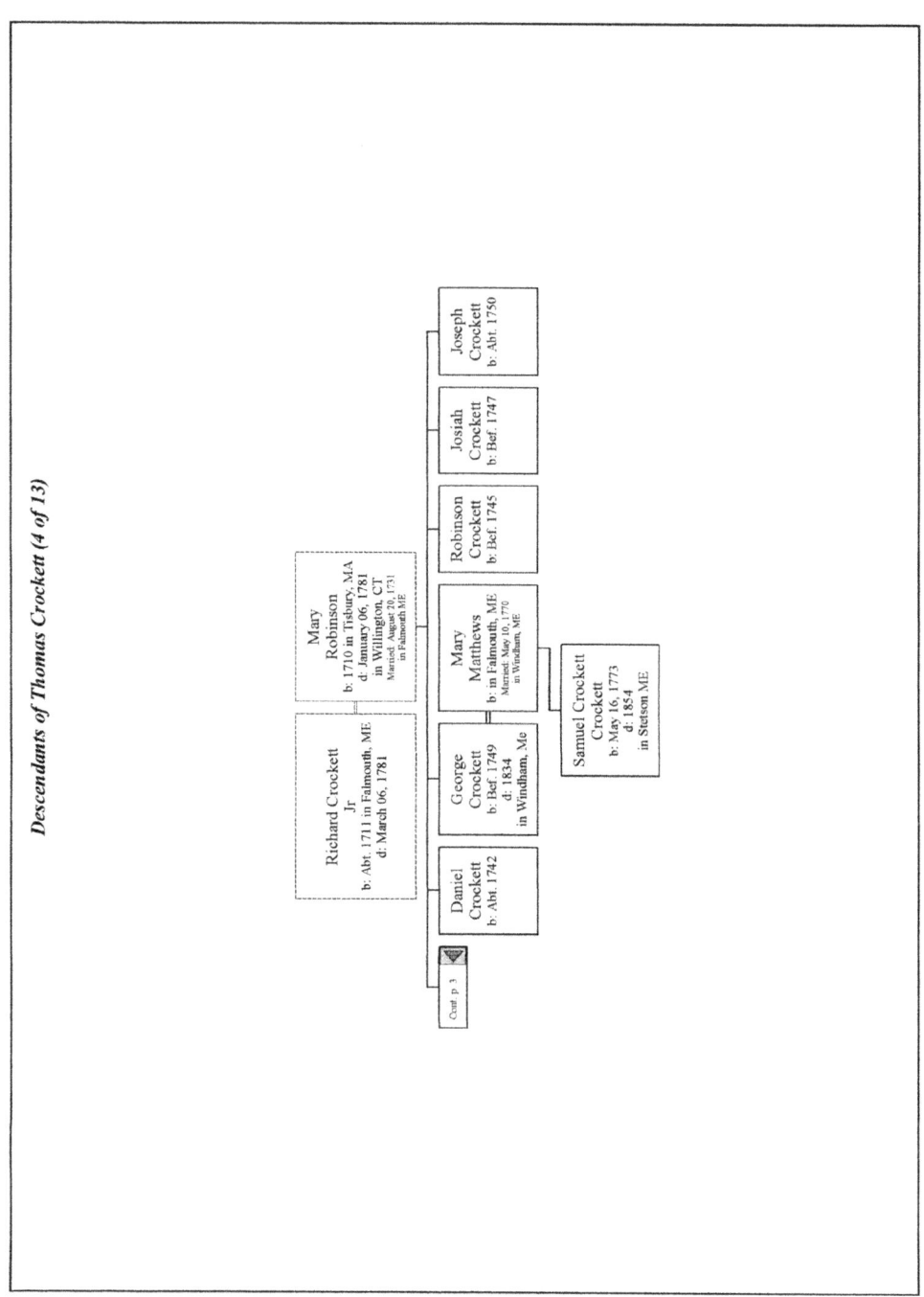

Descendants of Thomas Crockett – p. 4.

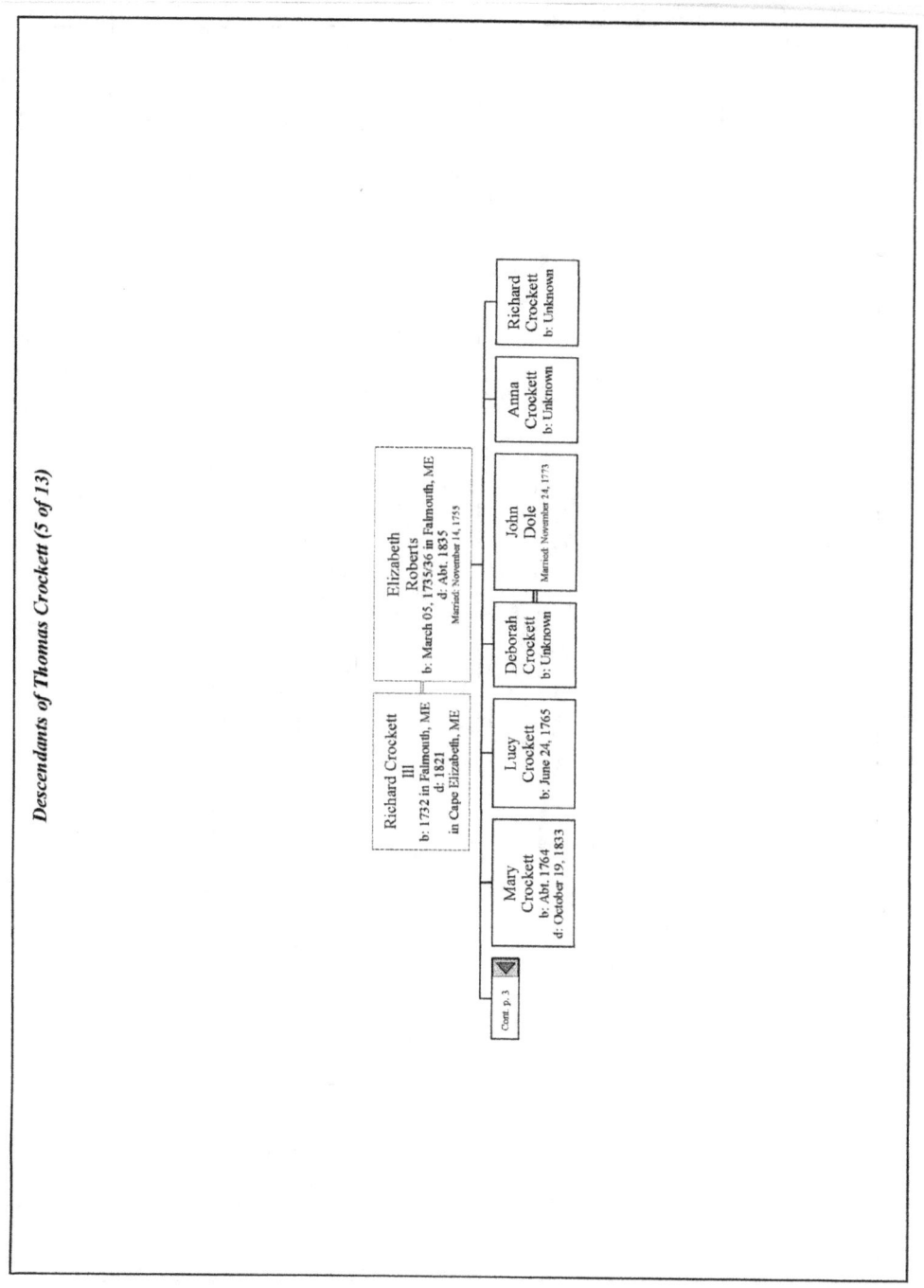

Descendants of Thomas Crockett – p. 5.

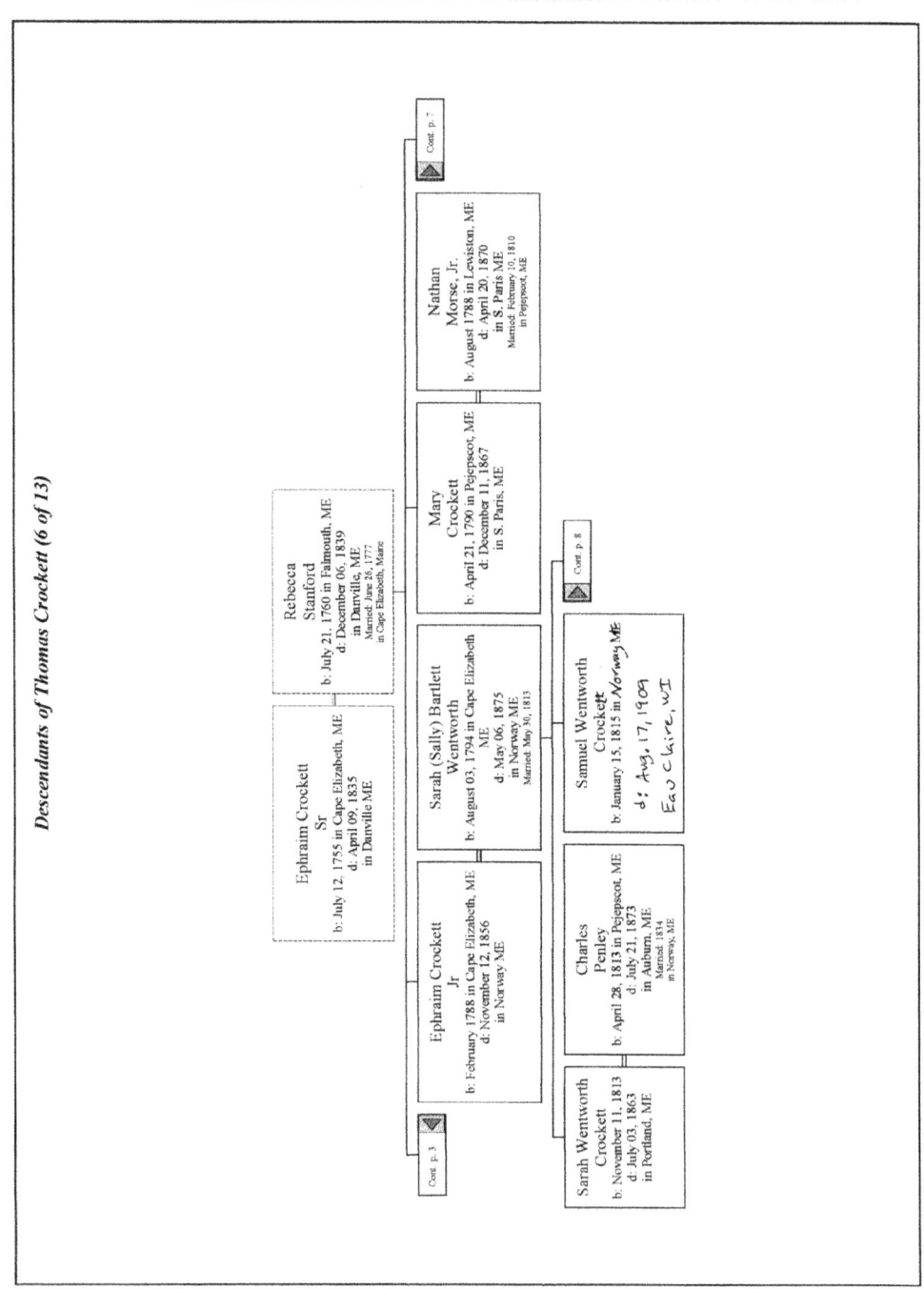

Descendants of Thomas Crockett – p. 6.

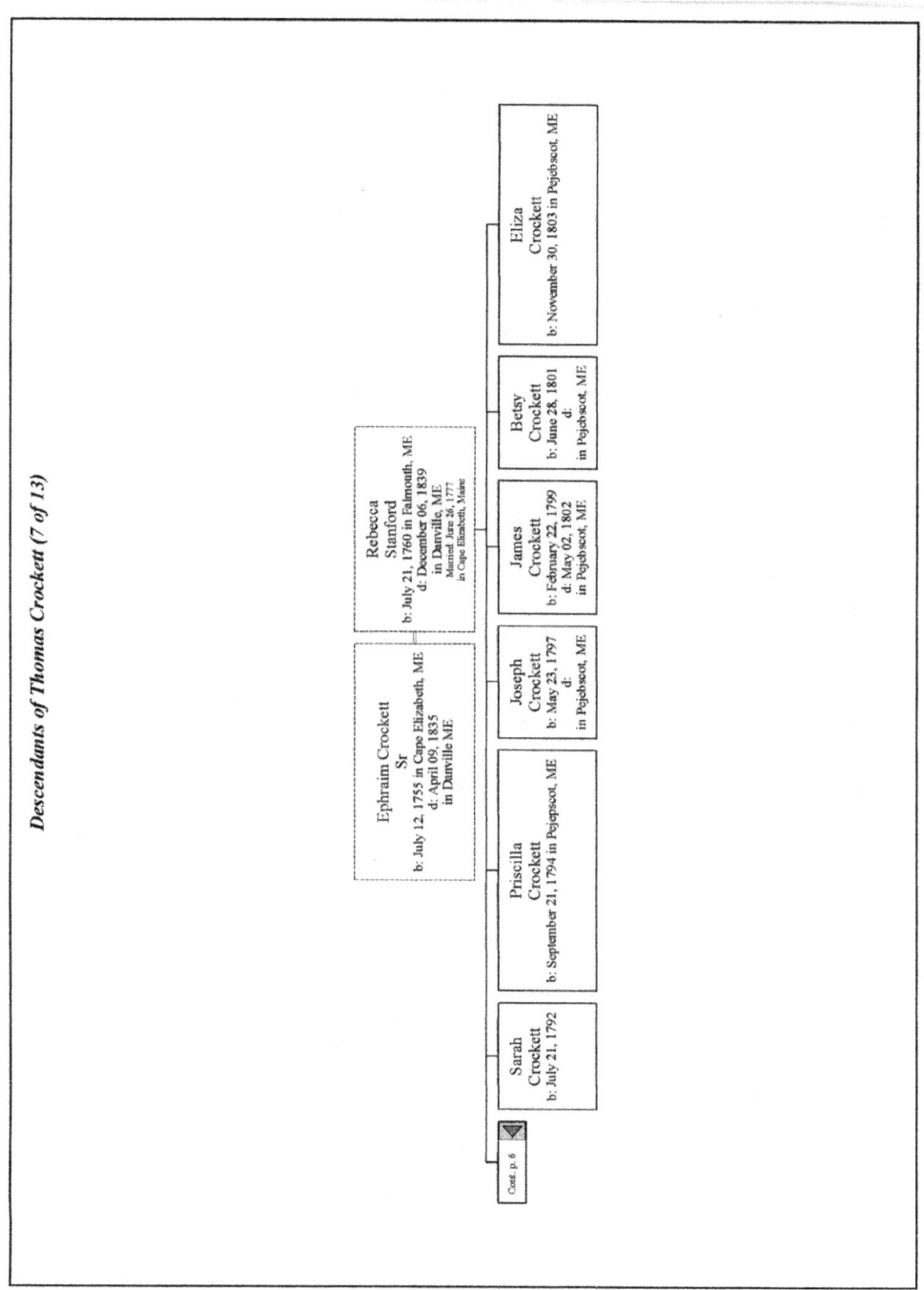

Descendants of Thomas Crockett – p. 7.

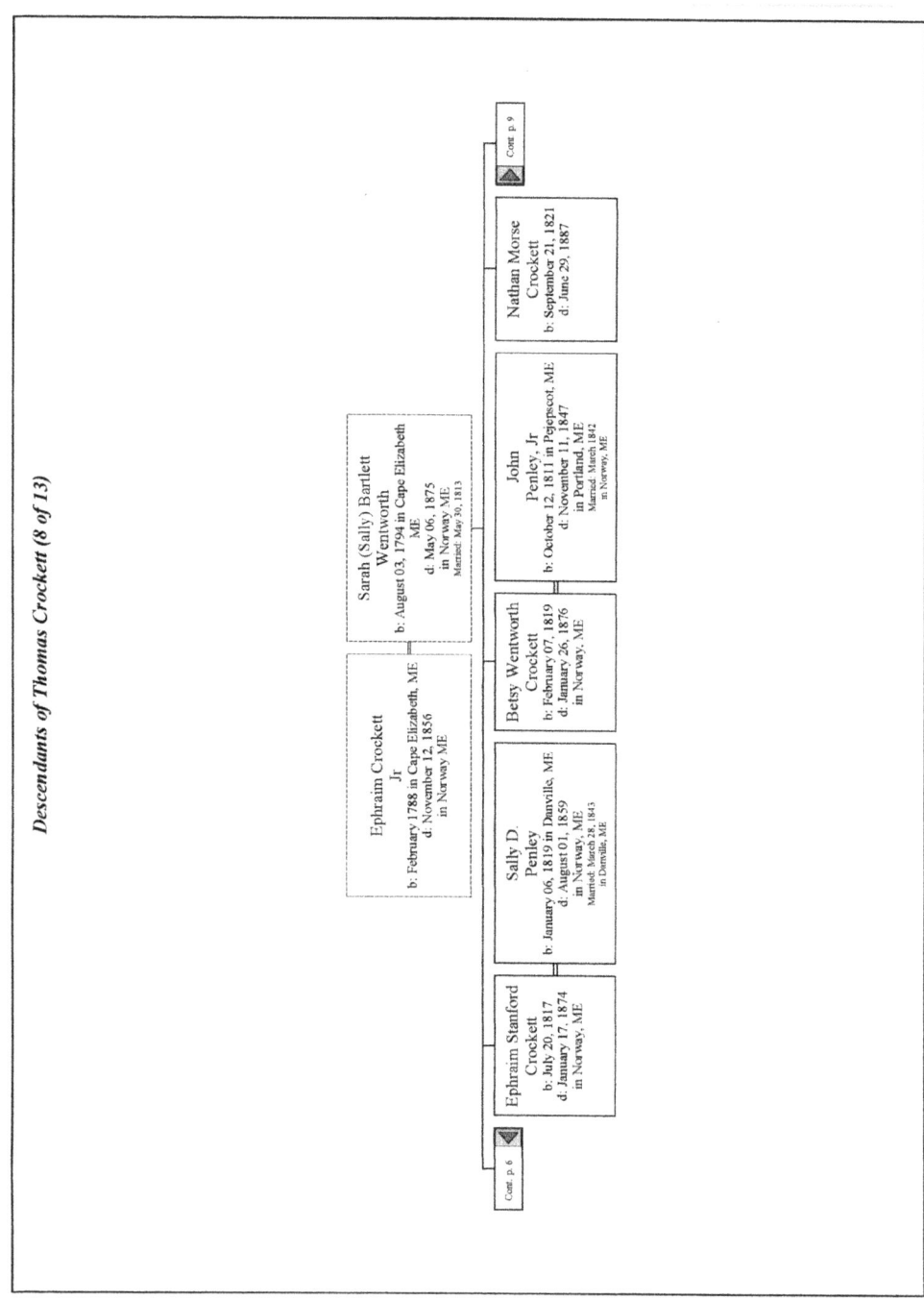

Descendants of Thomas Crockett – p. 8.

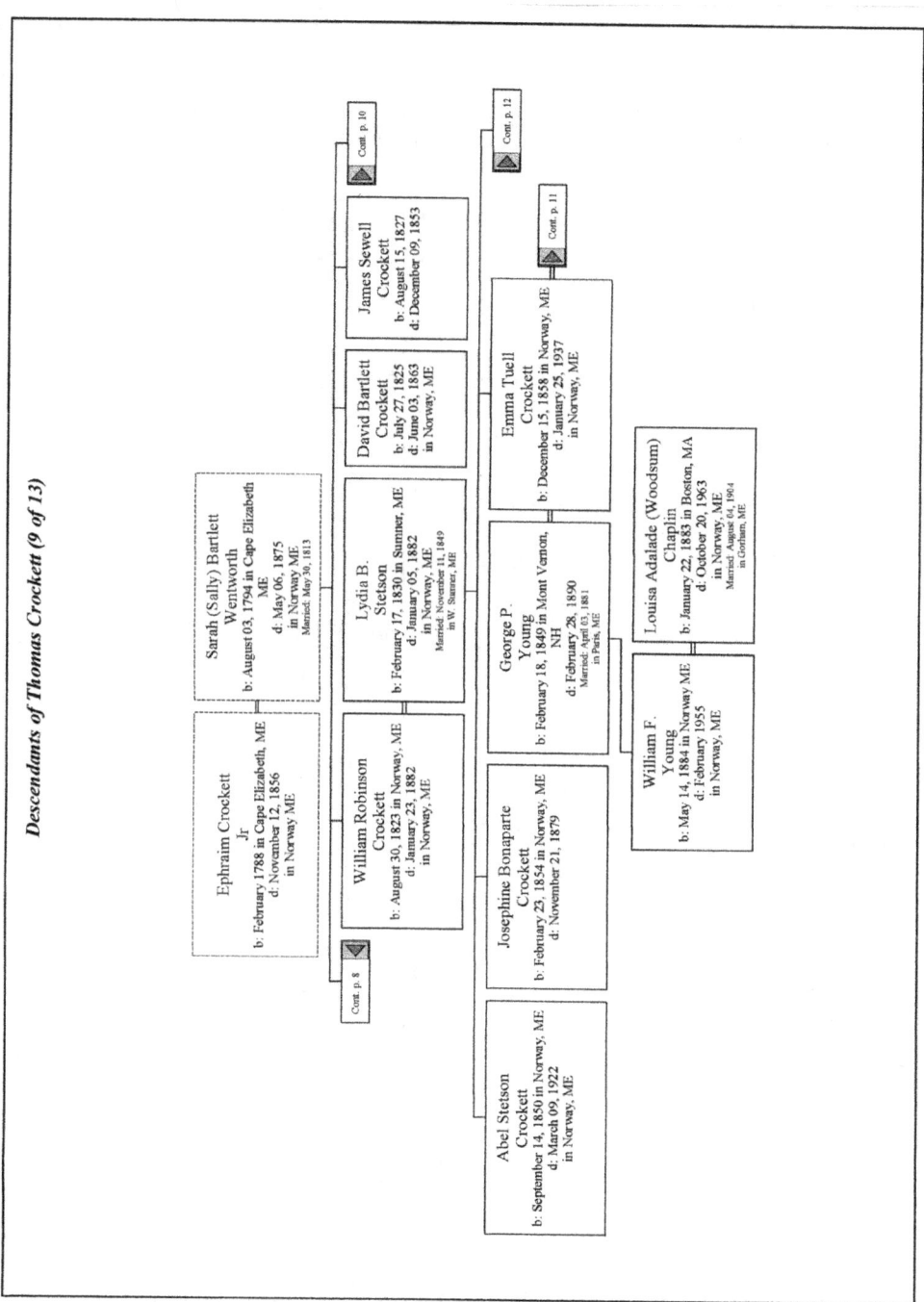

Descendants of Thomas Crockett – p. 9.

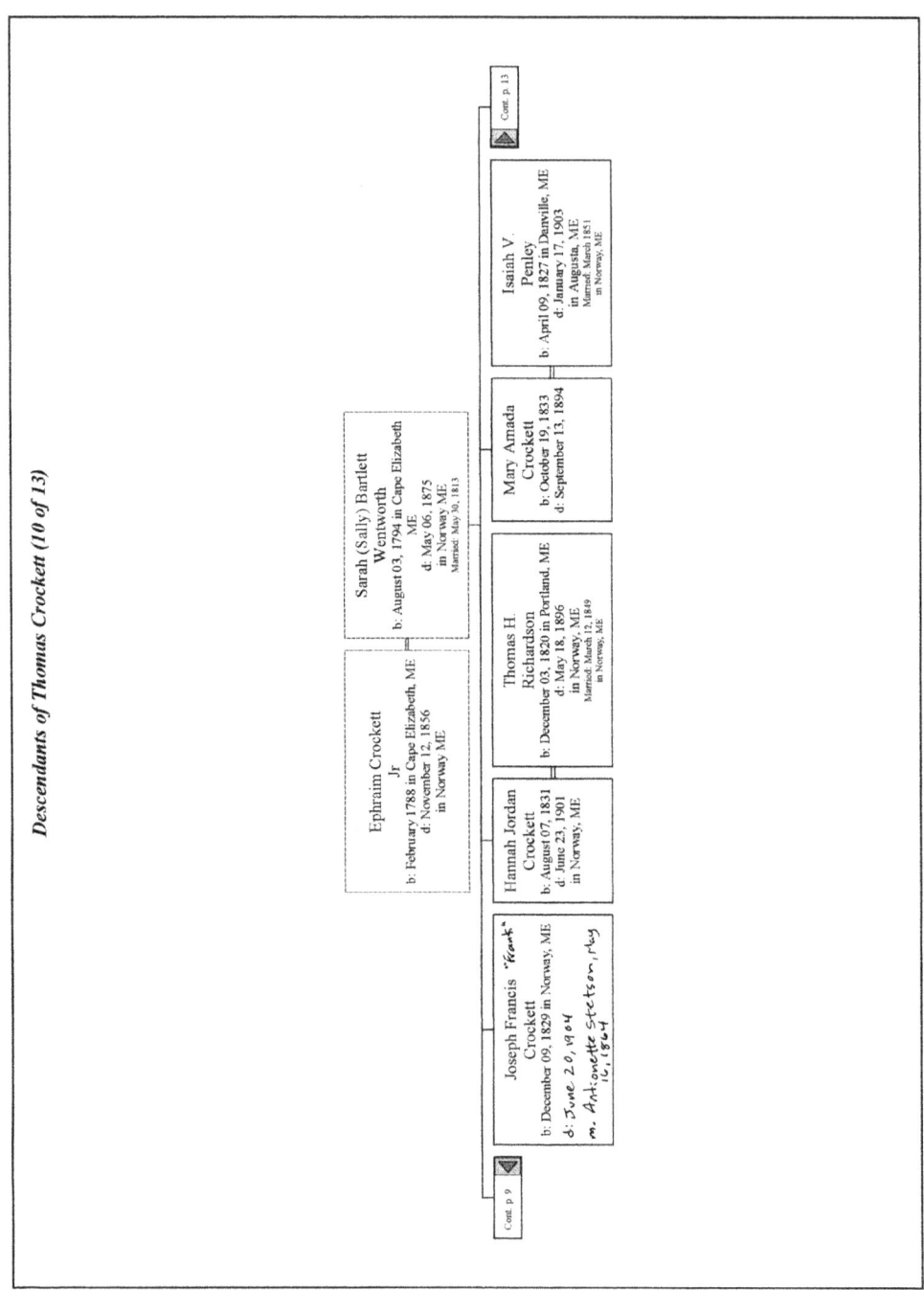

Descendants of Thomas Crockett – p. 10.

Descendants of Thomas Crockett (11 of 13)

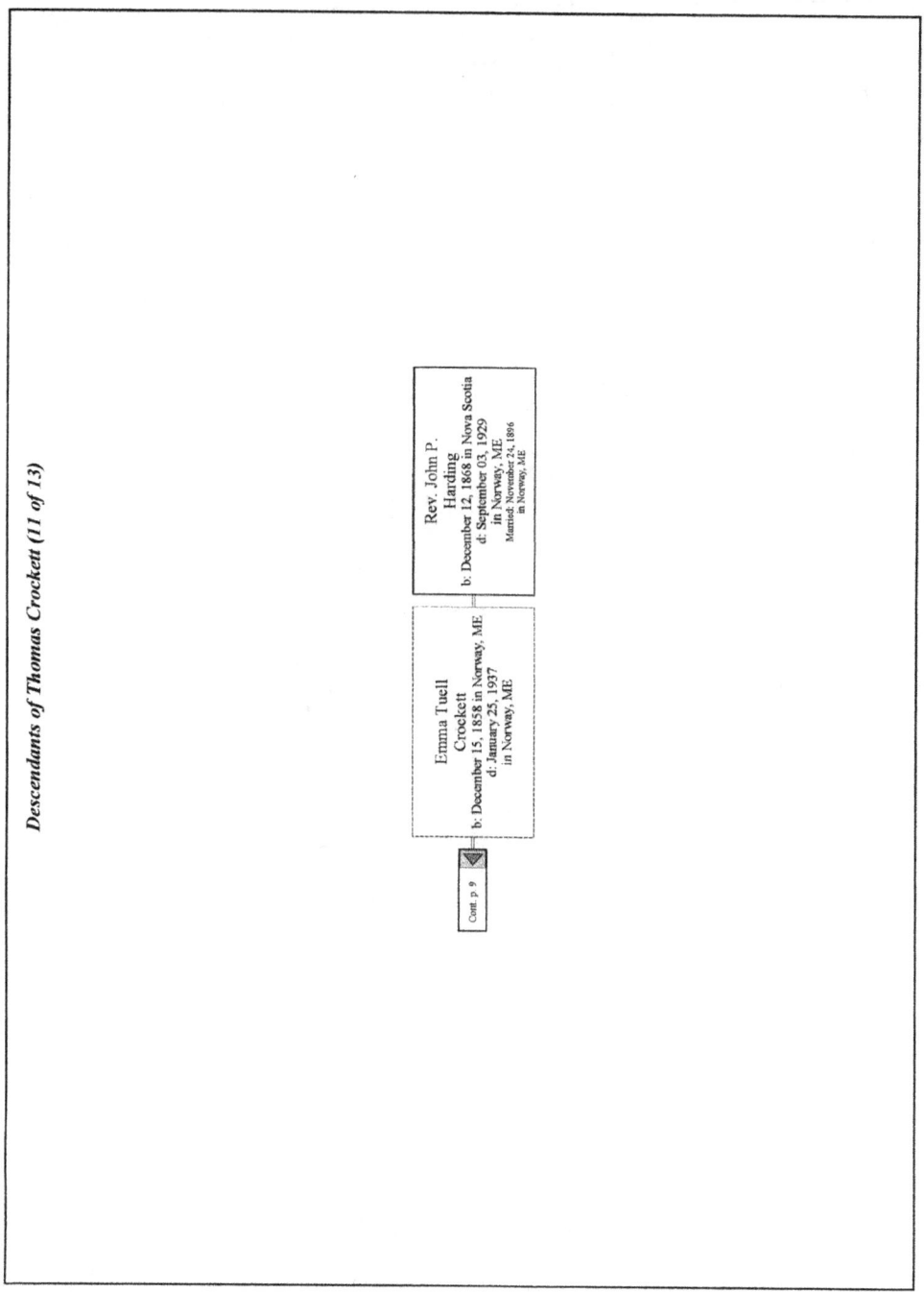

Descendants of Thomas Crockett – p. 11.

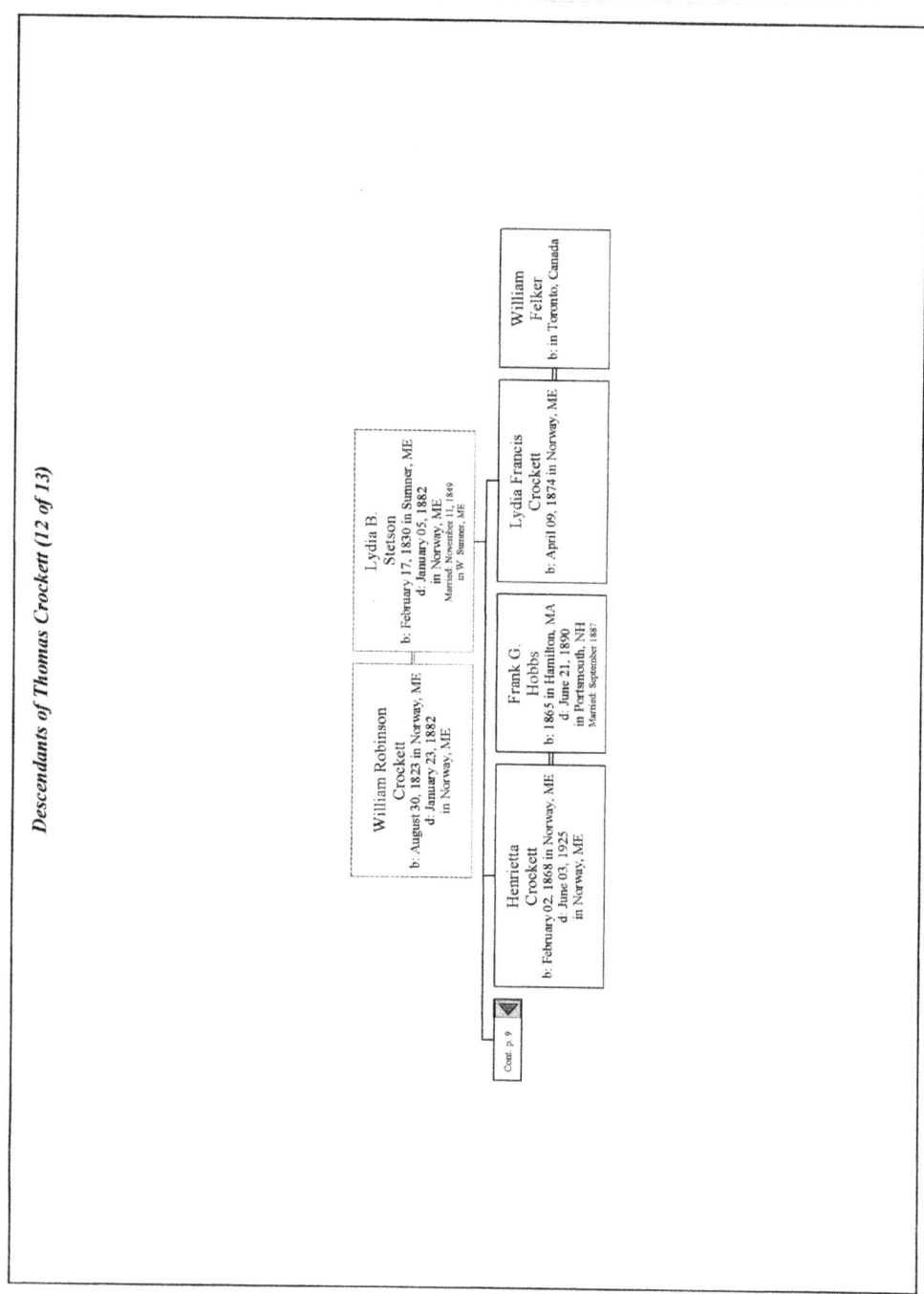

Descendants of Thomas Crockett – p. 12.

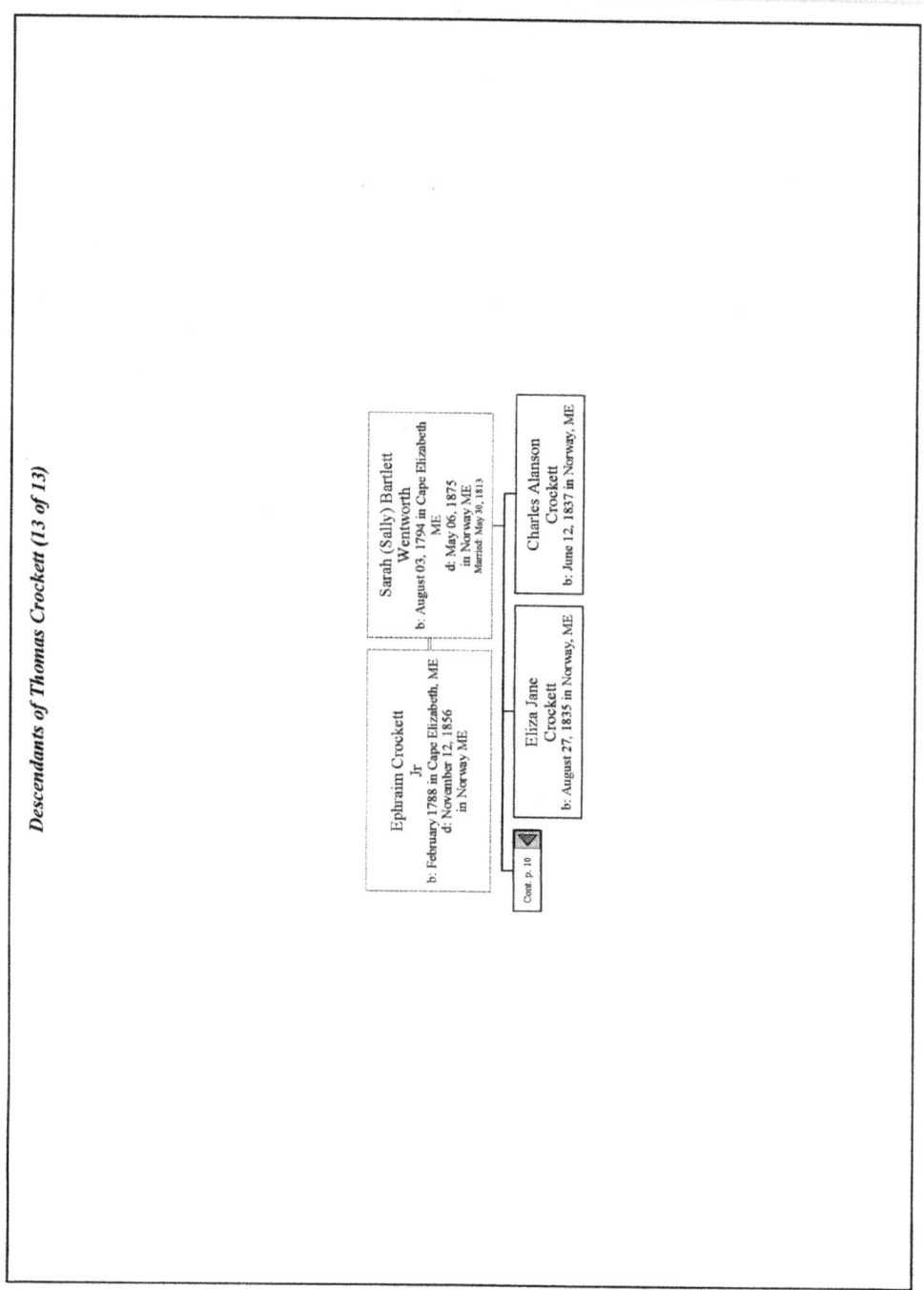

Descendants of Thomas Crockett – p. 13.

Index

Page numbers in italics refer to all images, including photos, postcards, charts, etc.
Page numbers in bold refer to maps.

A

Abbott, Lydia, 419
Aldrich, James Hibbard, 142
Aldrich, Mary Dyer (Penley) Churchill, 108, 115, 142, 142n201
Allard, Kermit, *358*
Allen, Bertha, 112
Allen, E.G., *223*
Allen, William Henry, 178
Ames, Samuel, 69–70
Andrews, Florence, 322, *358*, 360, *365*
Angell, Caroline E., 240, 240n245, 249
Annis, Annah (Batchelder), 307
Arlington National Cemetery, 268–269
Aroostook War, 97–100
Ashburton, Baron, 100
Atlantic and St. Lawrence Railroad, 110, 133
"Aunt Frances," 127n140, 146, 152, 159, 212, 256, 270–272, 304, *305*
"Aunt Mary." *See* Penley, Mary Amanda (Crockett)

B

Baptist Church, Madison, Maine, 305
Barnes, Charles P., 300
Batchelder, Abner, 283, 288, 307
Batchelder, Adelaide, 285n25
Batchelder, Charles Durham, 307
Batchelder, Grinlief, 307
Batchelder, Llewellyn, 283, 307
Batchelder, Luella, 264–265, 282, 284–285, 288–290, 305–309, 319, 422
Batchelder, Mary (York), 283, 288, 307
Beal, George, *135*
Beal, William, Jr., 101
Beals Hotel, 181, 182
Bean, Richard, *358*
Bearce, Henry M., 242, 245
Bennett, Daniel, 139
Bennett, Isaac, 51–52
Bennett, James, 148
B.F. Spinney & Co., 180–185, *196, 197*, 220–222, *223*
Bickford, Gene, 359–360
"A Birthday Jollification in School District No. 8" (Whitman), 218
black growth timber, 348–349
Blake, Jonathan, *135*
Blake, Sarah, 194
Blunt, Edmund, 23
Bodwell, Bailey, 51, 52–53
Bradbury, Bial Francisco, 247, 292, 293
Bradbury, Osgood N., 98–99, 133–134, 149–150, 166–167, 199, **210**, 246
browntail moth caterpillars, 296–297

C

Candage, Charles, 103, 108, 137, 141, 142n201, 146

Carpenter, William H., 145

Cathedral Pines Island, 95n45, 365. *See also* Penley Island

"Centennial history of the town of Sumner" (Handy), 91

Chaplin, Adalade Louise. *See* Young, Louise Adalade "Addie" (Chaplin)

Chaplin, Bertie, 285

Chaplin, Elroy Willis, 285, 288, 288n42, 308, 309

Chaplin, Etta Iola (Libby), 284–285, 284n20, 287–288, 288n41

Chaplin, Harry Elmer, 282, 285, 286, 288, 306, 319

Chaplin, Joanna (Stuart), 282, 282n6, 283, 307

Chaplin, John, 282–283, 282n8

Chaplin, Joseph, 286

Chaplin, Louise Adalade "Addie." *See* Young, Louise Adalade "Addie" (Chaplin)

Chaplin, Luella (Batchelder), 264–265, 282, 284–285, 288–290, 305–309, 319, 422

Chaplin, Myrtie, 285

Chaplin, Sidney Wiatt, 285, 288, 288n42, 308, 319

Chaplin, Washington, 282, 307

Chaplin, Willis Benjamin, 282, 284–290, 305–306, 307–308

Chapman, Albion P., 141

Chapman, Betsey Wentworth (Crockett) Penley, 70, 70n133, 108, 114, 115, *119*, 141

Charles Penley Farm, 76, 139

"Christmas Eve in School District No. 8" (Whitman), 216–217

Christmas Steamed Pudding recipe, 424

Churchill, Mary Dyer (Penley), 108, 115, 142, 142n201

Churchill, William, 142

Civil War, 130–137, 192, 205–206

"The Clark Tannery in 19th Century Amesbury" (Murphy), 180

Conant, Barbara, *358*

Cotton, Esther A.W. (Penley), 101, 108, 139, 146, 147n219

Cotton, Henry B., 139, 146–147, 147n219

the cow lane, 57, *57n100*, 292

Craig, Hope, 324, 324n139

Crane, A.R., 251, 252

Crockett, Abbie Jane. *See* Tubbs, Abbie Jane (Crockett)

Crockett, Abby Anna, 78

Crockett, Abel Stetson
   birth, 124, 146
   boarding with cousin Abbie Jane (Crockett) Tubbs, 269
   death, 270
   farming expertise shared with Bill Young, 296
   farming on Crockett homestead, 152
   farm laborer for John Rhodes, 258, 296n63
   move to Duluth, Minnesota, 158, 213, 213n158
   return to Norway, 247
   tenant farming, 155–156, 212

Crockett, Allie, 198–200, 211, 234–235, 268

Crockett, Ann, 29, *31*, 91n30

Index

Crockett, Antoinette (Stetson), 75, 90, 136, 152, 165–166, 242, 257, 268
Crockett, Augusta, 105n91
Crockett, Betsey Wentworth, 70, 70n133, 108, 114, 115, *119,* 141
Crockett, Charles Alanson, 75, 89, 117, 164
Crockett, Clara, 166, 166n278, 268
Crockett, David, 34, 44, 51
Crockett, David Bartlett, 75
Crockett, Edgar Little, 200, 211
Crockett, Eliza Jane, 75, 89, 117
Crockett, Ella, 116, 172–173, 175, 198–200, 211, 234–235, 268
Crockett, Emma Tuell. *See* Harding, Emma Tuell (Crockett) Young
Crockett, Ephraim (1644), *31*
Crockett, Ephraim, Jr.
  birth and death, *31, 33,* 33n6, 79, *93,* 130
  children of, 47–48, 71, 74–76
  early years in Pejepscot, 33–36
  Edward Little and, 16, 25, 37, *38,* 40–41
  homestead deed to Nathan Morse Crockett, 77–78
  images of, *28, 81*
  land split with Nathan Morse, Jr., **61–62**
  life in Norway, 64–74
  Lot 45 purchase with Josiah Hill, 37, *38,* **39**
  Lot 30 purchase with Nathan Morse, Jr., 57–58
  Lot 45 purchase with Nathan Morse, Jr., 40–41
  marriage to Sally, 47
  Military Land Bounty grant, 79–80, 79n159
  Norway Pine Grove Cemetery and, 79, 165, *169*

Crockett, Ephraim, Jr. (*continued*)
  relationship with Nathan Morse, Jr., 53–64
  relocation to Lee's Grant, 1, 29
  War of 1812 service, 50–53, 79
Crockett, Ephraim, Sr., 9, 29, 29n1, *31, 33, 35,* 45, 52n77, 73
Crockett, Ephraim Stanford
  Aroostook War service, 97–98, 100
  birth, 75, *93*
  children of, 108, 116
  death, *93,* 141
  genealogy of, 75, *93,* 176
  locket tintype of, *104,* 104n89
  Lot maps, **107, 118**
  marriage to Sally Penley, 75, *93,* 104
  near drowning, 64
  Norway Pine Grove Cemetery and, 161, *162*
  real estate transactions of, 100–101, 102–103, 102n74, 109, 115–116, 129, 147
Crockett, Hannah Jordan. *See* Richardson, Hannah Jordan (Crockett)
Crockett, Henrietta "Etta," 146, 152, 159, 210, 226, 256–257, 272, 310, 311
Crockett, James Sewall, 75, 115, 125, 125n138, 129, 164
Crockett, John Freeland, 108, 140, 161, 173, 198–199, 199n112
Crockett, Joseph Francis "Frank," 75, 90, 115, 136, 166, 257, 269
Crockett, Josephine Bonaparte, 146, 152, 154–155, 164–165
Crockett, Josephine (Knight), 155, 212, 213
Crockett, Joseph (son of Ephraim Sr.), 47
Crockett, Joshua, Jr., 51–52, 51n72, 71–72
Crockett, Joshua, Sr., 52, 52n77

447

Crockett, Joshua (Lieutenant), 52, 52n77
Crockett, Josiah Penley, 108, 116, 141, 161, 197, **210**, 210–211
Crockett, J.T., 153
Crockett, Judith (Pike), 54n85
Crockett, Lewis, 52, 71
Crockett, Lizzie Allison, 211
Crockett, Louisa Frances, 198–200, 211, 234–235, 268
Crockett, Lydia Frances, 127n140, 146, 152, 159, 212, 256, 270–272, 304, *305*
Crockett, Lydia (Stetson)
  birth, *31*, 90
  children of, 127n140, 146, 152
  death, *31*, 157, 211
  description of, 91–92
  gravestone of, *168*
  inheritance from father, 130
  marriage to William Robinson Crockett, *31*, 75, 90
  red geraniums tradition, 167n284
Crockett, Mahalon, 51n72, 109
Crockett, Martha (Pike), 51n72, 71–72
Crockett, Mary. *See* Morse, Mary (Crockett)
Crockett, Mary Amanda. *See* Penley, Mary Amanda (Crockett)
Crockett, Mary Jane, 129, 129n147
Crockett, Mary "Polly" Dennett (Stowell), 75, 78
Crockett, Mary (Robinson), 52n77
Crockett, Minerva Ella, 116, 172–173, 175, 198–200, 211, 234–235, 268
Crockett, Nancy (Twombly), 74, 100, 100n64, 105n91

Crockett, Nathan Morse, 75, 77–78, 79, 89, 109, 114–115, 136–137, 209n149
Crockett, Oscar Rufus, 161, 200, 211, 215, 215n166
Crockett, Rebecca (Stanford), *31*, 33, 45n43, 73
Crockett, Richard, II, 52n77
Crockett, Richard, III, 29n1, *31*, 33, 52n77, 53
Crockett, Richard, Jr., *31*
Crockett, Richard S., *31*
Crockett, Rose Emma, 125, 129, 129n146
Crockett, Salome (Frank), 75, 125, 125n138, 129, 129n146
Crockett, Samuel (son of Joshua, Sr.), 52
Crockett, Samuel Wentworth, 40, 74, 89, 100, 100n64, 102, 104–105, 105n91, 129
Crockett, Sarah Alamanza "Allie," 198–200, 211, 234–235, 268
Crockett, Sarah (Hamblin), 52
Crockett, Sarah Maria, 101
Crockett, Sarah "Sally" Bartlett (Wentworth)
  1870 census, 152
  childhood family history, 41–48
  children of, 47–48, 74–76
  death, 80, 153
  genealogy of, *93*, 176
  images of, *28*, *81*
  inheritance of, 77
  life in Norway, 64–74
Crockett, Sarah "Sally" Dingley (Penley)
  children of, 108, 116
  death, *93*, 140
  locket tintype of, *104*, 104n89
  marriage to Ephraim Stanford Crockett, 75, 104

Index

Crockett, Sarah "Sally" Dingley (Penley) (*continued*)
  purchase of Lot 44, 139–140
  reinterment to Norway Pine Grove Cemetery, 161, *162*

Crockett, Sarah Wentworth, 40n22, 47, 74, *93*, 108, 115, 138, *165*

Crockett, Thomas, 29–31, 91n30

Crockett, Warren Ephraim, 84, 200, 211, 234–235, 254–255, 268–269

Crockett, William Robinson
  birth, *31, 75,* 89
  brick house, building of, 120–124
  census records, 116–117, 152, 156–157
  children of, 127n140, 146
  Civil War and, 136–137
  death and will of, *31,* 157–159, 212–213
  descriptions of, 91–92
  gravestone of, *168*
  homestead purchase from Nathan Morse Crockett, 79, 89, 114–115
  Lot map of 1850, **118**
  Lydia Stetson, meeting of, 89–90
  Norway Grange and, 153
  real estate holdings at time of death, 159, **160**
  real estate transactions of, 146–149

Crockett family cemetery, 79, 129, 133, 138, 139, 140, 143, 153, 167

Crockett heirs, 172–173, **174**, 175, 197, 198–200, **210**, 211, 215, 234–235, 268–272

Crockett homestead
  back taxes and sale of black growth timber, 347–349

Crockett homestead (*continued*)
  barn fire, 316–318
  Bill and Addie Young on, 290–298
  brick house built by William Robinson Crockett, 120–124
  building of original house, 65–68
  cemetery on, 79, 129, 133, 138, 139, 140, 143, 153, 167
  1850 census of, 76–77, 116–117, 124
  as described by Osgood N. Bradbury, 149–150
  George P. Young's transformation to Fair View Farm, 213–215
  mortgaged to Abbie Jane (Crockett) Tubbs by Emma and George Young, 220
  photographs of, *66, 67, 122, 123, 148, 291, 293, 303, 304, 306, 355*
  William "Bill" Young as heir to two-thirds of, 259
  See also Young's Turkey Farm

Crockett Ridge Road, 427, 428–429

Crockett's Bridge, 52, *149,* 149n229

Crockett's Ledge, *32*

Crockett's Ridge
  descriptions by Charles F. Whitman, 216–219
  Emma Tuell (Crockett) Young Harding and, 246–249, 259–260, 276
  last descendants on, 26, 84
  stone wall on Ephraim Crockett's land, *56*
  tent caterpillar devastation on, 153–154
  "Will the Real Crockett's Ridge Please Stand Up?," 427–429

The Cross Road, 58, 60, **61**, 63

Cullinan, Walter F., 348

Cummings, E.W., **365, 366**

Cummings, Jonathan, 2n4, 2n5, 7
Cummings's Purchases, 4, 7–8

D

Danforth, Francis A., 246–247
Daniels, Mrs. Beryl, 360
Danville, 1, 16, 24, 29, 35, 87, 110. *See also* Pejepscot Claim
Davis, Amos, 12, *13*
Davis, Apphia D., 289
Davis, C.B., 365
Davis, Harriett (Young), 192
Davis, John, 147
"Dear Parent: A Biography and Letters of Edward Little" (Hodgkin), 18, 19, 23, 24, 49
Dewll, Samuel, 138
Dingley, Desire, 87n14, 92, 128
Dingley, Sarah "Sally" (Jordan), 87n14
Dingley, William, 44, 87n14
Dinsmore, Ansel, 153, 184n35, 209n149, 221, 242
Dinsmore, Fannie, 299, 300
Dinsmore, Horace G., 300
Dinsmore, Judith Crockett (Morse), 55, 55n97, 153, 209n149
Dinsmore, Mary A., 209n149
Dummer's Academy, 17, 18–19
Dunham, Emma "Gram," 311–315
Dunham, Mellie, 218, 218n179, 311–315
Durrell, Nicholas, 188
Durrell, Thomas, 188, 191–192

E

earthquake of 1870, 152

Edge, Anne, *31*
Edward Little High School, 24
Embargo Act of 1807, 48–49
Enforcement Act of 1809, 49
Enrollment Act of 1863, 136–137, 192
An Essay in Vindication of the Continental Colonies of America (Lee), 9

F

Fair View Farm, 213–215, 262, 265, 290–298
Fair View Jersey Farm, 298
Farnham, Albert P., 141, 141n195, 159, **160**, 172, 202, 216, 295
Farnham, Edith, 247, *295*
Farnham, Ella, 248, *295*
Farnham, Joe, *295*
Farnham, Sarah Belle (Penley), 141, 141n195, 143, 172, 216, 295
"Fatal Accident," 238–239
Felker, Lydia Frances (Crockett), 127n140, 146, 152, 159, 212, 256, 270–272, 304, *305*
Felker, William James, 271–272, 304
fire, Lynn, Massachusetts, 235–237
First Baptist Church of Franklin, Massachusetts, 263–264, 266
First Baptist Church of Madison, Maine, 266
First Baptist Church of Tiverton, Rhode Island, 263, 265–266
First Baptist Church of Warner, New Hampshire, 261, *262*
First Parish Church of Charleston, Massachusetts, 261
Ford, Henry, 312, *313*
"Four Musketeers," 377
Fourth of July Horse Trot, 232–233

Index

Foye, William, 41n26, 65, 65n116
Foye Brook, 65n116, 148
Foye's sawmill, 41n26, 65, 65n116, *151*
Frank, Salome, 75, 125, 125n138, 129, 129n146
Frechette, Gerald, 60n112
Frost, Jack, 359–360
Frost, Mrs., *358*
Frost, Sarah Elizabeth, 142, 226
Frosting recipe, 423
Fuller, Abigail (Weston), 194
Fuller, Abijah, 194
Fuller, Martha "Mattie" Wilkins, 194, 195–197, 196n100, 201, 208–209
Fuller, Mary Ward, 194, 194n91

G

Gaer, George I., 308
Ganong, Alan, 66–67
genealogy charts and lists, *31, 74–76, 93,* 108, 146, 176
Gerry, Ada L., 153, 158, 158n257, 212
Gerry, Emma J., 155
Gerry, John F., 152
Gerry, Josephine Bonaparte (Crockett), 146, 152, 154–155, 164–165
Gerry, Joseph W., 152–153, 152n, 154–155, 158n257
Gerry, Sarah, 152
Goodwin, Stuart W., 142n201, 161n262, 162, 166, 183, 184
The Governor's Academy, 17, 18–19
Graham Pudding recipe, 423
Gray Gables, 234–235
Greenhaigh, Elizabeth B., 158n257

Green Tomato Mincemeat recipe, 421
Greenwood, Alexander, 20, **21, 39**
Gunnison, Anne, *31*

H

Haley, Deborah, *31*
Hamblin, Sarah, 52
Hamlin, Hannibal, 131
Handy, Charles Edward, 91
Hanscom, Hepisbah, 43, 44, 176
Harding, Emma Tuell (Crockett) Young
  birth, *31,* 146, 171
  child and grandchildren of, 215–216, *266,* 292
  Crockett heirs and, 175, 198–199, 200
  death, *31,* 274–275, 320
  financial difficulties of, 267, 274, 316
  George P. Young and, 157, 185, 198–199, 201, 209, 210
  Heywood Club honorary member, 300n76
  influence of Richardson cousins, 177–178
  inheritance, 158, 171, 212–213, *256*
  John Harding, marriage to and relocations with, 252, 253–254, 257
  legacy on Crockett's Ridge, 1, 26, 276
  loss of multiple family members, 210–212
  new barn, financial assistance for, 297–298
  Norway move and life after George's death, 244–249
  pastoral calling of, 252, 263, 276
  photographs of, *170, 209, 264, 265, 270, 273*
  real estate transactions and ownership, 214–215, 219–220, 245, 246–247, 258–260

Harding, John Aberdeen
   birth and U.S. citizenship of, 250–251
   death, 267–268, 315–316
   meeting Emma Tuell Crockett Young, 249
   pastoral callings of, 251–252, 253–254, 261–264, 265–267, 305
   pastoral education of, 251, 253–254
   return to Norway, 257
Hard Sauce recipe, 425
Harmon, Hattie, 258
Harper, James W., 211
Harris, Oscar A., 207, 207n144
Heath, Andres, *358*
Hebron Academy, 251
Heywood Club, 299–302, 311, 313, 314, 352
Hilden, Lillian, 322, *323*
Hill, Josiah, Jr., 1, 36, 37, *38*, 40
"A History of Norway, Maine" (Whitman), *10, 11, 15*, 19, 20, 427
"The History of Norway, Maine" (Noyes), 37, 53
Hobbs, Amos, 2, 2n3, 4
Hobbs, Emma, *311*
Hobbs, Frank G., 226, 244
Hobbs, Frank Harriman, 232, 272, 272n333, 304, 310, *311,* 316, 320, **321**, 366
Hobbs, Fred, *311*
Hobbs, Henrietta "Etta" (Crockett), 146, 152, 159, 210, 226, 256–257, 272, 310, 311
Hobbs, Irene, *311*
Hobbs, Jeremiah, 2, 2n4, 4, 7
Hobbs, Louise, *311*
Hobbs, Mary Louise (Hunter), 272, 310, 316
Hobbs, Robert "Bob," *311*
Hodgkin, Douglas I., 18, 19, 23, 24, 49

Holt, Uriah, 20, **21**
Horne, Chester, 178–179, 180, 203
Horne, Herman L., 242
Horne, John L., 179, *179,* 179n19, 180–181, 221, 222
Houghton, Moses, 183–184
Howe, Freeland, 199–200, 221
Hunter, Mary Louise, 272, 310, 316

I

Independent Order of Odd Fellows (IOOF), 198, 199, 224, *225,* 225n203, 237, 239, 240–241

J

Jackson, Una, 419
John Penley Farm, 159, 219–220, 230–232, 259, 370
John Ring Farm, 188, 191
Johnson, Deborah, *368*
Johnson, Joshua, 86n9
Johnson, Mark, *368*
Johnson, Mary (Young), 192
Johnson, Paula (Palmer)
   with Addie in garden, *369*
   birth, 325
   "Four Musketeers," *377*
   recollects grandparents, 327
   red geraniums tradition, 168
   as young child on Young's Turkey Farm, 326, *326,* 327
   Young's Turkey Farm newspaper clippings, *337, 339*
   Young's Turkey Farm Open House, *358, 359*
Johnson, Robert, 286

Index

K

Kansas-Nebraska Act, 131
King, William, 50
King George of England, story of Norway land grant, 8–9
King's Woods, 16
Knight, Daniel, 25n86, 51, 54, 93
Knight, Josephine P., 155, 212, 213
Knight, Sally, 54
Knight, Sarah, 226n205
Knight, William, 146, 153, 214–215
Knightly, Howard A., 256, 259

L

Lake Pennesseewassee, 3, *4*, *32*, *149*, 154, *154*
Lapham, William B., 9, 98, 152, 182–183, 184, 198, 204–205, 222
Larson, Mary, 360
Latham Farm, 125, 129
League, Sarah B., 75
Lee, Arthur, 9–14, *10*
Lee, Eliza, 20
Lee, Francis Lightfoot, 9, 14, 15–16, 17, 19–20
Lee, Ludwell, 16n46, 20
Lee, Richard, 14
Lee's Grant
  boundaries of, 10–12
  history of, 4, **6**, 7–13
  land divide after Addie Young's death, 370–371
  Lot maps of, **61–62**, **96**, **106**, **107**, **118**, **160**, **173**, **174**, **260**, **321**, **373**
  peculiar history of Lot 45, 36–41
  surveys of, **13**, **20**, **21**, **39**
  tax exemption and back taxes, 15, 22

Lee's Grant (*continued*)
  tenant farming on, 14, 15–16
Lemon Pie Filling recipe, 423
Lemon Sponge Pie Filling recipe, 424
Lessley, Amasa, 2n5
Lessley, George, 2, 2n5, 4n9, 7
Lessley, George, Jr., 2n5
Libby, Etta Iola, 284–285, 284n20, 287–288, 288n41
Libby, Mary A., 288n42
Little, Edward
  birth and careers, 17, 18
  Drummer's Academy land purchase, 18–19
  financial difficulties, 19, 21n79, 22–24, 94
  letters to father Josiah Little, 19, 24, 58n105
  Lot 45 quitclaim deed with Ephraim Crockett, 40
  money management after death of father, 24–25
  purchases of Lee's Grant, 20, 36
  sale of lots on Lee's Grant, 20–22, 41, 57–58
Little, Joseph, 75
Little, Josiah, 16, 17, 19, 23, 24, 25, 37, 58n105, 94
Little, Mary, 24
Little, Michael, 17–18, 17n53, 18–19
Little, Moses, 16, 16n47, 16n49, 20
Little Pennesseewassee Pond, 52, 69, 72
Long, Joseph, 258
Lovejoy, Elijah Parish, 131
Luce, Stanley, 231
Lynn Conflagration, 235–237

M

Mabury, Francis A., 289

Madawaska War, 97–100
Maine, District of, 1, 2, 8, 10, 49
Maine, state of
   Civil War, 130–131
   statehood, 70, 130
   state turkey tagging, 349-351, 330–331
Maine Logging Camp, *82*
Maine State Turkey Growers Association, 330, 349–351
Masons (Freemasons), 189
Massachusetts, Commonwealth of
   debt at end of Revolutionary War, 3
   debt paid by Samuel Solley Wentworth, 45
   General Court of, 4–5, 7, 8
   land bounty grants, 2–3, 33–34, 43–44, 52, 251
   sale of Lee's Grant to Arthur Lee, 8–9
McAllister, Don, 131–132
McAllister, Norm, *358*
McLellan, Laura, 310
Merrill, Clarence, 245
Mesene, William, 296
Miller, Ella A., 288n42
Millett, Anson Joseph, 155
Millett, Ethelyn, 360
Millett, Harriet, 147
Millett, Israel, 21
Millett, John, 65n116, 146, 348
Millett, Josephine Bonaparte (Crockett), 146, 152, 154–155, 164–165
Millett, Justus, 155
Millett, Nathan, 180
Millett's sawmill, 65n116, 109, *151*
Millettville Road, 428
Missouri Compromise of 1820, 130

Montague, Mary Gertrude, 272, 304
Moody, Thankful, 86n9
Morgan, Susan Allen, 112, 177–178
Morse, Edwin A., 136–137, 153, 202, 242
Morse, Joseph, 147
Morse, Judith Crockett, 55, 55n97, 153, 209n149
Morse, Mary (Crockett)
   birth, 34
   death of daughter Mary, 70
   description of by Whitman, 64
   Lot Map, **107**
   relocation from Pejepscot to Lee's Grant, 29, 54, 55
   sale of estate and move to Paris, 143
Morse, Nathan, Jr.
   birth, 54
   death of daughter Mary, 70
   description of by Whitman, 64
   early years of marriage to Mary, 54–55
   land split of lots 45 and 30 with Ephraim Jr., **61–62**
   Lot map of 1850, **118**
   move to Paris, 143
   purchase of Lot 30 from Edward Little, 57
   purchases of Lot 45 with Ephraim Jr., 40–41, 54
   relationship with Ephraim Jr., 53–64
   relocation to Lee's Grant, 29
   sale of estate to Captain Penley, 143
Morse, Nathan, Sr., 54
Morse, Rick, 421
Morse, Sarah, 299
Morse, Sarah (Bacon), 54
Mother's Chocolate Cake recipe, 422

Index

Moulton, David, 317
Murphy, Tom, 180

N

Nathan Morse Farm, 143, 258–259, 316, 322
Needham, Evi, 102
Needham Road woodlots, 146–147, *148*
Nelson, John F., 192
"A New England Road" (postcard), 77
Newton Theological Seminary, 253, 253n279
Noble, Amos, 92, 94, 98
Noble, Fred, 258, 294, 296, 296n61
"Norage," 8, 8n19
North Easton Baptist Church, 253–254
North Pond, 41n26, 51, 65, 94, 109, 116, 147
North Pond Dam, *150, 151*
Norway, Lake, 3, *4, 32, 149,* 154, *154*
Norway, Maine
    B.F. Spinney & Co., 180–185, *196,* 197, 220–222, *223*
    Board of Selectmen, 351, *351*
    Centennial celebration, 224–225
    Civil War and, 131–132, 137
    earthquake of 1870, 152
    First Baptist Church, 249
    First Universalist Church, 240, 240n246, 249
    growth of, 71–72, 72n141
    land grants and purchases, 18th century, **6**
    map of 1880, **210**
    marketing stationary of 1928, *xxvi*
    in mid-1800s, 151
    postcard, *41*
    prohibition in, 151
    settlement of, 1–8
    snapshot of village in 1825, 70–71

Norway, Maine (*continued*)
    storm of 1907, *297*
    tannery, *179*
Norway Baptist Church, 251–253, 267, 275
Norway Board of Selectmen, 351, *351*
Norway Budget Committee, 351
Norway Farm Bureau, 350
Norway Grange, 153, 351
Norway High School, 246, 323, *324*
"Norway in the Forties" (Bradbury), 149–150, 166–167
Norway Pine Grove Cemetery, 161–169
    burial of Benning Wentworth, 207
    burial of Crocketts, 211, 213, 269, 270, 272
    burial of Hardings, 268, 275, 316
    burial of Hobbs, 311
    burial of Richardsons, 207
    burial of Youngs, 240, 364, 369
    Crockett family reinterment to, 79, 80, 161–162, 164–165
    Ephraim Crockett Jr.'s original gravestone, *169*
    establishment of, 162–163
    Jonathan Whitehouse, sexton, 166–167
    Penley family reinterment to, 165
    red geraniums tradition, 167–168, 167n284, 369
Norway Savings Bank robbery, 151
Norway Shoe Shop Company, 222, *223*
Norway Tanning Company, 179
"Norway Village in 1825" (Smith), 70–71
Noyes, Amos F., 133–134
Noyes, Bela, 102
Noyes, Claudius, 64
Noyes, David, 15, 37, 53, 64, 68–69, 70, 109

O

opiate usage in the 19th century, 203, 205

Orre, Bob, 360

The Oxford County Democrat, 237–238

Oxford County Trotting Horse-Breeders Association, 232–234

The Oxford County Trotting Horse-Breeders Association, 232–233

"Oxford Ferry Boy" (prize bull), 317

P

Packard, Harry A., 355–357

Palmer, Bill, *311*

Palmer, Jonathan, 121, *123*, 359n187

Palmer, Joyce (Nelson), 121, *127*, 168, 241

Palmer, Kurt
  birth, 325
  helping on farm, *335*, 359
  as young child on Young's Turkey Farm, *326, 327*
  "Four Musketeers," *377*
  Young's Turkey Farm newspaper clippings, *332, 333*

Palmer, Paula. *See* Johnson, Paula (Palmer)

Palmer, Rowena Mae
  birth, 325
  four generations photo, *364*
  "Four Musketeers," *377*
  marriage to Eldwin, 324n139
  Norway town assessor, 428
  red geraniums tradition, 168
  and Uncle Abe, 270
  as young child, *273, 273, 326, 327*
  Young's Turkey Farm and, *335, 337, 358, 359*

Palmer, William "Bill," 324–325, 324n139, 325–326

Palmer, Winona (Young)
  birth, 263, 293
  Cathedral Pines Island land development, 95n45, 365
  Crockett homestead house, 120, *122*
  divorce and move to Young's Turkey Farm, 325–326
  education and marriage, 323–325, 324n139, 324n140
  family artifacts kept by, 8, 42–43
  inheritance from Addie Young, 370
  Lemon Sponge Pie Filling recipe, 424
  photographs of, *265, 266, 294, 303, 306, 341, 358, 364*
  red geraniums tradition, 167–168, 167n284
  speaking of her grandfather's death, 186
  welcoming author into home, xiii–xv
  Young's Turkey Farm and, 273, 359

Paris, Maine, 17, 133, 136, 143, 162, 163, 209, 287

Parker, Sally, 45, 176

"Pasture Birches, Norway, Me" (postcard), *27*

Peaks Island, 305–306, *307*, 308, 319

Pejepscot Claim, 29, 34, 35, 42, 43–45, 47, 86

Pejepscot Patent, 18, 42, 44

Penley, Adrianne, 116, 138, 139

Penley, Betsey Wentworth (Crockett), 70, 70n133, 108, 114, 115, *119*, 141

Penley, Channing Robert, 143, 167

Penley, Charles
  birth and death, *93*
  children of, 108, 116
  death and inheritance, 139

Index

Penley, Charles (*continued*)
  Lot maps, **107, 118**
  marriage to Sarah Wentworth Crockett, 74, *93*
  real estate transactions, 77, 92–93, 94–97, 100, 101–102, 104–106, 115–116
  reinterment to Norway Pine Grove Cemetery, 165
  relocations to Auburn and Portland, 138–139
Penley, Charles F., 115
Penley, Charles Sewell, 104, 108, 117, 135–136, 142, 226, 294–295, 309, 310
Penley, Desire (Dingley), 87n14, 92, 128
Penley, Ephraim Crockett, 101, 108, 116, 132, 139
Penley, Esther A.W., 101, 108, 139, 146, 147n219
Penley, Esther (Fogg) Johnson, 86, 86n9
Penley, Francina, 101, 108, 116, 139
Penley, Harriet Jane, 143
Penley, Isadore, 115
Penley, Isaiah Vickery
  birth and death, *93*
  children of, 143, 167, 167n282
  Civil War draft, 136–137
  financial difficulties, 142–143, 172, 201–202
  inheritance from John Penley Sr., 143–144
  Lot map of 1874, **174**
  marriage to Mary Amanda Crockett, 75, *93*, 128
  real estate holdings in 1882, **160**
  real estate transactions, 159, 256
Penley, James, 86n9
Penley, James Jordan, 103, 104n86, 108

Penley, John, Jr., 103–104
  birth, *93*
  children of, 103–104, 104n86, 108
  death, *93*, 113–114, 113n–114n
  death of first wife, Mary Dyer Jordan, 103
  home on Lot 44, *119*
  Lot map of 1846, **107**
  marriage to Betsey Wentworth Crockett, *93*, 103
  real estate transactions of, 106
Penley, John, Sr. (Captain)
  birth, 86
  children of, 74, 128
  death, 138
  financial support of family, 103, 114, 142–143
  first wife, 87n14
  inheritance, 88, 138, 140, 141, 143–144
  Lot maps, **107, 118**
  photograph of, *88*
  real estate transactions, 102–103, 105, 116, 139–140, 143
  successes of, 84, 87–88
Penley, John III, 104, 104n86, 108
Penley, Joseph (brother of Captain Penley), 115
Penley, Joseph G. (nephew of Captain Penley), 115
Penley, Joseph (Sergeant, father of Captain Penley), 85–86
Penley, Josiah, 108
Penley, Laura Aramantha, 141n195, 143
Penley, Lizzie (Frost), 226, 226n205
Penley, Lovinia, 115
Penley, Mary Amanda (Crockett)
  birth, 75, *93*

457

Penley, Mary Amanda (Crockett) (*continued*)
  burial place of infant sons, 167, 167n282
  children of, 143
  death, *93, 247*
  Lot map of 1874, **174**
  marriage to Isaiah Vickery Penley, 128
Penley, Mary Dyer, 108, 115, 142, 142n201
Penley, Mary Dyer (Jordan), 103
Penley, Nathan, 108, 116, 132, 133, 134, 139, 202
Penley, Rebecca (Pavy), 86
Penley, Rufus Crockett, 108, 116, 132–133, 165
Penley, Rufus L., 108, 142
Penley, Sampson, 86
Penley, Sarah Belle, 141, 141n195, 143, 172, 216, 295
Penley, Sarah "Sally" Dingley. *See* Crockett, Sarah "Sally" Dingley (Penley)
Penley, Sarah Wentworth (Crockett), 40n22, 47, 74, *93*, 108, 115, 138, 165
Penley, Sewell Thomas, 143, 167
Penley, True Davis, 153, 217–218
Penley Corner Cemetery, 114, 138, 141, 142n201, 247
Penley Farm, 370
Penley Island, 95, 101, 143, 144, *365*, 370
Pennesseewassee, Lake, 3, *4, 32, 149, 154, 154*
Pike, Dennis, 310
Pike, Israel, 105
Pike, Luther, 105–106
Plantation No. 3, 17–18, 17n54, 19, 22
Plantation No. 4, 17
Pool, Joshua, 73
Pool, William A., 296

Poor, John A., 109–110
Preble Farm, 110, 112, 124–125, 145, 159
"Prosperous Farmer - Albert P. Farnham," 295

Q

Quimby, William, 60n111
Quinn, Jack, 352, 353, *353*

R

recipes, family, 421–425
Redemption (stallion), 227, 234, 242–243, 245
Reed/Read, Harriet C., 186, 186n44
remedies, family, 425
Revolutionary War
  Arthur Lee and, 8–9
  bounty land grants, 2–3, 33–34, 43–44, 52, 251
  debt left to Massachusetts, 3
  veterans, 2, 29, 42, 43, 44, 47, 51, 52, 73, 86, 87n14, 90, 90n29, 282, 283
Richardson, Albert, 115, 144, 159, 299
Richardson, Ann (Hanford) Jones, 112
Richardson, Calvin, 148–149, 153
Richardson, Edwina Maud, 144, 177–178, *178*, 180
Richardson, George Hanford, 144, 203–205
Richardson, Hannah Jordan (Crockett)
  birth, 75
  children of, 144, *178*
  cohabitation with Benning Wentworth, 205, 206–207
  divorce from Thomas Hanford Richardson, 207
  marriage to Oscar A. Harris, 207, 207n144

Richardson, Hannah Jordan (Crockett) (*continued*)
  marriage to Thomas Hanford Richardson, 75, 115, 144
  Norway Pine Grove Cemetery and, 165
  photographs of, *113, 145, 208*
  real estate transactions, 77, 145, 180
  as a young woman, 112–113
Richardson, Joshua, 110–112, 113, **118**, 125, 128, 129, 144
Richardson, Julia Ann, 144, 177–178, *178*, 180
Richardson, Nathaniel P., 144
Richardson, Thomas Hanford
  children of, 144, *178*
  Civil War draft, 136–137
  divorce from Hannah Jordan Crockett, 207
  Lot maps, **118, 160, 174**
  marriage to Hannah Jordan Crockett, 75, 115, 144
  on Preble Farm, 110, 112
  real estate transactions of, 128, 129, 144–145
Richardson, Thomas Putman, 144
"road to Millettville," 428
Roberts, Elizabeth, *31*
Roberts, Joseph, 47
Robinson, Addie (Titcomb) Thurston, 419, 421
Robinson, Mary, *31*
Rogers, Ava, 360
Roosevelt, Teddy, 255, 331–332
Ross, Harriet J., 86
Rough Riders, 254–255, 268
"Round the Pond Road," 428
Royall, Isaac, 44
Rust, Harry, 133, *135*
Rust, Henry, 2n1–2n5, 4–5, 11, 14–15, *135*
Rust's Purchase (Rustfield), 4, 5, 7–8, 11, 14–15
Ryerson, Colonel W., 52

S

Sanderson, Joseph, 148
sawmills
  Foye's, 41n26, 65, 65n116, *151*
  Maine Logging Camp and Saw Mill, *82*
  Millett's, 65n116, 109, *151*
Sawyer, Clarry (Young), 192
School District No. 8, 33, 92, 215–216, 218–219, 302
Script Warrant Act of 1855, 79
Smith, Elizabeth (Palmer), 273
Smith, Joshua, 20, **21**, 22
Smith, Mark P., 179
Smith, Sebastian, S., 70–71
"Social Circle Picnic in School District No. 8" (Whitman), 218–219
Spanish American War, 254–255
Spinney, B.F., 221–222, 236–237. *See also* B.F. Spinney & Co.
Stanford, Rebecca, *31,* 33, 45n43, 73
Stanley, Francis E., 230–232
Stanley, Freelan O., 230–232
Stanley Dry Plate Co., 230–232, 243–244
Staples, Ed, 167
Steep Falls, 203, *204*
Stephens, C.A., 246, 299
Stetson, Abel, 311
Stetson, Abel, Sr., 89, 90, 130
Stetson, Adeline (Howe), 227
Stetson, Antoinette, 75, 90, 136, 152, 165–166, 242, 257, 268
Stetson, Edward, 128

Stetson, Hannah (Benson), 90
Stetson, Hezekiah (Lydia's brother), 130
Stetson, Hezekiah (Lydia's grandfather), 90–91
Stetson, Lydia B. *See* Crockett, Lydia (Stetson)
Stetson, Olive (Prince), 90
Stetson, Rollin, 214n159, 227–228
Stevens, Jonas, 2, 2n2, 4
Stevens, Joseph, 2, 2n1, 4
Stinchfield, James, 4, 5
Stoddard, John L., 299–300
stone walls, 27, *56, 56,* 57, *59, 60*
Stowe, Harriet Beecher, 131
Stowell, Mary "Polly" Dennett, 75, 78
Strout, Perley, 288n41
Stuart, Joanna, 282, 282n6, 283, 307
Stuart, Joseph, 282n6, 283
Stuart, Joshua B., 286–287
Stuart, Nancy (Lombard), 282n6, 283
Stuart, Wentworth, 282n6, 283
"Study of the Penley Family," 86–87
Swift, Laura A., 75
Swift, Newton, 142

T

Taylor, Ellen, 139
Taylor, William, 139
tent caterpillars, 149, 153–154
"the Benevolent Literary Club," 299
"They Got Water!" (Packard), 355–357
Thibodeau, Tessa, *358*
Thomas, A.W., 299
Thurston, Addie, 299, 313
Thurston, Dean, *358*
Thurston, Stanley, 360, 421

Tongue property, 94, 102, 104–105, 116, 141, 159, 295
The Treaty of Ghent, 53
Tubbs, Abbie Jane (Crockett)
   burial in Norway Pine Grove Cemetery, 161
   Charles Whitman on, 140
   death, 269
   divorce from Charles N. Tubbs, 228–229
   genealogy of, 108, 176
   Lot map, **160**
   marriage to Charles N. Tubbs, 177
   real estate transactions, 159, 219–220, 231
   relocation to Waterville, 257
   schoolteacher certification, 175, 211
   See also Crockett heirs
Tubbs, Angiers, 176
Tubbs, Charles Newell, 176, 177, 211, 228–229
Tubbs, Christina Bird, 296n61
Tubbs, Elhanan B., 296
Tubbs, Idonia, 229, 257–258
Tubbs, Inez, 229
Tubbs, Jacob, 14, 16, 16n46, 110, 176
Tubbs, James, 176–177, 229
Tubbs, Oscar, 229, 257, 258n291
turkey tagging, 330–331, 349–350
Turple, James A., 288, 288n41
Turple, Marjorie, 288n41
Turple, Maurice, 288n41
Twombly, Nancy, 74, 100, 100n64, 105n91

U

"Uncle Tom's Cabin" (Stowe), 131
University of Maine at Orono Women's Rifle Club, 234n139, 323, *324*

Index

V

Vittum, Elkina Clough, 186n44, 190, 193, 232
Vittum, Harriett A., 186, 186n44
Vittum, Joseph Wentworth, 190, 193, 194, 232
Vittum, Stephen, 190
Vittum, William, 186n44, 190

W

Wagg, James, Jr., 29, 33
Wagg, James, Sr., 29, 29n1, 44
Wagg, Julia, 87n14
Wagg, Mary (Crockett), 29n1
War of 1812, 48–53, 283
Waterford Plantation, 7
Waterford Three Tiers, 4, 7–8
Weare, Abigail (Young), 192
Webster, Daniel, 100
Webster-Asburton Treaty, 100
Welsh Rarebit recipe, 422
Wentworth, Benning (son of Captain John Wentworth), 35, 42, 43–44, 43n35, 43n36, 45, 46–47, 87
Wentworth, Benning (son of William), 205–207
Wentworth, Betsey, 45, 47
Wentworth, Esther, 45
Wentworth, Foster, 177n8
Wentworth, John (Captain), 42, 42n28, 43
Wentworth, John (Lieutenant Governor of the Province of New Hampshire), 42
Wentworth, Margery (Pepperell), 42n28
Wentworth, Sally (Parker), 45, 176
Wentworth, Samuel, 206–207
Wentworth, Samuel Solley, 42, 43–44, 43n35, 45, 46, 77, 176
Wentworth, Samuel Solley, Jr., 45

Wentworth, Sarah "Sally" Bartlett. *See* Crockett, Sarah "Sally" Bartlett (Wentworth)
Wentworth, Stephen, 206
Wentworth, William (brother of Benning Wentworth), 206–207
Wentworth, William (Captain), 42n28
Wentworth, William (Elder), 42, 42n29
Wentworth, William (son of Samuel Solley), 45
"The Wentworth Genealogy," 42–43
Western State Normal and Training School, 279, 279n3, *280,* 318, 322
Whitehouse, Jonathan, 166–167
Whitman, Charles F.
  assisting George P. Young's divorce, 209
  "A Birthday Jollification in School District No. 8," 218
  "Christmas Eve in School District No. 8," 216–217
  on the Civil War, 132, 134, 135
  on Crocketts, 33, *56,* 63–64, 92, 140, 216–219, 235
  on himself, 217n174
  "A History of Norway, Maine," *10,* 11, 15, 19, 20, 427
  on John Horne, 179
  Norway Baptist Church and, 251
  on Norway Village, 72, 73
  on original settlers to Norway, 4, 14
  "Social Circle Picnic in School District No. 8," 218–219
  on tent caterpillar devastation, 153–154
  on Tubbs, 140, 177
  on Waterford Three Tiers, 7
  wife of, 209n149

Whitman, Mercy A., 70
Wildey Encampment No. 21, 198
Wilkins, Aaron, 16n46, 101, 120
Wilkins, David, 102
Williams, Lloyd, xvi, 57n101, 60n111
Williams, Pamela (Young), 57n101, 60n111, 322, 366, 366n196, 367
Wiltsie, Clarence, 161
Wiltsie, Inez (Tubbs) Tabor, 161
Witham, John, 35, 45
Wixson, Charles Wesley, 324n139
Wixson, Cheryl Ann, 364, *367*, 368
Wixson, Eldwin, Sr., 324n139
Wixson, Eldwin "Windy," Jr., 324n139, *358*
Wixson, Jennifer, *368*
Wixson, Lori, 119, 119n131
Wixson, Wesley, *119*, 119n131, 365
Wixson, William "Bill," *368*
Women's Federation of Clubs, 299
Woodbury, True, 45
Woodlawn Cemetery, 309
Woodstock, Maine, 3, 17–18, 17n54, 19, 22
Woodsum, Addie Louise. *See* Young, Louise Adalade "Addie" (Chaplin)
Woodsum, Charles S., 284–285
Woodsum, Jennie, 285
Woodsum, Susan (York), 284, 284n23
Wormeley, Robert, III, 12

Y

York, Georgianna (Hill), 285
York, Mary, 238, 307, 388
York, Nathaniel Folsom, 283
York, Paul, 285
York, Samuel, 283

Young, Aaron B., 188–189, 191, 192
Young, Abigail, 192
Young, Byron, 147, 322, 367n196
Young, Charles A., 189, 190n68, 229
Young, Charles H., 192
Young, Clarry, 192
Young, Dudley, Jr., 187–188, 187n48, 191–192
Young, Eddie, 189, 190n68
Young, Emma (sister of George P. Young), 189, 190n68
Young, Emma Tuell (Crockett). *See* Harding, Emma Tuell (Crockett) Young
Young, Florence (Andrews), 322, 358, 360, 365
Young, George P., 186–201
    appraisal of estate after death, 242–243
    as author's ancestral link to Crockett's Ridge, 26
    B.F. Spinney & Co. and, 184–185, 197–198
    birth, 186n43
    Charles F. Whitman on, 218
    child of, 215–216
    as co-executor of William Robinson Crockett's estate, 212–213
    conscription requirements and, 192, 194
    death, 186, 190, 238–241
    death of family members, 188–189, 190n68
    divorce from Martha "Mattie" Wilkins (Fuller) Young, 201, 208–209
    financial difficulties, 230–232, 239, 243–244
    Horse Trot and, 232–234
    letter to Rollin Stetson, 227–228
    life insurance policies, 239, 243, 244, 245, 246, 276, 297, 316
    loan from Stanley Dry Plate Co., 230–232, 243–244

Index

Young, George P., (*continued*)
   marriage to Emma Tuell Crockett, 157, 210
   marriage to Martha W. Fuller, 195–197, 196n100
   in Middleton, 193–194
   in Norway's Centennial celebration, 224–225
   photograph of, *186*
   real estate transactions, 165, 219–220
   trunk belonging to, 241
Young, George Willard "Jo Bill," 157, 214n159, 241, 322, 367n196
Young, George Willis
   birth, 262, 292–293
   helping on farm, *335*
   inheritance, 370
   marriage to Florence Andrews and move to old Morse Farm, 322
   as young child, *266, 294, 302, 303, 306*
   Young's Turkey Farm Open House, *358*
   Young's Turkey Farm truck deliveries, 340
Young, Harriet (Vittum), 189, 190–191, 192
Young, John C., 186, 188, 189, 190–191, 192
Young, Joseph, 187, 187n48, 187n49, 190n69
Young, Lewis A., 192
Young, Lillian (Hilden), 322, *323*
Young, Louise Adalade "Addie" (Chaplin)
   as author's ancestral link to Crockett's Ridge, 26
   cookbook, 419–426
   description by granddaughter Paula, 327
   final days of, 366–369
   Heywood Club and, 299–302, 352
   inheritance from Luella Chaplin, 319
   life on the Crockett homestead, 290–293

Young, Louise Adalade "Addie" (Chaplin) (*continued*)
   marriage to William Foss Young, 262, 279–281, 290
   newspaper clippings, *352, 353, 357, 361*
   parents of, 282, 286
   photographs of, *265, 278, 291, 303, 304, 306, 311, 312, 317, 334, 335, 358, 359, 367, 368, 369, 370*
   postcards sent to Bill, *363*
   purchase of real estate from Frank Hobbs, 366
   turkey business, establishment of, 318–319
   wedding anniversaries, *353, 353,* 361
   wedding dress and wedding book, *281*
   will of, 370–371
   Young's Cottage Lots and, 365–366
   See also Young's Turkey Farm
Young, Mark Edward, 189, 190n68
Young, Martha "Mattie" Wilkins (Fuller), 194, 195–197, 196n100, 201, 208–209
Young, Martha (Rennard), 193
Young, Mary, 192
Young, Nathaniel, Jr., 51–52
Young, Pamela, 57n101, 60n101, 322, 366, 366n196, 367
Young, Sally (Jacobs), 187
Young, Willard "Bud" Harding
   barn fire and, 316–317
   birth, 266, 293
   inheritance from Addie Young, 370
   lakefront property gifted to, 365
   life on the homestead, 302, *303, 306*
   marriage to Lillian Hilden, 322, *323*
   as young child, *266, 294, 358, 359*

Young, Willard "Bud" Harding (*continued*)
   Young's Turkey Farm Open House, 358–359

Young, Willard Norman
   birth, 323
   "Four Musketeers," *377*
   as young child on Young's Turkey Farm, *326,* 326–327, *327,* 359

Young, William "Bill" Foss
   as author's ancestral link to Crockett's Ridge, 26
   barn fire, 316–318
   birth, 215–216
   boarding with Fred Noble, 258
   building of new barn, 265
   death, 364
   description by granddaughter Paula, 327
   as a farmer, 344–347
   inheritance, 259, 320, **321**
   life on Crockett homestead, 290–298
   marriage to Louise Adalade "Addie" Chaplin, 262, 279–281, 290
   Norway Selectmen, 351

Young, William "Bill" Foss (*continued*)
   photographs of, *249, 297, 303, 306, 311, 359, 370*
   postcards from Addie, *363*
   wedding anniversaries, 353, *353,* 361
   See also Young's Turkey Farm

Young, Winona. *See* Palmer, Winona (Young)

Young's Cottage Lots, 365–366, **366**

Young's Turkey Farm
   Addie's marketing genius, 336–343
   back taxes, 347–349
   end of, 364–365
   establishment of, 318–320
   expansion of, 328–336
   newspaper clippings, *329, 331, 333, 335, 337, 338–339, 342–343, 345, 347, 350, 352, 353, 357, 360, 361*
   new well, 354–357
   Open House, 357–361
   photographs, *273, 326, 358, 372*
   stationery, *362*
   turkey tagging, 349–350

About the Author

Maine farmer and writer Jennifer Wixson is the 4th-great-granddaughter of Ephraim Crockett, Jr. and his wife Sally (Wentworth) Crockett, who settled Lot 45 on Lee's Grant in 1814. Jennifer's love of family history began in 1978 when she moved into the original Crockett homestead in Norway to live with her grandmother, Winona (Young) Palmer. Today, Jennifer is the proud owner of the ridge of land named for her ancestor and from which the Crockett Ridge Road takes its name. She currently lives with her husband Stanley Luce in Troy (Maine), where they garden, keep bees, and produce maple products.

Other Books by Jennifer Wixson

Fiction
Hens and Chickens
Peas, Beans and Corn
The Songbird of Sovereign
The Minister's Daughter
Maggie's Dilemma

Non-Fiction
Learning to SOAR!
Coming in 2025: *Into the Maine ~ One Maine Family's Quest for Land, 1630–1830.*

Back cover images: Studio portrait: Abel Stetson Crockett and his sister Emma (Crockett) Young Harding, circa 1920. (Courtesy of Joyce Palmer.) Photo: The old Crockett homestead circa 1970s, then home of Winona Y. Palmer. (Courtesy of Yvette Young). Colorized postcard, "Head of Lake Pennesseewassee from Crockett's Ledge, Norway, Me."

www.ingramcontent.com/pod-product-compliance
Lightning Source LLC
Chambersburg PA
CBHW051349070526
44584CB00025B/3696